Exchange Rate Forecasting: Techniques and Applications

Exchange Rate Forecasting: Techniques and Applications

Imad A. Moosa
Reader in Economics and Finance
La Trobe University

MACMILLAN
Business

First published 2000 by
MACMILLAN PRESS LTD
Houndmills, Basingstoke, Hampshire RG21 6XS
and London
Companies and representatives
throughout the world

ISBN 0–333–73644–3 hardcover

A catalogue record for this book is available
from the British Library.

10 9 8 7 6 5 4 3 2
09 08 07 06 05 04 03 02 01

Printed and bound in Great Britain
by Antony Rowe Ltd, Chippenham, Wiltshire

To Nisreen and Danny

Contents

List of Figures and Tables

FIGURES

TABLES

Currency Symbols

The following are the three-letter symbols of the currencies used in this book:

AUD	Australian dollar
CAD	Canadian dollar
CHF	Swiss franc
FRF	French franc
GBP	British pound
JPY	Japanese yen
NOK	Norwegian krone
USD	US dollar

Preface

Writing a book on exchange rate forecasting is not an easy task. There are at least two related problems concerning the subject matter and the targeted readership. The problem with the subject matter is that a book on exchange rate forecasting may concentrate on the techniques of forecasting, and in the extreme case it becomes a book on econometrics. It may, on the other hand, emphasise the applications and use of forecasts in business decision making, in which case less emphasis is placed on the econometrics and statistics of forecasting. This book encompasses both aspects of the subject matter, a feature that proved to be problematical, particularly in the presence of strict manuscript length constraints. I have, therefore, endeavoured to strike a balance between the two aspects at the cost of making the treatment of some topics look rather superficial. I must, for this reason, make it clear at the outset that this is not a textbook on econometrics. The basics of the econometric methods used to forecast exchange rates are explained within the constraints implied by the manuscript length and the objective of striking a balance between the two features mentioned above. In order to remedy this deficiency I have, whenever necessary, included a section referring the reader to other references that elaborate on the subject matter.

The second problem pertains to the choice of readership. Three classes of readers can be targeted by a book on exchange rate forecasting. The first are the well-established forecasters who are acquainted with the methods of forecasting. The second are the young forecasters who are developing their skills to become fully fledged forecasters. The third are not the forecasters, but rather the users of forecasts, the managers who take the decisions using forecasts as an input in the decision-making process. All of these classes are targeted to different extents. While readers belonging to the first class can overlook the material on the forecasting methods, they can benefit from the description of how their forecasts are used by the actual decision makers. Some of these forecasters can also benefit from the material on technical analysis and trading rules. For the forecasters who primarily use technical analysis, on the other hand, the book provides a broad survey of the econometric methods of forecasting and the economic models that explain, or attempt to explain, the behaviour of exchange rates. The second class of would-be readers are those forecasters who are not so experienced. The book provides a very accessible survey of what they should learn if they wish to become high-calibre forecasters. The third class of readers would benefit from the accessible treatment of some of the advanced topics such as neural networks and chaos. They should also benefit from the material on the applications of forecasts as well as the discussion of some of the philosophical aspects of forecasting.

At this stage it may be useful to outline the topics covered in this book in a chapter-by-chapter order. The book tries to strike a balance in two respects: between the techniques and applications, and between rigour and accessibility. Hence, the style of writing varies from one place to another, ranging between a very journalistic, simplified style and the rigorous exposition found in econometrics textbooks.

The book falls into 13 chapters. Chapter 1 provides the motivation for writing the book and deals with some preliminary and basic forecasting concepts. The chapter also deals with the expectations formation mechanisms and relates forecasting to expectation. Chapter 2 provides a more formal treatment of the role of forecasting in decision making, concentrating on financial decisions. It is shown that a large number of decision rules contain the expected exchange rate as a parameter, which means that a forecast is needed for decision making. These decision rules pertain to a number of financial operations, including speculation, hedging and capital budgeting. The chapter also describes some operations that do not need exchange rate forecasting since the decision rules do not include the expected exchange rate as a parameter.

The basic techniques of forecasting are dealt with in Chapters 3 and 4. Chapter 3 deals with the univariate time series techniques while Chapter 4 deals with the multivariate models, including single-equation models and multi-equation models. Chapter 5 describes market-based forecasting, which boils down to using the spot rate and the forward rate as forecasts. The discussion invariably leads to the random walk model, the unbiased efficiency hypothesis, as well as other concepts of market efficiency. Chapter 6 then deals with judgemental forecasting, discussing the role played by judgement in forecasting. In the same chapter, composite forecasting, that is the art of combining forecasts, is described and rationalised.

Chapter 7 departs from the fundamental models to deal with the technical models of forecasting. Technical analysis is rationalised and the tools of technical analysis are described. There is also a discussion of the economics of technical analysis. Chapter 8 is sort of an extension to Chapter 7, as it covers trading rules. Conventional trading rules are extended to deal with the complexities arising from the introduction of interest rates and allowing for the bid–offer spreads. Some fundamental trading rules are also described.

Chapter 9 provides a simplified treatment of two advanced topics: chaos and neural networks. It is shown that while these two topics have contrasting implications for forecasting, they are both based on the presumed presence of nonlinearity in the exchange rate determination process.

Chapter 10 deals with the issue of measuring forecasting accuracy. The chapter describes the general principles behind the measurement of forecasting accuracy, and this is followed by a presentation of the graphical and quantitative measures of accuracy. Chapter 11 then deals with the selection, implementation and monitoring of forecasts. Several important issues are discussed in this chapter, including the issue of why forecasters differ and the process whereby a choice is made between internal and external forecasters, as well as the criteria used to select an external forecaster. Chapter 12 presents five case studies that demonstrate how exchange rate forecasting is used in decision making.

The last word on exchange rate forecasting, as viewed in this book, comes in Chapter 13. The chapter starts with a recapitulation of the main issues and the motivation for writing the book. There is then a review of some of the vital questions raised in various chapters and some brief answers. The concluding remarks pertain to the future of exchange rate forecasting. The book ends on a happy note, suggesting that the apparent failure of exchange rate forecasting models will lead to better forecasting in the future.

Writing this book would not have been possible if it were not for the help and encouragement I received from family, friends and colleagues. My utmost gratitude must go to my small family who had to bear the opportunity cost of writing this book. My wife, Afaf, proved once again to be my best research assistant by producing, over a relatively short period of time, all of the diagrams shown in the book. Friends and colleagues have been supportive, directly or indirectly, by providing the intellectual and social environment that is conducive, among other things, to writing a book. I would, therefore, like to thank Mary Amiti, Prasad Bidakorta, Chongwoo Choe, Mardi Dungey, Harry Clarke, Iain Fraser, Gillian Hewitson, Sisira Jayasuriya, Pauline Kennedy, Liam Lenten, Rodney Maddock, Robert Pereira, Neil Perry, Param Silvapulle, Lee Smith, Rabee Tourky and Glenda Watson. I particularly benefited from discussion with some colleagues in the stimulating atmosphere of *the Eagle*, and for this reason I would like to thank Leon and Andre. Liam was particularly helpful with the extraction of data and the reading of the manuscript. Mardi was generous with her time as she helped me obtain data from *Datastream*. Two of my students at La Trobe University have been particularly helpful: Owen Guest and George Tawadros, and so they deserve to be mentioned here. An ex-student of mine, Hasan Tevfik, provided much-needed help in collecting data for which he must be thanked.

I would also like to thank friends and ex-colleagues who live far away but provide help via means of telecommunication, including Kevin Dowd, Bob Sedgwick, Sean Holly, Dave Chappell, Dan Hemmings, Ian Baxter,

Scott MacDonald, Razzaque Bhatti and Nabeel Al-Loughani. Last, but not least, I would like to thank Samantha Whittaker of Macmillan, who not only encouraged me to write this book but also kept providing positive feedback. Naturally, I am the only one responsible for any errors and omissions in this book.

IMAD A. MOOSA
Melbourne, April 1999

1: Expectation and Forecasting: An Overview

THE TALE OF A YOUNG TOURIST

John is a young British tourist who is planning his first trip to New York City in three months' time. For this purpose, he has been saving for long enough to accumulate a sufficient amount of cash to last him for the month or so he intends to spend in New York. The problem is that John's savings are in pounds while his expenditure in New York will be in dollars. Given that exchange rates fluctuate wildly, John is facing some sort of a dilemma. He wants to maximise the US dollar value of his pound savings. This value depends on the exchange rate between the pound and the dollar that is used to convert the savings into dollar spending money. So, John faces the problem of deciding when, and consequently at what exchange rate, he would convert his savings into US dollars. Assuming that the level of interest rates is low and the underlying amount is small, the interest rate factor will be ignored for the time being.

This situation arises because we live in an uncertain world where we have to make decisions whose outcomes depend on something that will happen in the future. Because of that, John has to base his decision on expectations or forecasts, implicitly or explicitly, consciously or otherwise. If he thinks that the dollar will appreciate during the next three months he will take a decision to buy his dollars now. If he thinks that the dollar will not start to appreciate until one month from now, then he will wait until then before converting his savings. If he expects the dollar to keep on depreciating over the next three months, he will wait until he embarks on his trip. He would then convert his pounds into dollars on departure to New York. If he thinks that the dollar will keep on depreciating even after that, he may consider two courses of action. The first course of action is to start converting pounds into dollars at the beginning of his trip and keep on doing that whenever the need for dollars arises. The second course of action is that he would not convert the pounds but rather use his credit card (assuming he has one) on his pound account in London. In all of these cases John acts on the basis of his expectations concerning the future path of the exchange rate. The outcome will depend on what actually happens to the exchange rate relative to John's expectation. Quantitatively, it will depend on the divergence between the value of the exchange rate John expects and the value that will actually materialise.

Before John acts on such a situation he will need to ask himself some questions. The first question is whether the exchange rate is going to rise or fall, that is whether the dollar is going to appreciate or depreciate (assuming that the exchange rate is measured as GBP/USD). The second question is by how much, which amounts to estimating (or forecasting) the expected change in the exchange rate. The third question concerns the timing of the change in the exchange rate. This means that John needs to form some expectations on the direction, magnitude and timing of the future changes in the exchange rate.

How would he form these expectations or forecasts? The first possibility is that John may act on the basis of his intuition and judgement, implying some mental consideration of the relationship between the future level of the exchange rate and its past history and/or the other variables that affect it, such as the inflation rate. This intuition-based expectation may even involve a belief, for example, that the expected appreciation of the dollar in the next three months is no more than 5 per cent. On the other hand, John may be a complete layperson who does not like such a brain-taxing activity as trying to work out the expected level of the exchange rate. If this is the case then he will base his expectation, and therefore decision, on the currency reports that can be found in the *Financial Times*, *Wall Street Journal*, and the financial and business pages of other daily newspapers. Or, let us assume that John is actually a graduate in economics with a strong background in quantitative analysis. He may in this case feed in some exchange rate data into a computer containing a forecasting package which will give him an answer like this: there is an 80 per cent chance that the dollar will appreciate by 5 per cent and a 20 per cent chance that it will appreciate by 2 per cent in the next three months. John may want to compare his forecast with that produced by a friend who actually works in this field or with the forecast produced by a financial adviser whom he has access to. He may then choose to act on the basis of his forecast, the forecast produced by the friend, the forecast produced by the financial adviser, or on the basis of a combination of them. Once he makes up his mind on which forecast to act, he will take a decision, implement it and wait for the outcome. Notice that the decision is taken now while the outcome will only materialise and become known in the future. If John decides to convert now at an exchange rate of 0.62, he will have made the wrong decision if in three months' time the exchange rate turns out to be 0.58. If, on the other hand, the exchange rate turns out to be 0.65, he will have made a sound decision.

This example shows how an individual could take a decision by acting on exchange rate forecasting. The forecast may be based on intuition, or on an actual analysis of data on the exchange rates and their determinants. The decision may also be based on a single forecast, more than one forecast, or a composite forecast. The decision may be based on a forecast that conveys something about the direction of the change within a certain time horizon or on a forecast that may say something about the magnitude of the change as well.

THE TALE OF A BUSINESS MANAGER

Mary is the general manager of a British trading company that imports beer from the continent. At present, the company owes its French supplier FRF500,000 which at the current exchange rate of 0.10 (GBP/FRF) is worth GBP50,000. This amount is due to be paid within three months. Mary is considering a decision whether or not to buy this amount of French francs forward to lock in the pound amount that needs to be paid in three months' time. By doing this, the exposure to the French franc would be covered.

Normally, a decision like this is taken if the French franc is expected to appreciate against the pound. If, for example, the franc appreciated such that the exchange rate became 0.12, the pound value of the amount would be GBP60,000. More precisely, such a decision will be taken if the spot exchange rate that is expected to prevail when the amount is due is higher than the current forward rate. Thus, this decision needs to be based on a forecast of the spot exchange rate prevailing at a particular point in time. What will Mary do to obtain this forecast? There are several possibilities. The first is that Mary may base the decision on her intuition and judgement as to the level of the spot exchange rate in three months' time. The second alternative is to obtain a forecast by reading the financial press or from the surveys published by Reuters if she has a Reuters screen in front of her or somewhere else on the premises. Another alternative is possible if the company has an economist, one of whose jobs is to forecast exchange rates. Yet another alternative is possible if the company subscribes to the services of a forecasting house, in which case the forecasts can be obtained from an external forecaster. In all cases a quantitative forecast may or may not be combined with intuition or judgement. Or it may be the case that more than one quantitative forecast may be combined with judgement. Once the forecast on which the decision is to be based has been determined, the decision is taken. The outcome of the decision (to hedge or not to hedge) that is taken at the present time depends on what the actual exchange rate turns out to be when the payables are due.

This example once again shows that forecasts can be obtained from the intuition and judgement of the business manager; by reading newspapers and magazines; and by utilising the services of a forecaster (an economist, a statistician, and so on) who is employed by the firm for this purpose. Forecasts can also be obtained by hiring the services of a forecasting house either on a regular subscription basis or on consultation basis whenever the need arises. The last source of forecasts gives rise to the problem of choosing between carrying out the forecasting function in-house and buying the forecasts from outside.

The problem faced by Mary is only one example of the problems faced by business managers that require exchange rate forecasting. Other problems pertaining to a variety of business decisions, financial and otherwise, may arise. This is because business firms operate in an uncertain world in which they have to take decisions whose outcomes depend on something that will happen in the future. Consider the following questions that are faced by business managers like Mary.

1. Should we take a long position on the Norwegian krone?
2. Is it profitable to borrow in a low interest currency and invest in a high interest currency short term?
3. Is it a good idea to change the currency composition of the securities portfolio?
4. Will it pay off to hedge our long exposure to the Japanese yen?
5. If we keep our prices at the same level, will our competitive position in foreign markets be affected?
6. Should we finance our short-term cash requirements in a single currency or a portfolio of currencies? If so, which currency or currencies?
7. We have received a proposal from one of our foreign subsidiaries which sounds appealing. Our foreign subsidiary is rather enthusiastic about this project. Should we go ahead with it?

All of these problems, which are listed in Table 1.1, require decisions that depend in whole or in part on exchange rate expectations. Hence, they should be based on exchange rate forecasting. The table shows the type of problems and the decision taken, given certain expectations or forecasts.

THE IMPORTANCE OF FORECASTING

So far, we have used the words 'expectation' and 'forecasting' interchangeably. So, do they mean the same thing? Not exactly: the connection is that forecasting is a formal method of generating expectations. The problem lies in defining the word 'formal'. Surely, if a forecast is based on some data analysis procedure then it is formal. But what about an expectation that is based on intuition and judgement? This is still a forecast if the intuition and judgement involve an actual analysis of the situation without the use of an exact formula or a rigorous model. In this case we refer to judgemental rather than quantitative (or scientific) forecasting. On the other hand, if the expectation is based on a 'hunch' of some sort, then it is not formal and the expectation does not constitute a forecast.

Forecasting is important and it is needed because we live, operate and make decisions in an uncertain world. One function of forecasting is to convert uncertainty into risk. Uncertainty is present when we do not know anything about the future, while risk is present when we have a probability distribution for the outcome. When we act upon this probability distribution,

Table 1.1 Some problems requiring exchange rate forecasting

Case	*Problem*	*Decision*
1	Spot speculation	Yes, if the krone is expected to appreciate against the base currency.
2	Uncovered interest arbitrage	Yes, if the low interest currency is not expected to appreciate by more than the interest differential.
3	Long-term portfolio investment	Yes, by shifting to the currencies that are expected to appreciate.
4	Hedging transaction exposure	Yes, if the yen is expected to depreciate.
5	Hedging economic exposure	Keep prices at the same level if the domestic currency is not expected to appreciate in such a way as to make the real exchange rate high enough to erode the competitive advantage.
6	Short-term financing	The decision depends on the overall expected rate of financing as compared with the domestic rate of financing. Yes, if the foreign currencies are expected to depreciate against the domestic currency.
7	Foreign direct investment	Yes, if the foreign currency is expected to appreciate by more than what is needed to offset other factors, producing a positive net present value.

the outcome of our decision may be good or bad depending on what actually happens in the future, which is beyond the decision maker's control. Hence, risk is present because there is a chance of sustaining losses by acting on the probability distribution resulting from the forecasting process. A probability distribution of the forecasts may take one of the following forms. It could be a single forecast with (perhaps an implicit) probability. It could be a number of single forecasts with various probabilities that sum up to 100 per cent (or 1). Or it could be a range of values with a probability that the exchange rate would fall within this range.

Although forecasting as a professional activity has flourished at an accelerating rate, it is often looked upon with scepticism both from within and outside the profession, that is by economists and non-economists who may be users or observers. The sceptics normally assert that forecasts have little value because they are invariably inaccurate, and so decision makers will do just as well or as badly by acting on the basis of tossing a coin. J. K. Galbraith, an eminent economist, put this view quite vividly when he once said: 'We have two forecasters, those who don't know and those who don't know that they don't know.' However, this argument is not valid. The focus on accuracy in a discussion of the value of forecasting is misplaced. Forecasting is useful because it reduces uncertainty and leads to better decisions. It makes the difference between basing a decision on an 'educated guess' and basing it on an 'uneducated guess'. But we have to bear in mind that forecasters do not possess a crystal ball that enables them to look into the future. Hence, forecasting errors are inevitable, and all the forecasters strive to do is to reduce the forecasting error by devising new, more powerful forecasting techniques and otherwise (such as resorting to forecast combination). Perhaps there is no better indication of the usefulness of forecasting than the fact that the forecasting industry has flourished since the early 1980s. The market for forecasts is currently worth hundreds of millions of dollars, this being the case despite the availability of free forecasts in the financial press and the reports produced by government bodies and international organisations. If acting on the basis of tossing a coin was just as good, why then would a business manager pay an annual subscription of something like USD30,000 to obtain forecasts? And why would another business manager employ a statistician, paying her an annual salary of USD200,000 to work out forecasts? Surely, it is cheaper to toss a coin.

The above argument is particularly valid when we consider the performance of foreign exchange forecasters in the first half of the 1980s. These forecasters failed miserably in predicting the timing of the beginning of the end for the dollar which started appreciating in 1980. The reason for the appreciation of the currency was a mix of contractionary monetary policy and expansionary fiscal policy that was implemented by the first Reagan Administration. This policy mix, coupled with the 1979 policy shift by the Federal Reserve System away from interest rate targeting, led to a high level of US nominal and real interest rates that propelled the dollar. Once the currency acquired the momentum, its behaviour started to resemble a bubble: it kept on appreciating because market participants kept on buying it on the belief that it would continue to appreciate. In mid-1982, exchange rate forecasters started telling their clients that the dollar would start depreciating 'in the second half of the year' or 'next month' or 'by the end of the year'. This was the case with forecasters employing a wide range of forecasting devices. They all failed miserably as the dollar did not start depreciating until March 1985. Eventually, and inevitably, they got it right. But on one occasion in 1984 the dollar appreciated significantly in one week that witnessed the negative economic fundamentals of a reduction in the prime lending rate and a downward revision of the GDP growth rate in the US. The forecasters failed miserably because they, probably without realising it, were dealing with a bubble. Still, we have not heard of a major forecasting house closing down because of this failure, although we have heard of mergers and takeovers in the forecasting industry. So, they must have produced better forecasts on other occasions, helping their clients reach good decisions.

In its issue of 1 August 1998, *The Economist* published an article entitled 'The perils of prediction' which cast significant doubt on the ability of forecasters to predict currency crises like the Asian crisis which started in 1997. The article concludes by saying that 'it seems near impossible to create models that neither miss too many crises that have occurred nor predict too many that never happen'. The same article cites Richard Portes, an academic economist, who describes these models as 'one of the most egregious examples of data mining in all of empirical economics'. The article received mixed reactions as reflected in the letters to the editor published in the 15 August issue. One of these reactions is that 'exact timing is far from the point of these models' and that under some conditions the models 'can prove very powerful' in the sense that they 'can be used to estimate not only the probability of a currency jump but also the new equilibrium level at which the currency might settle if such a jump should occur'. Another reaction is even more negative than the article itself. The commentator indicates that these models are 'financial tools which the world is better off without' since they can 'attract enough believers to become self-fulfilling'.

The fact remains, however, that exchange rate forecasting is needed and cannot be abandoned. Since the world has always been changing, forecasting has always been necessary. Many of the forecasting techniques that are used today and discussed in this book were developed in the 19th century (for example, regression analysis). Others were developed only recently (for example, structural time series analysis). Before the advent of modern forecasting techniques and the power of the computer, the manager's judgement was the only forecasting tool available. However, a decision maker is better off understanding quantitative forecasting techniques and using the forecasts they generate. Moreover, there is evidence that forecasts based on judgement only are not as accurate as those involving the application of quantitative techniques.

With the development of more sophisticated forecasting techniques and the advent of the computer, forecasting has become an even more important business activity. This statement is particularly true since the proliferation of the personal computer. This is made all the necessary by increased competition and the complexity of the world. Managers can now utilise very sophisticated data analysis techniques for forecasting purposes, and an understanding of these techniques has become essential for business managers. Quantitative forecasting, however, does not wipe out the need for good judgement. It is now accepted that the most effective forecaster is the one who is able to formulate a skilful mix of quantitative techniques and good judgement, avoiding the extremes of relying on either.

THE IMPORTANCE OF THE EXCHANGE RATE

This book is on exchange rate forecasting. Devoting a whole book to the forecasting of the exchange rate rather than other macroeconomic variables reflects the importance of this variable. It is not an exaggeration if one says that the exchange rate is the single most important macroeconomic variable in an open economy. This is so much the case in the present environment of deregulation and globalisation of financial markets. The exchange rate is important for countries (for macroeconomic policy purposes), for businesses (recall the dilemma Mary faced) and for individuals (recall the dilemma John faced).

THE EXCHANGE RATE AND MACROECONOMIC POLICY

The exchange rate is such an important macroeconomic policy variable that the debate is still raging about fixed versus flexible exchange rates. Recent developments in Europe and the move towards the European Monetary Union and a single currency point to the belief in the harm inflicted on the economy by sharp fluctuations in the exchange rate. Under a system of flexible exchange rates, central banks intervene in the market on a regular basis to 'smooth' and 'iron out' fluctuations in exchange rates. Sometimes they even intervene to accomplish the near-impossible objective of reversing an established market trend, and normally they fail spectacularly in this endeavour (recall the bitter experiences of the Bank of England in September 1992 and the Thai monetary authorities in July 1997).

The argument for central bank intervention embodies three propositions:

1. exchange rate fluctuations can be excessive;
2. exchange rate fluctuations have substantial adverse effect on economic activity;
3. central banks can smooth out exchange rate fluctuations by intervening in the foreign exchange market.

The first proposition actually implies the importance of exchange rate forecasting. The second proposition is that exchange rates create uncertainty that adversely affects the value of international trade and investment. Fluctuations in exchange rates can affect international trade in a number of ways. The first is that agents respond to uncertainty by reducing the volume of international transactions. The response may also involve a change in the composition of output and investment to reduce risk. Moreover, fluctuations in exchange rates may affect macroeconomic policy formation by changing policy trade-offs (see, for example, the International Monetary Fund, 1984). There is also some evidence that exchange rate uncertainty has a negative effect on exports and the allocation of resources (see, for example, Arize, 1995).

THE EXCHANGE RATE AND BUSINESS OPERATIONS

The exchange rate is very important for businesses, particularly under the present international environment. Business firms indulge in international operations to reap the benefits arising from the internationalisation or globalisation of trade and investment. One obvious benefit of international trade is the extension of the market for the firm's products beyond the national frontiers. The advantage of the globalisation of finance is to enhance the ability of business firms to diversify their financing and investment portfolios. However, there is no such thing as a 'free lunch' because there are risks associated with international operations. The risk that we are concerned with here is the foreign exchange risk that results from the effect of changes in exchange rates on sales, prices, costs and profits.

The best way to demonstrate the importance of the exchange rate for businesses is perhaps to present some real-life examples. These examples show why adverse exchange rate changes can demolish a business. The first example is that of the Beecham Group, a British company that in 1971 raised a Swiss franc loan. When the repayment of the loan became due in 1976, the pound had depreciated against the Swiss franc to the extent that made the pound value of the principal alone more than double its value in 1971. The depreciation of the pound gave rise to an additional cost of GBP12.6 million in principal repayment alone.

The second example is that of Laker Airlines, another British company that provided cheap transatlantic flights for British holidaymakers. During the 1970s this company purchased a number of DC-10 jet planes financed by borrowing US dollar funds. As the pound started to depreciate against the dollar in 1981, the demand for flights to America by British holidaymakers declined at a time when the company's debt in pound terms increased. The outcome of this chain of events was the inevitable plunge into bankruptcy.

Other examples demonstrate the effect of appreciating currencies. The appreciation of the US dollar in the first half of the 1980s resulted in a sharp loss of domestic and foreign market shares for some giant American companies such as Caterpillar and Eastman Kodak. The latter's pre-tax earnings were reduced by USD3.5 billion over the period 1980–1985 which witnessed a protracted appreciation of the US currency. It is interesting to note that the appreciation of the dollar during that period, and the consequent lobbying by these companies, led to the appointment of James Baker as the US Treasury Secretary in 1985, replacing Donald Regan. The reason for the replacement was different 'ideologies' with respect to intervention in the foreign exchange market. Regan was an investment banker and a firm believer in the power of the market, which made him oppose market intervention against the dollar. Baker, on the other hand, was a lawyer who had nothing against intervention that took off following the Plaza Accord of September 1985. In that meeting the treasurers and central bankers of the US, Japan, France, Germany and the UK met in the Plaza Hotel in New York City and agreed on a plan for concerted and co-ordinated intervention in the foreign exchange market to bring the dollar down. Subsequently, they implemented the agreement and the outcome was a spectacular success in achieving the stated objective. However, it seems that what achieved the objective was not the power of intervention as such, but rather that it reinforced (and not opposed) a market trend that had started six months earlier.

A more recent example of the importance of the exchange rate for business operations pertains to the effect of the Asian currency crisis on the companies operating in the region. By October 1997, several Australian companies with exposure to the region started conceding that their operations were affected. Investors started to sell the shares of these companies on a massive scale. Coca-Cola Amatil, which obtained 40 per cent of its profit from the Philippines and Indonesia, suffered a significant drop in its market value over a very short period of time for this reason.

The exchange rate is not important only for the operations of international firms, which are involved in international trade, investment and finance. Purely domestic firms are also exposed to foreign exchange risk. A firm that does not do any business with the outside world can lose a large portion of the domestic market if and when the appreciation of the domestic currency encourages foreign firms to enter the domestic market. Moreover, a domestic currency depreciation may, via a policy action, lead to a higher level of domestic interest rates, also affecting the operations of purely domestic firms.

THE EXCHANGE RATE AND PERSONAL DECISION MAKING

As for individuals, the exchange rate is also important, not only for the wealthy guys who have Swiss bank accounts. For example, a higher level of interest rates resulting from currency depreciation leads to larger mortgage payments. The depreciation may also attract foreign home buyers, causing a hike in house prices. Also, changes in exchange rates may determine which country is chosen for a holiday. The popularity of Bali as a destination for Australian holidaymakers increased significantly following the depreciation of the Indonesian currency in the second half of 1997. All of a sudden, Bali became better value for money than Hawaii as a destination for Australian holidaymakers. British holidaymakers started to invade South East Asia on a massive scale in 1998 as the weakness of Asian currencies and the strength of the pound made holidays in that part of the world good value for money.

EXCHANGE RATE FORECASTING: SOME PRELIMINARIES

In this section we describe and discuss some preliminary issues pertaining to exchange rate forecasting. These include the forms of exchange rate forecasting, the distinction between microeconomic and macroeconomic forecasting, the distinction between point and interval forecasting, the distinction between quantitative and judgemental forecasting, the forecasting techniques, the distinction between *ex post* and *ex ante* forecasting, the distinction between short-term and long-term forecasting, the forecasting process, and the computer software used for exchange rate forecasting.

FORMS OF EXCHANGE RATE FORECASTING

Exchange rate forecasting may take one of three forms. The first is the forecasting of event timing, that is forecasting the timing of an event of a once-and-for-all nature. This form of forecasting is mostly relevant to fixed exchange rates, more precisely to devaluation and revaluation of currencies under a system of fixed exchange rates. Realignment of exchange rates within the European Monetary System (EMS) is an example of such an event. Forecasting the timing of these realignments is an example of the forecasting of event timing.

The second form is forecasting event outcome. With reference to our example of the EMS realignment, this form of exchange rate forecasting is concerned with what actually happens in a realignment: which currency will be devalued, which currency will be revalued, and by how much?

In this book we are only concerned with the third form of exchange rate forecasting, which is time series forecasting. A time series is a sequence of values gathered at regular intervals of time. If S is the spot exchange rate and t is the present time then a time series on the spot exchange rate is $S_1, S_2, \ldots, S_t, S_{t+1}, \ldots, S_{t+n}$. If, at time t, we want to forecast the exchange rate at time $t+n$ (that is, we want to forecast the value of S_{t+n}) then n is called the forecast horizon.

At time t, S_{t+n} is a random variable. Time series forecasting involves finding the conditional distribution of S_{t+n}, given some information set, Ω_t, which is available at time t. The conditional mean of S_{t+n} is given by

$$\bar{S}_{t+n} = E(S_{t+n}|\Omega_t) \tag{1.1}$$

where E is the expected value operator. This equation says that the conditional mean (conditional upon the information set Ω_t) is the expected value of the exchange rate at time $t+n$, given the information set available at time t. The conditional mean represents a point forecast, that is a single forecast for a particular point in time. It is in fact the best forecast, the most likely value to be taken by S at time $t+n$. With the normality assumption, the conditional mean and variance can be used to determine an interval forecast, that is a range of values within which S_{t+n} is likely to fall with a given probability.

What does the information set Ω_t contain? If the information set includes the history of the exchange rate only, that is $\Omega_t = [S_1, S_2, \ldots, S_{t-1}, S_t]$, then what we have on our hands is univariate time series forecasting. If, on the other hand, the information set is $\Omega_t = [S_1, S_2, \ldots, S_{t-1}, S_t, X_1, X_2, \ldots, X_{t-1}, X_t]$, where $X_1, X_2, \ldots, X_t$ are explanatory variables that affect the exchange rate, then we have multivariate time series forecasting. Sometimes a model that is based on a univariate time series of the exchange rate is called a time series model while a model that is based on a multivariate time series is called an econometric model. A distinction may also be made between structural forecasting, which is based on an explicit theory, and non-structural forecasting, which is not. Structural forecasting is normally associated with econometric models while non-structural forecasting is associated with univariate time series models.

MICROECONOMIC VERSUS MACROECONOMIC FORECASTING

While microeconomic forecasting pertains to the forecasting of variables specific to one company or one sector (for example, car sales or the price of tomatoes), macroeconomic forecasting pertains to macroeconomic variables, one of which is the exchange rate. Therefore, exchange rate forecasting is macroeconomic forecasting. One problem with macroeconomic forecasting arises from the effect of structural breaks resulting, for example, from significant changes in the price of crude oil, inflation surges and policy shifts. This problem may make it necessary to combine the forecasts generated by a forecasting model with judgement, that is to modify the raw forecasts using the forecaster's judgement.

POINT VERSUS INTERVAL FORECASTING

Point forecasting implies that single forecast values are obtained for each point in time. Interval forecasting, on the other hand, provides a range of values within which the forecast value is likely to fall. Interval forecasts may be generated by calculating a confidence interval of one or two standard deviations around the point forecast. Alternatively, the interval emerges automatically when the forecaster generates conditional forecasts on the basis of a set of scenarios.

QUANTITATIVE VERSUS JUDGEMENTAL FORECASTING

Quantitative (or scientific) forecasting is based on some sort of a formal model. This kind of forecasting needs no input of judgement, since it is based on mechanical procedures that involve processing of data with varying degrees of sophistication. Judgemental (or qualitative) forecasting requires no explicit processing of the data and relevant information. It is based entirely on the forecaster's judgement or intuition although, to qualify as a forecast, the judgement must be based at least on a mental processing of historical data. Judgemental forecasting, therefore, is based on the same theoretical framework used in quantitative forecasting except that it is implicit, that is not represented by an explicit mathematical model. This means that judgemental forecasts are determined by subjective and often changing evaluation of the weights to be assigned to each of the causal factors. Because of this difference it is more difficult, if possible at all, to replicate judgemental forecasts than to replicate quantitative forecasts.

With respect to exchange rates, forecasting event timing and event outcome is normally judgemental forecasting while time series forecasting is predominantly quantitative forecasting. However, it is more often than not that quantitative forecasts are manipulated using the forecaster's judgement. For example, an econometric model may produce a forecast indicating that the US dollar will appreciate against the pound by 5 per cent over the next three months. The forecaster may have good reasons to believe that this is too much as judged by a similar previous episode. The forecaster then decides that the rate of appreciation should be cut in half to 2.5 per cent.

FORECASTING TECHNIQUES

Within quantitative forecasting techniques, there is a wide range of methods and models to choose from. The question may then arise as to the choice of the appropriate forecasting technique. The important consideration in this case is that the forecasts must lead to better decisions. The criterion is not that the technique utilises fancy econometrics or time series analysis but that it should produce a forecast that is accurate and timely. At one time, univariate time series models were rejected in favour of large-scale multi-equation models on the grounds that the former did not have any economic content, which made them unreliable. However, it has been repeatedly found that a cheap single-equation univariate model can outperform an expensive multi-equation structural econometric model. This finding has shifted interest to univariate models as a forecasting device. The underlying argument is that, for the purpose of forecasting, what matters is the accuracy of the forecasts, not the economic content of the model.

EX POST VERSUS EX ANTE FORECASTING

Distinction is normally made between in-sample (or within-sample) and out-of-sample forecasting. In-sample forecasting implies that the model is used to predict the value of the underlying variable (the exchange rate) within the sample period in which the model is estimated. Out-of-sample forecasting implies the opposite. Thus, out-of-sample forecasting may be *ex post* or *ex ante* forecasting. In *ex post* forecasting, observations on the dependent and the explanatory variables over the forecast period are known. *Ex post* forecasting is therefore unconditional forecasting. *Ex ante* forecasting is normally conditional forecasting, that is conditional on the values of the explanatory variables prevailing in the future. This is not necessarily the case, however. For example, suppose that a simple exchange rate forecasting model stipulates that the exchange rate depends entirely on the value of a key policy-determined interest rate. If the monetary authorities in the country concerned fix this rate at a preannounced level then its value is known with certainty. This value can then be used to forecast the exchange rate on *ex ante* basis.

A formal distinction between *ex ante*, *ex post*, conditional and unconditional forecasting may be made as follows. Assume that we have a sample period in which the model can be estimated, and that this period extends between a point in time, 1, and the present time t. The forecaster may choose to use the whole sample period for estimation, in which case there is no possibility for *ex post* or unconditional forecasting. This model can be used to forecast the exchange rate prevailing at $t + n$, which is *ex ante* and most likely conditional forecasting. If, on the other hand, the forecaster chooses to estimate the model over the period extending between 1 and $t - k$, such that $k < t$, then *ex post* forecasting is possible. The model can be used to forecast the exchange rate for the period between $t - k + 1$ and t, for which data on the exchange rate and the explanatory variables are available. Hence, this is unconditional forecasting, normally used to judge the accuracy of the model before it is used for *ex ante* forecasting.

SHORT-TERM VERSUS LONG-TERM FORECASTING

Exchange rate forecasting may be short-term or long-term forecasting. Short-term exchange rate forecasting is required for short-term operations such as money market investment and financing decisions. Long-term exchange rate forecasting is required, among other purposes, for foreign direct investment projects such as the establishment of a subsidiary in a foreign country. For this purpose, forecasts may be required for 10 years ahead. Forecasting critics are often cynical about long-term forecasting. They claim that economists like to forecast 30 years ahead because they (the forecasters) would not be around when the time comes to prove them wrong.

Sometimes, the forecast horizon is classified into the following:

1. immediate, that is, less than one month;
2. short-term, that is, one to three months;
3. medium-term, that is, between three months and two years;
4. long-term, that is, more than two years.

Forecasting less than one month ahead is required, for example, for daily trading in the foreign exchange market.

THE FORECASTING PROCESS

Four steps are involved in the forecasting process:

1. data collection;
2. data refinement;
3. model estimation;
4. forecast generation.

The first step is extremely important in the sense that the forecaster has to obtain high-quality and consistent data on exchange rates and the factors affecting them (the explanatory variables). No matter how sophisticated the forecasting technique is, the forecasts will not be accurate if the model is estimated on the basis of a faulty set of data, that is data with measurement errors. Data refinement includes such measures as determining the appropriate sample period, determining the explanatory variables to be included (as well as their definitions) and checking consistency if the data series are collected from different sources. For example, the appropriate sample period for estimating an exchange rate model under the present system should begin after 1973 when general floating started. Another example is that if data on interest rates and prices (as explanatory variables) are collected from different sources, with each source providing the data for part of the sample, then we have to make sure that the definitions of the variables are identical.

The third step is model estimation, which includes the specification, estimation and validation of the model. Several factors affect the choice of the model including, perhaps, the acceptance of the model by the decision maker (the manager) who may not be technically sophisticated. In fact, it should be the case that the forecaster is thought of as an adviser to the manager rather than someone who *monitors* an automatic decision-making device. This is why the acceptance of the model by the manager may be a factor playing a role in determining the chosen model. Once the model is estimated, forecasts can be generated. Often, the accuracy of the forecasts is checked against actual data from recent periods whose values are known. The (ex ante) forecasts can then be used for decision making.

COMPUTER SOFTWARE

Model estimation and forecast generation invariably require the use of a computer, unless we are talking about a judgemental forecast. What is also needed is software packages. There are two types of software packages that are of interest to forecasters. The first are general statistical and econometric packages that include regression analysis and other techniques used by forecasters to estimate models. Examples of these packages are MICROFIT, SHAZAM, EVIEWS, PC-GIVE, STAMP, SAS, WinRATS and SPSS. These packages also include spreadsheet programs such as Excel and Quatro Pro although, for forecasting purposes, these programs are less sophisticated than the previous ones. The second are purpose-designed forecasting packages such as Risk, Braincell, Crystal Ball, ForeCalc, ForecastPro, FuziCalc and SmartForecast.

WHICH EXCHANGE RATE?

This book is on exchange rate forecasting. It may, therefore, be useful at this stage to review the concepts of the exchange rate that are encountered in business decision making. We start with the concept of the bilateral exchange rate between two currencies, x and y. The exchange rate may be expressed as x/y to imply the price (in terms of x) of one unit of y. In this case a rise in the exchange rate implies an appreciation of y and a depreciation of x. This exchange rate may be inverted to obtain y/x, the price (in terms of y) of one unit of x. In this case a rise in the exchange rate indicates an appreciation of x and a depreciation of y. In practice, exchange rates are normally and most commonly expressed as the price of one US dollar, that is x/USD.

A bilateral exchange rate may be a spot rate or a forward rate. A spot rate, $S(x/y)$ or simply S, is the exchange rate applicable to transactions involving an immediate delivery of the currencies bought and sold. A forward exchange rate, $F(x/y)$ or simply F, is the exchange rate applicable to transactions involving delivery at some time in the future. Thus, F_t^{t+n} is the exchange rate applicable to a transaction initiated at time t for delivery at $t+n$.

The effective (or multilateral) exchange rate is an index of the value of a currency against several currencies. Let $x_1/y, x_2/y, \ldots, x_m/y$ be the bilateral exchange rates of currency y against the currencies $x_1, x_2, \ldots, x_m$. If there is a base period, 0, then the effective exchange rate of currency y at time t is calculated as

$$e_t = \sum_{i=1}^{m} w_i \left[\frac{(x_i/y)_t}{(x_i/y)_0} \right] \tag{1.2}$$

where w_i is the weight assigned to the exchange rate against currency x_i.

The concept of the real effective exchange rate is important for the evaluation of the economic risk faced by business firms. It is calculated by adjusting the (nominal) effective exchange rate as calculated above for prices. Let p be the price level in the country whose currency is y and $p_1, p_2, \ldots, p_m$ the price levels in the countries whose currencies are $x_1, x_2, \ldots, x_m$. The real effective exchange rate is calculated as

$$r_t = \sum_{i=1}^{m} w_i \left[\frac{(x_i/y)_t}{(x_i/y)_0} \left(\frac{p}{p_i} \right)_t \right] \tag{1.3}$$

where the price levels are measured as indices relative to the base period 0. Obviously, forecasting the real effective exchange rate requires an implicit or explicit forecasting of prices. This book deals mostly with the forecasting of the nominal bilateral exchange rate.

THE EXPECTATIONS FORMATION MECHANISMS

In economic theory a number of specifications have been used to represent the manner whereby agents (investors, and so on) form expectations. These specifications themselves can be used as forecasting models. All of these specifications are presented in terms of the logarithm of the (spot) exchange rate, which is denoted by the lower-case letter s. For this purpose, we shall use the letter E to denote the value expected to prevail in the future. This symbol does not necessarily imply that it is the mathematical expectation (the expected value).

STATIC EXPECTATIONS

We start by defining static expectations. Let the expectations formation mechanism be represented by

$$Es_{t+1} = \alpha s_{t-1} + (1 - \alpha) s_t \tag{1.4}$$

This specification tells us that the expected value of the exchange rate at time $t + 1$ is a weighted average of the current exchange rate and the rate in the previous period. If $\alpha = 0$, then

$$Es_{t+1} = s_t \tag{1.5}$$

which means that the expected value of the exchange rate is the current exchange rate. Thus, expectations are static.

EXTRAPOLATIVE EXPECTATIONS

Extrapolative or bandwagon expectations can be represented by the equation

$$E\Delta s_{t+1} = \beta\Delta s_t, \qquad \beta > 0 \tag{1.6}$$

where $\Delta s_{t+1} = s_{t+1} - s_t$. This specification implies that if a currency is depreciating then agents (investors, and so on) will expect it to continue to depreciate and vice versa. This kind of expectations formation mechanism produces destabilising speculation. If, on the other hand, $\beta < 0$, then the expectations formation mechanism will produce stabilising speculation. This is because the implication of a negative β is that when a currency is depreciating then it is expected to appreciate. The underlying assumption is that when a currency appreciates it is conceived to be overvalued and so it is sold and depreciation follows. This is destabilising speculation.

Another expectations formation mechanism that produces stabilising speculation is represented by the specification

$$E\Delta s_{t+1} = (1-\beta)\Delta s_t + \beta\Delta s_{t-1}, \qquad \beta > 0 \tag{1.7}$$

which is a simple form of a distributed lag specification.

ADAPTIVE EXPECTATIONS

Adaptive expectations, which is one of the oldest mechanisms used in economics, is represented by

$$Es_{t+1} = (1-\gamma)s_t + \gamma Es_t \tag{1.8}$$

where $0 < \gamma < 1$. This specification tells us that the expected exchange rate is a weighted average of the current actual exchange rate and the previous expected value. The specification can also be written as

$$E\Delta s_{t+1} = \gamma(Es_t - s_t) \tag{1.9}$$

which says that the expected change in the exchange rate is a fraction of the current period's error.

REGRESSIVE EXPECTATIONS

The regressive expectations model was popularised by Dornbusch (1976). This specification is written as

$$Es_{t+1} = (1 - \theta)s_t + \theta\bar{s}_t \tag{1.10}$$

where $\bar{s}_t$ is the long-run equilibrium exchange rate and $0 < \theta < 1$ is the speed at which the actual exchange rate converges on the equilibrium rate. The specification can also be written as

$$E\Delta s_{t+1} = -\theta(s_t - \bar{s}_t) \tag{1.11}$$

According to this specification, the expected change in the exchange rate is a fraction of the deviation of the current exchange rate from the equilibrium rate. If the current exchange rate is higher than the equilibrium rate then the exchange rate is expected to fall and vice versa. The long-run equilibrium rate can itself change. It is often assumed that it follows purchasing power parity, which means that it is determined by the inflation differential.

RATIONAL EXPECTATIONS

At one time, the adaptive expectations specification was used extensively in economics. The problem with this expectations formation mechanism is that it allows for systematic errors, that is agents forming expectations adaptively may consistently overestimate or underestimate the exchange rate expected to prevail in the future. Moreover, the adaptive expectations specification (and the other specifications for that matter) tell us that agents form expectations on the basis of the past history of the exchange rate. This excludes two pieces of information that can be useful in forming expectations. The first is the past history of the other factors that affect the exchange rate such as interest rates and inflation rates. The second is expectations concerning these variables. For example, if the Bank of England is expected to run an expansionary monetary policy in the future, then we should expect the pound to depreciate. The adaptive expectations hypothesis does not allow for this consideration, but the rational expectations hypothesis does. In fact, the rational expectations hypothesis implies that agents are rational in the sense that they utilise all available information to form expectations.

The rational expectations hypothesis does not imply that the forecast is necessarily correct. However, it implies that the expectations error is random. Hence, the specification may be written as

$$E(s_{t+1}|\Omega_t) = s_{t+1} + \xi_{t+1} \tag{1.12}$$

where ξ_{t+1} is a white-noise error term realised at $t+1$. Rational expectations thus implies the following: on the basis of the information set available at time t, Ω_t, the expected value of the exchange rate at time $t+1$ will be equal to the actual value plus a random error term (which may be positive or negative). It also tells us that the expected value of the exchange rate should converge on the mathematical expectation or the value generated by the true model. The mathematical expectation or simply the expected value of a random variable is a weighted average of all possible outcomes where the weight assigned to an outcome is equal to its probability.

The concept of rational expectations brings us to the issue of the rationality of forecasting or forecasts. This concept is best illustrated with this example. Suppose that, as part of a survey, you asked two people, an academic economist and a professional economist, to forecast the exchange rate over the next year. The rationality of forecasts requires the forecaster to collect and process all the relevant information. This process is costly, at least in terms of time. For an academic economist who gets paid for teaching and publishing papers, going through this exercise is not worthwhile, and so he would give a forecast from the top of his head, which is not rational. For the academic economist this does not matter because he has got nothing to lose. He is not going to act on the basis of this forecast, neither will his name be exposed as the 'guy with the terribly wrong forecast'. The professional economist, on the other hand, will do what she can, in terms of collecting and processing information, to arrive at what she believes is an optimal forecast. This is a rational forecast. The forecast may be wrong, or it may not be based on all of the information relevant to the forecast, but it is still rational if the economist is unaware of the existence of this information. She would do this because she acts on the basis of this forecast (by, for example, advising foreign exchange dealers) and so her job is at stake here. The academic economist may be aware of the existence of some relevant information but he will not make the effort to take advantage of this information. He may be busy revising a paper for a top journal, which is more important for his career than working out an accurate forecast for a survey. However, things would be completely different if this academic economist was indulging in this exercise as a part of a consultancy assignment. He would then endeavour to produce a rational forecast.

The rationality of forecasting and expectations is normally tested on the basis of survey data. The actual exchange rates are compared with the forecasts provided by the survey to find out if there is a systematic error. Frankel and Froot (1987) conducted one of the most important studies on the rationality of exchange rate forecasting and other issues pertaining to the expectations formation mechanisms. The results of this study reject rational expectations, static expectations and bandwagon expectations. The results also lend support to the proposition that expectations are formed in such a way as to result in stabilising speculation.

STYLISED FACTS ABOUT THE BEHAVIOUR OF EXCHANGE RATES

There are some stylised facts about the behaviour of exchange rates, which have important implications for their forecastibility. These stylised facts pertain to the behaviour of the exchange rate as a univariate time series or in relation to other variables.

The stylised facts are illustrated with graphs based on three data sets. The first data set is used to illustrate the random walk hypothesis. This set contains 600 daily observations on the GBP/USD exchange rate covering the period extending between 23 October 1995 and 6 March 1998. The second data set consists of a sample of pooled cross-section and time series (annual) data covering the period 1990–1996. This data set was obtained from the International Monetary Fund's *World Economic Outlook* (Statistical Appendix, October 1997). These data are on the effective exchange rates and other related variables for a number of countries. The related variables are the inflation rate (measured by changes in the GDP deflator), the current account, the (broad and narrow) money supply, and short-term interest rates. Data for the seven largest industrial countries only are used to describe the relationship between the exchange rate, on the one hand, and the money supply and the interest rate on the other. For the relationship between the exchange rate and either the inflation rate or the current account position, data for 17 countries are used (the big 7 plus 10 European countries). The third set of data covers Germany during the hyperinflationary period of January 1919–July 1923. This set of data is used to illustrate the effect of inflation and monetary growth on the exchange rate under hyperinflation. The price index is the wholesale price index, while the money supply is currency in circulation. This data set was obtained from Holtfrerich (1986).

THE RANDOM WALK HYPOTHESIS

The exchange rate follows approximately a random walk with little or no drift. This means that the period-to-period changes in the exchange rate are random and unpredictable. This proposition is consistent with the efficiency of the foreign exchange market in a weak sense. Figure 1.1 plots the level of the GBP/USD exchange rate using daily data over the period 23 October 1995 to 6 March 1998. The behaviour looks like a random walk with little or no drift. Figure 1.2 plots the corresponding percentage changes which look completely random. In fact the percentage changes resemble in behaviour the random numbers shown in Figure 1.3, which are generated from a standard normal distribution then scaled. Figure 1.4 plots an artificial exchange rate series generated from random numbers by assuming that each random number represents the change in the exchange rate. One can see that the behaviour of this artificial exchange rate series can be mistaken for the behaviour of an actual series. While the percentage changes in the exchange rate look random, the empirical evidence on the hypothesis that the exchange rate follows a random walk is not completely supportive.

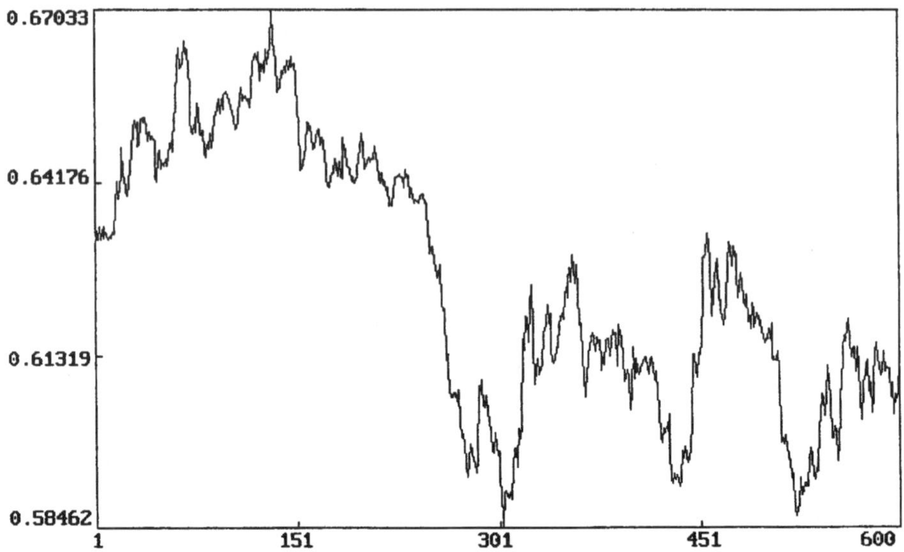

Figure 1.1 The GBP/USD exchange rate (daily data, 23 Oct 1995–6 March 1998)

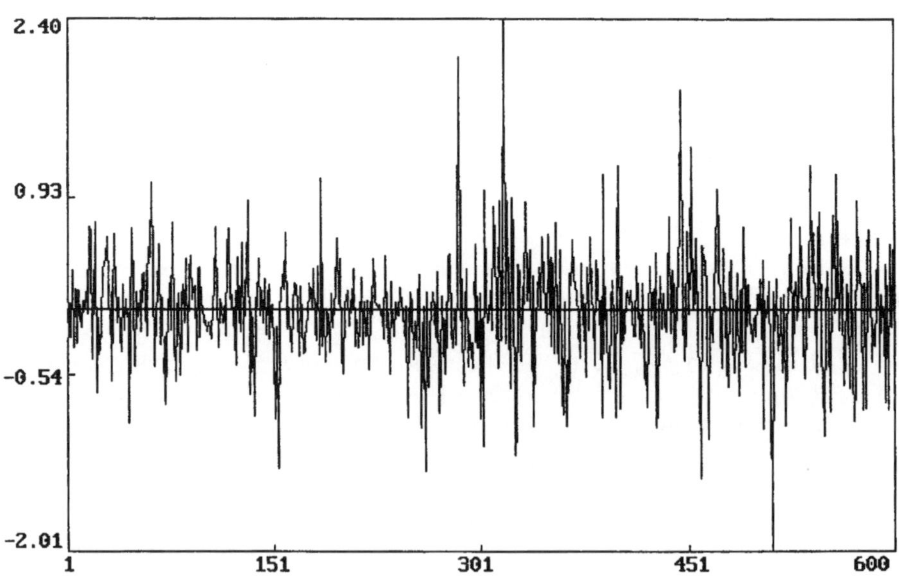

Figure 1.2 Percentage change in the GBP/USD exchange rate (daily data, 23 Oct 1995–6 March 1998)

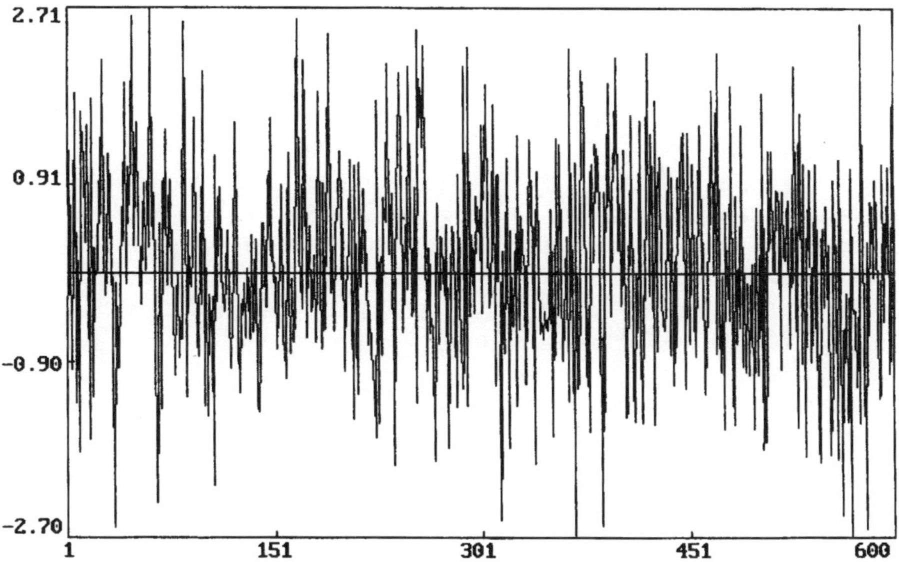

Figure 1.3 Random numbers

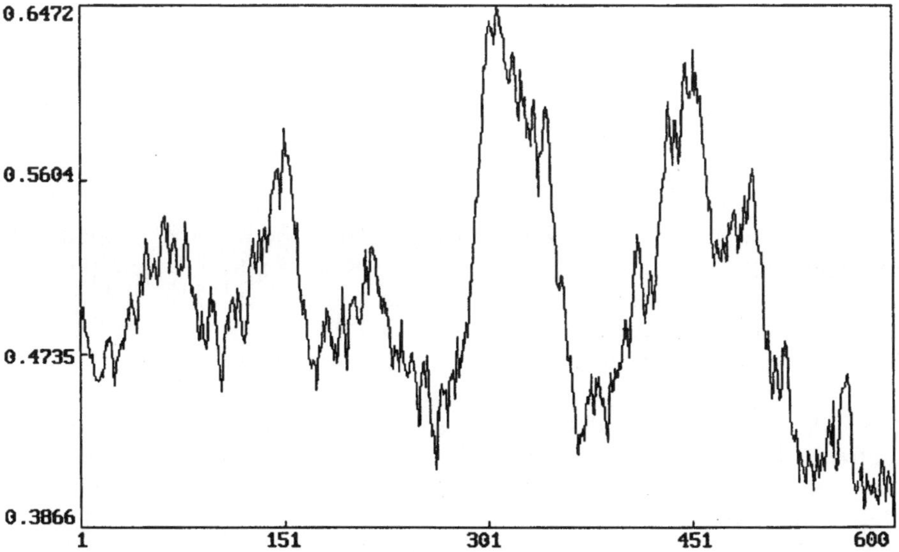

Figure 1.4 An artificial exchange rate series

If the exchange rate follows a random walk process, then by definition it is non-stationary. A stationary time series has a constant mean over time and it tends to fluctuate around this mean value. A non-stationary time series can be made stationary by differencing. This is obvious from the comparison of Figures 1.1 and 1.2. It must be made explicit that exchange rates are non-stationary under a system of floating exchange rates and normal inflationary conditions. In countries experiencing hyperinflation, the domestic currency depreciates so fast that the time series requires differencing twice to become stationary. This means that even the rate of change or the absolute change of the exchange rate is non-stationary. On the other hand, a fixed exchange rate is stationary, at least between two successive realignments.

Other univariate properties that are worthy of examination are normality, symmetry and seasonality, which pertain primarily to the change in the exchange rate. Estimates of the coefficients of skewness and kurtosis for the time series shown in Figure 1.2 provide no indication of deviation from normality and that the frequency distribution is rather symmetric (normality implies symmetry). This finding cannot be generalised, however. Moreover, (nominal) exchange rates rarely show any seasonal pattern. This is why we never hear about a seasonally adjusted exchange rate series.

SPOT AND FORWARD EXCHANGE RATES

Spot and forward exchange rates tend to move in the same direction by approximately the same amount, particularly if the movements are large. The implication of this observation is that it is not advisable to use the forward rate to predict the spot rate expected to prevail in the future, because it is unlikely to beat the random walk model. Again, the empirical evidence on this issue is mixed. This issue is discussed further in Chapter 5.

EXCHANGE RATES AND PRICES

It seems that there is no close correspondence between movements in exchange rates and movements in prices or inflation rates. This proposition casts doubt on the validity of the purchasing power parity (PPP) theory. The available empirical evidence indicates that PPP is valid only in the very long run and for countries experiencing hyperinflation. Figure 1.5 is a scatter diagram of the percentage change in the effective exchange rate on the inflation rate (GDP deflator) based on the second data set described earlier. Obviously, there is little correlation between the two variables. Compare this, however, with Figures 1.6 and 1.7 which show the relationship between the dollar/mark exchange rate and the German wholesale price index. The correlation is strongly negative, which supports PPP. This theory will be described in some detail in Chapter 4.

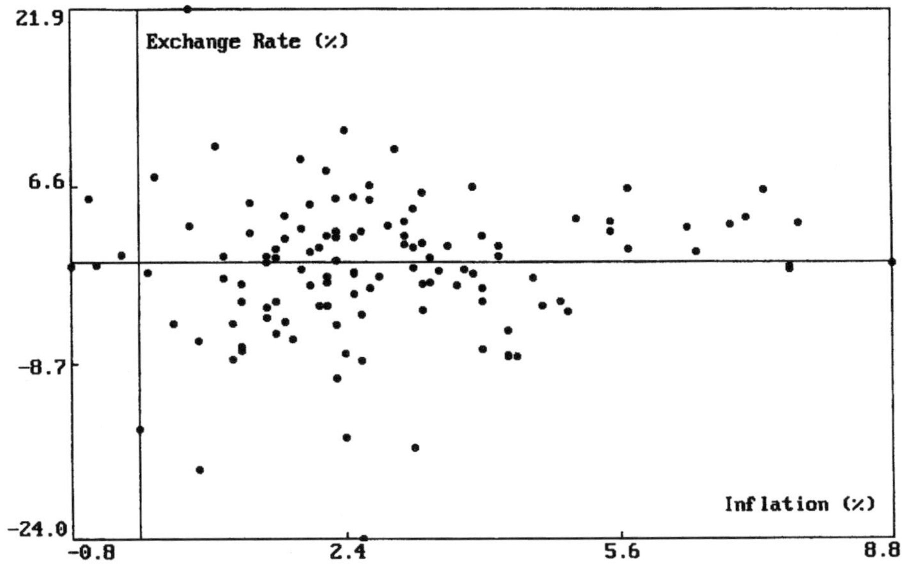

Figure 1.5 A scatter diagram of the change in the effective exchange rate on the inflation rate (pooled data)

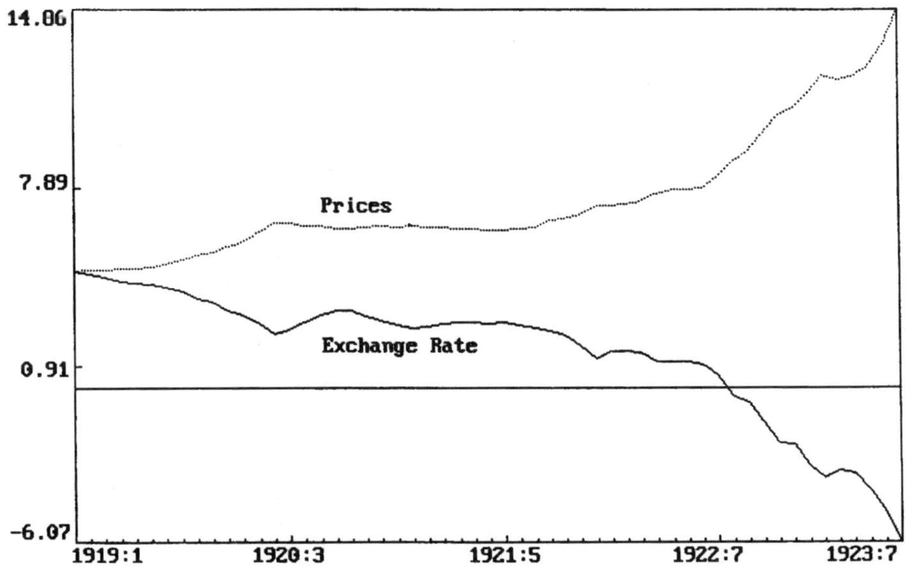

Figure 1.6 The dollar/mark exchange rate and prices (Germany, 1919–1923), logarithmic scale

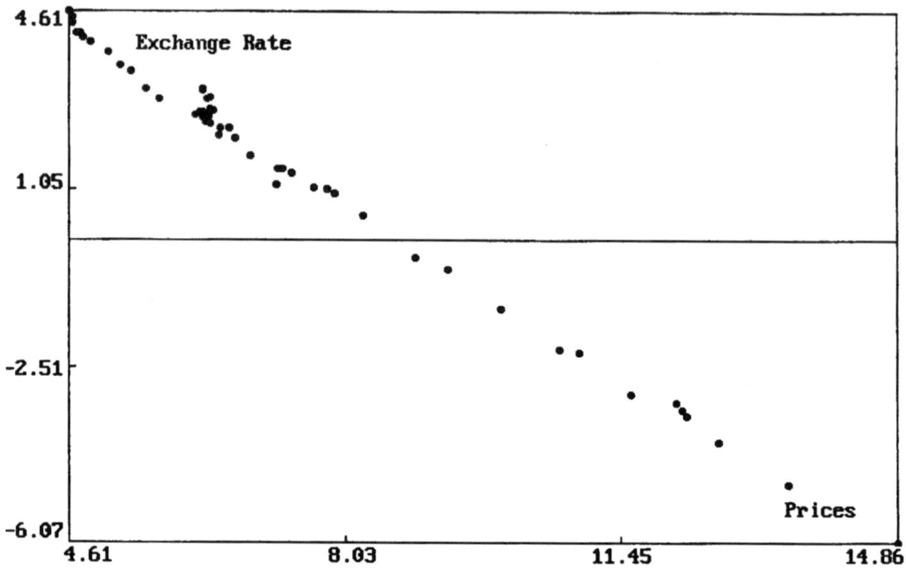

Figure 1.7 A scatter diagram of the dollar/mark exchange rate on prices (Germany, 1919–1923), logarithmic scale

THE EFFECT OF THE CURRENT ACCOUNT

The fourth stylised fact is that there has been a weak general tendency for countries experiencing sharp deterioration in the current account to experience depreciating currencies. For example, the US dollar appreciated considerably in the period 1981–1984 while the current account gap was widening. Figure 1.8 is a scatter diagram of the percentage change in the effective exchange rate on the current account balance. Again, there is little correlation. The relationship between the current account and the exchange rate will be encountered frequently in the discussion of the fundamental models of exchange rates discussed in Chapter 4.

THE EFFECT OF MONETARY GROWTH

Countries that experience rapid expansion of their money supplies also experience rapid depreciation of their currencies. The word 'rapid' must be emphasised here because this proposition seems to be valid for hyperinflation countries (for example, Germany in the 1920s). This proposition is a prediction of the monetary model of exchange rate determination that will be discussed in Chapter 4. Figures 1.9 and 1.10 show the relationship

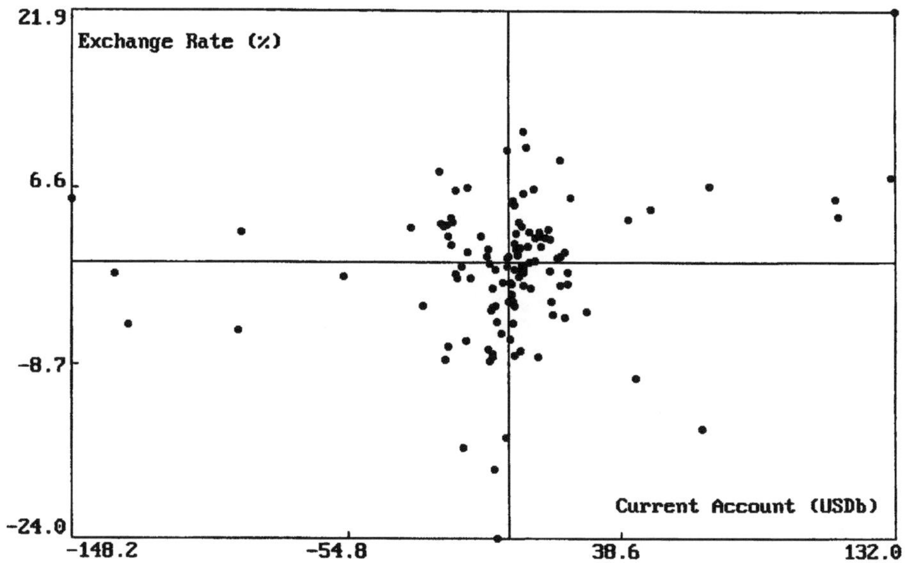

Figure 1.8 A scatter diagram of the change in the effective exchange rate on the current account position (pooled data)

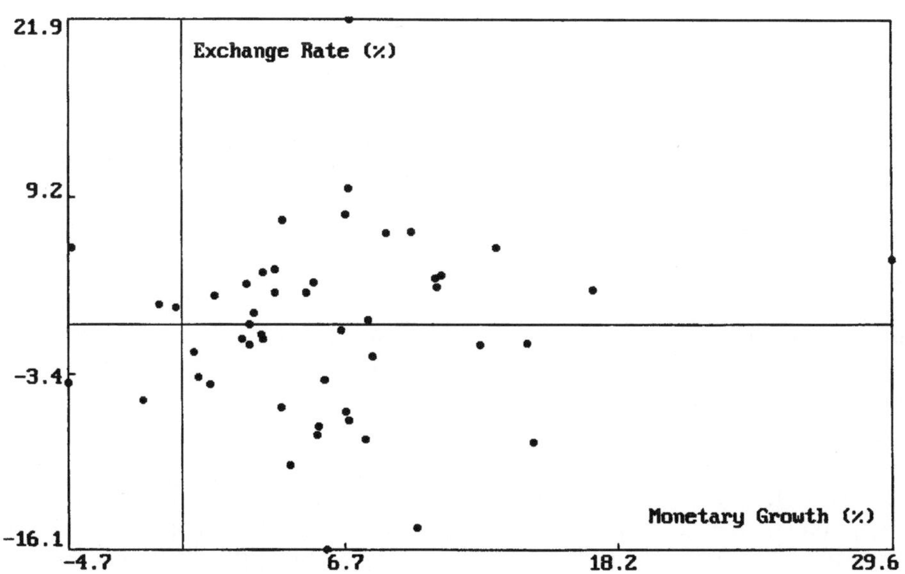

Figure 1.9 A scatter diagram of the change in the effective exchange rate on the monetary (M1) growth rate (pooled data)

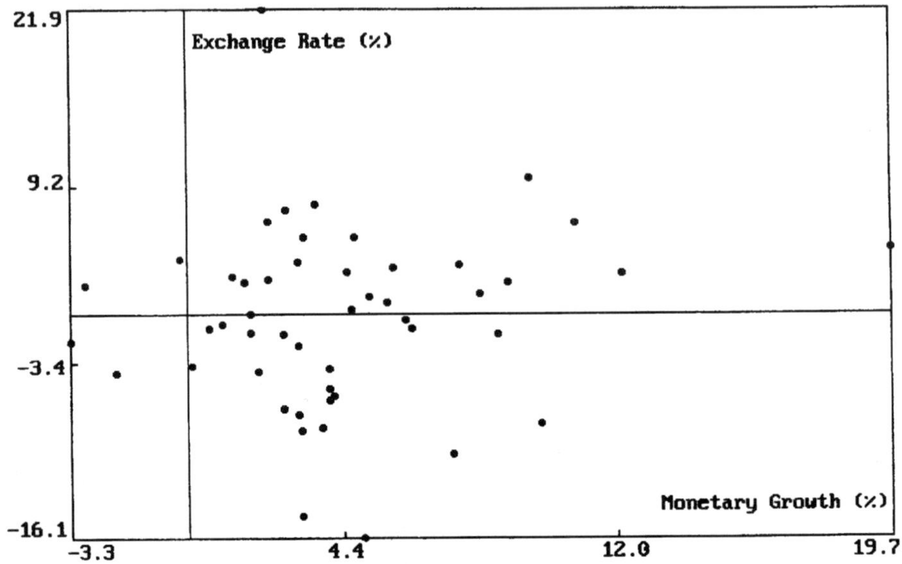

Figure 1.10 A scatter diagram of the change in the effective exchange rate on the monetary (M2) growth rate (pooled data)

between changes in the effective exchange rate and the rates of growth of narrow and broad money using a sample of pooled data from the period 1990–1996. Obviously, the correlation is very weak. The story told by Figure 1.11 is completely different, however. It shows how closely negative was the relationship between the money supply (defined as currency in circulation) and the mark/dollar exchange rate during the 1920s.

THE EFFECT OF INTEREST RATES

Exchange rates also do not seem to follow the prediction of uncovered interest parity in the sense that currencies offering higher interest rates tend to depreciate (with a time lag). In fact, common sense tells us that it should be the other way round, in that currencies offering higher interest rates tend to attract capital flows and consequently appreciate. The two stories are reconcilable, however. When the interest rate on a currency rises relative to the interest rate on another currency, the former tends to appreciate. As it appreciates further over time, investors start to believe that it is overvalued, and so they sell it, leading to its depreciation. Figure 1.12 shows that the relationship between the effective exchange rate and the interest rate is not that strong.

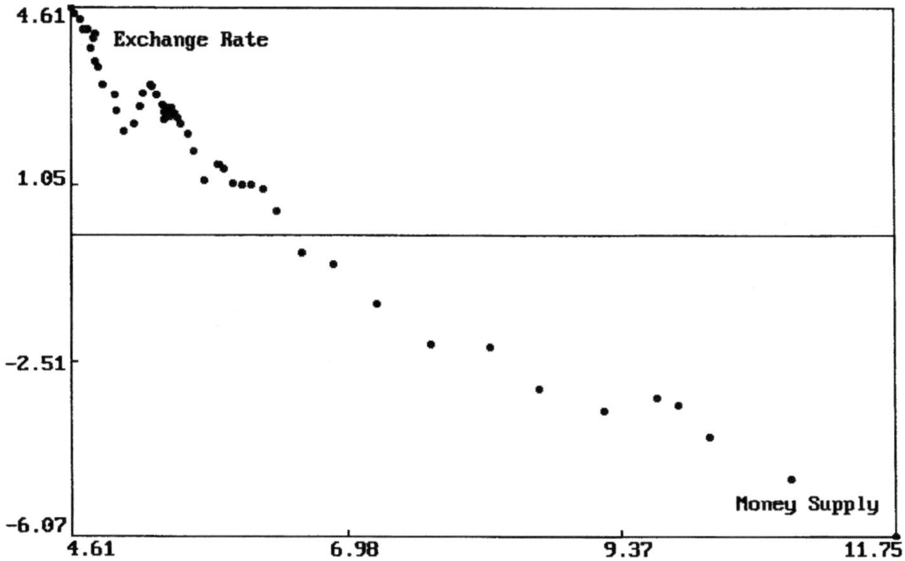

Figure 1.11 A scatter diagram of the dollar/mark exchange rate on the money supply (Germany, 1919–1923), logarithmic scale

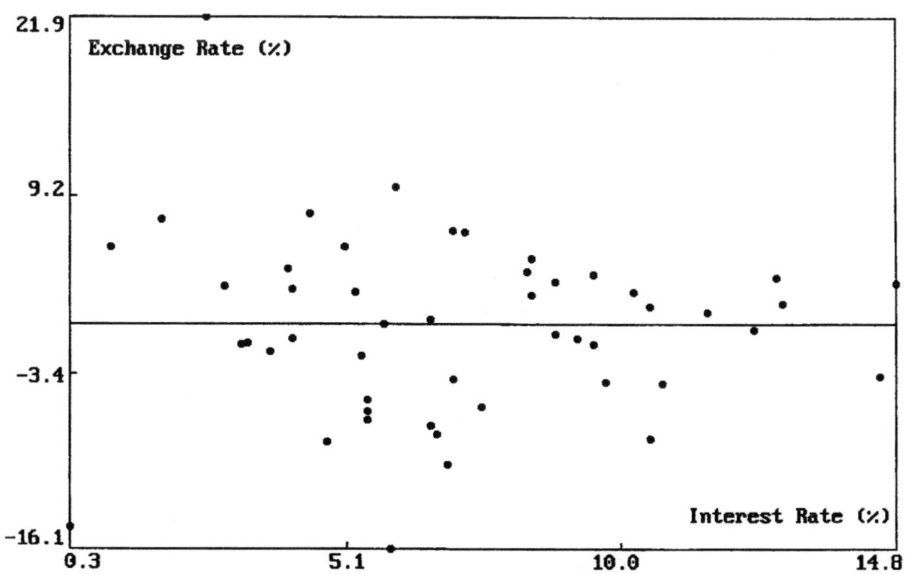

Figure 1.12 A scatter diagram of the change in the effective exchange rate on the interest rate (pooled data)

THE EFFECT OF NEWS

Finally, changes in exchange rates are thought to be unpredictable because they are determined by news, that is the unanticipated changes in the fundamental factors determining the exchange rate. Exchange rates are supposed to be as volatile or as stable as macroeconomic fundamentals. Some economists have even put forward the view that exchange rates move inexplicably, that they overshoot the overshooting equilibrium and that most short-term variability seems to be unrelated to news. Hence, they put forward the proposition that the proportion of exchange rate changes that are forecastable by the forward rate, the interest differential, survey data or models based on macroeconomic fundamentals appears to be not just low but almost zero. Frankel and Dornbusch (1988) argue that exchange rates must be reacting to something else, either economic factors that are unknown to the economist, as the equilibrium theorists will have it, or to irrelevant noise.

FINAL REMARKS

The implications of the stylised facts concerning the behaviour of the exchange rate are certainly not very sanguine as far as exchange rate forecasters are concerned. These stylised facts can hardly be the basis for writing a book on exchange rate forecasting! However, things are not really that bad if we take into account the following points and understand the caveats involved in this discussion.

The first point is that the figures on the relationship between the exchange rate and the variables discussed above may be misleading because they are pooled cross-section and time series data. Some of these relationships may, under certain conditions, be very useful as the basis of forecasting models. For example, the interest rate–exchange rate relationship can deliver a better message than what is delivered by Figure 1.12 if it is observed on a bilateral basis for specific currency combinations over a particular period of time. For some currencies the relationship works better if the nominal interest rate differential is replaced by the real interest rate differential. These relationships, it seems, cannot be generalised across time and countries but can be found useful in some cases. Currencies are affected differently by different factors over different periods of time. The relative sensitivity of the Australian dollar to interest rates and commodity prices varies considerably over time. In the second half of the 1980s it was sensitive to the interest rate factor, as it gained a lot of strength from a positive interest differential. In the 1990s, it has been more sensitive to commodity prices.

The second point is that an exchange rate is the price of a currency in terms of one or more currencies. Thus, this variable is affected by domestic and foreign factors. Some currencies are more sensitive than others to domestic factors and vice versa. The available evidence shows that the relative impact of international and domestic news varies considerably from one currency to another (see, for example, Dungey 1998).

Third, it is very important not to judge the relationship between the exchange rate and one determining factor while overlooking the role played simultaneously by other factors. For example, we may believe that the interest rate is an important factor for exchange rate determination, but an observation of the data does not reveal the presence of strong correlation between the two variables. This may not necessarily mean that the interest rate is not important. The lack of correlation may be due to the influence of other factors that work on the exchange rate in the opposite direction over the sample period. Some of these factors may be unquantifiable, which makes our scepticism of exchange rate forecasting even more profound.

Finally, it is true that the available formal empirical evidence on the behaviour of the exchange rate in relation to its past history and to other explanatory variables is not that favourable. However, some of these relationships have been shown to work reasonably well, and so we should not dismiss the viability of forecasting exchange rates altogether. We need exchange rate forecasting whether we like or not. If these relationships can help us arrive at forecasts that are less erroneous than otherwise (hence leading to better decisions) then exchange rate forecasting is an endeavour that we must not abandon. It remains to be seen for what specific reasons exchange rate forecasting is needed. This is the subject matter of the next chapter.

2: Exchange Rate Forecasting as an Input in the Decision-making Process

INTRODUCTION

Some economists claim (perhaps justifiably) that, in theory, it is difficult or even impossible to forecast exchange rates. In practice, the track record of exchange rate forecasters has not been so spectacular and perhaps even appalling. Why then do we need and want formal exchange rate forecasting? Why do we not just toss a coin and save the money and time spent on generating forecasts? The answer is simple: whether we like it or not decision making in business firms in general, and in international business firms in particular, requires exchange rate forecasting. It is invariably the case that, in situations requiring exchange rate forecasting, there is so much at stake that we are bound to feel uneasy about tossing a coin. How would a financial manager feel about making a decision on a position worth USD2 billion by tossing a coin? Not very happy, I suppose. The need for exchange rate forecasting to make (crucial) decisions is not limited to business firms. Government analysts and officials often encounter the same problem in their pursuit of economic policy.

In this chapter we describe some of the situations in which exchange rate forecasting is needed as an input in the decision-making process. Since forecasting is a formal method of generating expectations, it can be shown that forecasting is needed whenever a decision rule involves the expected exchange rate or the expected change in the exchange rate. The list of situations discussed in this chapter is not exhaustive. Moreover, most of these situations pertain to financial decision rules.

In the following analysis the assumption of risk neutrality is made: it is assumed that agents are indifferent between holding domestic and foreign assets and liabilities as long as the underlying prices, rates of return and financial costs are similar. Relaxing this assumption by introducing the risk premium (that is, assuming risk aversion) does not make any difference for the conclusions reached in this chapter on the need for forecasting. The decision rules can be modified by the introduction of the risk premium but they will still convey the same message: exchange rate forecasting is needed to act upon the decision rules.

The notation used in the following analysis is as follows. The letter E is used to denote the value of the underlying variable expected to hold in the future or the forecast value. It does not necessarily imply the mathematical expected value. This operator may be used with or without parentheses such that EX or $E(X)$ mean the expected value of X. The spot exchange rate between x and y may be denoted (x/y), $S(x/y)$ or simply S. The expected change in the spot exchange rate between t and $t+n$ is $\dot{S}_{t+n}(x/y)$ or $\dot{S}_{t+n}$. The forward exchange rate at time t for delivery at time $t+i$ is denoted $F_t^{t+i}(x/y)$, F_t^{t+i} or simply F. The corresponding forward spread is denoted $f_t^{t+i}(x/y)$, f_t^{t+i} or f. Profit realised from any operation is denoted π. Interest rates on currencies x and y are denoted i_x and i_y respectively. The subscripts b and a denote the bid and offer rates respectively. Finally, t denotes the present time while $t+n$ denotes a future date. Therefore, n is the forecasting horizon, which is also equal to the maturity of the underlying assets and liabilities or the holding period. Forecasting pertains to the exchange rate at time $t+n$, that is S_{t+n}, or to the path followed by the exchange rate between t and $t+n$. In the following analysis, the words 'expectation' and 'forecasting' may be used interchangeably.

SPOT SPECULATION

Speculation is the deliberate assumption of risk to obtain profit. In the case of spot speculation the risk arises from changes in the spot exchange rate. We will, for the purpose of the following analysis, ignore the interest rate factor by, for example, assuming that the interest rates on the two currencies are equal. This assumption is relaxed later when we discuss uncovered interest arbitrage.

THE SIMPLE CASE

Spot speculation entails selling an amount, K, of currency x, which is expected to depreciate, against currency y, which is expected to appreciate, and then reversing the operation in the future. Suppose that the present time is t such that the exchange rate is $(x/y)_t$. If y is expected to appreciate in the future such that $E(x/y)_{t+n} > (x/y)_t$, then a decision will be taken to sell an amount, K, of x to obtain $K/(x/y)_t$ of y. If the expectation (or the forecast) turns out to be correct such that $(x/y)_{t+n} > (x/y)_t$, then the amount $K/(x/y)_t$ of y is converted into x at $t+n$ to obtain $K(x/y)_{t+n}/(x/y)_t$. The net profit (in terms of currency x) is

$$\pi = K\left[\frac{(x/y)_{t+n}}{(x/y)_t} - 1\right] \tag{2.1}$$

where the term in square brackets is the percentage change in the spot exchange rate. Since $(x/y)_{t+n} > (x/y)_t$, it follows that $\pi > 0$. Notice that the decision is based on the forecast that y will appreciate which is represented by the inequality $E(x/y)_{t+n} > (x/y)_t$.

This forecast pertains to the direction of the change in the exchange rate only, that is it indicates that currency y will appreciate without saying by how much. Suppose now that the forecast has a quantitative element as well, such that $E(x/y)_{t+n} = \theta(x/y)_t$ where $\theta > 1$. If the forecast turns out to be accurate such that $(x/y)_{t+n} = \theta(x/y)_t$, and it is acted upon, then the resulting profit will be given by

$$\pi = K(\theta - 1) \tag{2.2}$$

Again, $\pi > 0$ because $\theta > 1$. The difference in this case is that the forecast does not only indicate that y will appreciate and that profit will be made but it also indicates the extent of the appreciation and hence the magnitude of the profit.

What if the forecast is not accurate, magnitude wise, such that $(x/y)_{t+n} = \lambda(x/y)_t$ where $\theta > \lambda > 1$? This means that the exchange rate has risen as the forecast indicated but not to the same extent. In this case profit will be lower, since $0 < K(\lambda - 1) < K(\theta - 1)$.

THE FORECAST AS A PROBABILITY DISTRIBUTION

If the forecast is given in terms of a probability distribution then the situation becomes as follows. Suppose that there are q forecasts given by $E(x/y)_{t+n,i}$ each materialising with a probability p_i. Consider two forecasts, $E(x/y)_{t+n,j}$ and $E(x/y)_{t+n,k}$ such that $E(x/y)_{t+n,j} < (x/y)_t < E(x/y)_{t+n,k}$. If the decision maker acts on the basis of the lower forecast, $E(x/y)_{t+n,j}$, which materialises with a probability p_j, then a decision will be taken to buy currency x and sell currency y since the forecast indicates that the former will appreciate. Conversely, if the decision maker acts on the basis of the higher forecast, $E(x/y)_{t+n,k}$, which materialises with a probability p_k, then a decision will be taken to buy currency y and sell currency x since the forecast indicates that the former will appreciate. If the decision is based on one forecast, then this naturally should be the forecast with the higher probability. Thus, if $p_j > p_k$ a decision will be taken to buy x and sell y and vice versa. The outcome will depend the deviation of the actual exchange rate at time $t + n$ from the forecast upon which the decision is made.

More appropriately, the decision is made on the basis of a weighted average of the forecasts where the weights are the probabilities. This is given by

$$E(x/y)_{t+n} = \sum_{i=1}^{q} E(x/y)_{t+n,i} \tag{2.3}$$

The outcome will depend on the actual exchange rate at $t + n$ in the same manner as before.

INTRODUCING THE BID–OFFER SPREAD

We will now introduce the bid–offer spread. Let the bid and offer exchange rates at time t be $(x/y)_{b,t}$ and $(x/y)_{a,t}$, such that

$$(x/y)_{a,t} = (1+m)(x/y)_{b,t} \tag{2.4}$$

where m is the bid–offer spread expressed as a percentage of the bid rate. In the presence of the bid–offer spread, the speculator buys currency y at the higher offer rate and sells it at the lower bid rate. If the forecast bid and offer rates are $E(x/y)_{b,t+n}$ and $E(x/y)_{a,t+n}$, and assuming that there is no change in the bid–offer spread between time t and time $t+n$, then

$$E(x/y)_{a,t+n} = (1+m)E(x/y)_{b,t+n} \tag{2.5}$$

To act on the basis of the forecast, a decision to buy y and sell x at time t will be taken if y is forecast to appreciate such that $E(x/y)_{b,t+n} > (x/y)_{a,t}$. If the forecast is accurate such that $(x/y)_{b,t+n} > (x/y)_{a,t}$ then the speculator can sell currency y at time $t+n$ at $(x/y)_{b,t+n}$ to realise profit (per unit of y) which is given by

$$\pi = (x/y)_{b,t+n} - (x/y)_{a,t} \tag{2.6}$$

or

$$\pi = (x/y)_{b,t+n} - (1+m)(x/y)_{b,t} \tag{2.7}$$

The profit realised is positive if

$$(x/y)_{b,t+n} - (1+m)(x/y)_{b,t} > 0 \tag{2.8}$$

or if

$$\frac{(x/y)_{b,t+n}}{(x/y)_{b,t}} > 1+m \tag{2.9}$$

which means that the operation will be profitable only if the percentage rise in the bid exchange rate is greater than the bid–offer spread. The forecast in this case must not only indicate the direction but also the magnitude of change. The decision to buy y and sell x at time t will be taken only if

$$\frac{E(x/y)_{b,t+n}}{(x/y)_{b,t}} > 1+m \tag{2.10}$$

Conversely, the decision to buy x and sell y at time t will be taken if

$$E(x/y)_{a,t+n} < (x/y)_{b,t} \tag{2.11}$$

If the expectation is realised such that $(x/y)_{a,t+n} < (x/y)_{b,t}$ then the speculator can sell currency x (buy currency y) at $(x/y)_{b,t+n}$ to realise profit that is given by

$$\pi = (x/y)_{b,t} - (x/y)_{a,t+n} \tag{2.12}$$

or

$$\pi = (x/y)_{b,t} - (1+m)(x/y)_{b,t+n} \tag{2.13}$$

For this profit to be positive, the following condition must be satisfied:

$$(1+m)(x/y)_{b,t+n} - (x/y)_{b,t} < 0 \tag{2.14}$$

or

$$\frac{(x/y)_{b,t+n}}{(x/y)_{b,t}} < \frac{1}{1+m} \tag{2.15}$$

which means that the operation will be profitable only if the bid exchange rate falls by a factor that is related to the bid–offer spread. Again, the forecast must indicate the direction and the magnitude of change. The decision to buy x and sell y will be taken only if

$$\frac{E(x/y)_{b,t+n}}{(x/y)_{b,t}} < \frac{1}{1+m} \tag{2.16}$$

The matter becomes more complicated if the bid–offer spread also changes between t and $t+n$. So let

$$(x/y)_{a,t} = (1+m_t)(x/y)_{b,t} \tag{2.17}$$

and

$$E(x/y)_{a,t+n} = [1+E(m_{t+n})]E(x/y)_{b,t+n} \tag{2.18}$$

A decision to buy x and sell y will be taken if

$$[1+E(m_{t+n})]E(x/y)_{b,t+n} < (x/y)_{b,t} \tag{2.19}$$

For this operation to be profitable, the following condition must be satisfied:

$$\frac{E(x/y)_{b,t+n}}{(x/y)_{b,t}} < \frac{1}{1+E(m_{t+n})} \tag{2.20}$$

which means that the change in the bid–offer spread must also be forecast.

UNCOVERED INTEREST ARBITRAGE

In describing spot speculation we ignored interest rates as parameters in the decision rule. We will now introduce interest rates. The decision rule described in the previous section is to buy a currency that is expected to appreciate and sell it later when it does. Suppose now that this is expected to happen at time $t+n$. When currency y is bought at time t and held until time $t+n$ the amount will not be held as idle (that is, as non-interest-bearing cash). Rather, it will be held as a deposit (or another short-term asset) earning the nominal interest rate i_y. The opportunity cost of holding currency y is the interest lost on holding currency x. If the position in y is financed by borrowing currency x, then there is an actual cost in the form of the interest paid to borrow currency x. If the interest rate factor is taken into account, the decision will not be taken unless currency y is expected to appreciate by more than the interest rate differential (the interest rate on currency x minus the interest rate on currency y).

Uncovered interest arbitrage is an operation that aims at making profit by utilising the interest rate differential on two currencies while paying attention to the expected change in the exchange rate. It is 'uncovered' because the long position (the position in the currency that is bought) is not covered but rather left open, which implies exposure to foreign exchange risk. This is why a decision on uncovered arbitrage requires exchange rate forecasting.

In the following analysis the interest rates are observed at time t, covering the period between t and $t+n$. The time subscript on i_x and i_y is, therefore, t: it is deleted for simplicity. To indulge in uncovered interest arbitrage by taking a short position on x and a long position on y the following steps must be followed. At time t, an amount, K, of currency x is borrowed at i_x for the period between t and $t+n$. This amount of currency x is converted into y at the current exchange rate, $(x/y)_t$, to obtain $K/(x/y)_t$ units of currency y. This amount of currency y is invested at i_y for the period between t and $t+n$. At time $t+n$, the amount obtained by investing in currency y (principal and interest) is $K(1+i_y)/(x/y)_t$. This amount is known with certainty at time t because it depends on $(x/y)_t$ and i_y, both of which are known then. What is not known in advance is the value of this amount in terms of currency x since it depends on the exchange rate expected to prevail at $t+n$, $(x/y)_{t+n}$. The expected value of this amount is $K(1+i_y)E(x/y)_{t+n}/(x/y)_t$. What also happens at $t+n$ is that the amount of x borrowed at time t and the accumulated interest must be repaid. This amount is equal to $K(1+i_x)$, which is known at t. Hence, the expected net profit is

$$E\pi = \frac{K(1+i_y)E(x/y)_{t+n}}{(x/y)_t} - K(1+i_x) \tag{2.21}$$

For this profit to be positive, in which case the decision to indulge in arbitrage is taken, the following condition must be satisfied:

$$\frac{E(x/y)_{t+n}}{(x/y)_t}\left[\frac{1+i_y}{1+i_x}\right] > 1 \tag{2.22}$$

which shows that the decision rule involves the expected exchange rate. If $S = x/y$, the underlying decision rule can be written as

$$\frac{ES_{t+n}}{S_t}\left[\frac{1+i_y}{1+i_x}\right] > 1 \tag{2.23}$$

By definition

$$\frac{ES_{t+n}}{S_t} = 1 + E\dot{S}_{t+n} \tag{2.24}$$

where $E\dot{S}_{t+n}$ is the expected change in the exchange rate during the time interval between t and $t+n$. It follows that the decision rule can be simplified to the following. A profitable uncovered arbitrage operation can be implemented by borrowing x and investing in y (going short on x and long on y) if

$$E\dot{S}_{t+n} > i_x - i_y \tag{2.25}$$

which tells us that uncovered arbitrage from x to y is profitable if the expected percentage change in the exchange rate is greater than the interest rate differential. If the forecast turns out to be accurate such that $E\dot{S}_{t+n} = \dot{S}_{t+n}$, then the profit made (as a percentage rate of return) will be equal to

$$\pi = \dot{S}_{t+n} - (i_x - i_y) \tag{2.26}$$

It is important to remember that the interest rates are known at time t. What is not known is the change in the exchange rate between t and $t+n$ because it depends on the exchange rate at $t+n$, which is not known at time t. This is where forecasting comes in. Table 2.1 shows the conditions under which a decision will be taken to indulge in uncovered interest arbitrage.

Notice that if the configuration of the expected change in the exchange rate and the interest differential is such that $E\dot{S}_{t+n} < i_x - i_y$, then uncovered arbitrage is still profitable. In this case however, a short position is taken on y and a long position is taken on x. If $E\dot{S}_{t+n} = i_x - i_y$, then uncovered interest parity (UIP) holds and arbitrage is not profitable. This is because arbitrage is triggered by the violation of an equilibrium condition, which in this case is UIP. A qualifying condition may be required for uncovered arbitrage to be profitable. For example, if the interest rate on y is higher than the interest rate on x, then uncovered arbitrage will be profitable as long as currency y appreciates or remains unchanged. In this case no qualifying condition is required. If currency y depreciates, then a qualifying condition for profitable arbitrage from x to y is that the latter depreciates by a smaller percentage than the interest rate differential. It is important to notice the following. The first column in Table 2.1 shows whether the interest differential (which is known at time t) is positive or negative. The second column shows the expected change in the exchange rate between t and $t+n$ which is unknown at time t. This is where exchange rate forecasting comes in.

Table 2.1 Conditions for profitable uncovered arbitrage

Interest rates	$E\dot{S}_{t+n}$	*Qualifying condition*	*Profitable arbitrage?*	*Short position*	*Long position*
$i_x < i_y$	$E\dot{S}_{t+n} > 0$	—	Yes	x	y
$i_x < i_y$	$E\dot{S}_{t+n} = 0$	—	Yes	x	y
$i_x < i_y$	$E\dot{S}_{t+n} < 0$	$\lvert E\dot{S}_{t+n}\rvert < \lvert i_x - i_y\rvert$	Yes	x	y
$i_x < i_y$	$E\dot{S}_{t+n} < 0$	$\lvert E\dot{S}_{t+n}\rvert > \lvert i_x - i_y\rvert$	Yes	y	x
$i_x < i_y$	$E\dot{S}_{t+n} < 0$	$E\dot{S}_{t+n} = i_x - i_y$	No*	—	—
$i_x = i_y$	$E\dot{S}_{t+n} > 0$	—	Yes	x	y
$i_x = i_y$	$E\dot{S}_{t+n} = 0$	—	No*	—	—
$i_x = i_y$	$E\dot{S}_{t+n} < 0$	—	Yes	y	x
$i_x > i_y$	$E\dot{S}_{t+n} > 0$	$E\dot{S}_{t+n} > i_x - i_y$	Yes	x	y
$i_x > i_y$	$E\dot{S}_{t+n} > 0$	$E\dot{S}_{t+n} < i_x - i_y$	Yes	y	x
$i_x > i_y$	$E\dot{S}_{t+n} > 0$	$E\dot{S}_{t+n} = i_x - i_y$	No*	—	—
$i_x > i_y$	$E\dot{S}_{t+n} = 0$	—	Yes	y	x
$i_x > i_y$	$E\dot{S}_{t+n} < 0$	—	Yes	y	x

* No arbitrage because UIP holds.

UNCOVERED ARBITRAGE IN THE PRESENCE OF BID–OFFER SPREAD

We now reconsider the uncovered arbitrage decision rule by taking into account the bid–offer spreads in both exchange and interest rates. Remember that a price taker in the foreign exchange market buys at the (higher) offer exchange rate and sells at the (lower) bid exchange rate of the market maker. A price taker in the money market borrows at the (higher) offer interest rate and lends at the (lower) bid interest rate of the market maker.

Uncovered arbitrage from x to y would, in this case, involve the following steps. At time t, an amount, K, of currency x is borrowed at the offer rate, i_{xa}. This amount is converted into currency y, buying it at the offer exchange rate, $S_{a,t}$, to obtain $K/S_{a,t}$ units of y. This amount is invested at the bid interest rate on y, i_{yb}. The foreign currency value of the invested amount at $t+n$ is $(K/S_{a,t})(1+i_{yb})$. At time $t+n$, the value of this amount in terms of currency x is $[KES_{b,t+n}/S_{a,t}](1+i_{yb})$. The value of the loan plus interest to be paid at $t+n$ is $K(1+i_{xa})$. The expected net profit on this operation is the difference between the amount expected to be received at $t+n$ and the amount borrowed plus interest. Thus, the expected profit is given by

$$E\pi = \frac{KES_{b,t+n}}{S_{a,t}}(1+i_{yb}) - K(1+i_{xa}) \tag{2.27}$$

For this profit to be positive

$$\frac{ES_{b,t+n}}{S_{a,t}}(1+i_{yb}) - (1+i_{xa}) > 0 \tag{2.28}$$

or

$$\frac{ES_{b,t+n}}{S_{b,t}(1+m)} > \frac{(1+i_{xa})}{(1+i_{yb})} \tag{2.29}$$

Thus

$$(1+E\dot{S}_{b,t+n})(1+i_{yb}) > (1+m)(1+i_{xa}) \tag{2.30}$$

By simplifying we obtain an approximate condition which implies the following decision rule: uncovered arbitrage from x to y is profitable if

$$E\dot{S}_{b,t+n} > i_{xa} - i_{yb} + m \tag{2.31}$$

It can be similarly demonstrated that uncovered arbitrage can be profitable by going short on y and long on x if

$$E\dot{S}_{a,t+n} < i_{xb} - i_{ya} - m \tag{2.32}$$

The conditions stated in Table 2.1 can be adjusted accordingly. The conditions can also be adjusted to allow for changes in the bid–offer spreads between t and $t+n$. The message, however, is essentially the same. The expected change in the exchange rate is a crucial factor in this decision-making process.

SPOT-FORWARD SPECULATION

Spot-forward speculation involves operations in both the spot and forward markets. Let F_t^{t+n} be the forward rate applicable to a forward contract initiated at time t for delivery at time $t+n$. If a speculator believes that the spot exchange rate prevailing at time $t+n$ will be higher than the forward rate then he will react by buying currency y forward at time t and selling it spot at time $t+n$ when the forward contract matures. The speculator will do this if

$$ES_{t+n}(x/y) > F_t^{t+n}(x/y) \tag{2.33}$$

By dividing both sides of the inequality by $S_t(x/y)$, we obtain

$$E\dot{S}_{t+n}(x/y) > f_t^{t+n}(x/y) \tag{2.34}$$

where f is the forward spread measured as the difference between the forward and spot rates as a percentage of the spot rate. Thus, the decision rule involves forecasting the spot exchange at time $t+n$ or the percentage change in the spot exchange rate between t and $t+n$. If the forecast is accurate such that $ES_{t+n}(x/y) = S_{t+n}(x/y)$, then profit (in terms of currency x) per unit of currency y is given by

$$\pi = S_{t+n}(x/y) - F_t^{t+n}(x/y) \tag{2.35}$$

If, on the other hand, the speculator believes that the spot rate at $t+n$ will be lower than the forward rate, then he will respond by selling currency y forward at t and buying it spot at $t+n$. Hence, the condition to indulge in spot-forward speculation is

$$ES_{t+n}(x/y) < F_t^{t+n}(x/y) \tag{2.36}$$

or

$$E\dot{S}_{t+n}(x/y) < f_t^{t+n}(x/y) \tag{2.37}$$

If the forecast is accurate such that $ES_{t+n}(x/y) = S_{t+n}(x/y)$, then profit (per unit of y) is given by

$$\pi = F_t^{t+n}(x/y) - S_{t+n}(x/y) \tag{2.38}$$

SPOT-FORWARD SPECULATION IN THE PRESENCE OF BID–OFFER SPREADS

If the bid–offer spreads in the spot and forward rates are taken into account then the problem becomes the following. If currency y is expected to appreciate, a speculator will buy it forward at the offer forward rate and sell it spot at the expected bid spot rate. Hence, the condition necessary to indulge in spot-forward speculation is

$$ES_{t+n}(x/y)_b > F_t^{t+n}(x/y)_a \tag{2.39}$$

By definition

$$F_t^{t+n}(x/y)_a = (1+m)F_t^{t+n}(x/y)_b \tag{2.40}$$

where m in this case is the bid–offer spread on the forward rate. Therefore, the condition becomes

$$ES_{t+n}(x/y)_b > (1+m)F_t^{t+n}(x/y)_b \tag{2.41}$$

The expected value of the profit is

$$E\pi = ES_{t+n}(x/y)_b - (1+m)F_t^{t+n}(x/y)_b \tag{2.42}$$

which is positive when

$$E\dot{S}_{t+n}(x/y)_b > f_t^{t+n}(x/y)_b + m \tag{2.43}$$

That is when the bid exchange rate is expected to rise by more than the sum of the forward spread and the bid–offer spread on the (bid) forward rate. Similar conditions can be derived for speculating by selling y forward at t. Allowance can also be made for changes in the bid–offer spreads between t and $t+n$.

FORWARD SPECULATION

It is possible to speculate by combining two offsetting forward transactions contracted at two different points in time but for the same delivery date, that is by using two forward contracts with two different maturities. Consider two futures contracts maturing at time $t+2$: one is a two-period contract initiated at time t to mature at time $t+2$ and the other is a one-period contract initiated at time $t+1$ to mature at time $t+2$. At time t, the speculator will indulge in forward speculation, by taking a long position on y, if

$$EF_{t+1}^{t+2} > F_t^{t+2} \tag{2.44}$$

where F_t^{t+2} is the two-period forward rate applicable to a forward contract initiated at t to mature at $t+2$ and F_{t+1}^{t+2} is the one-period forward rate applicable to a forward contract initiated at $t+1$ for delivery at $t+2$, both of which are measured as x/y. Thus, EF_{t+1}^{t+2} is the one-period forward rate expected to prevail at $t+1$. If this condition is satisfied, then the speculator can make profit by buying currency y on the two-period contract at t and selling the one-period contract at $t+1$. At $t+2$ the speculator will take delivery of currency y in accordance with the two-period contract and deliver to the counterparty in accordance with the one-period contract.

If we consider the three-period contract, then the speculator has even greater flexibility. She can speculate on the basis of the expected value of the one-period forward rate prevailing at $t+2$, EF_{t+2}^{t+3}, or the expected value of the two-period forward rate prevailing at $t+1$, EF_{t+1}^{t+3}. Suppose that both of these rates are expected to be higher than F_t^{t+3}. The speculator can buy an amount, K, of currency y at time t for delivery at time $t+3$ and sell it at $t+1$ and $t+2$ for delivery at $t+3$, acting on the expected values of the forward rates, F_{t+1}^{t+3} and F_{t+2}^{t+3}. Suppose also that she sells a fraction, w, of the amount at F_{t+1}^{t+3} and the rest of the amount, $1-w$, at F_{t+2}^{t+3}. The expected value of the profit is

$$E\pi = wK\left(EF_{t+1}^{t+3} - F_t^{t+3}\right) + (1-w)K\left(EF_{t+2}^{t+3} - F_t^{t+3}\right) \tag{2.45}$$

In general, if there are n periods then forward speculators can speculate on a set of forward rates ranging from the one-period rate expected to prevail at $t+n-1$ (one period before the maturity of the n-period contract) to the $(n-1)$-period rate expected to prevail at $t+1$ ($n-1$ periods before the maturity of the n-period contract). Again, if the speculator buys an amount at F_t^{t+n} and sells a fraction, w_i, at EF_{t+i}^{t+n} at time $t+i$ for $i=1$ to $i=t+n-1$ then the expected profit is

$$E\pi = \sum_{i=1}^{t+n-1} w_i K\left(EF_{t+i}^{t+n} - F_t^{t+n}\right) \tag{2.46}$$

It is obvious that the decision rule to indulge in forward speculation requires forecasting the forward exchange rates prevailing between t and $t+n$.

SPECULATION WITH OPTIONS

Let us consider call and put options on currency y. The call gives the holder the right to buy currency y at the exercise exchange rate, R (measured as x/y) while the put option gives the holder the right to sell the currency at the exercise exchange rate. Let us also assume for the time being that we are dealing with European options which can be exercised on the maturity of the contract only (that is on the expiry date of the option). A speculator will buy a call or sell a put if she expects currency y to appreciate and buy a put or sell a call if she expects the currency to depreciate.

Consider first the case of buying a call at time t which expires at time $t+n$. A speculator will do this if she expects the exchange rate at time $t+n$ to be higher than the exercise exchange rate, that is if

$$ES_{t+n} > R \tag{2.47}$$

If the forecast is accurate then the speculator can make profit by exercising the option at $t+n$, buying the currency at R and selling it spot at S_{t+n}, in which case the (gross) profit earned per unit of y is $S_{t+n} - R$. Based on the same forecast, the speculator may decide to sell a put. If the forecast is correct the holder of the put will not exercise and the speculator makes profit by keeping the premium paid to her (by the holder) up front.

If, on the other hand, the forecast indicates that the expected spot rate will be below the exercise exchange rate, then profit can be made by buying a put option. Thus, the condition required for buying a put option is

$$ES_{t+n} < R \tag{2.48}$$

If the forecast is accurate, then on the expiry date, the speculator buys currency y spot at S_{t+n} and sells it at the exercise exchange rate R, earning gross profit of $R - S_{t+n}$. Alternatively, the speculator can sell a call. If the forecast is accurate, the call will not be exercised and profit will be gained since the premium received up front can be kept.

Notice, however, the following. First, the forecast is not necessarily that currency y will appreciate or depreciate from the present level, but that it ends up higher or lower than the exercise exchange rate on the expiry date. The decision rule does not involve the current exchange rate, S_t. So, even if $S_{t+n} < S_t$, buying a call is still profitable as long as $S_{t+n} > R$. Similarly, if $S_{t+n} > S_t$, buying a put is still profitable as long as $S_{t+n} < R$.

Second, to make net profit when the speculator buys a call or a put, the difference between S_{t+n} and R must be greater than the premium, ρ. Hence, the decision rules can be modified to the following. The speculator will buy a call if

$$ES_{t+n} > R + \rho \tag{2.49}$$

in which case net profit will be $S_{t+n} - (R + \rho)$ if the forecast is accurate. On the other hand, a speculator will buy a put if

$$ES_{t+n} < R - \rho \tag{2.50}$$

in which case net profit will be $R - (S_{t+n} + \rho)$ if the forecast is accurate.

Third, the case is different for American options which can be exercised at any time between t and $t+n$. Suppose that $S_t = R$ so that the option is initially at the money. A forecast indicates that the exchange rate will rise between t and $t+k$ where $k < n$ and then decline to its present level at $t+n$ (that is, $ES_{t+n} = S_t$). If $ES_{t+k} > R + \rho$, then an American call option should be bought and exercised at $t+k$ to realise a net profit of $S_{t+k} - (R+\rho)$.

SPECULATION WITH COMBINED OPTION POSITIONS AND EXOTIC OPTIONS

We will consider two combined option positions, a short straddle and a long straddle. A short straddle involves selling a call and a put with the same exercise exchange rate. This position is taken when the underlying currency is not expected to move much. Suppose that at time t, $S_t = R$ and a forecast indicates that $ES_{t+n} = R$. In this case a short straddle position should be taken because if the forecast is accurate then neither the call nor the put will be exercised and profit will be realised that is equal to the premiums received for the two options.

If, on the other hand, $S_t = R$ and a forecast indicates that $ES_{t+n} > (R + \rho_c + \rho_p)$ or that $ES_{t+n} < (R - \rho_c - \rho_p)$, where ρ_c and ρ_p are the premiums on the call and the put respectively, then a long straddle position should be taken. If the first forecast is right, the call option is exercised while the put option is left to expire, in which case the profit will be $S_{t+n} - (R + \rho_c + \rho_p)$. If, on the other hand, the second forecast is right, then the put option is exercised while the call option is left to expire, in which case net profit will be $R - (S_{t+n} + \rho_c + \rho_p)$.

We now consider an example of exotic options, the average rate option. This option gives the right to sell an amount of the underlying currency at the exercise exchange rate if the average spot rate over the period between t and $t+n$ is less than the exercise exchange rate. Suppose that the average exchange rate, $\bar{S}$, is calculated on the basis of m observations taken at times $t+1, \ldots, t+2, \ldots, t+m$ where $m < n$. The average exchange rate is calculated as

$$\bar{S} = \frac{1}{m}\sum_{i=1}^{m} S_{t+i} \tag{2.51}$$

At time t, the exchange rate at $t+1, \ldots, t+2, \ldots, t+m$ is not known, and so it has to be forecast. Hence

$$E\bar{S} = \frac{1}{m}\sum_{i=1}^{m} ES_{t+i} \tag{2.52}$$

The option will be exercised if $\bar{S} < R$ in which case the holder can sell the underlying currency at R. If the speculator buys the currency spot at the average exchange rate, $\bar{S}$, then the profit realised is $R - (\bar{S} + \rho)$. Still better if the speculator buys the currency spot at S_{t+n}, where $S_{t+n} < \bar{S}$. The decision rule would be: buy an average rate option at time t if

$$\frac{1}{m}\sum_{i=1}^{m} ES_{t+i} < R \tag{2.53}$$

which obviously requires forecasting the spot exchange rate at several points in time between t and $t+n$.

HEDGING TRANSACTION EXPOSURE

Transaction exposure to foreign exchange risk arises because the domestic currency values of assets, liabilities, profits and other items are affected by changes in the exchange rate. A firm with international operations will invariably have foreign currency payables and receivables that are due at some time in the future. While the values of these payables and receivables may be known in foreign currency terms before they are due, their domestic currency values when they are due depend on the spot exchange rate prevailing then. An appreciation of the foreign currency against the domestic currency leads to an increase in the domestic currency value of payables and a decrease in the domestic currency value of receivables. If x is the domestic currency and y is the foreign currency, it follows that

$$EV_{x,t+n} = V_{y,t+n}E(x/y)_{t+n} \tag{2.54}$$

which says that the expected domestic currency value of an item is equal to its foreign currency value (which is known at time t) multiplied by the spot exchange rate expected to prevail at time $t+n$. Hence, exchange rate forecasting is required to get some idea about the expected value of payables and receivables.

Payables and receivables can be hedged by using a money market hedge, a forward market hedge and an options hedge. We will discuss these hedging instruments in turn.

MONEY MARKET HEDGING

A money market hedge of payables involves borrowing and lending such that the final product is equal to the amount of the payables in the foreign currency, y. Let this amount be K, which is due at time $t+n$. A money market hedge consists of the following steps:

1. At time t, an amount of the domestic currency, x, is borrowed. This amount is equal to $KS_t/(1+i_y)$.
2. The amount borrowed is converted into currency y at the spot exchange rate prevailing at time t to obtain $K/(1+i_y)$ units of currency y. This amount is the present value of the payables.
3. The present value of the payables is invested at i_y to obtain K units of currency y. This amount is realised at time $t+n$ when it is used to meet the payables.
4. At $t+n$ the loan becomes due. The amount of currency x that should be repaid is equal to $KS_t(1+i_x)/(1+i_y)$. This amount is known with certainty at time t, and this is the essence of hedging.

The decision whether or not to hedge depends on a comparison between the amount paid under the hedge decision, and the amount paid under the no-hedge decision. The latter implies that nothing is done until time $t+n$, and then the amount K is converted at the spot exchange rate prevailing at that time, S_{t+n}. At time t, this exchange rate is not known, and so the decision to hedge or not to hedge must be based on the expected value of this exchange rate. This makes hedging a speculative decision, although the objective is to avoid risk. The decision to hedge payables in the money market will be taken if

$$KS_t\left(\frac{1+i_x}{1+i_y}\right) < KES_{t+n} \tag{2.55}$$

or if

$$\bar{F}_t < ES_{t+n} \tag{2.56}$$

where $\bar{F}$ is the interest parity forward rate, that is the forward rate consistent with covered interest parity. This rate is calculated by adjusting the spot rate prevailing at time t for the interest rate differential, that is

$$\bar{F}_t = S_t\left(\frac{1+i_x}{1+i_y}\right) \tag{2.57}$$

Notice that the decision rule involves two variables: $\bar{F}_t$ which is known at time t, and S_{t+n} which is not. Thus, a forecast of the value of the spot rate prevailing at time $t+n$ is needed to implement this decision rule.

Similarly, it can be shown that a decision to hedge receivables in the money market will be taken if

$$\bar{F}_t > ES_{t+n} \tag{2.58}$$

A decision rule to hedge payables and receivables in the money market can also be formulated if allowance is made for the bid–offer spreads in exchange and interest rates. Thus, a decision to hedge payables will be taken if

$$KS_{a,t}\left(\frac{1+i_{xa}}{1+i_{yb}}\right) < KES_{a,t+n} \tag{2.59}$$

or if

$$\bar{F}_{a,t} < ES_{a,t+n} \tag{2.60}$$

Alternatively, a decision to hedge receivables will be taken if

$$KS_{b,t}\left(\frac{1+i_{xb}}{1+i_{ya}}\right) > KES_{b,t+n} \tag{2.61}$$

or if

$$\bar{F}_{b,t} > ES_{b,t+n} \tag{2.62}$$

Table 2.2 summarises the decision rules pertaining to hedging payables and receivables in the money market.

Table 2.2 Decision rules for money market hedging

	Payables	*Receivables*
Absence of bid–offer spreads		
$\bar{F}_t < ES_{t+n}$	Hedge	No-hedge
$\bar{F}_t > ES_{t+n}$	No-hedge	Hedge
Presence of bid–offer spreads		
$\bar{F}_{a,t} < ES_{a,t+n}$	Hedge	
$\bar{F}_{a,t} > ES_{a,t+n}$	No-hedge	
$\bar{F}_{b,t} > ES_{b,t+n}$		Hedge
$\bar{F}_{b,t} < ES_{b,t+n}$		No-hedge

FORWARD MARKET HEDGING

Forward market hedging implies that the foreign currency is bought (in the case of payables) and sold (in the case of receivables) forward in order to make the domestic currency values of the payables and receivables known at time t. Thus, a forward hedging of payables and receivables implies that the foreign currency amounts are converted at the forward rate. Again, the decision whether or not to hedge depends on a comparison between the domestic values of the payables and receivables under the hedge and no-hedge decisions. Under the no-hedge decision the domestic currency values are not known at time t because they depend on the spot exchange rate prevailing at time $t+n$. The decision depends on a comparison between the actual forward rate at time t and the spot rate expected to prevail at time $t+n$. Table 2.3 lists the decision rules for forward hedging in the presence and absence of bid–offer spreads. The need for exchange rate forecasting is obvious.

Table 2.3 Decision rules for forward market hedging

	Payables	*Receivables*
Absence of bid–offer spreads		
$F_t < ES_{t+n}$	Hedge	No-hedge
$F_t > ES_{t+n}$	No-hedge	Hedge
Presence of bid–offer spreads		
$F_{a,t} < ES_{a,t+n}$	Hedge	
$F_{a,t} > ES_{a,t+n}$	No-hedge	
$F_{b,t} > ES_{b,t+n}$		Hedge
$F_{b,t} < ES_{b,t+n}$		No-hedge

HEDGING WITH OPTIONS

Hedging with options differs from hedging in the money market or in the forward market in the sense that the outcome depends on whether or not the option is exercised. This in turn depends on whether the actual exchange rate prevailing when the option is exercised is higher or lower than the exercise exchange rate. Again, the decision to hedge payables (receivables) will be taken if the amount paid (received) under the hedge decision is smaller (larger) than the amount paid (received) under the no-hedge decision.

Let us for simplicity assume that we are dealing with European options which can be exercised only on the date of expiry which coincides with the date on which the payables or receivables fall due, that is $t+n$. Let us also assume that we have a probability distribution for the exchange rate expected to prevail on the expiry date. According to this probability distribution, the exchange rate assumes the values $S_{t+n,1}, \ldots, S_{t+n,m}$ with probabilities $p_1, \ldots p_m$. In general, a call option will be exercised if $S_{t+n,i} > R$, while a put option is exercised if $S_{t+n,i} < R$. Also assume that $S_{t+n,i} > R$ for $i = 1, 2, \ldots, k$ and $S_{t+n,i} < R$ for $i = k+1, \ldots, m$.

Let us start with the case of hedging an amount K of foreign currency payables due at $t+n$ by buying a call option with a premium ρ. For $i = 1, 2, \ldots, k$, the option will be exercised and the amount K is converted at R. The total cost of obtaining the amount K will be $K(R+\rho)$. This materialises with a probability of p_i for $i = 1, 2 \ldots, k$. For $i > k+1$, the option will not be exercised and the amount K is converted at the spot exchange rate, $S_{t+n,i}$. In this case the total cost of obtaining the amount K will be $K(S_{t+n,i} + \rho)$ which materialises with a probability p_i for $i > k+1$. Table 2.4 shows all of the possibilities. Hence, the expected value of the payables under the hedge decision is

$$EV = \sum_{i=1}^{k} K(R+\rho)p_i + \sum_{i=k+1}^{m} K(S_{t+n,i} + \rho)p_i \tag{2.63}$$

Under the no-hedge decision the amount will be converted at the spot exchange rates for $i = 1, \ldots, m$.

Table 2.4 Call option hedging with a probability distribution

$S_{t+n,i}$	*Exercise?*	*Value of payables (including premium)*	*Probability*
$S_{t+n,1}$	Yes	$K(R+\rho)$	p_1
$S_{t+n,2}$	Yes	$K(R+\rho)$	p_2
$\vdots$	$\vdots$	$\vdots$	$\vdots$
$S_{t+n,k}$	Yes	$K(R+\rho)$	p_k
$S_{t+n,k+1}$	No	$K(S_{t+n,k+1} + \rho)$	p_{k+1}
$S_{t+n,k+2}$	No	$K(S_{t+n,k+2} + \rho)$	p_{k+2}
$\vdots$	$\vdots$	$\vdots$	$\vdots$
$S_{t+n,m}$	No	$K(S_{t+n,m} + \rho)$	p_m

Hence, the expected value of the payables is

$$EV = \sum_{i=1}^{m} KS_{t+n,i}p_i \tag{2.64}$$

The decision to hedge payables will be taken if

$$\sum_{i=1}^{k} K(R+\rho)p_i + \sum_{i=k+1}^{m} K(S_{t+n,i}+\rho)p_i < \sum_{i=1}^{m} KS_{t+n,i}p_i \tag{2.65}$$

which involves knowing the probability distribution of the exchange rate expected to prevail at $t+n$.

Hedging receivables by buying a put option leads to a similar decision rule. Table 2.5 lists all of the possible outcomes. The expected value of the receivables under the hedge decision is

$$EV = \sum_{i=1}^{k} K(S_{t+n,i}-\rho)p_i + \sum_{i=k+1}^{m} K(R-\rho)p_i \tag{2.66}$$

Under the no-hedge decision the amount will be converted at the spot exchange rate for $i = 1, \ldots, m$. Hence, the expected value of the receivables is

$$EV = \sum_{i=1}^{m} KS_{t+n,i}p_i \tag{2.67}$$

Table 2.5 Put option hedging with a probability distribution

$S_{t+n,i}$	*Exercise?*	*Value of receivables (less premium)*	*Probability*
$S_{t+n,i}$	No	$K(S_{t+n,1}-\rho)$	p_1
$S_{t+n,2}$	No	$K(S_{t+n,2}-\rho)$	p_2
$\vdots$	$\vdots$	$\vdots$	$\vdots$
$S_{t+n,k}$	No	$K(S_{t+n,k}-\rho)$	p_k
$S_{t+n,k+1}$	Yes	$K(R-\rho)$	p_{k+1}
$S_{t+n,k+2}$	Yes	$K(R-\rho)$	p_{k+2}
$\vdots$	$\vdots$	$\vdots$	$\vdots$
$S_{t+n,m}$	Yes	$K(R-\rho)$	p_m

The decision to hedge receivables will be taken if

$$\sum_{i=1}^{k} K(S_{t+n,i} - \rho)p_i + \sum_{i=k+1}^{m} K(R - \rho)p_i > \sum_{i=1}^{m} KS_{t+n,i}p_i \tag{2.68}$$

which involves knowing the probability distribution of the exchange rate expected to prevail at $t + n$.

A relevant decision involves the choice between hedging methods, assuming that the decision to hedge is valid in all cases. A call option hedge of payables will be preferred if the expected amount paid under the option hedge is lower than the amount paid under the money market hedge or the forward hedge. A put option hedge of receivables will be preferred if the expected amount received under this hedge is larger than the amount received under a money market hedge or a forward hedge. Table 2.6 lists the decision rules for the choice of a hedge.

Table 2.6 Decision rules for the choice of a hedge

Condition	*Decision*
$\sum_{i=1}^{k} K(R + \rho)p_i + \sum_{i=k+1}^{m} K(S_{t+n,i} + \rho)p_i < KS_t\left(\frac{1 + i_x}{1 + i_y}\right)$	A call option hedge rather than a money market hedge is used for payables.
$\sum_{i=1}^{k} K(R + \rho)p_i + \sum_{i=k+1}^{m} K(S_{t+n,i} + \rho)p_i < KF_t$	A call option hedge rather than a forward market hedge is used for payables.
$\sum_{i=1}^{k} K(S_{t+n,i} - \rho)p_i + \sum_{i=k+1}^{m} K(R - \rho)p_i > KS_t\left(\frac{1 + i_x}{1 + i_y}\right)$	A put option hedge rather than a money market hedge is used for receivables.
$\sum_{i=1}^{k} K(S_{t+n,i} - \rho)p_i + \sum_{i=k+1}^{m} K(R - \rho)p_i > KF_t$	A put option hedge rather than a forward market hedge is used for receivables.

OTHER TECHNIQUES OF HEDGING TRANSACTION EXPOSURE

Other techniques of hedging transaction exposure also need exchange rate forecasting. Two of these techniques are (i) leading and lagging, and (ii) cross hedging. We start with leading and lagging. If the foreign currency is expected to appreciate, it would be a good idea to meet foreign currency payables sooner rather than later. This is called leading, and it is a good idea because the domestic currency value of the payables would be smaller than if the payment is made later. If, on the other hand, the foreign currency is expected to depreciate then it is a good idea to meet the payables later than sooner. This is called lagging. In this case lagging is a good idea because the domestic currency value of the payables will be smaller than if the payment is made sooner.

The other technique is cross hedging. Suppose that a company has some payables in foreign currency z. If this currency is expected to appreciate against the domestic currency x (that is if x/z is expected to rise) it would be a good idea to buy it forward at time t for delivery at time $t+n$. The problem is that forward contracts on this currency are not available. This problem can be circumvented if the exchange rates x/z and x/y are highly correlated where y is another foreign currency on which forward contracts are available. In this case currency y is bought forward at time t for delivery at time $t+n$. If z appreciates against x, so will y. If z and y appreciate in the same proportion, then the cross exchange rate y/z will be unchanged. The company takes delivery of y at $t+n$ and converts it spot into z to meet the payables. This problem requires the forecasting of the spot exchange rates $(x/z)_{t+n}$ and $(x/y)_{t+n}$ because the decision at time t is based on $E(x/z)_{t+n}$ and $E(x/y)_{t+n}$.

MEASUREMENT AND HEDGING OF ECONOMIC EXPOSURE

Economic exposure to foreign exchange risk arises from the effect of changes in the exchange rate on non-contractual or unplanned cash flows that pertain to sales in foreign markets, sales in domestic markets and input costs whether these are domestic or foreign. For example, a real appreciation of the foreign currency will lead to

1. an increase in domestic sales revenue;
2. an increase in foreign sales revenue;
3. an increase in the cost of imported raw materials and the cost of funding in foreign currencies.

If costs are more sensitive than revenues to changes in the real exchange rate, then the net result will be negative.

If a forecast indicates that the foreign currency will appreciate, the firm must do something about it. This invariably involves restructuring of operations. Depending on the conditions, some or all of the following measures may be taken:

1. increasing sales in new or existing foreign markets;
2. reducing the dependency on foreign suppliers of raw materials and intermediate products;
3. elimination of production facilities in foreign countries;
4. reducing the level of foreign currency debt.

Take, for example, the case of Laker Airlines that we came across in Chapter 1. Economic exposure could have been reduced by reducing dollar-denominated expenses and increasing dollar-denominated revenues. One may be justified to think either that the wrong exchange rate forecast was provided (which is more likely in this particular case) or that the right advice was provided but not utilised.

HEDGING TRANSLATION EXPOSURE

Translation exposure results from the effect of changes in the exchange rate on the values of items in a consolidated financial statement (balance sheet or income statement). Translation exposure is a source of concern because the translation method has an impact on the reported earnings per share and other vital financial indicators.

Translation exposure can be hedged via forward contracts. Suppose that currency x is the base currency of a company while currency y is the base currency of its foreign subsidiary. In constructing a consolidated balance sheet and income statement, the items in the financial statements of the subsidiary must be converted (translated) from currency y into currency x. The values of these items in terms of currency x depend on the exchange rate used for translation.

Suppose now that there is a forecast (available at time t) indicating that currency y will depreciate by the time the consolidated financial statements must be prepared (at time $t + n$). At a low exchange rate the values of the items on the subsidiary's statements will be very low, reflecting negatively on the consolidated financial statements. For example, the net income of the subsidiary will be lower, and so will the consolidated net income. One action to avoid this possibility is for the company to buy currency x forward against currency y. If the depreciation of y is realised, the drop in the net income of the subsidiary will be counterbalanced by the extra income realised by the company on the forward position.

SHORT-TERM FINANCING AND INVESTMENT DECISIONS

Short-term financing and investment decisions are concerned with financing and investment and in various currencies for periods, or using instruments with maturities, of less than one year. A decision rule is needed concerning the choice of the currency. This decision rule deals with two choice problems:

1. between the domestic currency and a foreign currency;
2. between one currency and a portfolio of currencies.

For the sake of argument it is assumed that the objective is to minimise the cost of financing and maximise the rate of return on investment. Let us deal with the financing decision first, assuming that x is the domestic currency and y is the foreign currency. Financing by borrowing currency x implies a cost of financing that is equal to the interest rate on x, that is i_x. Financing in a foreign currency implies that the cost of financing is equal to the foreign currency's effective financing rate, which has two components: the nominal interest rate on the foreign currency, i_y, and the percentage change in the spot exchange rate x/y between t and $t+n$. At time t, when the decision is taken, the percentage change in the exchange rate is unknown. Therefore, the expected value of the effective financing rate in currency y is

$$Er_y = i_y + E\dot{S}_{t+n} \tag{2.69}$$

The decision rule is the following: choose currency y rather than currency x for financing if

$$i_y + E\dot{S}_{t+n} < i_x \tag{2.70}$$

If two currencies have effective financing rates of r_y and r_z, then the effective financing rate of a two-currency portfolio is given by

$$r_p = w_y r_y + w_z r_z \tag{2.71}$$

where w_y and w_z are the weights assigned to the two currencies such that $w_y + w_z = 1$. The decision rule becomes as follows: choose the portfolio rather than currency x for financing if

$$w_y\left[i_y + E\dot{S}(x/y)_{t+n}\right] + w_z\left[i_z + E\dot{S}(x/z)_{t+n}\right] < i_x \tag{2.72}$$

If the portfolio contains m currencies $(y_1, \ldots, y_m)$, then the decision rule can be written as follows: choose the portfolio if

$$\sum_{j=1}^{m} w_j\left[i_j + E\dot{S}(x/y_j)_{t+n}\right] < i_x \tag{2.73}$$

The decision rule can be modified to take into account risk as measured by the standard deviation of the effective financing rate. For example, the objective may be to minimise the effective financing rate subject to bearing a maximum level of risk. No matter what the objective is, the decision (which is taken at time t) requires a forecast of the exchange rate or rates at $t+n$.

Decisions concerning short-term investment are based on the expected effective rate of return which is defined exactly as the effective financing rate except that the interest rate on currency y is now the lending rate rather than the borrowing rate. The objective would be to maximise the effective rate of return or to choose a portfolio of currencies with a higher effective rate of return than the interest rate on the domestic currency. Likewise, exchange rate forecasting is needed to implement this decision rule.

LONG-TERM FINANCING AND INVESTMENT DECISIONS

Consider a long-term financing decision by issuing zero coupon bonds with a maturity of n years. If the value of the bond issue is K domestic currency units, then the amount that has to be repaid on maturity is $K(1+i_x)^n$. Another alternative is to borrow by issuing foreign currency bonds. If an equivalent amount of currency y is raised, then the amount that has to be repaid is $K(S_{t+n}/S_t)(1+i_y)^n$. At time t, a decision will be taken to borrow by issuing bonds denominated in y if

$$\left(\frac{ES_{t+n}}{S_t}\right)(1+i_y)^n < (1+i_x)^n \tag{2.74}$$

The decision rule, therefore, requires a forecast of the exchange rate on the maturity of the bonds. If the bonds are straight bonds with annual coupon payments, the decision rule will require forecasting the exchange rate on each payment date between t and $t+n$.

Consider now a choice between investing in domestic and foreign shares over the period between t and $t+n$. Let $d(d^*)$ and $a(a^*)$ be the dividend yield and the rate of capital appreciation on domestic (foreign) shares. The decision rule will be as follows: choose foreign shares if

$$\left(\frac{ES_{t+n}}{S_t}\right)(1+d^*+a^*)^n > (1+d+a)^n \tag{2.75}$$

At time t, the parameters a, d, a^* and d^* may not be known. To implement the decision rule, these parameters must be forecast unless their historical values are used. This is irrelevant for the issue under consideration here, which is exchange rate forecasting. What is relevant is that the term ES_{t+n} appears in the decision rule, implying the need for exchange rate forecasting.

FOREIGN DIRECT INVESTMENT

The evaluation of foreign direct investment projects, by using such criteria as the net present value (NPV) and the internal rate of return (IRR), requires the conversion of the expected cash flows from foreign currencies into the domestic currency. Because of the exchange rate factor it is often the case that a project that is attractive in foreign currency terms may not be so in domestic currency terms.

Consider an n-year project costing X_t and producing cash flows $X_{t+1}, X_{t+2}, \ldots X_{t+n}$. The values of the capital cost and the cash flows in domestic currency terms are S_tX_t and $S_{t+1}X_{t+1}, S_{t+2}X_{t+2}, \ldots, S_{t+n}X_{t+n}$. Hence, the NPV of the project is

$$\text{NPV} = -S_tX_t + \frac{ES_{t+1}X_{t+1}}{1+i} + \frac{ES_{t+2}X_{t+2}}{(1+i)^2} + \cdots + \frac{ES_{t+n}X_{t+n}}{(1+i)^n} \tag{2.76}$$

where i is the discount rate. The IRR is given by r in the equation

$$-S_tX_t + \frac{ES_{t+1}X_{t+1}}{1+r} + \frac{ES_{t+2}X_{t+2}}{(1+r)^2} + \cdots + \frac{ES_{t+n}X_{t+n}}{(1+r)^n} = 0 \tag{2.77}$$

In general, a project is accepted if the NPV is positive or if the IRR is greater than the market interest rate. A decision to choose between two mutually exclusive projects is also based on the NPV and IRR. In this case the project with the higher NPV or IRR is chosen. To calculate the NPV and the IRR of a foreign direct investment project, exchange rate forecasting is needed.

PRICING AND STRATEGIC PLANNING

Pricing products that are sold in foreign markets is influenced by expected changes in the exchange rate. The foreign currency price of a product is its domestic currency price divided by the exchange rate. A firm may quote its prices in foreign currency terms, in which case what it receives in domestic currency terms depends on the exchange rate. Alternatively, it may quote its prices in domestic currency terms, in which case the foreign currency price will be determined by the exchange rate. If the foreign currency depreciates, the foreign currency price may rise to a level that will hurt the foreign market share of the exporting firm. Prices, therefore, have to be set while taking into account the expected exchange rate.

One aspect of strategic planning is the location of production facilities and the determination of export markets. One criterion for this strategic choice is based on purchasing power parity. Production facilities are located in countries whose currencies are expected to fall below the level implied by PPP, while the export markets are chosen so that revenue is earned in countries whose currencies are expected to appreciate above the level implied by PPP. This is because PPP provides some sort of indication for the equilibrium level of the exchange rate. Therefore, when a currency is above its PPP rate it is regarded as being overvalued. When it is below the PPP rate, it is regarded as being undervalued. Notice that the underlying assumption in this case is that exchange rates are measured in indirect quotation as the foreign currency price of one unit of the domestic currency.

CENTRAL BANK INTERVENTION AND MACROECONOMIC POLICY

Under the present system of managed floating, central banks intervene in the foreign exchange market by buying and selling currencies. The objective of intervention is either to smooth out fluctuations in the exchange rate, or to prevent the domestic currency from appreciating or depreciating excessively. Exchange rate forecasting is needed by the central bank in order to make the expected path of the exchange rate identical to the desired path. Whether or not this is possible in practice is debatable, but it is not our concern here.

The exchange rate is an important macroeconomic variable as revealed by the discussion in Chapter 1. It affects almost everything else in the economy: interest rates, growth, unemployment, inflation and the balance of payments. Thus, exchange rate forecasting is necessary for the formulation of macroeconomic policy.

DECISION RULES NOT REQUIRING EXCHANGE RATE FORECASTING

In this section we describe some operations and situations that do not require exchange rate forecasting. It will be demonstrated that these operations do not require exchange rate forecasting because the expected exchange rate does not appear as a variable in the decision rule. These are normally risk-free arbitrage operations which rarely arise in practice, because once they arise they will be exploited to the point of extinction.

TWO-POINT ARBITRAGE

Profitable two-point arbitrage opportunities arise when the exchange rate between two currencies is not the same in all financial centres. Assume that there are two financial centres A and B, and that the exchange rate between x and y in A is higher than the rate in B, that is

$$(x/y)_{t,A} > (x/y)_{t,B} \tag{2.78}$$

This means that currency y is more expensive in A than in B. A profitable arbitrage operation involves buying currency y in B and selling it in A. The decision is taken on the basis of the exchange rates prevailing at time t. Hence, this operation does not require any exchange rate forecasting.

THREE-POINT ARBITRAGE

A profitable three-point arbitrage operation will arise if the cross exchange rates are inconsistent. Consider three currencies: x, y and z. The cross exchange rates are inconsistent if

$$(x/y)_t \neq \frac{(x/z)_t}{(y/z)_t} \tag{2.79}$$

If

$$(x/y)_t > \frac{(x/z)_t}{(y/z)_t} \tag{2.80}$$

then it would be possible to make profit by buying currency z against currency x, buying currency y against currency z and finally buying currency x against currency y. If, on the other hand,

$$(x/y)_t < \frac{(x/z)_t}{(y/z)_t} \tag{2.81}$$

then it would be possible to make profit by going the other way round. That is, by buying currency y against currency x, buying currency z against currency y and finally buying currency x against currency z. Obviously, the decision rule does not involve any variable that is unknown at time t, and so this operation does not need any forecasting.

COVERED INTEREST ARBITRAGE

Covered interest arbitrage is similar to uncovered interest arbitrage except that the long position is covered by selling the underlying currency forward to eliminate foreign exchange risk. Consider the following choice problem in which an investor is faced with two alternatives. The first alternative is to invest in currency x, earning the interest rate on this currency, i_x. The second alternative is to convert currency x into currency y, invest in currency y to earn i_y and sell currency y at the forward rate, $F_t^{t+n}(x/y)$. At $t+n$, the first alternative brings $K(1+i_x)$ where K is the amount of x invested. The second alternative brings $(K/S_t)F_t^{t+n}(1+i_y)$. Investment in currency y is chosen if

$$\frac{KF_t^{t+n}}{S_t}(1+i_y) > K(1+i_x) \tag{2.82}$$

which also means that a profitable covered arbitrage operation can be conducted by going short on x and long on y. The opposite is also true. The decision rule can be simplified to the following: a profitable covered arbitrage operation can be conducted by going short on x and long on y if

$$f_t^{t+n} > i_x - i_y \tag{2.83}$$

that is if the forward spread is larger than the interest rate differential. Otherwise, a profitable covered arbitrage operation can be conducted by going short on y and long on x. Covered arbitrage will not be profitable if the forward spread is equal to the interest rate differential. If this is the case then covered interest parity (CIP) is said to hold. The decision rule is based on variables that are known at time t, and hence exchange rate forecasting is not needed for conducting this operation.

CHOOSING BETWEEN MONEY MARKET HEDGING AND FORWARD HEDGING

Suppose that the hedging decision rules tell us that both a money market hedge and a forward hedge are worthwhile, which of these should be chosen? Another decision rule is needed for this purpose: a money market hedge of payables is preferred to a forward market hedge if the interest parity forward rate is lower than the actual forward rate, that is if $\bar{F}_t < F_t$. On the other hand, a money market hedge of receivables is preferred to a forward market hedge if the interest parity forward rate is higher than the actual forward rate, that is if $\bar{F}_t > F_t$. Both of these variables are known at time t, and so there is no need for exchange rate forecasting.

CONCLUDING REMARKS

We have gone through a long list of the operations that require exchange rate forecasting as an input in the decision-making process. This list is not exhaustive, and a large number of situations may arise requiring decisions that are based on the expected exchange rate. However, the situations presented in this chapter do highlight the importance of exchange rate forecasting. In practice, operations like those presented in this chapter may involve billions of dollars, and a wrong or an improper decision may wipe out a whole company. Exchange rate forecasting leads to better decisions.

And although a hunch may prove to be more accurate than a formal forecast on a certain occasion, it is more likely that formal forecasting leads to better decisions on average.

Having established that exchange rate forecasting is needed for decision making, the next step is to study how forecasts are generated. We start with univariate time series techniques, which are the subject matter of the following chapter.

3: Univariate Time Series Techniques

INTRODUCTION

In this chapter we deal with univariate time series forecasting techniques: the methods and models that are based on the history of the variable to be forecast, which in this case is the exchange rate. The term 'univariate' implies that forecasting is based on a sample of time series observations of the exchange rate without taking into account the effect of the other variables such as prices and interest rates. The underlying rationale for this methodology is that the effect of other variables is embodied in, and reflected by, the actual behaviour of the exchange rate. If this is the case, then there is no need to take an explicit account of these variables. It is argued that these explanatory variables often suffer from measurement errors (for example, the current account), which are bound to have an adverse effect on the quality and the accuracy of the forecasts. Furthermore, since no explanatory variables are used, the forecasters avoid the problem of having to forecast the explanatory variables in order to be able to forecast the exchange rate. The data and the computational requirements of these methods and models are normally smaller than in the case of multivariate models. Subject to forecasting accuracy, it may be argued that the former are more cost-effective.

On the other hand, it is arguable that univariate time series techniques are not based on economic theory and so they are like 'black boxes'. While this criticism may be valid, forecasters are only interested in one thing, the accuracy of the forecasts, irrespective of whether or not they are based on economic theory. Remember that there are two objectives of model building: hypothesis testing and forecasting. If we are interested in forecasting only, then whether or not the model is based on economic theory is irrelevant. This is so much the case because there is no evidence that models based on economic theory have a better forecasting track record than univariate time series models. On the contrary, the large-scale macroeconomic models that were popular in the 1950s and 1960s have been replaced to a considerable extent with univariate time series models such as those based on the Box–Jenkins ARIMA methodology or Harvey's structural time series model. After all, one can argue that economists are yet to develop a satisfactory model of exchange rate determination, and so there is no incentive to be guided by the theory. In view of these arguments it seems more appropriate to let the data speak for themselves: this implies using theory-free univariate time series methods and models.

The univariate time series methods presented in this chapter include the averaging methods, the smoothing methods and time series decomposition. The following is a list of the methods and models that will be dealt with in this chapter.

AVERAGING METHODS

- The simple average method
- The single moving average method
- The double moving average method

SMOOTHING METHODS

- Single exponential smoothing
- Double exponential smoothing
- Holt's method
- Winter's method

UNIVARIATE TIME SERIES MODELS

- Box–Jenkins ARIMA models
- Harvey's structural time series model

THE FORECASTING SET-UP

The starting point is to put forward the forecasting set-up. We will for this purpose introduce different notation from what has been used so far to denote the forecast value, the hat notation. Thus, instead of using the symbol ES_{t+i} to denote the forecast value of the exchange rate at $t+i$, such that the forecast is made at the present time, t, we will use $\hat{S}_{t+i}$ to denote both the forecast and the fitted values.

For the purpose of illustrating the averaging and smoothing methods, the following forecasting set-up is used. A schematic representation of the set-up is provided by Table 3.1.

1. The reference point in time is the present time, t. This means that the forecast is generated at time t on the basis of the information available then. The actual value of the exchange rate at time t, S_t, is available.
2. At time t, observations on the exchange rate are available for points in time ranging from the most recent observation, S_t, to the oldest observation, S_1. Thus, the set of information available at time t is $[S_1, S_2, \ldots, S_k, \ldots, S_{t-1}, S_t]$.

Table 3.1 The forecasting set-up

Time	*Actual value*	*Ex post forecast*	*Ex post error*	*Ex ante forecast*
1	S_1	–	–	–
2	S_2	–	–	–
3	S_3	–	–	–
⋮	⋮	⋮	⋮	–
k	S_k	$\hat{S}_k$	$S_k - \hat{S}_k$	–
$k+1$	S_{k+1}	$\hat{S}_{k+1}$	$S_{k+1} - \hat{S}_{k+1}$	–
⋮	⋮	⋮	⋮	–
t	S_t	$\hat{S}_t$	$S_t - \hat{S}_t$	–
$t+1$	–	–	–	$\hat{S}_{t+1}$
⋮	⋮	⋮	⋮	⋮
$t+n$	–	–	–	$\hat{S}_{t+n}$

3. The forecaster chooses the first k observations to work out the forecasts and the remainder of the observations (between $k+1$ and t) to evaluate the (*ex post*) forecasting power of the model. In this case, the first subset of observations is known as the initialisation set, $[S_1, \ldots, S_k]$, while the second set is the test set, $[S_{k+1}, \ldots, S_t]$.
4. If the forecaster is happy with the *ex post* forecasting power of the model, then it can be used for generating *ex ante* forecasts. The forecasting error may be measured as the difference between the actual and forecast values or vice versa.

The forecasting set-up will be used to illustrate the averaging and smoothing methods. To illustrate time series decomposition and the univariate time series models, we will use a much simpler set-up to simplify the exposition. We will work on the basis of a sample of historical data ranging between S_1 and S_n such that S_t refers to the actual value of the exchange rate at any point in time.

AVERAGING METHODS

The assumption underlying averaging methods is that fluctuations in the exchange rate represent random departures from some smooth time path as represented by a curve. If it is possible to identify the smooth time path, or the curve, then it would be possible to produce forecasts by projecting the curve into the future.

THE SIMPLE AVERAGE METHOD

The simple average is obtained by finding the mean for all of the relevant values and then using this mean as a forecast for the next point in time. Suppose first that $k = t$, so that the initialisation set includes all of the available information. The forecast for time $t + 1$ is the average of the values of the exchange rate over the period extending between 1 and t.

$$\hat{S}_{t+1} = \frac{1}{t}\sum_{i=1}^{t} S_i \tag{3.1}$$

The forecast for $t + 2$ is calculated from a sample of $t + 1$ observations consisting of the observed t values and the forecast for $t + 1$. Hence

$$\hat{S}_{t+2} = \frac{1}{t+1}\left(\sum_{i=1}^{t} S_i + \hat{S}_{t+1}\right) \tag{3.2}$$

Similarly, the forecast for $t + n$ is calculated from a sample of $t + n - 1$ observations consisting of the original t values and the $n - 1$ forecasts for the period between $t + 1$ and $t + n - 1$. Hence

$$\hat{S}_{t+n} = \frac{1}{t+n-1}\left(\sum_{i=1}^{t} S_i + \sum_{j=1}^{n-1} \hat{S}_{t+j}\right) \tag{3.3}$$

Notice that in this case since actual observations are not available for the points in time $t + 1, \ldots, t + n$, the forecast values are used to calculate the simple average if, at time t, the forecast is required for points in time beyond $t + 1$. If the forecast is required for one period ahead only, that is for $t + 1$ only, then only the actual values of the exchange rate are used. Notice also that because the forecast values are used, the forecast is the same irrespective of the forecasting horizon. It is obvious from equations (3.1)–(3.3) that

$$\hat{S}_{t+1} = \hat{S}_{t+2} = \cdots = \hat{S}_{t+n} \tag{3.4}$$

Let us now assume that the forecaster wants to use the initialisation set only to generate the forecasts. Hence, the forecaster wants to use the information set $[S_1, \ldots, S_k]$ to calculate a set of in-sample forecasts over the period covered by the test set, that is the forecaster wants to calculate $[\hat{S}_{k+1}, \ldots, \hat{S}_t]$. The forecast for point in time $k + 1$ is calculated as the average of the actual values over the period extending between 1 and k.

Hence

$$\hat{S}_{k+1} = \frac{1}{k}\sum_{i=1}^{k} S_i \tag{3.5}$$

in which case the (in-sample) forecast error is

$$e_{k+1} = S_{k+1} - \hat{S}_{k+1} \tag{3.6}$$

Similarly, the forecast for point in time $k + 2$ is given by

$$\hat{S}_{k+2} = \frac{1}{k+1}\sum_{i=1}^{k+1} S_i \tag{3.7}$$

And, for the last observation corresponding to point in time t, the forecast is calculated as

$$\hat{S}_t = \frac{1}{t-1}\sum_{i=1}^{t-1} S_i \tag{3.8}$$

Thus, only actual values are used to calculate the average, but notice that the sample size changes. Only the first k observations are used to calculate the forecast for time $k + 1$, but $t - 1$ observations are used to calculate the forecast for t.

This forecasting method is very simple, but it may not always be appropriate. In general, this method is appropriate only if the observed time series has no trend and no seasonality.

THE SINGLE MOVING AVERAGE METHOD

A single moving average forecast is based on finding the average for a specified number of observations and using it as a forecast for the next period in time. This method will be preferable if the forecaster believes that more recent observations are more relevant to forecasting than old observations. The calculation of the moving average is based on a constant number of observations, and this is done by adding a new observation and dropping the oldest observation.

Assume that the forecaster wants to use a moving average of order k to forecast the exchange rate at time $k + 1$. The value of the moving average at time k, which is the average of the observations $S_1, \ldots, S_k$, is then used as the forecast for time $k + 1$.

Hence

$$\hat{S}_{k+1} = M_k = \frac{1}{k}\sum_{i=1}^{k} S_i \tag{3.9}$$

where M_k denotes the value of a moving average of order k at point in time k. Similarly, the value of the moving average (of order k) at point in time $k+1$ is used as the forecast for point in time $k+2$. Hence

$$\hat{S}_{k+2} = M_{k+1} = \frac{1}{k}\sum_{i=2}^{k+1} S_i \tag{3.10}$$

Notice that to calculate M_k we use k values of S ranging between S_1 and S_k. For M_{k+1} we also use k values, but in this case they range between S_2 and S_{k+1}. In general, to calculate M_{k+j} we use k values of S ranging between S_{j+1} and S_{k+j} or

$$\hat{S}_{k+j} = M_{k+j} = \frac{1}{k}\sum_{i=j+1}^{k+j} S_i \tag{3.11}$$

It is important to note the following observations about this method:

1. The process of calculation implies that equal weights are assigned to each observation.
2. The moving average method works best with stationary data, that is a time series whose mean value and statistical moments do not change over time. With trended data the forecasts do not catch up with the trend.
3. The method does not handle seasonality very well, although it does a better job than the simple moving average method. This may not be a problem if we believe that exchange rates do not exhibit seasonal behaviour.
4. The forecaster must determine the value of k, the order of the moving average, which measures the rate of response to changes in the underlying data pattern. The larger the order of the moving average the greater is the smoothing effect. Higher-order moving averages are less capable of reflecting fluctuations in the data series, while a low order is most desirable when there are sudden shifts in the level of the series. By using a low-order moving average a heavy weight is placed on recent history, which enables the forecast to catch up more rapidly with the current level. A high order is desirable when there are wide, infrequent fluctuations in the series. Notice that a moving average of order 1

implies that the last observation is taken as the forecast for the next point in time. A moving average of order 4 is useful for quarterly data because it can smooth out the seasonal effect. However, it cannot accommodate the trend or seasonal changes if it is used to forecast the next point in time. The same story goes for a moving average of order 12 when it is used to forecast monthly data.

THE DOUBLE MOVING AVERAGE METHOD

The double moving average method can be used to forecast a time series that has a linear trend, that is a time series that tends to increase or decrease in a linear manner over time. The first step is to calculate a set of observations on a moving average (of a given order) from the original data: this is called the single moving average. The process of calculation is as shown in the case of the single moving average method. Another set of observations on a moving average is then calculated from the observations on the single moving average: this is called the double moving average.

To calculate a double moving average of order k we need k observations on the single moving average. The first set of k observations on the single moving average covers the period between k and $2k-1$. Thus, the first observation on the double moving average can be calculated for time $2k-1$ as

$$M'_{2k-1} = \frac{1}{k}\sum_{i=k}^{2k-1} M_i \tag{3.12}$$

Similarly, the second observation on the double moving average can be calculated for time $2k$ as

$$M'_{2k} = \frac{1}{k}\sum_{i=k+1}^{2k} M_i \tag{3.13}$$

And, in general, the jth observation can be calculated for time $2k+j$ as

$$M'_{2k+j} = \frac{1}{k}\sum_{i=k+j+1}^{2k+j} M_i \tag{3.14}$$

Table 3.2 shows a time framework for the calculation of the observations on the single and double moving averages. Since $2k-1$ is the first point in time at which observations on both the single and the double moving averages are available, we will use it as a reference point for forecasting the

Table 3.2 A time framework for the calculation of single and double moving averages

Time	S_i	M_i	M'_i
1	S_1	–	–
2	S_2	–	–
3	S_3	–	–
⋮	⋮	⋮	⋮
k	S_k	M_k	–
$k+1$	S_{k+1}	M_{k+1}	–
$k+2$	S_{k+2}	M_{k+2}	–
⋮	⋮	⋮	⋮
$2k-1$	S_{2k-1}	M_{2k-1}	M'_{2k-1}
$2k$	S_{2k}	M_{2k}	M'_{2k}
$2k+1$	S_{2k+1}	M_{2k+1}	M'_{2k+1}
⋮	⋮	⋮	⋮
$2k+j$	S_{2k+j}	M_{2k+j}	M'_{2k+j}
⋮	⋮	⋮	⋮
t	S_t	M_t	M'_t

exchange rate in the periods ahead. These forecasts can be calculated from the single moving average M_{2k-1} and the double moving average M'_{2k-1}. First, we calculate the parameters a and b from the two moving averages. The parameter a is calculated from the equation

$$a_{2k-1} = 2M_{2k-1} - M'_{2k-1} \tag{3.15}$$

which illustrates the adjustment of the single moving average by the difference between the single and double moving averages. The parameter b, on the other hand, is calculated from the equation

$$b_{2k-1} = \frac{2}{k-1}(M_{2k-1} - M'_{2k-1}) \tag{3.16}$$

which defines the estimate of the trend from one point in time to the next. Notice that the parameters a and b have the same time subscript as the single and the double moving averages from which they are calculated. The forecast exchange rate for $2k+j$ is then calculated as

$$\hat{S}_{2k+j} = a_{2k-1} + jb_{2k-1} \tag{3.17}$$

which says that the forecast is equal to an adjusted smoothed value, a_{2k-1}, plus j times the trend component, b_{2k-1}. Therefore, the forecast for one period ahead is

$$\hat{S}_{2k} = a_{2k-1} + b_{2k-1} \tag{3.18}$$

Table 3.3 lists the values of the forecast exchange rates for points in time ranging between $2k$ and t where the forecasts are calculated from the single and double moving averages recorded at the reference point in time, $2k - 1$. At point in time $2k$, the forecasts for the periods ahead can be based on the moving averages observed at this point, M_{2k} and M'_{2k}. For this purpose we have to calculate new values for the parameters a and b and proceed in a similar way as before. The method can be modified by setting different orders for the single and double moving averages.

It is important to mention that, unlike the single moving average method, the double moving average method implies unequal weighting. Consider a simple example of using single and double moving averages of order 2. The single moving average at times 2 and 3 are given by

$$M_2 = \frac{1}{2}(S_1 + S_2) \tag{3.19}$$

$$M_3 = \frac{1}{2}(S_2 + S_3) \tag{3.20}$$

The double moving average (of order 2) at time 3 is given by

$$\begin{aligned} M'_3 &= \frac{1}{2}(M_2 + M_3) \\ &= \frac{1}{2}\left[\frac{1}{2}(S_1 + S_2) + \frac{1}{2}(S_2 + S_3)\right] \\ &= \frac{1}{4}S_1 + \frac{1}{2}S_2 + \frac{1}{4}S_3 \end{aligned} \tag{3.21}$$

Table 3.3 Actual and forecast exchange rates based on moving averages at $2k - 1$

Time	S_i	$\hat{S}_i$
$2k$	S_{2k}	$a_{2k-1} + b_{2k-1}$
$2k + 1$	S_{2k+1}	$a_{2k-1} + 2b_{2k-1}$
$\vdots$	$\vdots$	$\vdots$
$2k + j$	S_{2k+j}	$a_{2k-1} + jb_{2k-1}$
$\vdots$	$\vdots$	$\vdots$
t	S_t	$a_{2k-1} + (t - 2k)b_{2k-1}$

The forecast exchange rate at time 4 is calculated as

$$\hat{S}_4 = 2M_3 - M_3' + \frac{2}{2-1}(M_3 - M_3')$$
$$= -\frac{3}{4}S_1 + \frac{1}{2}S_2 + \frac{5}{4}S_3 \tag{3.22}$$

which implies unequal weighting, as heavier weights are assigned to more recent observations.

SMOOTHING METHODS

Smoothing methods are based on the same idea underlying the averaging methods. The objective is to identify a 'smooth curve' that represents the time path of the exchange rate and then project it into the future.

EXPONENTIAL SMOOTHING

Like the double moving average method, exponential smoothing is a technique that assigns heavier weights to more recent observations. The technique allows for a continual revision of the forecasts in the light of more recent experience.

Exponential smoothing is based on averaging (smoothing) past values of the exchange rate in a decreasing (exponential) manner. This effectively means that the observations are weighted, such that heavier weights are assigned to more recent observations. To examine this method formally let us assume that we want to forecast the exchange rate at time $k+1$ on the basis of the information available up to point in time k. The forecast is calculated as a weighted average of the actual exchange rate at time k and the previous forecast. This can be written as

$$\hat{S}_{k+1} = \alpha S_k + (1-\alpha)\hat{S}_k \tag{3.23}$$

where α is the smoothing constant which takes values ranging between zero and one. The equation can be rewritten as

$$\hat{S}_{k+1} = \hat{S}_k + \alpha(S_k - \hat{S}_k) \tag{3.24}$$

which says that the forecast value for $k+1$ is the previous forecast value plus a fraction of the forecast error for the previous point in time. Now since

$$\hat{S}_k = \alpha S_{k-1} + (1-\alpha)\hat{S}_{k-1} \tag{3.25}$$

by substitution we obtain

$$\hat{S}_{k+1} = \alpha S_k + \alpha(1-\alpha)S_{k-1} + (1-\alpha)^2\hat{S}_{k-1} \tag{3.26}$$

By repeated substitution we obtain

$$\begin{aligned}\hat{S}_{k+1} = &\alpha S_k + \alpha(1-\alpha)S_{k-1} + \alpha(1-\alpha)^2 S_{k-2} + \cdots \\ &+ (1-\alpha)^{k-1}S_1\end{aligned} \tag{3.27}$$

which shows that the forecast is a weighted average of the actual observations such that the weights decline exponentially as we use older observations.

To forecast the exchange rate by using exponential smoothing, the forecaster must determine the values of the smoothing constant, α, and the value of the initial forecast, $\hat{S}_k$. Let us start with the latter since it is more straightforward.

If we start at k, then the initial forecast can be calculated either as a weighted average of the past observed values, given the value of α, or we can even use a simple average for this purpose. If, however, we want to start at the beginning of the sample period, then we can utilise the assumption that $\hat{S}_1 = S_1$.

Now we discuss the determination of the smoothing constant. This parameter determines the extent to which the current observation (at time k) influences the forecast value. When the value of the smoothing constant is close to one, the new forecast ($\hat{S}_{k+1}$) will include a substantial adjustment for any error that occurred in the preceding forecast ($\hat{S}_k$). On the other hand, a value close to zero implies that $\hat{S}_{k+1}$ and $\hat{S}_k$ will be close to each other. If the forecaster wishes to make the forecasts stable, a small value of the constant must be used. If, on the other hand, the forecaster thinks that the forecasts must show a rapid response to changes in the behaviour of the exchange rate, then a larger value is more appropriate. Formally, the appropriate value of α can be determined by trying several values and then picking the one that gives the best results in terms of the forecasting errors.

It may be necessary at a certain stage to change the value of α, and this becomes necessary when the pattern of the data changes. This may be done by using a tracking system. Such a system contains a range of permissible forecast values in relation to the actual values (that is, permissible forecasting errors). As long as the values fall within this range, no change is necessary, but once a forecast falls outside the range then the system signals a need to change it.

One possible tracking system is based on the idea that if the forecasting method is doing well then it should not predominantly over- or underestimate the exchange rate. Therefore, out of k forecasts we should expect the number of underestimates or overestimates not to be significantly different from $k/2$.

Another technique that allows for continuous changes in the smoothing parameter is the adaptive-response-rate single exponential smoothing method (ARRSES). The method is described as being adaptive because the value of the parameter changes automatically when there is a change in the behaviour of the time series. This method is represented by the following set of equations:

$$\hat{S}_{k+1} = \alpha_k S_k + (1 - \alpha_k)\hat{S}_k \tag{3.28}$$

$$\alpha_{k+1} = \left|\frac{E_k}{D_k}\right| \tag{3.29}$$

$$E_k = \beta e_k + (1 - \beta)E_{k-1} \tag{3.30}$$

$$D_k = \beta|e_k| + (1 - \beta)D_{k-1} \tag{3.31}$$

$$e_k = S_k - \hat{S}_k \tag{3.32}$$

where β is a parameter assuming values between 0 and 1. The first equation allows the smoothing parameter to change over time, and this is why it has a time subscript. The second equation shows that the value of the smoothing constant at time $k + 1$ (which is used to forecast for $k + 2$) is calculated as the absolute value of the ratio of the smoothed error term to the smoothed absolute error term. The third and fourth equations show how the smoothed error term and the smoothed absolute error term are calculated by exponential smoothing. Finally, the last equation defines the error term as the difference between the actual and the forecast values.

The parameters E_k and D_k can be used to develop a tracking signal. The tracking signal is defined as

$$T_k = \frac{E_k}{D_k} \tag{3.33}$$

The tracking signal as defined above indicates non-random errors (with a 95 per cent confidence) when the value of T_k exceeds 0.51 for a β of 0.1 or 0.74 for a β of 0.2.

DOUBLE EXPONENTIAL SMOOTHING: BROWN'S METHOD

The double exponential smoothing technique, which is also known as Brown's method, is used for forecasting time series data that have a linear trend. The technique is rather similar to the double moving average technique in the sense that it requires the calculation of two parameters, a and b, from a single and a double exponentially smoothed values of the exchange rate.

Let A_k be the single exponentially smoothed value and A'_k the double exponentially smoothed value for point in time k. These values are calculated as

$$A_k = \alpha S_k + (1 - \alpha)A_{k-1} \tag{3.34}$$

$$A'_k = \alpha A_k + (1 - \alpha)A'_{k-1} \tag{3.35}$$

The parameters a and b for point in time k are calculated as

$$a_k = 2A_k - A'_k \tag{3.36}$$

$$b_k = \left(\frac{\alpha}{1 - \alpha}\right)(A_k - A'_k) \tag{3.37}$$

The forecast exchange rate j periods ahead with point k being the reference point is calculated as

$$\hat{S}_{k+j} = a_k + jb_k \tag{3.38}$$

EXPONENTIAL SMOOTHING ADJUSTED FOR TREND: HOLT'S METHOD

This is also known as Holt's two-parameter method. In this case the trend and slope are smoothed directly by using different smoothing constants for each. The exponentially smoothed series is calculated from an equation that is similar to single exponential smoothing except that a term is added for the trend. This equation is written as

$$A_k = \alpha S_k + (1 - \alpha)(A_{k-1} + T_{k-1}) \tag{3.39}$$

where T is the trend, which is estimated by taking the difference between two successive exponential smoothing values. The equation used for estimating the trend at time k is written as

$$T_k = \beta(A_k - A_{k-1}) + (1 - \beta)T_{k-1} \tag{3.40}$$

Hence, the forecast for $k + j$ is calculated as

$$\hat{S}_{k+j} = A_k + jT_k \tag{3.41}$$

EXPONENTIAL SMOOTHING ADJUSTED FOR TREND AND SEASONAL VARIATION: WINTER'S METHOD

The smoothing methods that have been described so far cannot handle seasonal data. If the underlying time series is stationary, then single exponential smoothing is appropriate. If the time series has a linear trend then either Brown's or Holt's methods are appropriate. If the time series has a seasonal pattern then Winter's method is more appropriate. We do not normally think of exchange rates as exhibiting seasonal behaviour. However, it is arguable that some fundamental factors that affect the exchange rate (such as the current account) do exhibit seasonal behaviour that may be transmitted to the exchange rate.

According to Winter's method the exponentially smoothed series is calculated as

$$A_k = \alpha\left(\frac{S_k}{N_{k-L}}\right)(1-\alpha)(A_{k-1}+T_{k-1}) \tag{3.42}$$

where N is the seasonal estimate and L is the length of seasonality (for example the number of months or quarters in a year). This equation is similar to the corresponding equation in Holt's method except that the value of the exchange rate at time k is divided by the seasonal factor lagged L periods. The objective of this adjustment is to remove the seasonal effect that may be present in the time series. The trend is estimated from the equation

$$T_k = \beta(A_k - A_{k-1}) + (1-\beta)T_{k-1} \tag{3.43}$$

while the seasonal factor is estimated from the equation

$$N_k = \gamma\left(\frac{S_k}{A_k}\right) + (1-\gamma)N_{k-L} \tag{3.44}$$

where γ is the smoothing constant for the seasonal factor. The forecast exchange rate at time $k+j$ is then calculated as

$$\hat{S}_{k+j} = (A_k + jT_k)N_{k-L+j} \tag{3.45}$$

TIME SERIES DECOMPOSITION

The objective of time series decomposition is to identify the components of the underlying time series. Once they are identified they can be forecast individually and then combined to produce a forecast of the total series. These components are the trend, the cycle, the seasonal component and the random component. The trend describes the long-run behaviour of the time series and can be increasing, decreasing or unchanged. This is particularly valid for exchange rates. When a currency appreciates over a long period of time, its exchange rate (measured as the value of one unit of the currency in terms of another currency) exhibits an increasing trend. When it depreciates, the exchange rate exhibits a decreasing trend. And when it is stable over time, the trend is unchanged. The cyclical component represents the short-run ups and downs of the underlying time series. The seasonal component represents periodic fluctuations caused by seasonal factors. Finally, the random or the irregular component is the difference between the total time series and the combined effect of the trend, cycle and seasonal component. Time series decomposition is based on removing seasonality first, then the trend and then the cycle. Any residual is assumed to be the random component.

The following illustration is based on a consideration of the value of the exchange rate at time t, where t is any point in time within the sample period, ranging between 1 and n. In general it is assumed that the time series on the exchange rate has the following specification:

$$S_t = f(\mu_t, \phi_t, \gamma_t, \varepsilon_t) \tag{3.46}$$

where μ is the trend, ϕ is the cycle, γ is the seasonal component and ε is the random component. The equation is written as a functional relationship because it could take two forms: additive and multiplicative. These are written as

$$S_t = \mu_t + \phi_t + \gamma_t + \varepsilon_t \tag{3.47}$$

and

$$S_t = \mu_t \times \phi_t \times \gamma_t \times \varepsilon_t \tag{3.48}$$

Since the multiplicative specification can be transformed into an additive specification by taking logs, we will initially deal with the additive specification.

The process of the decomposition consists of the following steps.

STEP 1

Calculate a moving average whose order is equal to the length of seasonality. For example, for quarterly data calculate a four-period (quarter) moving average. This moving average is used to remove the seasonal and random components. Hence

$$M_t = \hat{\mu}_t + \hat{\phi}_t \tag{3.49}$$

where a hat denotes the estimated value of the component.

STEP 2

Subtract the moving average from the original time series to isolate the seasonal and random components. This is done by centring the moving average. Hence

$$\hat{\gamma}_t + \hat{\varepsilon}_t = S_t - M_t \tag{3.50}$$

A word is warranted on centring the moving average. For example, a three-period moving average, which is calculated from the observations for points in time 1, 2 and 3, is centred at point in time 2. Similarly, a three-period moving average, which is calculated from the observations at points in time 2, 3 and 4, is centred at point in time 3. Hence, the three-period moving average is centred at 2, 3, 4 and so on. A problem, however, arises by trying to centre a moving average of an even order such as 4. For example, if the moving average is calculated from observations 1, 2, 3 and 4, it should be centred at point 2.5, and so on. To overcome this problem, we calculate a four-period single moving average and then a two-period double moving average. The latter can then be centred at 3, 4, 5, and so on.

STEP 3

The seasonal component can extracted by averaging $S_t - M_t$ for each of the seasons. The implication here is that the seasonal component varies from one season to another within one year but it is constant for the same season across all years. This is a description of deterministic seasonality. However, seasonality may be stochastic in the sense that seasonal factors change over time. This technique cannot handle stochastic seasonality, unlike the structural time series model which will be discussed later.

The seasonal component associated with season i can be calculated as

$$\hat{\gamma}_i = \frac{1}{L}\sum_{i=1}^{L}(S_t - M_t)_i \tag{3.51}$$

where L is the seasonal factor for each of the periods making up the complete length of the seasonality (for example over the four quarters).

STEP 4

Identify the appropriate form of the trend (for example, linear or exponential), and then estimate it. The trend can then be estimated by regression. For example, a linear trend can be estimated from a linear regression equation in which the dependent variable is the exchange rate and the explanatory variable is time. Hence

$$\hat{\mu}_t = a + bt \tag{3.52}$$

where a and b are estimated from the linear regression equation

$$S_t = a + bt \tag{3.53}$$

Again, this is a definition of a deterministic time trend. If the trend is stochastic in the sense that it changes over time then another technique must be used to estimate this component. One possibility is to use the Hodrick–Prescott (HP) filter. Stochastic trends can also be handled by the structural time series model which we will describe later.

STEP 5

Subtract the trend from the sum of the trend and the cycle to obtain the cycle. Hence

$$\hat{\phi}_t = M_t - \hat{\mu}_t \tag{3.54}$$

STEP 6

The random component can then be extracted by subtracting the three components from the original time series. Hence

$$\hat{\varepsilon}_t = S_t - (\hat{\mu}_t + \hat{\phi}_t + \hat{\gamma}_t) \tag{3.55}$$

STEP 7

To calculate a forecast for a particular point in time, we add the estimated trend for that point in time to the estimated cycle and the estimated seasonal component. Hence

$$\hat{S}_{t+j} = \hat{\mu}_{t+j} + \hat{\phi}_{t+j} + \hat{\gamma}_{t+j} \tag{3.56}$$

While estimating the trend and the seasonal component is straightforward (if they are stationary), the estimation of the cyclical component is not so. Unfortunately, exchange rate behaviour is such that the cyclical component is more important than the seasonal component. In any case, a preliminary examination of the data is required to get a rough idea about the components that should be included in the model and other features such as the specification of the trend. Figure 3.1 shows some of these patterns. We shall later present structural time series analysis, which is a more powerful technique for dealing with these problems.

If we want to deal with the original data without resorting to logarithmic transformation, then we use the ratio-to-moving average method which involves division rather than subtraction. The equations of the model change to the following:

$$S_t = \mu_t \times \phi_t \times \gamma_t \times \varepsilon_t \tag{3.57}$$

$$M_t = \hat{\mu}_t \times \hat{\phi}_t \tag{3.58}$$

$$\hat{\gamma}_t \times \hat{\varepsilon}_t = \frac{S_t}{M_t} \tag{3.59}$$

$$\hat{\phi}_t = \frac{M_t}{\hat{\mu}_t} \tag{3.60}$$

$$\hat{\varepsilon}_t = \frac{S_t}{\hat{\mu}_t \times \hat{\phi}_t \times \hat{\gamma}_t} \tag{3.61}$$

$$\hat{S}_{t+j} = \hat{\mu}_{t+j} \times \hat{\phi}_{t+j} \times \hat{\gamma}_{t+j} \tag{3.62}$$

THE BOX–JENKINS METHODOLOGY: ARIMA MODELLING

ARIMA models are a class of models that can produce forecasts based on detecting patterns in historical data. This methodology is appropriate if the observations of a time series are statistically dependent on each other. The method is based on an iterative approach of identifying a possible model specification from a general class of models. Once this model is estimated it is checked against the historical data. If the model fits well it is used for forecasting; otherwise a new model specification is selected. If the model fits well, the residuals must be small and random.

AUTOREGRESSIVE MODELS

An autoregressive model of order p, or AR(p), is specified as

$$S_t = \phi_0 + \phi_1 S_{t-1} + \phi_2 S_{t-2} + \cdots + \phi_p S_{t-p} + e_t \tag{3.63}$$

where e is the error term and the ϕ are coefficients.

(a) No trend, no cycle and no seasonal component

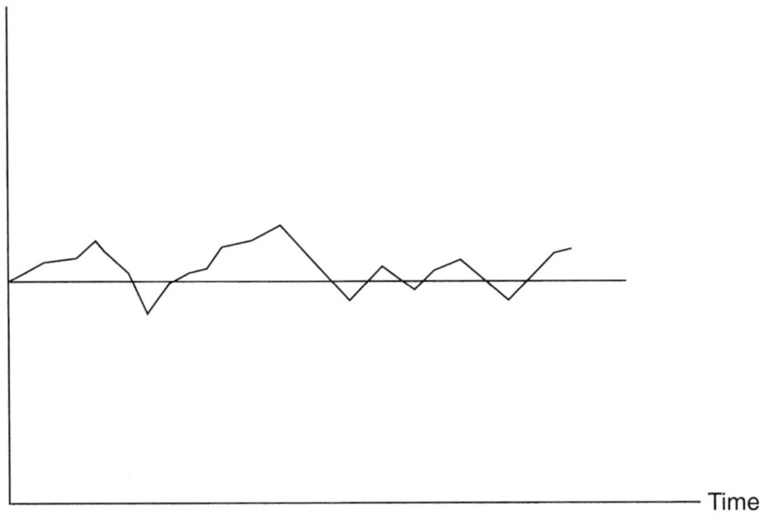

(b) Increasing linear trend

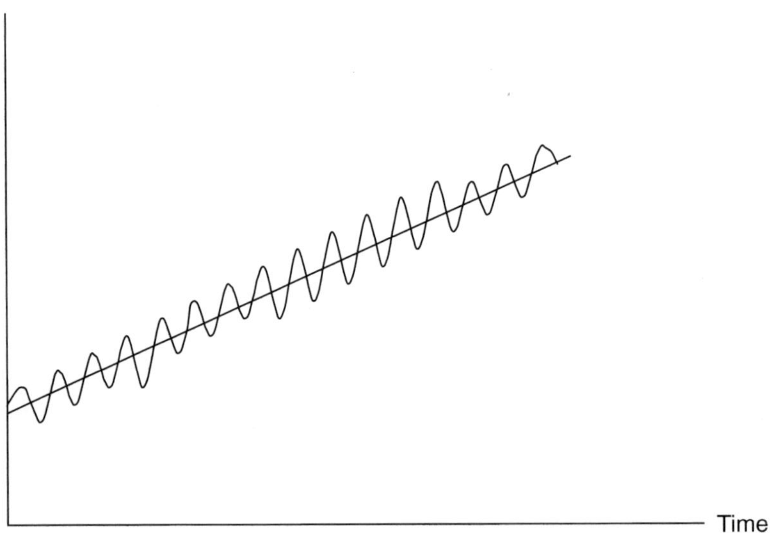

Figure 3.1 Some possible time series patterns

(c) Increasing exponential trend

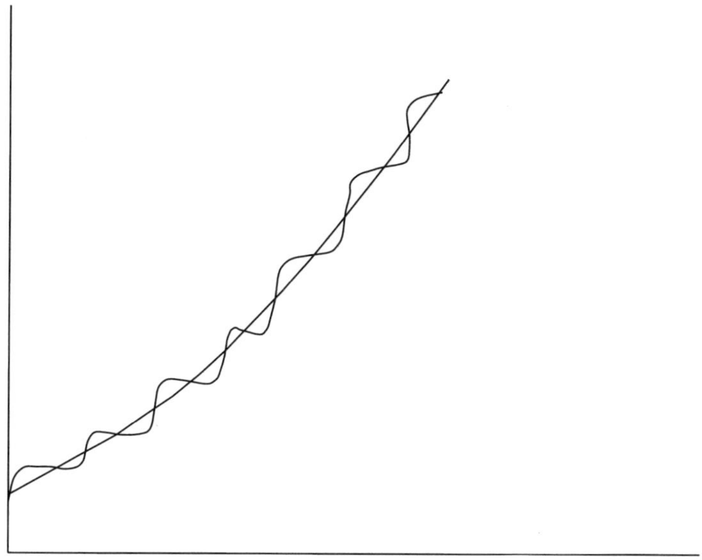

(d) Stochastic trend

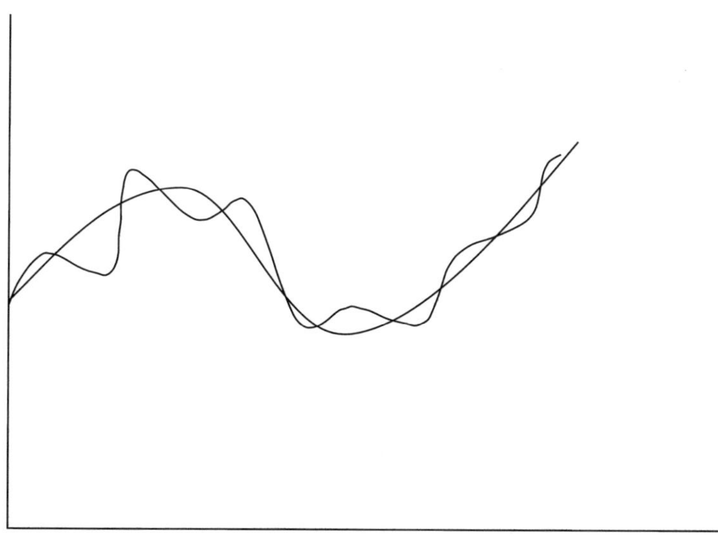

Figure 3.1 Some possible time series patterns (cont.)

(e) Seasonality (additive, deterministic)

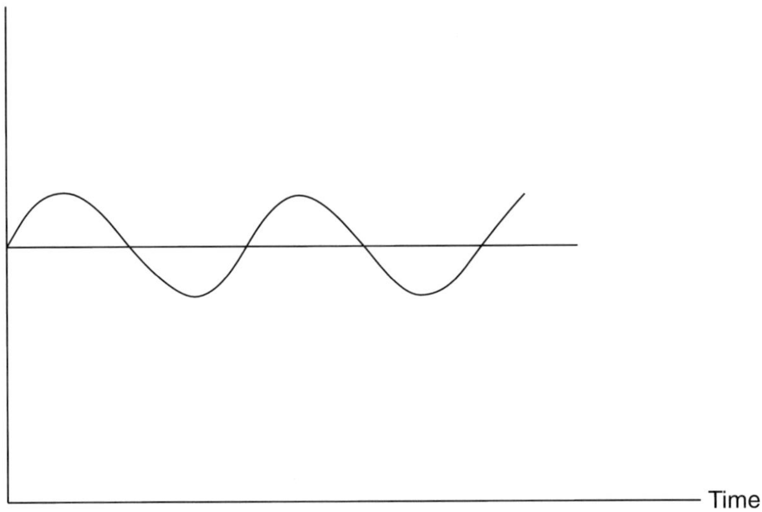

(f) Cycle

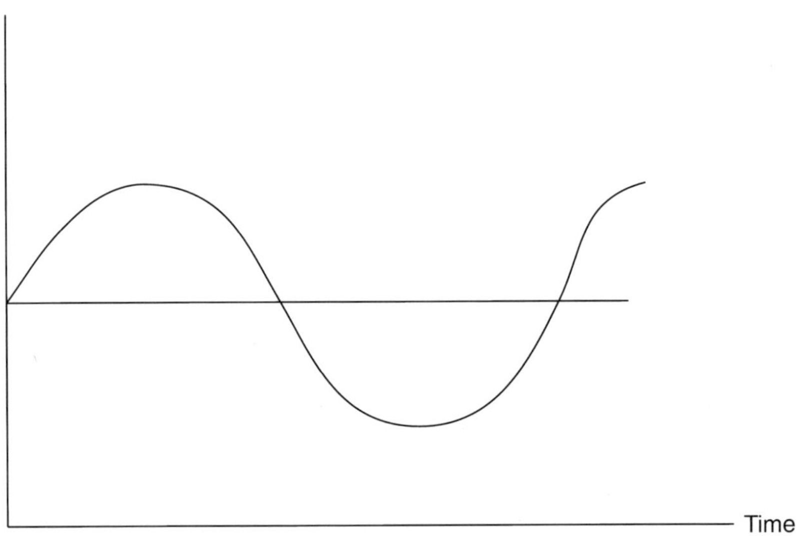

Figure 3.1 Some possible time series patterns (cont.)

In an autoregressive model the dependent variable is determined by its lagged values. Thus, AR(1) and AR(2) models are written as

$$S_t = \phi_0 + \phi_1 S_{t-1} + e_t \tag{3.64}$$

$$S_t = \phi_0 + \phi_1 S_{t-1} + \phi_2 S_{t-2} + e_t \tag{3.65}$$

MOVING AVERAGE MODELS

A moving average model of order q, or MA(q), is written as

$$S_t = \theta_0 + e_1 - \theta_1 e_{t-1} - \theta_2 e_{t-2} - \cdots - \theta_q e_{t-q} \tag{3.66}$$

Hence, the MA model specifies the dependent variable in terms of the lagged values of the error term. It is customary to show the coefficients with negative signs even though they can be either negative or positive. The sum of the coefficients does not have to be equal to one. Thus, MA(1) and MA(2) models are written as

$$S_t = \theta_0 + e_t - \theta_1 e_{t-1} \tag{3.67}$$

$$S_t = \theta_0 + e_t - \theta_1 e_{t-1} - \theta_2 e_{t-2} \tag{3.68}$$

MIXED MODELS: ARMA AND ARIMA

A mixed ARMA (autoregressive moving average) model is a model which specifies the dependent variable to be determined by a mixture of autoregressive and moving average processes. An ARMA(p, q) model may be written as

$$S_t = \mu + \phi_1 S_{t-1} + \phi_2 S_{t-2} + \cdots + \phi_p S_{t-p} + e_t - \theta_1 e_{t-1} - \theta_2 e_{t-2} - \cdots - \theta_q e_{t-q} \tag{3.69}$$

If S is non-stationary (as it is normally the case), then this model is known as an autoregressive integrated moving average model, ARIMA(p, d, q), where d denotes the number of differencing required to make the time series stationary. It is invariably the case that the exchange rate requires differencing once to achieve stationarity. The above model therefore is ARIMA(p, 1, q). The corresponding ARMA(p, q) or ARIMA(p, 0, q) is written in first differences as

$$\Delta S_t = \mu + \phi_1 \Delta S_{t-1} + \phi_2 \Delta S_{t-2} + \cdots + \phi_p \Delta S_{t-p} + e_t - \theta_1 e_{t-1} - \theta_2 e_{t-2} - \cdots - \theta_q e_{t-q} \tag{3.70}$$

Hence, an ARMA(p, q) model is equivalent to an ARIMA(p, 0, q) model. Table 3.4 provides a list of specifications for some ARIMA models.

Table 3.4 Some special ARIMA models

Model	*Specification*	*Remarks*
ARIMA(0, 0, 0)	$S_t = \mu + e_t$	No autoregressive or moving average processes
ARIMA(0, 1, 0)	$S_t = S_{t-1} + e_t$ $\Delta S_t = e_t$	No autoregressive or moving average processes when the model is written in first differences
ARIMA(1, 0, 0) or AR(1)	$\Delta S_t = \phi_0 + \phi_1 \Delta S_{t-1} + e_t$	Stationary autoregressive model of order one
ARIMA(0, 0, 1) or MA(1)	$\Delta S_t = \theta_0 + e_t - \theta_1 \Delta e_{t-1}$	Stationary moving average model of order one
ARIMA(1, 0, 1) or ARMA(1, 1)	$\Delta S_t = \mu + \phi_1 \Delta S_{t-1} + e_t - \theta_1 e_{t-1}$	Simple mixed model for a stationary variable
ARIMA(1, 1, 1)	$S_t = \mu + \phi_1 S_{t-1} + e_t - \theta_1 e_{t-1}$	Simple mixed model for a non-stationary variable

FORECASTING WITH ARIMA MODELS

Three steps are involved in forecasting with ARIMA models:

(1) Model Identification

The first step is to determine whether or not the series is stationary. Exchange rates are non-stationary and so they have to be made stationary. In this step, the forecaster must determine the value of the parameter d which is normally one for exchange rates. This is followed by identifying the form of the model to be used. The identification process involves a comparison of the autocorrelation and partial autocorrelation coefficients with the theoretical distributions of these coefficients. The autocorrelation and partial autocorrelation functions relate the coefficients to the lag length. The autocorrelation coefficient between S_t and S_{t-k}, r_k, is calculated as

$$r_k = \frac{\text{Cov}(S_t, S_{t-k})}{\sqrt{\text{Var}(S_t)\text{Var}(S_{t-k})}} \tag{3.71}$$

where $\text{Cov}(S_t, S_{t-k})$ is the covariance between S_t and S_{t-k} and $\text{Var}(S_t)$ is the variance of S_t. The partial autocorrelation coefficient between S_t and S_{t-k} is calculated on the assumption that the lagged values at other lag lengths are unchanged.

If the exchange rate is non-stationary of order 1, the autocorrelation function will not show a sign of decay. The shapes of the autocorrelation and partial autocorrelation functions determine the specification of the model. In general the forecaster should identify the autocorrelation coefficients that drop off exponentially to zero. If the autocorrelation coefficient drops off exponentially to zero, an AR process is indicated. If the partials drop off to zero, an MA model is indicated. If both do that a mixed ARIMA model is indicated. By counting the number of autocorrelation and partial autocorrelation coefficients which are significantly different from zero, the forecaster can determine the order of the AR and/or the MA process. Table 3.5 lists the possibilities while Figure 3.2 shows the possible patterns of the autocorrelation and partial autocorrelation functions. It remains the fact, however, that identifying mixed models involves some degree of trial and error. This is why testing the model is important.

Table 3.5 Behaviour of autocorrelation and partial autocorrelation functions for some ARIMA models

Autocorrelation function	*Partial autocorrelation function*	*AR*	*MA*
Exponential decay or damped sine wave	Single spike at first lag	1	0
Single spike at first lag	Exponential decay or damped sine wave	0	1
Spike at first lag followed by exponential decay or damped sine wave	Spike at first lag followed by exponential decay or damped sine wave	1	1
Spike at first lag followed by exponential decay or damped sine wave	Spike at first two lags followed by exponential decay or damped sine wave	2	1
Spike at first two lags followed by exponential decay or damped sine wave	Spike at first lag followed by exponential decay or damped sine wave	1	2
Spike at first two lags followed by exponential decay or damped sine wave	Spike at first two lags followed by exponential decay or damped sine wave	2	2

(2) Model Estimation and Testing

The regression coefficients are estimated by using nonlinear least squares, which is an iterative estimation method. Preliminary estimates are used as a starting point then the estimates are improved until the final estimated

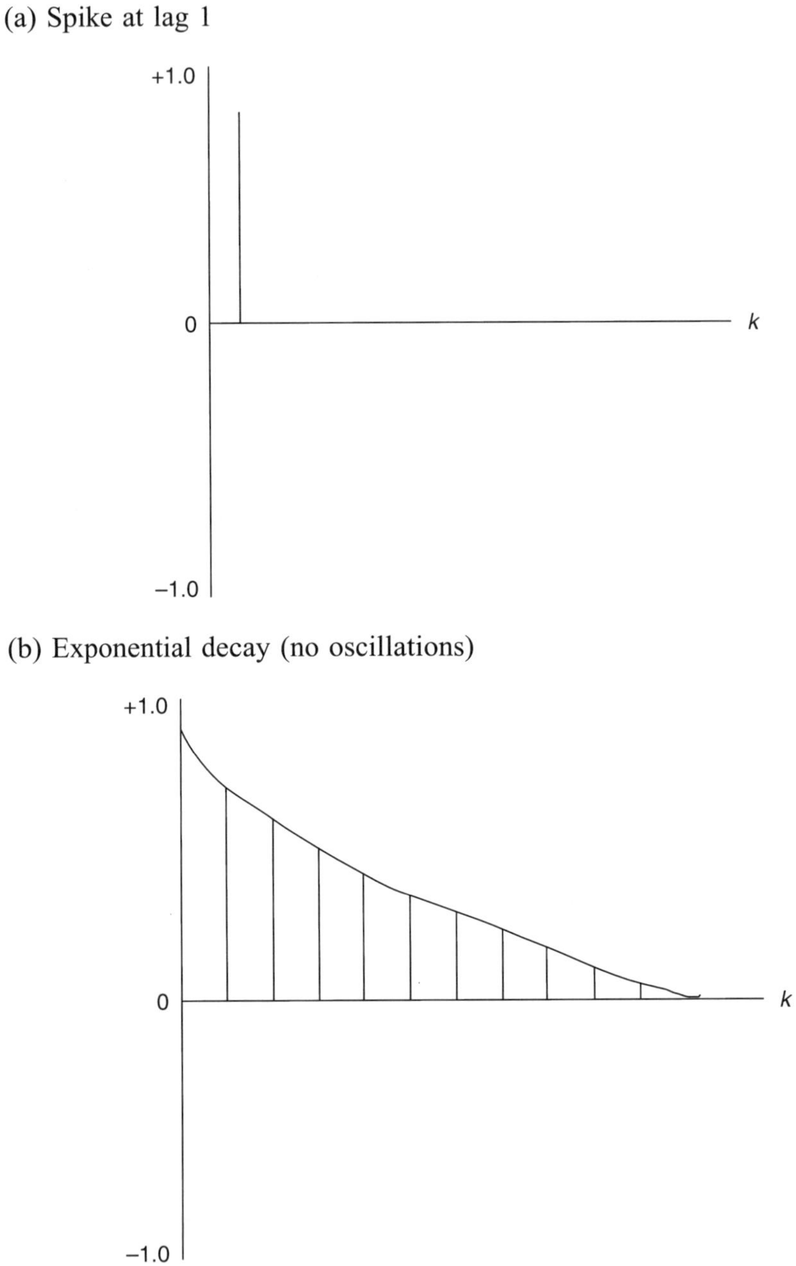

Figure 3.2 Patterns of autocorrelation and partial autocorrelation functions

(c) Exponential decay (with oscillations)

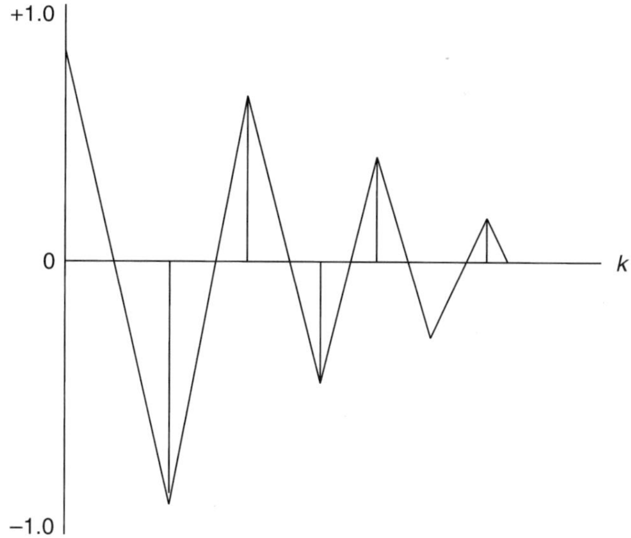

(d) Damped sine wave

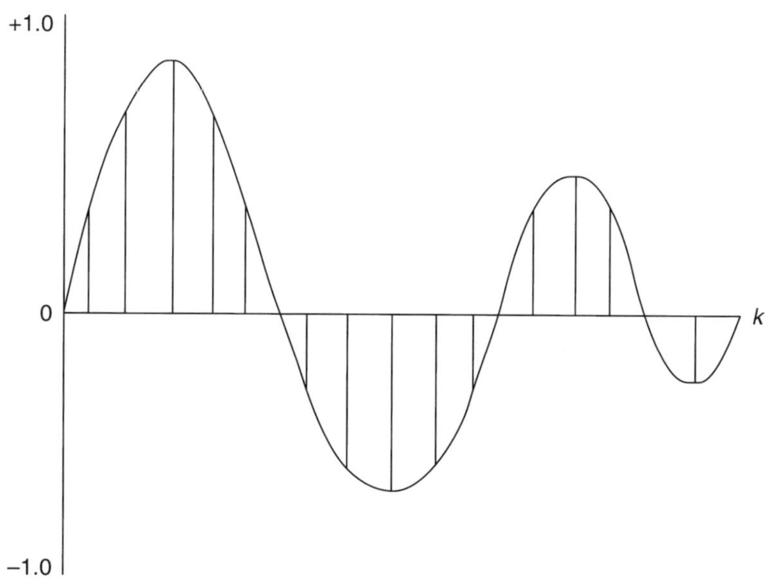

Figure 3.2 Patterns of autocorrelation and partial autocorrelation functions (cont.)

values are obtained. Once the model has been estimated we may check its adequacy by examining the error term, in particular the autocorrelation coefficients of the error term. If a few lags are significantly different from zero, then the model is inadequate. The Box–Pierce Q statistic can also be used. The test statistic is calculated as

$$Q = (n - d) \sum_{k=1}^{m} r_k^2 \tag{3.72}$$

where n is the number of observations of the original time series, m is the maximum lag used and d is the degree of differencing (normally one for exchange rates). The test statistic is distributed as χ^2 with $m - p - q$ degrees of freedom. If the test statistic is significant then the model is inadequate. In this case the forecaster should go back to the first step.

(3) Forecasting

Once the model has been estimated and tested it can be used to forecast the exchange rate one or several periods into the future. The computation of the forecast $\hat{S}_{t+j}$ can be done recursively using the estimated ARIMA model. This involves first computing a forecast one period ahead, $\hat{S}_{t+1}$ and using this forecast to compute $\hat{S}_{t+2}$ and so on. We start by calculating a one-period-ahead forecast for the first difference, $\hat{\Delta S}_{t+1}$. Since

$$\begin{aligned} \Delta S_{t+1} = &\mu + \phi_1 \Delta S_t + \phi_2 \Delta S_{t-1} + \cdots + \phi_p \Delta S_{t-p+1} \\ &+ e_{t+1} - \theta_1 e_t - \theta_2 e_{t-1} \cdots - \theta_q e_{t-q+1} \end{aligned} \tag{3.73}$$

The forecast can be calculated by taking the conditional expected value of $\hat{\Delta S}_{t+1}$, which is given by

$$\begin{aligned} \hat{\Delta S}_{t+1} &= E(\Delta S_{t+1} | \Delta S_t, \ldots) \\ &= \mu + \phi_1 \Delta S_t + \phi_2 \Delta S_{t-1} + \cdots + \phi_p \Delta S_{t-p+1} \\ &\quad - \theta_1 \hat{e}_t - \theta_2 \hat{e}_{t-1} - \cdots - \theta_q \hat{e}_{t-q+1} \end{aligned} \tag{3.74}$$

where $\hat{e}_t, \ldots$ are the observed residuals. By using the one-period forecast we could obtain a two-period forecast as

$$\begin{aligned} \hat{\Delta S}_{t+2} &= E(\Delta S_{t+2} | \Delta S_t, \ldots) \\ &= \mu + \phi_1 \hat{\Delta S}_{t+1} + \phi_2 \Delta S_t + \cdots + \phi_p \Delta S_{t-p+2} \\ &\quad - \theta_2 \hat{e}_t \cdots - \theta_q \hat{e}_{t-q+2} \end{aligned} \tag{3.75}$$

The process is repeated until the j period forecast is obtained

$$\begin{aligned}\hat{\Delta S}_{t+j} =& \mu + \phi_1 \hat{\Delta S}_{t+j-1} + \cdots + \phi_j \Delta S_t + \cdots + \phi_p \Delta S_{t-p+j} \\ &- \theta_j \hat{e}_t - \cdots - \theta_q \hat{e}_{t-q+j}\end{aligned} \tag{3.76}$$

A forecast of the original series (the level of the exchange rate) can be obtained by summing the forecasts for the first differences. Hence

$$\hat{S}_{t+j} = S_t + \hat{\Delta S}_{t+1} + \hat{\Delta S}_{t+2} + \cdots + \hat{\Delta S}_{t+j} \tag{3.77}$$

TIME SERIES ANALYSIS: HARVEY'S STRUCTURAL TIME SERIES MODEL

The structural time series model of Harvey (1985, 1989) is used to decompose an observed time series into unobserved components. These components can be forecast individually and combined to produce a forecast for the total series. This model arguably represents the main features of a time series by considering its various constituent components. The model may be written as

$$S_t = \mu_t + \phi_t + \gamma_t + \varepsilon_t \tag{3.78}$$

where S_t is the observed exchange rate (or its logarithm), μ_t is the trend component, ϕ_t is the cyclical component, γ_t is the seasonal component and ε_t is the random component. Although this equation looks identical to the one considered under time series decomposition, there is a big difference. This model postulates general specifications for the processes generating the components, thus allowing for any possibility such as the presence of stochastic (rather than deterministic) trend and seasonality. The trend, cyclical and seasonal components are assumed to be uncorrelated while ε_t is assumed to be white noise.

The trend component, which represents the long-term movement in a series, is assumed to be stochastic and linear. This component can be represented by

$$\mu_t = \mu_{t-1} + \beta_{t-1} + \eta_t \tag{3.79}$$

$$\beta_t = \beta_{t-1} + \zeta_t \tag{3.80}$$

where $\eta_t \sim NID(0, \sigma_\eta^2)$, and $\zeta_t \sim NID(0, \sigma_\zeta^2)$. μ_t is a random walk with a drift factor, β_t, which follows a first-order autoregressive process as represented by equation (3.80). This process collapses to a simple random walk with drift if $\sigma_\zeta^2 = 0$, and to a deterministic linear trend if $\sigma_\eta^2 = 0$ as well. If, on the other hand, $\sigma_\eta^2 = 0$ while $\sigma_\zeta^2 \neq 0$, the process will have a trend which changes relatively smoothly.

The cyclical component, which is assumed to be a stationary linear process, may be represented by

$$\phi_t = a\cos\theta t + b\sin\theta t \tag{3.81}$$

where t is time and the amplitude of the cycle is given by $(a^2 + b^2)^{1/2}$. In order to make the cycle stochastic, the parameters a and b are allowed to evolve over time, while preserving continuity is achieved by writing down a recursion for constructing ϕ before introducing the stochastic elements. By introducing disturbances and a damping factor we obtain

$$\phi_t = \rho(\phi_{t-1}\cos\theta + \phi_{t-1}^*\sin\theta) + \omega_t \tag{3.82}$$

$$\phi_t^* = \rho(-\phi_{t-1}\sin\theta + \phi_{t-1}^*\cos\theta) + \omega_t^* \tag{3.83}$$

where ϕ_t^* appears by construction such that ω_t and ω_t^* are uncorrelated white noise disturbances with variances σ_ω^2 and $\sigma_{\omega^*}^2$ respectively. The parameters $0 \leq \theta \leq \pi$ and $0 \leq \rho \leq 1$ are the frequency of the cycle and the damping factor on the amplitude respectively. The period of the cycle, which is the time taken by the cycle to go through its complete sequence of values is $2\pi/\theta$ (Harvey, 1989, p. 38). The stochastic cycle in equations (3.82) and (3.83) collapses to an AR(1) process when $\theta = 0$ or π. In order to make numerical optimisation easier, the constraint $\sigma_\omega^2 = \sigma_{\omega^*}^2$ is imposed.

While there are a number of different specifications for seasonality (see Harvey, 1989, Chapter 2), the trigonometric specification is the most preferred. For an even s, where s is the number of seasons per year (four for quarterly data), the seasonal component is written as

$$\gamma_t = \sum_{j=1}^{s/2} \gamma_{j,t} \tag{3.84}$$

$\gamma_{j,t}$ is given by

$$\gamma_{j,t} = \gamma_{j,t-1}\cos\lambda_j + \gamma_{j,t-1}^*\sin\lambda_j + \kappa_{j,t} \tag{3.85}$$

$$\gamma_{j,t}^* = -\gamma_{j,t-1}\sin\lambda_j + \gamma_{j,t-1}^*\cos\lambda_j + \kappa_{j,t}^* \tag{3.86}$$

where $j = 1, \ldots, s/2 - 1$, $\lambda_j = 2\pi j/s$ and

$$\gamma_{j,t} = -\gamma_{j,t-1} + \kappa_{j,t}, \quad j = s/2 \tag{3.87}$$

where $\kappa_{j,t} \sim NID(0, \sigma_\kappa^2)$ and $\kappa_{j,t}^* \sim NID(0, \sigma_{\kappa^*}^2)$. Again, the assumption $\sigma_\kappa^2 = \sigma_{\kappa^*}^2$ is imposed. One advantage of this specification is that it allows for smoother changes in the seasonals (Harvey and Scott, 1994, p. 1328).

The extent to which the trend, seasonal and cyclical components evolve over time depends on the values of σ_η^2, σ_ζ^2, σ_κ^2, σ_ω^2, θ and ρ which are known as the hyperparameters. These parameters can be estimated by maximum likelihood in the time or frequency domain once the model has been written in a state space form (Harvey, 1989, Chapter 4). The frequency domain estimation is much faster but it provides slightly different results because the procedure is based on an approximation to the frequency domain likelihood function. When these parameters have been estimated via the Kalman filter, it is indeed possible to obtain estimates of the unobserved components. The following is a brief description of the state space representation and the estimation method.

The model can be written in state space form as

$$S_t = \mathbf{Z}_t'\mathbf{A}_t + \varepsilon_t \tag{3.88}$$

$$\mathbf{A}_t = \mathbf{B}_t\mathbf{A}_{t-1} + \mathbf{v}_t \tag{3.89}$$

Equations (3.88) and (3.89) are the measurement and transition equations respectively in which $\mathbf{Z}_t$ is an $m \times 1$ fixed vector, $\mathbf{A}_t$ is an $m \times 1$ unobservable state vector and $\mathbf{B}_t$ is a non-stochastic $m \times m$ matrix. Equation (3.89) tells us that the state vector is updated each period, and that it is also subject to serially uncorrelated random disturbances (represented by the $m \times 1$ vector $\mathbf{v}_t$) with zero mean and variance covariance matrix $\mathbf{M}_t$. Once the model is written in state space form, estimates of the parameters of the model can be obtained by maximum likelihood, using the Kalman filter to update the estimated values of the unobserved components. If $\mathbf{a}_{t-1}$ is an estimate of $\mathbf{A}_{t-1}$ and $\mathbf{R}_{t-1}$ is its covariance matrix, then the optimal (minimum mean square error) linear projection of $\mathbf{a}_t$ and $\mathbf{R}_t$ at time $t-1$ are given by

$$\mathbf{a}_{t|t-1} = \mathbf{B}\mathbf{a}_{t-1} \tag{3.90}$$

and

$$\mathbf{R}_{t|t-1} = \mathbf{B}\mathbf{R}_{t-1}\mathbf{B} + \mathbf{M}_t \tag{3.91}$$

The Kalman filter updates $\mathbf{a}_{t|t-1}$ with the new information contained in S_t according to a process which can be described by the equations

$$\mathbf{a}_t = \mathbf{a}_{t|t-1} + \mathbf{R}_{t|t-1}\mathbf{Z}_t(S_t - \mathbf{Z}_t'\mathbf{a}_{t|t-1})/k_t \tag{3.92}$$

$$\mathbf{R}_t = \mathbf{R}_{t|t-1} - \mathbf{R}_{t|t-1}\mathbf{Z}_t\mathbf{Z}_t'\mathbf{R}_{t|t-1}/k_t \tag{3.93}$$

where

$$k_t = \mathbf{Z}_t'\mathbf{R}_{t|t-1}\mathbf{Z}_t + \sigma_\varepsilon^2 \tag{3.94}$$

Equation (3.92) tells us that the predictor, $\mathbf{a}_{t|t-1}$, is updated by incorporating the prediction error, $S_t - \mathbf{Z}_t'\mathbf{a}_{t|t-1}$, weighted by the Kalman gain, $\mathbf{R}_{t|t-1}\mathbf{Z}_t/k_t$. Likewise, equation (3.93) shows that the covariance matrix, $\mathbf{R}_t$, is updated such that its new value is equal to the old value less $\mathbf{Z}_t'\mathbf{R}_t|t-1$ weighted by the Kalman gain.

Model validation is based on measures of goodness of fit (R^2, R_d^2 and Akaike's information criterion, *AIC*) and the diagnostics for serial correlation (*Q*), normality (*N*) and heteroscedasticity (*H*). The following is a brief description of these statistics (for more details see Koopman *et al.*, 1995).

Let the residuals be ν_t where $t = d+1, \ldots, T$ and T is the sample size. Also let the prediction error variance (PEV) be represented by $\tilde{\sigma}^2$ which is the variance of the one-step-ahead prediction error in the steady state. The coefficient of determination can, therefore, be defined as

$$R^2 = 1 - \frac{(T-d)\tilde{\sigma}^2}{\sum_{t=1}^{T}(S_t - \bar{S})^2} \tag{3.95}$$

where S is the original exchange rate series (the dependent variable) and $\bar{S}$ is its mean. Harvey (1989) argues that for trended time series data, R_d^2 is a more appropriate measure of the goodness of fit. This measure is calculated as

$$R_d^2 = 1 - \frac{(T-d)\tilde{\sigma}^2}{\sum_{t=2}^{T}(\Delta S_t - \overline{\Delta S})^2} \tag{3.96}$$

where $\overline{\Delta S}$ is the mean of the first difference of S. A negative R_d^2 implies that the estimated model is worse than a simple random walk plus drift model. Another measure of goodness of fit that is used for comparative purposes is Akaike's information criterion (*AIC*) which is calculated as

$$AIC = \log \tilde{\sigma}^2 + 2m/T \tag{3.97}$$

where m is the number of hyperparameters plus the number of non-stationary components.

The diagnostic test for serial correlation is the Ljung–Box (1978) Q statistic. It is calculated on the basis of the first n autocorrelation coefficients of the residuals as

$$Q(n,q) = T(T+2)\sum_{t=j}^{n}\frac{r_j^2}{T-n} \tag{3.98}$$

where r is the autocorrelation coefficient. In this case Q is distributed as $\chi^2(q)$ where $q = n + 1 - k$ and k is the number of estimated parameters.

The diagnostic for normality, N, is the Bowman–Shenton (1975) test statistic which measures the extent of departure of the third and fourth moments from their expected values under normality. The third and fourth moments are measures of skewness and kurtosis respectively (for a normal distribution they have values of 0 and 3). The test statistic is calculated as

$$N = \left(\frac{T-d}{6}\right)b_1 + \left(\frac{T-d}{24}\right)(b_2-3)^2 \tag{3.99}$$

where b_1 is the square of the third moment and b_2 is the fourth moment. The test statistic is distributed as $\chi^2(2)$.

Finally, H is a diagnostic for heteroscedasticity that is calculated as

$$H(h) = \sum_{t=T-h+1}^{T}\nu_t^2 \bigg/ \sum_{t=d+1}^{d+1+h}\nu_t^2 \tag{3.100}$$

which is the ratio of the squares of the last h residuals to the squares of the first h residuals where h is the closest integer to $T/3$. Thus, a high (low) value of the statistic indicates an increase (decrease) in the variance over time.

If the model is found to be satisfactory, the forecasts of the components and the total series can be computed. The forecasts are generated recursively. For more details, see Harvey (1989) and Koopman *et al.* (1995).

COMPUTER SOFTWARE

Several computer software packages can be used to implement the forecasting techniques surveyed in this chapter. The following is a brief description of these packages and what they can be used for. It must be emphasised, however, that this list is not by any means exhaustive: it is rather selective.

EXCEL

Excel and similar spreadsheet programs can be used to implement the averaging and smoothing methods. Since these programs are not purpose-designed forecasting packages, a full understanding of the mathematical foundations of the techniques is required for implementing them on these programs. For the same reason, these programs cannot offer automatic determination of the order of the moving average or the selection of the optimal model in general. Working with these programs on these techniques can, therefore, be cumbersome and time consuming. For simple problems, however, these programs can do a good job.

FORECAST PRO

Forecast Pro is a spreadsheet, purpose-designed forecasting package that produces forecasts automatically and evaluates them. It also allows for batch forecasting, that is it automatically allows the forecaster to prepare univariate forecasts for up to ten series. The extended edition of the program, Forecast Pro XE, allows the same routines to be carried out on up to 100 series. The package contains the following routines.

Averaging Methods

The program allows three options: 'automatic', 'moving average' and 'random walk'. The option 'automatic' determines the order of the moving average using as a criterion the minimisation of error over the sample period. The 'moving average' option allows the user to select the order of the moving average. The 'random walk' option sets the order of the moving average to one, so that the forecast is the last observed value.

Exponential Smoothing

One feature of Forecast Pro is that it views Harvey's structural time series model as an extension of exponential smoothing. The program views exponential smoothing as an approximate Kalman filter. It allows automatic model selection from simple exponential smoothing, Holt's method and Winter's method, and tries both additive and multiplicative specifications. The optimal model selected on the basis of the minimisation of Schwartz's Bayesian information criterion, SBC.

To estimate the model parameters, the program uses an iterative search to minimise the sum of squared errors over the sample period. The output contains lower and upper confidence limits for exponential smoothing forecasts.

ARIMA Models
Forecast Pro offers automatic algorithms that allow the forecaster to build ARIMA models quickly and easily. The program determines the order of differencing necessary to make the time series stationary. This is followed by the estimation of a group of candidate models. Each of these models is tested and the one that is selected has the minimum SBC. Thus, the program offers automatic identification but it also allows for manual identification. By default, a constant term is used only when the model does not include differencing.

SMARTFORECASTS

SmartForecasts is another spreadsheet program that can be used to implement a range of forecasting techniques. The program offers the following facilities:

1. Forecasting using moving average and exponential smoothing methods. The latter include single exponential smoothing, double exponential smoothing and Winter's exponential smoothing.
2. Batch forecasting of a large number of time series.
3. The calculation of basic statistics, autocorrelation and cross-correlation functions. The basic statistics include the mean, standard deviation, coefficient of variation, minimum and maximum values, order statistics, range and median.
4. Additive and multiplicative time series decomposition as well as seasonal adjustment.
5. Multi-level forecasting of a group of related data series and its total using bottom-up and top-down models.
6. Automatic forecasting using event adjustment models to reflect the effects of special events.

MICROFIT

Although Microfit is not a univariate time series package it can be used to perform the following tasks that pertain to the forecasting techniques presented in this chapter:

1. Calculation of simple and moving averages.
2. Estimating and plotting autocorrelation functions.
3. Estimating linear and HP trends.
4. Estimating ARIMA models without allowing for model identification. Although Microfit is not designed to estimate ARIMA models this task can be done by estimating an autoregressive model and specifying a moving average process of a certain order for the error term. The identification stage is unavailable.

SHAZAM

Shazam is an econometric package that can also be used to estimate ARIMA models. The ARIMA command involves three stages:

1. The identification stage reports the autocorrelation and partial autocorrelation functions, which can be inspected to determine the specification of the model.
2. The estimation stage reports the parameters of the estimated model as well as diagnostic tests to check the validity of the model.
3. The forecasting stage, which provides point forecasts and confidence intervals.

STAMP

STAMP (Structural Time Series Analyser, Modeller and Predictor) is a computer program written especially to handle structural time series models. The program can be used to estimate these models, testing them and using them to forecast time series. It also has additional features such as data manipulation and transformation.

STAMP 5.0 allows the user to input time series and estimate univariate time series models. The user can choose a model with any combination of the components: a trend (which consists of a level and a slope), a cycle, a seasonal component and a random component. For the trend the user can choose between deterministic and stochastic levels and slopes, and the same for the seasonal component which can be trigonometric, dummies or deterministic (fixed). A choice can be made between three cycles at three different frequencies. The program also plots the components and shows the estimation results of the final state vector with plots of the separate components.

As far as forecasting is concerned, the program allows for out-of-sample forecasting when the model is estimated over a part of the sample period. In this case it reports the results of tests of predictive accuracy and structural breaks. When the model is estimated over the whole sample period, it can be used to forecast the time series on *ex ante* basis. For more details, see Koopman *et al.* (1995).

EVIEWS

Unlike Shazam, which is a command-driven package, EVIEWS is a menu-driven econometric package that can be used to estimate and evaluate ARIMA models. Like Shazam, it allows for the identification, estimation and forecasting stages.

FURTHER READING

The treatment of the univariate time series techniques is rather general, intended only to provide some sort of indication on what methods and models are available. For the interested reader there are a number of excellent references which may be resorted to.

Makridakis *et al.* (1983) provide a comprehensive treatment of univariate time series forecasting techniques. Averaging and smoothing methods are discussed in Chapter 3, and time series decomposition is described in Chapter 4. ARIMA models are described in Chapters 8 and 9 while Chapter 10 deals with multivariate ARIMA models (not described in this book). The original reference on ARIMA models is the book by Box and Jenkins of which there is now a third edition (Box *et al.*, 1994). Bowerman and O'Connell (1987) also deal with ARIMA modelling in Chapters 2, 3 and 4. Diebold (1998a) presents a general treatment of modelling trends, seasonality and cycles in Chapters 4, 5, 6 and 7. Two good general references on univariate time series analysis are Mills (1990) and Harvey (1993). Harvey's structural time series model is dealt with comprehensively in Harvey (1989) and briefly in Koopman *et al.* (1995).

4: Multivariate Time Series Models

AN OVERVIEW

The univariate time series methods and models described in Chapter 3 are based on one time series containing observations on the exchange rate to be forecast over a particular period of time. This chapter deals with multivariate time series models which, as the name implies, involve more than one time series. The time series may relate to various exchange rates to be forecast jointly or to an exchange rate and its determining variables. These models take the following forms.

SINGLE-EQUATION ECONOMIC MODELS

Single-equation economic models are also known as single-equation econometric models or reduced-form models. These models consist of a single equation that specifies the exchange rate (as the dependent variable) to be a function of some explanatory variables. They are 'economic' models because they are based on economic theory, unlike the models described in Chapter 3. They are 'econometric' models because they are estimated by using some econometric method such as OLS. They are 'reduced-form' models because the single equation explains the dependent (endogenous) variable in terms of other (exogenous) explanatory variables.

SINGLE-EQUATION STRUCTURAL TIME SERIES MODELS

A single equation structural time series model is similar to Harvey's (1989) structural time series model, which was described in the previous chapter, except that it contains explanatory variables. In such a model, the exchange rate is determined by its time series components as well as some explanatory variables.

MULTI-EQUATION ECONOMIC MODELS

These models, also known as simultaneous-equation models, consist of more than one equation that contain explanatory variables. Other than the exchange rate equation, some equations are specified to explain other endogenous variables in terms of exogenous and predetermined variables. The model may include some definitional relationships and identities.

SINGLE-EQUATION ECONOMIC MODELS: SPECIFICATION AND FORECASTING

A single-equation model is specified such that the exchange rate (or its rate of change) depends on one or more explanatory variables as envisaged by economic theory. In general, a single-equation model may be specified as

$$S_t = f(X_{1,t}, X_{2,t}, \ldots, X_{n,t}) \tag{4.1}$$

which tells us that the value of the exchange rate at point in time t depends on the values of the explanatory variables $X_1, X_2, \ldots, X_n$. The exchange rate and the explanatory variables may be measured in natural logarithms. The explanatory variables may include anything that influences the exchange rate such as prices, interest rates, the money supply and the balance of payments position. These variables are postulated to affect the exchange rate in a number of theoretical models such as purchasing power parity, uncovered interest parity, the flow model and the monetary model. The variables may also be composite variables, that is X may be the relative money supply as in the monetary model of exchange rate determination. Moreover, some of these variables may have a different time subscript such as $t+1$ or $t-1$, which means that leads and lags may be involved. This will be the case if the exchange rate at time t depends on the future or the lagged values of a variable (that is, $X_{1,t+1}$ and $X_{2,t-1}$ respectively). The functional relationship given by equation (4.1) is invariably specified as a linear equation. Therefore, it can be written as

$$S_t = a_0 + a_1 X_{1,t} + a_2 X_{2,t} + \cdots + a_n X_{n,t} \tag{4.2}$$

where a_0, a_1, ..., a_n are parameters that measure the magnitude and direction of the influence of each explanatory variable on the exchange rate. a_0 is a constant term that reflects the autonomous component of the exchange rate, that is the component of the exchange rate time series that is unrelated to any of the explanatory variables $X_1, \ldots, X_n$. A random error term is normally added to the equation to reflect the unexplained variation in the exchange rate. The estimation of equation (4.2) by a regression-based econometric method on the basis of historical data produces numerical values for the coefficients $a_0, a_1, \ldots, a_n$. Once these estimates are obtained, forecasting is carried out by estimating the value of the exchange rate at time $t+1$ and beyond, which can only be obtained if we know, or assume, the future values for the explanatory variables. Thus

$$S_{t+1} = a_1 X_{1,t+1} + a_2 X_{2,t+1} + \cdots + a_n X_{n,t+n} \tag{4.3}$$

We will now illustrate how single-equation models can be used to generate forecasts. For this purpose, we use the simple two-variable model

$$S_t = \alpha + \beta X_t + \varepsilon_t \tag{4.4}$$

where $\varepsilon_t \sim N(0, \sigma^2)$. We start by considering unconditional forecasting which assumes that X_{t+1} is known at time t. The best forecast of S at $t+1$, $\hat{S}_{t+1}$, is given by

$$\hat{S}_{t+1} = E(S_{t+1}) = \alpha + \beta X_{t+1} \tag{4.5}$$

The forecast error is given by

$$\hat{e}_{t+1} = \hat{S}_{t+1} - S_{t+1} \tag{4.6}$$

This forecast error has two desirable properties: zero mean and minimum variance among all possible forecasts based on linear equations. The first property is obvious because the mean is

$$E(\hat{e}_{t+1}) = E(\hat{S}_{t+1} - S_{t+1}) = E(-\varepsilon_{t+1}) \tag{4.7}$$

The variance of the forecast error is

$$\sigma_f^2 = E\left[(\hat{e}_{t+1})^2\right] = E\left[(\hat{\varepsilon}_{t+1})^2\right] = \sigma^2 \tag{4.8}$$

Since $e \sim N(0, \sigma^2)$, a significance test can be performed on the forecast value of S by calculating the normalised error

$$\lambda = \frac{\hat{S}_{t+1} - S_{t+1}}{\sigma} \tag{4.9}$$

where $\lambda \sim N(0, 1)$. A 95 per cent confidence interval can be constructed because

$$\text{prob}\left[-\lambda_{0.05} \leq \frac{\hat{S}_{t+1} - S_{t+1}}{\sigma} \leq \lambda_{0.05}\right] = 0.95 \tag{4.10}$$

where $\lambda_{0.05}$ can be obtained from the normal distribution tables. Therefore, the confidence interval can be written as

$$\hat{S}_{t+1} - \lambda_{0.05}\sigma \leq S_{t+1} \leq \hat{S}_{t+1} + \lambda_{0.05}\sigma \tag{4.11}$$

A very important point must be mentioned here. A single-equation model may produce poor forecasting results even though it has a high R^2 and significant t-statistics. This will happen, for example, when there is a structural break. On the other hand, a model with low R^2 and insignificant t-statistics may produce good forecasting results if the dependent variable exhibits little variation.

We will now deal with conditional forecasting when the value of the explanatory variable X is unknown. Consider the model represented by equation (4.4) but in this case we have the following:

$$\hat{X}_{t+1} = X_{t+1} + u_{t+1} \tag{4.12}$$

$$\varepsilon_t \sim N(0, \sigma^2) \tag{4.13}$$

$$u_t \sim N(0, \sigma_u^2) \tag{4.14}$$

$$E(\varepsilon_t u_t) = 0 \tag{4.15}$$

$$E\left[\left(\hat{X}_{t+1} - X_{t+1}\right)\left(\hat{\beta} - \beta\right)\right] = E\left[\left(\hat{X}_{t+1} - X_{t+1}\right)(\hat{\alpha} - \alpha)\right] = 0 \tag{4.16}$$

where $\hat{\alpha}$ and $\hat{\beta}$ are the OLS estimates of α and β respectively. Thus

$$\hat{S}_{t+1} = \hat{\alpha} + \hat{\beta}\hat{X}_{t+1} \tag{4.17}$$

The forecast error is given by

$$\hat{e}_{t+1} = \hat{S}_{t+1} - S_{t+1} = (\hat{\alpha} - \alpha) + (\hat{\beta}\hat{X}_{t+1} - \beta X_{t+1}) - \varepsilon_{t+1} \tag{4.18}$$

Hence

$$E(\hat{e}_{t+1}) = 0 \tag{4.19}$$

It can be shown that the forecast error variance in this case is larger than before, producing a wider confidence interval. This is because forecasting X leads to a larger forecasting error. For more details, see Pindyck and Rubenfeld (1991, Chapter 8).

PROBLEMS WITH SINGLE-EQUATION MODELS

There are several problems associated with forecasting by using single-equation economic models. These problems are discussed in turn.

THE 'BLACK BOX' PROBLEM

A single-equation model is called a reduced-form model because it explains the value of the exchange rate in terms of other variables without telling us how these explanatory variables are determined. This is like feeding information into a 'black box' and obtaining forecasts without knowing what goes on inside. For example, a model that postulates the exchange rate to be determined by the interest rate differential implicitly assumes that interest rates are determined by factors outside the model. The model implicitly precludes the possibility of the influence running from the exchange rate to interest rates. This may not be necessarily the case as causality could run in the opposite direction. For example, when the domestic currency comes under pressure and starts to depreciate the monetary authorities may opt to support the currency by raising interest rates. In this case, causality runs from the exchange rate to the (domestic) interest rate. Second, the model is a 'black box' in the sense that it does not readily explain the (transmission) mechanism whereby interest rates affect exchange rates. It is more plausible to think of the exchange rates and interest rates as being determined simultaneously, two products of the working of one system.

It must be mentioned that univariate time series models are even more of 'black boxes' than single-equation multivariate models. The former do not even tell us what factors determine the exchange rate, apart from its past history. The 'black box' problem can, however, be dealt with by specifying a multi- or simultaneous equation model.

CONDITIONAL FORECASTING

Forecasts may be conditional on the future values of the explanatory variables. If this is the case, the forecast exchange rate depends on the accuracy of the forecasts of the explanatory variables. For example, forecasting the exchange rate on the basis of the (theoretical) relationship between the exchange rate and inflation requires a knowledge of future inflation rates. We may assume these levels on the basis of past behaviour and monetary policy stance or by obtaining an official forecast, such as the forecast implicit in the budget. But it still remains true that the forecast depends on what future values are assigned to the explanatory variables. This problem is also encountered (in fact it is even more acute) in the case of multi-equation models. On the other hand, the problem is not encountered in the case of univariate models, simply because they do not contain explanatory variables.

DATA FREQUENCY

If we want to forecast exchange rates on a daily basis, the explanatory variables must be available on a daily basis to estimate the relationship. This is not always the case. Prices are available on a monthly basis only, while national income figures are available on a quarterly basis only. Thus, we cannot use a model, in which the exchange rate is determined by the inflation rates, to forecast exchange rates on a daily basis. Daily forecasts are what is needed for day-to-day trading in the foreign exchange market. Again, this problem is not encountered in the case of univariate time series models.

STRUCTURAL CHANGES

The assumption underlying this forecasting technique is that the relationship as estimated from historical data will remain valid over the forecasting horizon, implying that the estimated coefficients are constant over time. Hence, the model needs to be modified to take into account structural changes in the relationship. One way to do this is to re-estimate the model using only the most recent data. The model may also be estimated in a time-varying parametric framework. This problem is encountered in all models, since all models are estimated from historical data.

MEASUREMENT ERRORS

There are measurement errors in some explanatory variables. For example, the balance of payments position is measured with a significant 'errors and omissions' item. It can be argued, however, that the decisions affecting exchange rates are taken on the basis of published data even if measurement errors are present in the data. This problem is not encountered in the case of univariate models because there are no explanatory variables. The underlying principle of univariate models is that the behaviour of the exchange rate reflects changes in all of the explanatory variables, including qualitative variables.

QUALITATIVE VARIABLES

A bigger problem arises when some of the explanatory variables are qualitative in nature such as 'market sentiment' or 'market psychology'. This problem can be tackled either by a quantitative adjustment of the forecasts derived from an econometric model, or by resorting to judgemental forecasting.

THEORETICAL FOUNDATIONS: PURCHASING POWER PARITY

We have seen that a single-equation model is determined by economic theory. It is economic theory that tells us what $X_1, X_2, \ldots, X_n$ are. The objective of this section and the following sections is to present an overview of some of the most common theories that specify what the variables should be. In this section we deal with the theory of purchasing power parity (PPP). For a full survey of the theory of and the empirical evidence on PPP, see Moosa and Bhatti (1997).

ABSOLUTE PPP

Purchasing power parity is a theory that describes the relationship between prices and exchange rates. In its simplest and most strict form (known as absolute PPP) it can be written as

$$P = SP^* \tag{4.20}$$

where P and P^* are the domestic and foreign price levels respectively and S is the exchange rate measured as the domestic currency price of one unit of the foreign currency. This version of PPP can be specified as a model of exchange rate determination by writing it as

$$S = \frac{P}{P^*} \tag{4.21}$$

Thus, as domestic prices rise relative to foreign prices, S will rise (the domestic currency will depreciate) and vice versa. The PPP equation may be written in a functional form as

$$S = a + b\left(\frac{P}{P^*}\right) \tag{4.22}$$

where a and b are constant coefficients that can be estimated by regression and $b > 0$. Equation (4.22) says that the spot exchange rate is a linear function of the price ratio. In a testable logarithmic form the PPP relationship may be written as

$$s_t = a + b(p_t - p_t^*) \tag{4.23}$$

where lower-case letters are used to indicate natural logarithms and t is a time subscript. By relaxing the assumption of symmetry, that is that the domestic and foreign prices have equal (absolute) effects on the exchange rate, the PPP model may be written as

$$s_t = a + b_1 p_t + b_2 p_t^* \tag{4.24}$$

where $b_1 > 0$ and $b_2 < 0$.

RELATIVE PPP

The relative version of PPP may be written in terms of rates of change as

$$\dot{S} = \dot{P} - \dot{P}^* \tag{4.25}$$

where a dot indicates the rate of change of the underlying variable. Hence, $\dot{S}$ is the rate of change of the exchange rate, $\dot{P}$ is the domestic inflation rate and $\dot{P}^*$ is the foreign inflation rate. This equation represents a comparative statics hypothesis on the relationship between the exchange rate and inflation differentials, stipulating that the rate of change of the exchange rate should be equal to the inflation differential. If $\dot{P} > \dot{P}^*$, then $\dot{S} > 0$, which implies domestic currency depreciation and vice versa. In other words, the country with the higher inflation rate should have a depreciating currency and vice versa. Thus, while absolute PPP describes the relationship between exchange rates and prices at a particular point in time, relative PPP describes the movement of the exchange rate from one level to another under the influence of changes in prices (that is, inflation). In a testable logarithmic form it can be written as

$$\Delta s_t = a + b(\Delta p_t - \Delta p_t^*) \tag{4.26}$$

or in an unrestricted form as

$$\Delta s_t = a + b_1 \Delta p_1 + b_2 \Delta p_t^* \tag{4.27}$$

where $b_1 > 0$ and $b_2 < 0$.

Relative PPP allows us to calculate the value of the exchange rate compatible with PPP. Between two points in time 0 and 1, relative PPP implies that

$$\frac{S_1}{S_0} = \frac{P_1/P_1^*}{P_0/P_0^*} \tag{4.28}$$

or

$$S_1 = S_0 \left[\frac{P_1/P_1^*}{P_0/P_0^*} \right] = S_0 \left[\frac{P_1/P_0}{P_1^*/P_0^*} \right] \tag{4.29}$$

Equation (4.29) can be written as

$$S_1 = S_0 \left[\frac{1 + \dot{P}}{1 + \dot{P}^*} \right] \tag{4.30}$$

Equations (4.29) and (4.30) tell us the following: starting from a base time period, 0, with an exchange rate, S_0, the exchange rate at time 1, S_1, will differ from S_0 by a factor reflecting domestic and foreign inflation rates. Thus, the two equations can be used to calculate the exchange rate consistent with PPP, or what may be called the PPP rate. The underlying idea is that if PPP held during the period between 0 and 1, in the sense that relative inflation is the only factor determining the exchange rate, then there would be no deviation from the PPP rate. Deviation, however, arises because of the effect of factors other than inflation on the exchange rate. In general, the exchange rate consistent with PPP (some sort of an equilibrium exchange rate) may be calculated as

$$\bar{S}_t = S_0 \left[\frac{P_t}{P_t^*} \right] \tag{4.31}$$

where prices are measured as indices relative to the same base period, 0.

EX ANTE PPP

Ex ante PPP is based on intertemporal speculation in commodity markets. Its specification is similar to that of relative PPP, except that the expected, rather than the actual, values of the variables are used. The relationship is written as

$$\dot{S}^e = \dot{P}^e - \dot{P}^{*e} \tag{4.32}$$

where the superscript e indicates the expected value of the underlying variable. In a logarithmic form, it can be written as

$$\Delta s^e = \Delta p^e - \Delta p^{*e} \tag{4.33}$$

Notice that because equation (4.33) is written in terms of the expected values of the variables, the time subscripts on the variables (which are not shown for simplicity) should be $t+1$. This implies that expectation is made at time t for the values prevailing at time $t+1$.

Ex ante PPP has the same testable form as relative PPP if the hypothesis of rational expectations is used to replace the expected values of the variables with the actual values. This hypothesis tells us that the expected values are equal to the actual values plus or minus a random error term. For more elaboration on the rational expectations substitution, see Moosa and Bhatti (1997).

MODIFICATION OF THE PPP MODEL

Because of the effect of variables other than prices in the short run, the PPP model may be modified by including other explanatory variables. The inclusion of these variables may be necessary to account for deviations from PPP.

The first of these modifications was suggested by Balassa (1964) who was sceptical of the validity of PPP as a theory that explains the determination of the equilibrium exchange rate. His productivity bias hypothesis rests on the proposition that the ratio of non-traded goods prices to traded goods prices tends to be higher in developed countries than in developing countries. Consequently, the PPP exchange rate calculated on the basis of consumer prices tends to underestimate the true equilibrium value of the currency of the developed country that has a higher level of productivity. The PPP equation must be modified by including productivity levels as explanatory variables. Hence the modified PPP equation becomes

$$s_t = a + b(p_t - p_t^*) + c(\nu_t - \nu_t^*) \tag{4.34}$$

where $\nu(\nu^*)$ is the domestic (foreign) productivity level. This hypothesis is used to explain the persistent appreciation of the yen against the dollar over a long period of time.

Another modification rests on the proposition that the failure of PPP is due to the interaction between exchange rates, interest rates and prices in goods and asset markets. The underlying argument is that arbitrage is rather costly in goods markets and less so in assets markets. Consequently, exchange rates are affected by short-run fluctuations arising from highly volatile assets markets and by long-run effects from interrelated goods markets. Thus, PPP is unlikely to hold without due consideration given to interest rates. The modified model would become

$$s_t = a + b(p_t - p_t^*) + c(i_t - i_t^*) \tag{4.35}$$

where $i(i^*)$is the domestic (foreign) interest rate.

A third modification of PPP can be obtained by using the terms of trade as an explanatory variable. An improvement in a country's terms of trade, that is a rise in the price of exports relative to the price of imports, leads to an appreciation of the domestic currency. In the case of some countries, like Australia, the terms of trade are very sensitive to changes in commodity prices. Hence, commodity prices can be used as an explanatory variable as well.

THEORETICAL FOUNDATIONS: COVERED AND UNCOVERED INTEREST PARITY

Covered interest parity (CIP) is an arbitrage relationship based on covered arbitrage. Covered arbitrage is a profit-seeking activity that works as follows: an arbitrager borrows a currency x (say the domestic currency), converts the proceeds into another currency y (say a foreign currency), and invests in currency y while selling it forward. This process is triggered by a certain configuration of the spot exchange rate, the forward exchange rate, and the interest rates on the two currencies. Covered arbitrage is triggered only if the configuration of interest and exchange rates is such that the covered interest parity condition is violated. Arbitrage itself affects supply and demand, forcing changes in the exchange and interest rates until the equilibrium condition is restored. When this happens, arbitrage is no longer profitable. The equilibrium condition implied by covered interest parity requires an equality between the domestic return and the covered foreign return. This condition can be written as

$$1 + i = \frac{F}{S}(1 + i^*) \tag{4.36}$$

where F is the forward rate. In a more simplified form the condition can be written as

$$i - i^* = f \tag{4.37}$$

where $f = (F - S)/S$ is the forward spread, defined as the difference between the spot and forward rates as a ratio of the spot rate. The equilibrium condition tells us that the currency that offers a lower interest rate must be selling at a premium while the currency offering a higher interest rate must be selling at a discount.

Uncovered interest parity (UIP) is similarly derived from uncovered arbitrage. This is a similar operation except that the long position is not covered in the forward market. Rather, currency conversion takes place at the spot exchange rate prevailing on the maturity date of the investment. This rate is naturally unknown at the time when the decision to indulge in uncovered arbitrage is made. Hence, the decision must be based on the spot exchange rate expected to prevail on the maturity date of the investment, S^e. The UIP condition can be written as

$$1 + i = \frac{S^e}{S}(1 + i^*) \tag{4.38}$$

which says that the gross domestic return must be equal to the expected gross uncovered foreign return. The condition may be written in a more simplified form as

$$i - i^* = \dot{S}^e \tag{4.39}$$

which says that the exchange rate must change by a percentage that is equal to the interest rate differential. The condition tells us that the currency offering a lower interest rate must be expected to appreciate, while the currency offering a higher interest rate must be expected to depreciate. This is an important implication for exchange rate forecasting, as the interest rate differential may be used as a forecaster of the exchange rate. Although it may sound odd, it makes a lot of sense, for no one would want to hold a currency that offers a low interest rate and is expected to depreciate. CIP and UIP, as we are going to see later, are important components of the monetary model of exchange rate determination. For more on CIP and UIP, see Moosa and Bhatti (1997) and Moosa (1998).

THEORETICAL FOUNDATIONS: THE FLOW MODEL

The flow model of exchange rate determination postulates that the exchange rate is determined by trade and capital flows as recorded on the balance of payments. In fact this model views the balance of payments and the foreign exchange market to be related to the extent that a balance of payments deficit is a reflection of excess demand for the foreign currency while a surplus reflects excess supply. The exchange rate in this model is determined as an equilibrium price in the foreign exchange market by the forces of supply and demand. Supply and demand are determined by three important factors: relative income levels, relative price levels and the interest rate differential. Hence, the model may be written in a testable logarithmic form as

$$s_t = a_1(y_t - y_t^*) + a_2(p_t - p_t^*) - a_3(i_t - i_t^*) \tag{4.40}$$

where a_1, a_2 and a_3 are positive constants. Notice that the predictions of this model are as follows:

1. If domestic income grows faster than foreign income, imports will grow faster than exports. The resulting deterioration in the balance of payments leads to domestic currency depreciation (higher s).
2. If the domestic price level rises faster than the foreign price level, domestic goods will be less attractive than foreign goods. Exports will decrease while imports will increase. The resulting deterioration in the balance of payments leads to domestic currency depreciation (higher s).
3. If the interest rate differential rises, domestic financial assets become more attractive than foreign financial assets. The resulting capital inflows will lead to an improvement in the balance of payments and domestic currency appreciation (lower s).

The flow model is criticised on the grounds that it only considers flow equilibrium, not stock equilibrium. It does not explain, for example, what constitutes the accumulation of foreign assets.

THEORETICAL FOUNDATIONS: THE FLEXIBLE-PRICE MONETARY MODEL

While the flow model is based on the proposition that the supply and demand for currencies are determined by trade and capital flows, the monetary model is an asset model. Thus, the monetary model considers the supply and demand for currencies to be determined by stock (rather than flow) equilibrium in the money market. In essence, the model tells us that since the exchange rate is the price of one 'money' in terms of another, it must be determined by the relative supplies of, and demands for, the two 'monies'.

The flexible-price monetary model, which was developed by Frenkel (1976) and Bilson (1978), assumes that PPP holds continuously, implying that it is valid in the short run and in the long run as well. The simplest version of the monetary model can be derived by assuming that there is a stable demand for money function of the form

$$M_d = kPY \tag{4.41}$$

where M_d is the quantity of money demanded, P is the price level, Y is real income and k is a positive constant. Assuming also an exogenous money supply, equilibrium in the money market (which requires equality between the demand for money and the exogenously determined money supply) yields

$$P = \frac{M}{kY} \tag{4.42}$$

where M is the money supply. If PPP holds then $S = P/P^*$. By substituting equation (4.42) into the PPP equation, we obtain

$$S = \frac{M}{kP^*Y} \tag{4.43}$$

The model tells us that the exchange rate will rise (the domestic currency will depreciate) when there is an increase in the money supply, a decrease in income and a decrease in the foreign price level. The model also tells us that there is a proportional relationship between the money supply and the exchange rate, that is a 10 per cent rise in the money supply, *ceteris paribus*, leads to a 10 per cent rise in the exchange rate. This prediction follows from a combination of the quantity theory of money and PPP, both of which embody the property of proportionality. The quantity theory of money postulates that an increase in the money supply leads to a proportional increase in the price level. PPP then tells us that this rise in the price level leads to a proportional rise in the exchange rate.

This simple version of the model can be extended by specifying a foreign demand for money function of a similar form. Thus

$$M_d^* = k^* P^* Y^* \tag{4.44}$$

By combining the equilibrium conditions in the domestic and foreign money markets we obtain

$$\frac{M}{M^*} = \frac{kPY}{k^* P^* Y^*} \tag{4.45}$$

By substituting PPP ($S = P/P^*$) into equation (4.45) and rearranging we obtain an equation representing the monetary model. This equation is written as

$$S = \frac{M/M^*}{(k/k^*)(Y/Y^*)} \tag{4.46}$$

This version of the monetary model tells us that the exchange rate is determined by the relative money supply and relative income. A rise in the domestic money supply relative to the foreign money supply leads to a (proportional) rise in the exchange rate (domestic currency depreciation). On the other hand, a rise in domestic income relative to foreign income leads to domestic currency appreciation.

THE ROLE OF INTEREST RATES IN THE MONETARY MODEL

Interest rates can be incorporated in the monetary model by respecifying the demand for money functions. For the purpose of the following exposition, time subscripts will be specified for the variables. The following semi-log demand for money functions are often used for this purpose:

$$m_{d,t} - p_t = \beta_1 y_t - \beta_2 i_t \tag{4.47}$$

$$m_{d,t}^* - p_t^* = \beta_1 y_t^* - \beta_2 i_t^* \tag{4.48}$$

where β_1 and β_2 are positive constants and lower-case letters denote the natural logarithms of the underlying variables except for interest rates (i and i^*). For simplicity, we have imposed the assumption of symmetry, that is equality of the income elasticities (β_1) and interest semi-elasticities (β_2) of the demand for money. By combining the demand for money equations with the equilibrium conditions in the money market and PPP, we obtain

$$s_t = (m_t - m_t^*) - \beta_1(y_t - y_t^*) + \beta_2(i_t - i_t^*) \tag{4.49}$$

which means that there is a positive relationship between s and $i - i^*$, that is a rise in the domestic interest rate relative to the foreign interest rate causes a depreciation of the domestic currency. Thus, the predictions of the monetary model with respect to the effect of income and interest rate on the exchange rate are exactly the opposite to the predictions of the flow model.

Notice that by relaxing the assumption of symmetry, the foreign demand for money function can be written as

$$m^*_{d,t} - p^*_t = \beta^*_1 y^*_t - \beta^*_2 i^*_t \tag{4.50}$$

in which case the flexible-price monetary model becomes

$$s_t = (m_t - m^*_t) - \beta_1 y_t + \beta^*_1 y^*_t + \beta_2 i_t - \beta^*_2 i^*_t \tag{4.51}$$

The model can also be written in a general testable form by relaxing the assumption of proportionality to obtain

$$s_t = \alpha m_t - \alpha^* m^*_t - \beta_1 y_t + \beta^*_1 y^*_t + \beta_2 i_t - \beta^*_2 i^*_t \tag{4.52}$$

in which case proportionality is represented by the null hypothesis $\alpha = \alpha^* = 1$, while symmetry is represented by the hypotheses $\beta_1 = \beta^*_1$ and $\beta_2 = \beta^*_2$.

THEORETICAL FOUNDATIONS: EXTENSIONS TO THE FLEXIBLE-PRICE MONETARY MODEL

The monetary model represented by equation (4.49) can be modified in several ways. The resulting specifications are presented in turn.

INTRODUCING CIP

By substituting equation (4.37) into equation (4.49), we obtain

$$s_t = (m_t - m^*_t) - \beta_1 (y_t - y^*_t) + \beta_2 f_t \tag{4.53}$$

Equation (4.53) tells us that the spot exchange rate is determined not only by the relative money supply and relative income but also by the forward spread. The relationship is positive, implying that a currency that sells at a forward premium should be expected to appreciate.

INTRODUCING UIP

UIP can be written in a logarithmic form as

$$i_t - i_t^* = \Delta s_{t+1}^e \tag{4.54}$$

By substituting equation (4.54) into equation (4.49) we obtain

$$s_t = (m_t - m_t^*) - \beta_1(y_t - y_t^*) + \beta_2 \Delta s_{t+1}^e \tag{4.55}$$

where Δs^e is the expected change in the exchange rate. Equation (4.55) tells us that a currency will appreciate or depreciate if it is expected to appreciate or depreciate. This is because if a currency is expected to depreciate, traders will sell it, leading to its depreciation, and vice versa.

Equation (4.55) can be used to derive the rational expectations version of the monetary model. The equation can be rewritten as

$$\begin{aligned} s_t = &(1+\beta_2)^{-1}(m_t - m_t^*) - (1+\beta_2)^{-1}\beta_1(y_t - y_t^*) \\ &+ \beta_2(1+\beta_2)^{-1} s_{t+1}^e \end{aligned} \tag{4.56}$$

If expectations are rational, then by forward iteration it can be shown that equation (4.56) can be expressed in the forward solution form as

$$s_t = (1+\beta_2)^{-1} \sum_{j=0}^{\infty} \left[\frac{\beta_2}{1+\beta_2}\right]^j \left[\left(m_{t+j}^e - m_{t+j}^{*e}\right) + \beta_1\left(y_{t+j}^e - y_{t+j}^{*e}\right)\right] \tag{4.57}$$

INTRODUCING *EX ANTE* PPP

Another modification is obtained by substituting *ex ante* PPP, as represented by equation (4.33), into equation (4.55) to obtain

$$s_t = (m_t - m_t^*) - \beta_1(y_t - y_t^*) + \beta_2\left(\Delta p_{t+1}^e - \Delta p_{t+1}^{*e}\right) \tag{4.58}$$

where Δp^e (Δp^{*e}) is the expected change in the domestic (foreign) price level, that is the expected domestic (foreign) inflation rate. Equation (4.58) tells us that the exchange rate is also dependent on expected inflation rates. Thus, if it is expected that domestic inflation will be higher than foreign inflation, then the domestic currency should depreciate (s rises). Furthermore, if inflationary expectations are triggered mainly by expectations concerning monetary growth then relative expected monetary growth ($\Delta m^e - \Delta m^{*e}$) can replace ($\Delta p^e - \Delta p^{*e}$) in equation (4.58). Hence

$$s_t = (m_t - m_t^*) - \beta_1(y_t - y_t^*) + \beta_2\left(\Delta m_{t+1}^e - \Delta m_{t+1}^{*e}\right) \tag{4.59}$$

where Δm^e (Δm^{*e}) is the expected change in the domestic (foreign) money supply. Equations (4.58) and (4.59) tell us that expectations play a role in exchange rate determination but these expectations are induced by monetary factors. The current level of the exchange rate is affected not only by the current levels of the domestic and foreign money supplies, but also by the money supplies expected to prevail in the future.

INTRODUCING THE DISTINCTION BETWEEN TRADED AND NON-TRADED GOODS

Moosa (1994) has suggested another specification of the monetary model that allows for the distinction between traded and non-traded goods. This modification comes in response to the argument that PPP is valid for traded goods only. In this case PPP takes the form

$$S = \frac{P^T}{P^{T*}} \tag{4.60}$$

where P^T (P^{T^*}) is the domestic (foreign) price of traded goods. Let the price levels be (logarithmic) weighted averages of the prices of traded goods (P^T and P^{T^*}) and the prices of non-traded goods (P^N and P^{N^*}) such that

$$P = (P^N)^\gamma (P^T)^{1-\gamma} \tag{4.61}$$

$$P^* = (P^{N^*})^\gamma (P^{T^*})^{1-\gamma} \tag{4.62}$$

It follows that

$$\frac{P}{P^*} = \frac{S}{(P^T/P^N)^\gamma/(P^{T*}/P^{N*})^\gamma} \tag{4.63}$$

Equation (4.63) can be written in logarithmic form as

$$p_t - p_t^* = s_t - \gamma(g_t - g_t^*) \tag{4.64}$$

where $g = \log(P^T/P^N)$. Thus, the final equation of the monetary model is

$$s_t = (m_t - m_t^*) - \beta_1(y_t - y_t^*) + \beta_2(i_t - i_t^*) + \gamma(g_t - g_t^*) \tag{4.65}$$

which tells us that the relative internal price structure affects the exchange rate such that a rise in the relative price of traded goods in the home country in comparison with that of the foreign country brings about a depreciation of the domestic currency.

THEORETICAL FOUNDATIONS: THE STICKY-PRICE MONETARY MODEL

One of the major criticisms of the flexible-price monetary model is the postulation that PPP holds in the short run and in the long run. This postulation is based on the (classical) assumption of perfect price flexibility: this is why the versions of the monetary model presented so far fall under the so-called flexible-price monetary model. However, the empirical evidence does not support short-run PPP, in the sense that there are significant and persistent deviations from the PPP exchange rate in the short run. On the basis of this evidence, it has been suggested that the empirical failure of the monetary model is due (at least in part) to the failure of short-run PPP (see, for example, Lane, 1991).

To overcome this problematic feature of the monetary model, Dornbusch (1976) developed a monetary model by relaxing the assumption of short-run PPP, although the assumption that PPP holds in the long run was maintained. This model assumes that prices are sticky in the short run because goods markets adjust more slowly to monetary shocks than financial markets. Accordingly, this model is also described as being a 'hybrid' model, in the sense that it encompasses the Keynesian property of fixed prices in the short run and the classical property of flexible prices in the long run.

The structure of the sticky-price monetary model is as follows. First, PPP holds in the long run only, which means that PPP determines the long-run equilibrium level of the exchange rate. Hence, long-run PPP may be written as

$$\bar{s}_t = \bar{p}_t - \bar{p}_t^* \tag{4.66}$$

where a bar indicates the long-run equilibrium value of the underlying variable. Thus

$$\bar{s}_t = (\bar{m}_t - \bar{m}_t^*) - \beta_1(\bar{y}_t - \bar{y}_t^*) + \beta_2(\bar{i}_t - \bar{i}_t^*) \tag{4.67}$$

In the short run the exchange rate, s, may deviate from the equilibrium level, $\bar{s}$, but the former will tend to converge on the latter in the long run. Thus, the expected change in the exchange rate depends on the deviation of the current rate from the long-run rate. The adjustment mechanism is described by the equation

$$\Delta s_{t+1}^e = \theta(\bar{s}_t - s_t) \tag{4.68}$$

where θ is a (positive) adjustment coefficient. Equation (4.68) tells us that if the current exchange rate is above its long-run level ($s > \bar{s}$), the former will be expected to fall and vice versa. The speed of adjustment is measured by the value of the adjustment coefficient. The process continues until the two rates converge. By combining equation (4.68) with UIP we obtain

$$i_t - i_t^* = \theta(\bar{s}_t - s_t) \tag{4.69}$$

Equation (4.69) can be manipulated to obtain

$$s_t = \bar{s}_t - \frac{1}{\theta}(i_t - i_t^*) \tag{4.70}$$

Combining equations (4.70) and (4.67) we obtain

$$s_t = (\bar{m}_t - \bar{m}_t^*) - \beta_1(\bar{y}_t - \bar{y}_t^*) + \beta_2(\bar{i}_t - \bar{i}_t^*) - \frac{1}{\theta}(i_t - i_t^*) \tag{4.71}$$

If we assume that the current values of the explanatory variables are long-run equilibrium values, then

$$s_t = (m_t - m_t^*) - \beta_1(y_t - y_t^*) - \beta_3(i_t - i_t^*) \tag{4.72}$$

where $\beta_3 = -(\beta_2 - 1/\theta)$. This specification of the sticky-price model is similar to the specification of the flexible-price model represented by equation (4.49) except that the coefficient on the interest rate differential is negative. The reason for this difference is simple. In the flexible-price monetary model the interest rate differential reflects the expected inflation differential. Therefore, a rise in the domestic interest rate relative to the foreign interest rate implies a higher expected domestic inflation rate, leading to a depreciation of the domestic currency, that is, a rise in s. In the sticky-price model, the interest rate differential reflects relative liquidity positions. In this case, a rise in the domestic interest rate indicates a relative shortage of liquidity in the domestic money market, which gives rise to capital inflows and hence domestic currency appreciation, that is, a fall in s.

THEORETICAL FOUNDATIONS: OTHER MODELS OF EXCHANGE RATES

Economists have come up with other exchange rate determination models by modifying and extending the monetary model. These extensions and modifications are based on the relaxation of some assumptions and/or the introduction of new determining variables. These models will be presented in turn.

THE REAL INTEREST DIFFERENTIAL MODEL

This model, which was developed by Frankel (1979a), is identical to the sticky-price monetary model except that the real interest differential is added as an additional explanatory variable. The model draws upon the sticky-price model by assuming that PPP fails to hold in the short run but that it is valid in the long run. The only difference lies in the expectations formation mechanism. The mechanism used in this model postulates that the expected change in the exchange rate depends on two factors: the deviation of the current rate from the long-run equilibrium rate and the expected inflation differential (as in the flexible-price model). Thus

$$\Delta s_{t+1} = \theta(\bar{s}_t - s_t) + (\Delta p^e_{t+1} - \Delta p^{*e}_{t+1}) \tag{4.73}$$

By combining equation (4.73) with uncovered interest parity and rearranging we obtain

$$\bar{s}_t = s_t + \frac{1}{\theta}\left[(i_t - \Delta p^e_{t+1}) - (i^*_t - \Delta p^{*e}_{t+1})\right] \tag{4.74}$$

If $\bar{s}$ is determined as in the flexible-price model then

$$\bar{s}_t = (m_t - m^*_t) - \beta_1(y_t - y^*_t) + \beta_2(\Delta p^e_{t+1} - \Delta p^{*e}_{t+1}) \tag{4.75}$$

By combining equations (4.74) and (4.75) we obtain

$$\begin{aligned} s_t = {} & (m_t - m^*_t) - \beta_1(y_t - y^*_t) + \beta_2(\Delta p^e_{t+1} - \Delta p^{*e}_{t+1}) \\ & - \frac{1}{\theta}\left[(i_t - \Delta p^e_{t+1}) - (i^*_t - \Delta p^{*e}_{t+1})\right] \end{aligned} \tag{4.76}$$

THE HOOPER–MORTON MODEL

Hooper and Morton (1982) argue that the most serious deficiency of the monetary model is that it overlooks the role of the current account in the exchange rate determination process. Thus, they introduce the current account as another explanatory variable. The current account, however, does not influence the exchange rate directly but only indirectly through its effect on exchange rate expectation. The Hooper–Morton model is based on the postulation that there is an equilibrium level of the real exchange rate, which is compatible with equilibrium in the current account. But at any point in time, the equilibrium exchange rate is determined by the cumulative sum of past and present current account balances, that is

$$q_t = f(c_t, c^*_t) \tag{4.77}$$

where q is the real exchange rate and c (c^*) is the domestic (foreign) cumulative current account position. This implies that changes in the cumulative current account positions give rise to changes in the market expectation of the long-run real exchange rate, which in turn give rise to expected changes in the nominal exchange rate. If, for example, there is a rise in the cumulative current account surplus, an upward adjustment in the real (and hence in the nominal) value of the currency would be required. The equation representing this model would thus look like

$$\begin{aligned} s_t =&(m_t - m_t^*) - \beta_1(y_t - y_t^*) + \beta_2(\Delta p_{t+1}^e - \Delta p_{t+1}^{*e}) \\ &- \beta_3(i_t - i_t^*) - \beta_4(c_t - c_t^*) \end{aligned} \tag{4.78}$$

THE PORTFOLIO BALANCE MODEL

The monetary model may be viewed as being restrictive in the sense that money is the only asset available. The portfolio balance model has been proposed to remedy this deficiency. This model relaxes the assumption that financial assets are perfect substitutes, in which case UIP does not hold because of the existence of a risk premium. This model tells us that the ratio of domestic bonds to foreign bonds is determined by their relative returns. The latter is defined by the sum of the interest rate differential and the expected change in the exchange rate. The model can eventually be written as an equation in which the exchange rate depends on the relative return as well as the stocks of domestic and foreign bonds. Thus

$$s_t = -a_1(i_t - i_t^* - \Delta s_{t+1}^e) + a_2(b_t - b_t^*) \tag{4.79}$$

where b (b^*) is the stock of domestic (foreign) bonds. We also have

$$\begin{aligned} s_t - \bar{s}_t =& -\left(\frac{1}{\theta}\right)\left[(i_t - \Delta p_{t+1}^e) - (i_t^* - \Delta p_{t+1}^{*e})\right] \\ &+ \left(\frac{1}{\theta}\right)(i_t - i_t^* - \Delta s_{t+1}^e) \end{aligned} \tag{4.80}$$

which tells us that the exchange rate deviates from its long-run value by an amount proportional to the real interest rate differential and the risk premium. If the equilibrium exchange rate is determined by the basic monetary model, then

$$\begin{aligned} s_t =&(m_t - m_t^*) - \beta_1(y_t - y_t^*) + \beta_2(\Delta p_{t+1}^e - \Delta p_{t+1}^{*e}) \\ &- \frac{1}{\theta}\left[(i_t - \Delta p_{t+1}^e) - (i_t^* - \Delta p_{t+1}^{*e})\right] + \frac{1}{\theta}(i_t - i_t^* - \Delta s_{t+1}^e) \end{aligned} \tag{4.81}$$

Notice that in the standard monetary model, PPP ensures that the real interest differential is zero while UIP ensures that the risk premium is zero. This means that equation (4.81) reduces to equation (4.58). By combining equations (4.81) and (4.79) we obtain

$$\begin{aligned} s_t = &(m_t - m_t^*) - \beta_1(y_t - y_t^*) + \beta_2(\Delta p_{t+1}^e - \Delta p_{t+1}^{*e}) \\ &- \frac{1}{\theta}\left[(i_t - \Delta p_{t+1}^e) - (i_t^* - \Delta p_{t+1}^{*e})\right] + \frac{1}{\theta a_1}\left[a_2(b_t - b_t^*) - s_t\right] \end{aligned} \tag{4.82}$$

Solving equation (4.82) for s, we obtain

$$\begin{aligned} s_t = &\frac{1}{\theta a_1 + 1} + \frac{\theta a_1}{\theta a_1 + 1}(m_t - m_t^*) - \frac{\theta a_1 \beta_1}{\theta a_1 + 1}(y_t - y_t^*) \\ &+ \frac{a_1(\theta\beta_2 + 1)}{\theta a_1 + 1}(\Delta p_{t+1}^e - \Delta p_{t+1}^{*e}) \\ &- \frac{a_1}{\theta a_1 + 1}(i_t - i_t^*) + \frac{1}{\theta a_1 + 1}(b_t - b_t^*) \end{aligned} \tag{4.83}$$

which tells us that an excess supply of domestic bonds relative to foreign bonds leads to domestic currency depreciation.

THE CURRENCY SUBSTITUTION MODEL

Currency substitution is the tendency of individuals and businesses to alter the composition of their money holdings between domestic and foreign currencies. An important implication of currency substitution is that the more highly substitutable domestic and foreign currencies are, the more volatile exchange rates may be in response to even small changes in the underlying economic fundamentals.

It is possible to embody the effect of currency substitution in the monetary model. This is done by respecifying the demand for money functions to the following:

$$m_{d,t} - p_t = \beta_1 y_t - \beta_2 i_t - \beta_3 \Delta s_{t+1}^e \tag{4.84}$$

$$m_{d,t}^* - p_t^* = \beta_1 y_t^* - \beta_2 i_t^* + \beta_3 \Delta s_{t+1}^e \tag{4.85}$$

Notice that the coefficient on the expected change in the exchange rate is negative in the demand for domestic money equation (4.84) and positive in the demand for foreign money equation (4.85). β_3 is a measure of the elasticity of demand for foreign and domestic money with respect to the expected change in the exchange rate. It is also a measure of the elasticity of substitution between domestic and foreign currency. If we combine equations (4.84) and (4.85) via PPP ($s = p - p^*$) we obtain

$$s_t = (m_t - m_t^*) - \beta_1(y_t - y_t^*) + \beta_2(i_t - i_t^*) + 2\beta_3\Delta s_{t+1}^e \tag{4.86}$$

Since $i_t - i_t^* = \Delta p_{t+1}^e - \Delta p_{t+1}^{*e} = \Delta m_{t+1}^e - \Delta m_{t+1}^{*e}$, it follows that

$$s_t = (m_t - m_t^*) - \beta_1(y_t - y_t^*) + \beta_2(\Delta m_{t+1}^e - \Delta m_{t+1}^{*e}) + 2\beta_3\Delta s_{t+1}^e \tag{4.87}$$

If $\Delta s_{t+1}^e = \Delta m_{t+1}^e - \Delta m_{t+1}^{*e}$, then

$$s_t = (m_t - m_t^*) - \beta_1(y_t - y_t^*) + (\beta_2 + 2\beta_3)(\Delta m_{t+1}^e - \Delta m_{t+1}^{*e}) \tag{4.88}$$

Equation (4.88) is similar to equation (4.59) with respect to the effect on the exchange rate of $(m - m^*)$ and $(y - y^*)$. The difference lies in the effect of inflationary expectations resulting from expected monetary growth.

SINGLE-EQUATION MODELS: SOME ECONOMETRIC ISSUES

In this section we discuss some issues pertaining to the estimation and testing of single-equation models before using them for forecasting. Three issues will be discussed in turn: (i) dynamic specification; (ii) modelling with integrated variables; and (iii) diagnostics and goodness of fit measures.

DYNAMIC SPECIFICATION

We have seen that the PPP hypothesis can be represented by a static model that is written in levels (equations 4.23 and 4.24). We called this model absolute PPP. The hypothesis can also be represented by a dynamic model which is written in first differences (equations 4.26 and 4.27), which we called relative PPP. The question that arises here concerns the choice of the specification to be used for forecasting the exchange rate on the basis of the PPP model.

As a general rule, dynamic models are more useful for forecasting, particularly for short-run forecasting. It can be shown, however, that even the static model representing absolute PPP is a special (and very restrictive) case of a general autoregressive distributed lag (ADL) model. Let us write this model as

$$s_t = \alpha + \sum_{i=0}^{m} \beta_i p_{t-i} + \sum_{i=0}^{m} \gamma_i p_{t-i}^* + \sum_{i=1}^{m} \delta_i s_{t-i} + \varepsilon_t \tag{4.89}$$

where ε is an error term. If $m = 1$ the model reduces to

$$s_t = \alpha + \beta_0 p_t + \beta_1 p_{t-1} + \gamma_0 p_t^* + \gamma_1 p_{t-1}^* + \delta_1 s_{t-1} + \varepsilon_t \tag{4.90}$$

Various model specifications of PPP can be derived from equation (4.90) by imposing certain restrictions on the parameters of the equation. If $\beta_1 = \gamma_1 = \delta_1 = 0$, then the model reduces to

$$s_t = \alpha + \beta_0 p_t + \gamma_0 p_t^* + \varepsilon_t \tag{4.91}$$

which is the static model to represent absolute PPP. If, on the other hand, $\beta_1 = -\beta_0$, $\gamma_1 = -\gamma_0$ and $\delta_1 = 1$, then we will end up with the specification

$$\Delta s_t = \alpha + \beta_1 \Delta p_t + \gamma_1 \Delta p_t^* + \varepsilon_t \tag{4.92}$$

which is the specification used to represent relative PPP. If $\beta_1 = \gamma_1 = 0$, then the model reduces to

$$s_t = \alpha + \beta_0 p_t + \gamma_0 p_t^* + \delta s_{t-1} + \varepsilon_t \tag{4.93}$$

which is the partial adjustment model as applied to PPP.

For simplicity, we will use the restricted version of the PPP equation to derive the error correction model (see Hendry *et al.*, 1984). We start with the equation

$$s_t = \beta_0 (p - p^*)_t + \beta_1 (p - p^*)_{t-1} + \delta_1 s_{t-1} + \varepsilon_t \tag{4.94}$$

Equation (4.94) can be reparameterised to obtain

$$\Delta s_t = \beta_0 \Delta (p - p^*)_t + (\beta_1 + \beta_0)(p - p^*)_{t-1} + (\delta_1 - 1) s_{t-1} + \varepsilon_t \tag{4.95}$$

or

$$\Delta s_t = \beta_0 \Delta (p - p^*)_t + (\delta_1 - 1)\left[s_{t-1} - \theta (p - p^*)_{t-1}\right] + \varepsilon_t \tag{4.96}$$

where $\theta = (\beta_0 + \beta_1)/(1 - \delta_1)$. In equation (4.96), θ represents the long-run response and the term $\left[s_{t-1} - \theta(p - p^*)_{t-1}\right]$ is the error correction term. The parameter β_0 measures the impact effect while $(\delta_1 - 1)$ is a measure of the feedback effect. If $\theta = 1$, then the model reduces to

$$\Delta s_t = \beta_0 \Delta (p - p^*)_t + (\delta_1 - 1)\left[s_{t-1} - (p - p^*)_{t-1}\right] + \varepsilon_t \tag{4.97}$$

which is the special case of long-run proportionality (or homogeneity in linear models). This dynamic representation is superior to the partial adjustment model for at least three reasons:

1. as Hendry (1980) puts it, it provides a general lag structure that does not impose too specific a shape on the model;
2. it avoids the spurious regression problem of Granger and Newbold (1974); and
3. if the error correction model is the appropriate specification, the partial adjustment model will suffer from serial correlation.

Wickens and Breusch (1988) have suggested that several alternatives to standard partial adjustment and error correction models can be derived by imposing certain restrictions on a general autoregressive distributed lag model of the form

$$s_t = \sum_{i=1}^{m} \alpha_i s_{t-i} + \sum_{i=0}^{n} \beta_i x_{t-i} + \varepsilon_t \tag{4.98}$$

where x is any variable determining the exchange rate which, in the case of the PPP model, is $(p - p^*)$. Obviously, equation (4.98) shows the short-run dynamics only. The long-run response of the exchange rate to the price ratio, θ, can be estimated from equation (4.98) as

$$\theta = \frac{\sum_{i=0}^{n} \beta_i}{1 - \sum_{i=1}^{m} \alpha_i} \tag{4.99}$$

Thus, additional calculations are required for the value and the variance of θ. A more convenient and more direct procedure is to rewrite equation (4.98) utilising a variant of the Bewley (1979) transformation. By subtracting $(\sum \alpha_i)s_t$ from both sides of equation (4.98), rearranging and renormalising, we obtain

$$s_t = -\lambda \sum_{i=1}^{m} \alpha_i \Delta_i s_t + \lambda \left(\sum_{i=0}^{n} \beta_i \right) x_t - \lambda \sum_{i=1}^{n} \beta_i \Delta_i x_t + \lambda \varepsilon_t \tag{4.100}$$

where $\Delta_i s_t = s_t - s_{t-1}$, $\Delta_i x_t = x_t - x_{t-i}$ and $\lambda = 1/(1 - \sum \alpha_i)$ such that $\theta = \lambda(\sum \beta_i)$. Another specification involves first differences only and is given by

$$s_t = -\lambda \sum_{i=0}^{m-1} \left(\sum_{j=i+1}^{m} \alpha_j \right) \Delta s_{t-i} + \lambda \left(\sum_{i=0}^{n} \beta_i \right) x_t$$
$$- \lambda \sum_{i=0}^{n-1} \left(\sum_{j=i+1}^{n} \beta_j \right) \Delta x_{t-i} + \lambda \varepsilon_t \quad (4.101)$$

It is also possible to obtain a specification containing the *i*th differences of *s* and *x*. This is given by

$$s_t = \sum_{i=1}^{m} \phi_i \Delta^i s_t + \theta x_t + \sum_{i=1}^{n} \gamma_i \Delta^i x_t + \lambda \varepsilon_t \quad (4.102)$$

where $\Delta^i x_t = \Delta \Delta^{i-1} x_t = \Delta^{i-1} x_t - \Delta^{i-1} x_{t-1}$, and the same applies to *s*.

Another specification that can be used to calculate the average lag in the response of *s* to *x* can be written as

$$s_t = -\lambda \sum_{i=1}^{m} i\alpha_i \Delta s_t + \lambda \sum_{i=2}^{m} \alpha_i (i\Delta s_t - \Delta_i s_t) + \lambda \left(\sum_{i=0}^{n} \beta_i \right) x_t$$
$$- \lambda \sum_{i=1}^{n} i\beta_i \Delta x_t + \lambda \sum_{i=2}^{n} \beta_i [i\Delta x_t - \Delta_i x_t] + \lambda \varepsilon_t \quad (4.103)$$

Wickens and Breusch (1988) compare these specifications with the standard partial adjustment model

$$s_t = \alpha_1 s_{t-1} + \beta_0 x_t + \varepsilon_t \quad (4.104)$$

which can be rewritten as

$$s_t = \frac{-\alpha_1}{1-\alpha_1} \Delta s_t + \frac{\beta_0}{1-\alpha_1} x_t + \frac{\varepsilon_t}{1-\alpha_1} \quad (4.105)$$

They show that equation (4.105) is a special (limited dynamics) case of equation (4.102).

MODELLING WITH INTEGRATED VARIABLES

Integrated variables are non-stationary variables that require differencing to achieve stationarity, which may be necessary to avoid the risk of obtaining a spurious relationship. Exchange rates and their determinants are invariably integrated variables.

The classical approach to modelling relationships involving integrated variables is to model these relationships in first differences, in which case standard asymptotic theory applies, and inference on the magnitudes of the estimated coefficients can be derived on the basis of conventional t-statistics. The problem with this approach, however, is that it implicitly rules out the possibility of the existence of a relationship between the levels of the variables. Moreover, it leads to the loss of information embodied in the levels. That is why differencing may not be an appropriate strategy.

One alternative is to apply the Engle–Granger (1987) two-step method to estimate an error correction model that may take the parsimonious form

$$\Delta s_t = \gamma + \delta \Delta x_t + \theta(s_{t-1} - \beta x_{t-1}) + \varepsilon_t \qquad (4.106)$$

where β is the cointegrating parameter estimated from the cointegrating regression $s_t = \beta x_t + u_t$, which represents the long-run relationship between the exchange rate and its determining factor, x. The Engle–Granger two-step method is appealing because of its simplicity, but it may result in severe biases in small samples.

Wickens and Breusch (1988) argue that the error correction model is just another way of rewriting equation (4.97), but that it is not 'particularly convenient'. To estimate the long-run as well as the short-run dynamics, it would be better to use (4.100) or (4.102), which for this case becomes

$$s_t = \phi_1 \Delta s_t + \theta x_t - \gamma_1 \Delta x_t + u_t \qquad (4.107)$$

They also argue that in the case of non-stationary variables it is necessary to include the lags in s and x to achieve full efficiency of the estimate of the long-run coefficient. In fact, they assert that it is possible to misspecify the dynamic structure of the models with non-stationary variables by omitting higher-order lags or differenced terms.

Another alternative to the error correction model estimated along the lines suggested by Granger and Engle is to estimate the following equation

$$\Delta s_t = \gamma + \delta \Delta x_t + \alpha_1 s_{t-1} + \alpha_2 x_{t-1} + \varepsilon \qquad (4.108)$$

where α_2 is implicitly equal to $-\theta\beta$ in equation (4.106). Sims *et al.* (1990) have shown that the standard asymptotic distribution theory applies to all of the coefficients in equation (4.108). It can also be shown that estimating equation (4.106) directly by nonlinear least squares is equivalent to estimating equation (4.108) by OLS.

The general principle behind these methods is that improved estimates of the long-run coefficients can be obtained by incorporating short-run dynamics. The generalised two-sided estimator (GTS) utilises the information in the leads and lags of the error correction term and the explanatory variable(s). The underlying model is written as

$$s_t = \beta x_t + \sum_{i=-k}^{k} \delta_i (s - \beta x)_{t-i} + \sum_{i=-k}^{k} \gamma_i \Delta x_{t-i} + \varepsilon_t \tag{4.109}$$

which has the property that the error term, ε_t, is free of the nuisance parameters. Equation (4.109) incorporates disequilibrium dynamics, as represented by leads and lags of the error correction term $(s - \beta x)$, and shock dynamics, as represented by leads and lags of changes in the explanatory variable x_t (Lim and Martin, 1995).

The Phillips–Loretan (1991) estimator is based on an equation similar to equation (4.109) except that it does not include leads of the error correction term. This equation can be derived by imposing the restrictions $\delta_i = 0, \forall i < 0$ on equation (4.109) to obtain

$$s_t = \beta x_t + \sum_{i=0}^{k} \delta_i (s - \beta x)_{t-i} + \sum_{i=-k}^{k} \gamma_i \Delta x_{t-i} + \varepsilon_t \tag{4.110}$$

which can be estimated by nonlinear least squares to obtain superconsistent and asymptotically efficient estimates.

Likewise, the Saikkonen (1991) estimator, which is equivalent to the estimator proposed by Stock and Watson (1993), is based on an equation that can be derived by imposing the restrictions $\delta_i = 0, \forall i$ on equation (4.109). Thus, we have

$$s_t = \beta x_t + \sum_{i=-k}^{k} \gamma_i \Delta x_{t-i} + \varepsilon_t \tag{4.111}$$

which can be estimated by OLS to produce superconsistent and asymptotically efficient estimates.

DIAGNOSTICS AND GOODNESS OF FIT MEASURES

Two questions arise in this respect. First, when we estimate a dynamic model starting with a general lag, how do you choose the final, parsimonious model specification? In other words, which lags do we include and which ones do we exclude? The second question is that once the model has been estimated how do we confirm its validity before we use it for forecasting? The answer to both questions lies in a battery of diagnostic tests and goodness of fit measures, which are used to validate the model just like we use the Box–Pierce test to confirm, or otherwise, the validity of an ARIMA model.

There is one important point that must be mentioned here. Econometric model building has two objectives: hypothesis testing and forecasting. In the case of hypothesis testing, we are mainly interested in testing the statistical significance of the relationships among variables. For example, the PPP model can be used to test the hypothesis that prices determine exchange rates. In this case we are concerned mostly with a finding, or otherwise, of significant t-statistics subject to a finding that the model is free of serial correlation as judged, for example, by the Durbin–Watson (DW) statistic. If, on the other hand, we want to use the model to forecast the exchange rate then what is important is the explanatory and predictive value of the model. One may argue that the two things go together, that is explanatory variables that produce significant t-statistics also produce high explanatory power. This is not the case, however. Suppose that domestic and foreign prices are so highly correlated that the PPP model exhibits multicollinearity. This multicollinearity will produce high standard errors and low (or insignificant) t-statistics for the estimated coefficients, but it will not affect the explanatory power of the model as indicated by R^2. Thus, this model can be used to generate forecasts, although it does not adequately show the magnitude and direction of the effects of prices on the exchange rate. Naturally, the same thing can be said about univariate time series models.

A common method for arriving at a parsimonious specification is the general-to-specific methodology. The idea is to start with a dynamic model with a general lag structure (such as that represented by equation 4.98) then eliminate the insignificant lags subject to some goodness of fit and diagnostic test statistics. Since these tests are well known, the following is a brief description of the test statistics. Details can be found in Cuthbertson *et al.* (1992) and in Pesaran and Pesaran (1997).

THE COEFFICIENT OF DETERMINATION

The coefficient of determination (R^2) measures the explanatory power of the model. It is calculated as the ratio of the explained sum of squares to the total sum of squares of the dependent variable.

THE ADJUSTED COEFFICIENT OF DETERMINATION

The adjusted coefficient of determination ($\bar{R}^2$) is the coefficient of determination adjusted for the degrees of freedom. The relationship between R^2 and $\bar{R}^2$ is

$$1 - \bar{R}^2 = \left(\frac{n-1}{n-k}\right)(1 - R^2) \tag{4.112}$$

where n is the number of observations and k is the number of regressors.

THE F-STATISTIC

The F-statistic is used to test the statistical significance of the regressors other than the intercept term. It has an F-distribution with $k - 1$ and $n - k$ degrees of freedom under the null that all of the coefficients on the regressors are zero.

THE DURBIN–WATSON (DW) STATISTIC

The Durbin–Watson statistic is used to test for first-order serial correlation when the model does not include a lagged dependent variable. A value of 2 indicates a complete absence of serial correlation.

DURBIN'S *h*-STATISTIC

When the model includes a lagged dependent variable then it is more appropriate to use Durbin's *h*-statistic. Under the null hypothesis of no serial correlation it is distributed as a standard normal variate.

GODFREY'S TEST OF SERIAL CORRELATION

There are two versions of this test, which are asymptotically equivalent: the Lagrange multiplier (LM) version and the F-version. These have a χ^2 distribution and F-distribution respectively (see Godfrey 1978a, b). In both cases the null is that there is no serial correlation.

RAMSEY'S RESET TEST OF FUNCTIONAL FORM

This is a test of linear versus quadratic specifications, which has an LM and F-versions. The null hypothesis is that the specification is linear.

TESTING FOR NORMALITY OF THE RESIDUALS

The Jarque–Bera test (Jarque and Bera, 1980; Bera and Jarque, 1981) can be used for testing the normality of the residuals where the null hypothesis is that the residuals are normally distributed. The failure of a model to pass this test does not necessarily mean that the model is misspecified: it may just indicate the presence of outliers, in which case dummy variables may be used.

TESTING FOR HETEROSCEDASTICITY

A test for heteroscedasticity may be based on a regression of the squares of the residuals on the squares of the estimated values of the dependent variables. The null hypothesis is that the errors are homoscedastic, that is they have equal error variances. Another test for heteroscedasticity has been suggested by Breusch and Pagan (1979).

AKAIKE INFORMATION CRITERION (*AIC*)

This is a model selection criterion that is based on the statistical fit as given by the maximised value of the log-likelihood function. It is calculated as

$$AIC = \log(\tilde{\sigma}^2) + \frac{2k}{n} \tag{4.113}$$

where $\tilde{\sigma}^2$ is the maximum likelihood estimate of the variance of the error terms, k is the number of freely estimated parameters and n is the sample size. The lower the value of *AIC* the better is the statistical fit of the model.

SCHWARZ BAYESIAN CRITERION (*SBC*)

This criterion is calculated as

$$SBC = \log(\tilde{\sigma}^2) + \left(\frac{\log n}{n}\right)k \tag{4.114}$$

Again, the lower the value of *SBC* the better the statistical fit of the model.

HANNAN–QUINN CRITERION (*HQC*)

This criterion is calculated as

$$HQC = \log(\tilde{\sigma}^2) + \left(\frac{2\log\log n}{n}\right)k \tag{4.115}$$

Once more, the lower the value of *HQC* the better the statistical fit of the model.

SINGLE-EQUATION STRUCTURAL TIME SERIES MODELS

Single-equation structural time series models are similar to the ones studied in Chapter 3 except that they contain explanatory variables. Hence, the exchange rate is portrayed as being determined by its components as well as the explanatory variables that may include a lagged dependent variable.

The general model may be written as

$$s_t = \mu_t + \phi_t + \gamma_t + \mathbf{X}_t'\mathbf{B} + \varepsilon_t \tag{4.116}$$

where $\mathbf{X}_t$ is a vector of explanatory variables and $\mathbf{B}$ is a vector of unknown coefficients. If, for example, the only explanatory variable is the interest rate differential, the model can be written as

$$s_t = \mu_t + \phi_t + \gamma_t + b(i_t - i_t^*) + \varepsilon_t \tag{4.117}$$

which says that the exchange rate is determined by its components (trend, cycle, seasonal component and random components) as well as the interest rate differential. The underlying idea is that if the explanatory variables are only partially successful in explaining the exchange rate then there is a role for the components which may in this case explain the behaviour of the omitted variables. If, on the other hand, the explanatory variables are completely successful in explaining the exchange rate then the trend would reduce to a constant while the cycle and the seasonal components become unnecessary.

This model can be estimated along the same lines used to estimate the univariate structural time series model. The model is written in state space form so that it can be estimated by maximum likelihood using the Kalman filter to update the estimates. The state vector would look different as it will contain the coefficients on the explanatory variables.

MULTI-EQUATION ECONOMIC MODELS

Multi-equation models solve the 'black box' problem associated with single-equation models. These models consist of a number of equations which may represent the whole macroeconomy or a sub-sector of the macroeconomy. The idea is that if the equation determining the exchange rate contains endogenous variables, which are determined jointly with the exchange rate by the working of the system, then the model should contain equations that describe how these variables are determined. These models have the advantage of showing how the effect of the endogenous fundamental variables is transmitted to the exchange rate. Obviously, this desirable feature can only be achieved at a much higher cost in terms of the data and estimation requirements of these models, some of which may contain hundreds of equations. One argument against multi-equation models is that a specification error in one of the equations in the system will spill over to the rest of the system.

The following is a simple multi-equation model. The model consists of the following equations:

$$\Delta s_t = \alpha_0 + \alpha_1 \Delta p_t + \alpha_2 \Delta p_t^* + \alpha_3 i_t + \alpha_4 i_t^* \tag{4.118}$$

$$\Delta p_t = \beta_0 + \beta_1 \Delta p_t^m + \beta_2 \Delta m_t + \beta_3 (y_t - \bar{y}_t) \tag{4.119}$$

$$i_t = \gamma_0 + \gamma_1 \Delta p_{t+1}^e \tag{4.120}$$

$$y_t - \bar{y}_t = \delta_0 + \delta_1 \Delta m_t + \delta_2 \Delta g_t \tag{4.121}$$

$$\Delta p_t^e = \frac{1}{2}(\Delta p_t + \Delta p_{t-1}) \tag{4.122}$$

The model consists of four behavioural equations and one definitional equation containing five endogenous variables, six exogenous variables and one predetermined (lagged) variable. The endogenous variables are the following:

Δs	first log difference of the exchange rate
Δp	domestic inflation rate
i	domestic interest rate
y	actual output (income)
Δp^e	expected domestic inflation rate

The exogenous variables which are determined outside the model are the following:

Δp^*	foreign inflation rate
i^*	foreign interest rate
Δp^m	first log difference of import prices
Δm	first log difference of the money supply
$\bar{y}$	potential output (income)
Δg	first log difference of government expenditure

The first equation tells us that the exchange rate is determined by domestic and foreign inflation and interest rates. It is, therefore, a modified PPP equation that allows for the short-run effect of interest rates. The second equation explains the domestic inflation rate in terms of import prices, the money supply and the output gap, that is the difference between actual output and potential output. The latter is exogenous because it is assumed to be determined by the growth of the labour force, capital and technology. The third equation explains the determination of the domestic interest rate by the expected inflation rate. This is simply the Fisher equation. The fourth equation explains the determination of the deviation of actual output from potential output by the monetary and fiscal stimuli in the economy. The final equation is a definitional equation which tells us that the expected inflation rate is calculated as a two-period moving average of the actual inflation rate. A reduced-form equation for the exchange rate can be obtained by substitution. Thus

$$\Delta s_t = \alpha_0 + \alpha_1\left[\beta_0 + \beta_1 \Delta p_t^m + \beta_2 \Delta m_t + \beta_3(\delta_0 + \delta_1 \Delta m_t + \delta_2 \Delta g_t)\right] + \alpha_2 \Delta p_t^* + \alpha_3\left[\gamma_0 + \frac{\gamma_1}{2}(\Delta p_t + \Delta p_{t-1})\right] + \alpha_4 i_t^* \quad (4.123)$$

which can be expanded to obtain

$$\begin{aligned}\Delta s_t = &\left[\alpha_0 + \alpha_1\beta_0 + \alpha_1\beta_3\delta_0 + \alpha_3\gamma_0 + \frac{\alpha_3\gamma_1\beta_0}{2} + \frac{\alpha_3\gamma_1\beta_3\delta_0}{2}\right] \\ &+ \left[\alpha_1\beta_1 + \frac{\alpha_3\gamma_1\beta_1}{2}\right]\Delta p_t^m \\ &+ \left[\alpha_1\beta_2 + \alpha_1\beta_3\delta_1 + \frac{\alpha_3\gamma_1\beta_2}{2} + \frac{\alpha_3\gamma_1\beta_3\delta_1}{2}\right]\Delta m_t \\ &+ \left[\alpha_1\beta_3\delta_2 + \frac{\alpha_3\gamma_1\beta_3\delta_2}{2}\right]\Delta g_t \\ &+ \alpha_2\Delta p_t^* + \frac{\alpha_3\gamma_1}{2}\Delta p_{t-1} + \alpha_4 i_t^* \end{aligned} \quad (4.124)$$

This equation can be used to forecast the exchange rate following the estimation of the structural equations of which the model consists. For this purpose the methods of two-stage least squares or three-stage least squares must be used. Another version of multi-equation models is the vector autoregression (VAR) model. In this case all of the variables are regarded as endogenous and jointly determined.

EMPIRICAL EVIDENCE

In what has become a landmark study, Meese and Rogoff (1983a) compared the forecasting power of several of the models outlined so far in this chapter with that of the simple random walk, various univariate time series models, and a VAR model. The conclusion emerging from this study is that no model could outperform the random walk at any forecast horizon. This led Meese and Rogoff to conclude by saying 'given our finding that the random walk model almost invariably has the lowest root mean square error over all horizons and across all exchange rates, we can unambiguously assert that the other models do not perform significantly better than the random walk model'. In another study, Meese and Rogoff (1983b) investigated the possibility that the forecasting performance of these models may have been affected by simultaneous equation bias. They demonstrated this proposition by using VAR models to show that the instruments used in their previous study were not truly exogenous. The results this time showed that it is possible to beat the random walk model for horizons longer than 12 months. One possible interpretation of this finding is that although the exchange rate behaves like a random walk in the short run, its path is determined by economic fundamentals in the long run. Krugman (1993, p. 7) commented cynically on the forecasting power of economic models by saying that 'it became difficult to present another set of weak regression results without embarrassment', adding that 'the theory of exchange rate determination never recovered from the empirical debacle of the early 1980s'.

Some economists tried to enhance the forecasting power of the economic models by including a lagged dependent variable to allow for dynamic adjustment. By doing so, Somanath (1986) was able to outperform the random walk model. On the other hand, Boothe and Glassman (1987) did the same but their results confirmed the findings of Meese and Rogoff. Boughton (1984, 1987) has also shown that it is possible to outperform the random walk model by using a portfolio balance model. However, Pentecost (1991) argues that the inclusion of a lagged dependent variable as an explanatory variable effectively transforms the model into a random walk with additional explanatory variables.

Other economists have tried to improve the forecasting performance of economic models by allowing for nonlinearities. Studies of this sort have been carried out by Wolff (1987a, b) and by Schinasi and Swamy (1989). The results of these studies are mixed but they show the possibility of outperforming the random walk model.

The poor forecasting performance of the single-equation models has led some economists to suggest that multi-equation models are more appropriate for capturing the co-movements of exchange rates and other variables in response to exogenous shocks. This argument is based on the proposition that these models invariably have endogenous variables (such as interest rates and prices) among their explanatory variables. For example, Papell (1988) argues that the price and exchange rate dynamics inherent in Dornbusch's (1976) overshooting model cannot be modelled by using single-equation techniques. Gandolfo *et al.* (1990) similarly argue that since the exchange rate is just one of the endogenous variables of an economy-wide model, its determination occurs in conjunction with the determination of the other endogenous variables in a general setting where all variables interact. They recommend that only by moving away from single-equation models towards economy-wide models can one hope to beat the random walk model. They also show that their model of the Italian economy outperforms the random walk model in forecasting the exchange rate of the lira against the dollar out of sample.

COMPUTER SOFTWARE

Three computer programs are commonly used to estimate models and generate forecasts: Microfit, Shazam and Eviews. Since they provide rather similar facilities, I will concentrate on a brief description of the first, Microfit. Full details are found in Pesaran and Pesaran (1997).

Microfit 4 is a self-contained interactive econometric analysis package that provides many useful features. It has an extensive data processing and preliminary analysis menu as well as graphics facilities. It has two main options for estimating and testing single-equation models and multi-equation models. Under single-equation methods, several options are available. OLS estimation is allowed with a variety of assumptions about the behaviour of the residuals, including autoregressive processes, moving average processes and ARCH/GARCH processes. Other options include recursive regression, rolling regression, nonlinear regression, the Phillips–Hansen estimation method, autoregressive distributed lag models, and logit and probit models. Multi-equation options include unrestricted VARs, cointegrated VARs and seemingly unrelated regressions. A variety of goodness of fit measures and diagnostics are provided as well as a forecasting facility.

To estimate single and multi-structural time series equations with and without explanatory variables, STAMP 5.0 is used. It provides an excellent forecasting facility, allowing static and dynamic forecasting. It even allows *ex ante* forecasting if a multi-univariate-equation model is used (seemingly unrelated time series equation).

FURTHER READING

Most of the forecasting books have a chapter or two on regression analysis but these are inadequate. Possibly the most comprehensive econometrics and time series analysis book is Hamilton (1994). This book deals with various estimation and testing methods, and it contains a chapter on forecasting. A more accessible book with a particular emphasis on forecasting is Pindyck and Rubinfeld (1991). Pesaran and Pesaran (1997) contains a brief but a useful exposition of the econometrics underlying Microfit 4. On single- and multi-structural time series equations, see Harvey (1989) and Koopman *et al.* (1995).

5: Market-based Forecasting: The Spot and Forward Exchange Rates

INTRODUCTION

This chapter deals with market-based forecasting that involves using the current spot and forward exchange rates to forecast the spot rate at some future point in time. This is called market-based forecasting because the forecasters (the spot and forward rates) are provided by the spot and forward foreign exchange markets.

Market-based forecasting rests on two hypotheses: the random walk hypothesis and the unbiased efficiency hypothesis. The random walk hypothesis tells us that period-to-period changes in the spot exchange rate are random and unpredictable. The spot exchange rate tomorrow is as likely to be above today's level as to be below it. Hence, the best forecast for tomorrow's exchange rate is today's rate. The unbiased efficiency hypothesis tells us that the current spot rate is an unbiased and efficient forecaster of the spot exchange rate prevailing on the maturity date of the forward contract. This is because the exchange rate supposedly reflects the market's expectation of the level of the spot rate in the future. The importance of these forecasters (the spot and the forward exchange rates) is that they are used as benchmarks to evaluate the forecasting performance of the models presented in the previous two chapters. The question is always whether or not a particular model can outperform the random walk model or the forward rate. The two hypotheses also have implications for market efficiency. The random walk model implies that the spot market is weakly efficient, while the unbiased efficiency hypothesis implies efficiency of both the spot and forward markets. All of these issues will be discussed in this chapter.

THE SPOT RATE AS A FORECASTER: THE RANDOM WALK MODEL

Assume that we have a sample of observations on the spot exchange rate covering the period between point in time 1 and the present time, t. Hence, we have the observations $S_1, S_2, \ldots, S_t$. Using the spot rate as a forecaster implies that

$$\hat{S}_{t+1} = S_t \tag{5.1}$$

The rationale underlying this forecaster is the random walk model which can be represented by the equation

$$S_t = S_{t-1} + \varepsilon_t \tag{5.2}$$

Equation (5.2) is a representation of the hypothesis that the exchange rate at t will differ from the exchange rate at time $t-1$ by an error term which has the following properties:

$$E(\varepsilon_t) = 0 \tag{5.3}$$

$$E(\varepsilon_t \varepsilon_{t-j}) = \sigma_\varepsilon^2 \qquad \text{for } j = 0 \tag{5.4}$$

$$E(\varepsilon_t \varepsilon_{t-j}) = 0 \qquad \text{for } j \neq 0 \tag{5.5}$$

Equations (5.3)–(5.5) tell us that the error term is a white noise, having a zero mean and a constant variance, and that it is serially uncorrelated. According to the random walk hypothesis, the behaviour of the exchange rate resembles the behaviour of a drunken person. If you look for a drunken person try the place where this person was last seen. Likewise, if you want to forecast the exchange rate try its last observed value for a forecast.

The random walk model as described by equation (5.2) may be modified to allow for a drift factor. Hence, it can be written as

$$S_t = \alpha + S_{t-1} + \varepsilon_t \tag{5.6}$$

where α is the drift factor. The forecast exchange rate is, therefore, given by

$$\hat{S}_{t+1} = \alpha + S_t \tag{5.7}$$

Equations (5.2) and (5.6) can be rewritten in terms of the changes in the exchange rate as

$$\Delta S_t = \varepsilon_t \tag{5.8}$$

$$\Delta S_t = \alpha + \varepsilon_t \tag{5.9}$$

Equations (5.8) and (5.9) imply that period-to-period changes in the exchange rate are random and unpredictable. This is because the exchange rate changes as traders react to newly arriving information. Since information arrives in a random manner, it follows that the exchange rate moves randomly.

Let us now see how to calculate the forecasting error variance. The forecast for time $t+1$ is

$$\hat{S}_{t+1} = E(S_{t+1}|S_t, \ldots, S_1) \tag{5.10}$$

Since $S_{t+1} = S_t + \varepsilon_{t+1}$ is independent of $S_{t-1}, \ldots, S_1$, it follows that

$$\hat{S}_{t+1} = S_t + E(\varepsilon_{t+1}) = S_t \tag{5.11}$$

Likewise, the forecast exchange rate at $t+2$ is given by

$$\begin{aligned}\hat{S}_{t+2} &= E(S_{t+2}|S_t, \ldots, S_1) = E(S_{t+1} + \varepsilon_{t+2}) \\ &= E(S_t + \varepsilon_{t+1} + \varepsilon_{t+2}) = S_t\end{aligned} \tag{5.12}$$

In general

$$\hat{S}_{t+j} = S_t \tag{5.13}$$

Hence, the forecast value is the same irrespective of how far into the future we are forecasting (that is, irrespective of the value of j). However, the forecasting error variance increases as the value of j increases. To demonstrate this proposition we start by calculating the one-period-ahead forecasting error as

$$e_1 = S_{t+1} - \hat{S}_{t+1} = S_t + \varepsilon_{t+1} - S_t = \varepsilon_{t+1} \tag{5.14}$$

The variance of the forecasting error is given by

$$E\left(\varepsilon_{t+1}^2\right) = \sigma_\varepsilon^2 \tag{5.15}$$

Similarly, the forecasting error two periods ahead is

$$e_2 = S_{t+2} - \hat{S}_{t+2} = S_t + \varepsilon_{t+1} + \varepsilon_{t+2} - S_t = \varepsilon_{t+1} + \varepsilon_{t+2} \tag{5.16}$$

and its variance is given by

$$E\left[(\varepsilon_{t+1} + \varepsilon_{t+2})^2\right] = E\left(\varepsilon_{t+1}^2\right) + E\left(\varepsilon_{t+2}^2\right) + 2E(\varepsilon_{t+1}\varepsilon_{t+2}) \tag{5.17}$$

Since ε_{t+1} and ε_{t+2} are independent, it follows that

$$E\left[(\varepsilon_{t+1} + \varepsilon_{t+2})^2\right] = E\left(\varepsilon_{t+1}^2\right) + E\left(\varepsilon_{t+2}^2\right) = 2\sigma_\varepsilon^2 \tag{5.18}$$

It also follows that the variance of the forecasting error j periods ahead is $j\sigma_{\varepsilon}^2$. Thus, the confidence interval for the forecasts will widen as j increases. This is shown in Figure 5.1.

The same conclusion is reached when we consider a model of random walk with drift. The forecast for one period ahead is given by

$$\hat{S}_{t+1} = E(S_{t+1}|S_t, \ldots, S_1) = S_t + \alpha \tag{5.19}$$

Similarly, the forecast for j periods ahead is given by

$$\hat{S}_{t+j} = S_t + j\alpha \tag{5.20}$$

The one-period forecasting error is given by

$$e_1 = S_{t+1} - \hat{S}_{t+1} = S_t + \alpha + \varepsilon_{t+1} - S_t - \alpha = \varepsilon_{t+1} \tag{5.21}$$

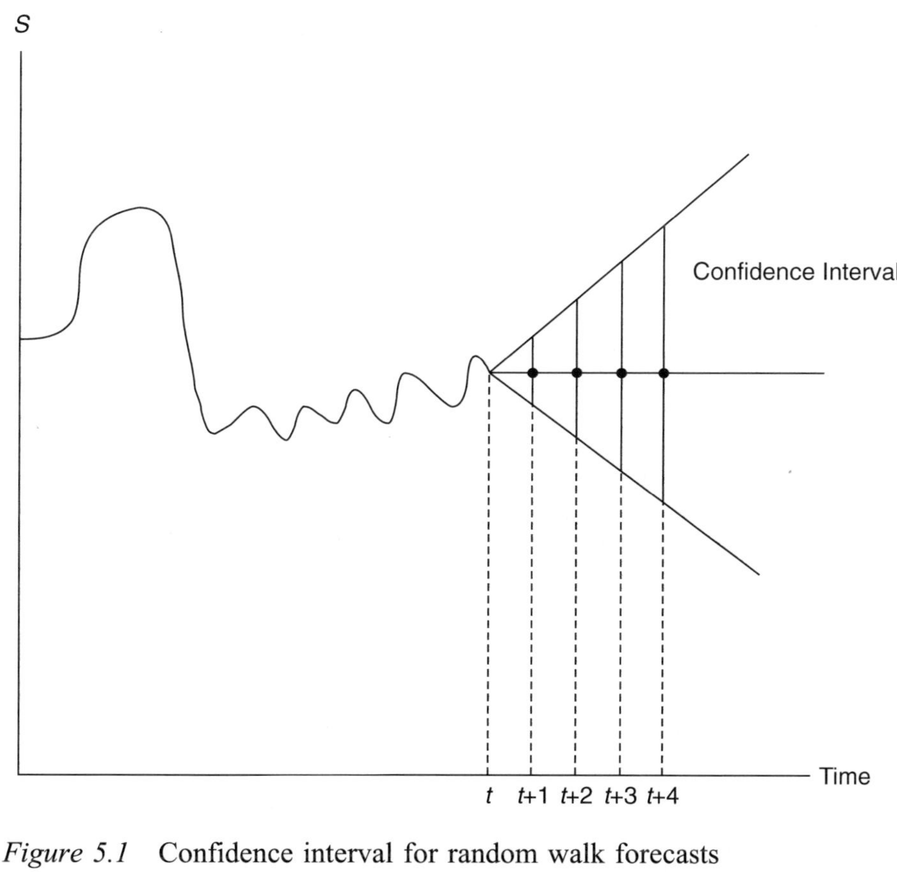

Figure 5.1 Confidence interval for random walk forecasts

and so it has the same variance as before. Again, the forecasting error increases with j. The confidence interval for forecasts from a random walk plus a drift model is represented by Figure 5.2.

SOME MODIFICATIONS

The first modification is required if the data are trended. The forecast is adjusted by adding the difference between the last actual observation and the one before it. Hence

$$\hat{S}_{t+1} = S_t + (S_t - S_{t-1}) \tag{5.22}$$

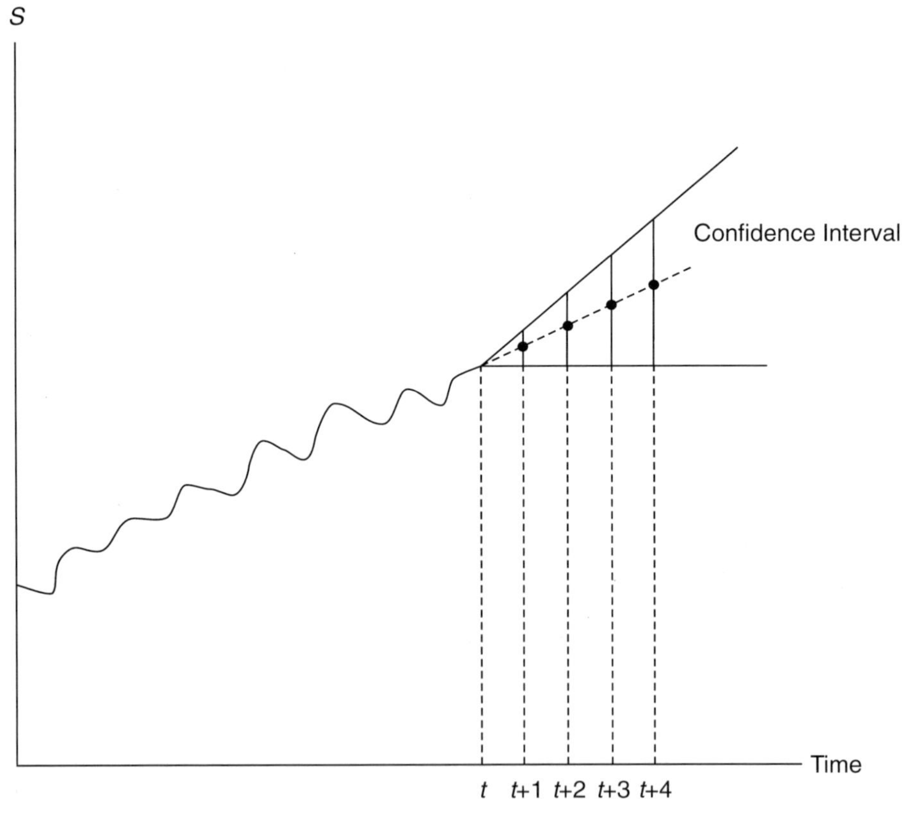

Figure 5.2 Confidence interval for forecasts from random walk with drift

The rate of change of the exchange rate may be more appropriate than the absolute change $(S_t - S_{t-1})$. The forecast is therefore calculated as

$$\hat{S}_{t+1} = S_t \left[\frac{S_t}{S_{t-1}} \right] \tag{5.23}$$

It may be even better to adjust the last actual observation by using an average of past absolute changes or rates of change. If two periods are used then we have

$$\hat{S}_{t+1} = S_t + \frac{1}{2}[(S_t - S_{t-1}) + (S_{t-1} - S_{t-2})] \tag{5.24}$$

and

$$\hat{S}_{t+1} = S_t \left[\frac{1}{2} \left(\frac{S_t}{S_{t-1}} + \frac{S_{t-1}}{S_{t-2}} \right) \right] \tag{5.25}$$

Equation (5.25) may be modified by using a geometric average to obtain

$$\hat{S}_{t+1} = S_t \left[\sqrt{\left(\frac{S_t}{S_{t-1}} \right) \left(\frac{S_{t-1}}{S_{t-2}} \right)} \right] \tag{5.26}$$

By using n periods we have

$$\hat{S}_{t+1} = S_t + \frac{1}{n} \left[\sum_{i=0}^{n} S_{t-i} - S_{t-i-1} \right] \tag{5.27}$$

$$\hat{S}_{t+1} = S_t \left[\frac{1}{n} \sum_{i=0}^{n} \left(\frac{S_{t-i}}{S_{t-i-1}} \right) \right] \tag{5.28}$$

$$\hat{S}_{t+1} = S_t \left[\prod_{i=0}^{n} \left(\frac{S_{t-i}}{S_{t-i-1}} \right) \right]^{\frac{1}{n}} \tag{5.29}$$

THE FORWARD RATE AS A FORECASTER: THE UNBIASED EFFICIENCY HYPOTHESIS

The unbiased efficiency hypothesis can be illustrated with the help of the following example of speculation on the relationship between the spot and forward exchange rates. If a speculator believes that the n-period forward exchange rate will be lower than the spot rate prevailing at time $t + n$, it will be profitable to buy (the foreign currency) forward and sell spot when the forward contract matures at $t + n$. Let S_{t+n} be the spot rate prevailing at time $t + n$ where t is the present time, and F_t^{t+n} be the forward rate agreed upon at time t for delivery at time $t + n$. If the speculator is correct, he or she will make profit amounting to the difference between the selling rate and the buying rate. Hence

$$e_{t+n} = S_{t+n} - F_t^{t+n} \tag{5.30}$$

If this speculator acts on the basis of public information, then there is no reason why other speculators do not do the same thing to obtain the same profit as the first speculator. If this happens, the resulting increase in the demand for forward contracts will raise the forward rate and reduce profit until the latter disappears. At time t, when the decision to speculate is taken, S_{t+n} is not known, which means that the speculator has to act on the basis of his or her expectation with respect to the spot exchange rate. Hence, the speculator will buy forward at time t and sell spot at time $t + n$ if the expected value of the spot exchange rate is higher than the forward rate, that is if

$$E(S_{t+n}) > F_t^{t+n} \tag{5.31}$$

Speculation will come to an end when

$$E(S_{t+n}) = F_t^{t+n} \tag{5.32}$$

or if profit is expected to be zero, that is

$$E(e_{t+n}) = 0 \tag{5.33}$$

The term representing speculative profit, e_{t+n}, is also the forecasting error where the forward exchange rate is used as a forecaster of the spot rate. Market efficiency will hold in general if the forward exchange rate is an unbiased and efficient forecaster of the spot exchange rate. Unbiasedness means that, on average, the forward rate will be equal to (and that it will not systematically underestimate or overestimate) the spot exchange rate prevailing on the maturity date of the forward contract. Efficiency of forecasting means that it is not possible to improve the forecast by utilising information other than what is embodied in the forward rate. This is why this kind of efficiency is known as unbiased efficiency.

In more general terms, equation (5.32) can be rewritten as

$$E(S_{t+n}) = a + bF_t^{t+n} + \varepsilon_t \tag{5.34}$$

where ε_t is an error term. For market efficiency, the following conditions must be satisfied: (i) $a = 0$, (ii) $b = 1$ and (iii) ε_t is completely random. This is also called simple efficiency, but we will use the term 'unbiased efficiency'. General efficiency is obtained by relaxing the restriction $a = 0$. The difference between simple efficiency and general efficiency is the existence or otherwise of a risk premium, which in equation (5.34) is represented by a. Unbiased efficiency implies that $a = 0$, an indication that agents (traders or market participants) are risk neutral, that is they are indifferent between foreign and domestic currency assets if these assets offer the same return. If, on the other hand, $a \neq 0$ then agents are not risk neutral but rather risk averse, requiring a risk premium to switch from one currency to another.

While equations (5.32) and (5.34) are written in terms of the levels of the forward rate and the expected spot rate, they can be rewritten in terms of the forward spread, f, and the expected change in the spot exchange rate, $\dot{S}$. Hence, the unbiased efficiency hypothesis may be written as

$$E(\dot{S}_t^{t+n}) = f_t^{t+n} \tag{5.35}$$

where $\dot{S}_t^{t+n}$ is the percentage change in the exchange rate between t and $t+n$ and f_t^{t+n} is the forward spread. Equation (5.35) tells us that the expected change in the spot exchange rate between t and $t+n$ is equal to the forward spread for a forward contract maturing at $t+n$. General efficiency, on the other hand, is given by

$$E(\dot{S}_t^{t+n}) = a + bf_t^{t+n} \tag{5.36}$$

What is the implication for forecasting of this hypothesis? If the unbiased efficiency hypothesis holds then forecasters can be judged on the basis of their performance relative to the forward rate. If the general efficiency hypothesis holds such that there is a risk premium, then forecasters will be expected to outperform the forward rate. The benchmark in this case should be a risk-premium-adjusted forward rate. If neither simple efficiency nor general efficiency hold then the forward rate is not a good criterion to evaluate the forecasting performance. This is because the forward rate does not, in this case, reflect the market's implicit forecast.

EMPIRICAL EVIDENCE AND RATIONALISATION

Figure 5.3 shows the spot rate and the lagged three-month forward rate of the pound against the dollar (GBP/USD) over the period 1986–1998. It can be readily observed that the turning points in the spot rate occur before the turning points in the lagged forward rate. It seems that the forward rate follows rather than leads the spot rate.

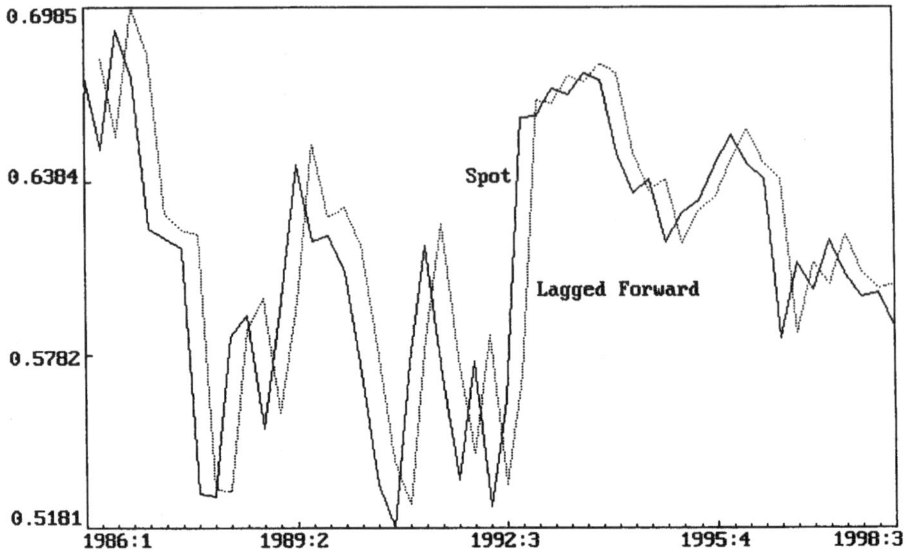

Figure 5.3 GBP/USD: spot and lagged three-month forward rate

In general, the available empirical evidence provides no support for unbiased efficiency. Several factors have been identified to account for this bias, including the presence of political risk, foreign exchange risk, purchasing power risk and interest rate risk. Other factors include the irrationality of expectations and the effect of news, that is the unanticipated changes in the economic variables affecting the foreign exchange market.

While the evidence on this issue is mixed, it is invariably the case that more recent studies using more sophisticated techniques have produced unfavourable results. The results are also sensitive to model specification. Results based on models specified in levels are more supportive than those based on differenced data. In general, it is agreed now that unbiased efficiency does not hold, and that a risk premium does exist. However, it is likely the case that the risk premium is not detected because it changes signs and averages zero. This implies that the risk premium is time varying and can only be detected by using a TVP regression.

If the forward rate is not an unbiased forecaster of the future spot rate how can we explain the bias? Several explanations have been put forward, and these are discussed in turn.

COVERED INTEREST PARITY

According to CIP, the forward rate does not reflect exchange rate expectation but rather the interest rate differential. Thus, bias will result if the differential does not reflect exchange rate expectation.

THE RISK PREMIUM

The risk premium arises out of risk aversion in the sense that market participants do not switch from one currency to another without requiring a risk premium. However, the counter-argument is that if foreign exchange risk can be diversified away, then there will be no need for a risk premium. Several models have been advanced to represent and estimate the risk premium, including the mean-variance optimisation model (Frankel, 1979b, 1982), Fama's (1984) decomposition model, Lucas' (1982) model, the ARCH model (for example, Domowitz and Hakkio, 1985), the GARCH model (Bollerslev, 1986), and the state space model (Wolff, 1987a).

IRRATIONALITY OF EXPECTATIONS

Several studies have been conducted using exchange rate expectations survey data with respect to the information available at the time of the expectation formation. These studies fall into two categories. The first category is concerned with testing the efficiency of survey-based data with respect to the information available to agents at the time of the expectation formation. For this purpose, the forward premium is decomposed into expectational and risk premium components, and the survey data are used to discern if the forward rate bias is due to the risk premium or to irrational expectations. The second category is concerned with modelling the expectations formation mechanism. The objective in this case is to find out whether the expectation formation mechanism is adaptive, extrapolative or regressive. It is important to know whether the foreign exchange market is dominated by chartists or fundamentalists. The empirical evidence on this issue is mixed (see, for example, Dominguez, 1986; Froot and Frankel, 1986, 1989; Frankel and Froot, 1987; Liu and Maddala, 1992; MacDonald, 1992).

THE PESO PROBLEM

The term 'peso problem' was devised to describe the situation surrounding the Mexican peso prior to its devaluation in the third quarter of 1976. Since the devaluation had been expected for many years prior to that, the peso was traded at a forward discount. As long as devaluation did not take place, if a researcher were to use data from the period before devaluation the forward exchange rate would appear to be a biased forecaster. Krasker (1980) argues that the bias in this case does not imply market inefficiency but rather deviations of the sampling distribution from normality.

GOVERNMENT INTERVENTION

Government intervention can affect the forecasting power of the forward rate in two ways. First, if the central bank is a big player in the foreign exchange market and it is not motivated by accounting profit, then the forward rate can be supported at a level that bears no relationship to the future spot rate. Second, the central bank can use monetary policy to influence domestic interest rates. If covered interest arbitrage is active the forward rate reflects domestic monetary policy as well as exchange rate expectations. The counter-argument is that risk neutral agents will exploit expected speculative profit at the expense of the central bank.

TRANSACTION COSTS

The effect of transaction costs is to create a wedge between the current forward rate and the future spot rate. Hence, the coefficient restriction $a = 0$ in equation (5.34) will not hold.

POLITICAL RISK

One source of political risk is changes in government. The underlying argument is that elections provide news about the probability of pursuing different economic policies. A change in the governing party may change the relative value of the country's assets and therefore the forward rate bias. The bias tends to increase when the government is likely to impose tax or change the rules and regulations governing the repatriation of capital.

EXCHANGE, PURCHASING POWER AND INTEREST RATE RISK

Foreign exchange risk arises because of deviations from uncovered interest parity, that is when the exchange rate changes by an amount that is different from the interest rate differential. The purchasing power risk arises from changes in the inflation rate and hence it can be measured by the standard deviation of the inflation rate. Similarly, the interest rate risk arises from changes in the interest rate differential, and hence it can be measured by the standard deviation of the differential. These risks lead to exchange rate bias.

DIFFERENCES IN REAL INTEREST AND EXCHANGE RATES

If market agents are able to anticipate real exchange rate movements and differences in the real interest rates across countries, then the forward rate will differ from the future spot rate. Levine (1989), for example, concluded on the basis of his empirical results that the risk premium is not the only factor that explains the bias.

THE EFFECT OF NEWS

News in this strand of literature refers to the unanticipated components of the fundamental variables that affect the exchange rate. For example, it is arguable that an announced high rate of monetary expansion may not lead to currency depreciation if the rate is lower than what was anticipated. Alternatively, an announced low rate of monetary expansion may lead to depreciation of the currency if it is higher than what was anticipated. The explanation for this scenario is that a lower (higher) than anticipated monetary expansion implies improvement (deterioration) in the ability of the monetary authorities to control the money supply, which has positive (negative) implications for the domestic currency. In both cases the news or the unanticipated component is measured by the difference between the actual value and the expected value of the fundamental variable.

A simple news model may be derived as follows. Let the exchange rate be determined by the following equation which relates the percentage change in the exchange rate to a vector of fundamental variables, z:

$$\Delta s_{t+1} = \gamma z_{t+1} + \varphi_{t+1} \tag{5.37}$$

where φ is an error term. When agents form rational expectations at time t we obtain

$$\Delta s^e_{t+1} = \gamma z^e_{t+1} \tag{5.38}$$

By subtraction we obtain

$$\Delta s_{t+1} - \Delta s^e_{t+1} = \gamma\left(z_{t+1} - z^e_{t+1}\right) + \varphi_{t+1} \tag{5.39}$$

which says that the forecasting error is driven by news about the fundamental variables that determine the exchange rate. By incorporating the general efficiency hypothesis ($\Delta s^e_{t+1} = a + bf_t$) we obtain

$$\Delta s_{t+1} = a + bf_t + \gamma\left(z_{t+1} - z^e_{t+1}\right) + \varphi_{t+1} \tag{5.40}$$

which shows that the percentage change in the exchange rate is determined by the risk premium, a, the forward spread, f, and the news.

OTHER CONCEPTS OF MARKET EFFICIENCY

The concept of market efficiency was initially developed for the stock market but it is equally applicable to the foreign exchange market and indeed to markets in general, financial or otherwise. In an efficient market, prices reflect all available information. The implication of this definition is that it is not possible to predict price movements from available information since this information is already reflected in prices. Since the arrival of information is random, and given that new information is reflected in prices very quickly, the period-to-period changes in prices tend to be random. Another implication is that it is not possible to earn abnormal (higher) returns via active trading as compared to what can be obtained from a passive buy and hold strategy.

There are three levels of efficiency that are defined with reference to the contents of the underlying information set. These concepts are explained with reference to the foreign exchange market. Hence, we refer to exchange rates rather than prices.

WEAK EFFICIENCY

In a weakly efficient market, the current level of the exchange rate reflects all the information contained in its the past behaviour. This is obviously a limited set of information as it excludes other relevant variables that affect the exchange rate. If the foreign exchange market is weakly efficient then this means that the future behaviour of the exchange rate cannot be predicted from its past behaviour. This postulation casts doubt on the reliability and usefulness of univariate time series models, technical forecasting, and mechanical trading rules.

SEMI-STRONG EFFICIENCY

In this case, the information set contains not only the past behaviour of the exchange rate, but also all publicly available information. In the case of the foreign exchange market, publicly available information pertains to the variables that affect exchange rates, economic and otherwise. Economic news as released by the authorities (central banks and treasuries) is publicly available, since it is reported by the media as soon as it is released. This information includes statistics and analyses pertaining to the variables that affect the exchange rate such as the ones appearing in the models described in Chapter 4. Relevant information also includes various reports and analyses prepared by the media and financial institutions and made publicly available. Non-economic factors include such things as cabinet reshuffles, changes in governments, political and military developments, and so on. If the foreign exchange market is efficient in this sense, then even research into the fundamental factors affecting the exchange rate will not help us predict its future behaviour. This level of efficiency casts doubt on the reliability not only of univariate time series models but also multivariate economic models that are built on the basis of some underlying economic theory.

STRONG EFFICIENCY

In this case, exchange rates reflect all available information, including private and insider information. It is normally argued that this level of efficiency is not applicable to the foreign exchange market because, unlike the stock market, insider information is not important. However, it is not difficult to come up with examples of insider and private information pertaining to the foreign exchange market. Insider information may be obtained by having dinner with an official of the central bank who (privately) transmits his or her knowledge of plans for intervention in the foreign exchange market, or plans to change the exchange rate arrangement. Insider information can also be transmitted by Treasury officials who are aware of hitherto unreleased information pertaining to changes in economic policy that are bound to affect the exchange rate. Private information may arise when, for example, an analyst develops a profitable trading rule that is not revealed as public information. If the foreign exchange market is efficient in this sense, then not even insider and private information can help us forecast the future behaviour of the exchange rate or to make abnormal profit.

REFINEMENTS AND IMPLICATIONS

The arguments underlying the concept of efficiency have been refined in two ways. The first is that because collecting information is a costly process market participants will not choose to be completely informed. Hence, even in an efficient market, prices do not fully reflect all information. The second point concerns the heterogeneity of market participants. Because these participants are heterogeneous with respect to their wealth, expectations, risk aversion and forecasting accuracy, market prices will reflect a mixture of diverse opinions, with each opinion weighted by the amount of funds backing it.

The implication of the above assertions is that tests of market efficiency involve testing a joint hypothesis. A rejection of the market efficiency hypothesis may be attributed to two factors. The first is the failure of agents to use the information to make abnormal profit. The second is that there is something wrong with the test. There is a disagreement on what constitutes abnormal profit, which makes tests of market efficiency difficult to formulate and interpret.

CROSS-SECTIONAL EFFICIENCY AND COINTEGRATION

Cross-sectional efficiency is a concept that arose from the cointegration literature popularised by Engle and Granger (1987). The idea is simple: two variables are said to be cointegrated if they are linked by a long-run relationship such that they cannot drift too far apart. Moreover, deviations from the equilibrium values implied by the equilibrium relationship are only possible in the short run.

Let S_1 and S_2 be the (non-stationary) spot exchange rates of two currencies measured against a numeraire such as the US dollar. A long-run (or a cointegrating) relationship between these two spot exchange rates can be written as

$$S_{1,t} = a_0 + a_1 S_{2,t} + \varepsilon_t \tag{5.41}$$

where $S_{1,t} \sim I(1)$, $S_{2,t} \sim I(1)$ and $\varepsilon_t \sim I(0)$. According to this relationship, the value of $S_{1,t}$ should be determined in relation to the value of $S_{2,t}$ while allowing for the possibility of deviations in the short run. In the long run, however, the error term should revert to a mean value of zero, in which case the value of $S_{1,t}$ should be determined exactly in relation to the value of $S_{2,t}$ as defined by equation (5.41). Given the existence of such a long-run relationship, the following error correction model can be derived:

$$\Delta S_{1,t} = b_0 \Delta S_{2,t} + b_1(S_{1,t-1} - a_0 - a_1 S_{2,t-1}) \tag{5.42}$$

where $b_1 < 0$. The term in parentheses is the error correction term, which is an expression of the deviation from the long-run equilibrium condition at time $t-1$. This model tells us that short-run (that is, period-to-period) changes in $S_{1,t}$ are determined by short-run changes in $S_{2,t}$ as well as the previous period's deviations from the long-run equilibrium condition represented by equation (5.41). For example, if $S_{1,t-1}$ was below the equilibrium value implied by the long-run equilibrium condition, then we should expect it to rise, that is $\Delta S_{1,t}$ should be positive. The implication of this line of reasoning is that information available at time $t-1$ can be used to predict the value of the exchange rate at time t, which is inconsistent with market efficiency. Thus, cross-sectional market efficiency requires that the exchange rates not be cointegrated. In general, the empirical evidence seems to support this hypothesis (see, for example, Tronzano, 1992 and Copeland, 1991).

Baillie and Bollerslev (1989) argue that the presence of a first-order error correction model (representing the dynamic relationship between asset prices) indicates the part of the price (or exchange rate) changes that would be predictable. This implies that the disequilibrium error (from a cointegrating relationship linking prices or exchange rates) is an important component in next period's change and this can be interpreted as a violation of weak-form efficiency.

Inconsistency between cointegration and efficiency arguably arises out of two conflicting assertions: (i) changes in prices cannot be predicted in efficient markets, and (ii) a deviation of prices from a cointegrating relationship implies predictable future changes.

AN ALTERNATIVE INTERPRETATION

The proposition of inconsistency between a finding of cointegrating exchange rates and market efficiency has been challenged on two grounds. The first is that the restriction only applies to genuinely different assets (see, for example, Copeland, 1991, p. 187). This challenge, however, rests on the concept of 'genuinely different assets', which is very loose as it is not easy to draw the dividing line between different assets. Granger (1986) uses the example of gold and silver, but it can always be argued that these two assets are not genuinely different and that they belong to the family of precious metals. Copeland (1991), on the other hand, mentions two cases in which inconsistency between cointegration and efficiency is not valid: (i) two fixed exchange rates, and (ii) the prices of a derivative security and the underlying asset.

The second challenge to the proposition of inconsistency is more fundamental. Dwyer and Wallace (1992) argue that the 'alleged inconsistency' of cointegration and market efficiency relies on a definition of efficient markets in which changes in asset prices are unpredictable. The argument goes as follows: if efficient markets are defined as those in which there are no risk-free returns above the opportunity cost available to agents, given transaction costs and information, then efficiency does not preclude cointegration. Several pieces of work are cited to support this argument. First, Sims (1984) derives a connection between market efficiency and unpredictability of prices at high frequencies on the assumption that changes in information are relatively more important at high frequencies while changes in the fundamentals are more important at low frequencies. Since cointegration is a relationship at the zero frequency, the connection between unpredictability and cointegration seems to be loose. Second, LeRoy (1989) argues that there is no obvious reason to be particularly interested in unpredictability. Third, Fama (1990) points out that changes in stock prices can be predictable in an efficient stock market, clarifying his earlier paper on market efficiency. To sum up, Dwyer and Wallace (1992, p. 325) put forward the proposition that there is no inconsistency between market efficiency and cointegration, given that efficiency is defined to imply the lack of arbitrage opportunities.

6: Judgemental and Composite Forecasting

The forecasting techniques described in the previous chapters involve the manipulation of historical data to produce forecasts. The discussion so far implies that the forecaster's judgement is not involved in generating forecasts. This is not the case, however. On the contrary, sound judgement is an essential component of good forecasting techniques. Moreover, the assumption so far is that forecasts are derived from a single method or model. For example, a forecast can be derived from a PPP model, from an ARIMA model or from exponential smoothing. Nothing has been said about combining the forecasts derived from two different methods or models.

In this chapter both of these assumptions are relaxed. By considering judgemental forecasting, we relax the assumption that the forecast is derived from a model or a mechanical method without using the forecaster's judgement. And by considering composite forecasting we find out whether or not some benefit (in terms of forecasting accuracy) is gained by combining the forecasts derived from different models and methods.

JUDGEMENTAL FORECASTING: AN OVERVIEW

In a sense, all forecasts are judgemental. Since forecasts pertain to future events, some element of human judgement is always involved in making inductive inferences. Forecasting is a day-to-day activity of the human brain. We generate forecasts continuously through time as we contemplate the outcomes of frequently encountered situations. Consider, for example, the following situations when a forecast is required to answer the questions arising out of them. The following are some typical questions:

1. Who will win the World Cup final?
2. Will she go out with me?
3. Will I get the job I was interviewed for yesterday?
4. Will I get to the station before the train leaves?

These are only four of an endless list of questions that arise in our daily lives, each of which requires forecasting. In all of these situations judgemental forecasts are generated. You do not construct a formal model and use a computer to forecast whether or not she will accept your invitation for dinner. This will be the case even if you are a brilliant mathematician and/or a computer wizard. You will, however, process all available information to generate a forecast, since her decision (which you are trying to forecast) matters to a considerable extent.

In generating a forecast on whether or not your date is going to materialise, you might deliberately overlook some important pieces of information because they point to a negative outcome that you find hard to contemplate. In this case what is generated is not a jugdemental forecast, but rather wishful thinking or wishful expectation. This indeed reminds me of the 'prediction' made by the arrogant manager of an unknown team in the 1982 World Cup tournament that was held in Spain. That manager, whose team reached the World Cup final for the first (and last) time, made the 'forecast' that his team would reach the final, making the additional remark that he did not care which other team joined his team on the occasion (implying naturally that the other team would lose anyway). This manager disregarded several pieces of information, including the fact that his team was in a very difficult group. This forecast cannot be regarded as a judgemental forecast, not even an irrational forecast. It is wishful thinking. Needless to say, that team was knocked out of the tournament in the first round. Ironically, when this manager was interviewed following his team's exit from the tournament, he made another (long-term) 'forecast'. He declared, 'we will win the World Cup even if we have to wait one million years!'

It is arguable that judgemental forecasting may be used in situations involving dating and football, but not when it comes to business decisions. This is not the case, however, because forecasts are often made on judgemental basis. An economist, who normally uses formal models to forecast exchange rates, may resort to judgemental forecasting on some occasions. For example, this economist could be attending a meeting with his superiors in which he is (unexpectedly) asked to give a view on a certain currency. This economist cannot excuse himself from the meeting to go and generate forecasts from the forecasting model on his computer. Rather, he will respond with a quick (very quick) brain-storming session whereby he comes up with an answer. Naturally, the view must represent a rational forecast, because this economist has his job in the balance. In other situations the unavailability of data, measurement problems and other reasons may force this economist to resort to judgemental forecasting.

Even when this economist has the time to prepare forecasts based on the formal model stored on his computer, judgement is still important. The economist will have to use his judgement in deciding on the model he uses, the data, the time horizon, the estimation method and several other factors that affect the forecasting accuracy. Indeed, two equally good econometricians are very likely to produce highly divergent forecasts because of differences in judgement. This is why the forecasting accuracy of foreign exchange forecasting services could differ considerably. This is a point that will be discussed in detail in Chapter 12.

Judgemental forecasting also appears in situations when a consensus forecast is reached in a meeting of senior management. Suppose that a meeting is held to consider a decision whether or not to hedge foreign-currency receivables to be realised in six months. This decision naturally depends on the behaviour of the exchange rate between the domestic currency and the foreign currency in which the receivables are denominated. The chairman of the meeting may start by asking the participants where they expect that exchange rate to be six months from now, and they come up with different answers. The problem in this case is that group dynamics can distort the process and result in a consensus forecast that may not be carefully thought out by all participants. In this case the Delphi method may become useful. This method is described at a later stage.

Apart from the situations described above, the role judgement plays in forecasting may take the following forms:

1. Judgemental forecasting is an integral part of the decision-making process.
2. Judgemental manipulation of the forecasts produced by using a formal model.
3. Judgement regarding the writing of scenarios to generate conditional forecasts.

Each one of these roles will be discussed in the following three sections.

JUDGEMENTAL FORECASTING AS PART OF THE DECISION-MAKING PROCESS

Decision theory addresses the elements that comprise the decision-making function of business executives. In this sense, forecasts are made as part of the planning or decision-making process. The concepts of expected value and utility are important for decision making. The tree diagram is also used to help the decision maker visualise complex situations and make rational decisions.

Phillips (1987) states three principles that govern the decision-making process:

1. Probabilities represent the decision maker's degree of belief such that zero means no chance of occurring and one represents certainty.
2. The utility (or expected utility) is a function of the expected value of the outcome and the risk of this outcome as measured by the standard deviation.
3. A decision maker chooses the course of action that maximises utility.

Let us explain the concepts of expected value and decision tree with the following example that involves a situation that frequently arises. Suppose that there is an American company which owes a British company an amount of GBP1,000,000 payable in six months from the present time. Suppose that the current six-month forward rate (USD/GBP) is 1.68 and that the spot rate is 1.65. The company must consider a decision whether or not to hedge this position. The hedge decision implies that the American company will pay USD1,680,000 when the payment falls due six months from now. Hedging may be a good or a bad course of action, depending on whether the exchange rate ends up higher or lower than the forward rate when the payment is due. If the pound appreciates, so that the exchange rate ends up higher than the forward rate on the payment date, hedging will be a good decision because the company will pay a smaller amount in dollar terms than under the no-hedge decision. Conversely, if the pound depreciates, hedging will not be a good idea because the company will pay a larger amount than under the no-hedge decision. Obviously, the decision involves a forecast, and this forecast may be judgemental, generated by the decision maker as part of the overall decision-making process in a brain-storming session or sessions.

Let us imagine that the decision maker generates the following judgemental forecasts: there is a probability of 0.4 that the pound will appreciate to 1.75 and a probability of 0.6 that it will depreciate to 1.60. The following outcomes are possible:

1. The pound appreciates under the hedge decision, in which case the company has to pay USD1,680,000 rather than USD1,750,000, making a net gain of USD70,000.
2. The pound depreciates under the hedge decision, in which case the company has to pay USD1,680,000 rather than USD1,600,000, making a net loss of USD80,000.
3. The pound appreciates under the no-hedge decision, in which case the company has to pay USD1,750,000 rather than USD1,680,000, making a net loss of USD70,000.
4. The pound depreciates under the no-hedge decision, in which case the company has to pay USD1,600,000 rather than USD1,680,000, making a net gain of USD80,000.

The decision tree corresponding to this problem is shown in Figure 6.1. If the decision maker feels comfortable about his or her judgemental exchange rate forecasts, then the decision will be based on the expected value of the outcome, that is the payoff. Under the hedge decision the payoff can be either a gain of USD70,000 or a loss of 80,000 with probabilities of 0.4 and 0.6 respectively. This means that the expected value of the payoff is −20,000. Under the no-hedge decision, the payoff can be either −70,000

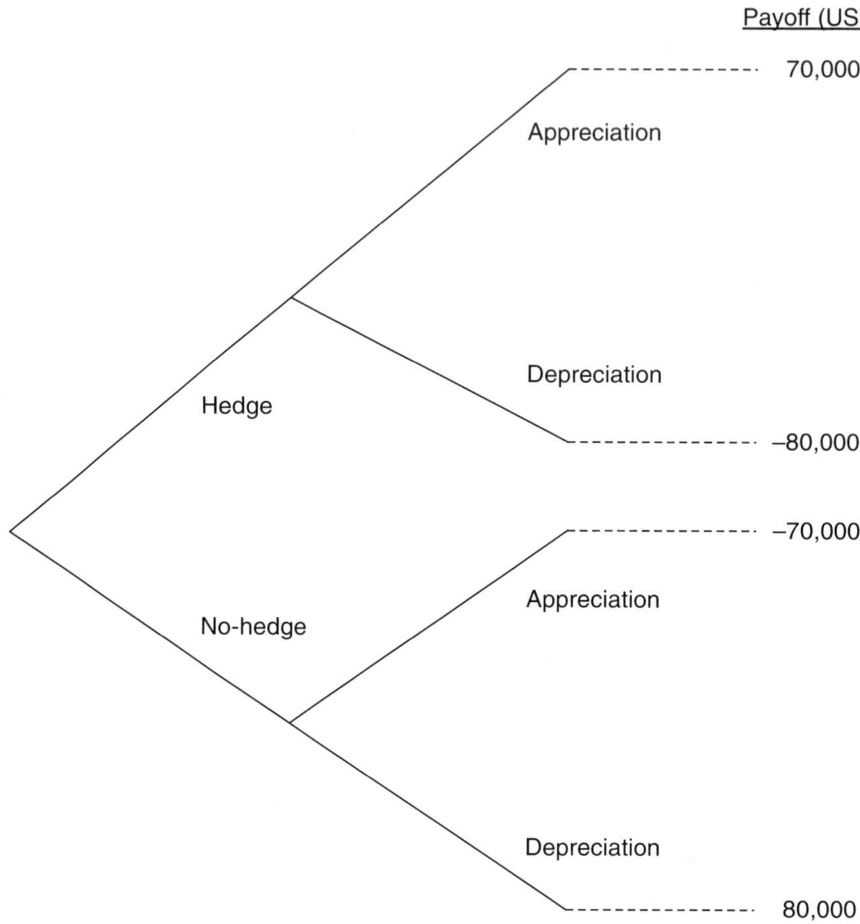

Figure 6.1 Decision tree for hedging

or 80,000 with probabilities of 0.4 and 0.6 respectively. This means that the expected value of the payoff is 20,000. The decision maker, under these conditions, will choose the no-hedge decision.

Let us now consider a more complicated problem resulting in a more complicated decision tree. A business manager with the base or domestic currency being the pound is considering a short-term financing decision whereby he chooses either purely foreign currency financing or mixed currency financing such that the domestic currency component is 50 per cent. Three foreign currencies are under consideration: the US dollar, the Japanese yen and the German mark. The objective underlying the decision is to minimise the effective financing rate over the borrowing period. Since

Table 6.1 The effective financing rate under two scenarios

Currency	*Effective financing rate (1)*	*Effective financing rate (2)*
USD	5.5	10.5
JPY	4.5	12.5
DEM	8.5	13.5
GBP	9.0	9.0

the effective financing rate in a foreign currency depends on the change in the exchange rate over the borrowing period, its value is not known in advance. To calculate a possible value of the effective financing rate in each foreign currency a forecast of the exchange rate of the foreign currency against the pound is required. Again, this forecast may be judgemental, generated as part of the overall decision-making process. Suppose that the decision maker decided to come up with two probabilistic judgemental forecasts for each currency, which means that each effective financing rate will have two values under scenarios 1 and 2 (with probabilities of 0.4 and 0.6 respectively). Table 6.1 shows the expected values of the financing rate for each foreign currency based on the judgemental forecasts. Notice that the effective financing rate in the domestic currency (the pound) is known with certainty because it is equal to the domestic interest rate.

The decision maker has in front of him the following alternatives:

1. Financing with a single foreign currency, which could be the dollar, the yen or the mark.
2. Financing with a portfolio of the three foreign currencies. The portfolio can be equally weighted or unequally weighted. In the latter case the following weights are assigned to the three currencies: dollar (50 per cent), yen (30 per cent) and mark (20 per cent).
3. Financing with a mixed domestic–foreign currency portfolio that contains one foreign currency. The portfolio consists of 50 per cent domestic currency and 50 per cent foreign currency.
4. Financing with a portfolio of 50 per cent domestic currency and 50 per cent foreign currencies. The foreign currency component can be either equally weighted or unequally weighted (as in 2).

The decision tree for this problem is shown in Figure 6.2. The expected values of the effective financing rate under all of the possible options are given in Table 6.2. If the decision maker's objective is to minimise the effective financing rate then the choice will fall on financing with a single foreign currency, the US dollar.

There seems to be something missing from this decision-making process. Financing with the US dollar produces an effective financing rate of 8.5, but

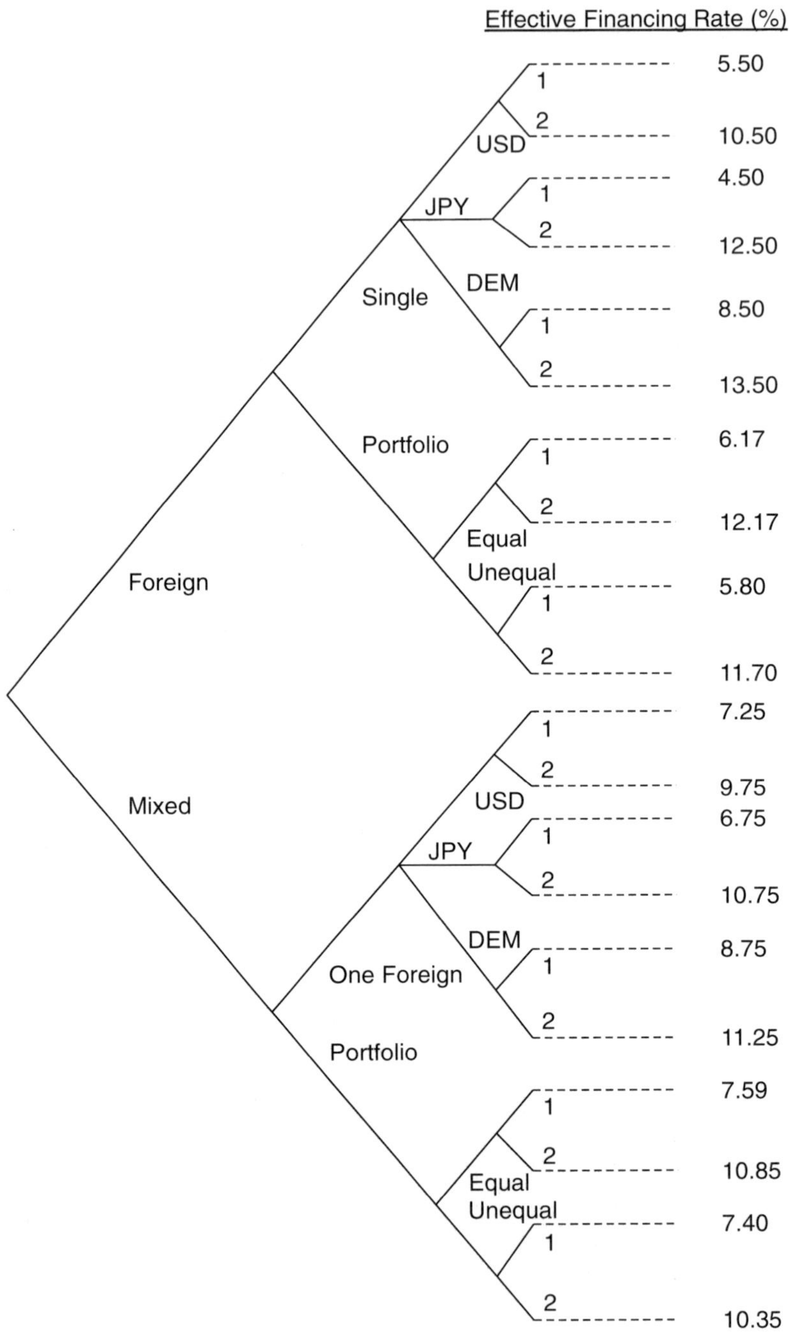

Figure 6.2 Decision tree for short-term financing (1)

Table 6.2 Expected values of effective financing rate

Financing method	*Expected value*
Single foreign currency (USD)	8.50
Single foreign currency (JPY)	9.30
Single foreign currency (DEM)	11.50
Foreign currency portfolio (Equal)	9.77
Foreign currency portfolio (Unequal)	9.34
Mixed financing with one foreign currency (USD)	8.75
Mixed financing with one foreign currency (JPY)	9.15
Mixed financing with one foreign currency (DEM)	10.25
Mixed financing with equal portfolio	9.55
Mixed financing with unequal portfolio	9.17

not with certainty, while financing with the domestic currency (the pound) only produces an effective financing rate of 9 per cent that is known with certainty. If the decision maker is risk averse then he will choose to finance with the domestic currency. Choosing the dollar as the currency of financing means running the risk of getting an effective financing rate of as high as 10.5 per cent. This is where the concept of utility comes in. More appropriately, the decision depends on the decision maker's utility, which in this case depends not only on the expected value of the effective financing rate but also on risk, the latter being measured by the standard deviation of the effective financing rate.

Why utility matters can be seen in the following example. Suppose that the effective financing rate in the domestic currency is 9 per cent and that foreign currency financing produces two possibilities: 12 per cent or 6 per cent with equal probabilities. If the decision maker chooses foreign currency financing then, depending on the outcome, the decision maker will be three percentage points better off or worse off. If the decision maker regards the disutility derived from being three percentage points worse off to be greater than the utility derived from being three percentage points better off, he will choose domestic currency financing. This kind of utility function implies risk aversion. Notice that the expected value of foreign currency financing is also 9 per cent. In this situation the following propositions can be stated:

1. If the decision maker chooses domestic currency financing, then he is risk averse.
2. If the decision maker chooses foreign currency financing, then he is a risk lover.
3. If the decision maker is indifferent between the two modes of financing, then he is risk neutral.

Table 6.3 Interest and exchange rates

Currency	*Interest rate (per cent)*	*Exchange rate (currency/GBP)*
USD	8	1.6500
JPY	6	215.00
DEM	9	2.8500

Let us consider the following, more comprehensive, example. The decision maker wants to choose one of the three foreign currencies for financing. The interest rates and current exchange rates on the three currencies are presented in Table 6.3.

In order to calculate the effective financing rate, the decision maker must generate forecasts for the levels of the three exchange rates at the end of the financing period. The decision maker chooses to use his judgement to generate the forecast. Since there is a high level of uncertainty, the decision maker formulates four scenarios with probabilities 0.1, 0.2, 0.3 and 0.4. Table 6.4 shows the values of the exchange rates at the end of the financing period under the four scenarios. The corresponding values of the effective financing rates (calculated roughly as the sum of the interest rate and the percentage change in the exchange rate) are also shown in the table. The decision tree for this problem is shown in Figure 6.3.

What will be the decision? On the basis of minimising the effective financing rate, the decision maker should choose the yen and be indifferent between the dollar and the mark. But when utility is taken to depend on risk as well, the picture changes. The decision maker will not be indifferent between the dollar and mark because the effective financing rate in the dollar is more volatile and therefore more risky. Choosing the dollar means running the risk of getting an effective financing rate of 12.03. Second, although the yen offers a lower effective financing rate, it is more risky than the other two currencies. Thus, given the choice between the dollar and the mark, the decision maker will definitely choose the mark. The choice between the yen and mark depends on the decision maker's utility function and his attitude towards risk.

Let us now consider the following decision-making problem concerning the choice of foreign currency investment. In this case the decision maker wants to maximise the expected value of the effective rate of return subject to the associated risk. Like the effective financing rate, the effective rate of return is roughly equal to the interest rate plus the expected change in the exchange rate.

Let us assume that the expected utility is a linear function of the ratio of the expected value of the effective rate of return to its standard deviation as

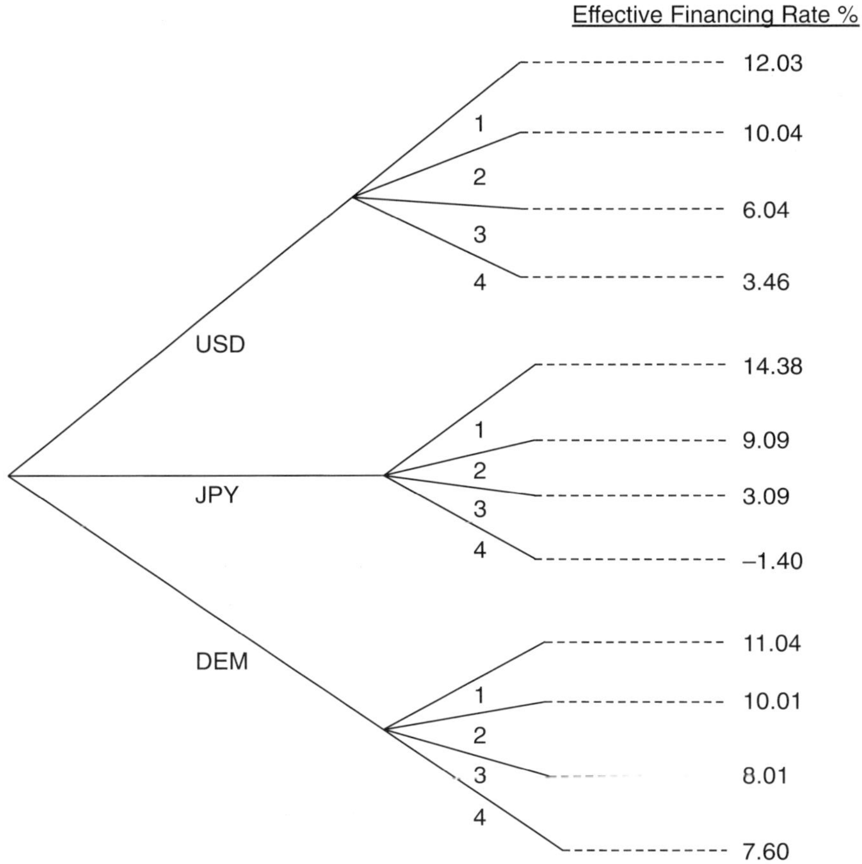

Figure 6.3 Decision tree for short-term financing (2)

Table 6.4 Exchange rates and effective financing rates

Currency	*Scenario 1 (0.4)*	*Scenario 2 (0.3)*	*Scenario 3 (0.2)*	*Scenario 4 (0.1)*	*Expected value*
Exchange rate					
USD	1.5710	1.6170	1.6830	1.7284	1.6229
JPY	198.38	208.55	221.45	232.20	209.43
DEM	2.7930	2.8215	2.8785	2.9070	2.8301
Financing rate					
USD	13.03	10.04	6.04	3.46	9.78
JPY	14.38	9.09	3.09	−1.40	8.96
DEM	11.04	10.01	8.01	7.60	9.78

Table 6.5 Expected values and standard deviations of effective rates of return

Currency	*Expected value*	*Standard deviation*	*Ratio*
USD	10	4	2.5
JPY	8	4	2.0
DEM	9	3	3.0
Portfolio A	15	6	2.5
Portfolio B	15	5	3.0
Portfolio C	7	2	3.5

reported in Table 6.5. This is effectively a measure of the rate of return per unit of risk, where the latter is taken to be one percentage point of the standard deviation. The objective, therefore, is to maximise the ratio of the expected rate of return to the standard deviation. This objective implies the following:

1. The decision maker is indifferent between the US dollar and portfolio A, although portfolio A offers a significantly higher expected rate of return.
2. The decision maker is indifferent between the German mark and portfolio B although the expected rate of return on the latter is higher by 6 percentage points.
3. Japanese yen investment is inferior to all other investments although it offers a higher expected rate of return than portfolio C.
4. The decision maker will choose portfolio C although it offers the lowest expected rate of return.
5. The expected utility derived from these alternatives in a descending order is the following: portfolio C; portfolio B and the German mark; Portfolio A and the US dollar; and the Japanese yen.

To make coherent and consistent preferences, judgement needs to be made about probability and utility. What is important in this case is not to make a point forecast but rather a range of forecasts. It is arguable though that any particular scenario for the future value of the exchange rate (and therefore the effective rate of return) has associated with it a small probability since there could be an infinite number of possibilities. It is normally the case, however, that only a few outcomes are anticipated, making probabilities irrelevant and perhaps misleading. Phillips (1987) provides a counter-argument to this proposition. The expected utility rule provides a relative comparison of the options derived from the possibilities under consideration. What matters, therefore, is the relative magnitudes of

Table 6.6 Effective financing rates and associated probabilities

Currency	*Scenario 1*	*Scenario 2*	*Scenario 3*	*Scenario 4*
USD	13.0	10.0	6.0	3.0
JPY	14.0	9.0	4.0	2.0
DEM	11.0	10.0	8.0	3.0
Probability (i)	0.40	0.30	0.20	0.10
Probability (ii)	0.24	0.18	0.12	0.06
Normalised probability (ii)	0.40	0.30	0.20	0.10

probabilities, not their absolute values. Hence, even though the list of possibilities is not exhaustive and absolute probabilities sum to less than one, the expected utility rule can still be applied to see which option is the most attractive.

In fact, it is possible to tackle this problem by normalising the probabilities if they do not add up to one. Consider the following example in which the decision maker tries to minimise the effective financing rate by considering three currencies: the US dollar, the Japanese yen and the German mark. The relevant information is presented in Table 6.6. Assume first that the four scenarios account for all possible outcomes. In this case we have a set of probabilities (i) that add up to one. Assume now that the decision maker believes that the four scenarios account for 60 per cent of the possible outcomes. In this case we have a set of probabilities (ii) that do not add up to one, but rather to 0.60.

Normalised probabilities for the set (ii) can be calculated by dividing each probability by the sum of the probabilities. These probabilities, which are shown in the last row of Table 6.6, are exactly equal to the probabilities in the first set. Since the two sets of probabilities are identical, the expected values of the effective financing rates will also be identical. Thus, whether the decision maker uses the set of probabilities (i), which accounts for all eventualities or the normalised probabilities of set (ii), which do not account for all eventualities, the results are the same. The decision maker will come up with the same order of preference: the German mark (9.3), the US dollar (9.7) and the Japanese yen (10.0).

JUDGEMENTAL MANIPULATION OF FORECASTS

The forecasting procedures considered so far rely on the manipulation of historical data to estimate a model that is then used to extrapolate the data into the future to generate forecasts. The underlying assumption here is that what has been a valid representation of the process generating exchange rates will be valid in the future. This assumption precludes possible shifts and structural breaks in the relationship. In some circumstances the forecasts are manipulated by the forecaster on the basis of his or her judgement after consideration of unusual circumstances of the situation or after recognising that the past history is not an accurate predictor of the future. The amount of judgement injected into the forecasting process tends to be higher when the historical data are few in number or are judged to be partially irrelevant. In the extreme case, it may be the forecaster's opinion that there are no historical data that are directly relevant to the forecasting process, in which case the forecast will be purely judgemental.

Consider the following example. Assume that the exchange rate is determined by the linear model

$$S_t = \alpha + \beta X_t + \varepsilon_t \tag{6.1}$$

A forecast is then derived by estimating the model to obtain

$$\hat{S}_{t+1} = \alpha + \beta X_{t+1} \tag{6.2}$$

If the forecaster believes that $\hat{S}_{t+1}$ is an underestimation of the actual exchange rate prevailing at $t+1$ because of an upward shift in the relationship, then the actual model, which cannot be picked by the historical data, is

$$S_t = (\alpha + \gamma) + \beta X_t + \varepsilon_t \tag{6.3}$$

in which case the forecast is

$$\hat{S}_{t+1} = \alpha + \gamma + \beta X_{t+1} \tag{6.4}$$

Since γ cannot be estimated from the historical data, the forecaster will have to use his judgement to assign values to this parameter. This situation may arise, for example, when there is an expected increase in the demand for the US dollar that reflects an impending increase in US stock prices.

The same problem arises when there are qualitative or unquantifiable variables such as 'sentiment' or 'military tension'. In this case the actual model will be

$$S_t = \alpha + \beta X_t + \delta Z_t + \varepsilon_t \tag{6.5}$$

where Z is a qualitative or an unquantifiable variable. The forecast is given by

$$\hat{S}_{t+1} = \alpha + \beta X_{t+1} + \delta Z_{t+1} \tag{6.6}$$

Since equation (6.6) cannot be estimated from historical data, the forecaster must use his judgement to assign values to the term δZ_{t+1}. This situation arises particularly when there are bubbles, such as the bubble which characterised the appreciation of the US dollar in the first half of the 1980s. The model will consistently underestimate the future value, which requires a judgemental upward adjustment. Notice, however, that the same kind of adjustment can be used with univariate time series models.

Research has shown that when historical data are available, judgemental manipulation may reduce the accuracy of the forecasts produced by a model. This may be attributed to some bias on the part of the forecaster. McNees (1990) provides evidence indicating that forecasters may go too far in the manipulation of their raw forecasts. The evidence also reveals that judgemental revision is not beneficial in the case of long-term forecasts.

THE ROLE OF JUDGEMENT IN SCENARIO WRITING

Conditional forecasting on the basis of econometric models requires the availability of some scenarios if the forecaster is not certain about what is going to happen to the variables affecting the exchange rate. This is almost always the case when forecasts are generated from a multivariate model, but not when a univariate model is used. For example, the PPP model tells us that the percentage change in the exchange rate is determined by the domestic and foreign inflation rates. In order to forecast the percentage change in the exchange rate the forecaster needs to input the values of the inflation rates that are unknown at the time when the forecaster is trying to generate the forecasts. Hence, the forecaster needs to assign one or more values to each of the two inflation rates. Each pair of values form a single scenario. Scenarios are constructed almost invariably on the basis of judgement.

Scenarios are descriptions of alternative hypothetical futures that allow the forecaster to assess potential developments. They do not describe what the future will look like but rather what possible futures one might expect. One reason for contemplating various scenarios is that the process sets no boundaries for thinking.

The *Concise Oxford Dictionary* defines the word ‘scenario’ as an ‘imagined sequence of future events’. In the forecasting literature, there are two popular definitions of scenario. Khan (1965) defines scenarios as ‘hypothetical sequences of events constructed for the purpose of focusing attention on causal processes and decision points’. The second definition is suggested by Mitchell *et al.* (1979). According to the second definition a scenario is ‘an outline of one conceivable state of affairs, given certain assumptions about the present and the course of events in the intervening period’. Jungermann and Thuring (1987) distinguish between the two definitions on the basis of their emphasis on the course of events between the initial state and the final state. In Khan's definition the emphasis is on the explication of the chain of actions and events and their causal relations. The definition of Mitchell *et al.*, on the other hand, emphasises the depiction of the situation at the time horizon, given certain assumptions about the preceding period. Hence, Jungermann and Thuring call the first definition a 'chain scenario' and the second definition a 'snapshot scenario'. Furthermore, they list the following properties of a scenario:

1. It is hypothetical in the sense that it describes some possible future.
2. It is selective in the sense that it represents one possible state of some complex state of affairs.
3. It is bound in the sense that it consists of a limited number of states, events, actions and consequences.
4. It is connected in the sense that its elements are conditionally or causally related.
5. It is assessable in the sense that it can be judged with respect to its probability and/or desirability.

Ducot and Lubben (1980) have suggested the following three criteria for classifying scenarios:

1. Scenarios are either explanatory or anticipatory. Explanatory scenarios are forward-directed, in the sense that they start from some assumed final state of affairs and explore what consequences might result. Anticipatory scenarios are backward-directed, in the sense that they start from a final state of affairs and ask for the possible events that could produce these effects.
2. Scenarios are either descriptive or normative. Descriptive scenarios present potential futures irrespective of their desirability or otherwise. Normative scenarios take an explicit account of values and objectives.
3. Scenarios are trend or peripheral. A trend scenario extrapolates the normal surprise-free course of events or state of affairs that one might expect if no particular action is taken, A peripheral scenario depicts trend-breaking surprising or unsurprising developments.

Geschka and Reibnitz (1983) have suggested a scenario-writing process that consists of the following steps:

1. Defining and structuring the task, specifying the area of interest and identifying the major relevant features of this area.
2. Describing important external factors and their influences on the area of interest. These factors form the influence fields.

3. Identifying major descriptors for each field and making assumptions about their future trends.
4. Checking the consistency of the possible combinations of alternative assumptions regarding the critical descriptors and identifying assumption bundles.
5. Combining assumptions with the trend assumptions regarding the uncritical depictors, resulting in a scenario for each field.
6. Making assumptions with respect to possible interfering events and their probabilities as well as their impacts on the field.
7. Assessing the impact of the field scenarios on the area of interest and its depictors. Respective scenarios are constructed.
8. Identifying strategies that could promote or impede the developments described in the scenarios.

Jungermann and Thuring (1987) assume the following steps in the cognitive activity of a person embarking on the task of writing scenarios:

1. The relevant problem will be activated within the world knowledge of the individual.
2. A mental model is constituted on the basis of the activated problem knowledge that includes those elements and relations of the domain that are needed for the specific task.
3. Inferences are drawn by simulating the mental model.
4. Scenario knowledge is composed by selecting those inferences that seem most relevant, probable, interesting or whatever criteria might be.

AN EXAMPLE: SCENARIOS FOR A PPP FORECASTING MODEL

Scenario writing involves defining the particulars of an uncertain future by writing a 'script' for the variables that affect the exchange rate. A 'most likely' scenario is normally written along with one or more less likely but possible scenarios. The scenario-writing process is often followed by a discussion to obtain a solid consensus or alternative scenarios. For example, the scenario may be written by the chief economist and discussed by the management team.

Consider the PPP model

$$\dot{S}_t = \alpha + \beta \dot{P}_t + \gamma \dot{P}_t^* + \varepsilon_t \tag{6.7}$$

which implies a forecast that is given by

$$\hat{\dot{S}}_{t+1} = \alpha + \beta \dot{P}_{t+1} + \gamma \dot{P}_{t+1}^* \tag{6.8}$$

Table 6.7 Scenarios for a PPP model

Scenario	*Domestic inflation*	*Foreign inflation*	$\dot{P}_{t+1}$	$\dot{P}^*_{t+1}$	*Probability*
1	High	High	10	12	0.4
2	High	Low	10	4	0.3
3	Low	High	3	12	0.2
4	Low	Low	3	4	0.1

The scenarios pertain to the values of the inflation rates at time $t + 1$. Table 6.7 shows four possible scenarios with probabilities ranging between 0.4 and 0.1.

Given the four scenarios, four different point forecasts can be generated. The expected value of the percentage change in the exchange rate can be calculated as a weighted average of these four values with the weights being the probabilities of the four scenarios.

JUDGEMENTAL FORECASTING: FINAL REMARKS

There is no question about the fact that judgemental forecasting is used in business decision making. In fact some expert advice is often based on judgemental forecasting. This does not mean that a forecaster can say anything and claim it to be a forecast. Rather, the forecaster endeavours to produce a rational forecast by collecting and processing all available information pertaining to the situation under consideration. The processing of this information, however, will not take place in a computer, but rather in the forecaster's head. The forecast will not be generated by an exact formula, but by the 'balance of probabilities' as judged by the forecaster's brain.

This is why judgemental forecasting may be perceived as lacking objectivity. Wharton Econometrics Forecasting Associates (WEFA) states explicitly on its web page that its forecasts are not judgemental. The following statement is explicitly made:

> Unlike many other exchange rate forecasts, our projections are not based on intuitive judgement. They are derived from models tempered with analytic and country expertise.

This is to give the impression that a lot of effort is put into the process of generating the forecasts and that they are based on scientific methods, not on 'witchcraft'. But it remains to be true that while these forecasts are based on rigorous and highly complex econometric models, judgemental manipulation of the forecasts is resorted to. The analytic and country experts perform two functions, both of which pertain to judgemental forecasting. First, they write the scenarios needed to generate conditional forecasts. Second, they manipulate the forecasts generated by econometric models when these forecasts do not make sense.

It is most likely that a client of a forecasting service will be less impressed by judgemental forecasts than by formal forecasts, at least *ex ante*. In general, judgemental forecasts may be considered to be inferior for a number of commonly held beliefs. The following are examples:

1. Forecasting is a scientific endeavour, and science must be based on mathematical modelling. Judgemental forecasting is not scientific, probably close to being a collection of subjective 'hunches'.
2. Formal forecasting methods that are based on rigorous methodologies allow auditing, replication and verification. Judgemental forecasting does not allow these exercises.
3. Judgemental forecasting is more prone to personal bias, and so it is less objective than formal forecasting.

Despite these perceptions, resorting to judgemental forecasting is sometimes inevitable. Moreover, it may be the case that formal forecasts are no better than judgemental forecasts, *ex post*.

COMPOSITE FORECASTING: AN OVERVIEW

Composite forecasting involves the combination of two or more forecasts derived from different models to produce the final forecast. One reason for doing this is to reduce the forecasting error via diversification and to combine views to obtain collective knowledge. The underlying forecasts can be judgemental forecasts or formal forecasts derived from econometric models. By combining two or more forecasts the objective is to arrive at a consensus forecast.

The principle of diversification underlying the motto 'do not put all of your eggs in one basket', normally used in portfolio selection, is the prime reason for composite forecasting. It is the case, however, that combining forecasts derived from vastly different techniques produces better results than combining forecasts derived from similar techniques. This means, for example, that better results are obtained by combining two forecasts generated by a PPP model and an ARIMA univariate model than by combining two forecasts derived from a PPP model and the unbiased efficiency model.

Composite forecasting and the principle behind it also explain why many firms subscribe to several forecasting services using different techniques to generate their forecasts. When these forecasts are obtained they are pooled and combined internally in order to arrive at a composite forecast that may be taken to be a consensus forecast. This is also what the financial media do to arrive at a consensus forecast.

The Delphi method can be used to arrive at a consensus forecast in situations in which the group effect may distort the forecasts. This method may be used to generate a consensus judgemental forecast from a group of executives and analysts belonging to the same company. Suppose that the company is contemplating a decision to hedge foreign currency payables, a decision that depends on the movement of the underlying exchange rate. The participants in this exercise are initially asked to forecast the exchange rate individually and reply in writing, stating the forecast and the reasoning behind it. The person running the exercise summarises the forecasts and the comments and sends them to all of the participants. The participants are then able to read the reactions of the others and respond in two ways: either to stick to their original views and defend them or to modify them on the basis of the views put forward by the other participants. This process continues until it is believed that many views have been developed and that every view is carefully considered. At this stage the participants are invited to attend a meeting to debate their views. At the end of the process a clear consensus forecast should emerge.

There are mixed views in the academic literature on composite forecasting. Armstrong (1989) claims that the results of over 200 studies demonstrate that combining forecasts produces consistent but little gains in accuracy. He further adds that this line of research does not define well the conditions under which combining forecasts is most effective nor how the methods should be combined in each situation. Mahmoud (1989) argues that although the amount of research on combining forecasts is substantial, relatively little is known about when and how managers combine forecasts. A positive view is presented by Clemen (1989) who claims that the primary conclusion of research on composite forecasting is that forecasting accuracy can be substantially improved by combining forecasts.

METHODS OF COMBINING FORECASTS

Consider the following four exchange rate forecasting models: the PPP model, an ARIMA (2, 1, 0) model, the forward rate model and the random walk model. The forecasts derived from these models are represented by the following set of equations:

$$\hat{S}_{t+1} = a + bP_{t+1} + cP^*_{t+1} \tag{6.9}$$

$$\hat{S}_{t+1} = \alpha + \beta S_t + \gamma S_{t-1} \tag{6.10}$$

$$\hat{S}_{t+1} = F_t \tag{6.11}$$

$$\hat{S}_{t+1} = S_t \tag{6.12}$$

Denote the composite forecast by $\hat{S}_C$ and the four forecasts by $\hat{S}_P$, $\hat{S}_A$, $\hat{S}_F$ and $\hat{S}_R$. The composite forecast can be the simple average of the four individual forecasts, in which case it is calculated as

$$\hat{S}_C = \frac{1}{4}\left[\hat{S}_P + \hat{S}_A + \hat{S}_F + \hat{S}_R\right] \tag{6.13}$$

Otherwise, it can be calculated as a weighted average, in which case it is given by

$$\hat{S}_c = w_P\hat{S}_P + w_A\hat{S}_A + w_F\hat{S}_F + w_R\hat{S}_R \tag{6.14}$$

where

$$w_P + w_A + w_F + w_R = 1 \tag{6.15}$$

In general, if there are k individual forecasts, then the composite forecast is calculated as

$$\hat{S}_C = \sum_{i=1}^{k} w_i \hat{S}_i \tag{6.16}$$

where

$$\sum_{i=1}^{k} w_i = 1 \tag{6.17}$$

It is important to bear in mind that composite forecasting is useful only if there is no forecast encompassing. A forecast is said to encompass another if it incorporates (or encompasses) all the relevant information in the latter. Consider a regression of the actual value of the exchange rate on two forecasts, $\hat{S}_P$ and $\hat{S}_A$

$$S_{t+j} = \alpha_P\hat{S}_{P,t+j} + \alpha_A\hat{S}_{A,t+j} + \varepsilon_{t+j} \tag{6.18}$$

Testing for forecast encompassing is based on testing coefficient restrictions. If $(\alpha_p, \alpha_A) = (1, 0)$, the PPP forecast encompasses the ARIMA forecast. Alternatively, if $(\alpha_P, \alpha_A) = (0, 1)$, the ARIMA forecast encompasses the PPP forecast. Because of the non-stationarity of the exchange rate it may better to specify the regression in terms of changes as follows:

$$S_{t+j} - S_t = \alpha_P(\hat{S}_{P,t+j} - S_t) + \alpha_A(\hat{S}_{A,t+j} - S_t) + \varepsilon_{t+j} \tag{6.19}$$

The same coefficient restriction tests apply in this case.

The question that arises now is how to determine the weights. This question deals with the different methods of combining forecasts. The following methods are used to combine forecasts.

COMBINING FORECASTS WITH EQUAL WEIGHTS

This is the case described by equation (6.13). This method avoids the need to select which forecasts are better, and so it treats good and bad forecasts on equal footing.

COMBINING FORECASTS WITH PERFORMANCE WEIGHTS

In this case heavier weights are assigned to the more accurate forecasts over the sample period.

THE VARIANCE–COVARIANCE METHOD

Consider a composite forecast obtained by combining the PPP and ARIMA forecasts. This is expressed as

$$\hat{S}_{C,t+j} = w\hat{S}_{P,t+j} + (1 - w)\hat{S}_{A,t+j} \tag{6.20}$$

The composite forecasting error is also a weighted average of the two individual forecasting errors. Thus

$$e_{C,t+j} = we_{P,t+j} + (1 - w)e_{A,t+j} \tag{6.21}$$

The variance of the composite forecasting error is

$$\sigma_C^2 = w^2\sigma_p^2 + (1 - w)^2\sigma_A^2 + 2w(1 - w)\sigma_{P,A}^2 \tag{6.22}$$

where σ_C^2 is the variance of the error of the composite forecast, σ_P^2 is the variance of the forecasting error of the PPP model, σ_A^2 is the forecasting error of the ARIMA model and $\sigma_{P,A}^2$ is the covariance of the forecasting errors of the two models. The optimal value of the weight, w, is given by

$$w = \frac{\sigma_A^2 - \sigma_{P,A}^2}{\sigma_A^2 + \sigma_P^2 - 2\sigma_{P,A}^2} \tag{6.23}$$

The variances and covariances can be estimated from the sample. For example, the covariance can be calculated as

$$\sigma_{P,A}^2 = \sum_{t=1}^{N} e_{P,t+j}\, e_{A,t+j} \tag{6.24}$$

where N is the sample size. If the covariance is zero then equation (6.23) reduces to

$$w = \frac{\sigma_A^2}{\sigma_A^2 + \sigma_P^2} \tag{6.25}$$

It is obvious that if $\sigma_P^2 \rightarrow 0$, $w \rightarrow 1$ which means that the whole weight is assigned to the PPP forecast.

COMBINING FORECASTS WITH REGRESSION WEIGHTS

The weights in this case are estimated as coefficients in a regression equation of the actual values on the forecasts. The regression equation is written as

$$S_{t+j} = \beta_0 + \beta_1 \hat{S}_{P,t+j} + \beta_2 \hat{S}_{A,t+j} + \varepsilon_{t+j} \tag{6.26}$$

A problem arises when one of the coefficients turns out to be negative. It is possible though to impose the restrictions $\beta_0 = 0$ and $\beta_1 + \beta_2 = 1$. It is also possible to impose the restrictions that the coefficients are positive. Granger and Ramanathan (1984) have shown that the unrestricted version produces better results and that the composite forecast will be unbiased even if the individual forecasts are biased.

Several variations to the regression method can be introduced. For example, if there is a reason to believe that the relative accuracy of the individual forecasts change over time then it is possible to estimate time-varying regression coefficients. We may also estimate the regression by allowing the residuals to follow autoregressive or moving average processes. Another modification involves taking a weighted average of the simple average combination and the regression. Finally, the regression equation may be specified as being nonlinear.

CONSENSUS FORECASTS

It is often the case that composite forecasting is used to obtain some sort of a consensus forecast. Different forecasters have different information and capabilities, and this is why they differ. By combining forecasts it may be possible to arrive at some sort of a consensus forecast. The media often report consensus forecasts by combining individual forecasts produced by various forecasters.

Four types of studies have dealt with consensus forecasting. These studies have produced the following definitions of consensus forecasts:

1. Some studies define the consensus forecast as the mean or median value of the individual forecasts (for example, McNees, 1987 and Zarnowitz, 1985).
2. Agnew (1985) argues that forecasts are highly correlated across forecasters, so that calculating a mean gives little cancellation. Instead, he uses optimal pooling, using regression weights that are gradually updated over time.
3. The consensus forecast may be defined on the basis of some properties of the distribution of forecasts across forecasters. Lahiri and Teigland (1987) and Schnader and Stekler (1991) suggest that consensus requires a distribution of forecasts which is unimodal, systematic and at least as peaked as the normal density function.
4. Some studies track the dispersion of forecasts or the forecasting errors over time with a view to testing for significance. Significant patterns indicate that forecasters are not alike. Examples of these studies are Stekler (1987) and Batchelor (1990).

7: Technical Analysis

DEFINITION AND UNDERLYING PRINCIPLES

Technical analysis can be defined as the study of exchange rates (and other financial prices) based on supply and demand. Technical analysts (also called technicians or chartists) record, normally in chart form, historical exchange rates and try to deduce from the pictured history the probable future trend. The basic idea is that exchange rates as observed in the foreign exchange market are determined by supply and demand, and this is all that is needed to be known.

Technical analysis is widely used, particularly when there is little change in the economic fundamentals that affect exchange rates, and particularly for trading over short periods (for example, daily or intra-day trading). The growing popularity of technical analysis is due largely to dissatisfaction with the fundamental models of exchange rate determination that have been shown to have low explanatory and predictive power. The behaviour of exchange rates since the advent of floating in the early 1970s has been characterised by significant deviations from the equilibrium rate implied by fundamental models such as PPP or the monetary model. Because these models produce some sort of an equilibrium exchange rate, any jump in the exchange rate above this value will be interpreted as a bearish sign. Conversely, technical analysis views the jump as a bullish sign as long as there is no sign indicating a trend reversal.

Technical analysis is based on the postulation that exchange rates do not move randomly but rather they move in repeated and identifiable patterns. The exchange rate series that is recorded over time reflects all available information on which supply and demand decisions are based. This information pertains to economic fundamentals as well as to other non-quantifiable factors such as expectations, sentiment and psychology. It is these factors that lead to the emergence of the patterns observed by technical analysts. This postulation does not go without a challenge, however. For example, Cootner (1964) and Malkeil (1990) argue that the apparent cycles in stock prices (and financial prices in general) are no more regular than the run of chance, and that they can be replicated by the toss of a coin. The argument goes further, as Malkeil puts forward the proposition that although market history tends to repeat itself, it does so with too many variations to be predictable. Recall Figure 1.4 that shows an artificial exchange rate series generated from random numbers. One can easily identify some of the patterns to which technical analysts give certain interpretations.

Technical analysis is based on three principles. The first of these principles is that all of the factors affecting exchange rates are discounted: they are reflected in the actual behaviour of exchange rates as shown on a chart. These factors include economic, political, psychological and other factors. Unlike fundamental analysts, technical analysts believe that it is futile to study fundamental variables to determine the intrinsic value of a currency. In the 1980s, the US dollar appreciated persistently in the face of negative economic fundamentals such as slower economic growth and lower interest rates. PPP measures of the intrinsic values of currencies almost invariably indicate overvaluation or undervaluation of currencies. In the second half of 1998 no one could explain the strength of the pound and the weakness of the Australian dollar. Trying to trace out the movement of exchange rates on the basis of fundamental factors may be futile for at least two reasons: measurement errors and unavailability of high-frequency data on variables such as prices, output and the balance of payments. Hence, intra-day changes in exchange rates cannot be governed by economic fundamentals.

The movements of exchange rates simply reflect changes in the forces of supply and demand. Technical analysts do not pay attention to, or try to find out, what causes changes in supply and demand. They are only interested in what happens, not in why or how it happens. Hence, the argument goes, the study of exchange rate movements is all that matters. This explains the motto of 'sell on good news' because if the actual events are as expected then they are already reflected in the level of the exchange rate. Based on this news, therefore, we should not expect any further rise. Figure 7.1 illustrates how changes in the forces of supply and demand produce a time path for the exchange rate. The initial exchange rate is S_1, determined by the intersection of the supply and demand curves $(Sf)_1$ and $(Df)_1$. As the demand curve shifts to the right, the exchange rate rises to S_2 and then to S_3. As the supply curve shifts to the right, the exchange rate falls to S_4 and then to S_5. Finally, as the demand curve shifts back to $(Df)_2$ and $(Df)_3$ the exchange rate falls further to S_6 and then to S_7.

The second principle is that exchange rates move in trends and that trends persist. The supply and demand balance sets a trend in motion, and this trend remains intact until it ends. For example, if a currency is appreciating it will continue to appreciate until there is a clear reversal. The same is true if a currency is depreciating. When a car is heading north, it cannot all of a sudden reverse direction to go south: it has to reduce speed first, and may even have to stop. The reduction in speed or stopping is the signal that there is a reversal of the direction. The same is true of the movements of exchange rates. When a currency appreciates its exchange rate goes up, creating a trend. The trend will persist until the movement slows and gives warning before finally reversing and moving downwards, and this is when a new trend is created. The motto 'the trend is your friend' is true because

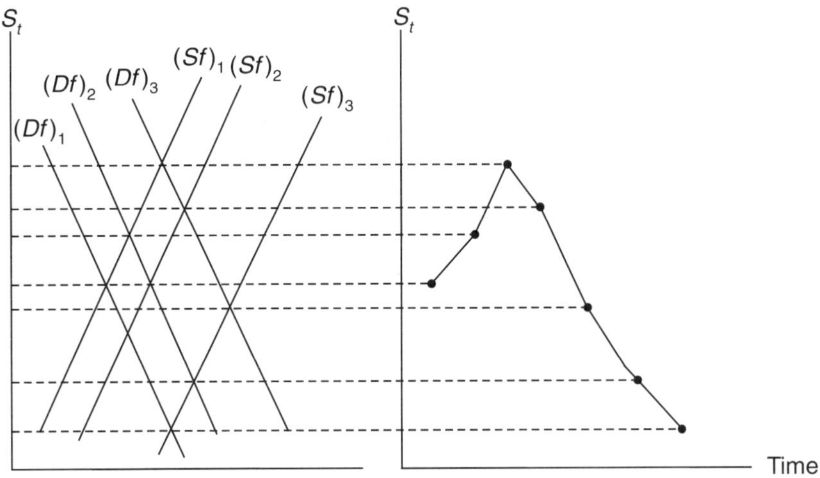

Figure 7.1 Time path generated by shifting supply and demand curves

once begun it is likely to continue, and by following it a trader is likely to make money.

The third principle is that market behaviour is repetitive. This is because human nature means that people react to similar situations in a consistent manner. Since the foreign exchange market is a reflection of the actions of people (the traders), technical analysts study these actions to determine how people react under certain conditions and thus how exchange rates move. In other words, technical analysts analyse the recurrence of similar characteristics in an attempt to identify major peaks and troughs in exchange rates. Technical analysts do that by examining patterns on charts. These patterns have meanings that can be interpreted in terms of probable future movements in exchange rates.

Technical analysis is based on the study of historical data on the underlying exchange rate. These data may be intra-day, daily, weekly, monthly or even quarterly. What determines the frequency of the data used is the objective of the trader. Normally, monthly data indicate the long-term trend, weekly data represent the intermediate-term trend, while daily data show the short-term trend.

THE DOW THEORY AND THE ELLIOTT WAVE THEORY

Two theories of technical analysis that attempt to describe the movement of financial prices are the Dow theory and the Elliott wave theory. These two theories are described briefly in this section.

THE DOW THEORY

Between 1900 and 1902 Charles Dow wrote a number of editorials in the *Wall Street Journal* which later came to be known as the Dow theory. William Hamilton, another editor of the *Wall Street Journal*, developed the work in another series of editorials. The first formalised account of the Dow theory was written by Rhea (1932a, b).

The Dow theory deals with the determination of trends in financial markets. The first basic assumption of the theory is that the market discounts all information, implying that current prices (or exchange rates) must reflect all information (related to the fundamental variables). The market is characterised by the presence of three trends: primary trends, secondary reactions and minor trends. Primary trends represent long-term trends. Secondary reactions interrupt the trend, acting in the opposite direction, which means that they are corrective. A secondary reaction may be called a 'temporary decline' if it is a downward correction in a bull market and a 'temporary recovery' if it is an upward correction in a bear market. Minor trends are day-to-day fluctuations. All of these types of movements occur simultaneously, resembling the tide, waves and ripples respectively. Figure 7.2 shows a representation of the primary trends and the secondary reactions in bull and bear markets (ignoring the minor trends).

The Dow theory further postulates that primary upward trends in bull markets have three phases. A bull market begins with a reaction (by expert traders) against the panic selling at the end of a bear market. The second phase starts when other traders join, motivated by capital gains. The final phase witnesses rampant speculation as the less experienced public join in. Primary downward trends work exactly the other way round. In a true bull market the low after each secondary reaction must be higher than the previous low, and vice versa.

While the Dow theory has gained wide acceptance, it has been criticised on several grounds. The first criticism is that the theory is frequently late in giving signals. A bull market is indicated only when the market breaks above the previous secondary top. Hence, significant profitable opportunities may be missed as a result of waiting to be sure of the onset of the bull market. The second criticism is that the theory provides no precise definition for the extent and duration of the primary trends and the secondary reactions. Moreover, the theory does not provide short-term trend signals, and it can give wrong signals.

THE ELLIOTT WAVE THEORY

The Elliott wave theory, due to Ralph Elliott, attempts to predict rather than confirm market reversals. According to this theory financial markets follow

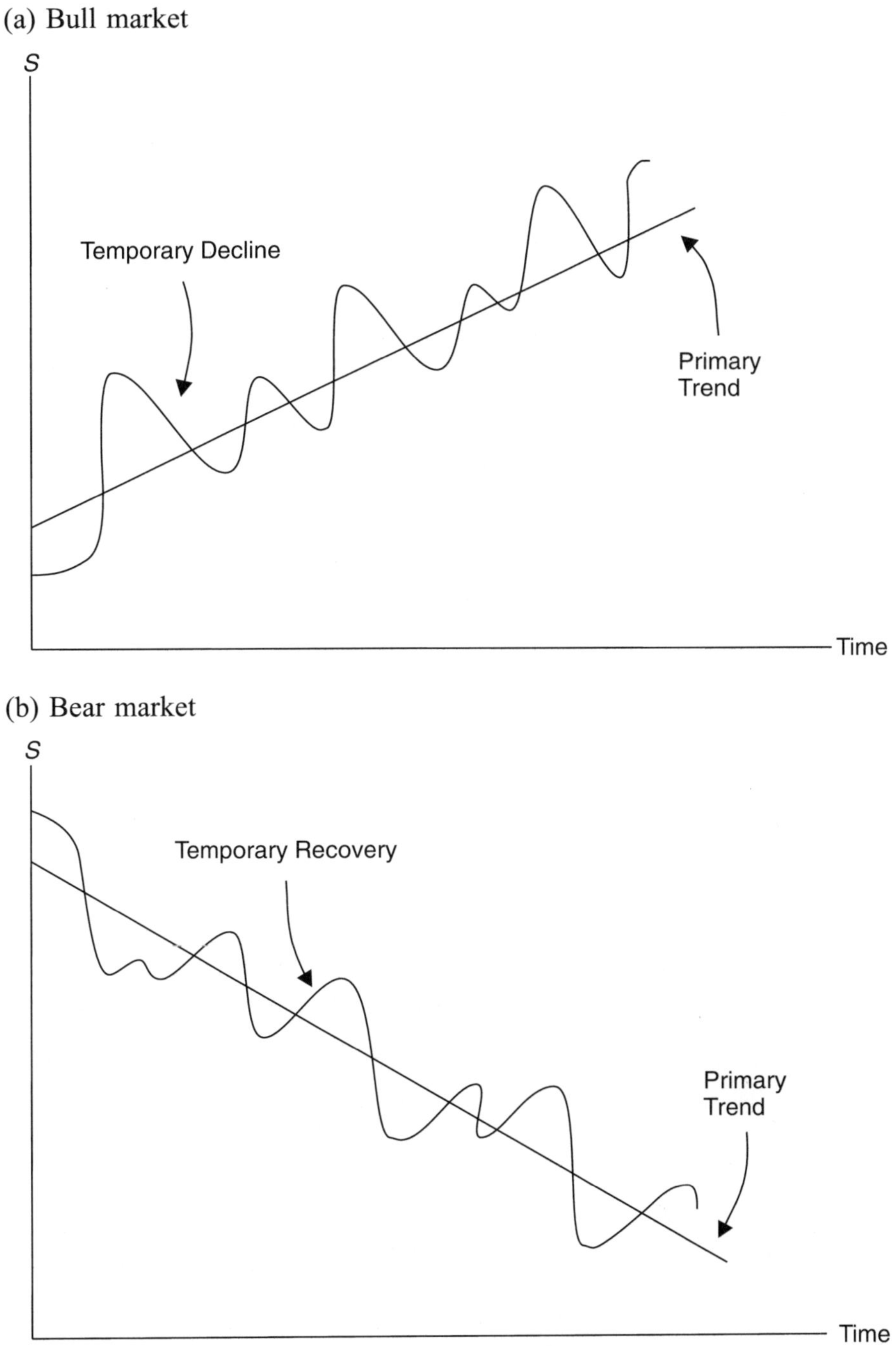

Figure 7.2 Bull and bear markets in the Dow theory

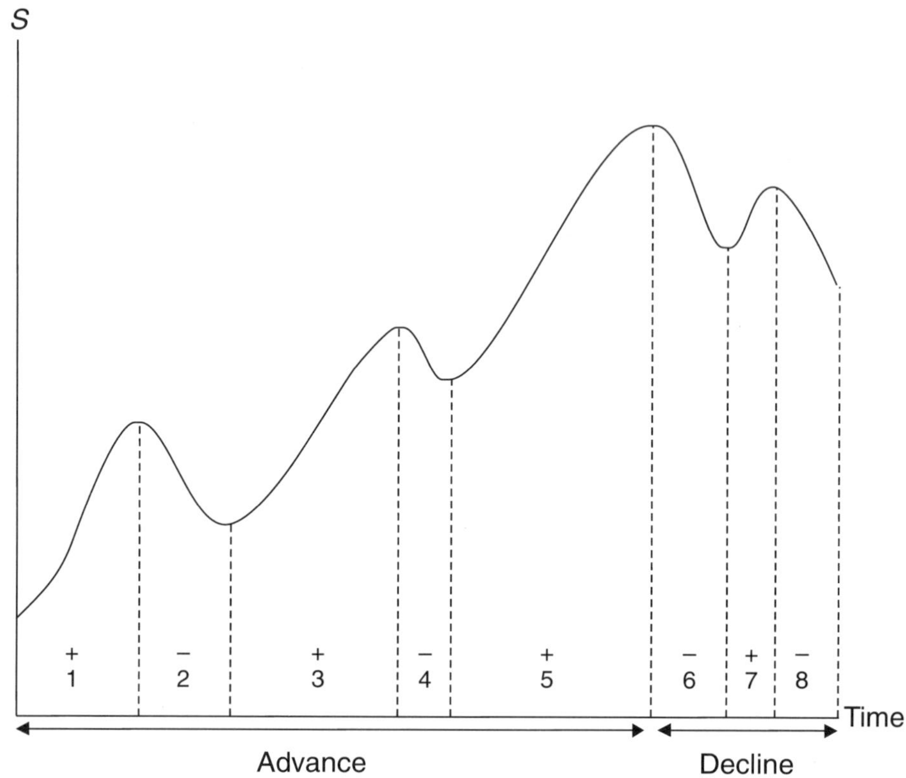

Figure 7.3 The Elliott wave theory

a repetitive cycle of a five-wave advance followed by a three-wave decline as shown in Figure 7.3. A wave is a move either from a trough to a peak (upward wave) or from a peak to a trough (downward wave). These waves are indicated by the + and – signs in Figure 7.3. The first set of five waves consists of three upward waves separated by two downward waves. The second set of waves consist of two downward waves separated by an upward wave.

The underlying idea is that a correction (as shown by the decline in Figure 7.3) does not run to five waves. Figure 7.4(a) represents a genuine bull market. The five-wave advance is followed by a three-wave decline and this is followed by another five-wave advance and so on. Figure 7.4(b) is a representation of how a bull market changes to a bear market. The five-wave advance is followed by a five-wave decline. The following three-wave advance proves to be a temporary rally after which the market keeps on declining.

(a) Bull market

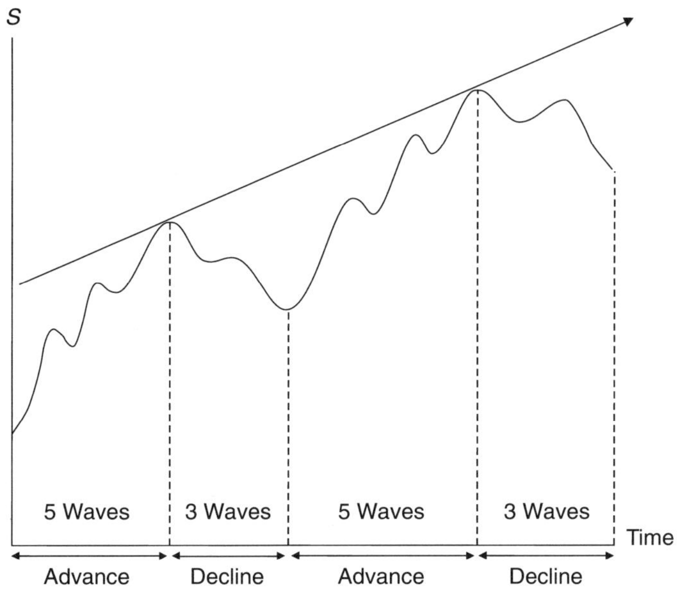

(b) Bear market

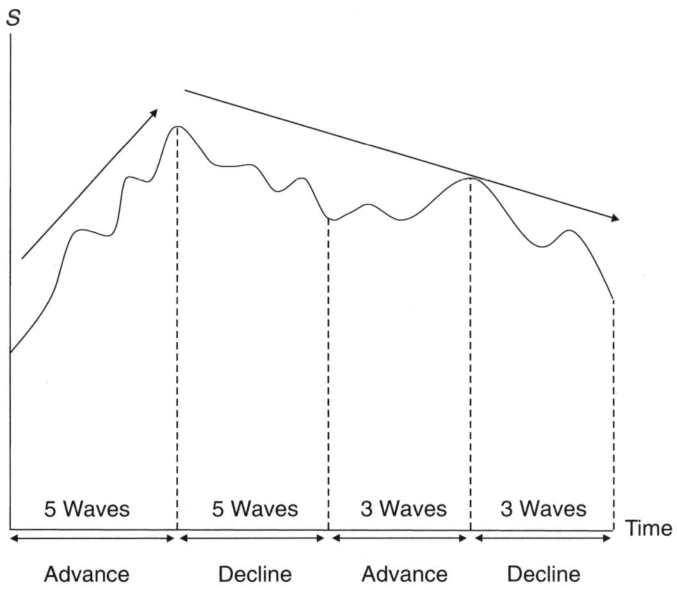

Figure 7.4 Elliott waves in bull and bear markets

TYPES OF CHARTS

The technical analyst's main tool is the chart. Four types of charts are used: bar charts, line charts, point and figure charts and Japanese candlestick charts. These charts are described in turn.

BAR CHARTS

Bar charts are by far the most commonly used type of chart. In a bar chart, a vertical line that ranges from the period's lowest level of the exchange rate to its highest represents each time period. A horizontal tick indicates closing level. Thus, for each time period we require three levels of the exchange rate to construct a bar chart.

Constructing a bar chart is easy as shown in Figure 7.5. The level of the exchange rate is measured on the vertical axis, while time is measured on the horizontal axis. The time period may be an hour, a day, a week and so on. For each time period, the high, low and closing levels are plotted. A bar is a vertical line that connects the highs and lows, while a horizontal tick that intersects with the bar indicates the closing level. Sometimes, the opening level is also plotted. In this case two horizontal ticks are used: a tick to the left indicates the opening level while a tick to the right indicates the closing level.

LINE CHARTS

Line charts plot one observation for every time period, normally the closing level of the exchange rate. The points are connected by a smooth line (or curve) to form the time path of the exchange rate. The right-hand side of the diagram in Figure 7.1 describes a line chart. A line chart representing actual data is shown in Figure 1.1.

Line charts have the advantage (over bar charts) of speed and simplicity, but this is achieved at the cost of losing some information. For example, if a line chart plots the daily closing exchange rates, then the information embodied in the intra-day exchange rates is lost. This may be justified on the grounds that the closing rate is the most important and representative of each day. This problem can be circumvented by plotting the exchange rate at intervals more frequent than one day.

POINT AND FIGURE CHARTS

Although point and figure charts are not as widely used as bar and line charts, they have been in existence since around 1800. The most important difference between a bar chart and a point and figure chart is that the latter

(a) High–low–close chart

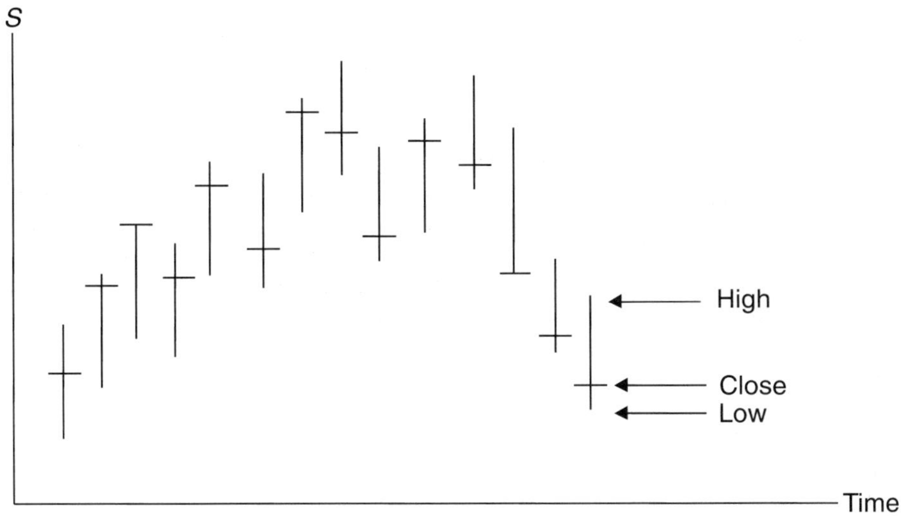

(b) High–low–close–open chart

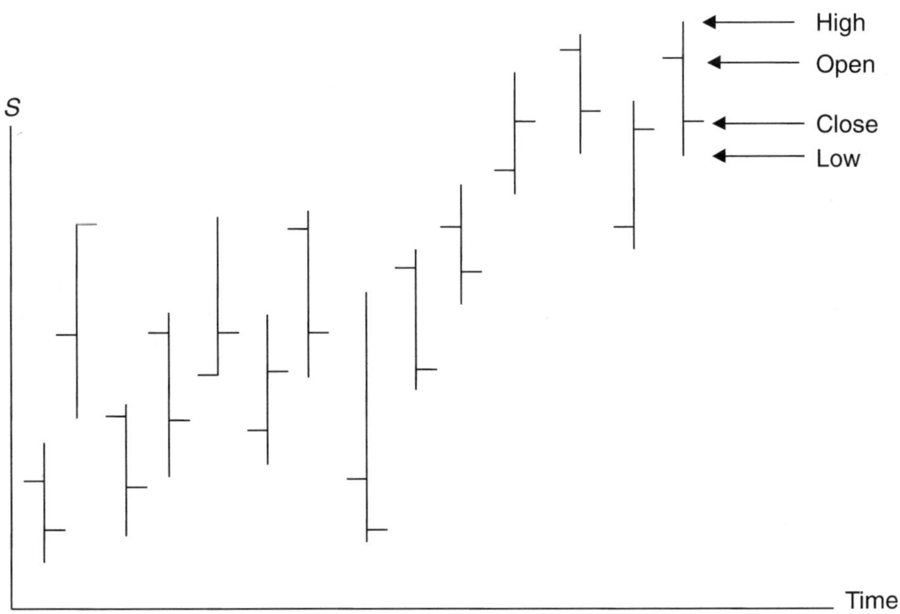

Figure 7.5 Bar charts

has no time dimension, or at least that the time periods are not spaced out evenly. Time is not taken into account when exchange rates are plotted.

Unlike line and bar charts, point and figure charts do not show small rate movements. Entries are made on a point and figure chart only when there is a 'significant change' in the exchange rate. What is significant depends on the underlying exchange rate and the technical analysts using them. For example, if the underlying exchange rate is the JPY/USD rate then a significant change may be 2 yen. Thus, if the exchange rate rises from 130 to 131.5, it will not be recorded, because it is less than 2. However a change from 130 to 132.5 will be recorded.

Figure 7.6 represents a point and figure chart. Entries are made with X's when the exchange rate rises and with O's when it falls. The six X's in the first column show a rise in the exchange rate from S_1 to S_2, that is six significant changes upwards. When the exchange rate stops rising and starts to fall a new column is started. Thus, the three O's in the second column indicate a fall in the exchange rate back to S_3. By repeating this process over and over again the chart can be used to highlight major market trends. The height of the column indicates the persistence of an upward trend (X) and a downward trend (O). A trend reversal is indicated by the move from one column to a new one to the right.

JAPANESE CANDLESTICK CHARTS

Although candlestick charts have been used by Japanese traders for centuries, they have only recently captured the attention of international traders. Candlestick charts are easy to construct as shown in Figure 7.7. Each line represents the trading activity of one period (an hour, a day, a week and so on) and shows opening, high, low and closing levels of the exchange rate. The main body (the thick part) of the candlestick line represents the range between the period's opening and closing exchange rates. If the closing exchange rate is higher than the opening level then the main body is white (empty). If, on the other hand, the closing exchange rate is lower than the opening exchange rate then the main body is black (filled). The thin lines above and below the main body are called shadows: they show the high and low exchange rates for the period. A long white body is considered bullish, since the exchange rate closes near the high of the period in a wide range. A long black body is viewed bearish since the exchange rate moves within a wide range and closes near the low of the period. When the opening and closing exchange rates are the same then the body is neither white nor black. In this case it is called a doji line. Because these charts require an opening as well as a closing rate, they cannot be used to represent spot exchange rates for which the opening levels are not normally available. However, they can be used to represent movements of exchange rates implicit in the futures currency contracts.

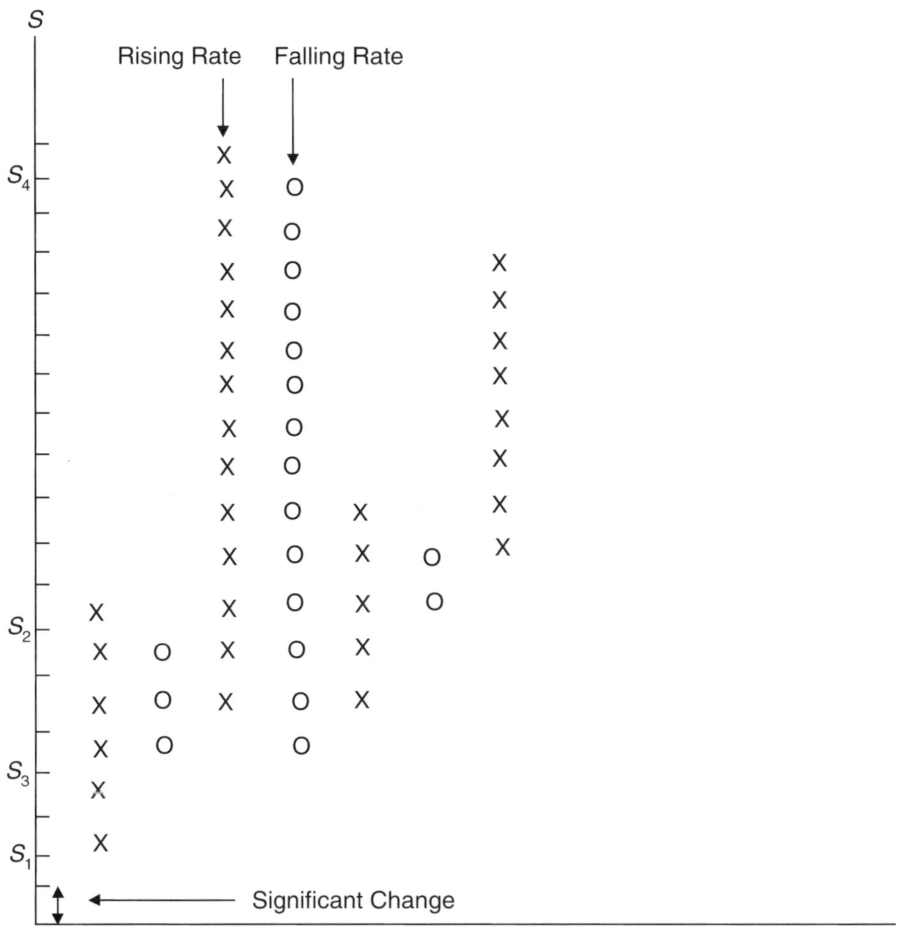

Figure 7.6 A point and figure chart

Candlestick lines can take a variety of shapes depending on the relationship between the opening, high, low and closing levels of the exchange rate. Figure 7.8 shows some of these lines. We will consider the reversal and continuation patterns later.

CHART FORMATIONS: TRENDLINES AND CHANNELS

One of the principles that technical analysis is based on is that exchange rates move in trends. The trends can be upward, downward or sideways as illustrated by Figure 7.9. An upward trend is characterised by successively higher highs and higher lows. A downward trend occurs on successively

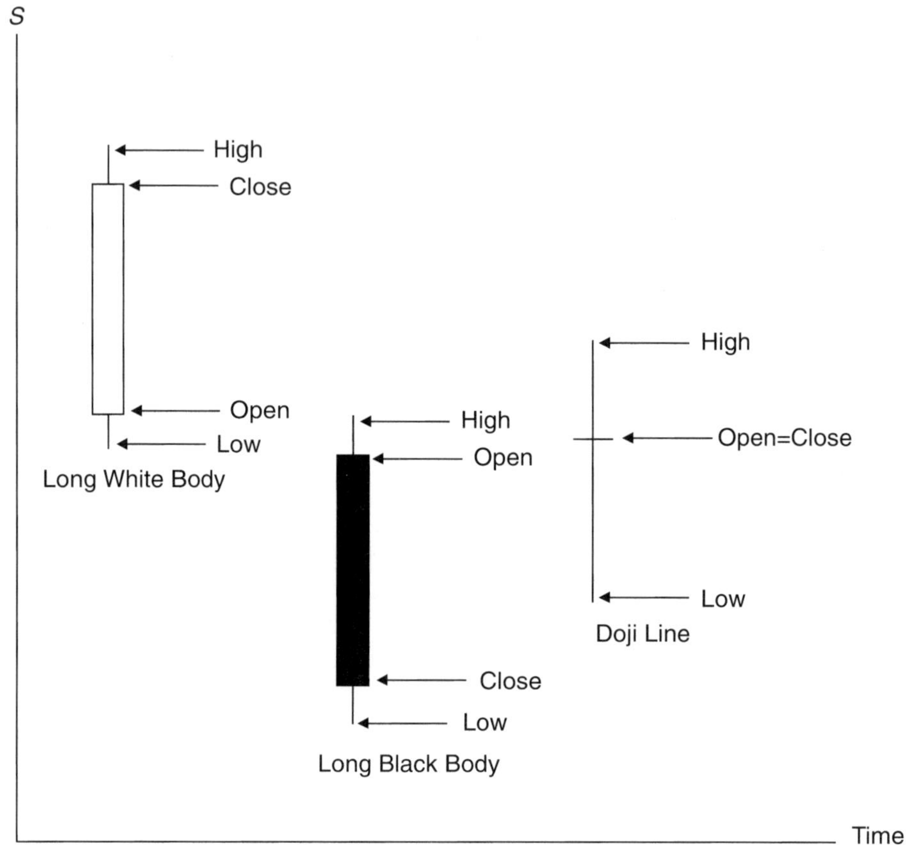

Figure 7.7 Japanese candlestick chart

lower highs and lower lows. A sideways trend reflects horizontal exchange rate movements. Traders can make profit by determining the trend and then following it until it is reversed. A long position is taken when there is an upward trend and a short position is taken when there is a downward trend.

Drawing a trendline is easy. A trendline is simply a straight line that connects a series of exchange rates, either tops or bottoms. An upward trend appears at the bottom of the exchange rate pattern (or time path) as shown in Figure 7.9(a). On the other hand, a downward trendline is a straight line that connects a series of tops as shown in Figure 7.9(b). It appears at the top of the exchange rate pattern.

Two factors determine the significance of the trendline: the number of points that the trendline goes through and the length of the time the trendline persists without being penetrated. The significance of an upward trendline is enhanced whenever the exchange rate moves back towards it

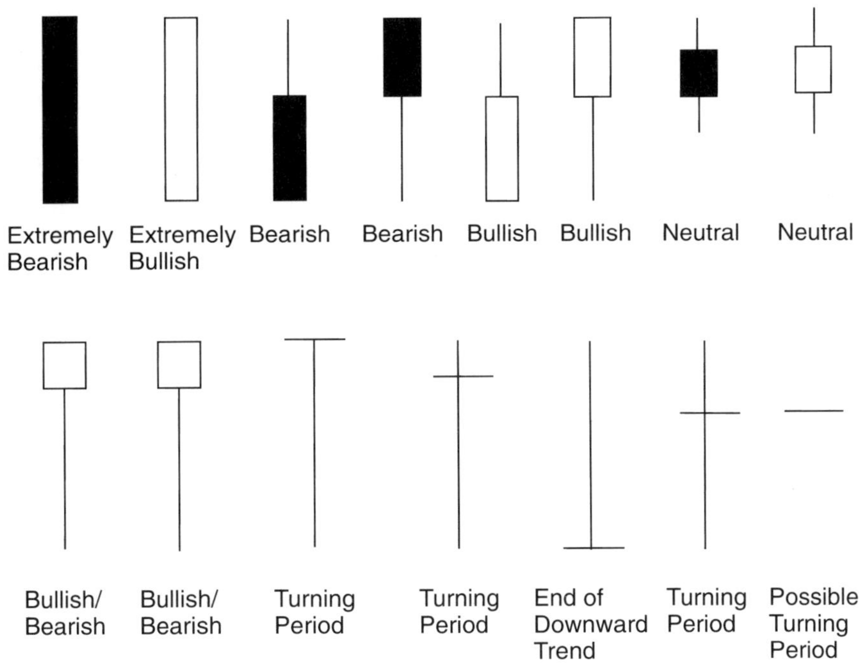

Figure 7.8 Candlestick lines

and renews its advance. Likewise, the significance of a downward trendline is enhanced whenever the exchange rate moves back towards it and declines. The length of the trendline indicates the period of time that the exchange rate remains above or below a trendline. The longer the period, the greater the significance of the trendline. Some technical analysts also believe that the angle of the trendline adds to its significance.

TRENDLINE PENETRATION

Once a trendline has been established, a change in the direction of the trend is signalled when the exchange rate breaks through the trendline as shown in Figure 7.10. Two criteria are used to determine the validity of a trendline penetration. The first is the extent of the penetration, that is the extent by which the exchange rate moves past the trendline. For example, if the closing exchange rate for the day is 3 per cent lower (for an upward trend) or higher (for a downward trend) then the penetration is valid. Some technical analysts also use a time filter, that is if the exchange rate closes above an upward trendline or below a downward trendline for two days in a row, then there is a valid penetration, which means that the exchange rate is

(a) Upward trend

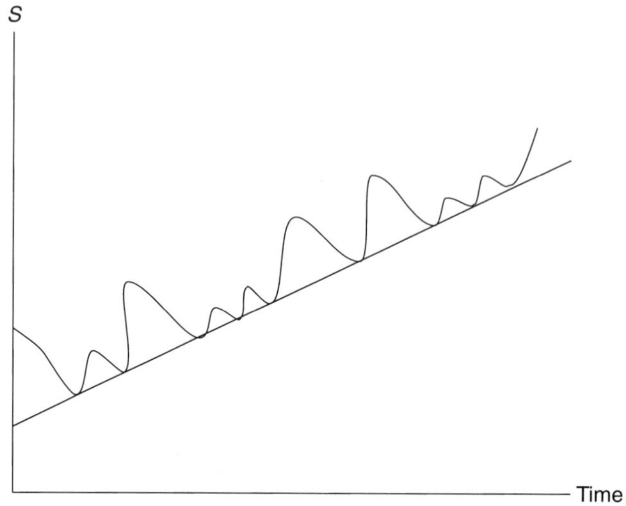

(b) Downward trend

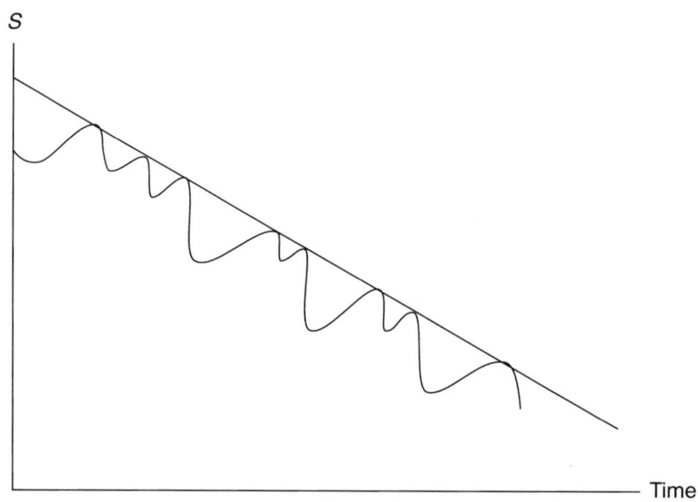

Figure 7.9 Trends

(c) Sideways trend

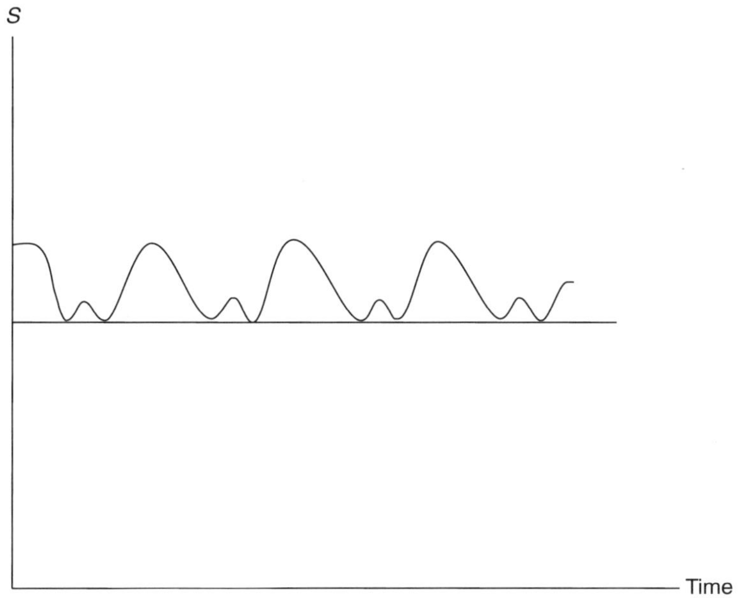

Figure 7.9 Trends (cont.)

likely to continue its trend reversal. Once a valid penetration occurs, the exchange rate will move at least as far as the maximum distance it was on the opposite side of the trendline.

TREND CHANNELS

It often happens that the exchange rate repeatedly moves about the same distance away from the trendline before returning to it. In situations like these a straight line can be drawn connecting the tops of the rallies in an upward trend or the bottoms of declines in a downward trend. This line is often parallel to the trendline and is called a channel line. The channel line and the trendline create a trend channel, a range within which the exchange rate moves. Figure 7.11 illustrates trend channels in upward and downward trends.

Trend channels can be used to determine profit-taking levels. For example, in an upward trend the currency is sold when the exchange rate reaches the upper level of its trend channel. Moreover, by observing exchange rate movements within the two boundary lines of the trend channel it is possible to find warning signals that the trend direction is changing. If, in an upward trend channel, the exchange rate rises from the trendline but fails to reach the upper channel line, then this would signal a

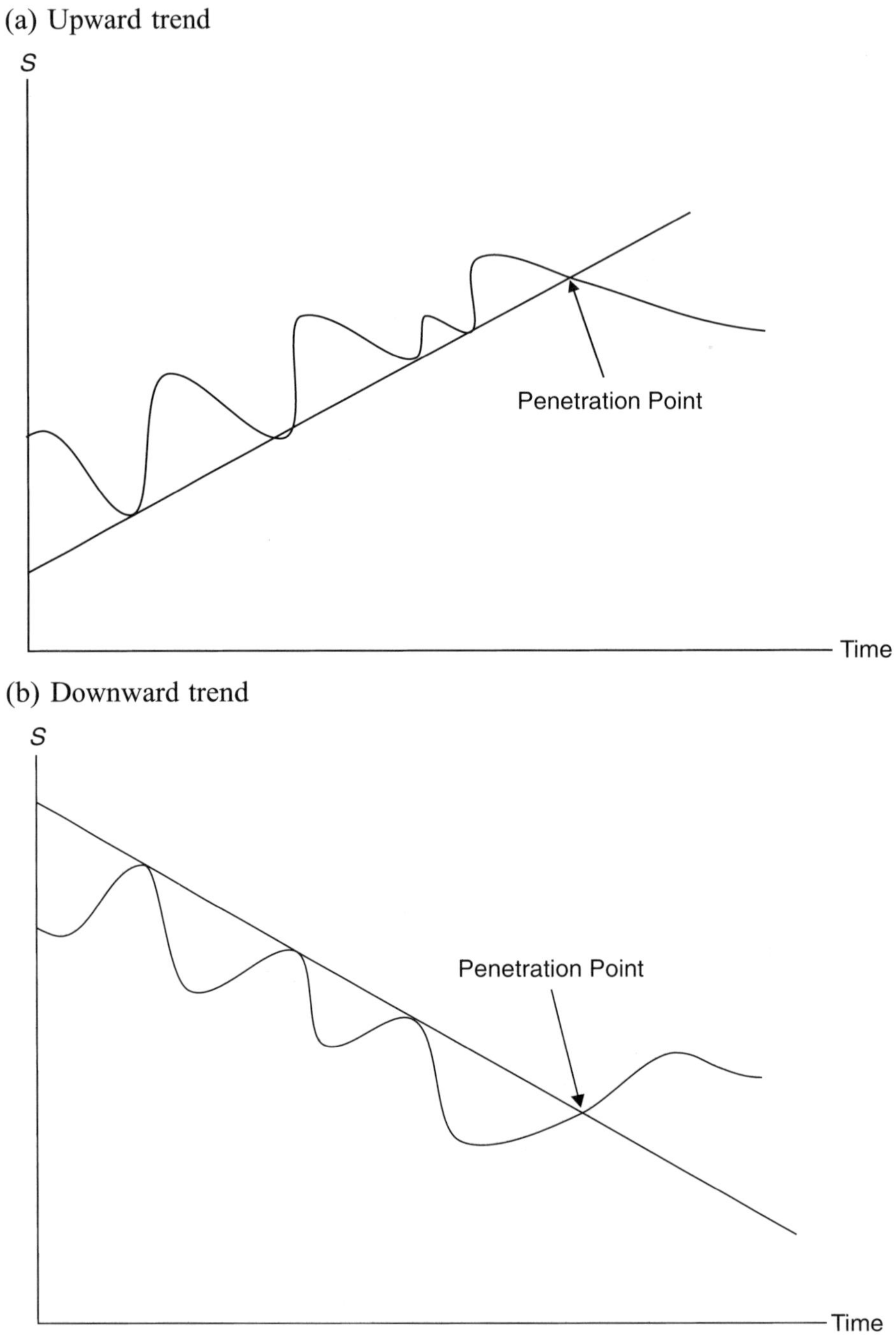

Figure 7.10 Trendline penetration

(a) Upward trend

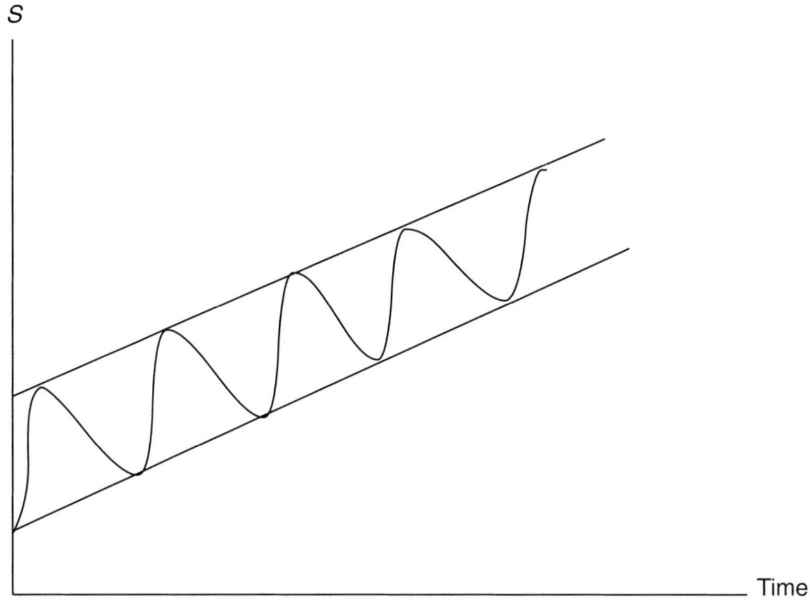

(b) Downward trend

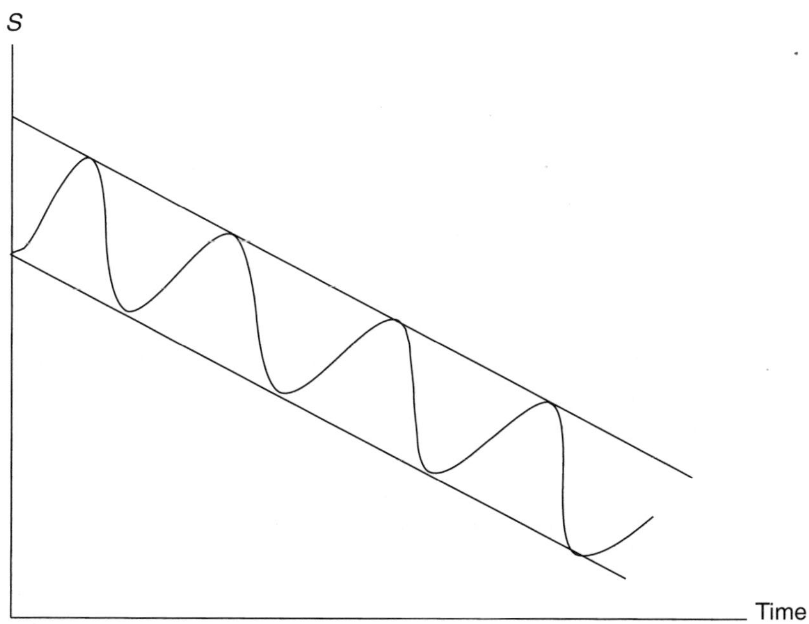

Figure 7.11 Trend channels

deterioration of the trend and the probability that the lower line would be broken. Frequently, the distance from the top of the failed rally to the channel line is equal to the distance by which the next move downwards penetrates the trendline. Also, if the exchange rate breaks through the upper line in an upward trend channel, an acceleration of the existing upward trend is signalled. At this point, some traders will take additional (long) positions. On the other hand, if the exchange rate moves through the bottom line of a downward trend channel, the existing downward trend appears to be picking up pace. The currency is sold short at this point.

THE FAN

A fan is obtained by drawing three trendlines in a fan-like appearance. To draw a fan in an upward trend the following steps are followed (Figure 7.12). First, an initial trendline is drawn connecting the lows. Then the trendline is penetrated or broken and the exchange rate moves to a lower point from which it rises back to the bottom of the trendline. A second trendline is then drawn from the beginning of the first trendline. The exchange rate once again declines and breaks through the second trendline, creating a new low, then it rises to the bottom of the second trendline. The third and final trendline is drawn from the low beginning at the first trendline and the low just created. When the exchange rate subsequently falls and breaks through the third trendline, a reversal in the exchange rate is signalled. Similarly, a downward trending fan can be drawn. In this case a reversal is indicated by the breaking of the third trendline.

SUPPORT, RESISTANCE, RETRACEMENT AND SPEED RESISTANCE LINES

The terms ‘support’ and ‘resistance’ are almost synonymous with demand and supply respectively. Support is a level of the exchange rate at which there is adequate demand for the currency to stop the exchange rate from moving downwards, moving upwards instead. Resistance is a level of the exchange rate at which there is a significant supply of the currency, causing the exchange rate to stop moving upwards, moving downwards instead (Figure 7.13). In an upward trend both support and resistance levels rise as illustrated in Figure 7.14. Typically, support levels hold while resistance offers temporary halts to upward movements in exchange rates. Resistance levels are repeatedly broken until the upward trend is broken. In a downward trend, both support and resistance levels move lower. Typically, resistance levels hold while support levels temporarily stop downward exchange rate movements. Support levels are repeatedly broken until the downward trend is broken.

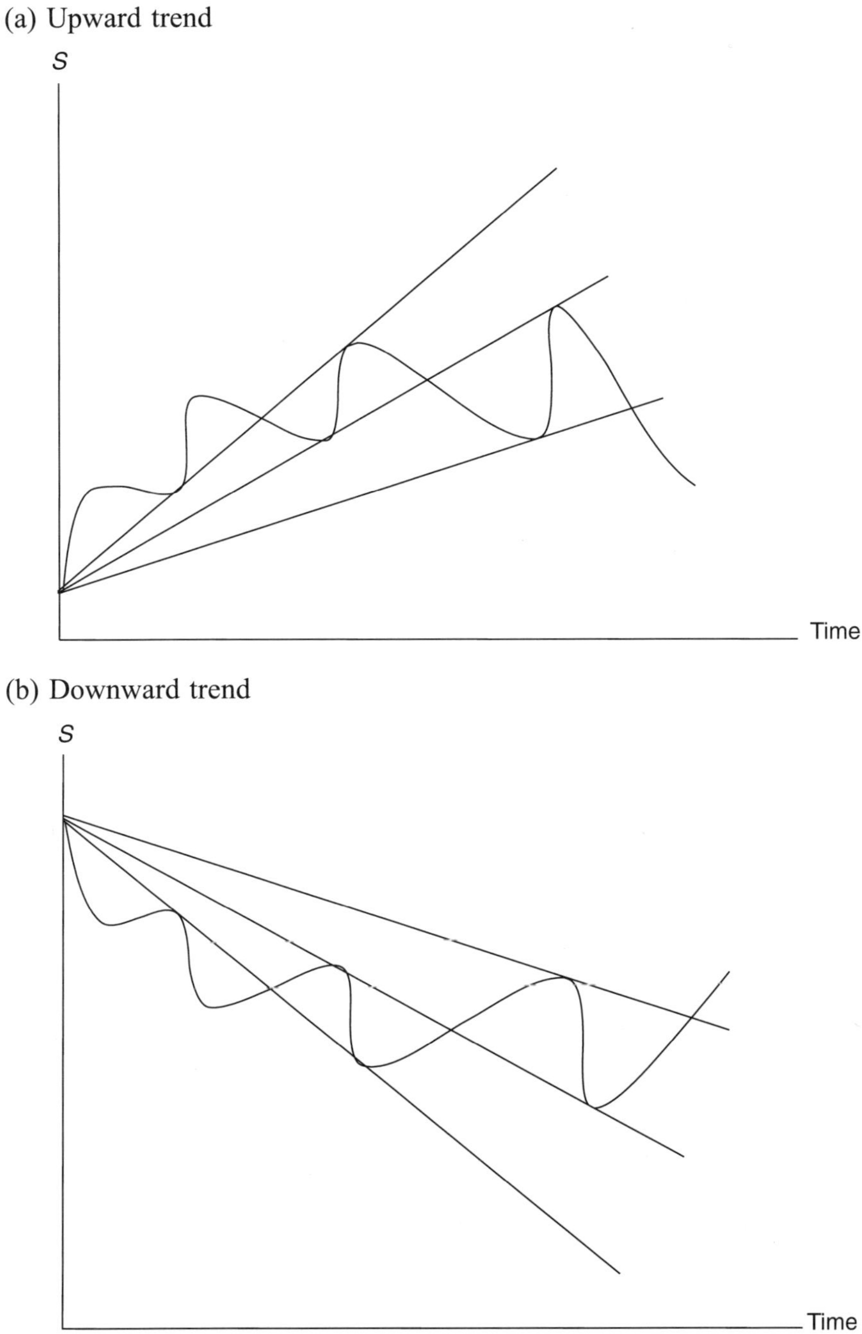

Figure 7.12 The fan

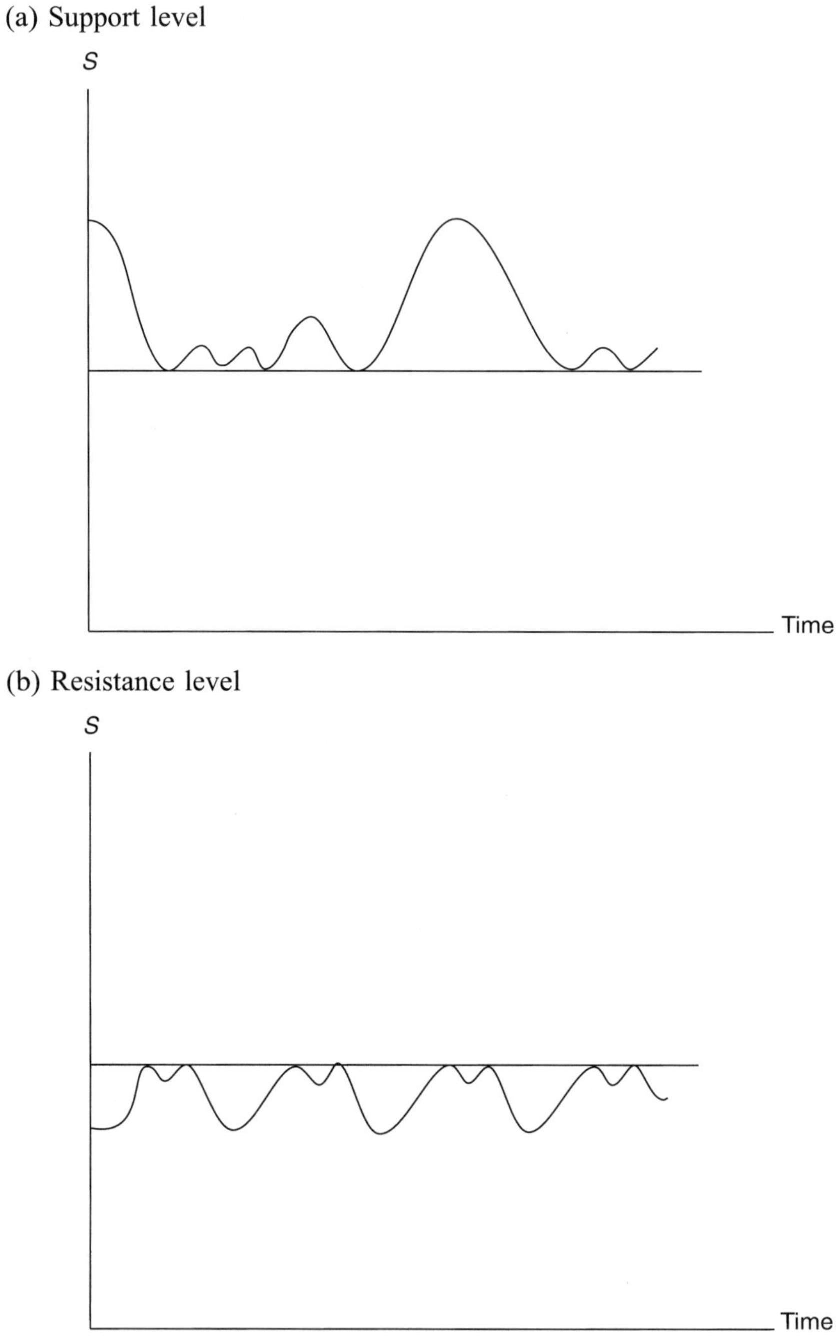

Figure 7.13 Support and resistance levels

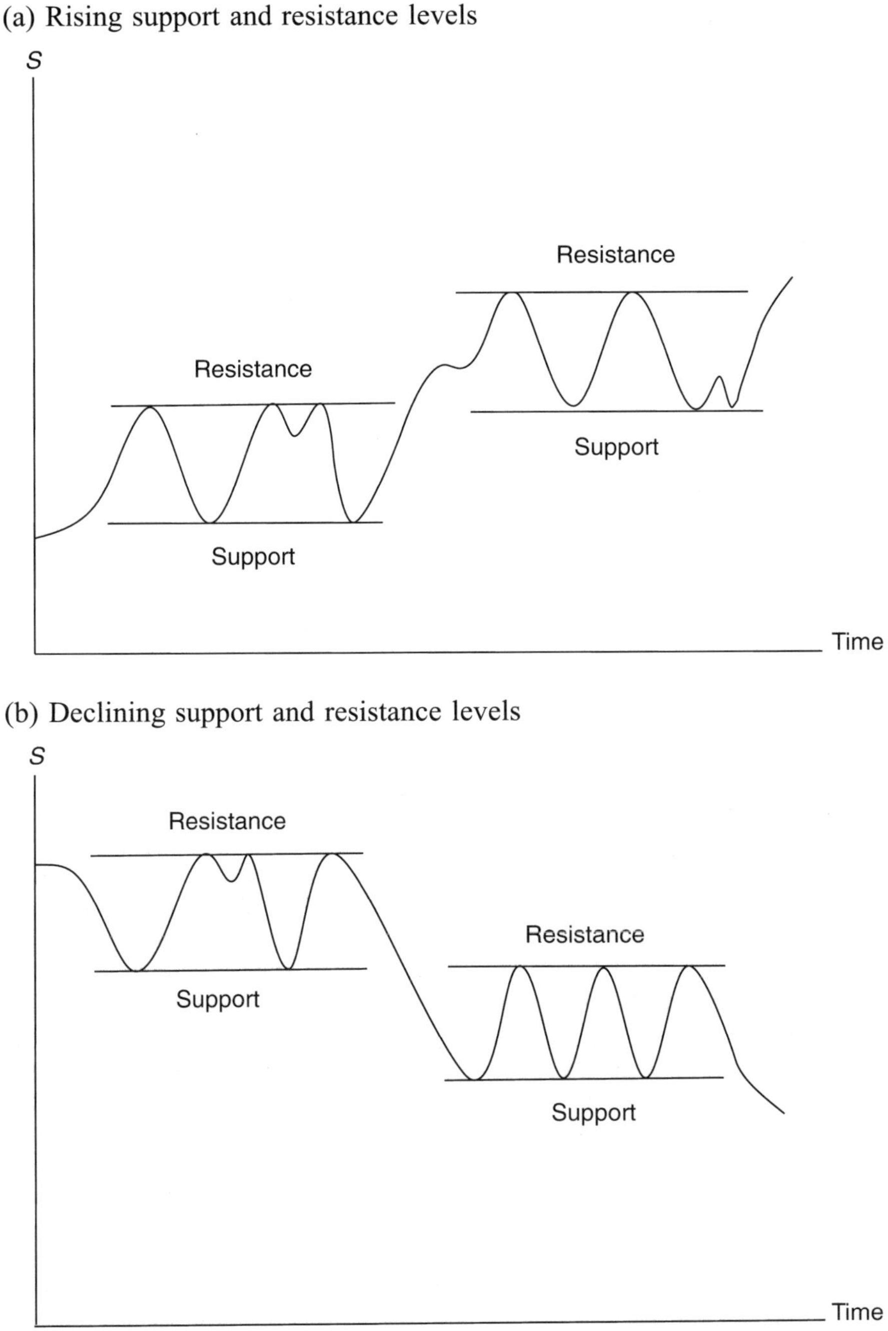

Figure 7.14 Changing support and resistance levels

Technical analysts have discovered that exchange rates often find support or resistance at round numbers such as 10, 15, 20, and so on. These numbers act as psychological levels at which advances or declines come to an end. For example, the exchange rate between the US dollar and the Japanese yen (JPY/USD) may show resistance at 150. Once this is broken then 155 will become the new resistance level while 150 becomes the support level. Because of this observation, traders who take decisions on the basis of technical analysis do not place trading orders or protective stop-loss orders at round numbers. Technical analysts advise that in an upward trend it is better to place buy orders just above round numbers and stop-loss orders just below round numbers. On the other hand, it is advisable to short sell in a downward trend, placing sell orders just below and stop-loss orders just above the appropriate round number.

Resistance levels and support levels often change roles, and this is what is called role reversal. In an upward trend, resistance levels often become support levels after they are broken significantly as shown in Figure 7.15(a). In a downward trend the opposite occurs as support levels frequently become resistance levels as shown in Figure 7.15(b). The likelihood of role reversal is greater when (i) the volume of trading at the support or resistance levels is significant; (ii) the time period over which the exchange rate is near the support or resistance level is long; and (iii) trading occurred at that level recently.

Trend reversal can be detected in conjunction with the resistance and support levels. A reversal of an upward trend occurs when the exchange rate cannot penetrate a resistance level. Figure 7.16(a) shows that a reversal of an upward trend occurs when the exchange rate is unable to penetrate the resistance level. Figure 7.16(b) shows the reversal of a downward trend occurs when the exchange rate is unable to penetrate the support level. It is to be kept in mind that a trend reversal is not signalled by the first failure to break through the resistance level in an upward trend or a support level in a downward trend. Rather, a reversal pattern must fully develop before one gets the signal that the trend has changed. Reversal patterns will be described later.

PERCENTAGE RETRACEMENTS

After the exchange rate moves upwards or downwards for some time, it usually moves in the opposite direction, retracing (or correcting) a portion of the previous move. Subsequently, the exchange rate continues moving along the original trend. Often, the exchange rate retraces between one-third and two-thirds of its previous move before it continues on the original trend.

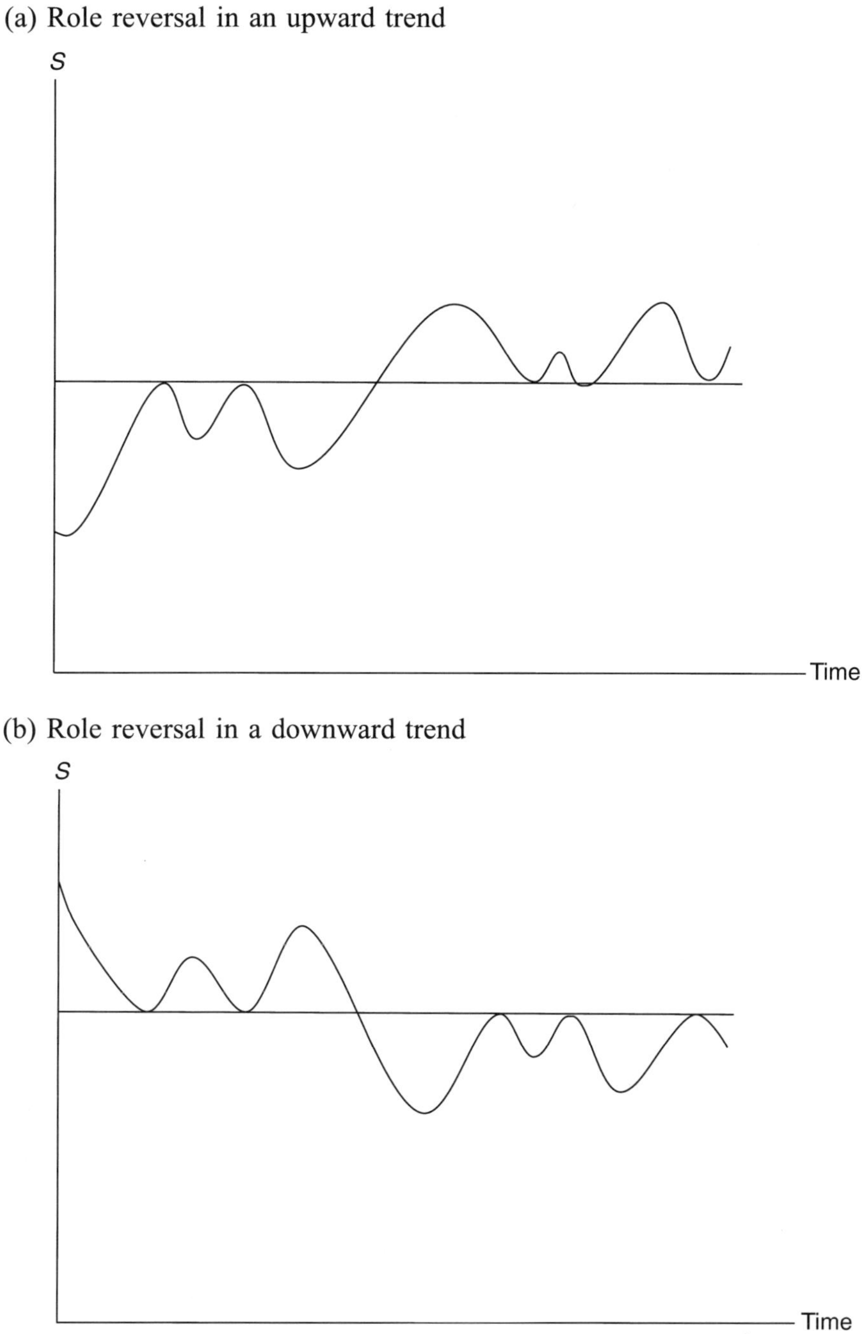

Figure 7.15 Role reversal of support and resistance levels

(a) Reversal of an upward trend

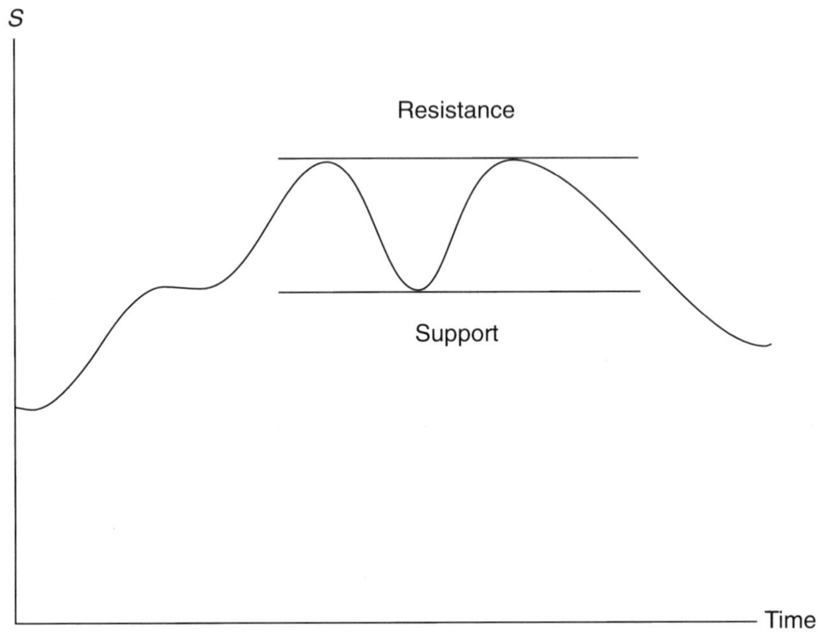

(b) Reversal of a downward trend

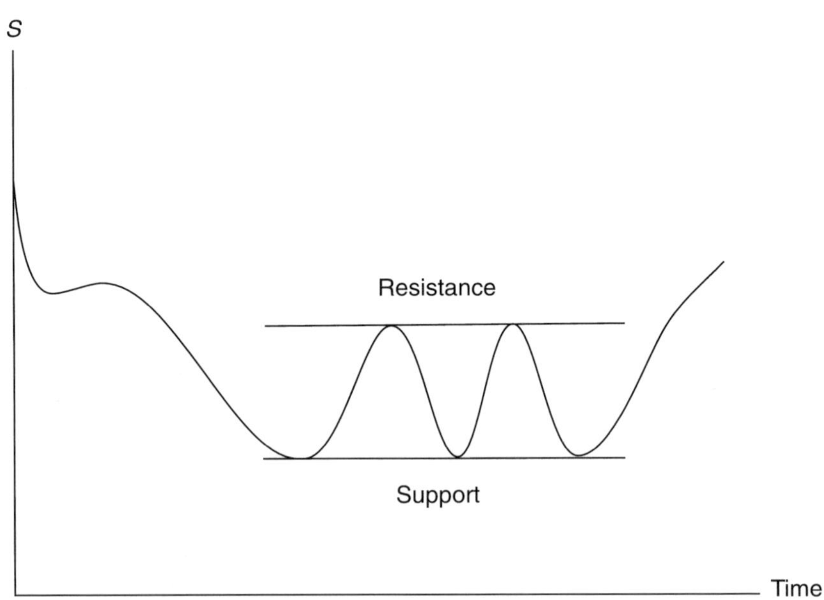

Figure 7.16 Trend reversal

Figure 7.17 illustrates percentage retracements. Some traders consider a retracement of between 33 per cent and 50 per cent to be a buying opportunity in an upward trend and a selling opportunity in a downward trend. The two-thirds level is critical. If the exchange rate moves past the two-thirds retracement level, a trend reversal is likely.

SPEED RESISTANCE LINES

Speed resistance lines (or speed lines for short) are based on a theory that trends are divided into thirds. Unlike percentage retracements that look at exchange rate movements just in terms of thirds, speed resistance lines measure the rate at which a trend moves up or down.

In an upward trend, speed lines are constructed by dividing the vertical distance from the beginning of the trend to the highest point on the chart. This distance is then divided into thirds. Two trendlines are drawn as illustrated in Figure 7.18(a). The first trendline is drawn from the beginning of the trend to one-third of the way up the vertical distance. The second trendline is drawn from the beginning of the trend to two-thirds of the way up the vertical distance. Figure 7.18(b) similarly shows how speed lines are constructed for a downward trend. If in an upward trend the exchange rate makes a new peak and starts to retrace some of its upward movement then it will frequently stop at the two-thirds speed line. If this does not happen then the exchange rate is likely to move to the one-third line. If it is not held at the one-third line then a trend reversal is signalled.

REVERSAL PATTERNS

While the trend is changing, identifiable chart patterns often develop. The reversal patterns help identify when the exchange rate is changing directions either from upwards to downwards or vice versa. The importance of reversal patterns is that they help a currency trader make sound decisions involving selling a currency before considerable depreciation and cover short positions prior to considerable appreciation. Technical analysts have identified a number of reversal patterns. Some of these patterns appear frequently while others are rarely observed. Some are very reliable while others do not result in the exchange rate movement one anticipates. Figure 7.19 shows some of these patterns.

What causes a trend to change direction? It is the interaction of the forces of supply and demand for the underlying currency. The forming of a market top and the subsequent reversal occur as a result of supply overcoming demand, or excess supply. This is known as distribution. The opposite occurs when demand overcomes supply, which is called accumulation.

(a) Upward trend

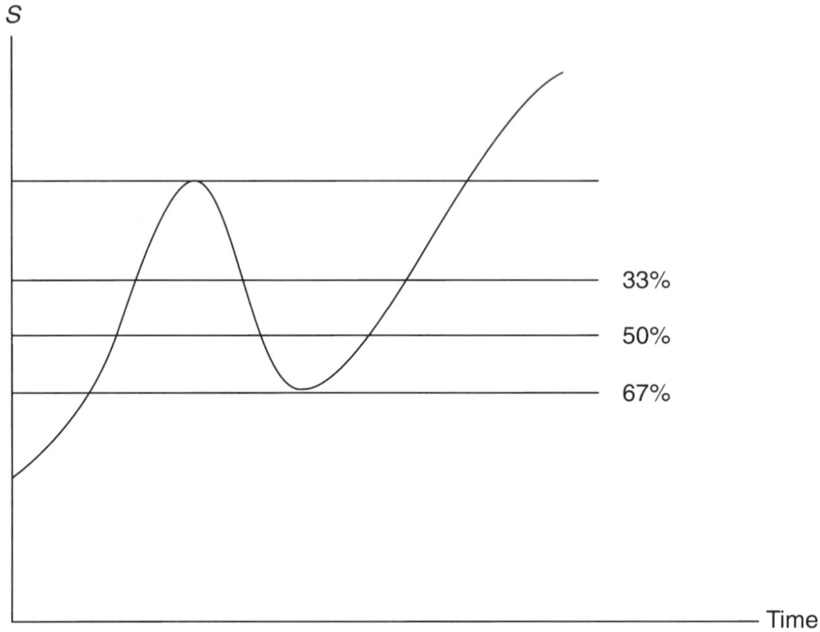

(b) Downward trend

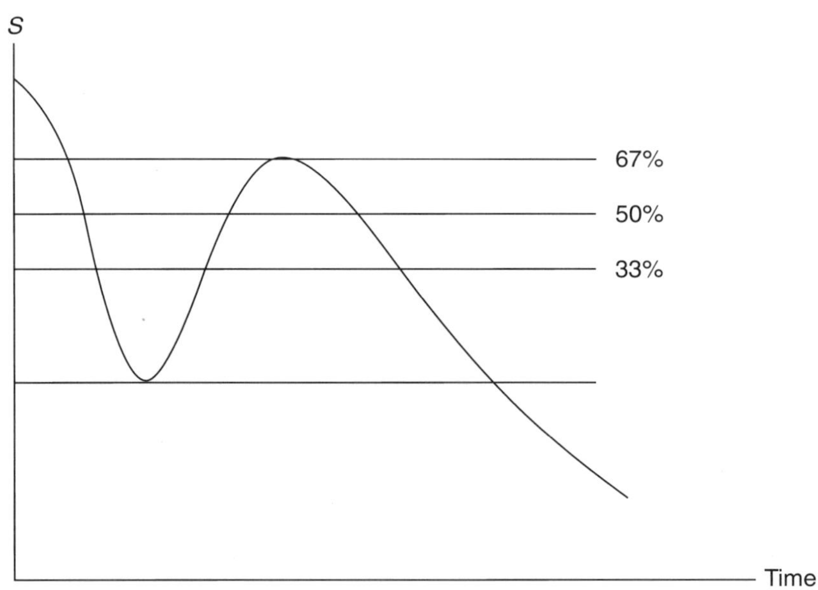

Figure 7.17 Percentage retracements

(a) Upward trend

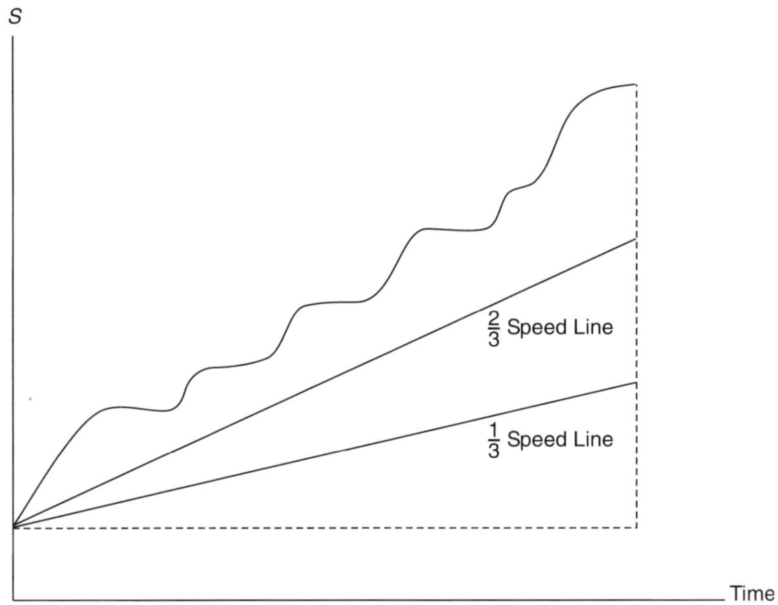

(b) Downward trend

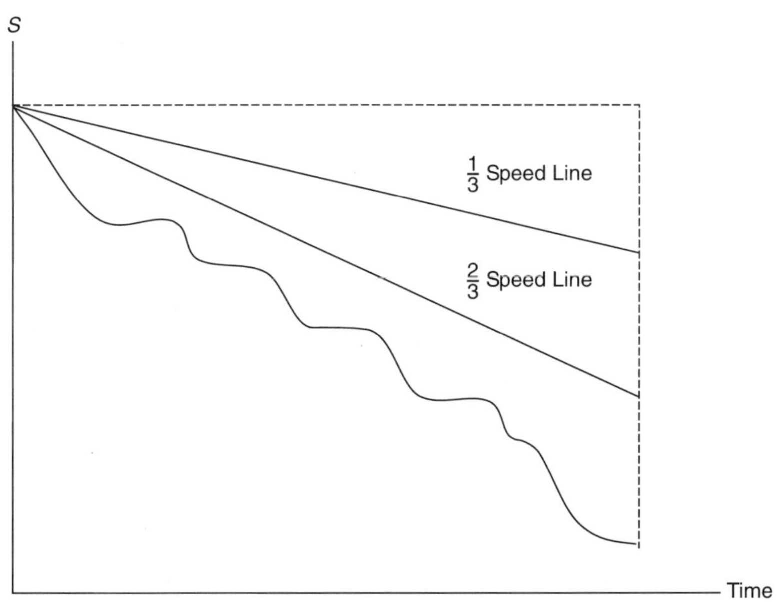

Figure 7.18 Speed resistance lines

(a) Head and shoulders

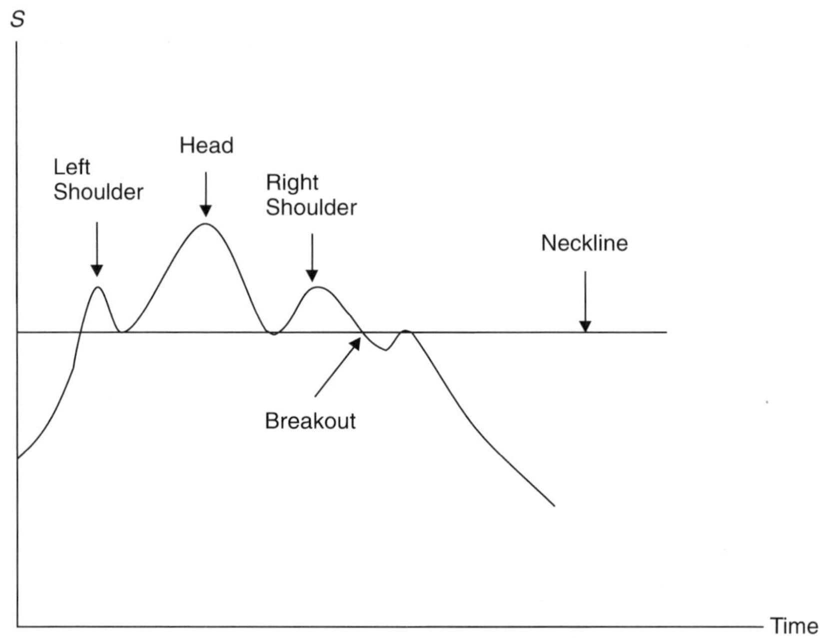

(b) Inverse head and shoulders

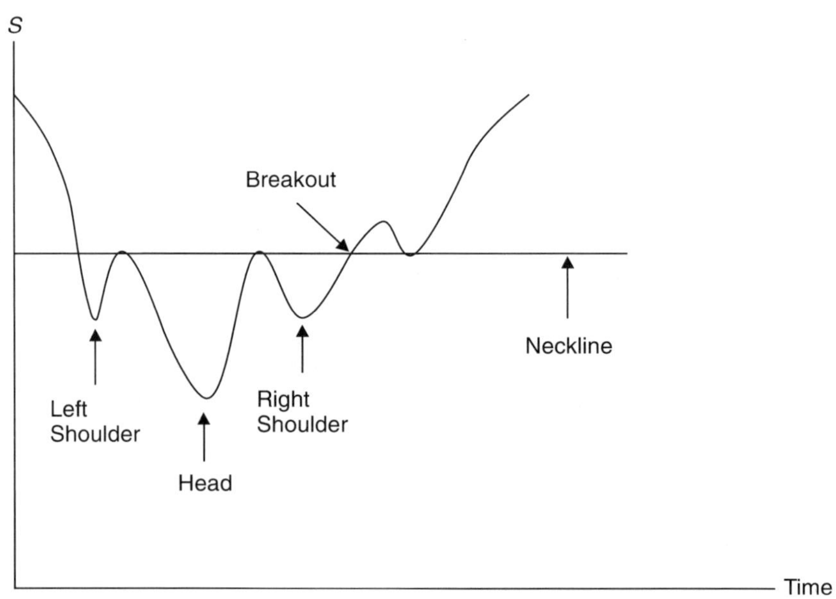

Figure 7.19 Reversal patterns

(c) Ascending triangle

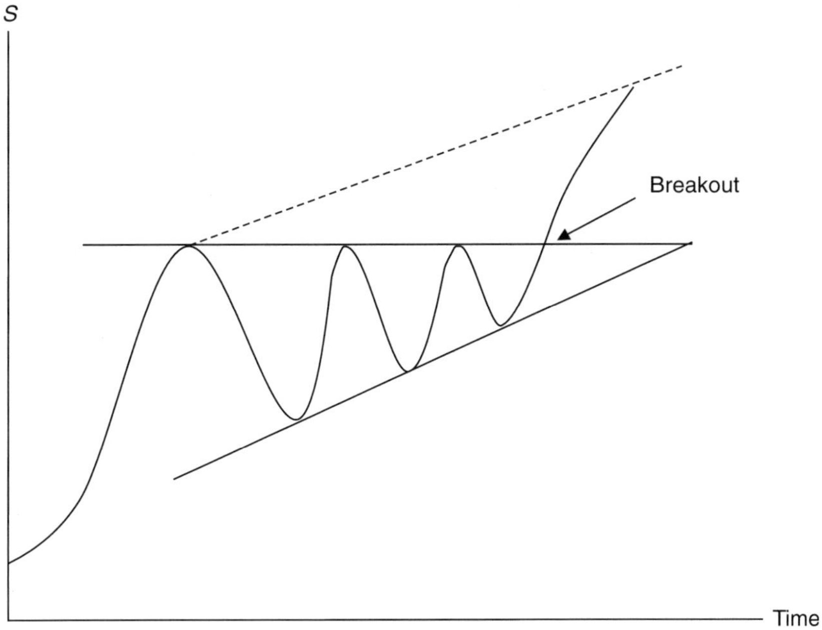

(d) Descending triangle

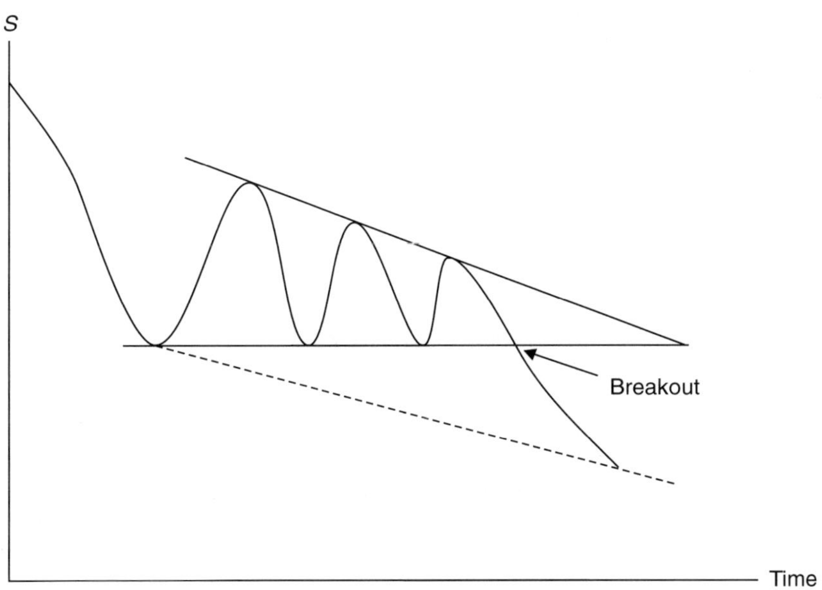

Figure 7.19 Reversal patterns (cont.)

(e) Bullish rectangle

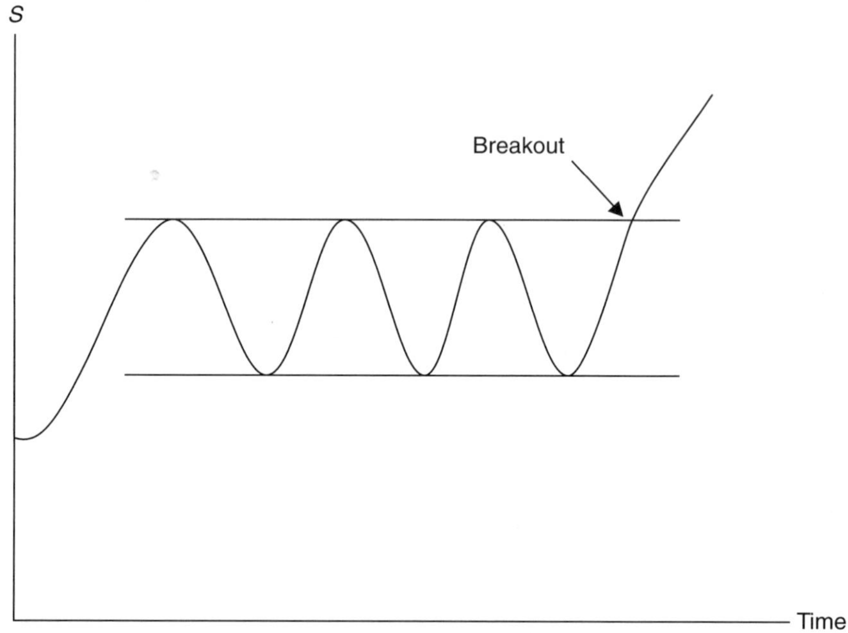

(f) Bearish rectangle

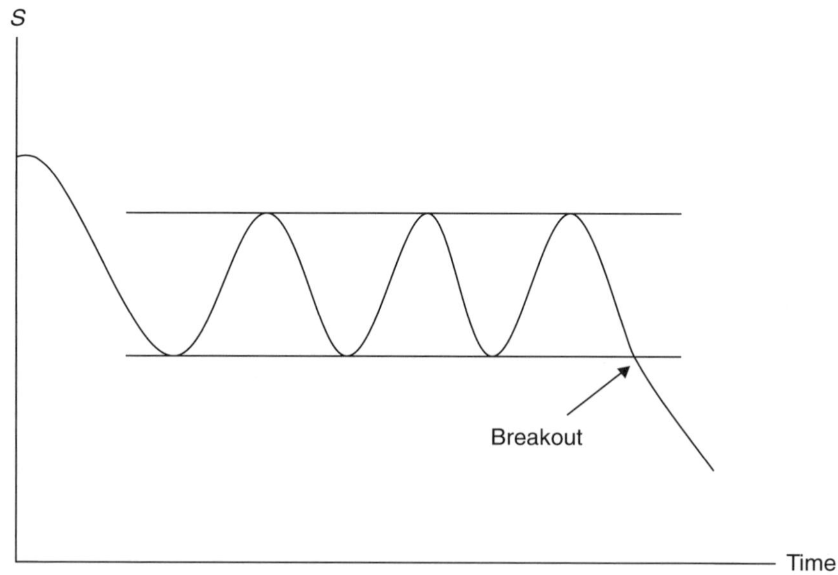

Figure 7.19 Reversal patterns (cont.)

(g) Double top

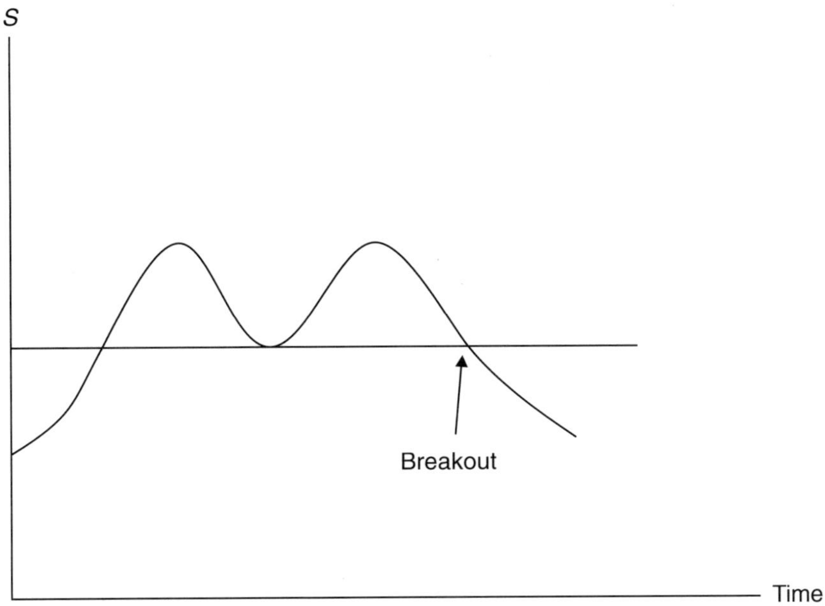

(h) Double bottom

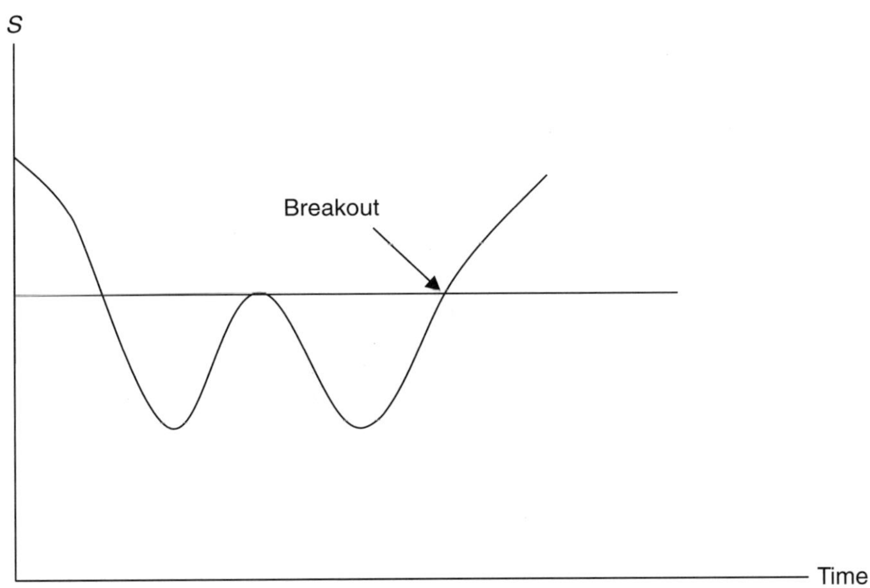

Figure 7.19 Reversal patterns (cont.)

(i) Triple top

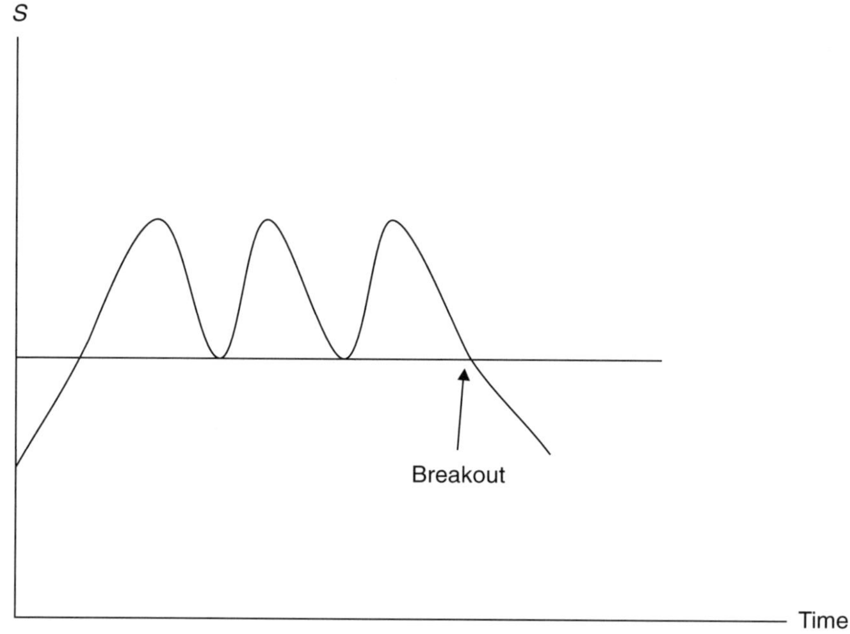

(j) Triple bottom

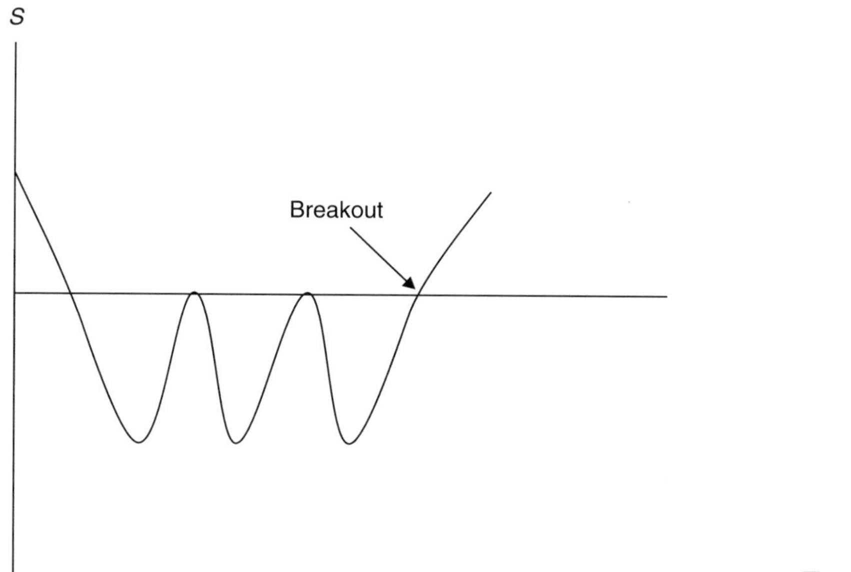

Figure 7.19 Reversal patterns (cont.)

(k) Rising wedge

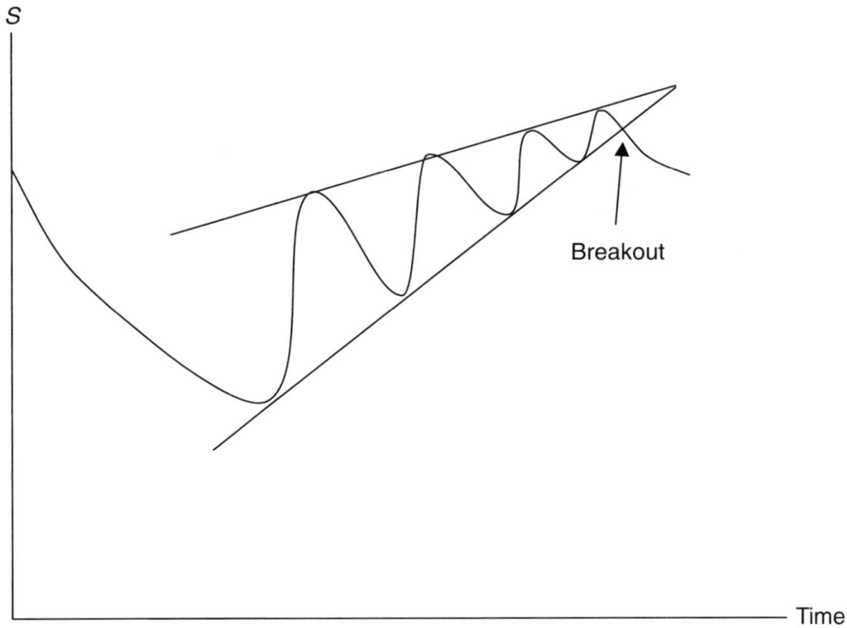

(l) Falling wedge

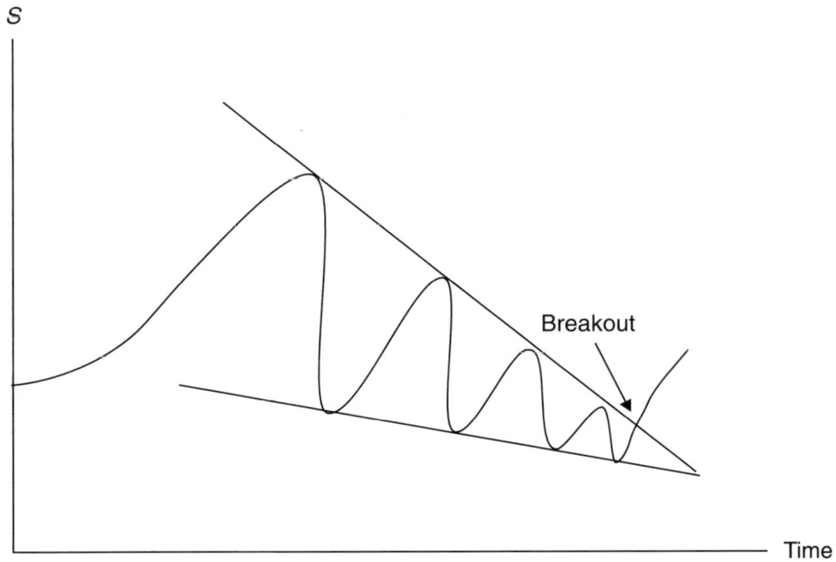

Figure 7.19 Reversal patterns (cont.)

(m) Diamond

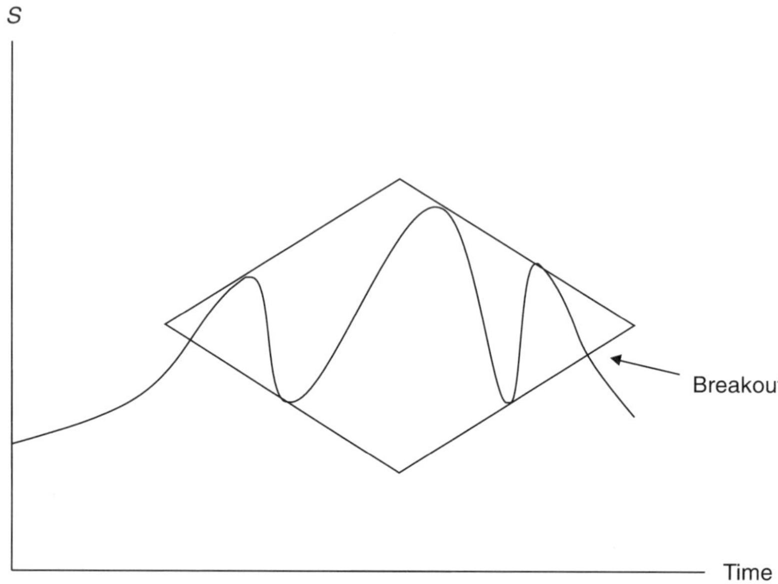

Figure 7.19 Reversal patterns (cont.)

In both cases excess supply or excess demand builds up gradually, and the exchange rate moves back and forth in a sideways fashion in a manner that leads to the development of a reversal pattern until a complete reversal is accomplished. The greater the time it takes for a reversal pattern to develop the more reliable the signal generated.

HEAD AND SHOULDERS

The head and shoulders formation (also called head and shoulders top) is one of the most common and most reliable chart patterns. The left shoulder is typically formed at the end of an extensive advance. After the exchange rate drops from the peak of the left shoulder it rises to a new high and then declines to near the low of the left shoulder, forming the head. A final advance to a peak lower than the head is followed by a decline to form the right shoulder. This completes the pattern. A neckline can be drawn linking the bottoms of the left and right shoulders. A sign of trend reversal is generated when the exchange rate crosses the neckline downwards. After moving lower, the exchange rate may move up again to the neckline before it continues to decline. Once the neckline is broken the exchange rate is expected to move the same distance from the top of the head to the neckline. A reverse head and shoulders pattern indicates a trend reversal from downwards to upwards.

TRIANGLES

Triangles can be ascending or descending. An ascending triangle occurs when the exchange rate moves between a horizontal top boundary line and an upward-sloping bottom boundary line. This arises when demand is growing but continues to meet supply at a certain exchange rate. Once supply is absorbed, the exchange rate breaks out of the pattern and moves up rapidly. A descending triangle occurs the other way round.

Triangles appear regularly on daily charts, but they are less frequent on weekly charts. They provide profitable trading opportunities in the sense that an ascending triangle suggests a bullish outlook while the descending triangle suggests a bearish outlook. An indication of how far up or down the exchange rate will move once it breaks out of the triangle is indicated by drawing a line parallel to the upper or lower boundary line (the dotted line). The exchange rate then moves up or down until this line is reached.

RECTANGLES

A rectangle pattern consists of a sideways movement in the exchange rate that is contained within two horizontal or near horizontal lines. The area in between is called a trading area or trading range. Rectangles are formed when there is consistent supply of a currency at a certain exchange rate and demand at a certain lower exchange rate. When the exchange rate reaches the lower level, the currency is purchased, driving up the exchange rate until such time as it reaches the upper boundary and traders are ready to sell and drive the exchange rate back to the lower boundary. This occurs repeatedly until one side or the other gives way and the pattern is broken in one direction or the other. A closing exchange rate outside the rectangle implies the direction of the exchange rate movement. Bullish and bearish rectangles are shown in Figures 7.19(e) and 7.19(f) respectively.

Some short-term traders make trades within well-defined rectangles. They buy when the exchange rate reaches the bottom boundary line and sell short when the exchange rate reaches the upper boundary line. To minimise losses in the event of a pattern breakout they also place a stop-loss order whenever they buy or short sell just outside the lower or upper boundary lines. If the pattern is broken they are stopped out at a small loss and they quickly place a new order on the direction of the breakout.

DOUBLE TOPS AND BOTTOMS

A double top pattern is formed when the exchange rate reaches a certain level, turns down, then rises again to near the previous peak and then moves down a second time to below the valley between the two peaks. A double bottom is the same as a double top except that it is upside down.

There are two ways to confirm a double top or a double bottom formation. One way is to wait until the exchange rate goes below the low level of the valley between the two peaks (or above the high between the two valleys for the double bottom). Another way is to use time. As a yardstick peaks should be one month apart and the valley at least 15 per cent lower than the top peak level. In both cases the exchange rate is expected to move in the direction of the reversal at least the distance from the valley to the peak.

TRIPLE TOPS AND BOTTOMS

These formations are similar to double tops and bottoms except that they have three tops and bottoms. These are shown in Figures 7.19(i) and 7.19(j) respectively.

RISING AND FALLING WEDGES

Wedges are characterised by exchange rates fluctuating between two converging boundary lines. For a rising wedge the boundary lines slope upwards with the lower line being steeper. For a falling wedge the boundary lines slope downwards with the upper boundary line being steeper. On a daily chart a wedge takes about three weeks or more to complete. When the exchange rate breaks through the lower line of a rising wedge it usually falls in earnest. In this case a sell signal is generated. When the exchange rate breaks through the upper boundary of a falling wedge a buy signal is generated.

DIAMOND

The diamond pattern is a combination of two triangles. The formation starts when the exchange rate swings wider, then narrower. The pattern is completed when one of the boundary lines of the second triangle is broken. On a breakout, the exchange rate should move a minimum distance equal to the distance from the top to the bottom of the formation.

CONTINUATION PATTERNS

A continuation (or consolidation) pattern can be defined as a sideways movement that temporarily interrupts an upward or a downward move in the exchange rate. These patterns occur when the exchange rate moves up or down too fast and reaches a level at which the demand or supply that produced the move is completely absorbed. At that point three things can occur. First, the exchange rate can reverse its trend, in which case a reversal pattern is likely to develop. Second, the exchange rate can decline or rise to a support level before building up steam again. Third, the exchange rate can move sideways, creating a continuation pattern from which to base a further move in the direction of the trend. The most reliable formations are shown in Figure 7.20. These will be described in turn.

FLAGS

A flag pattern represents a pause in a quick, almost vertical, up or down move in the exchange rate. In a flag the exchange rate moves sideways forming a flag-like pattern, breaks out from that pattern and then continues in the same direction as before. Flags appear regularly on daily charts and take about four weeks to complete. Because of that they are unlikely to be observed in weekly or monthly charts. They typically appear at the halfway point of an upward or downward move. Therefore, one may expect the exchange rate to move about the same distance after the breakout from the flag pattern as it did just prior to the pattern.

SYMMETRICAL TRIANGLES

In a symmetrical triangle, the exchange rate swings in a narrow range between a downward sloping and an upward sloping boundary lines that are fairly symmetrical. On a valid upward breakout the exchange rate is expected to continue until it reaches a line drawn parallel to the lower boundary line. The opposite is valid for a downside breakout.

HEAD AND SHOULDERS CONTINUATION PATTERNS

Head and shoulders continuation patterns are inverted relative to the direction of the trend before their appearance. When the exchange rate is trading lower, a head and shoulders formation pattern appears similar to a head and shoulders top. In an upward trend a head and shoulders continuation pattern appears like a reverse head and shoulders pattern.

BULLISH REVERSAL PATTERNS IN CANDLESTICK CHARTS

Figure 7.21 shows bullish reversal patterns in Japanese candlestick charts. These patterns are described in turn.

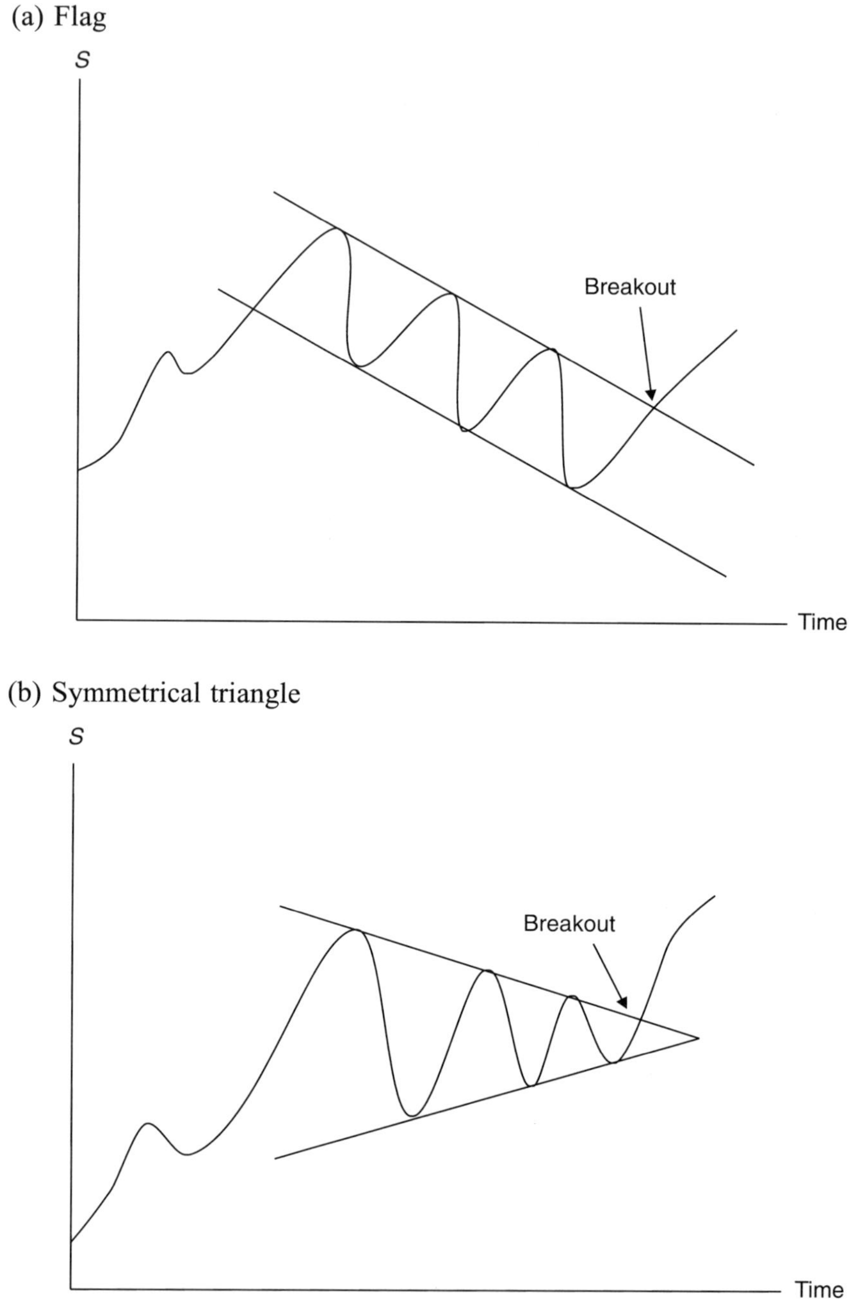

Figure 7.20 Continuation patterns

(c) Bullish head and shoulders continuation pattern

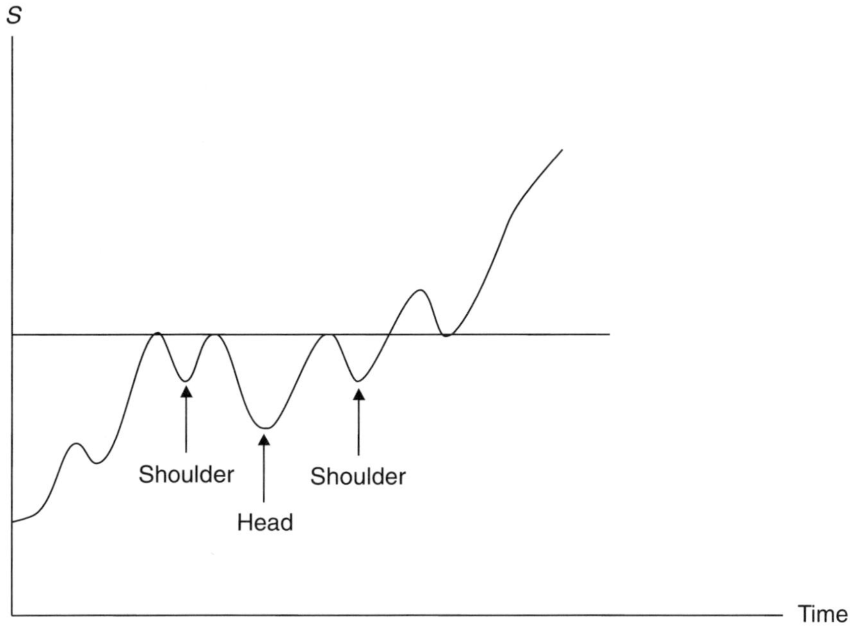

(d) Bearish head and shoulders continuation pattern

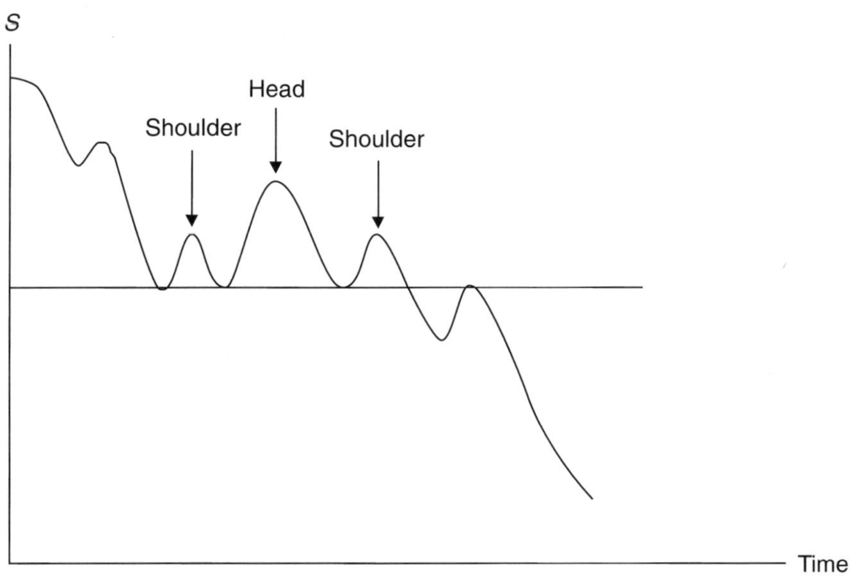

Figure 7.20 Continuation patterns (cont.)

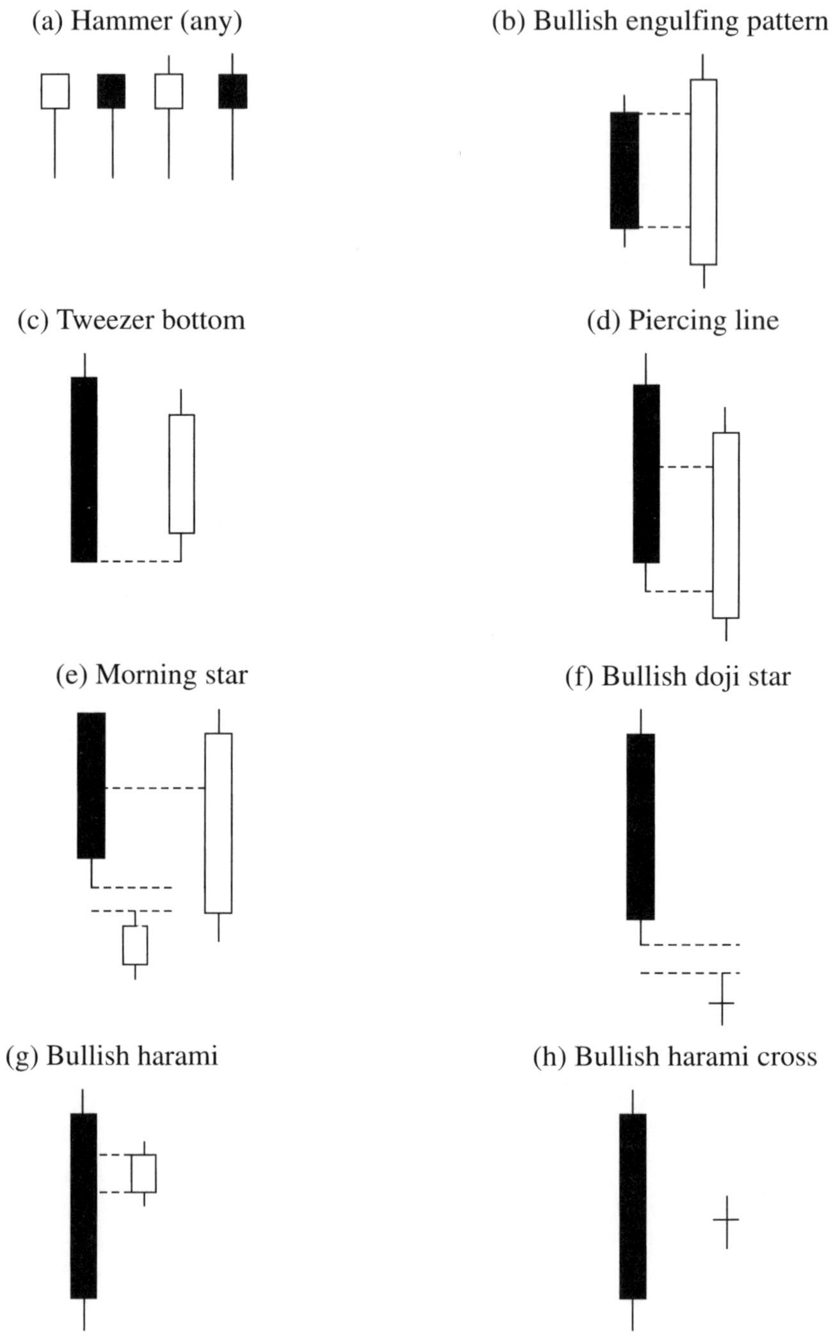

Figure 7.21 Bullish reversal patterns in candlestick charts

(i) Bullish meeting lines

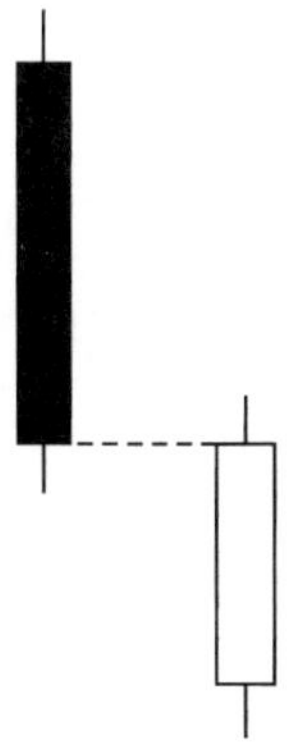

Figure 7.21 Bullish reversal patterns in candlestick charts (cont.)

HAMMER

A hammer occurs when the exchange rate rises from an intra-period sell-off to close near the open. This puts the main body, black or white, at the upper end of the period's trading range with little or no upper shadow. The lower shadow must be at least twice the length of the main body for the pattern to be considered legitimate.

BULLISH ENGULFING PATTERN

This pattern occurs when the exchange rate moves lower than the previous period's close and then rises to close above the previous period's open. Thus, the current period's white main body engulfs the previous period's black main body. Only the main body is important in this case, while the shadows are ignored.

TWEEZER BOTTOM

This pattern is simply two consecutive periods with matching lows. It is not important whether the main body is black or white, and there is no requirement regarding the length of the shadow lines. All that matters is that the lows for the two periods are the same.

PIERCING LINE

This pattern occurs when the exchange rate is lower on the opening as compared with the previous period and then retraces to close above the mid-point of the previous period's black body. The pattern consists of a period with a black main body followed by a period with a white main body. The second period's main white body should have the following characteristics: the open is lower than the previous period's low and the close is higher than the centre of the previous period's black main body.

MORNING STAR

A morning star pattern develops over three periods. In the first period the exchange rate closes lower than the opening level, which results in a black main body. In the second period, the exchange rate opens lower than the previous period but closes higher in a narrow trading range, creating a narrow white body. In the third period, the exchange rate continues to move higher to close above the midpoint of the first period's black main body.

BULLISH DOJI STAR

This pattern occurs when the exchange rate opens lower than the previous close and then closes at the same exchange rate as the open.

BULLISH HARAMI

In this pattern the main body for the current period falls within the main body of the previous period. It does not matter whether the main bodies are both black, both white or have different colours. If a harami pattern occurs in a downward trend, it is viewed as a bullish reversal signal.

BULLISH HARAMI CROSS

This is the same as the harami chart formation except that the open and close are the same in the second period. If a harami cross pattern occurs in a downward trend it is viewed as a bullish reversal sign.

BULLISH MEETING LINES

This pattern occurs when the exchange rate goes lower on the open and closes unchanged from the previous period. Hence, a black main body in the first period is followed by a white main body in the second period.

BEARISH REVERSAL PATTERNS IN CANDLESTICK CHARTS

Some bearish reversal patterns are illustrated in Figure 7.22. These patterns are described in turn.

HANGING MAN

This pattern occurs when the exchange rate rises from an intra-period sell-off to close near the open. This puts the main body (which can be black or white) at the upper end of the previous period's trading range with little or no upper shadow. The lower shadow must be at least twice the length of the main body for the pattern to be valid. Whether a pattern is a hanging man or a hammer depends on when it appears: if it forms after a downward trend, it is a hammer. Regardless of whether the pattern is called a hanging man or a hammer it signals a reversal in the trend.

BEARISH ENGULFING PATTERN

This pattern occurs when the exchange rate opens higher than the previous period's close and then closes below the previous period's open. Thus, the current period's black main body engulfs the previous period's white main body. Only the main body is important in this pattern: the upper and lower shadows are ignored.

TWEEZER TOP

This is simply two consecutive periods with matching highs. It is not important whether the candle lines have white or black main body (or simply doji lines). All that matters is that the highs for the two periods are the same.

DARK CLOUD COVER

This pattern occurs when the exchange rate edges higher on the opening and then retraces to close below the midpoint of the previous period's white body. Thus, a period with a white main body is followed by a period with a black main body. In the second period, the open is higher than the previous period's high, and the close is lower than the centre of the previous period's white main body.

UPSIDE GAP TWO CROWS

This pattern occurs when the exchange rate meets resistance on two consecutive days after rising higher. A period having a white main body is followed by two periods with black main bodies. There is an upside gap between the white main body and the first black main body.

EVENING STAR

This pattern develops over three periods. In the first period, the exchange rate closes higher than the open, resulting in a white main body. In the second period the exchange rate opens higher, creating an upside gap and closing lower after trading in a relatively narrow range (a small main body). In the third period the exchange rate continues to move lower and closes below the midpoint of the first period's white main body.

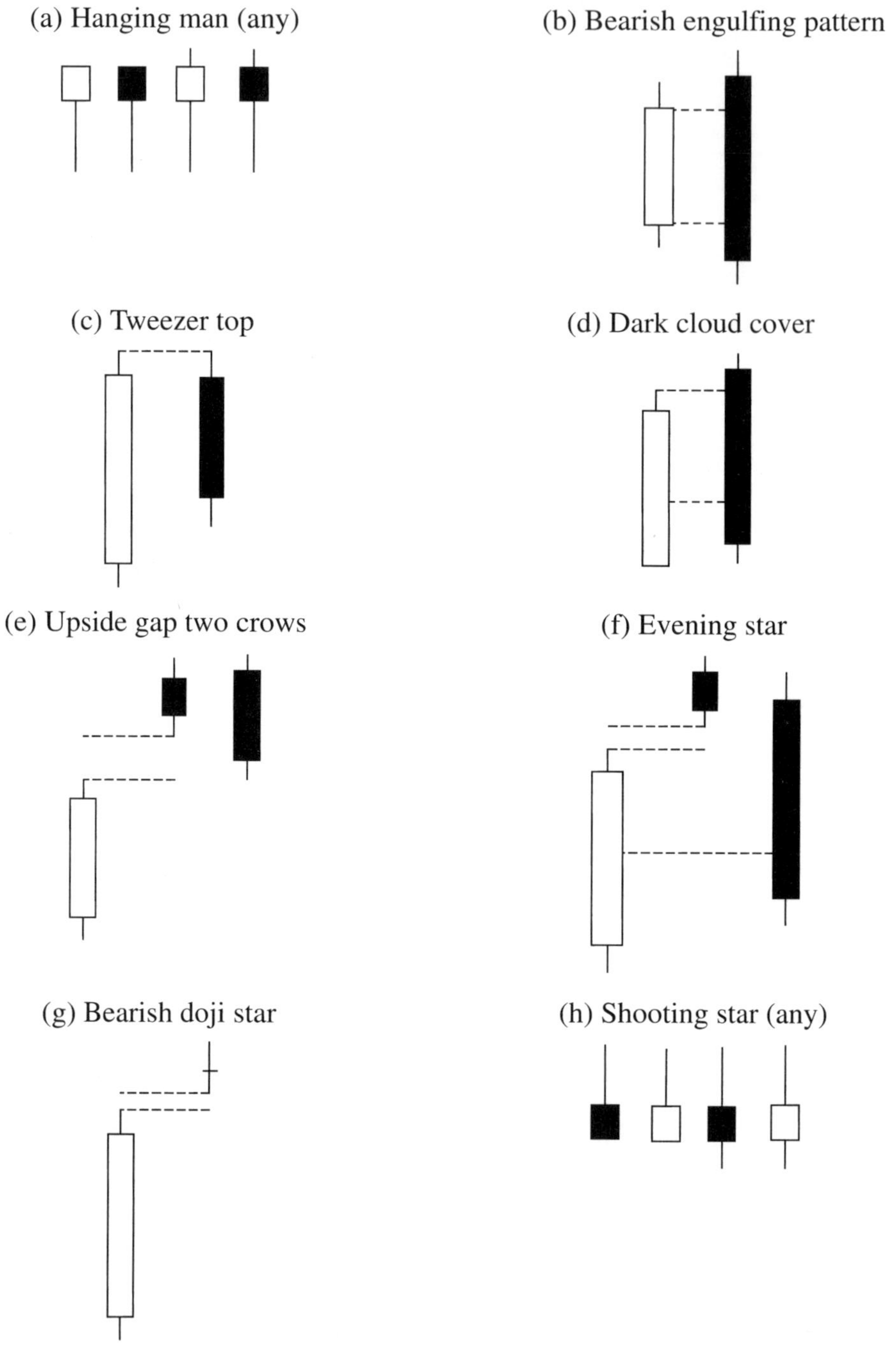

Figure 7.22 Bearish reversal patterns in candlestick charts

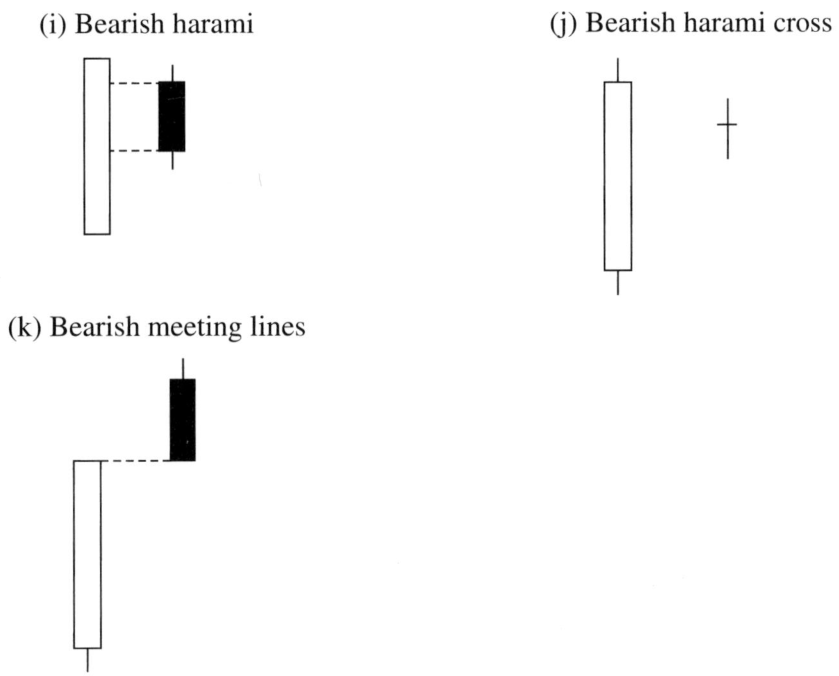

Figure 7.22 Bearish reversal patterns in candlestick charts (cont.)

BEARISH DOJI STAR

This pattern occurs when the exchange rate rises on the open and then closes at the same level as the open.

SHOOTING STAR

This is a period having a small main body that can be either black or white, at the lower end of the exchange rate range with a long upper shadow.

BEARISH HARAMI

The main body for the current period falls within the main body of the previous period. It does not matter whether the main bodies are black, white or have different colours. What is important is when the pattern occurs: if it occurs in an upward trend it is considered a bearish reversal pattern.

BEARISH HARAMI CROSS

This pattern is the same as the bearish harami pattern, except that the open and close levels are the same for the second period. If it occurs in an upward trend it is considered a bearish reversal pattern.

BEARISH MEETING LINES

This pattern occurs when the exchange rate rises on the open and then closes unchanged from the previous period. A white main body in the first period is followed by a black main body in the second period.

CONTINUATION PATTERNS IN CANDLESTICK CHARTS

Some continuation patterns are shown in Figure 7.23. These patterns are described in turn.

WINDOW

A window is simply a gap, which is an area on a chart where no actual trading takes place. An upside window is considered to be bullish while a downside window is considered to be bearish.

UPSIDE TASUKI GAP

An upside Tasuki gap pattern develops over three periods. In the first period the exchange rate closes above the opening level, resulting in a white main body. In the second period the exchange rate rises on the open with a gap, and then closes higher, resulting in a white main body. In the third period, the exchange rate opens within the main body of the second period and then closes lower without filling the gap. This suggests that only a temporary setback has occurred and that the exchange rate will continue higher. In this sense the gap acts as a support level.

RISING THREE METHODS

This pattern occurs when a long white main body is followed by three or more small white or black main bodies and then a long black main body which makes a new high close. It appears after a rally and presents an opportunity for some profit taking before the rally continues.

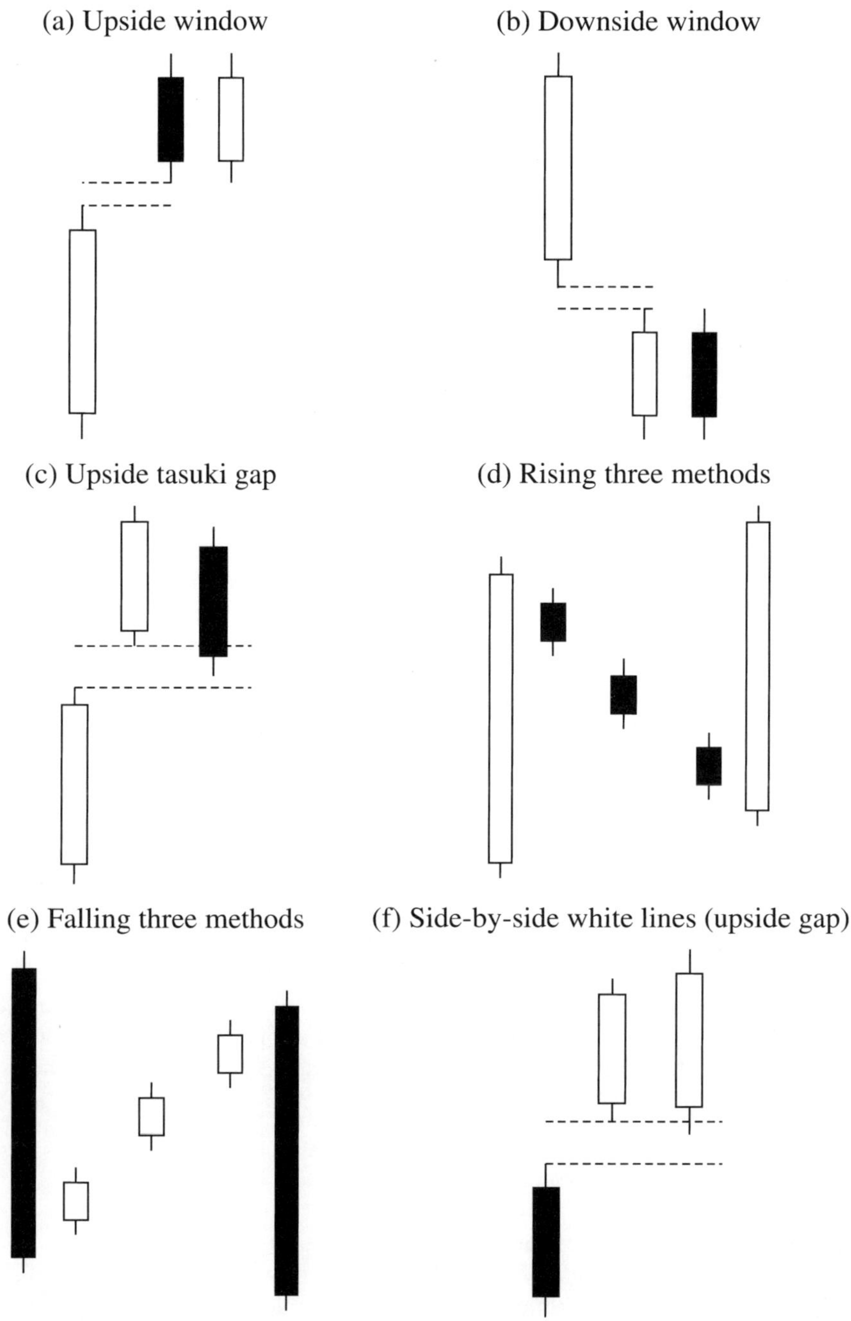

Figure 7.23 Continuation patterns in candlestick charts

(g) Side-by-side white lines (downside gap)

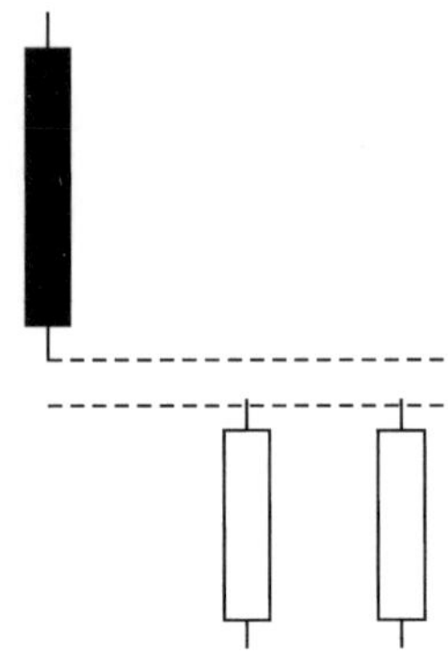

Figure 7.23 Continuation patterns in candlestick charts (cont.)

FALLING THREE METHODS

This pattern occurs when a long black body is followed by three or more small white or black main bodies, and then a long black main body which makes a new low close. It appears after a sharp downward trend and represents an opportunity for short covering before the drop in the exchange rate continues.

SIDE-BY-SIDE WHITE LINES (UPSIDE GAP)

This pattern develops over three periods. In the first period the main body can be either white or black. The exchange rate rises, leaving a gap on the opening of the second period and then closes higher. In the third period the exchange rate opens at the same opening level as in the second period and closes higher. The inability of the exchange rate to fill the gap indicates a strong support level.

SIDE-BY-SIDE WHITE LINES (DOWNSIDE GAP)

This pattern develops over three periods. In the first period the main body can be either white or black. The exchange rate moves down, creating a gap on the opening of the second period and then closes higher. In the third period the exchange rate closes at the same closing level as in the second period after having risen from the open. The inability to fill the gap indicates a strong resistance level.

QUANTITATIVE TECHNICAL INDICATORS

Quantitative technical indicators have numerical values that can be calculated from certain equations. The numerical values are interpreted to derive buy and sell signals. Three quantitative technical indicators are described in turn: oscillators, the relative strength index and the stochastics.

OSCILLATORS

Oscillators serve many purposes but they are primarily designed to give a clearer picture of market action. They are useful particularly because they can be used irrespective of whether the exchange rate is moving on an upward trend, a downward trend or sideways. Many other technical indicators are not useful when the exchange rate is moving sideways.

Oscillators are typically constructed with lower and upper boundaries, such as -1 to $+1$ or 0 to 100. Oscillator readings range between lower and upper boundaries. Typically, highs and lows in the oscillators correspond to the highs and lows in the exchange rate. There are three kinds of oscillators.

The first kind are momentum oscillators, which are designed to measure the speed or the rate of change in the exchange rate. Hence, a momentum oscillator measures the acceleration or deceleration in the exchange rate. The value of a k-period momentum oscillator at a particular point in time is calculated as

$$O_t^k = S_t - S_{t-k} \tag{7.1}$$

where k may also be called the order of the momentum oscillator. When the momentum oscillator goes up in the current time period it means that the exchange rate rose by more or declined by less than k periods ago. Similar interpretations are assigned to flat and downward movements in momentum oscillators. One of the benefits of momentum oscillators is that they lead exchange rate movements at market turning points. A momentum oscillator flattens out while the current exchange rate trend is still in effect.

The second kind are the rate of change oscillators. A rate of change oscillator of order k is calculated as

$$O_t^k = \frac{S_t}{S_{t-k}} \tag{7.2}$$

It is normally the case that this value is multiplied by 100, in which case the oscillator will fluctuate above and below the 100 level.

The third kind are the moving average oscillators. A moving average oscillator is calculated as the difference between two moving averages of different orders. This is useful for at least two reasons: (i) to identify divergences, (ii) to make moving average crossovers easy to see. Moving average oscillators are described in Chapter 8 as moving average trading rules.

Once the values of the oscillator have been calculated they are plotted along with upper and lower boundaries as well as the midpoint line. The midpoint is zero for a -1 to $+1$ range and 50 for a range of 0–100. Once this is done, then the following interpretations are possible.

1. When the oscillator crosses the midpoint line a signal is given that the exchange rate will move in the direction of the crossing. If the oscillator moves through the midpoint line it is bullish. On the other hand, if the oscillator declines through the midpoint line, it is bearish.
2. When the exchange rate makes a high, corrects and then makes a new high while the oscillator makes a high, corrects and does not make a new high, a bearish divergence occurs. It suggests that the exchange rate is likely to go lower. On the other hand, when the exchange rate makes a low, corrects and then makes a new low, while the oscillator makes a low, a correction and does not make a new low, then a bullish divergence occurs. The implication is that the exchange rate is likely to go up.
3. Extremely high readings suggest an overbought position and are therefore viewed as bearish. Extremely low readings are interpreted as indicating oversold positions, that is bullish. Since oscillators can remain at extreme readings for long periods of time, it is best to recognise extreme readings as periods of market vulnerability and not as specific buy and sell signals.

THE RELATIVE STRENGTH INDEX

The relative strength index (*RSI*) is designed to deal with some problems associated with oscillators. The first of these problems is that the oscillator may move erratically due to a sharp change in the exchange rate some time ago. For example, a ten-day oscillator may give a misleading high or low reading if the exchange rate rose or declined sharply ten days ago. The second problem is that there is no way of telling how high or low the exchange rate should go in order to be interpreted as a buy or sell signal. The third problem pertains to the data requirements: a massive amount of data is required to calculate an oscillator. The *RSI* circumvents all of these problems.

The *RSI* is calculated as follows:

$$RSI = 100 - \frac{100}{1 + RS} \tag{7.3}$$

where

$$RS = \frac{\frac{1}{n}\sum_{t=1}^{n} \Delta S_t^+}{\frac{1}{n}\sum_{t=1}^{n} |\Delta S_t^-|} \tag{7.4}$$

where n is the number of periods over which the *RSI* is calculated, ΔS_t^+ is a positive change and $|\Delta S_t^-|$ is the absolute value of a negative change. Notice that, for the purpose of this calculation, when $\Delta S_t \geq 0$, then $|\Delta S_t^-| = 0$, and when $\Delta S_t \leq 0$, then $\Delta S_t^+ = 0$. For example, if we consider a ten-day period ($n = 10$), *RS* is calculated by dividing the average of the positive changes by the average of the absolute value of the negative changes over the ten-day period.

The *RSI* is calculated by keeping the number of observations constant. As we move from one point in time to the next, the old observation is dropped while a new observation is added. To update the *RSI* each period, the previous up and down averages are multiplied by $n - 1$ and the new up and down values are added to calculate *RS*. Hence we have

$$RS_{t+1} = \frac{(n-1)\frac{1}{n}\sum_{t=1}^{n} \Delta S_t^+ + \Delta S_{t+1}^+}{(n-1)\frac{1}{n}\sum_{t=1}^{n} |\Delta S_t^-| + |\Delta S_{t+1}^-|} \tag{7.5}$$

and

$$RSI_{t+1} = 100 - \frac{100}{1 + RS_{t+1}} \tag{7.6}$$

The *RSI* may be interpreted as follows:

1. Extreme *RSI* readings signal the likelihood of major tops or bottoms, but the exact level for such indication is debatable. It is sometimes recommended that a rise above 70 indicates that a major top is likely while a decline below 30 suggests a high probability of a major bottom.
2. The chart patterns presented earlier are equally applicable to the *RSI* as they are to exchange rate data. Often, a triangle or a head and shoulders pattern can be seen in the *RSI*. The same breakout rules apply to the *RSI*.

3. A top failure swing occurs when the index rises above 70, declines to a lower level (fail point), rises again but failing to reach 70 and then falls to lower than the prior lower level, which again is a fail point. At this point a sell decision should be taken. This is illustrated in Figure 7.24(a). A bottom failure swing is shown in Figure 7.24(b).
4. Support and resistance lines are often apparent on the *RSI* before the exchange rate data. Breaking of support and resistance is interpreted in the same way as in the exchange rate chart.
5. Divergence between the exchange rate and the *RSI* suggests that the exchange rate will be reversing. If the exchange rate is rising or flat and the *RSI* is decreasing, then a downward turn is expected. If, on the other hand, the exchange rate is declining or flat and the *RSI* is increasing, then an upward turn should be expected.

THE STOCHASTICS

The stochastics is a measure of the velocity of exchange rate changes. The underlying idea is that as the exchange rate increases, the closing level has the tendency to be near to the high of the period. Similarly, as the exchange rate decreases, the closing level has the tendency to be near the low for the period. The stochastics, K, is calculated as

$$K = \frac{S_C - S_L}{S_H - S_L} \times 100 \qquad (7.7)$$

where S_C is the latest closing level of the exchange rate, S_L is the low level for the last n periods and S_H is the high during the last n periods. n is normally chosen to be between 5 and 21. K can be smoothed, typically by using a three-period moving average, to obtain another measure, D. Both K and D are then plotted on the same chart. The stochastics has the following interpretations:

1. A bearish divergence is illustrated in Figure 7.25(a). It occurs when the exchange rate makes a high then corrects, moving lower and subsequently reaches a higher high. At the same time D makes a high followed by a lower high. The sell signal is indicated when the K line moves below the D line. Figure 7.25(b) illustrates the case of a bullish divergence.
2. Readings of 0 and 100 on the K line do not mean that the exchange rate has reached a bottom or top respectively. Rather they suggest significant weakness and strength. When a reading of 0 is reached, the K line frequently moves up to the 20–25 level and then declines to near 0.

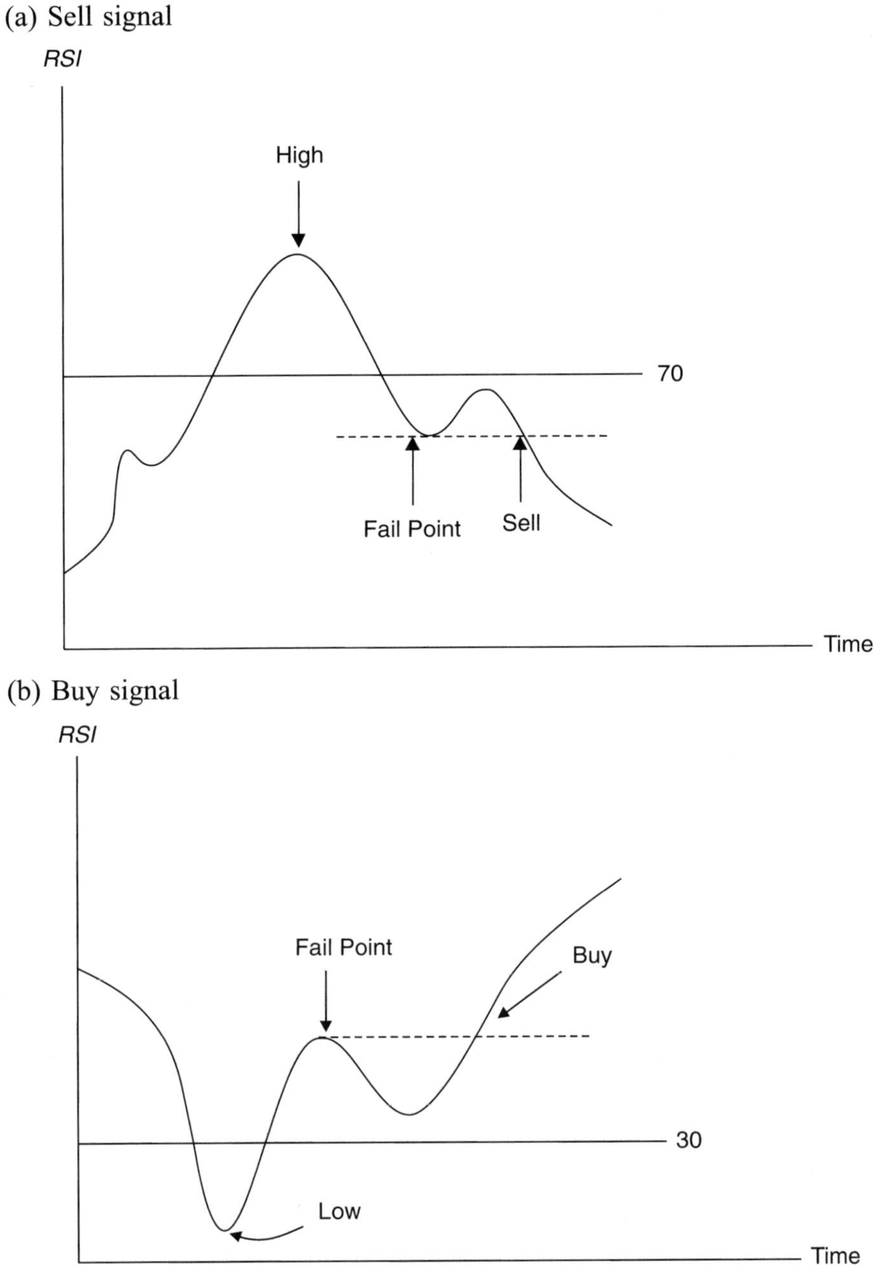

Figure 7.24 Buy and sell signals generated by the *RSI*

When the *K* line moves up from that area, one can expect a minor rally. Likewise, when the *K* line reaches 100, the *K* line often drops to the 75–80 range and then moves back up to or near the 100 level. On the next decline a minor drop is likely.

3. When the line has been moving in one direction for many periods then suddenly reverses direction sharply in one period (2 to 12 per cent) a warning signal is given. The exchange rate is likely to reverse direction in one or two periods.

THE ECONOMICS OF TECHNICAL ANALYSIS

Economists have been studying technical analysis with increasing enthusiasm, perhaps because of the failure of fundamental models as explanatory and predictive tools. In studying technical analysis economists seek to address three issues: (i) the extent to which technical analysis is used in practice to predict exchange rate movements; (ii) the forecasting power of technical models as opposed to fundamental models; and (iii) the role technical analysts play in exchange rate determination.

The first question has frequently been raised in the literature. Traditionally, economists have rejected the propositions put forward by technical analysts, since they believe that economic fundamentals are the only determinants of exchange rates. Given the notion of market efficiency, old information (particularly that which is publicly available) must be useless because it is already incorporated in the current exchange rate. Malkiel (1990, p. 154) puts forward the cynical view that 'technical strategies are usually amusing, often comforting, but of no real value'. But if this is the case, why is it that technical analysts are still in demand by financial institutions? Malkiel (1990, Chap. 6) has a ready answer: they are hired by brokers largely in order to generate trades and hence commissions. Allen and Taylor (1993) put forward the counter-argument that even if this is the case, 'the results of this policy manifest themselves as self-fulfilling chartist strategies'. The fact remains, however, that the failure of fundamental models has forced economists to take technical analysis more seriously.

The studies on the extent of the use of technical analysis have produced results showing extensive use of this technique for exchange rate forecasting, particularly for short-term forecasting. Allen and Taylor (1989, 1990) and Taylor and Allen (1992) present evidence on the use of technical analysis based on a survey of some 240 foreign exchange dealers in London. The survey revealed a broad consensus regarding the weights given to technical analysis at different time horizons. At short horizons, ranging from intra-day to weekly, 90 per cent of the participants reported using

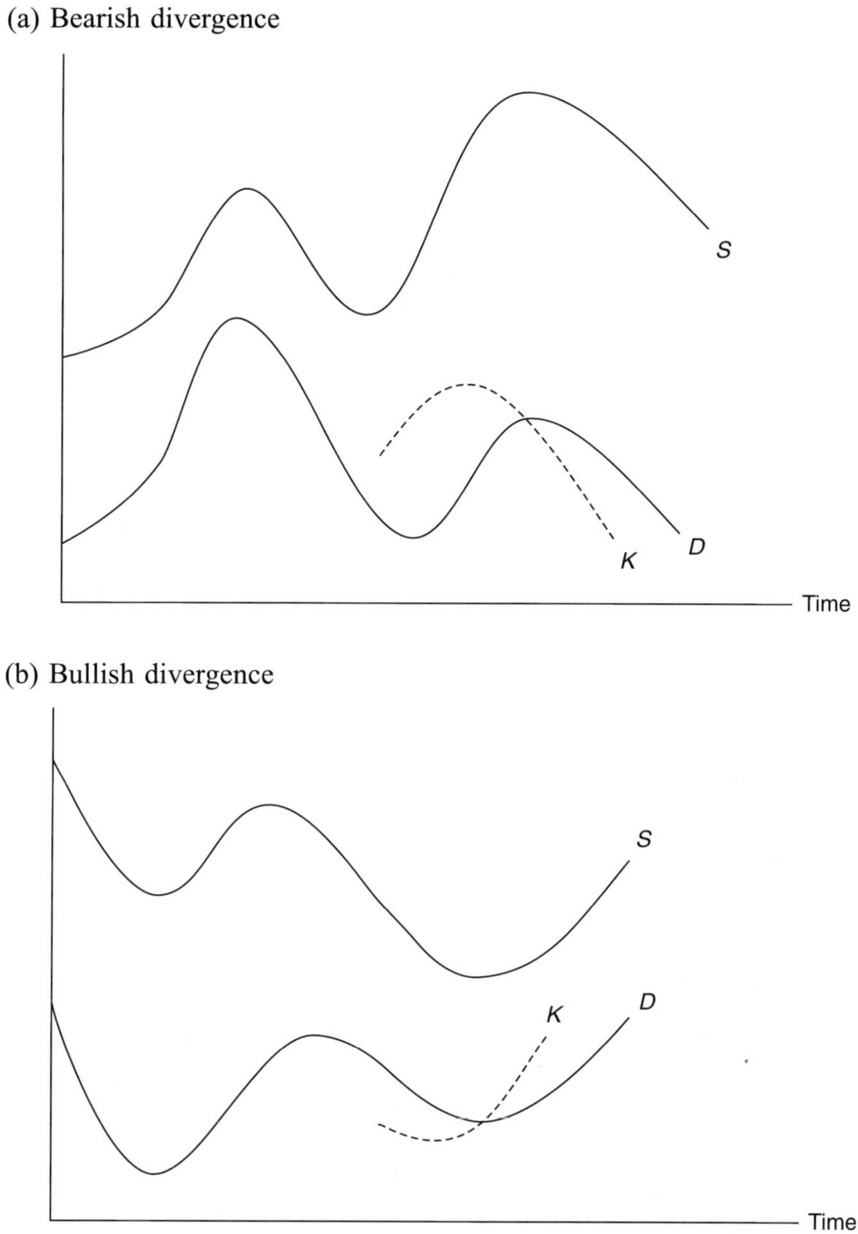

Figure 7.25 Bearish and bullish divergence as indicated by the stochastics

technical analysis. Some 60 per cent of the participants said that they regarded technical analysis at least as important as fundamental analysis. The results also revealed that at long horizons the weight given to technical analysis is greater. There was a very small minority (2 per cent) who claimed never to have used fundamental analysis. The overall conclusion that can be derived from the survey is that technical analysis and fundamental analysis are complementary.

More recently, Lui and Mole (1998) conducted a similar survey involving 153 foreign exchange dealers in the Hong Kong market. This survey revealed that a very high proportion of the respondents placed some weight on both technical and fundamental analysis at all time horizons. At shorter horizons, however, there exists a skew towards reliance on technical analysis. Moreover, a view was reflected that technical analysis is only slightly more useful than fundamental analysis in predicting trends but significantly more useful in predicting turning points.

A number of economists have studied the forecasting accuracy of technical analysis in comparison with fundamental analysis. Allen and Taylor (1990) have found that some individual technical forecasts outperformed the random walk model, VAR models and ARIMA models for the one-week and four-week horizons. However, they reported a large degree of heterogeneity among technical forecasts. Neftci (1991) compared technical analysis to the Wiener–Kolmorgrove prediction theory and concluded that technical analysis might capture some information ignored by the latter. LeBaron (1991) and Brock *et al.* (1992) found that moving average and other technical models are of value in making prediction.

Goodman (1979, 1980) studied the profitability of exchange rate forecasts provided by forecasting services using technical analysis and fundamental analysis. The results revealed that technical forecasts outperformed the forward rate in qualitative tests while the forward rate outperformed fundamental forecasts. Taylor (1994) applied a channel rule to futures data, finding it to be 'surprisingly profitable'. Chang and Osler (1995) developed an algorithm to identify head and shoulders patterns. By analysing this algorithm they obtained profit that is 'statistically and economically meaningful'. Curcio and Goodhart (1991) conducted a controlled experiment in which students traded currencies with and without the help of computer software for technical analysis. They showed that although there was no significant difference in the profit, the variance of the profit was lower for the group utilising the software. Finally, Pilbeam (1995) studied the profitability and variability of trades based on technical and fundamental forecasts and found that there was little reason to prefer technical analysis to fundamental analysis and vice versa.

Recently, there has been a tendency among economists to assign some role to the activity of technical analysts in the process of exchange rate determination. This is legitimate particularly over short periods and in the absence of major changes in the fundamentals. Under these conditions, acting on technical analysis becomes a self-fulfilling prophecy. When a trader is convinced, by a certain chart pattern, that the exchange rate is going to rise after a long decline (that is a trend reversal upwards is expected) he will buy the currency, with the resulting increase in demand causing the exchange rate to rise as indicated by the chart. The opposite is also true.

The behaviour of traders who act on the basis of fundamental analysis and those who act on the basis of technical analysis may differ drastically. Fundamental analysts watch deviations from an equilibrium level of the exchange rate as implied by a fundamental model. If the exchange rate is above the equilibrium level the currency is sold, which should lead to a currency depreciation. This is not necessarily the case, however. If technical analysts believe that there is no indication of a trend reversal they will keep on buying it, lending support to the currency. What happens to the exchange rate depends on the net effect of the forces of supply and demand by fundamental analysts and technical analysts. The same argument is valid if the exchange rate falls below the equilibrium value.

Several economists have formalised the idea put forward in the preceding paragraph. Goodhart (1988) puts forward the proposition that exchange rate misalignment is determined by the balance of the predictions of technical analysts and fundamental analysts. Likewise, Frankel and Froot (1990b) suggest a model based on the same idea to explain the sharp rise in the demand for the dollar in the first half of the 1980s. The explanation provided on the basis of this model is that the increase in the demand for the dollar is the overwhelming role of technical analysts during that period. Kirman (1991) presents an extension of the Frankel–Froot model.

The issue of technical versus fundamental analysis is far from over. The consensus view is that fundamental analysis is the only way to analyse exchange rate movements in the long run, but in the short run technical analysis can be more important. Allen and Taylor (1993) suggest a 'scientific explanation' for why technical analysis is important in the short run. The argue that technical analysts may 'get a feel' for local approximations to processes which are too complex to be captured by fundamental models. This postulation is dealt with formally by Clyde and Osler (1997) in a paper entitled 'Charting: Chaos Theory in Disguise?' The authors show that technical analysis may represent crude but useful ways of exploring nonlinear qualities in data. They further propose that technical analysis may be restated in terms of attractors and may be viewed as equivalent to nonlinear prediction methods. They also present evidence in support of this hypothesis in the form of an application of a head and shoulders pattern identification algorithm to high-dimension nonlinear data, resulting in successful pattern identification and prediction.

COMPUTER SOFTWARE AND FURTHER READING

Drawing charts can be carried out by utilising some widely used programs such as Excel, which provides some excellent graphics capabilities. Some examples of these capabilities are provided by Figures 7.26–7.30. Figures 7.26–7.29 are daily bar charts using 150 observations ending on 23 September 1998 for four exchange rates. Figure 7.30 is a monthly candle-stick chart of the JPY/USD exchange rate ending in August 1998.

There are a large number of software packages designed specifically for technical analysis. These packages may be used to plot all types of charts and calculate the quantitative technical indicators. Most of these charts are designed for stock markets and futures markets but they can be used for the

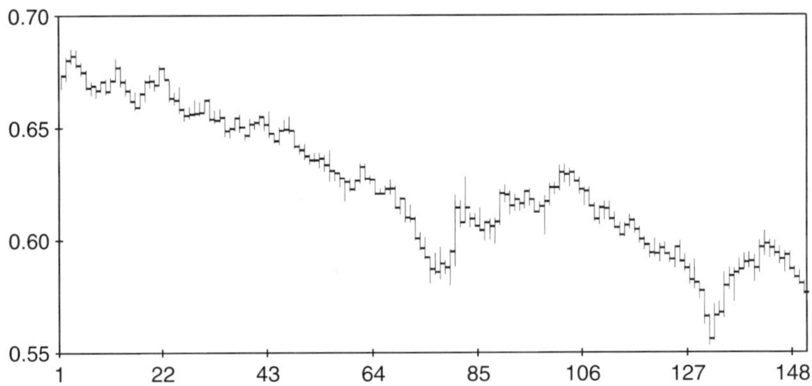

Figure 7.26 USD/AUD daily bar chart

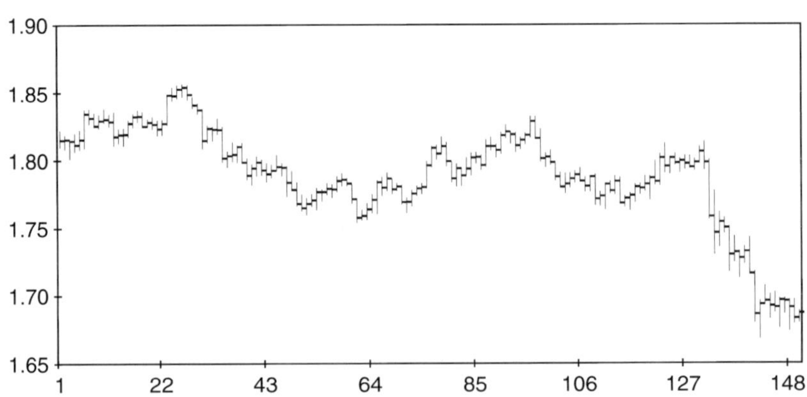

Figure 7.27 DEM/USD daily bar chart

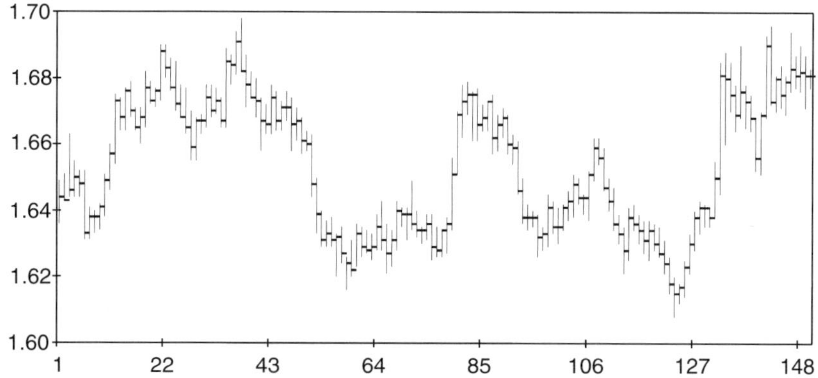

Figure 7.28 USD/GBP daily bar chart

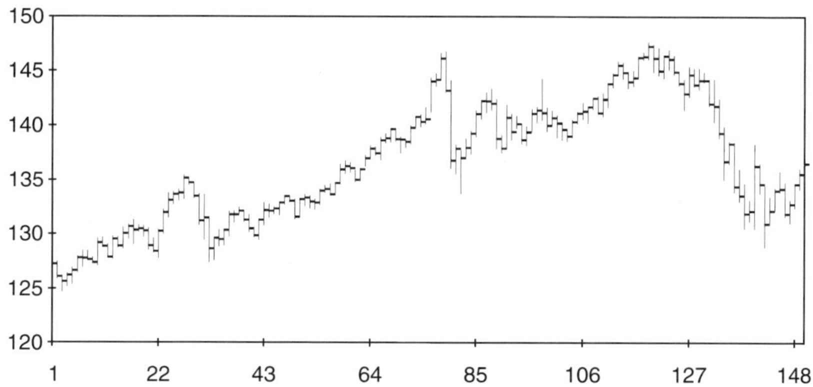

Figure 7.29 JPY/USD daily bar chart

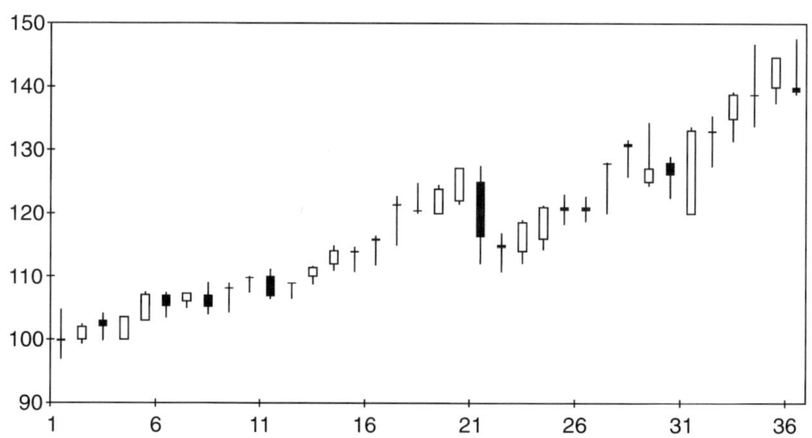

Figure 7.30 JPY/USD monthly candlestick chart

foreign exchange market. The three most common of these packages are MetaStock, The Technician, and Telescan Analyzer. A description of technical analysis software packages is available in the *Individual Investor's Microcomputer Resource Guide* which is published annually by the American Association of Individual Investors.

Books dealing with technical analysis are plentiful. General technical analysis is found in Colby and Meyers (1988), Wilder (1978), Pring (1991) and Schwager (1984). The Dow theory is dealt with in Sheimo (1989), while the Elliott wave theory is discussed in Prechter and Frost (1990) and Prechter (1980). Nison (1991) provides a comprehensive treatment of Japanese candlestick charts and Burke (1990) deals with point and figure charts.

8: Trading Rules

INTRODUCTION

Trading rules are devices used by traders in financial markets to obtain buy and sell signals according to some predetermined criteria. Although trading rules are normally associated with technical analysis, it is possible to devise some rules that are based on fundamental analysis, that is on economic models. Hence, we may distinguish between technical rules and fundamental rules. In technical rules a buy signal is indicated if it is established that an upward trend will continue, and a sell signal is indicated if a downward trend is perceived to continue for some time in the future. If the trading rule is based on the concept of an equilibrium exchange rate then a currency is bought when it is undervalued (the exchange rate is below the equilibrium level) and sold when it is overvalued (above the equilibrium level). In fundamental rules the buy and sell signals are extracted from the behaviour of the underlying trend of the exchange rate series or they are indicated by deviations from an equilibrium or a 'fair value' of the exchange rate. Thus, trading rules based on technical analysis and fundamental analysis may lead to contrasting decisions as we will see later.

The objective of this chapter is to describe the basic technical trading rules as well as their modifications, and to present the empirical evidence on the profitability or otherwise of trading strategies based on these rules. We will also describe some fundamental trading rules and compare them with the technical rules. We start with a description of the first type of technical trading rules: filter rules.

SIMPLE FILTER RULES

Filter rules were initially developed by Alexander (1961) who applied them to the stock market. A similar attempt was made by Fama and Blume (1966). Subsequently, filter rules were applied to other financial markets, including the foreign exchange market. The latter attempts have been made by several economists including Dooley and Shafer (1976, 1983) and Sweeney (1986, 1988).

A filter rule works as follows. A currency is bought when it appreciates (that is, when the exchange rate rises) by a certain percentage from its most recent trough (that is bottom, or low value). On the other hand a currency is sold when it depreciates by a certain percentage from its most recent peak (that is, top or high value). Thus, an x per cent filter rule (where x is a small number) works as follows: a currency is bought when the exchange rate rises by x per cent from its most recent trough and it is sold when the exchange rate declines by x per cent from its most recent peak. The process is subsequently repeated when the exchange rate reaches a trough and starts to rise. When $x = 1$ we have on our hands a 1 per cent filter rule. Similarly, we could have 2.5 per cent, 5 per cent and 10 per cent filter rules.

The idea underlying filter rules is very simple. When a currency appreciates by x per cent, then it should (according to the rationale behind these rules) appreciate further, and so it should be bought. Alternatively, when a currency depreciates by x per cent then it should keep on depreciating, and so it should be sold. Figure 8.1 illustrates how an x per cent rule works. The exchange rate reaches a trough at point A. Once it has risen by x per cent from its level at point A, the currency is bought and the long position is held until the exchange rate reaches a peak at point B. Once it has declined by x per cent from its level at B the currency is sold. Obviously, this buy–sell transaction is profitable since the currency is sold

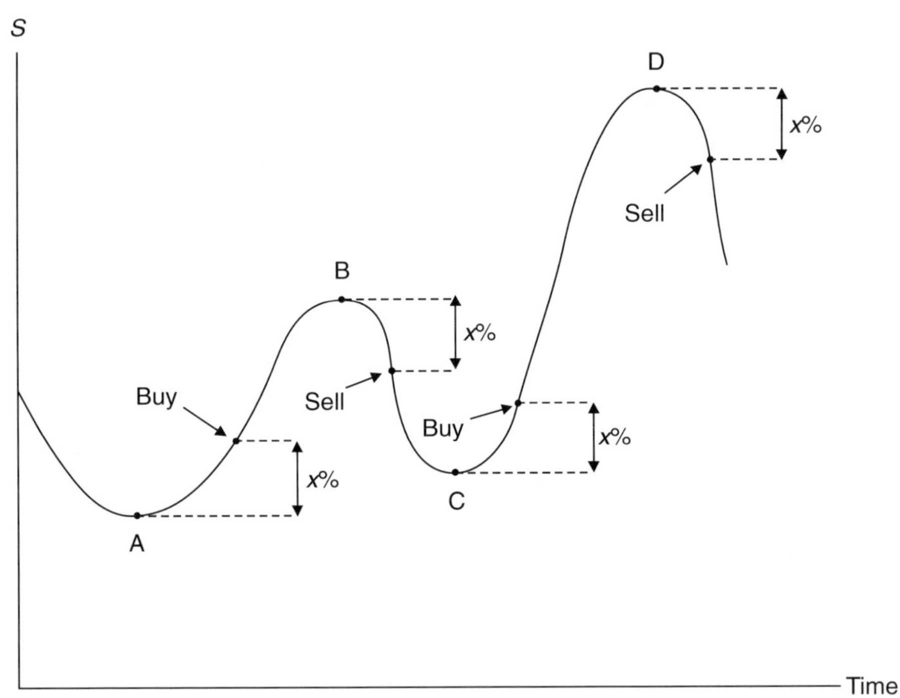

Figure 8.1 x per cent filter rule

at a higher exchange rate than the one at which it is bought. The operation is then repeated. Once the exchange rate has risen by x per cent from its trough at point C it is bought and held until it declines by x per cent from its peak at point D.

Filter rules implicitly assume the existence of an equilibrium exchange rate. But being technical, they do not define this equilibrium rate or how it is reached. Filter rules are designed to catch a breakout from the bands represented by the dashed lines in Figure 8.1. Within the band the currency is assumed to be trading at around its equilibrium value (that is, the exchange rate is around its equilibrium level). But as new information is absorbed the exchange rate breaks out, presumably towards its new equilibrium value. The filter rule is designed to catch the exchange rate at the breakpoint as it moves from the old equilibrium value to the new equilibrium value that falls within the following band. The breakpoint is represented by the lower dashed line on the downturn and the upper dashed line on the upturn. In an efficient market, this is not possible since the exchange rate would adjust to new information too quickly to allow any trader to capture it.

Of course it would be more profitable to buy at A and sell at B, that is exactly at the peak and trough. But these turning points cannot be determined, *ex ante*. So, the question is why wait x per cent, why not buy immediately after the trough and sell immediately after the peak? The answer is that waiting for the x per cent move is necessary to make sure that the exchange rate will keep on rising from the trough and keep on falling from the peak.

The simple x per cent filter rule can be modified in at least two ways. First, it is possible to allow for short selling of the currency, that is borrowing the currency and selling it when there is a bearish sign. Starting from point B, if the trader does not already have a (long) position on the currency, then when the exchange rate falls by x per cent the trader could take a short position and wait. When the exchange rate rises by x per cent from its trough at point C, then the currency is bought and the short position is covered. The other modification results in an x–y filter. In this case the currency is bought when the exchange rate rises by x per cent from its trough and sold when the exchange rate falls by y per cent from its peak, such that $x > y$ or $x < y$. If, for example, the exchange rate behaves in an asymmetric way, such that it rises by more than it falls, then an x–y filter with $x > y$ may be more appropriate. To illustrate this proposition, let us assume that $x = 3$ and $y = 1$. The x–y filter works as follows: the currency is bought when the exchange rate rises by 3 per cent from its trough and it is sold when it falls by 1 per cent from its peak. The implication of this rule is that we need a larger percentage increase to make sure that the exchange rate will keep on rising than the percentage decline needed to make sure that the exchange rate will keep on declining.

FORMAL REPRESENTATION OF FILTER RULES

The working of the filter rule depends on the recognition of peaks and troughs (*ex post*) in the exchange rate series. Assume that the exchange rate is observed at points in time $t-m$, $t-m+1$, ..., t, $t+1$. The value of the exchange rate at time t, S_t, defines a trough if

$$S_{t+1} - S_t > 0 \tag{8.1}$$

and

$$S_{t-i} - S_{t-i-1} < 0 \qquad \text{for } i = 0, 1, \ldots, m-1 \tag{8.2}$$

Equations (8.1) and (8.2) imply that for S_t to define a trough the necessary condition is that $\Delta S_{t+1} > 0$, while the sufficient condition is that $\Delta S_{t-i} < 0$ for $i = 0, 1, \ldots, m-1$. On the other hand, S_t defines a peak if

$$S_{t+1} - S_t < 0 \tag{8.3}$$

and

$$S_{t-i} - S_{t-i-1} > 0 \qquad \text{for } i = 0, 1, \ldots, m-1 \tag{8.4}$$

Equations (8.3) and (8.4) imply that for S_t to define a peak the necessary condition is that $\Delta S_{t+1} < 0$, while the sufficient condition is that $\Delta S_{t-i} > 0$ for $i = 0, 1, \ldots, m-1$. The buy and sell signals generated by an x per cent filter rule are then identified as follows. If there is a trough at S_t, then a buy signal emerges at S_{t+i} if

$$S_{t+i} = (1+x)S_t \tag{8.5}$$

where x is measured as a decimal, not as a percentage. On the other hand, if there is a trough at S_t, then a sell signal emerges at S_{t+i} if

$$S_{t+i} = (1-x)S_t \tag{8.6}$$

It may be the case that S_{t+i} is not observable at a particular point in time because the exchange rate assumes discrete values. This is particularly valid if the rule is based on low-frequency data. For example, if the peak in the USD/GBP rate is 1.6500, then a 5 per cent filter rule implies that the pound should be sold at 1.5675. However, the exchange rate may decline directly from 1.5700 to 1.5500, in which case the value 1.5675 will not be recorded. The trader can still follow the rule by selling at 1.5500. Therefore, the buy and sell signals may be more appropriately defined in terms of inequalities:

a buy signal is generated when $S_{t+i} \geq (1+x)S_t$ and a sell signal is generated when $S_{t+i} \leq (1-x)S_t$. We will, however, use the conditions as represented by equations (8.5) and (8.6).

The representation of the x–y filter rule is similar. The buy signal is given when the exchange rate rises by x per cent from the trough as represented by equation (8.5). The sell signal, on the other hand, is given when the exchange rate falls by y per cent from its most recent peak. This is represented by equation (8.6) with y replacing x.

THE EFFECT OF THE FILTER SIZE

What determines which filter size is the most profitable? Notice that reducing the filter size has two implications: transaction costs will be higher, and there will be a higher probability that we do not have a genuine trend on our hands.

Let us examine this issue by looking at Figure 8.2, which traces the time path of an exchange rate. The exchange rate reaches a trough at point A (time t_1), after which it starts to rise until it reaches a peak at point C

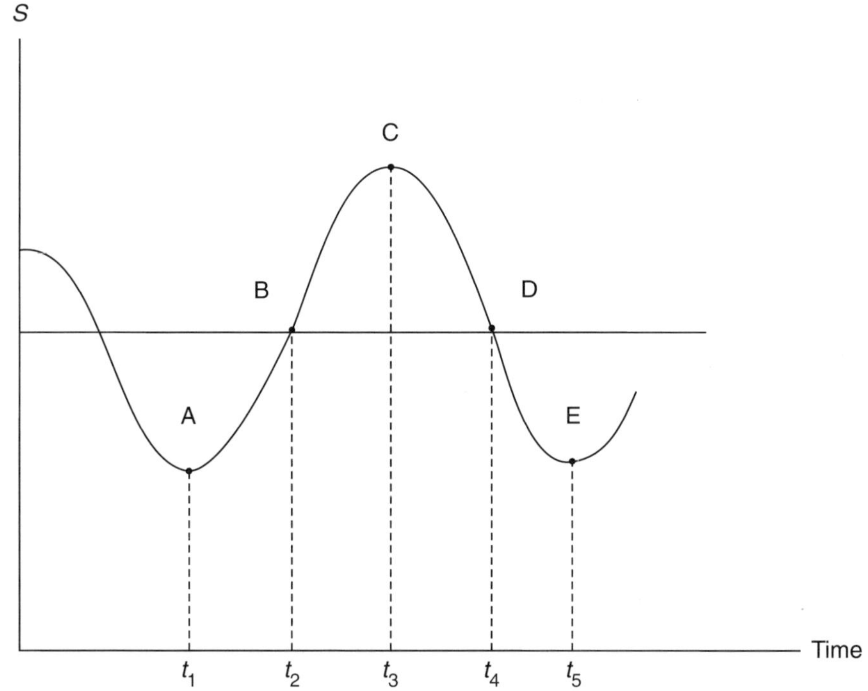

Figure 8.2 The effect of the filter size

(time t_3), then it declines again until it reaches another trough at point E (time t_5). The following possibilities, illustrated in Figure 8.3, are readily observable:

1. The filter rule will be profitable if the filter size leads to a buy signal between A and B and a sell signal between C and D.
2. The filter rule will be unprofitable if the filter size leads to a buy signal between B and C and a sell signal between D and E.
3. The filter rule will lead to a breakeven if the filter size leads to a buy signal at point B and a sell signal at point D.

The filter size may also lead to buy signals falling between B and C and sell signals between C and D, or buy signals falling between A and B and sell signals falling between D and E. In these cases we have *x–y* filters, which may lead to profit, loss or breakeven. These situations are illustrated in Figure 8.4. It is also possible that a filter size may result in a loss even though it is used in a bull market, and in profit even though it is used in a bear market. These situations are illustrated in Figure 8.5.

(a) Profitable *x*% filter

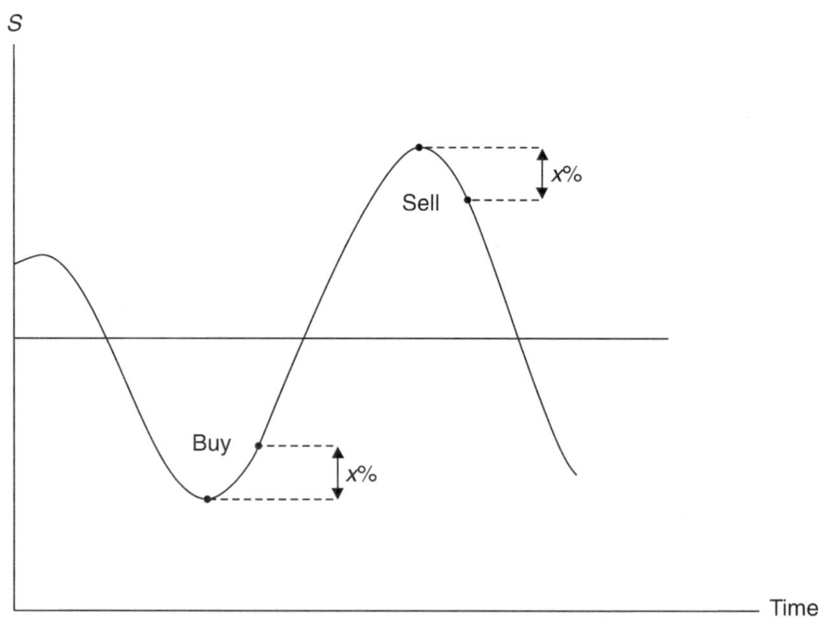

Figure 8.3 Profitable and unprofitable filter sizes (1)

(b) Unprofitable $x\%$ filter

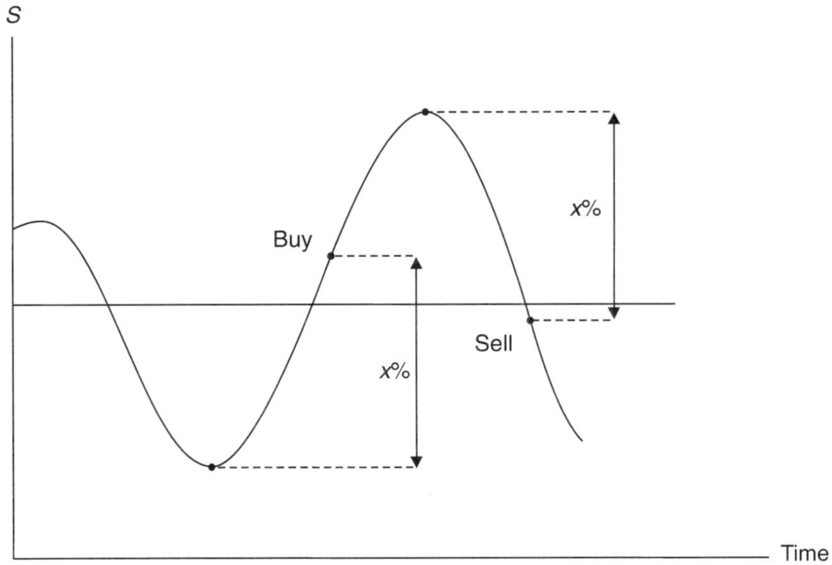

(c) Breakeven $x\%$ filter

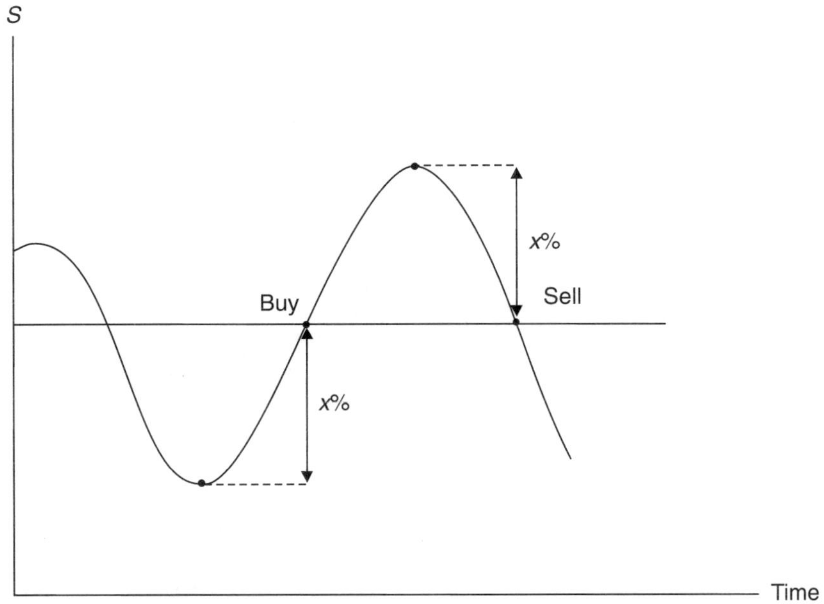

Figure 8.3 Profitable and unprofitable filter sizes (1) (cont.)

(a) Profitable *x–y* filter

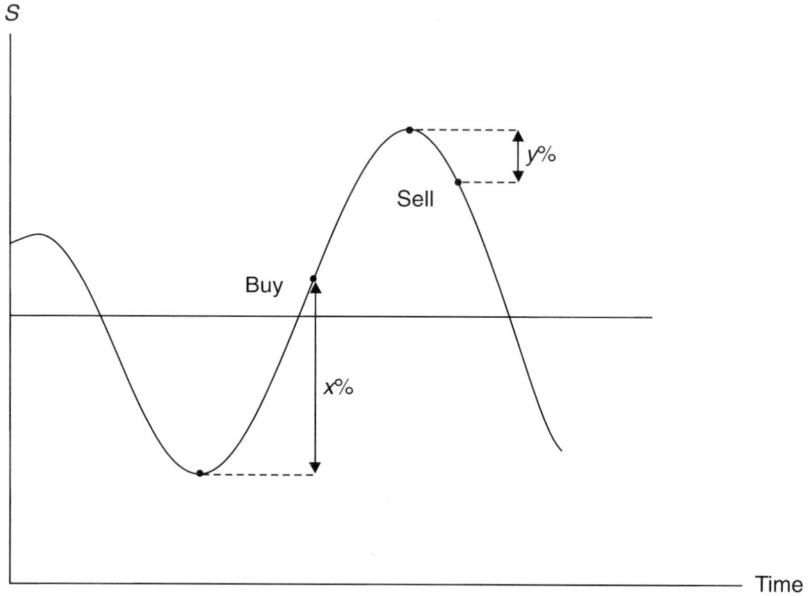

(b) Unprofitable *x–y* filter

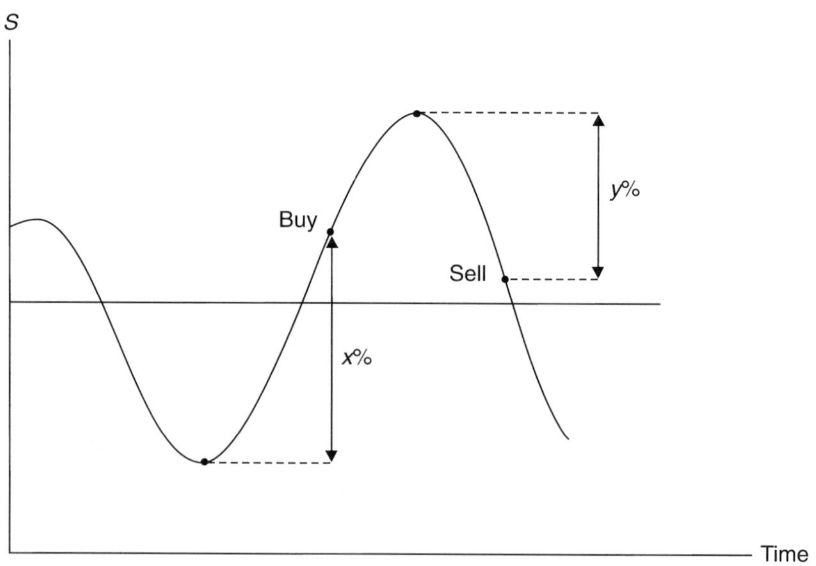

Figure 8.4 Profitable and unprofitable filter sizes (2)

(c) Breakeven *x–y* filter

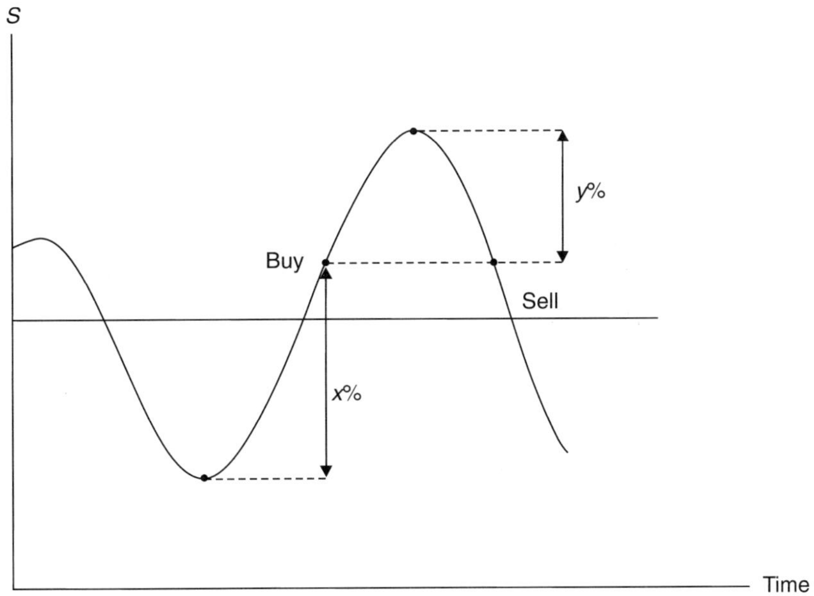

(d) Profitable *x–y* filter

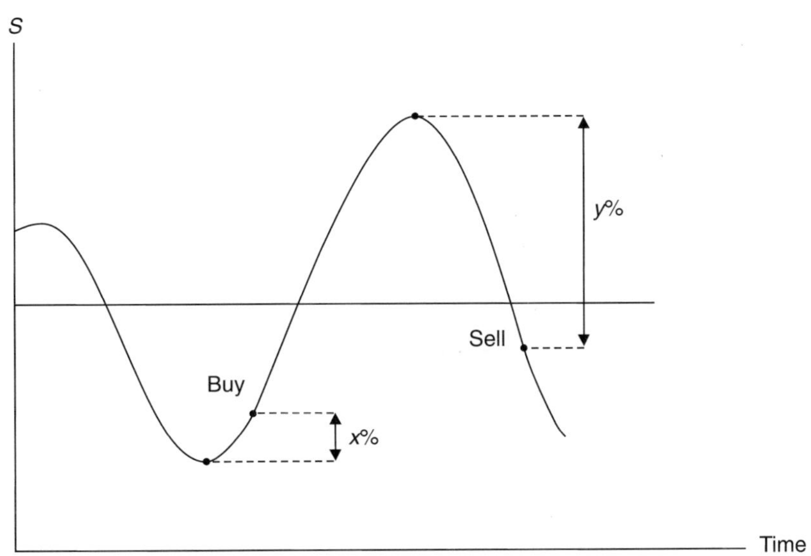

Figure 8.4 Profitable and unprofitable filter sizes (2) (cont.)

(e) Unprofitable x–y filter

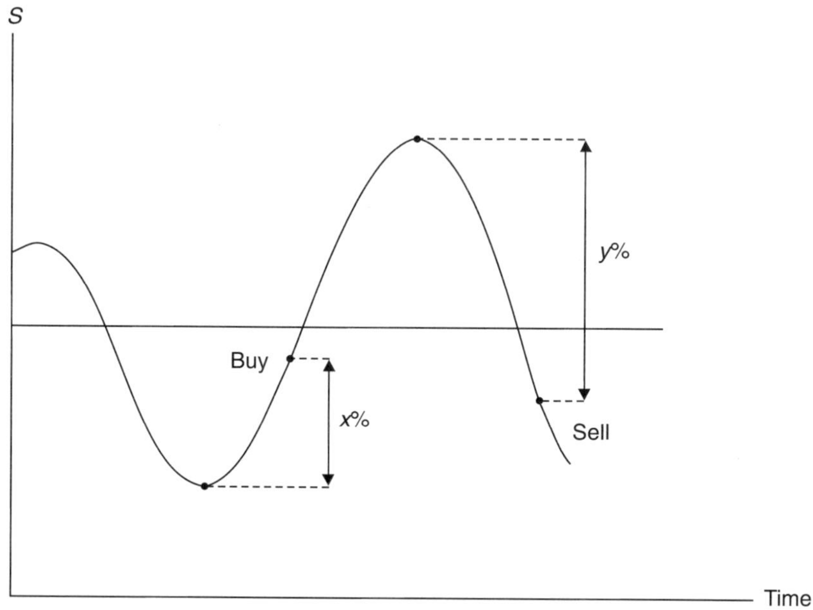

(f) Breakeven x–y filter

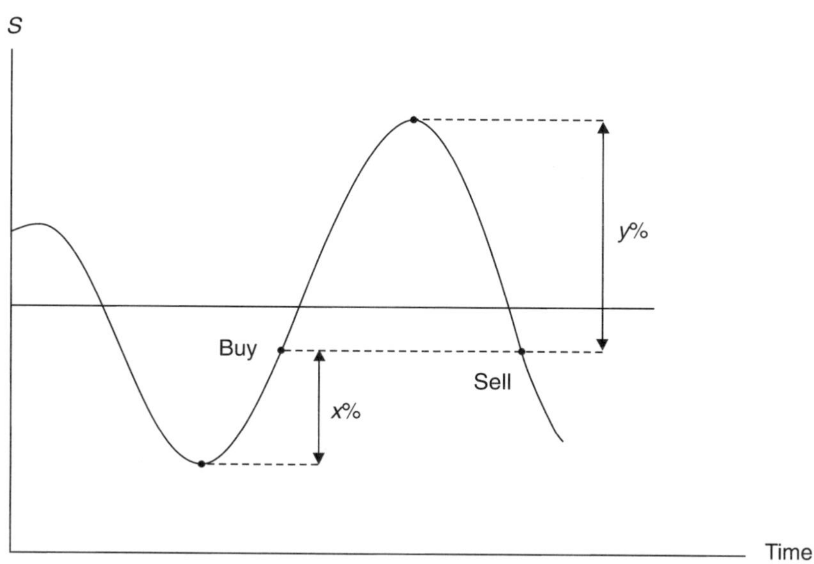

Figure 8.4 Profitable and unprofitable filter sizes (2) (cont.)

(a) Unprofitable filter in a bull market

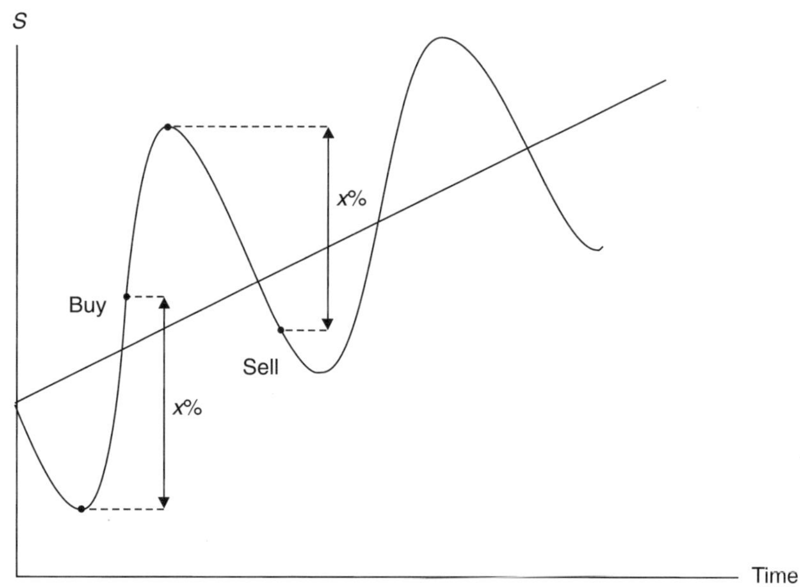

(b) Profitable filter in a bear market

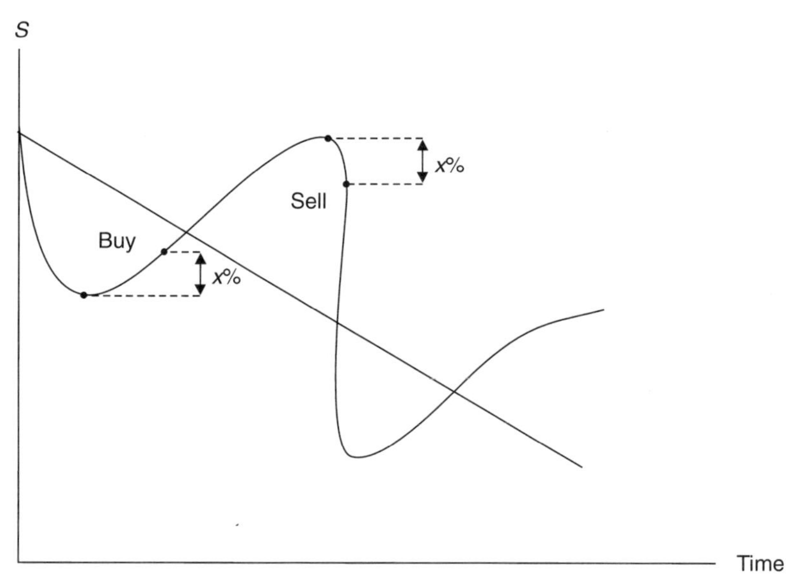

Figure 8.5 Filter rules in bull and bear markets

Let us now consider the issue for an x per cent rule in a more rigorous manner. It is assumed that the trough occurs at point in time t, while the peak occurs at point in time $t+n$ as shown in Figure 8.6. Hence, the buying rate will be $(1+x)S_t$, while the selling rate will be $(1-x)S_{t+n}$. It is further assumed that it takes the exchange rate j time periods to rise by x per cent from the trough and k time periods to fall by x per cent from the peak. Hence, the buying rate will prevail at time $t+j$, while the selling rate will prevail at $t+n+k$. Finally, it is assumed that the exchange rates corresponding to the peak and trough are related by the equation

$$S_{t+n} = (1+\theta)S_t \tag{8.7}$$

where θ is some sort of a measure of the amplitude of the exchange rate cycle. This means that we can express the selling rate in terms of the rate prevailing at the peak as $(1-x)(1+\theta)S_t$. The profit realised by buying the currency at $(1+x)S_t$ and selling it at $(1-x)(1+\theta)S_t$ is given by

$$\pi = [(1-x)(1+\theta) - (1+x)]S_t \tag{8.8}$$

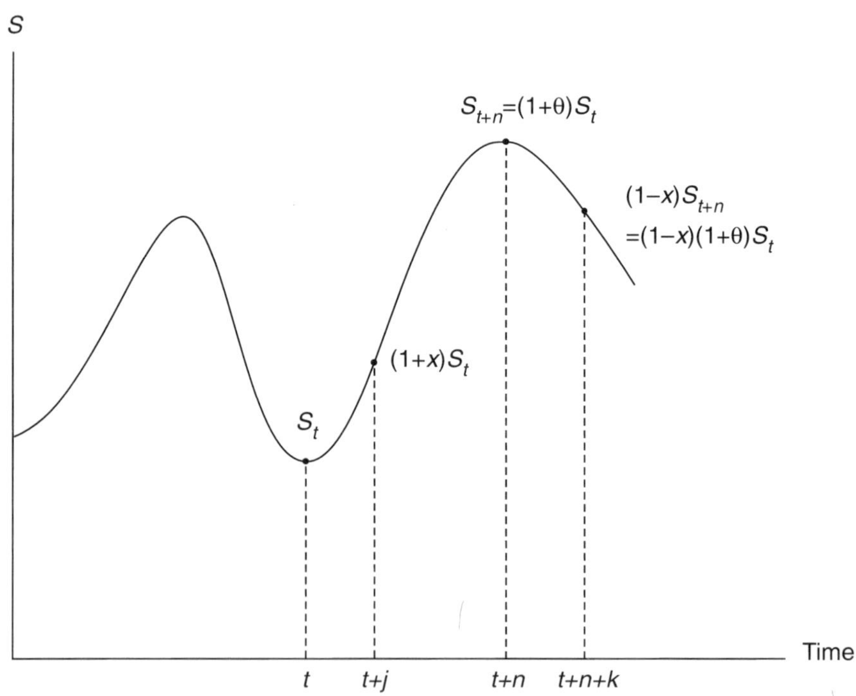

Figure 8.6 The analytics of filter rules

which means that the trading rule will be profitable if

$$(1-x)(1+\theta) > (1+x) \tag{8.9}$$

or if

$$1+\theta > \frac{1+x}{1-x} \tag{8.10}$$

The condition represented by equation (8.10) says that the exchange rate must rise by a minimum percentage (that is related to the filter size) between the trough and the peak in order for the rule to be profitable. This is illustrated in Figure 8.7, which shows that after the exchange rate rises by x per cent above the trough (giving a buy signal) it follows two alternative time paths: A and B. If it follows time path A it reaches a peak at $(1+\theta)S_t$ and gives a sell signal when it reaches the level $(1-x)(1+\theta)S_t$. In this case the operation is profitable. When it follows time path B, it reaches a peak at $(1+\lambda)S_t$ where $\lambda < \theta$. Hence the sell signal is given at $(1-x)(1+\lambda)S_t$, which makes the operation unprofitable.

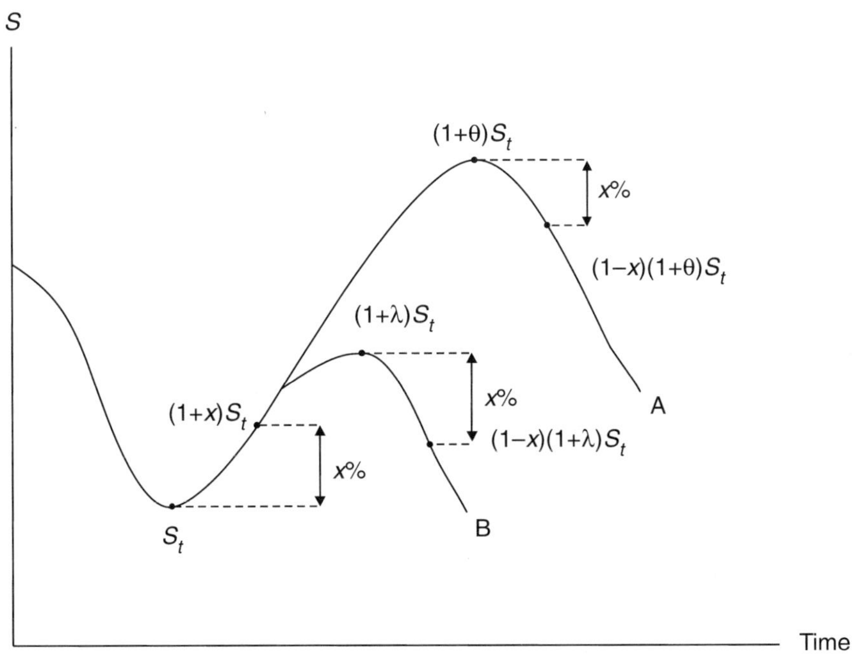

Figure 8.7 Profitable and unprofitable time paths

Table 8.1 Breakeven filter sizes corresponding to θ (per cent)

θ	1	2	3	4	5	6	7	8	9	10
x	0.48	0.99	1.48	1.96	2.44	2.91	3.38	3.85	4.31	4.76

The breakeven filter size is given by the equation

$$x = \frac{\theta}{2+\theta} \tag{8.11}$$

Table 8.1 reports the breakeven filter sizes corresponding to values of θ ranging from 1 to 10 per cent. This means that if the exchange rate rises by 5 per cent from trough to peak, then the breakeven filter size is 2.44 per cent. Notice that if θ is small then

$$x \approx \frac{\theta}{2} \tag{8.12}$$

Any filter size greater than $\theta/2$ will produce a loss while a filter size smaller than $\theta/2$ will produce profit.

Similar conclusions can be derived for an x–y filter. The filter size will be profitable if

$$1+\theta > \frac{1+x}{1-y} \tag{8.13}$$

The breakeven filter size is given by

$$\frac{1+x}{1-y} = 1+\theta \tag{8.14}$$

which can be satisfied by a combination of values for x and y. For example, if $\theta = 0.05$ (5 per cent), then possible breakeven filter sizes are 1–3.8 per cent and 3–1.9 per cent.

FILTER RULES WITH BID–OFFER SPREADS AND INTEREST RATES

We will now examine the effect, on the size and profitability of filters, of some factors that are normally overlooked in the literature on filter rules. We arrive at more complicated expressions for the breakeven filter sizes by allowing for bid–offer spreads and by introducing the role of interest rates. These modifications will be discussed in turn.

INTRODUCING THE BID–OFFER SPREAD IN THE EXCHANGE RATE

If we allow for the bid–offer spread in exchange rates, then the trader will buy at the offer rate and sell at the bid rate. Let the subscripts b and a denote the bid and offer rates respectively. Assuming that there is no change in the bid–offer spread between the buying and selling dates, the profit realised from an x per cent filter is calculated as

$$\pi = (1 - x)(1 + \theta)S_{b,t} - (1 + x)S_{a,t} \tag{8.15}$$

Assuming that the profit as calculated from equation (8.8) is based on the mid-rate, which is the average of the bid and offer rates, it follows that profit derived from the filter rule in the presence of the bid–offer spread is lower than otherwise. This is because $S_{b,t} < S_t$ and $S_{a,t} > S_t$. The explanation is very simple: the bid–offer spread is a form of transaction costs, which is bound to reduce the profitability of any operation. In the presence of the bid–offer spread, therefore, a filter rule will be profitable if

$$(1 - x)(1 + \theta)S_{b,t} > (1 + x)S_{a,t} \tag{8.16}$$

By definition we have

$$S_{a,t} = (1 + m)S_{b,t} \tag{8.17}$$

where m is the bid–offer spread measured in percentage terms. The condition for a profitable filter rule thus becomes

$$(1 - x)(1 + \theta)S_{b,t} > (1 + m)(1 + x)S_{b,t} \tag{8.18}$$

which means that the filter is profitable if

$$1 + \theta > (1 + m)\left[\frac{1 + x}{1 - x}\right] \tag{8.19}$$

By comparing the condition represented by (8.19) with the condition represented by (8.10), it is obvious that a higher value of θ is needed to satisfy (8.19) than to satisfy (8.10). The condition for a breakeven filter is

$$1 + \theta = (1 + m)\left[\frac{1 + x}{1 - x}\right] \tag{8.20}$$

which can be solved for x to obtain

$$x = \frac{\theta - m}{2 + \theta + m} \tag{8.21}$$

Table 8.2 Breakeven filter sizes corresponding to θ and m

θ	1	1	5	5	10	10
m	0.2	0.8	0.2	0.8	0.2	0.8
x	0.40	0.10	2.34	2.04	4.66	4.36

Equation (8.21) shows that the bid–offer spread plays a role in the determination of the size of breakeven filter. Table 8.2 shows the size of the breakeven filter for some values of θ and m. Thus, for each value of θ, the filter must be smaller than without the bid–offer spread. The higher the value of the spread the smaller the filter.

INTRODUCING INTEREST RATES

We now introduce the effect of interest rates on the profitability of filter rules. It is unfortunate, and perhaps strange, that the literature on the profitability of filter rules in the foreign exchange market has largely ignored the effect of interest rates. It seems that the reason for this neglect is the direct extrapolation of the technique from the stock market (where there is no explicit role for interest rates) to the foreign exchange market. But this neglect of interest rates necessarily implies that what is traded is cash rather than interest-bearing bank deposits. It is likely the case that long periods of time elapse between the generation of a buy and a sell signal. While the trader is waiting for a sell signal, it is unlikely that he or she will be sitting on a big cash position that does not earn interest. Rather, the position will be held as on call deposit, earning something like the overnight rate. Moreover, if the filter rule involves short positions, then the interest rate charged on borrowed funds will constitute a transaction cost. Hence, the interest rates on the currencies bought and sold must be an important factor in the determination of the profitability or otherwise of a filter of a certain size. Another reason for the neglect of the effect of interest rates is perhaps the belief that the interest rate differential is only a small part of the total cost or profit, and so it can be ignored for practical purposes. Again, there is no reason to believe that this is the case.

Let us initially introduce the interest rates without making any distinction between the bid and offer interest rates (or the lending and borrowing rates). We will also assume no bid–offer spread in exchange rates. Consider a trader who is buying and selling a foreign currency with an interest rate i^* against a domestic currency with an interest rate i. With reference to Figure 8.6, applying a filter rule, which involves taking short and long positions, requires the following steps:

1. At time $t+j$ the trader gets a buy signal. He reacts by going short on (that is, borrowing) the domestic currency and going long on (buying with the proceeds) the foreign currency. The amount of the foreign currency obtained (for each unit of the domestic currency) is

$$X_1 = \frac{1}{(1+x)S_t} \tag{8.22}$$

2. The amount of foreign currency obtained is invested at the foreign interest rate, i^*, for a duration falling between $t+j$ and $t+n+k$, that is for $n+k-j$ periods, to obtain

$$X_2 = \frac{1}{(1+x)S_t}(1+i^*)^{n+k-j} \tag{8.23}$$

3. When the sell signal is given at $t+n+k$, the foreign currency is sold at $(1-x)(1+\theta)S_t$ to obtain an amount of the domestic currency that is given by

$$X_3 = \frac{(1-x)(1+\theta)S_t}{(1+x)S_t}(1+i^*)^{n+k-j} \tag{8.24}$$

4. At $t+n+k$ the short position must be covered, that is the loan (principal and interest) must be repaid. The amount due is calculated as

$$X_4 = (1+i)^{n+k-j} \tag{8.25}$$

The operation is then completed. The profit realised from the operation is given by

$$\pi = X_3 - X_4 = \frac{(1-x)(1+\theta)S_t}{(1+x)S_t}(1+i^*)^{n+k-j} - (1+i)^{n+k-j} \tag{8.26}$$

Thus, the operation is profitable if

$$\frac{(1-x)(1+\theta)}{(1+x)}(1+i^*)^{n+k-j} - (1+i)^{n+k-j} > 0 \tag{8.27}$$

or if

$$1+\theta > \left(\frac{1+x}{1-x}\right)\left[\frac{(1+i)}{(1+i^*)}\right]^{n+k-j} \tag{8.28}$$

Table 8.3 Breakeven filter sizes corresponding to θ, i, i^* and $n+k-j$

θ	5	5	10	10
i	5	10	5	10
i^*	4	2	4	2
$n+k-j$	60	180	60	180
x	2.4	0.5	4.7	2.8

The breakeven filter size is therefore given by

$$x = \frac{(1+\theta)(1+i^*)^{n+k-j} - (1+i)^{n+k-j}}{(1+\theta)(1+i^*)^{n+k-j} + (1+i)^{n+k-j}} \tag{8.29}$$

Table 8.3 shows the breakeven filter size for combinations of θ, i, i^* and $n+k-j$ (measured in days, if we are considering daily data). For a constant θ, the filter size declines as the interest rate differential $(i-i^*)$ rises and as the period between the buy and sell signals gets longer.

INTRODUCING THE BID–OFFER SPREAD IN EXCHANGE AND INTEREST RATES

We will now introduce the bid–offer spread in both interest and exchange rates. The operation involves the following steps:

1. At time $t+j$ the trader gets a buy signal. He reacts by going short on the domestic currency and going long on the foreign currency. Since he buys the foreign currency at the offer exchange rate, the amount of the foreign currency obtained is

$$X_1 = \frac{1}{(1+x)S_{a,t}} \tag{8.30}$$

2. The amount of foreign currency obtained is invested at the foreign bid interest rate, i_b^*, for a duration falling between $t+j$ and $t+n+k$, that is for $n+k-j$ periods, to obtain

$$X_2 = \frac{1}{(1+x)S_{a,t}}(1+i_b^*)^{n+k-j} \tag{8.31}$$

3. When the sell signal is given at $t+n+k$, the foreign currency is sold at $(1-x)(1+\theta)S_{b,t}$ to obtain an amount of the domestic currency that is given by

$$X_3 = \frac{(1-x)(1+\theta)S_{b,t}}{(1+x)S_{a,t}}(1+i_b^*)^{n+k-j} \tag{8.32}$$

4. At $t+n+k$ the short position must be covered. The amount due is calculated as

$$X_4 = (1+i_a)^{n+k-j} \tag{8.33}$$

The operation is then completed. The profit realised from the operation is given by

$$\pi = X_3 - X_4 = \frac{(1-x)(1+\theta)S_{b,t}}{(1+x)(1+m)S_{b,t}}(1+i_b^*)^{n+k-j} - (1+i_a)^{n+k-j} \tag{8.34}$$

Thus, the operation is profitable if

$$\frac{(1-x)(1+\theta)}{(1+x)(1+m)}(1+i_b^*)^{n+k-j} - (1+i_a)^{n+k-j} > 0 \tag{8.35}$$

or if

$$1+\theta > \left[\frac{(1+x)(1+m)}{(1-x)}\right]\left[\frac{(1+i_a)}{(1+i_b^*}\right]^{n+k-j} \tag{8.36}$$

The breakeven filter size is therefore given by

$$x = \frac{(1+\theta)(1+i_b^*)^{n+k-j} - (1+m)(1+i_a)^{n+k-j}}{(1+\theta)(1+i_b^*)^{n+k-j} + (1+m)(1+i_a)^{n+k-j}} \tag{8.37}$$

Since $i_b^* < i$, $i_a > i$ and $m > 0$, it follows that the breakeven filter as given by equation (8.37) is smaller than what is given by equation (8.29). It is also clear that the right-hand side of (8.36) is greater than the right-hand side of (8.28). The implication is that the exchange rate must rise more than in the case without bid–offer spreads to produce a profitable filter. This is because the bid–offer spread is a transaction cost.

MOVING AVERAGE RULES

The moving average rule is a mechanical trading rule that is based on buy–sell signals derived from the behaviour of the exchange rate relative to one or more moving averages of a certain order. Suppose that we observe the exchange rate, S_t, over discrete time intervals, $t = 0, 1, 2, 3, \ldots, T$.

A moving average of order (length) q at time t can be measured as

$$M_t(q) = \frac{1}{q}\sum_{i=0}^{q-1} S_{t-i} \tag{8.38}$$

This is called the simple moving average and it is in essence the moving arithmetic mean. This is the moving average most widely used by technical analysts because it easy to calculate and at the same time it is fairly effective.

The weighted moving average is used rather than the simple moving average if it is believed that more relevant information is embodied in the most recent observations. A weighted moving average is calculated by assigning heavier weights to more recent observations. Notice that the implicit assumption in the calculation of the simple moving average is that all observations convey the same information, and so they are equally weighted. The weighted moving average is calculated as

$$M_t(q) = \frac{1}{q}\sum_{i=0}^{q-1} w_i S_{t-i} \tag{8.39}$$

A special case of the weighted moving average is the exponentially smoothed moving average in which each weight is a fixed proportion of the preceding weight. The exponentially smoothed moving average is calculated as

$$M_t(q) = \frac{1}{q}\sum_{i=0}^{q-1} \alpha(1-\alpha)^i S_{t-i} \tag{8.40}$$

where $0 < \alpha < 1$. This means that the current exchange rate is assigned a weight of α, while the previous period's exchange rate is assigned a weight of $\alpha(1-\alpha)$, and so on.

THE SINGLE AND DOUBLE MOVING AVERAGE RULES

According to the single moving average rule, buy and sell signals are indicated by the intersection of the time paths of the exchange rate and a moving average of some order. This proposition can be illustrated with the help of Figure 8.8 that shows the theoretical behaviour of the exchange rate and the moving average (S_t and M_t respectively). Prior to t_1 the moving average is above the exchange rate, that is $S_t < M_t$ or $S_t - M_t < 0$. This relationship is reversed following the intersection at t_1 where $S_t > M_t$ or $S_t - M_t > 0$. At t_1, there is an intersection of the moving average and the

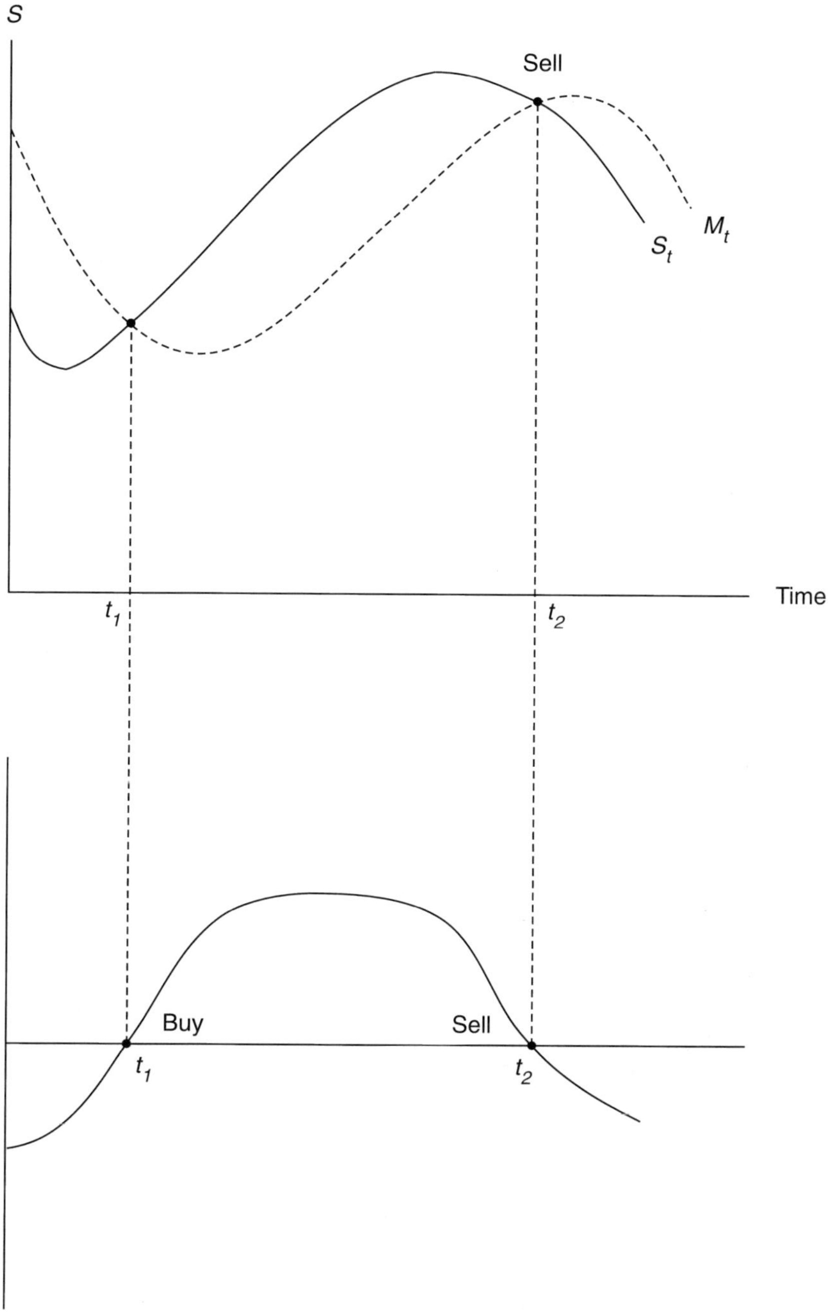

Figure 8.8 The single moving average rule

exchange rate such that the former cuts the latter from above. This is a buy signal. At points in time after t_2 (at which the moving average cuts the exchange rate from below) the relationship is reversed once more, that is $S_t < M_t$ or $S_t - M_t < 0$. This is a sell signal. Therefore, the single moving average rule implies that the trader should buy at t_1 and sell at t_2. This buy–sell transaction is obviously profitable as shown in the diagram, since the sell exchange rate is higher than the buy exchange rate. The buy and sell signals are also indicated by the behaviour of the difference between the exchange rate and the moving average, which is shown in the lower part of Figure 8.8. The buy signal is indicated when the difference cuts the horizontal axis from below and the buy signal is indicated when the former cuts the latter from above.

The rule can be generalised as follows:

1. Buy when the moving average cuts the exchange rate from above, that is when

$$S_t = M_t \quad \text{or} \quad S_t - M_t = 0 \tag{8.41}$$

and

$$S_{t-1} < M_{t-1} \quad \text{or} \quad S_{t-1} - M_{t-1} < 0 \tag{8.42}$$

2. Sell when the moving average cuts the exchange rate from below, that is when

$$S_t = M_t \quad \text{or} \quad S_t - M_t = 0 \tag{8.43}$$

and

$$S_{t-1} > M_{t-1} \quad \text{or} \quad S_t - M_t > 0 \tag{8.44}$$

The exchange rates indicated by the points of intersection may not be observable, in which case the buy and sell rates are those observed immediately after the intersection. If this is the case then the conditions represented by (8.41) and (8.43) may be rewritten as inequalities of the form

$$S_t \geq M_t \quad \text{or} \quad S_t - M_t \geq 0 \tag{8.45}$$

and

$$S_t \leq M_t \quad \text{or} \quad S_t - M_t \leq 0 \tag{8.46}$$

In terms of the lower part of Figure 8.8, a buy signal is indicated by a change in the sign of the difference from negative to positive, and a sell signal is indicated by a change in the sign from positive to negative. The quantity $(S_t - M_t)/M_t$ can be used as a quantitative technical indicator. If this quantity is more than a certain percentage (about 3.5 per cent) then the exchange rate is rising faster than normal, implying significant bullishness. If, on the other hand, it is lower than 3.5 per cent, then a significant bearishness is suggested. Figure 8.9 shows the behaviour of the GBP/USD exchange rate using 100 daily observations ending on 6 March 1998 with a 10-day moving average superimposed. Figure 8.10 shows the behaviour of the difference between the exchange rate and the moving average where the intersection points with the horizontal axis indicate buy and sell signals.

The double moving average rule works in exactly the same way except that the buy and sell signals are indicated by the intersection of two moving averages: a short moving average M_t^s and a long moving average, M_t^ℓ. The double moving average rule may be stated as follows:

1. Buy when the long moving average cuts the short moving average from above, that is when

$$M_t^s = M_t^\ell \quad \text{or} \quad M_t^s - M_t^\ell = 0 \tag{8.47}$$

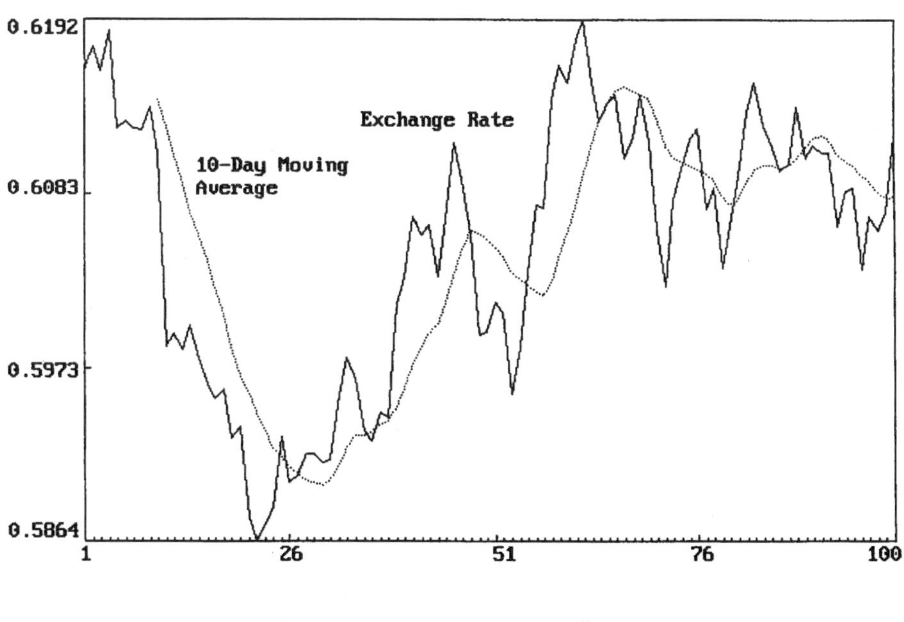

Figure 8.9 The GBP/USD exchange rate (daily observations ending 6 March 1998)

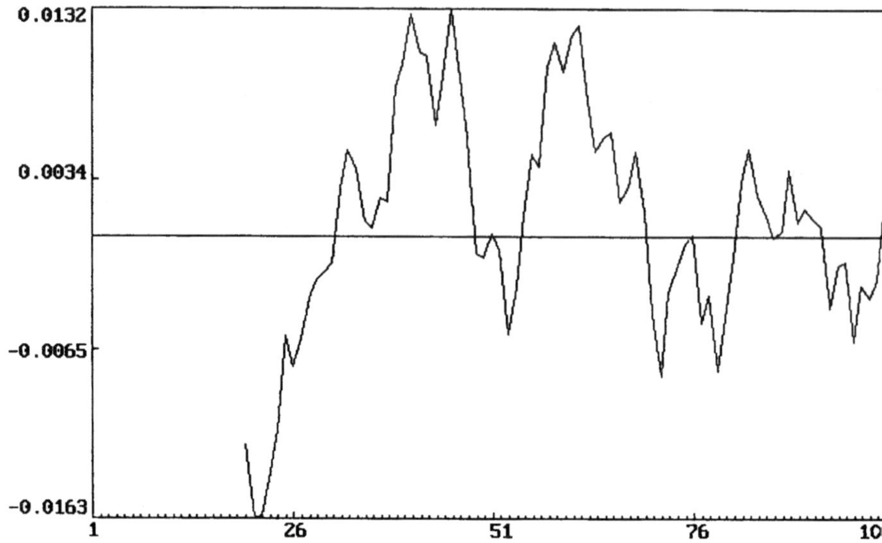

Figure 8.10 Difference between the GBP/USD exchange rate and the 10-day moving average

and

$$M^s_{t-1} < M^\ell_{t-1} \quad \text{or} \quad M^s_{t-1} - M^\ell_{t-1} < 0 \tag{8.48}$$

2. Sell when the long moving average cuts the short moving average from below, that is when

$$M^s_t = M^\ell_t \quad \text{or} \quad M^s_t - M^\ell_t = 0 \tag{8.49}$$

and

$$M^s_t > M^\ell_t \quad \text{or} \quad M^s_t - M^\ell_t > 0 \tag{8.50}$$

Figure 8.8 can be used to illustrate the double moving average rule by replacing M_t and S_t with M^ℓ_t and M^s_t respectively. Figure 8.11 shows a 10-day and a 20-day moving average for the same data set shown in Figure 8.9. Figure 8.12 shows the behaviour of the difference between the short moving average and the long moving average ($M^s_t - M^\ell_t$). Again, the points of intersection with the horizontal axis indicate buy and sell signals.

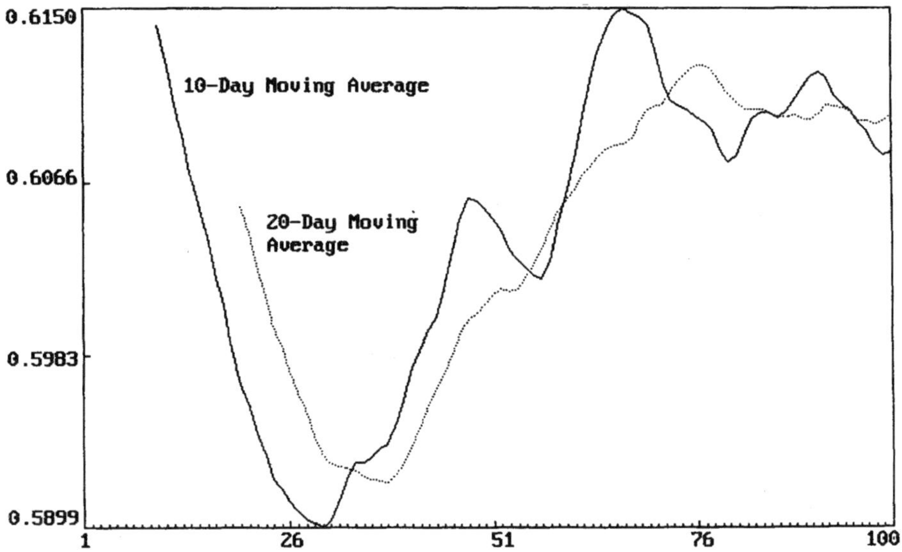

Figure 8.11 10-day and 20-day moving averages of the GBP/USD exchange rate

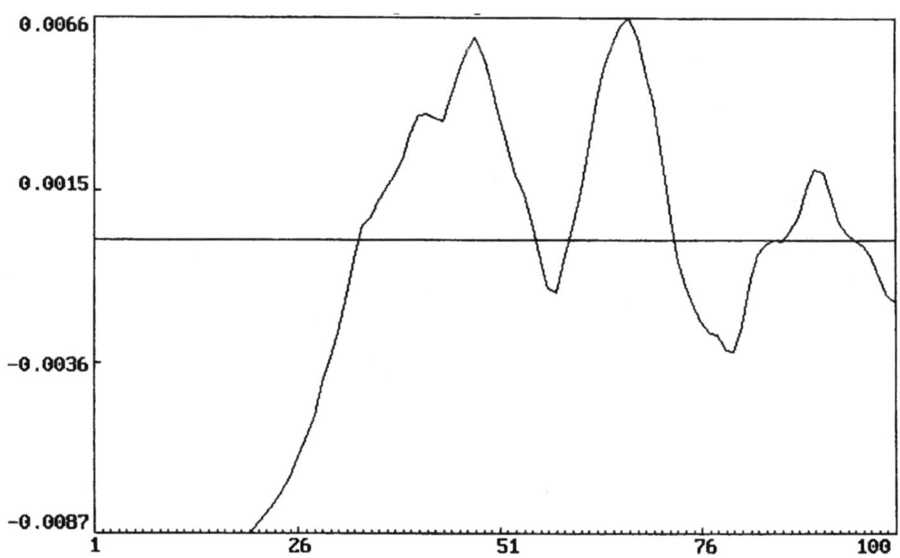

Figure 8.12 Difference between the 10-day and 20-day moving averages

TRADING RULES BASED ON QUANTITATIVE TECHNICAL INDICATORS

It is possible to devise trading rules on the basis of the quantitative technical indicators we came across in Chapter 7. Hence, we may have an oscillator rule, an *RSI* rule and a stochastics rule. These rules, which are illustrated in Figure 8.13, work as follows.

OSCILLATOR RULE

Buy when the oscillator cuts the midway line from below and sell when the former cuts the latter from above.

RSI RULE

Buy when the *RSI* line goes below 30 and sell when it goes above 70.

STOCHASTICS RULE

Buy when the K line touches 0 and sell when it touches 100.

FUNDAMENTAL TRADING RULES

Fundamental trading rules are based on one or more economic models that describe the relationship between the exchange rate and its determining factors. The profitability or otherwise of these rules, therefore, depends on the validity of the underlying economic models. These models presumably define an equilibrium exchange rate, and the trading rule is based on deviations of the actual rate from the equilibrium rate. The trading rule generates a buy signal when the currency is undervalued (that is, when the exchange rate is below the level predicted by the model) and a sell signal when the currency is overvalued. The underlying idea is that if the currency is undervalued, it is likely to appreciate and if it is overvalued then it is likely to depreciate. The rule may have a quantitative dimension, that is a buy signal is given if the exchange rate is below its equilibrium level by x per cent and a sell signal is given when the exchange rate is above its equilibrium level by x per cent. Figure 8.14 describes the working of a fundamental rule that is based on the behaviour of the actual and the equilibrium exchange rates (S and $\bar{S}$). The latter may be fixed or changing.

Formally, the equilibrium level of the exchange rate is determined by a vector of variables, X. Thus

$$\bar{S}_t = f(X_t) \tag{8.51}$$

(a) Oscillator rule

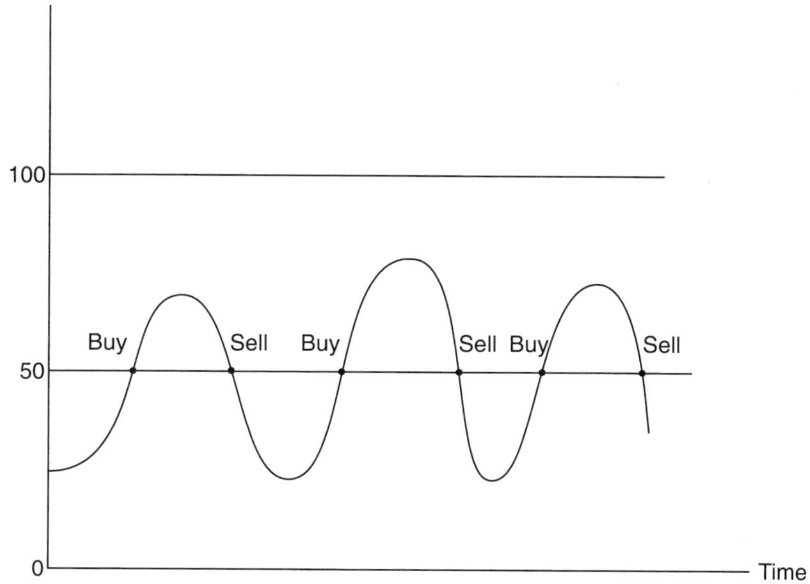

(b) *RSI* rule

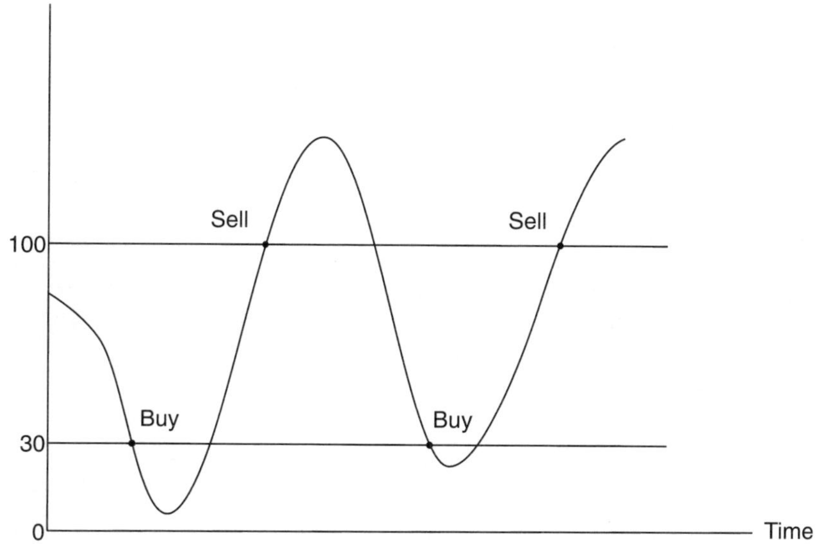

Figure 8.13 Trading rules based on quantitative technical indicators

(c) Stochastics rule (K line)

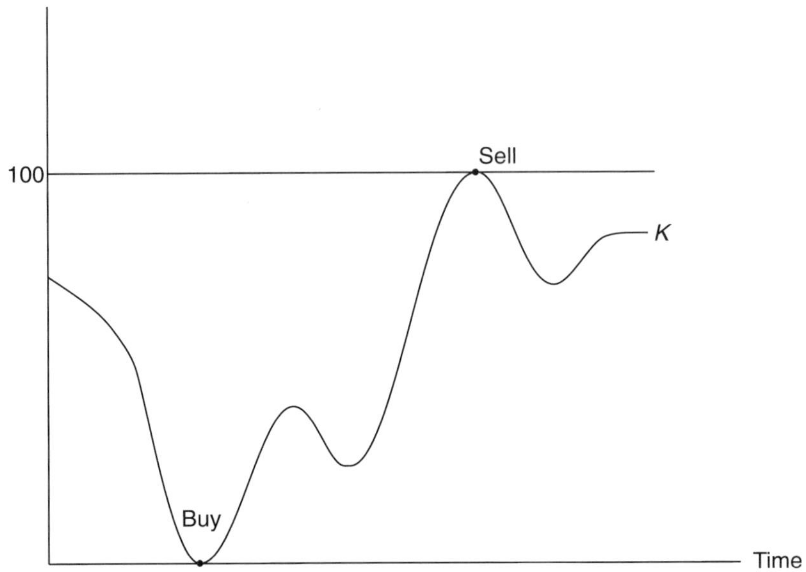

Figure 8.13 Trading rules based on quantitative technical indicators (cont.)

The current level of the exchange rate may deviate from the equilibrium level because of random shocks that tend to have a temporary effect. Hence, the current level of the exchange rate may be represented by

$$S_t = \bar{S}_t + \varepsilon_t \tag{8.52}$$

where ε_t is a random term. Thus, the currency is undervalued when $S_t < \bar{S}_t$ and overvalued when $S_t > \bar{S}_t$. If a quantitative dimension is added to the rule then a buy signal is generated when the exchange rate is lower than the equilibrium rate by a certain percentage, say x. Hence, the buy signal is generated when

$$S_t = (1 - x)\bar{S}_t \tag{8.53}$$

while the sell signal is generated when

$$S_t = (1 + x)\bar{S}_t \tag{8.54}$$

(a) Fixed equilibrium rate

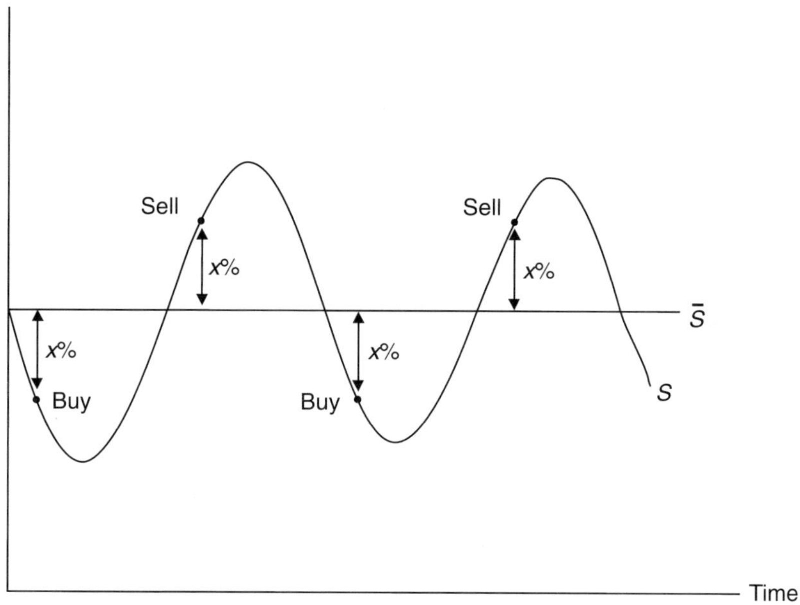

(b) Changing equilibrium rate

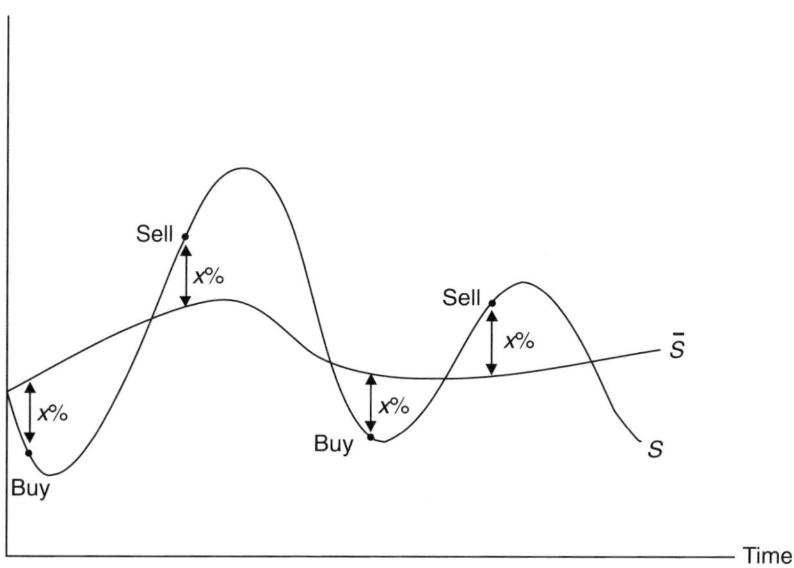

Figure 8.14 An *x* per cent fundamental rule

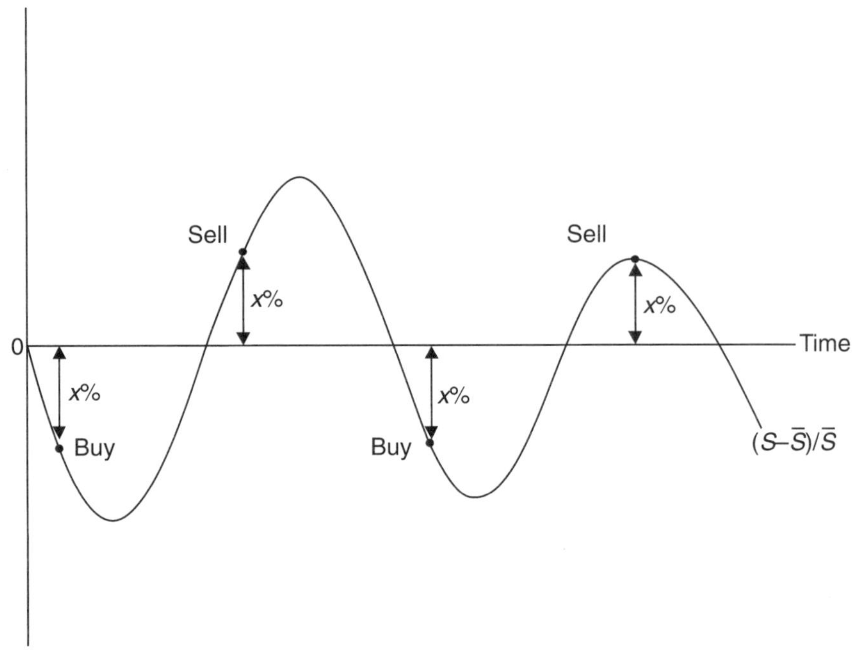

Figure 8.15 An x per cent fundamental rule based on the deviation of the actual rate from the equilibrium rate

Alternatively, the conditions for buy and sell signals can be written respectively as

$$S_t - (1 - x)\bar{S}_t = 0 \tag{8.55}$$

and

$$S_t - (1 + x)\bar{S}_t = 0 \tag{8.56}$$

The conditions for the buy and sell signals as represented by (8.55) and (8.56) are derived graphically from the behaviour of the difference between the actual rate and the equilibrium rate. This is shown in Figure 8.15, which shows that buy and sell signals are generated whenever S deviates from $\bar{S}$ by x per cent.

The question that arises here is how to determine the equilibrium level of the exchange rate. This naturally depends on the vector of explanatory variable, X, as postulated by various economic models. This is why we may have the following trading rules.

PURCHASING POWER PARITY (PPP) RULE

This rule is based on an equilibrium exchange rate that is determined, according to PPP, by prices or inflation rates. Hence, the equilibrium exchange rate is calculated as

$$\bar{S}_t = S_0 \left[\frac{1 + \dot{P}_t}{1 + \dot{P}_t^*} \right] \tag{8.57}$$

where 0 is a base period and the dot implies the rate of change between 0 and t. Hence, $\dot{P}$ is the domestic inflation rate while $\dot{P}^*$ is the foreign inflation rate. Since prices are not volatile and move smoothly over time, this rule does not generate many buy and sell signals over a short period of time. This is because once the exchange rate is overvalued or undervalued according to PPP, it tends to remain so for a long time, as the process of mean reversion is rather slow. Hence, this rule can only be used for trading over long periods of time.

UNCOVERED INTEREST PARITY (UIP) RULE

In this rule the equilibrium exchange rate is determined according to uncovered interest parity, that is by the interest rate differential. Thus, the equilibrium exchange rate is calculated as

$$\bar{S}_t = S_{t-1} \left[\frac{1 + i_{t-1}}{1 + i_{t-1}^*} \right] \tag{8.58}$$

where i is the domestic interest rate and i^* is the foreign interest rate. Since interest rates change more frequently than prices, this rule can be used over a short period of time.

THE FORWARD RATE RULE

This rule is based on the unbiased efficiency hypothesis that the forward rate is an unbiased and efficient forecaster of the spot exchange rate. On average, the spot exchange rate should be equal to the forward rate prevailing in the previous period. Hence, the equilibrium exchange rate must be calculated according to the equation

$$\bar{S}_t = F_{t-1} \tag{8.59}$$

where F_{t-1} is the forward exchange rate in the previous period.

MIXED FUNDAMENTAL RULES

A mixed fundamental rule can be devised by using two or more of the rules in combination. Suppose, for example, that a trader believes that the exchange rate is determined by a combination of inflation rates, interest rates and the forward rate. Suppose further that the trader has certain weights in mind as to the effect of each of these variables on the exchange rate. In a mixed PPP–UIP–forward rate rule the equilibrium exchange rate is determined by the equation

$$\bar{S}_t = w_1\left[S_0\left(\frac{1+\dot{P}_t}{1+\dot{P}_t^*}\right)\right] + w_2\left[S_{t-1}\left(\frac{1+i_{t-1}}{1+i_{t-1}^*}\right)\right] + w_3F_{t-1} \quad (8.60)$$

where w_1, w_2 and w_3 are the weights assigned respectively to PPP, UIP and the forward rate in the determination of the equilibrium exchange rate respectively such that $w_1 + w_2 + w_3 = 1$.

COMPARING FUNDAMENTAL AND TECHNICAL RULES

By comparing an x per cent fundamental rule with a y per cent filter rule, it can be demonstrated that they can lead to inconsistent decisions as well as different levels of profitability. For simplicity we will assume that, between the trough and the peak, the exchange rate rises by a percentage, θ, which is greater than either x or y.

Four possibilities are illustrated in Figure 8.16, assuming that the equilibrium exchange rate is constant. In Figure 8.16(a) the fundamental rule gives a buy signal earlier than the filter rule, but the two rules turn out to be equally profitable. In Figure 8.16(b) the use of a large filter produces an unprofitable filter rule at a time when the fundamental rule is profitable. In Figure 8.16(c) the technical rule is more profitable than the fundamental rule, while in Figure 8.16(d) the fundamental rule is more profitable than the filter rule.

MEASURING THE PROFITABILITY OF TRADING RULES

The objective of this exercise is to find out whether or not a trader can outperform the market by following this trading rule, that is whether or not the trader can achieve a higher rate of return by following the trading rule than by adopting the passive strategy of buy and hold. Thus, we need a method whereby comparable rates of return can be calculated. This method is illustrated below.

(a) Equally profitable

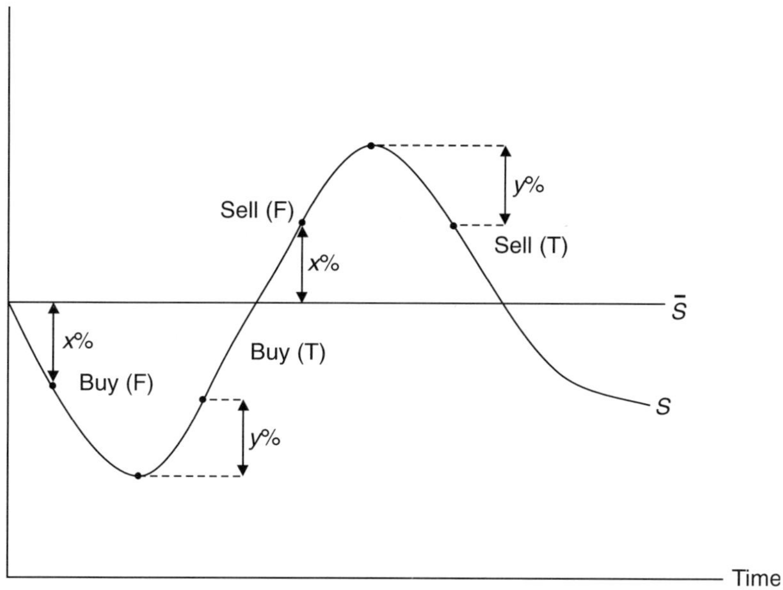

(b) Profitable fundamental rule and unprofitable technical rule

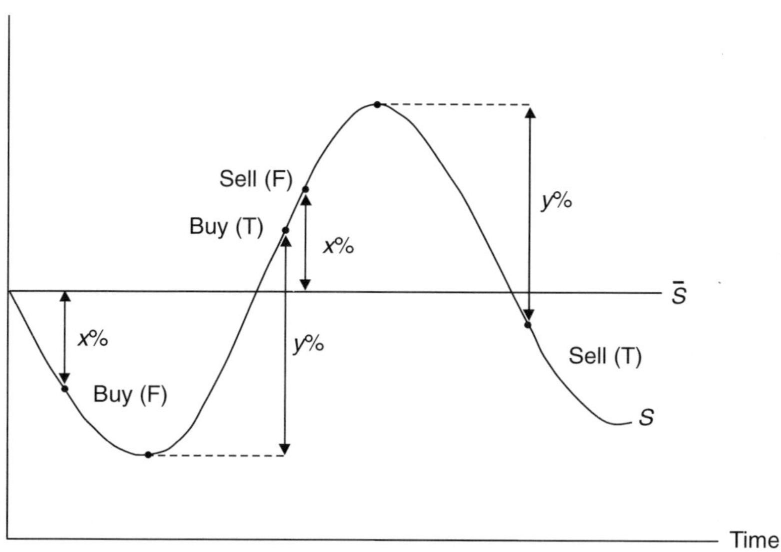

Figure 8.16 Comparing an x per cent fundamental rule with a y per cent technical rule (constant equilibrium rate)

(c) Technical rule more profitable

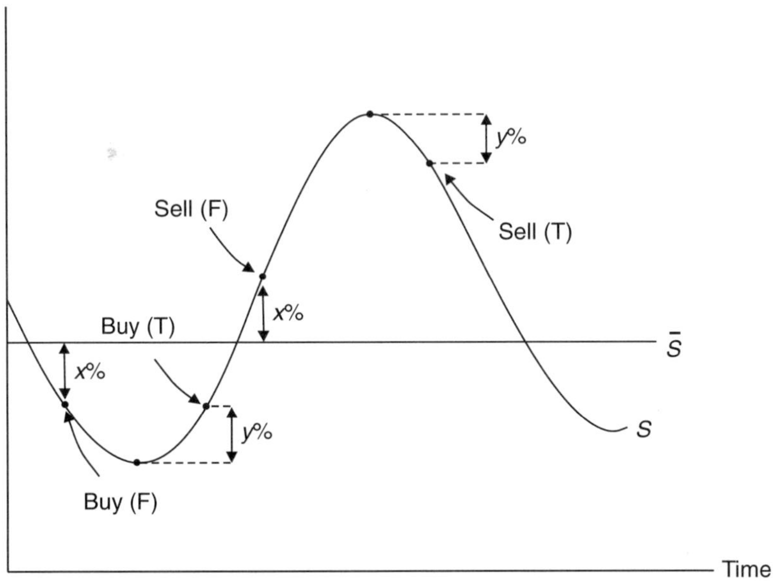

(d) Fundamental rule more profitable

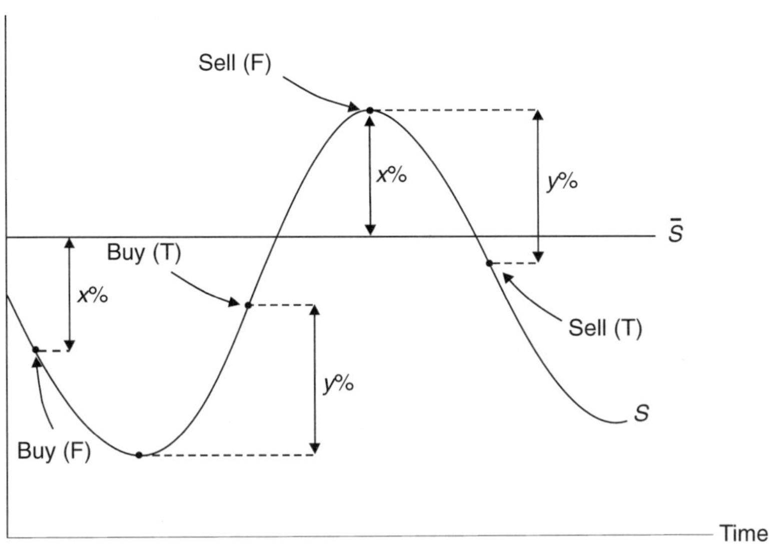

Figure 8.16 Comparing an *x* per cent fundamental rule with a *y* per cent technical rule (constant equilibrium rate) (cont.)

For simplicity we will ignore the bid–offer spread and the interest rate differential. If, by adopting the trading rule, the buying takes place at time 1 and the selling takes place at time 2, the rate of return over the period extending between 1 and 2, R_1^2, is given by

$$R_1^2 = \frac{S_2}{S_1} - 1 \tag{8.61}$$

which can be generalised to buying and selling at any two points in time, t and $t + k$, as

$$R_t^{t+k} = \frac{S_{t+k}}{S_t} - 1 \tag{8.62}$$

Now, let us imagine that an initial amount of (domestic currency) capital, X_0, is allocated to currency trading. Assume that over some period of time the rule gives a buy signal at 1 and a sell signal at 2, followed by a buy signal at 4 and a sell signal at 7. If this is the case then the value of the accumulated (domestic currency) capital at time 7 is given by

$$X_7 = X_0\left(1 + R_1^2\right)\left(1 + R_4^7\right) \tag{8.63}$$

Equation (8.63) can be generalised for m buy and sell signals occurring over a time period extending between $t = 0$ and $t = T$ as follows:

$$X_T = X_0 \prod_{i=1}^{m} R_i \tag{8.64}$$

where $R_i = R_{T-s}^{T-k}$ and $R_m = R_{T-\ell}^{T}$ such that $s > k$ and $k > \ell$. The underlying assumption is that the first buy and sell transactions take place at times $T - s$ and $T - k$ respectively, while the last of these transactions take place at $T - \ell$ and T respectively.

If brokerage fees are charged to the seller at the rate of τ per cent of the value of the transaction, then

$$X_T = X_0 \prod_{i=1}^{m} R_i(1 - \tau) \tag{8.65}$$

In both cases (with or without brokerage fees), the rate of return on the entire period can be calculated from the values of the capital at the beginning and the end of the period as

$$R_{T-s}^{T} = \frac{X_T}{X_0} - 1 \tag{8.66}$$

On the other hand, a buy and hold strategy implies that the foreign currency is bought and sold only once. If the buy and sell exchange rates correspond to the first buy exchange rate and the last sell exchange rate applicable to the trading rule then

$$X_T = X_0 R_{T-s}^T \tag{8.67}$$

If brokerage fees are charged then

$$R_{T-s}^T = \frac{S_T(1-\tau)}{S_{T-s}} - 1 \tag{8.68}$$

By comparing the rates of return realised from the trading rule and the buy and hold strategy it is possible to determine whether or not it is a good idea to adopt the rule. The same methodology can be used to determine the optimal filter size or the order of the moving average from historical data. These are the size or the order producing the highest rate of return.

EMPIRICAL EVIDENCE ON THE PROFITABILITY OF TRADING RULES

A large number of studies have been conducted to find out whether or not mechanical trading rules are profitable. The motivation for these studies has been largely the investigation of the efficiency of financial markets. For, if financial markets were efficient, mechanical trading rules could not consistently produce profit over and above what is produced by a passive buy and hold strategy. Put differently, if the market is efficient and uncovered interest parity holds then the interest rate costs of a trading strategy based on a trading rule should on average eliminate profit. The evidence on this issue has been rather mixed.

In the early applications of filter rules to the stock market, the evidence was rather inconsistent. Alexander (1961, 1964) presented evidence for the ability of mechanical trading rules to 'beat the market', although transaction costs would consume all of the profit. In contrast, Fama and Blume (1966) concluded that filter rules did not produce any profit. Following the Fama–Blume study, the mainstream academic view was that mechanical trading rules did not work. In fact, Fama (1970) dismissed technical analysis as a futile undertaking. In a more recent study, Brock *et al.* (1992) considered the performance of various simple moving average rules in the absence of transaction costs. They concluded that the rules identify periods in which it is wise to be in the market, when returns are high and volatility is low.

Studies applying filter rules to the foreign exchange market using daily data produced some evidence for the profitability of these rules. These studies include Cornell and Dietrich (1978), Dooley and Shafer (1983) and Logue *et al.* (1978). Sweeney (1986) used a risk-adjusted test to present evidence for the profitability of filter rules. Some evidence has also been found for the profitability of moving average rules in the foreign exchange market. Surajaras and Sweeney (1992) found that single and double moving average rules produced significant out-of-sample profit that was on average larger than what is produced by following a filter rule. Moreover, Bilson (1981) and Sweeney and Lee (1990) found profit from trading rules in the forward foreign exchange market. Further favourable but indirect evidence is provided by Engle and Hamilton (1990) who demonstrated that the dollar from the early 1970s to the late 1980s was susceptible to 'long swings' or largely uninterrupted trends which are susceptible to mechanical trading rules. It remains the case, however, that the optimal filter rule size could not be chosen *ex ante*, and that there are often important elements of riskiness in that substantial subperiod losses are often generated.

In a recent study, Allen and Karjalainen (1999) crticised these studies on the grounds that the *ad hoc ex post* specification of trading rules can lead to biased test results. They argue that genetic algorithms can be used to derive trading rules that are not *ad hoc* but in a sense optimal. They further argue that this approach avoids the potential bias caused by *ex post* selection 'because the rules are chosen by a machine learning algorithm using price data available before the start of the test period'. However, their results confirm those of previous studies, suggesting that markets are efficient in the sense that it is not possible to make money after transaction costs by using technical trading rules.

9: Recent Developments: Chaos and Neural Networks

INTRODUCTION

This chapter deals with some recent developments that are not specifically related to exchange rate forecasting. Rather, they are new developments that originated in the biological and physical sciences and then were imported to economics and finance. These two topics are dealt with in one chapter not because they are inherently related, but because they are new developments that have some implications for exchange rate forecasting. Indeed, the two topics have completely contrasting implications for exchange rate forecasting. Chaos theory tells us that if the process generating exchange rates is chaotic then it is deterministic but unpredictable. Conversely, enthusiastic proponents of neural networks as a forecasting technique claim that it is superior to conventional techniques when it comes to forecasting economic and financial variables, including exchange rates. The conclusions derived from the discussion of these two topics and the implications for exchange rate forecasting are completely the opposite.

We start with a discussion of chaos theory. Recent years have witnessed an explosion of interest in this subject by scholars from various disciplines. The interest has even engulfed the public media. This may sound really strange, given that this topic is extremely demanding when it comes to the level of mathematics required to handle it. The public interest is perhaps due to the association between chaos and the movement of financial variables (such as stock prices and exchange rates) of which the public has become a close observer. In order to be accessible to the non-specialist, the exposition of chaos presented in the following sections is extremely simplified. In fact, the treatment may even look superficial for the specialist reader. It is believed, however, that running the risk of conceiving the exposition as being superficial is worthwhile, given the objective of making the material accessible to most readers. In any case this book is not intended for highly sophisticated mathematicians and econometricians.

CHAOS THEORY: BACKGROUND

Chaos theory provides an analysis of phenomena or processes that are too irregular to be predictable. A chaotic process is a deterministic process that looks random. Like many other techniques, the study of chaos or chaotic behaviour originated in mathematics and pure science, then was imported to economics and finance. In these fields, the study of chaos has been motivated by the desire to find out whether or not some natural phenomena are governed by as yet undiscovered laws. Scientists have noticed that some phenomena, like planetary motion, are governed by stable laws but others, such as weather patterns, are not. Hence, the question is whether or not the weather phenomena are random. This question has motivated a 'search for the truth' because it has become apparent that what was once thought to be random is in fact chaotic. A variable or a process is said to show a chaotic behaviour when its evolution or time path seems to be random when in fact it is deterministic. This time path is generated by a deterministic nonlinear equation.

It is perhaps useful at this stage to say something about the history of chaos. The first recognition of chaotic dynamics is attributed by Weiss (1991) to Henri Poincaré, a French mathematician who was engaged in some work on celestial mechanics some 100 years ago. Poincaré put forward the intuitive idea that dynamical systems governed by nonlinear equations of motion are nonlinear. He was, however, unable to explore the idea formally because the mathematics of his time was not adequately advanced to handle this topic.

For a long time after Poincaré, interest in the topic died down. Then in the 1960s and 1970s, mathematicians and scientists resumed their interest in the subject. A mathematician by the name of Stephen Smale used differential topology to create theoretical models. Edward Lorenz, a meteorologist, devised a simple system of equations to simulate the weather which produced extreme sensitivity to changes in the initial conditions. A biologist named Robert May used the logistic difference equation to model population level at a successive periods of time. This is exactly the same model we will use later on in this chapter to generate chaotic behaviour in exchange rates.

Ever since, mathematicians have been engaged in developing a theory of nonlinear and chaotic systems, while scientists in a number of fields (physics, biology, meteorology) have been discovering chaotic phenomena. At one point in time, it was recognised that mathematicians and scientists were working on the same things. Needless to say, the growth of computer power has contributed to a significant extent to the understanding of chaotic and nonlinear processes in general.

Economists joined the bandwagon when they found out that chaos could explain some economic and financial phenomena that conventional models have not been able to handle. For example, economists have reached the conclusion that the empirical evidence on the forecasting power of the fundamental exchange rate models is not sanguine. This dismal conclusion was reached when it became apparent that these models were not capable of explaining what seems to be an erratic behaviour of exchange rates. The reaction of economists to this state of affairs has not been uniform. On the one hand, some economists explained this behaviour in terms of news. The news approach invariably leads to the conclusion that exchange rates are not forecastable, since they are determined by news, which is by definition unforecastable. On the other hand, some economists have kept on attempting to model the erratic movements of exchange rates. It is obvious that exchange rates are not generated by simple deterministic processes. Economists, therefore, have followed two approaches to model (and forecast) exchange rates. The first approach is to attribute the complicated behaviour of exchange rates to the role played by numerous factors that must be incorporated in the underlying model. Hence, complex models have been built for this purpose. The second approach is based on the assumption that there is an underlying trend but that there are random errors. In fact, it has become a prevailing wisdom that exchange rate movements are dominated by noise and so the objective is to understand the nature of this noise and predict its effect on exchange rates. These two approaches have produced little success in exchange rate forecasting.

What seems to be the problem with these approaches is the assumption of linearity. The implication of this assumption is that exchange rates respond in a linear manner to changes in the determining variables, or that they are generated by univariate linear processes. The tendency to use linear relationships is reinforced by the importance of linear regression techniques in this methodology, and the unavailability (until recently) of the tools required to explore nonlinear specifications. There is, however, no reason why we should believe that this is the case. If exchange rates are generated by nonlinear processes then, given certain conditions, the behaviour would look completely random, as it is in reality. This is a nonlinear chaotic behaviour: it is deterministic and not stochastic. Clyde and Osler (1997) suggest that 'the concentration on linearity to the exclusion of all other functional specifications is like taking the bet that the unidentified animal in the next room is an elephant instead of one of any of the other species of animals'.

DETERMINISTIC AND STOCHASTIC MODELS

If the value of a variable at a particular point in time can be obtained from a deterministic equation, and given the availability of some information, then forecasting this variable should not be a problem. In this case the behaviour is determined for all points in time. Put differently, if a variable is determined by a deterministic process, its value at any point in time uniquely determines its value at subsequent points in time. Take, for example, the simple (deterministic) autoregressive model whereby the value of the exchange rate at time t is determined:

$$S_t = aS_{t-1} \tag{9.1}$$

If the value of a is known then the value of S at any point in time in the future can be forecast with certainty. This is like the motion of planets. Figure 9.1 shows the behaviour of the exchange rate over time as determined by equation (9.1) for an initial value of 0.50 and values of a equal to 1.02, 0.95 and 1. When the value of a is 1, the behaviour of the exchange rate resembles what happens under a system of fixed exchange rates.

Deterministic models may even contain explanatory variables. Consider the deterministic model

$$S_t = aS_{t-1} + bX_t + cX_{t-1} \tag{9.2}$$

where X is an explanatory variable that is determined by the equation

$$X_t = \beta X_{t-1} \tag{9.3}$$

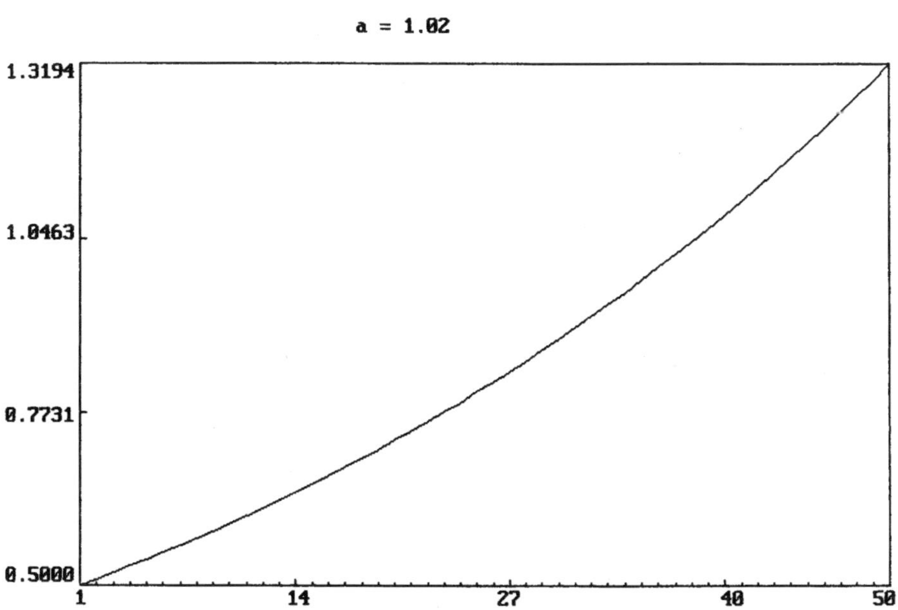

Figure 9.1 The behaviour of the exchange rate as generated by a deterministic model

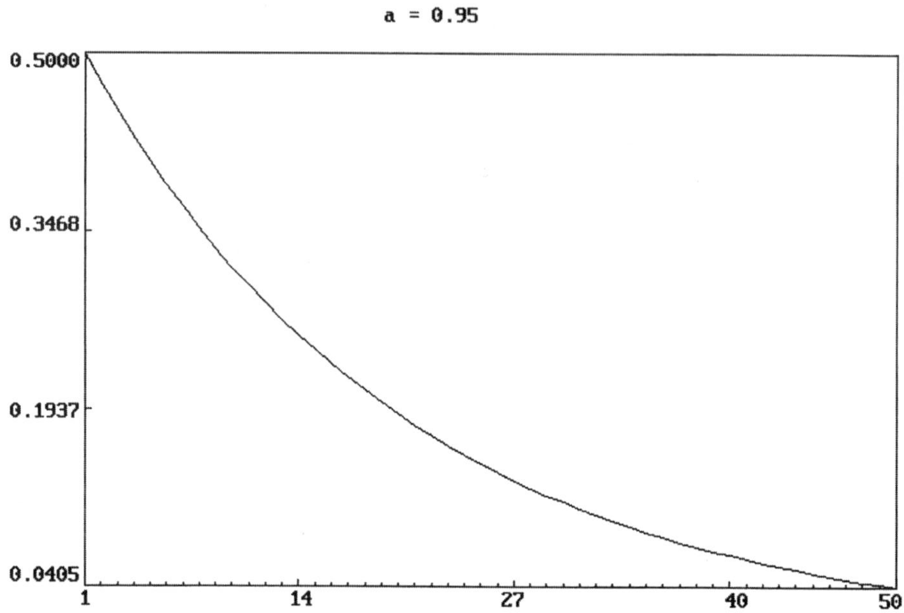

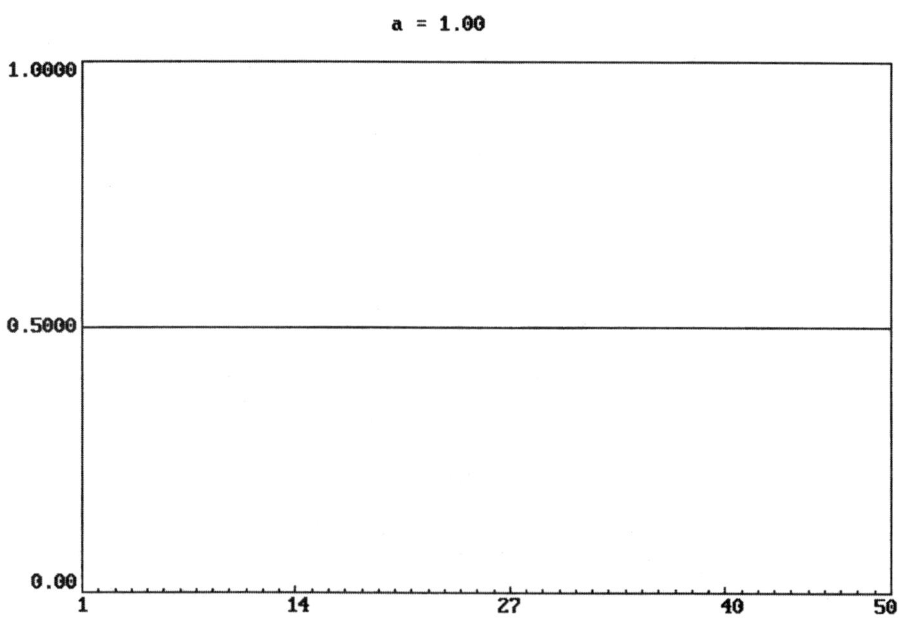

Figure 9.1 The behaviour of the exchange rate as generated by a deterministic model (cont.)

By substituting equation (9.3) into equation (9.2) we obtain

$$S_t = aS_{t-1} + (b\beta + c)X_{t-1} \tag{9.4}$$

Again, if the values of the coefficients a, b, c and β are known, then it is possible to forecast the exchange rate at any point in time. The behaviour of the exchange rate under this model will be determined by the behaviour of the explanatory variable X.

By examining the behaviour of the exchange rate shown in Figure 9.1, we immediately reach the conclusion that exchange rates cannot be generated by deterministic models like those represented by equations (9.1) and (9.4). Exchange rates are volatile and erratic, not smooth, stable and well behaved as in Figure 9.1. Economists have traditionally used stochastic models to represent exchange rates by including stochastic error terms with white noise properties. The stochastic counterpart of the model represented by equation (9.1) is

$$S_t = aS_{t-1} + \varepsilon_t \tag{9.5}$$

where ε_t is the error term. Given that this term is by definition unforecastable, it follows that the exchange rate can only be forecast with a forecasting error that is now represented by ε_t. Notice that if $a = 1$, then the model reduces to the simple random walk without drift model, which is often used to represent the behaviour of the exchange rate (recall the stylised facts presented in Chapter 1). Figure 9.2 shows what the behaviour of the exchange rate looks like (starting with an initial value of 0.50) when a stochastic model rather than a deterministic model is used to represent it. This behaviour looks more like the actual behaviour of exchange rates. Figure 9.3 shows the decomposition of the overall series, S_t, as shown in Figure 9.2, into a deterministic component, aS_{t-1} and a stochastic component, ε_t.

The stochastic equivalent of the model containing an explanatory variable is represented by

$$S_t = aS_{t-1} + bX_t + cX_{t-1} + \varepsilon_t \tag{9.6}$$

and

$$X_t = \beta X_{t-1} + \xi_t \tag{9.7}$$

Hence

$$S_t = aS_{t-1} + (b\beta + c)X_{t-1} + (\varepsilon + b\xi)_t \tag{9.8}$$

where we have a composite stochastic component, $(\varepsilon + b\xi)_t$, with white noise properties.

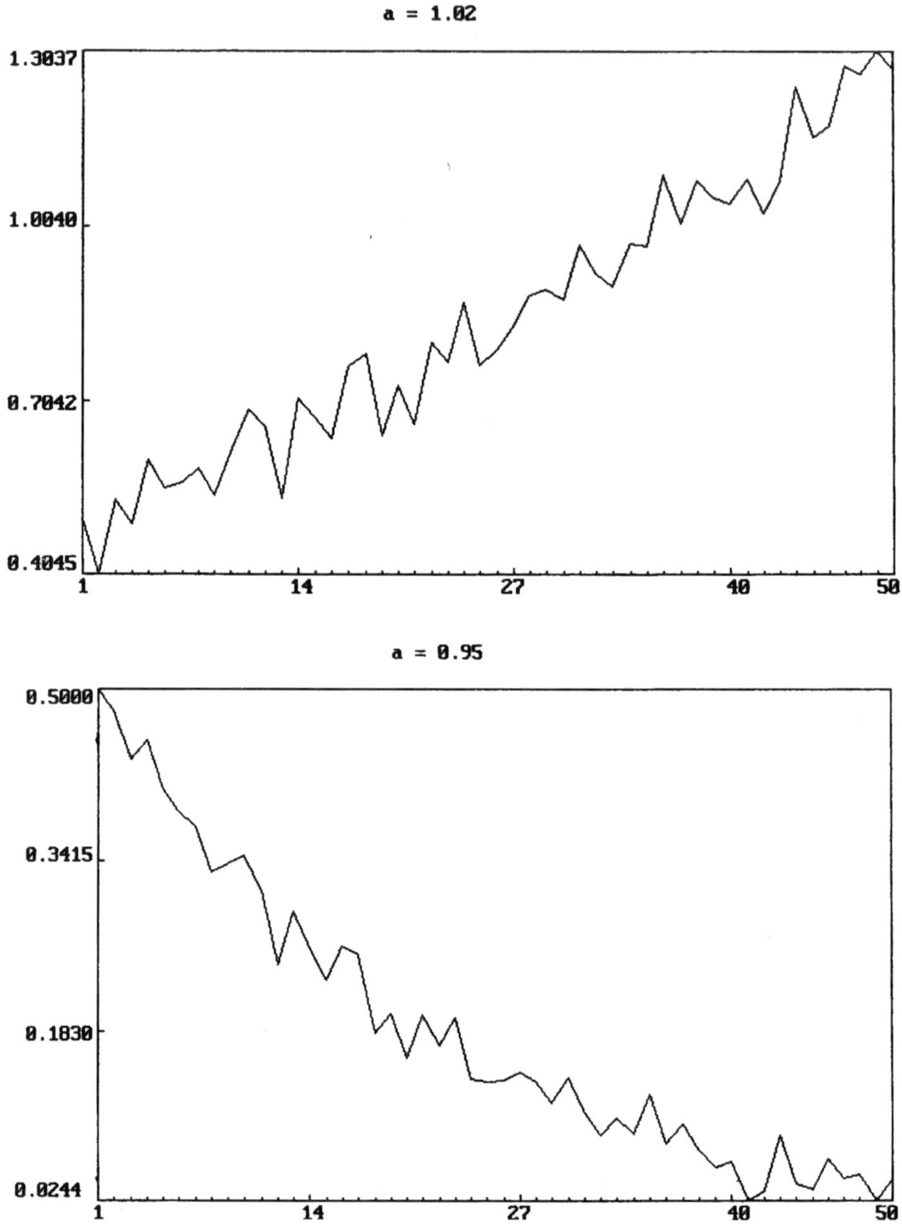

Figure 9.2 The behaviour of the exchange rate as generated by a stochastic model

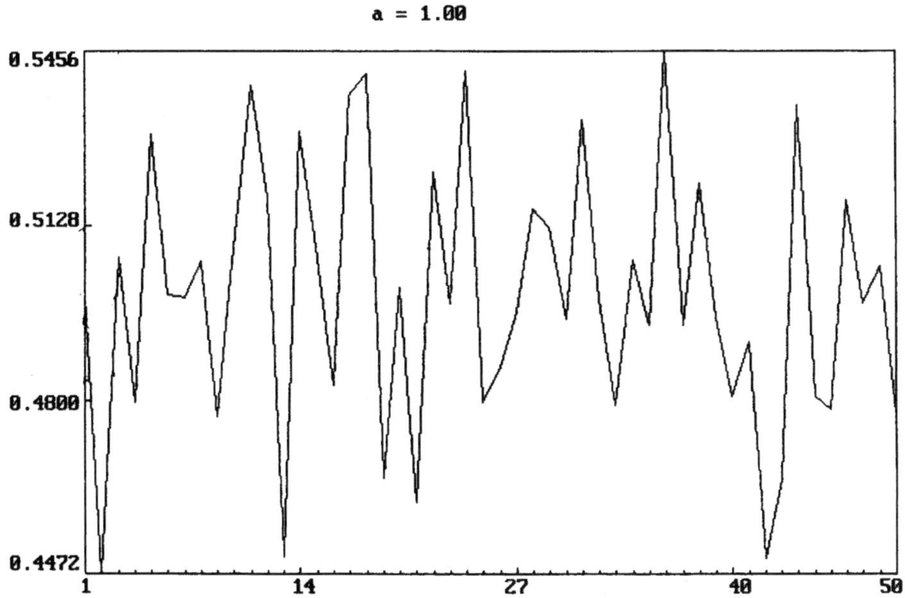

Figure 9.2 The behaviour of the exchange rate as generated by a stochastic model (cont.)

NONLINEAR AND CHAOTIC MODELS

To start with, it may be useful to state at the outset that while chaotic models are necessarily nonlinear, not all nonlinear models are chaotic. What we will show in this section is that the same nonlinear model may and may not produce chaotic behaviour.

The chaos literature has provided another alternative to explain the behaviour of the exchange rate. It can be shown that the random behaviour produced by the introduction of the stochastic error term can also be produced by a simple deterministic nonlinear model. Notice that both the stochastic and deterministic models described above are linear (in variables). The simplest nonlinear model that can produce chaotic behaviour is represented by the logistic function

$$S_t = kS_{t-1}(1 - S_{t-1}) \tag{9.9}$$

Copeland (1994, pp. 392–3) shows that this representation can be derived from the regressive expectations representation, which is a component of the exchange rate overshooting model. It can be shown that this equation

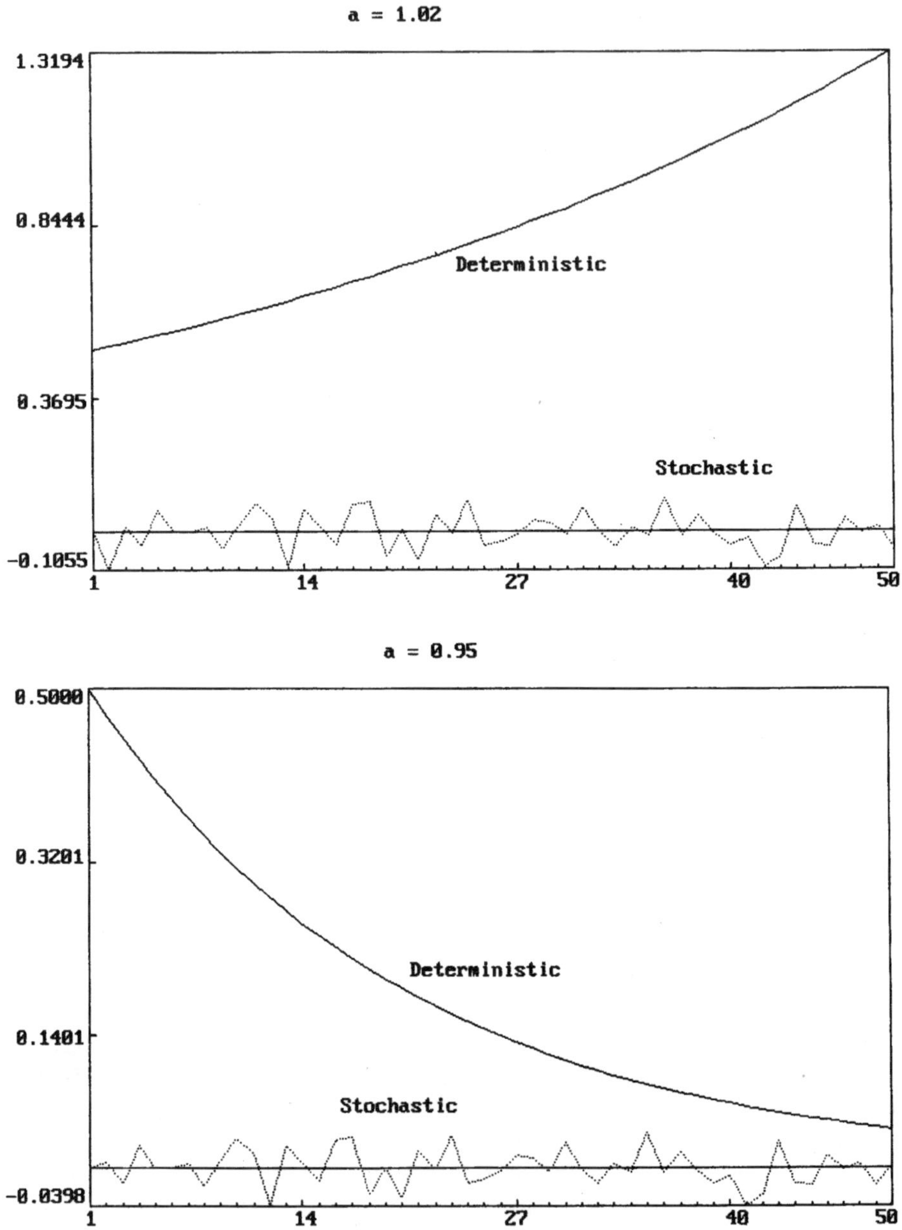

Figure 9.3 Decomposition of the exchange rate series into deterministic and stochastic components

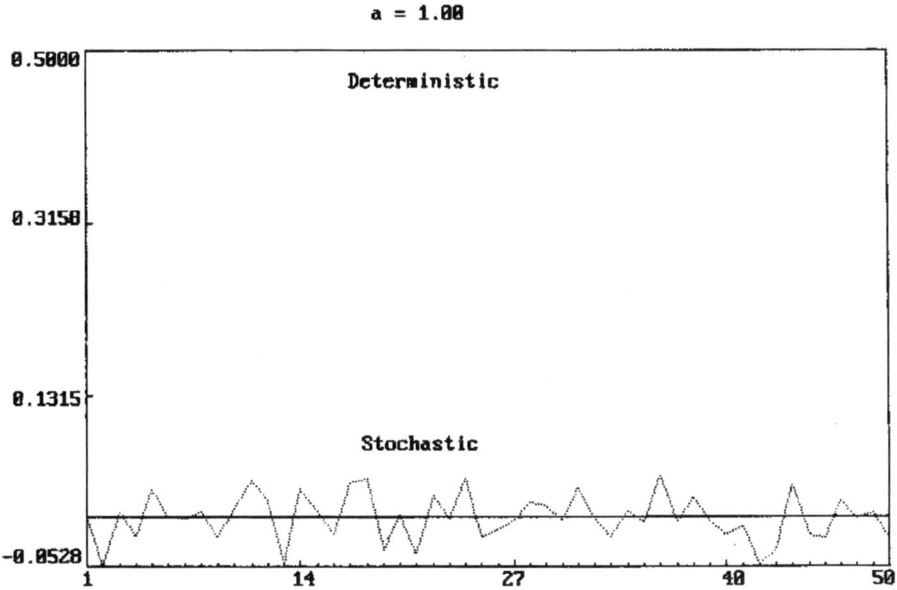

Figure 9.3 Decomposition of the exchange rate series into deterministic and stochastic components (cont.)

can generate a variety of time paths for the exchange rate depending on the value of the tuning parameter, k, and the initial value of the exchange rate, S_0.

Figures 9.4 and 9.5 show the time paths of the exchange rate as generated by equation (9.9) for the initial values of $S_0 = 0.25$ and $S_0 = 0.50$ respectively. In each case 12 different values are assigned to k, ranging between 0.5 and 4. It is obvious that the time path of the exchange rate depends on the value of k in both cases. In fact, the behaviour of the exchange rate depends on the range within which the value of k falls. The following ranges can be distinguished.

THE RANGE 0–1

When the value of k falls in the range 0–1, the exchange rate converges on zero. In this range the exchange rate is unsustainable, a scenario that can be ruled out as a valid description of the actual behaviour of exchange rates. Figures 9.4(a) and 9.5(a) show that the exchange rate starts at the initial value then falls rapidly towards zero.

THE RANGE 1–2

At a range between 1 and 2, the exchange rate converges smoothly on some equilibrium value. The pattern of convergence, as shown in Figures 9.4(b) and 9.5(b), is described as being 'monotonic'. The implication of this behaviour is that equilibrium is restored following any real disturbance. Notice, however, the difference in the behaviour, which is attributed to difference in the initial values of the exchange rate (0.5 and 0.25 respectively). In Figure 9.5(b) the exchange moves upwards, since it is below the equilibrium value of 0.33, until it converges on it. In Figure 9.4(b), the exchange rate moves downwards since it is above the equilibrium value of 0.33, again converging on it. This difference in behaviour is also evident when $k = 2$ as shown in Figures 9.4(c) and 9.5(c). Notice in particular that the behaviour of the exchange rate in Figure 9.4(c) is similar to the behaviour derived from the deterministic model represented by equation (9.1) as shown in Figure 9.1(c).

THE RANGE 2–3

When k assumes values within the range 2–3, the exchange rate starts to exhibit stable cycles that converge on the long-run equilibrium level. In Figures 9.4(d) and 9.5(d) the exchange rate moves in cycles initially and then converges on the equilibrium value of 0.64. As the value of k increases, the number of cycles also increases, and it takes the exchange rate longer periods to converge. For example, when $k = 2.99$ there is no convergence after 50 periods as shown in Figures 9.4(e) and 9.5(e).

THE RANGE 3–3.68

At a range between 3 and 3.68, the exchange rate moves in cycles without convergence on an equilibrium value. The pattern of these cycles, however, is highly sensitive to the value of k. When $k = 3.4$ as shown in Figures 9.4(f) and 9.5(f), the cycles exhibit increasing amplitudes initially, but this instability is only temporary. Shortly afterwards, a regular two-period cycle is established and sustained indefinitely. As the value of k increases further, different cycles are obtained. At $k = 3.47$, the exchange rate moves in a four-period cycle as shown in Figures 9.4(g) and 9.5(g). See also what happens to the periodicity of the cycle at $k = 3.6$ as shown in Figures 9.4(h) and 9.5(h).

THE RANGE 3.68–4

When k assumes values between 3.68 and 4 chaotic behaviour starts to appear. At $k > 3.68$ the cycles are no longer stable and the patterns of the time path become endless. Chaotic behaviour is evident when k assumes the values of 3.75, 3.95 and 3.99. Notice, however, how the behaviour changes drastically by increasing the value of k from 3.99 to 4. At $k = 4$ the behaviour is not chaotic and not cyclical.

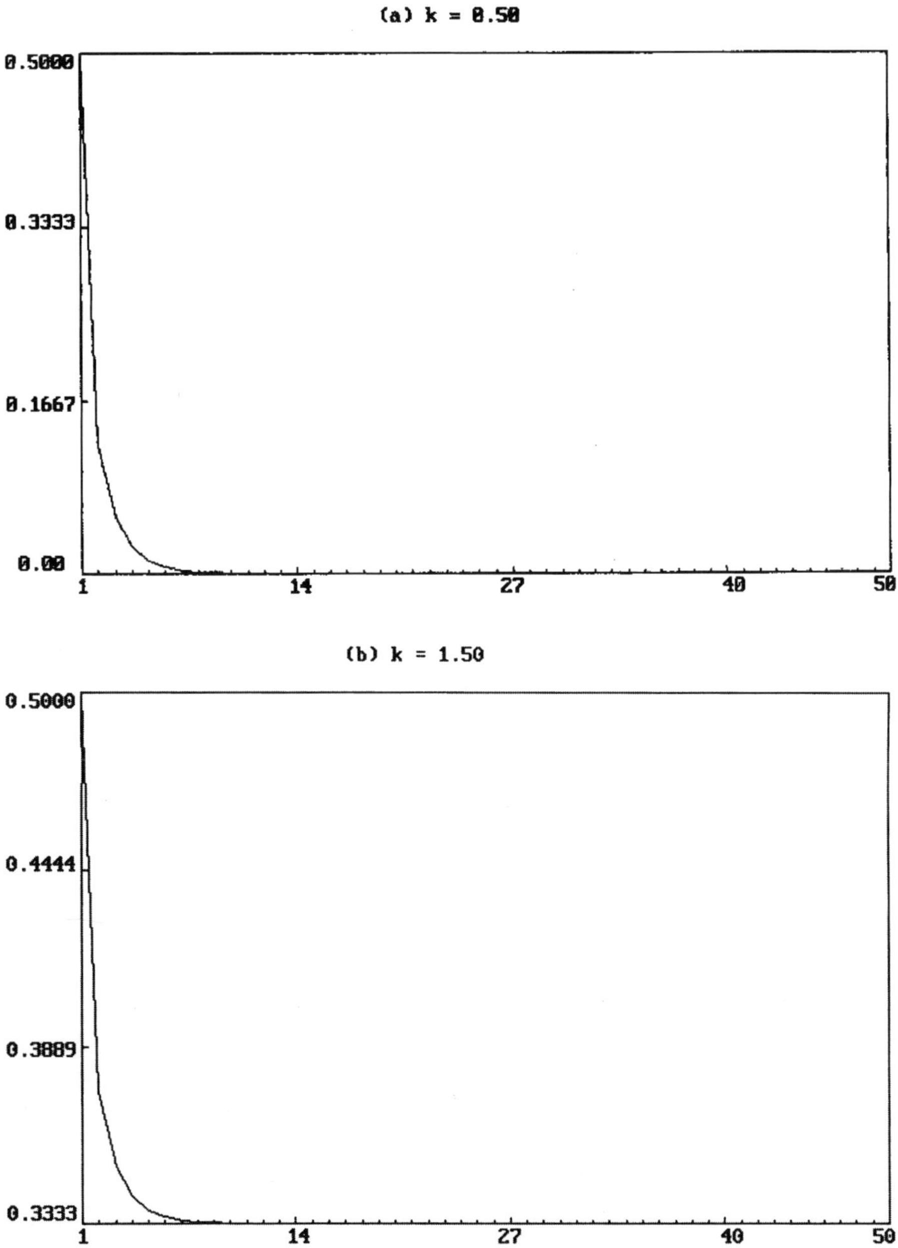

Figure 9.4 The behaviour of the exchange rate as generated by a nonlinear logistic function (initial value = 0.50)

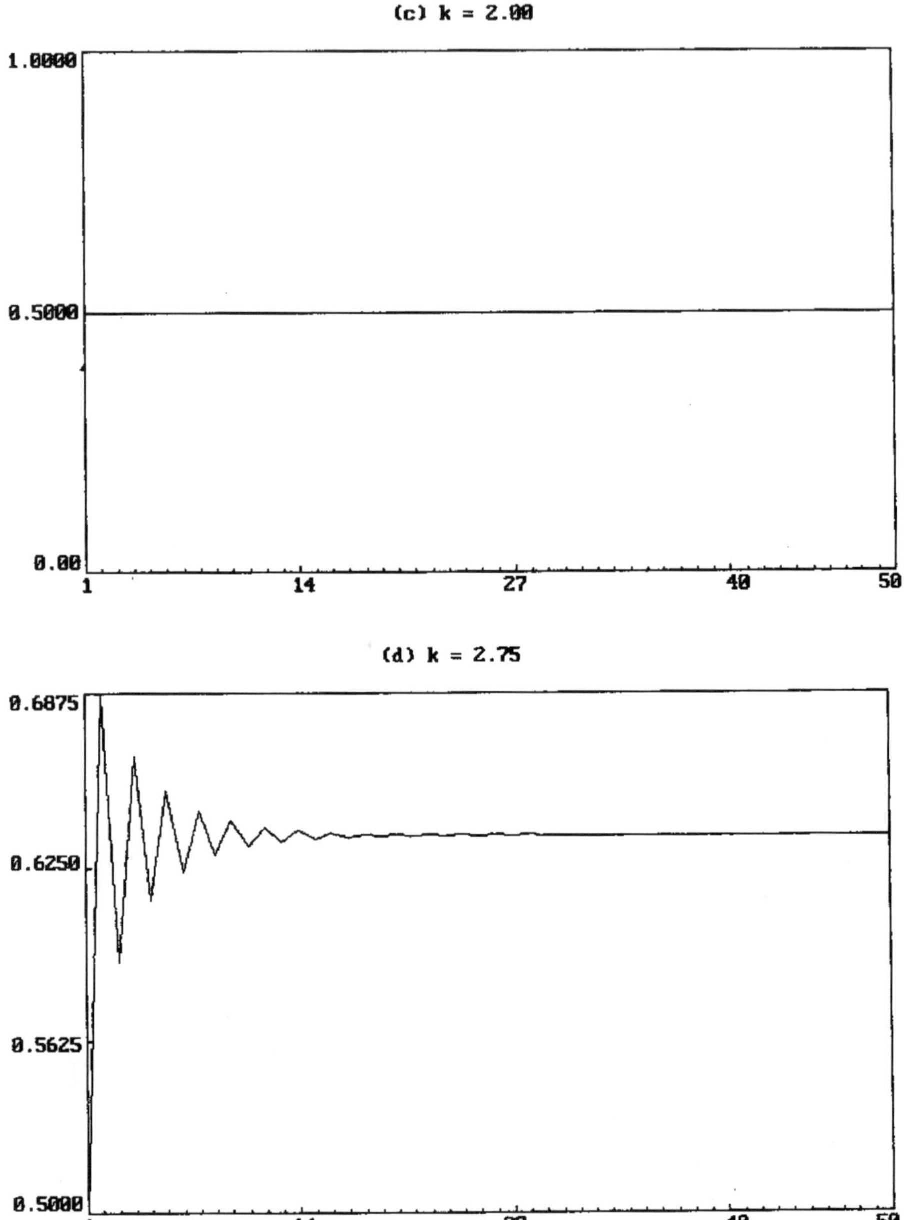

Figure 9.4 The behaviour of the exchange rate as generated by a nonlinear logistic function (initial value = 0.50) (cont.)

(e) k = 2.99

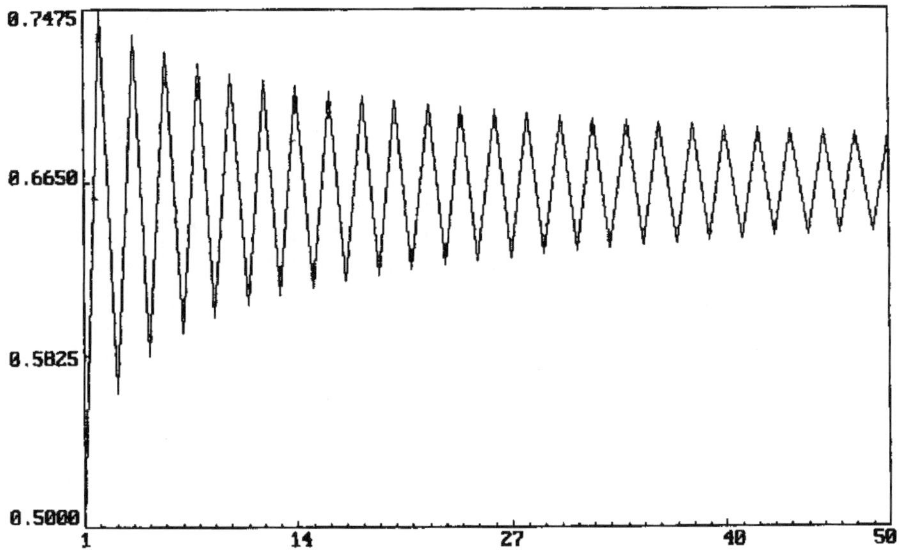

(f) k = 3.40

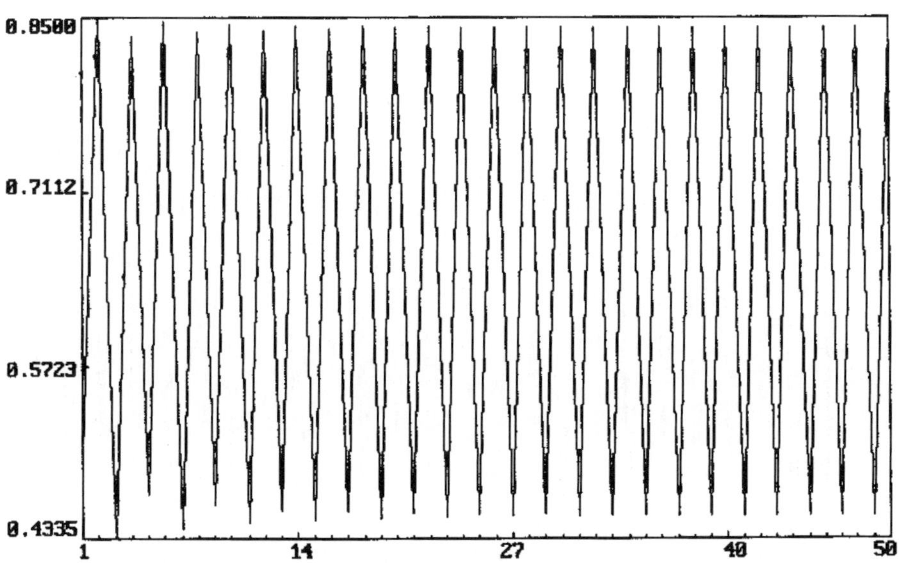

Figure 9.4 The behaviour of the exchange rate as generated by a nonlinear logistic function (initial value = 0.50) (cont.)

(g) k = 3.47

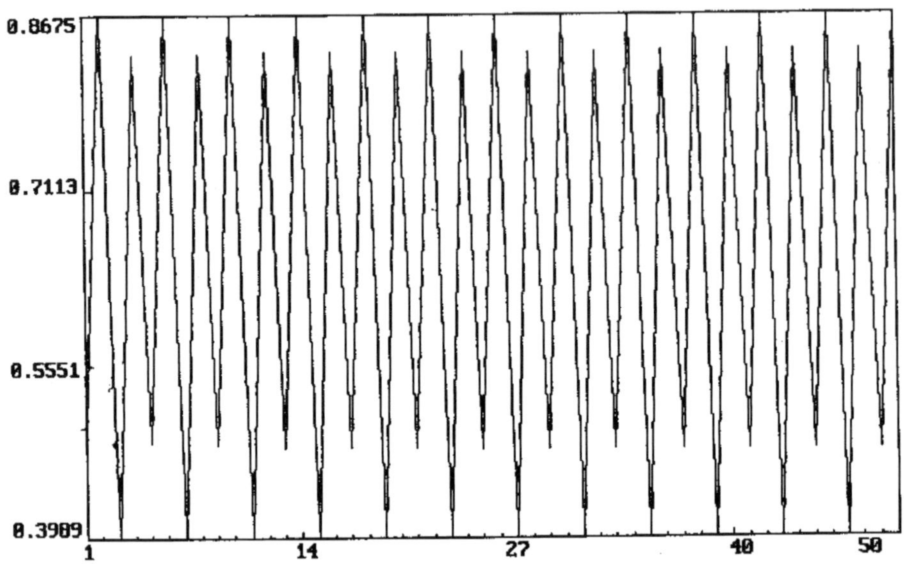

(h) k = 3.60

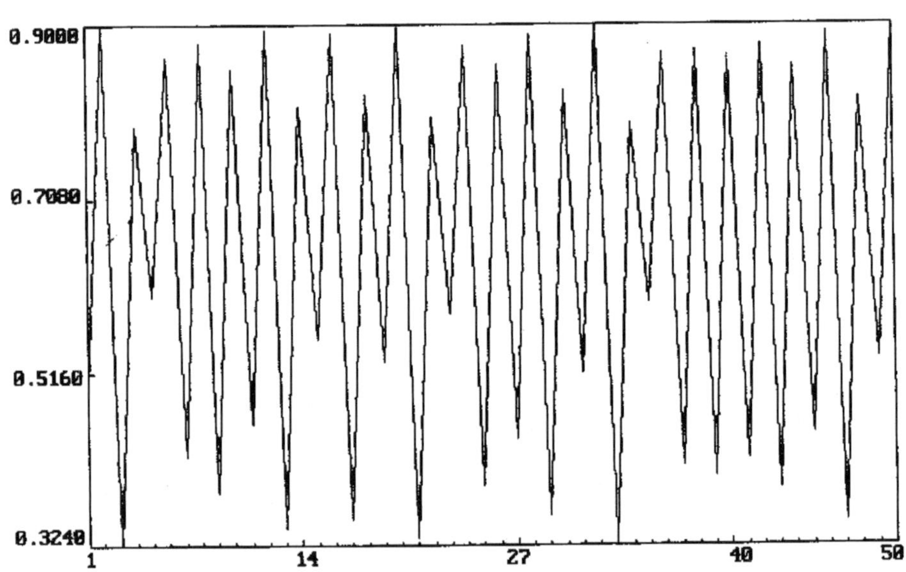

Figure 9.4 The behaviour of the exchange rate as generated by a nonlinear logistic function (initial value = 0.50) (cont.)

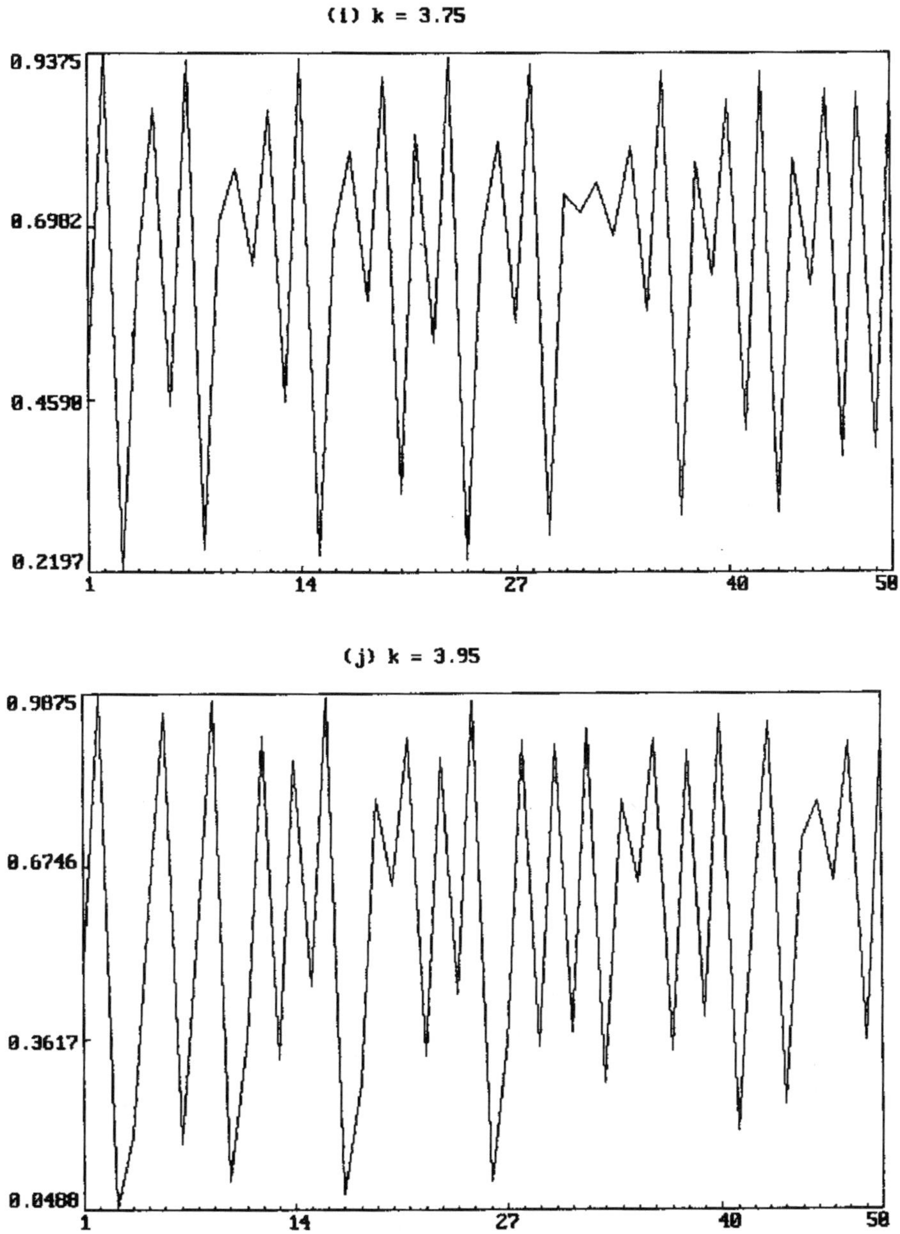

Figure 9.4 The behaviour of the exchange rate as generated by a nonlinear logistic function (initial value = 0.50) (cont.)

(k) k = 3.99

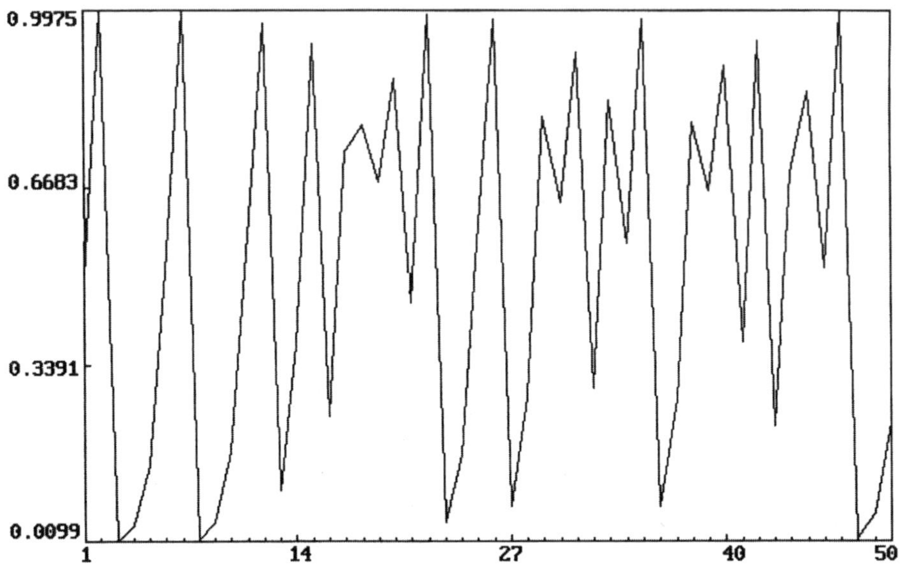

(l) k = 4.00

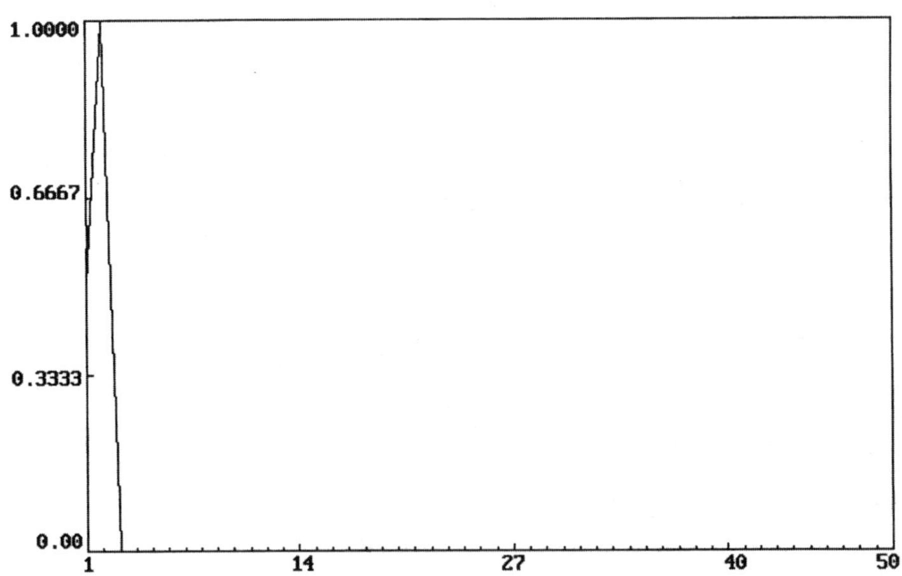

Figure 9.4 The behaviour of the exchange rate as generated by a nonlinear logistic function (initial value = 0.50) (cont.)

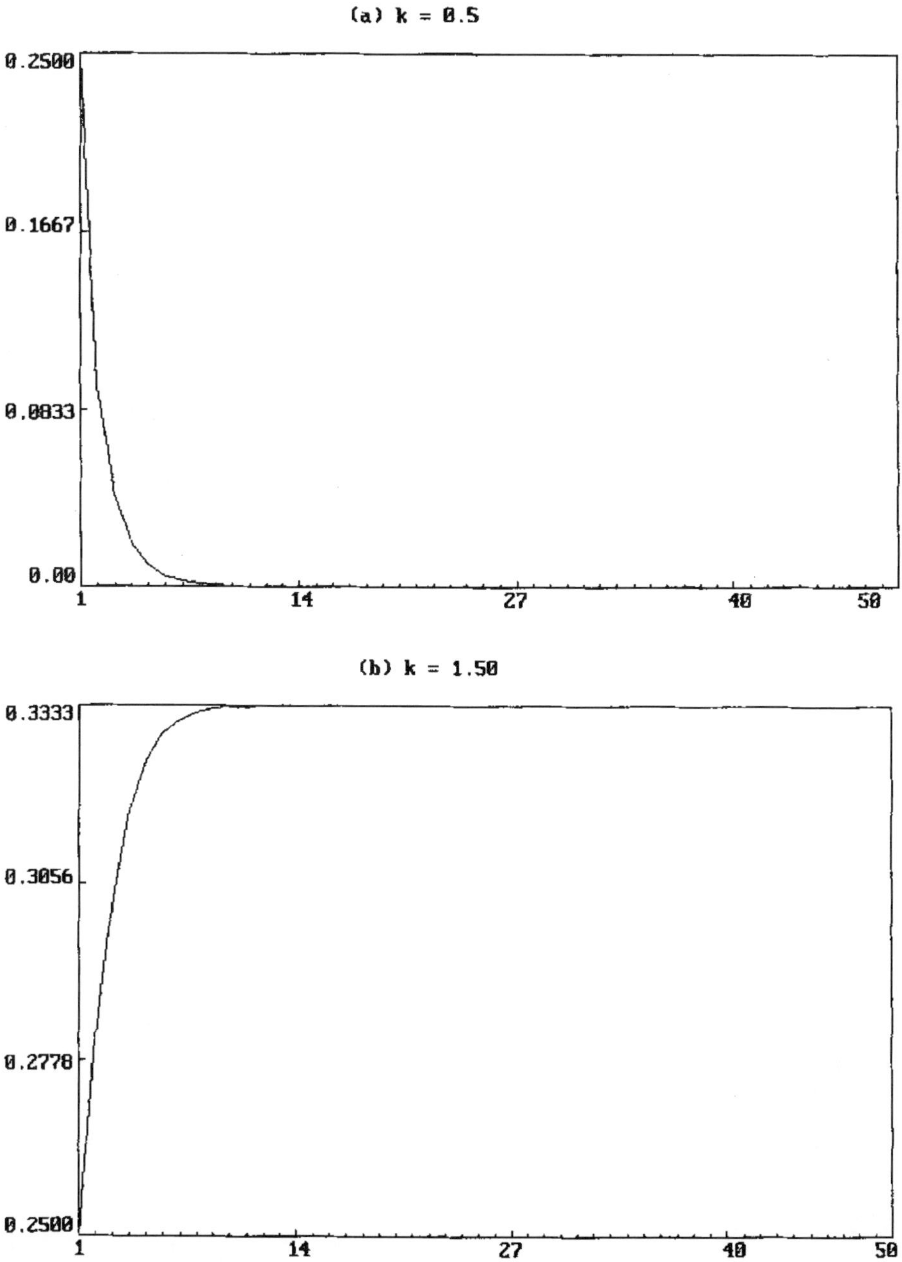

Figure 9.5 The behaviour of the exchange rate as generated by a nonlinear logistic function (initial value = 0.25)

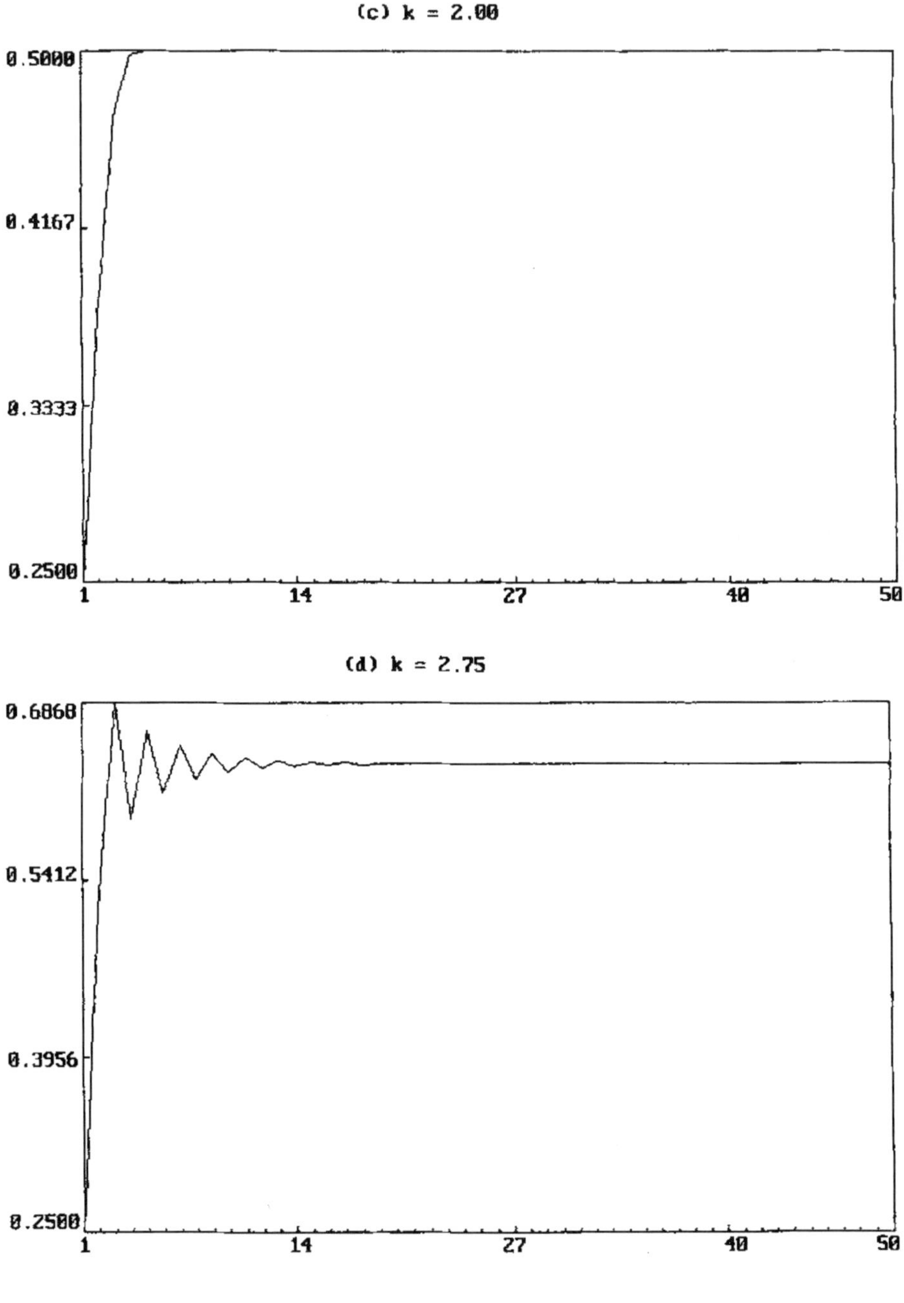

Figure 9.5 The behaviour of the exchange rate as generated by a nonlinear logistic function (initial value = 0.25) (cont.)

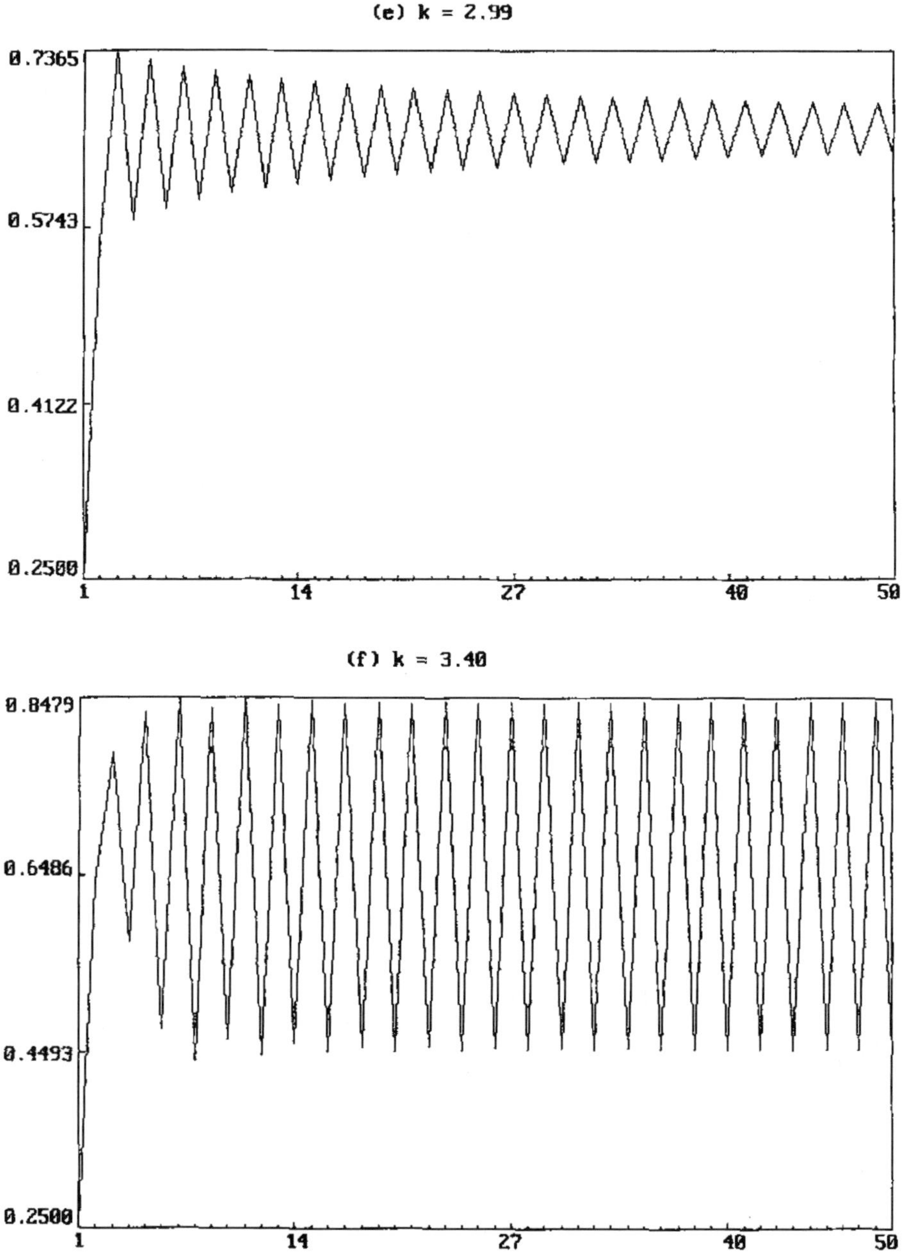

Figure 9.5 The behaviour of the exchange rate as generated by a nonlinear logistic function (initial value = 0.25) (cont.)

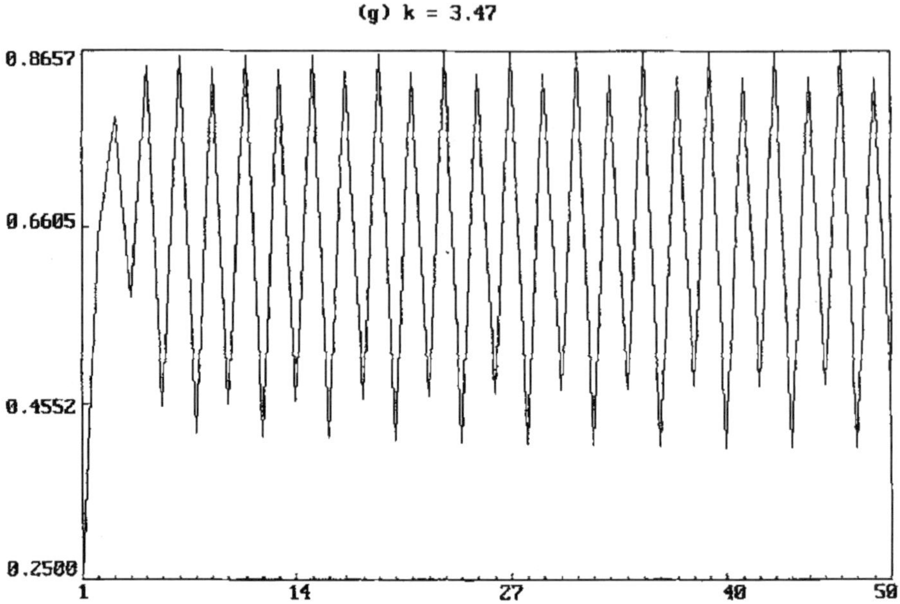

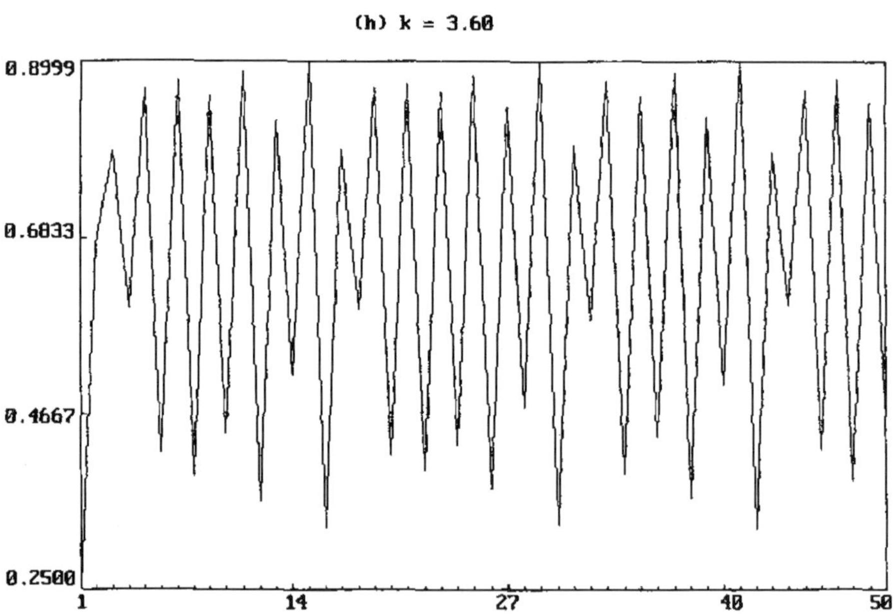

Figure 9.5 The behaviour of the exchange rate as generated by a nonlinear logistic function (initial value = 0.25) (cont.)

(i) k = 3.75

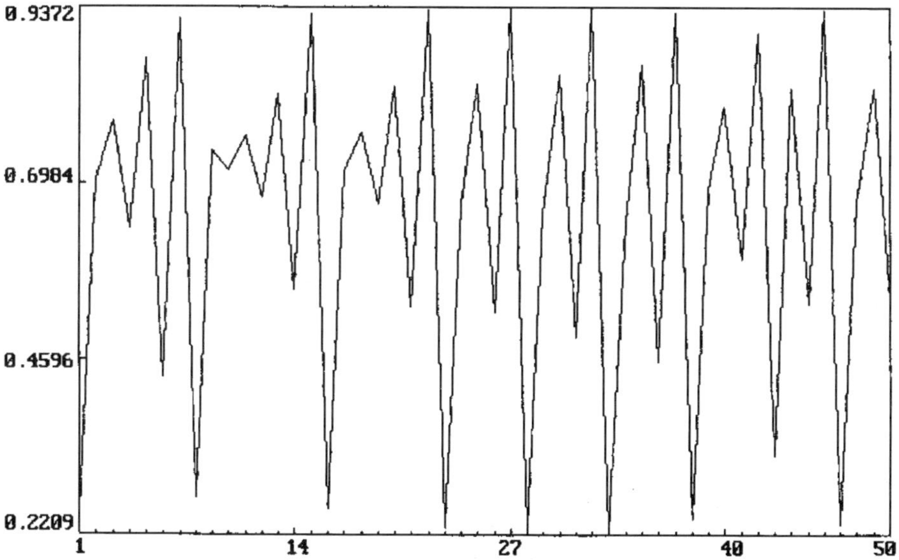

(j) k = 3.95

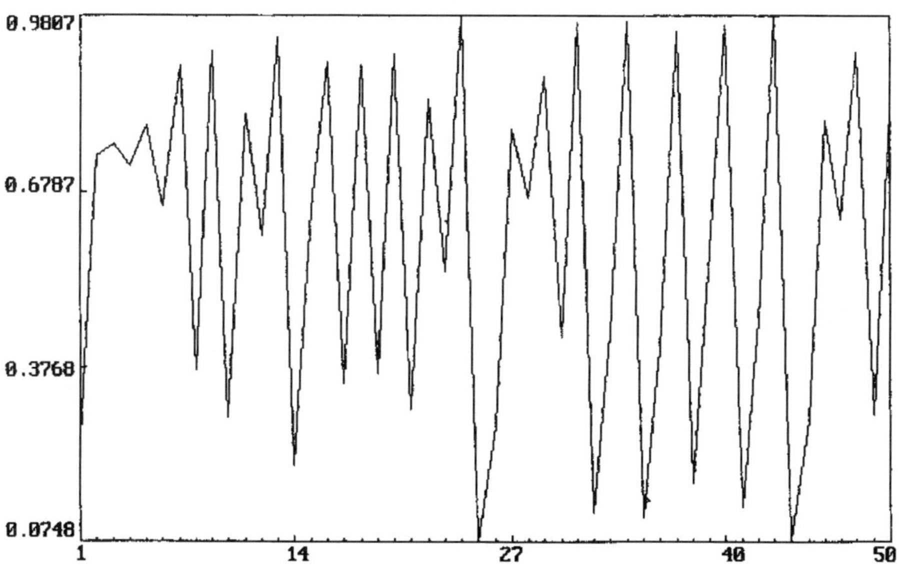

Figure 9.5 The behaviour of the exchange rate as generated by a nonlinear logistic function (initial value = 0.25) (cont.)

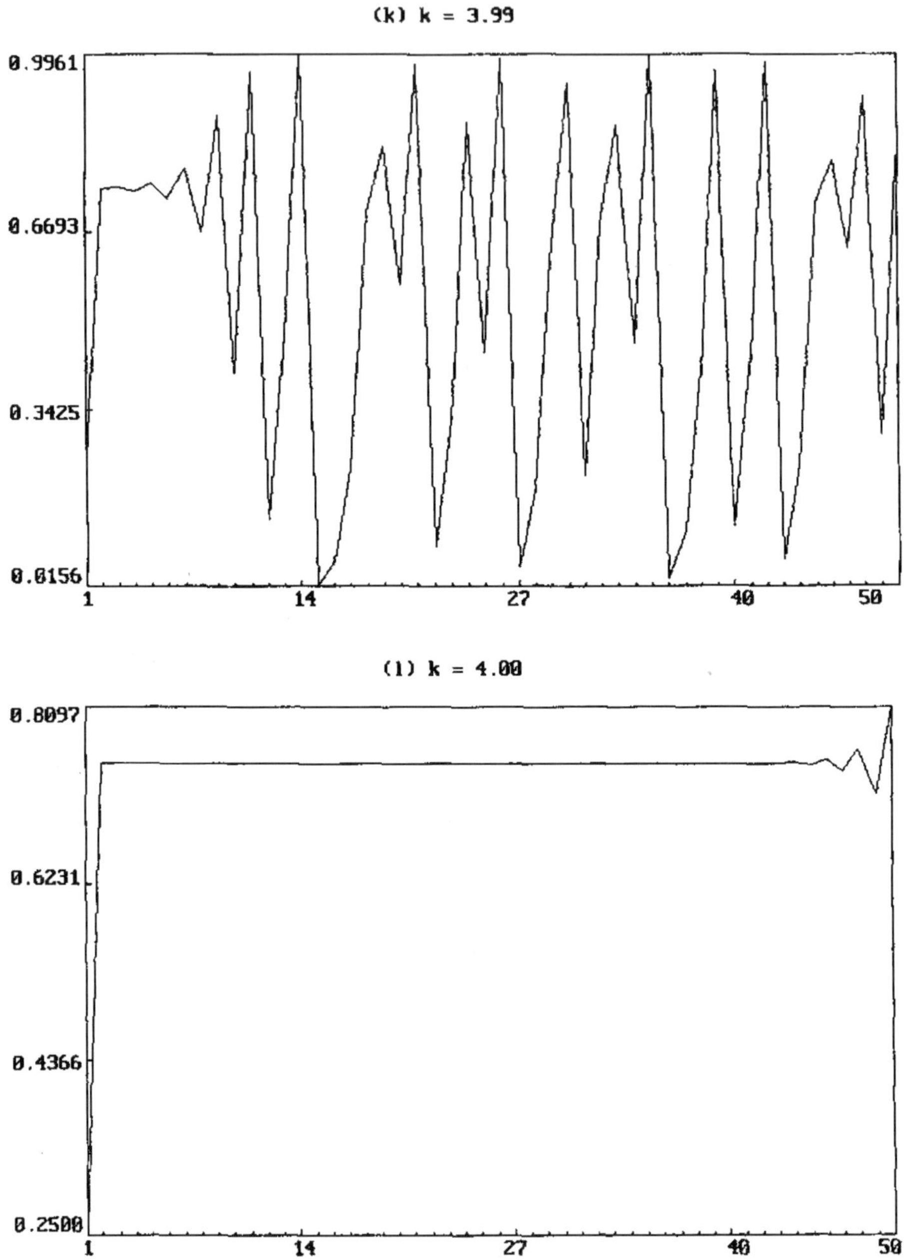

Figure 9.5 The behaviour of the exchange rate as generated by a nonlinear logistic function (initial value = 0.25) (cont.)

SUMMARY OF THE POSSIBILITIES

It is possible to summarise the possibilities as the value of k increases.

1. For values between 0 and 1, the exchange rate converges on zero.
2. For values between 1 and 3, the exchange rate converges on a certain non-zero value.
3. Above 3, cycles start to appear. As the value of k increases, the process moves from two-period cycles to four-period cycles and so on.
4. Above the range giving rise to cycles, chaos starts to appear within the range of up to 4. Within this range there is a small interval over which a stable three-period cycle appears.

SENSITIVITY TO THE INITIAL CONDITION AND THE TUNING PARAMETER

It is obvious that the behaviour of the exchange rate over time is sensitive to the initial value of the exchange rate (S_0) and the value of the tuning parameter, k. Indeed, it is extremely sensitive, and this is obviously more evident in the following case, which is illustrated in Figure 9.6. Starting with $S_0 = 0.30$ and $k = 3.68$, it is obvious that there is a chaotic behaviour as shown in Figure 9.6(a). Look now what happens as the initial value is changed slightly to 0.299. Figure 9.6(b) shows that while the behaviour is still chaotic, it is completely different from what is shown in Figure 9.6(a). This is amazing, considering the small change in the initial value of the exchange rate. Consider now what happens if the initial value is restored to 0.30 but the value of k is changed slightly to 3.679. Again, the small change in the value of k produces a significant change in the behaviour of the exchange rate (Figure 9.6(c)). Finally, Figure 9.6(d) shows what happens as both S_0 and k are changed. The change in the behaviour as a result of changing the initial value of the exchange rate and the value of the tuning parameter will be more pronounced for longer time periods. Figure 9.6 shows the behaviour over 100 time periods only.

NON-CHAOTIC, NONLINEAR BEHAVIOUR

Naturally, not all nonlinear models are capable of producing chaotic behaviour. Consider, for example, the nonlinear equation

$$S_t = aS_{t-1}^2 \qquad (9.10)$$

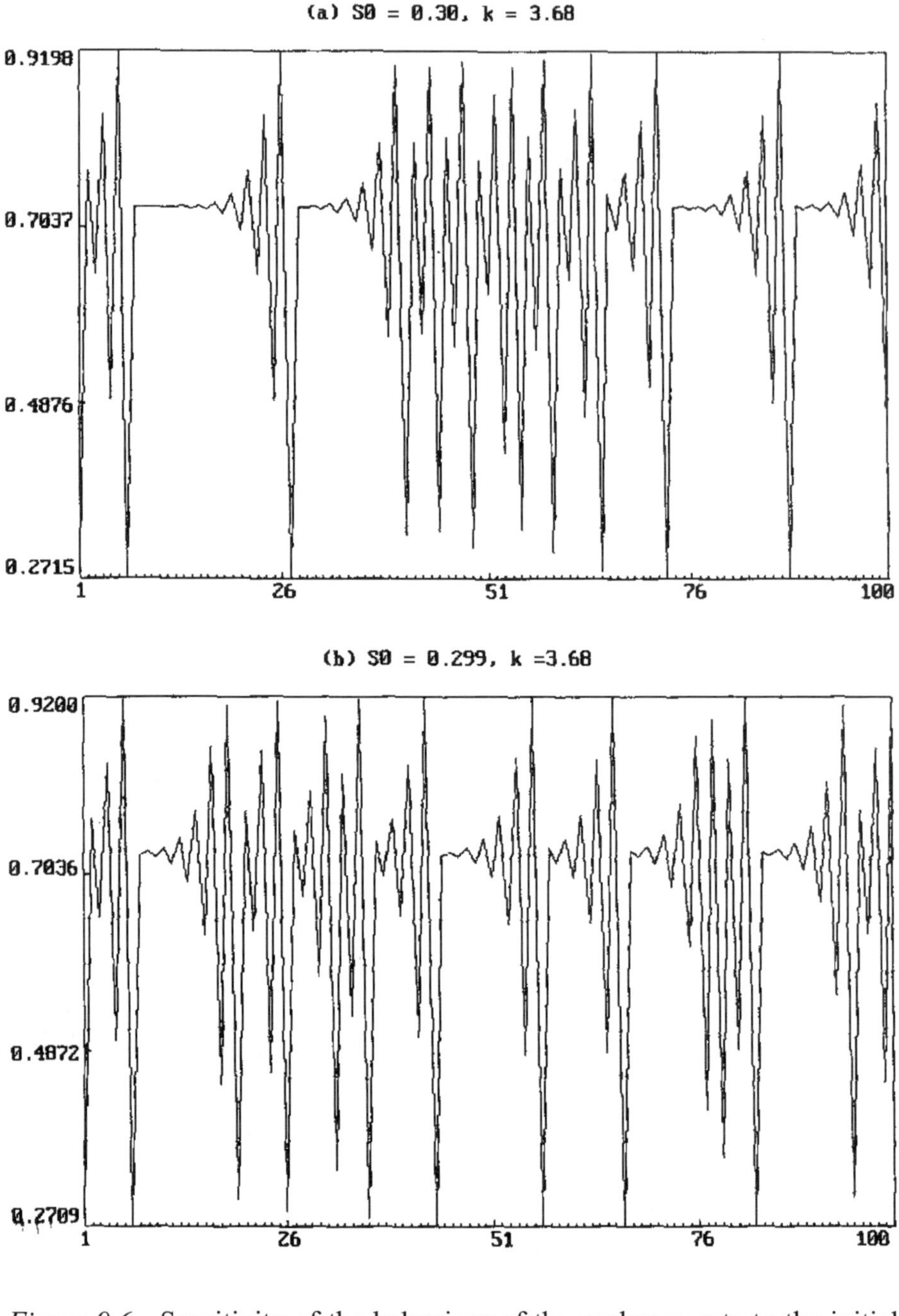

Figure 9.6 Sensitivity of the behaviour of the exchange rate to the initial value and the tuning parameter

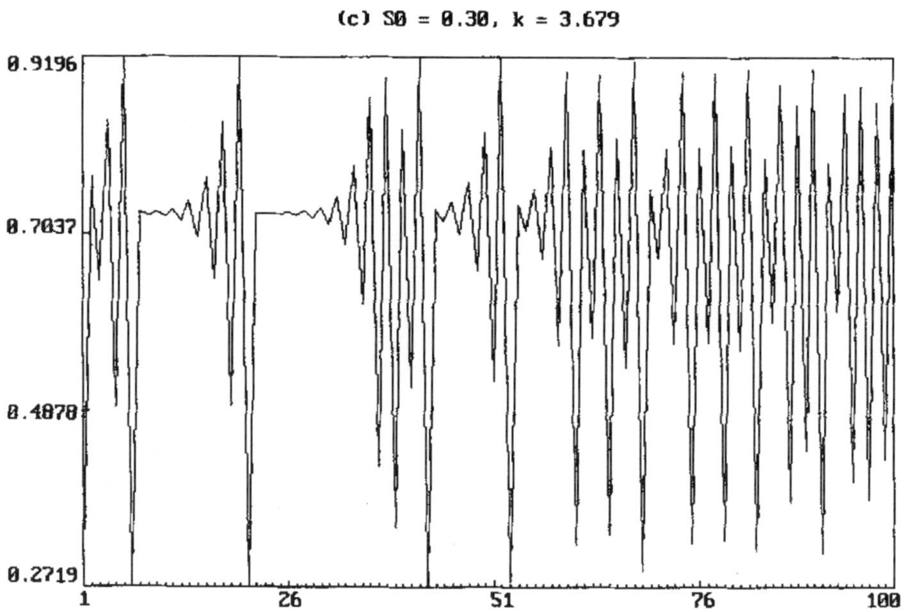

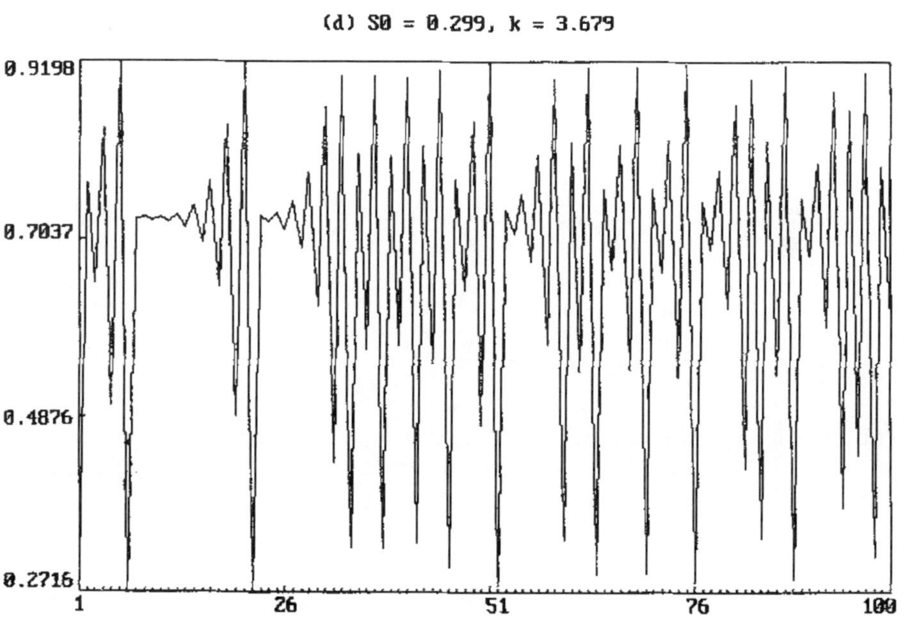

Figure 9.6 Sensitivity of the behaviour of the exchange rate to the initial value and the tuning parameter (cont.)

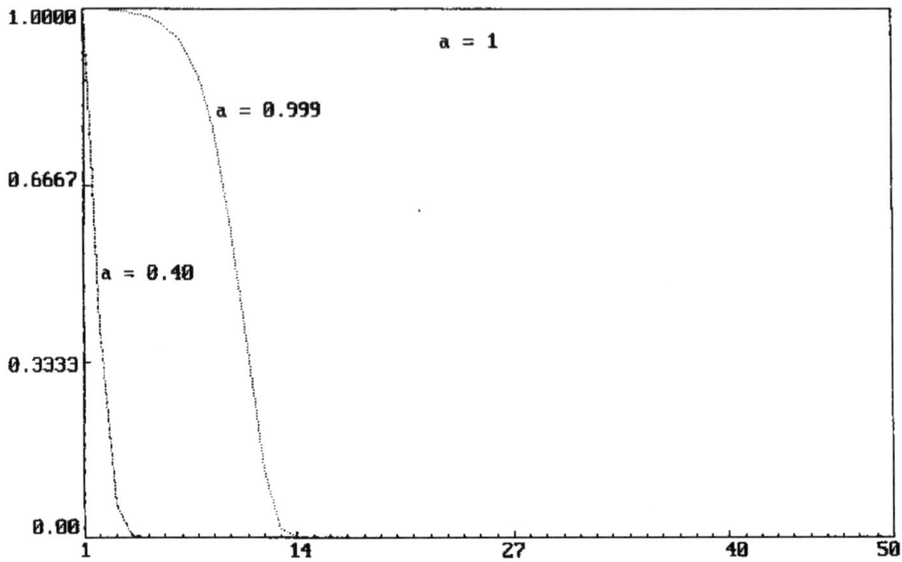

Figure 9.7 Non-chaotic, nonlinear behaviour of the exchange rate

Figure 9.7 shows the values of behaviour of S for an initial value of 1.00. Three values are assigned to a: 1, 0.999 and 0.40. While the value of 1 produces a horizontal line, the other two values produce a pattern of exponential decay as the exchange rate converges on the value of zero. The only difference is the speed of convergence, which is determined by the value of the parameter a.

A COMPARISON BETWEEN CHAOTIC AND STOCHASTIC PROCESSES

The easiest way to compare the behaviour of a stochastic process with that of a chaotic process is to generate observations from these two processes and examine them visually. Figure 9.8 shows the behaviour of these processes. Figure 9.8(a) plots observations generated from the same logistic function used earlier by specifying values for S_0 and k equal to 1 and 3.75 respectively. Figure 9.8(b), on the other hand, plots random numbers between 0 and 1. The behaviour of the two time series look rather similar: the chaotic process looks as random as the stochastic process. However, do not jump to conclusions yet.

Let us now examine the behaviour of the two processes in terms of the phase portrait (or the phase space), which is a (scatter) plot of the value assumed by the exchange rate in one period against its value in the previous period. The phase portraits for the chaotic process and the stochastic process are shown in Figure 9.9. They are remarkably different. The points in the phase portrait of the chaotic process fall on a smooth curve (an attractor) represented by the equation $S_t = 3.75S_{t-1}(1 - S_{t-1})$. On the other hand, the points in the phase portrait of the stochastic process are all over the place. While, on the surface, the behaviour of the two processes looks similar as in Figure 9.8, they are in fact completely different as shown in Figure 9.9. They have to be different because the chaotic process is deterministic, that is represented by an exact equation.

One big difference between stochastic and chaotic processes is the following. Stochastic processes are 'noisy', and so statisticians have developed various smoothing methods to deal with them. These methods are not appropriate for chaotic processes. Unlike stochastic processes, chaotic processes contain important information that can be lost by smoothing. It could be the case, however, that a process may exhibit a mixture of a nonlinear behaviour and noise. Analysis of these processes must consider both the nonlinear effect and the residual noise.

How does a chaotic process generated by a nonlinear equation compare with a deterministic process generated by a linear equation such as equation (9.1)? Take, for example, the equation $S_t = 0.996S_{t-1}$. The behaviour of the exchange rate generated by this equation (for an initial value of 1.00) is shown in Figure 9.10(a), while a phase portrait is shown in Figure 9.10(b). The points in this case fall on a straight line. Figure 9.11 further shows that the behaviour of the exchange rate in this case is not as sensitive to changes in the initial value and the coefficient a. In Figure 9.11(a) three initial values are used (1.0, 0.8 and 0.6) but the behaviour is similar: in all cases the exchange rate converges on a value close to zero. When different values for the parameter a are used as in Figure 9.11(b) the only difference is the speed of convergence.

SOURCES OF NONLINEARITY

A question that arises is the following. If chaotic behaviour requires nonlinearity, then a nonlinear structure must be present for economic and financial time series (like exchange rates) to be chaotic. If so, what is the source of nonlinearity in these series?

To understand nonlinearity in exchange rate movements we must understand the concept of feedback effects. According to the stabilising speculation hypothesis, when the exchange rate gets too high the underlying currency is sold, pulling the exchange rate down, and when it is low the currency is bought, leading to a reversion in the direction of the exchange rate. This is an example of feedback effect which can be linear or nonlinear.

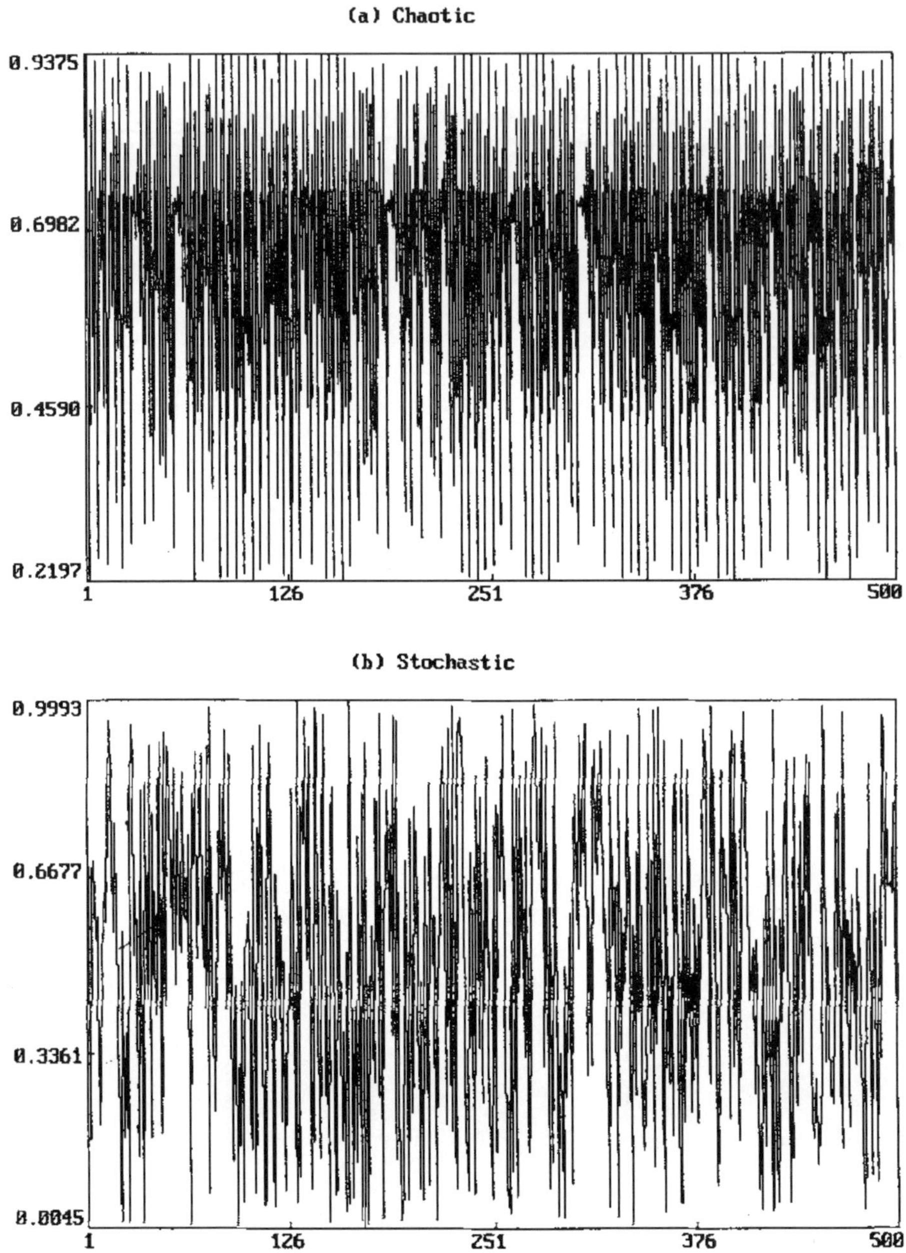

Figure 9.8 The behaviour of chaotic and stochastic processes

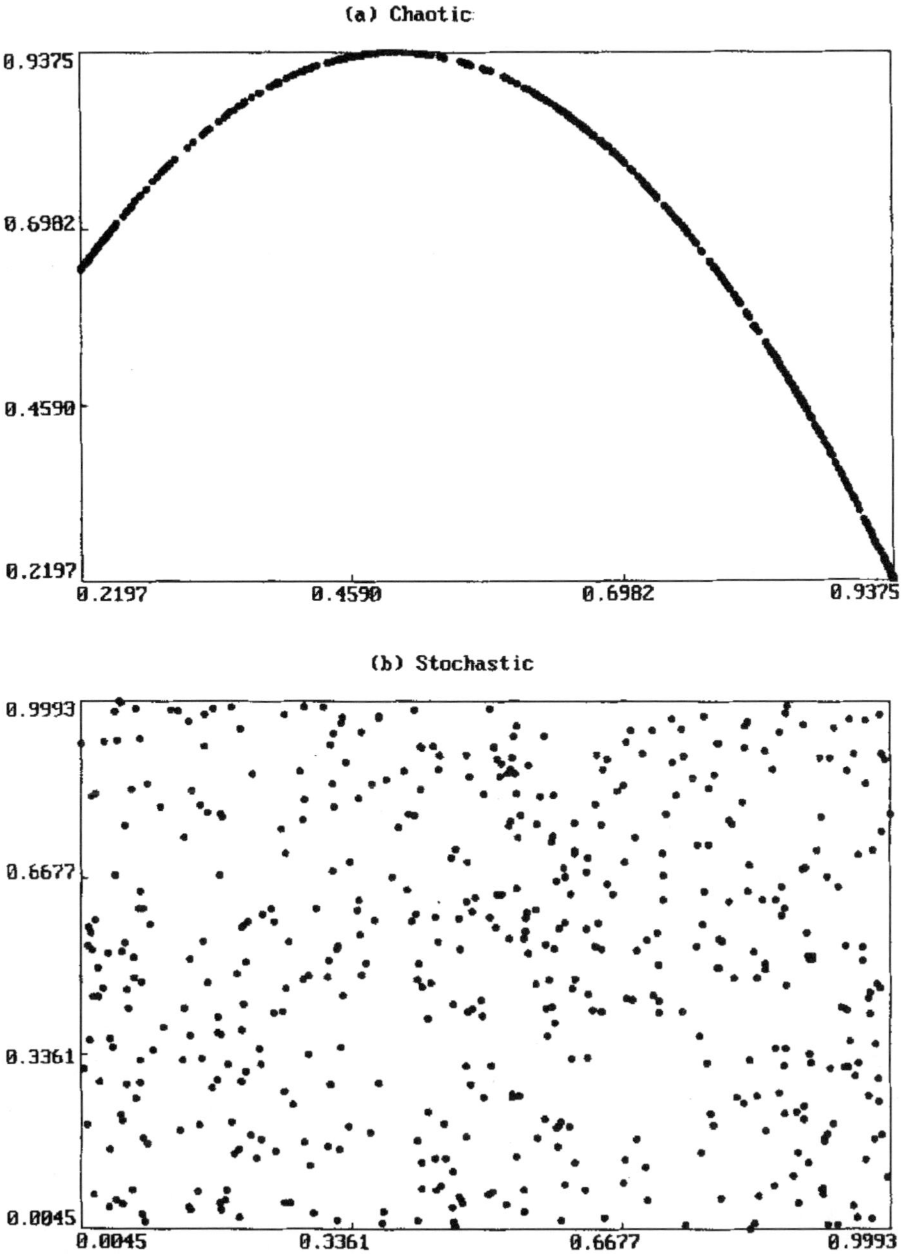

Figure 9.9 Phase portraits of chaotic and stochastic processes

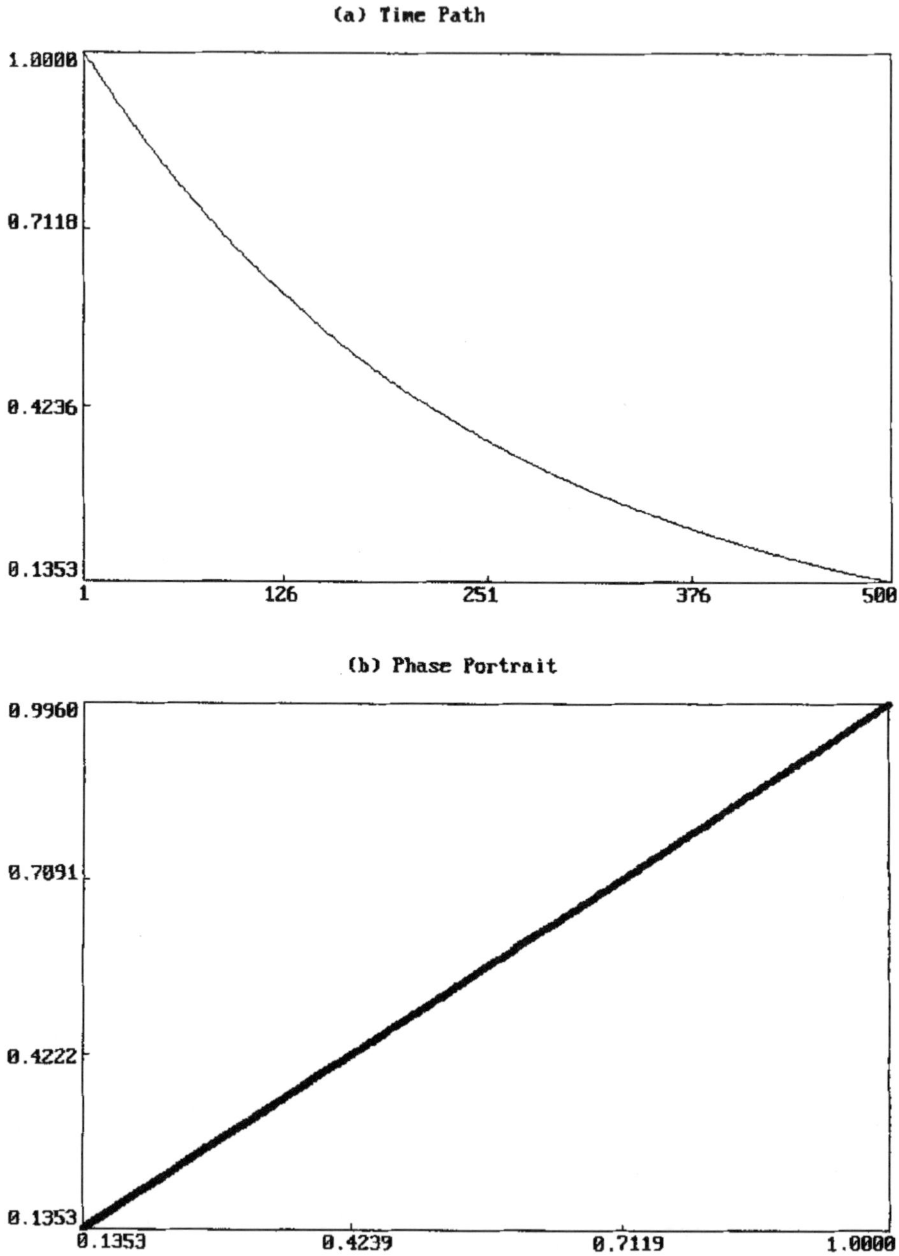

Figure 9.10 The behaviour of the exchange rate as generated by a linear deterministic model

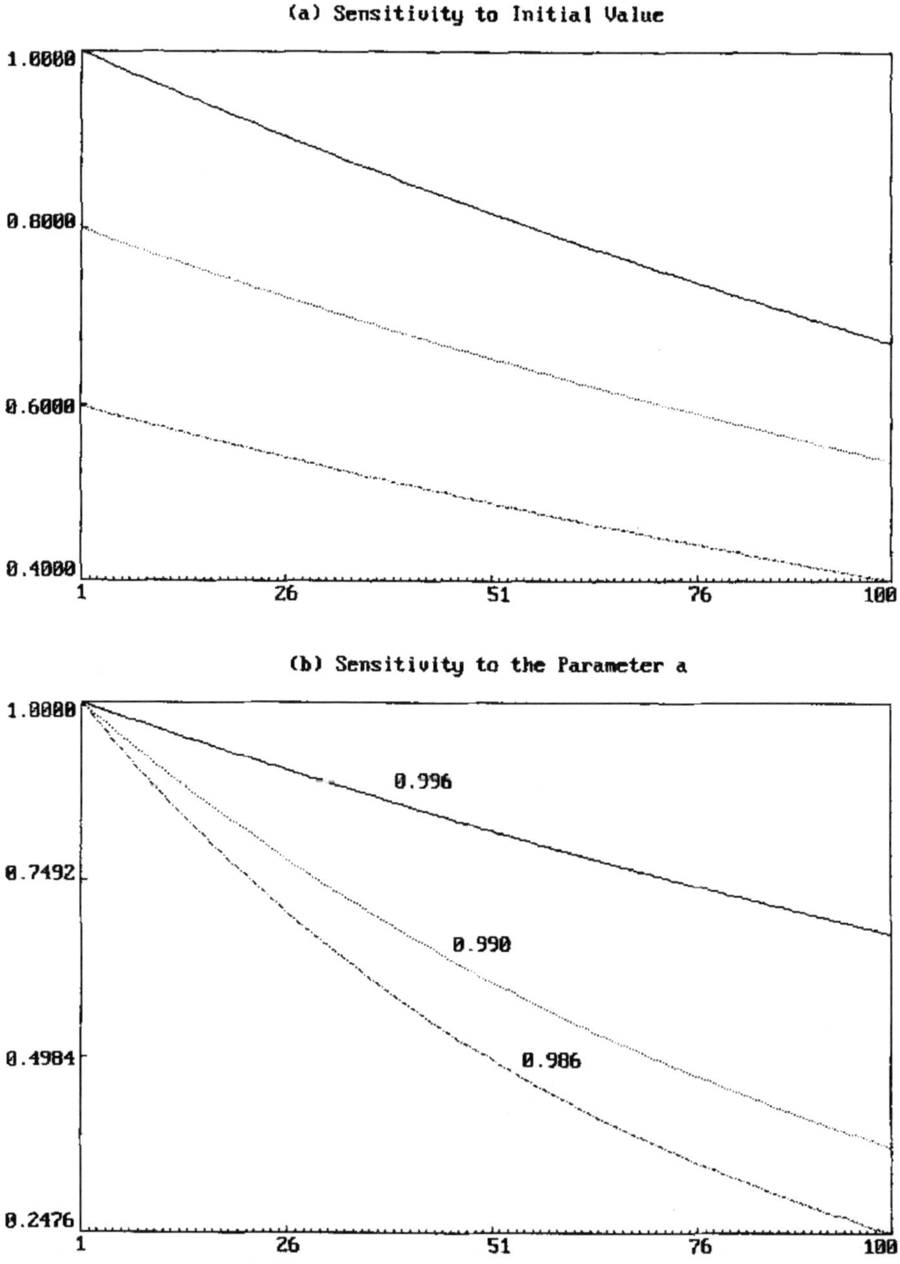

Figure 9.11 Sensitivity of the behaviour of the exchange rate as generated by a linear deterministic model

Linear feedback implies adjustments, which are proportional to the amount by which the exchange rate is above or below its equilibrium value. By a sequence of such adjustments, the exchange rate is forced back in line. The problem is that a linear feedback effect cannot generate the random (or random-looking) exchange rate movements that we observe in reality.

On the other hand, nonlinear feedback effects mean that corrections are not proportional. Savit (1988) argues that one source of nonlinear reaction is market psychology that causes overreaction to bad news. Nonlinear feedback can be explained in terms of equation (9.9) which can be rewritten as

$$S_t = kS_{t-1} - kS_{t-1}^2 \tag{9.11}$$

The nonlinear term, kS_{t-1}^2, generates negative feedback that competes with the linear term kS_{t-1}, and under some conditions helps to stabilise exchange rate fluctuations. For example, if $k > 1$ but not too large and $0 < S_0 < 1$, then $0 < S_t < 1$ for any value of t. On the other hand if $S_t = kS_{t-1}$ then $S_t \approx k^t$, which means that the process becomes explosive.

Interest in nonlinear models has grown because they can generate a wide variety of behaviour. Linear models can generate four types of behaviour only: (i) oscillatory and stable, (ii) oscillatory and explosive, (iii) non-oscillatory and stable, and (iv) explosive. Nonlinear models can generate a behaviour characterised by sudden bouts of volatility and occasional large movements. This is the type of behaviour that can be observed during currency crises.

Notice that nonlinearities and chaos can be illustrated by using a model that contains explanatory variables. Let the exchange rate at time t be determined by one or more explanatory variables as in the functional relationship

$$S_t = f(X_t) \tag{9.12}$$

where X is a single variable or a vector of explanatory variables. Suppose now that X is generated by the nonlinear difference equation

$$X_t = g(X_{t-1}) \tag{9.13}$$

As $t \rightarrow \infty$, there are four possibilities (as we have seen before): (i) the unrealistic case; (ii) convergence on a constant value; (iii) convergence on a limit cycle; and (iv) convergence on a 'strange attractor'. The last case describes chaotic behaviour in the exchange rate derived from the chaotic behaviour in the explanatory variable. The 'strange attractor' will be a 'non-degenerate attractor' because of the sensitivity to the initial condition (that is, the initial value of the exchange rate or, in this case, the explanatory variable).

Some theoretical models have been suggested in the literature to show that under certain conditions the behaviour of exchange rates will be nonlinear and perhaps chaotic. One of these models, which is the model presented earlier, is derived by adjusting the regressive expectation formation mechanism to take into account the speculative and hedging activity of exporters (Copeland, 1994). De Grauwe and Vansanten (1990) have developed an exchange rate model in which the introduction of nonlinearities results in chaotic behaviour. Finally, Liao (1997) developed a model in which the exchange rate exhibits nonlinear and chaotic behaviour as a result of the interaction of the activities of speculators and the central bank.

IMPLICATIONS OF CHAOS FOR FORECASTING

The implications of chaos for forecasting are very dismal. They amount to the proposition that forecasting chaotic processes is either impossible or so erroneous that the forecasts are rendered useless. The proposition is evident from the following implications, which will be valid if (for the time being) we assume that exchange rates are generated by chaotic processes.

1. We know by now that every forecast has to start from some point in time when the value of the exchange rate is known. Because of the sensitivity to the initial value, any slight measurement error is likely to produce unlimited divergence between the forecast and actual values as time passes. Any error in specifying an initial condition (even a very small error due, for example, to computer rounding in the 100th decimal place) can give rise to forecasts whose behaviour bears no relevance to the behaviour of the actual values. Put differently, any small error in the initial value will lead, after some time, to very large forecasting errors although it is possible to calculate the exchange rate from a deterministic equation. This will be invariably the case because it is not possible to perform numerical computations to infinite precision.
2. There is even a bigger problem as we are unlikely to know the generating process. We may have evidence indicating that exchange rates are chaotic, but this will not necessarily tell us anything about the generating nonlinear equation. The logistic equation we used in this chapter to generate chaotic behaviour is not the only equation capable of doing so. It is sometimes argued, however, that it may not be necessary to know the generating equation. All we need is to identify the attractor from the plot of a phase portrait. Once this attractor is identified, it is possible to derive forecasts by applying local polynomial mapping. One can simply identify the current position on the attractor and then infer the evolution over time of points near the current point (Clyde and Osler, 1997).

3. If we assume that we know the generating equation and that we have a somewhat precise measure of the initial condition, this will only produce somewhat accurate forecasts over a short period of time. But as long as there are rounding errors, no matter how small they are, these will accumulate so rapidly as to make long-run forecasts too erroneous to be useful. Meteorologists have long recognised the hazards of long-term weather forecasting, a lesson that economists have yet to learn. Economists who argue for the feasibility of forecasting from the phase portrait admit this eventuality. Clyde and Osler (1997) concede that 'as the forecasting horizon is stretched out, the evolution of nearby points spreads out over the attractor, and predictive power is finally reduced to zero'.
4. The conclusion on the inability to forecast chaotic processes can be reached from a different perspective. Chaos can be viewed as the culmination of a sequence of changes in the cyclical behaviour of a nonlinear function. A chaotic process is necessarily aperiodic, that is it does not repeat itself. Given that periodicity implies forecastability and vice versa, it follows that chaotic processes are not forecastable.

On the other hand, it has been suggested that there is a link between chaos and technical analysis. Clyde and Osler (1997) argue that technical analysis may be related in terms of attractors and strange attractors. They also suggest that technical analysis may allow prediction on systems of higher dimensions than nonlinear models do at this time. For example, a head and shoulders pattern may be an attractor of a very high dimension. In fact, it is claimed that technical analysis may be equivalent to nonlinear predictive methods which are based on the phase portrait and polynomial mapping.

Evidence for the hypothesis that exchange rates are chaotic provides both relief and frustration. It provides relief because it explains the erratic behaviour of exchange rates. On the other hand, it is a source of frustration because it implies the difficulty or impossibility of forecasting exchange rates. This evidence is examined in the following section.

TESTING AND EMPIRICAL EVIDENCE

Chaotic behaviour can potentially explain fluctuations in financial markets that appear to be random. So, there is a need to test for the presence of chaos. If chaos is present then linear forecasting methods will not work, to say the least.

There is no doubt that changes in exchange rates are very erratic. Given a sample of data, how can we detect the presence of chaos, if it is present in the data? Remember that a necessary condition for chaos is that the generating process is nonlinear. Therefore, testing for chaos has to start with testing for nonlinearity.

The bulk of exchange rate (univariate or multivariate) models assume linearity. Conventional analysis, which implicitly assumes linearity, is based on the concept of correlation. Take, for example, a simple linear autoregressive model. A requirement for the validity of this model as a representation of the exchange rate generating process is that the residuals of the model (the difference between the actual values and the values estimated by the model) are not serially correlated. This is because serial correlation simply implies the presence of information in the residuals, which can be utilised to improve the model. The absence of serial correlation is a property of independent, identically distributed (IID) residuals that economists look for and sometimes assume. However, if the residuals are not serially correlated, this may not necessarily imply the absence of dependence. It could be the case that they are linearly independent, but that they are dependent in a nonlinear manner. Well, it may be possible to detect this dependence by measuring the correlation between the squares of the residuals. This, however, will be the case only if the nonlinear dependence takes the form of correlation between the squares of the residual. What is needed here is a test which is capable of detecting nonlinear dependence, if it is present, without specifying the nature of this dependence.

Economists have for some time now dropped the assumption of IID residuals by using the autoregressive conditional heteroscedasticity (ARCH) model due to Engle (1982), or its other variants, such as the GARCH model or the EGARCH model. These models seem to fit the behaviour of financial variables very well, including the property of volatility clustering (periods of extreme turbulence followed by periods of extreme calm). If the ARCH models do not fit well then we need to test for general nonlinearity. Three tests are used in the literature: the correlation dimension, the *BDS* test and the Lyapunov exponent test. These tests are described (rather superficially) in turn.

CORRELATION DIMENSION

The correlation dimension test is due to Grassberger and Procaccia (1983). This test is based on the significant difference in the behaviour of a chaotic process and a stochastic process as shown in Figure 9.9. The correlation dimension is calculated by constructing n histories of filtered data (obtained either by first differencing or by fitting an autoregressive model). An n history is a point in n-dimensional space where n is called the 'imbedding dimension'. The correlation integral $C_n(\varepsilon)$ is then calculated: this is the fraction of pairs of points that are close to each other, in the sense that they are not far away from each other by more than ε.

The correlation dimension is the slope of the curve obtained by plotting $\log C_n(\varepsilon)$ on $\log(\varepsilon)$. For small values of ε, the slope is calculated as

$$\upsilon_n = \lim_{\substack{\varepsilon \to 0 \\ n \to \infty}} [\log C_n(\varepsilon) / \log(\varepsilon)] \tag{9.14}$$

If υ_n does not increase with n, the data are nonlinear and possibly chaotic. For a random process the correlation dimension is ∞.

THE BDS TEST

The *BDS* test, which is also based on the concept of the correlation dimension, is due to Brock *et al.* (1987). The null hypothesis is that the series is IID. The test statistic is calculated as

$$W_n(\varepsilon) = \frac{\sqrt{N}[C_n(\varepsilon) - C_1(\varepsilon)^n]}{\sigma_n(\varepsilon)} \tag{9.15}$$

where N is the sample size and $\sigma_n(\varepsilon)$ is an estimate of the standard deviation under the null hypothesis. The test statistic is asymptotically distributed as $N(0, 1)$. A rejection of the null hypothesis implies nonlinearity.

THE LYAPUNOV EXPONENT TEST

This is a test for the necessary and sufficient conditions for chaos: the necessary condition being nonlinearity, while the sufficient condition is sensitivity to the initial condition. A necessary and a sufficient condition for chaos is that the largest Lyapunov exponent is strictly positive.

The simplest representation of the concept of the Lyapunov exponent is the following. Assume a ball that contains the initial values with a radius $r(0)$ at time $t = 0$. When the system evolves through time, the ball would become an ellipsoid. Let the ith principal axis of the ellipsoid at time t have length $r_i(t)$, then the ith Lyapunov exponent is given by

$$\lambda_i = \lim_{t \to \infty} [(\log r_i(t) - \log r_i(0))/t] \tag{9.16}$$

If $\lambda_i > 0$ for at least one i, the process can be identified as being chaotic.

THE RESULTS

Empirical tests on the presence of chaos in economic time series have proliferated (Sayers (1991) provides a survey). Brock (1986) had earlier provided evidence against chaos in macroeconomic time series. The initial work on chaos in financial markets was done on stock markets, including studies by Merville and Pieptea (1989) and Eldridge *et al.* (1993).

The presence of nonlinearity in exchange rates has been studied by a number of economists but the results turned out to be ambiguous. For example, Hsieh (1989) and Kugler and Lenz (1991) detect nonlinearities for several exchange rates but these nonlinearities can be explained by a GARCH model. Studies conducted by Diebold and Nason (1990) and Meese and Rose (1990, 1991) use non-parametric estimation of nonlinear models but they do not reach any significant improvement over the linear models, including the random walk model. One study producing favourable results has been carried out by Bajo-Rubio *et al.* (1997) who tested (using the correlation dimension and the Lyapunov exponents tests) for the presence of deterministic chaos in the Spanish peseta–US dollar exchange rates (spot and forward). The results of this study reveal the presence of chaotic behaviour. This finding was used to derive short-term forecasts, which were found to be superior to those obtained from a random walk model. This conclusion must be treated with caution, however. Once a time series is determined to be chaotic, there is no method for discovering the underlying mechanism from which it is derived.

In another study, Chappell and Eldridge (1997) examined the behaviour of the exchange rate between the pound and the European currency unit (ECU) during the time before the UK joined the exchange rate mechanism of the European Monetary System and during the time of its membership. It was found that during the membership period a GARCH(1,1) model fit the data very well but during the period before membership there was evidence for significant nonlinearity and the possibility of a chaotic process. These results are based on the three tests described in this section. Further evidence for chaos in the foreign exchange market is provided by Liao (1997) who used the correlation dimension test and Laypunov exponent test to examine the exchange rates of five Asian countries. The results reveal that these exchange rates exhibit chaotic behaviour.

In considering the weight of the evidence, the following conclusions can be drawn:

1. Evidence based on the correlation dimension and related tests points to the presence of nonlinearities in the behaviour of exchange rates.
2. There is little evidence for chaos.
3. The residuals from correctly specified ARCH or GARCH models show little sign of any remaining nonlinearity. This implies that these models may provide an adequate and a valid representation of the behaviour of exchange rates.

ARTIFICIAL NEURAL NETWORKS: AN OVERVIEW

One more reason why chaos and neural networks are dealt with in one chapter is that both of the techniques are based on nonlinear models.

Sometimes a comparison is made between the forecasting power of an artificial neural network model incorporating noise and that of a chaotic process generated from a logistic equation. It is often claimed that the former is superior (see, for example, Qi, 1996). Like the study of chaotic processes, one of the motivations for using neural networks to forecast exchange rates is the inadequacy of linear models.

An artificial neural network (ANN) is a representation of a nonlinear non-parametric model. The procedure allows the data to determine the structure and parameters of the model without any restrictive assumptions. In other words, it is a technique that allows the data to speak for themselves rather than introducing parameter restrictions based on preconceived ideas and hypotheses. It can be shown that neural network modelling is related to conventional statistical methods, including linear regression, logit and probit models, principal components, and latent variable models (see Qi, 1996). ANNs can be viewed as being a special class of nonlinear parametric models where the process of 'learning' or 'training' is equivalent to the estimation of parameters. ANNs have attracted the attention of scholars from a variety of fields because of their (alleged?) power in recognising patterns of behaviour. This is also the reason why the technique has attracted the attention of practitioners, particularly those following and attempting to forecast the behaviour of financial prices, including exchange rates.

Work on ANNs has been inspired by the structure and functioning of the nerve cells in the brain. It is therefore based on the basic anatomy of the human nerve cell or the 'neuron'. This work originated in mathematical modelling, motivated by the desire to model the functioning of the human brain. Subsequently, it has been applied to a variety of fields, including economics and finance.

An ANN can be thought of as a system connecting a set of inputs to a set of outputs in a possible nonlinear way. The approach is non-parametric in character. The links between inputs and outputs are typically made via one or more hidden layers of neurons. The number of layers and neurons (or units) and the weights attached to mappings from neuron to neuron are chosen to give the best possible fit to a set of training data using some sort of training algorithm which can take on a large number of iterations to converge. The underlying idea is that this process resembles the way the brain learns.

ANN STRUCTURE

The structure of an ANN is defined by its architecture, which describes the processing elements and their interconnections, and its activation (or transfer) function. We start by describing the processing element, the neuron, then we move on to describe the collection of neurons that comprises a neural network.

We start with a brief lesson in biology. A biological neuron operates by receiving signals from other neurons through some connections. These connections are called 'synapses'. What happens next depends on whether a combination of these signals is in excess of a certain level, which is called the threshold or the activation level. If it is, the receiving neuron will 'fire' by sending a signal to the neurons that are connected to it. In general, signals may cause 'excitations' or 'inhibitions' to a neuron firing, which is represented by a generation of an electrical impulse. It is believed that thinking is the collective effect of the presence or absence of firing in the pattern of synaptic connection between neurons.

ANNs are artificial models of the biological neural networks. Therefore, we move on to describe an artificial or a model neuron, which from now on will be called a 'unit'. An artificial neuron, as shown in Figure 9.12, consists of multiple inputs (in this case four inputs, $x_1, \ldots, x_4$) and a single output, y. Each input has a weight that is assigned to it ($w_1, \ldots, w_4$). The unit calculates a weighted sum of the inputs then sends it to a transfer function

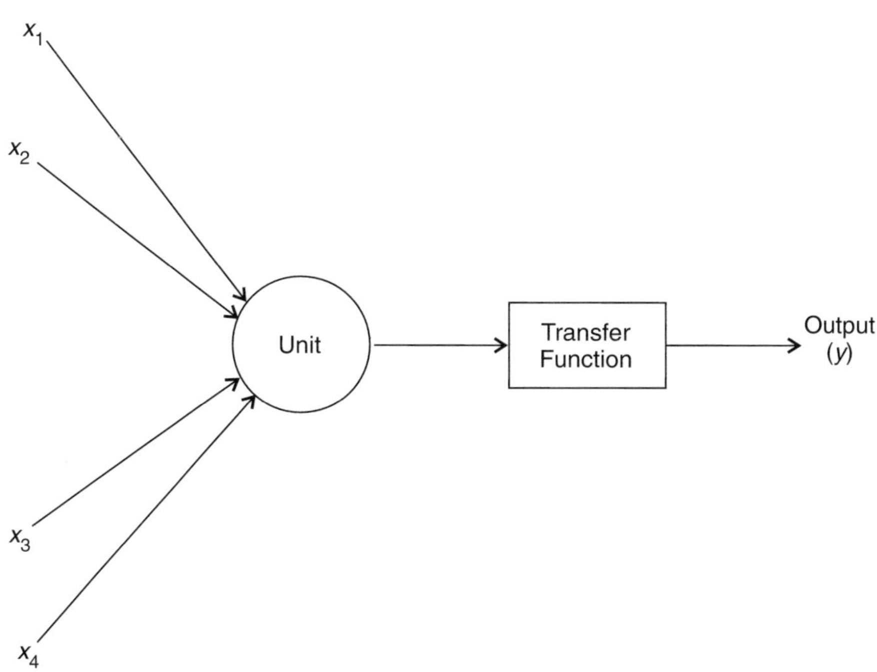

Figure 9.12 The working of an artificial neuron (unit)

(or a squasher) to smooth out the output. The output is sent either to another unit or to the outside world.

ANNs may take several shapes but the most common type is the multilayer feedforward backpropagation or simply the feedforward network. This ANN consists of layers of units, as shown in Figure 9.13, which again assumes four inputs and a single output. In each layer, inputs are connected either to a preceding layer or they come from the outside world. On the other hand, outputs are connected either to a succeeding layer or to the outside world. The following layers can be distinguished:

1. The input layer is connected to the external world on the input side. The function of this layer, whose units have no transfer functions, is to distribute signals from the outside world to the other layers.
2. The output layer is connected to the outside world on the output side. Its function is to collect the features detected from the signals and use those features to produce a response.

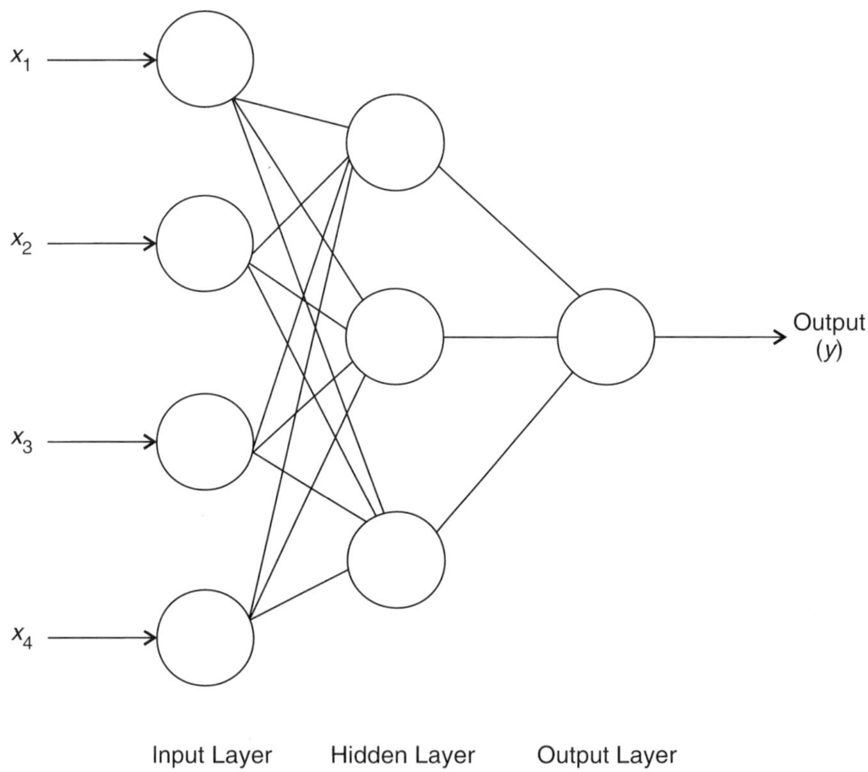

Figure 9.13 A feedforward ANN

3. The layers in between (one in this example) are called intermediate, hidden or middle layers. These layers have no input or output connection with the outside world. They perform the function of detecting features of the signals they receive. They also provide the link between input and output layers.

The network maps inputs into outputs in such a way as to make the signals flow in one direction only, that is from the input layer to the middle layer to the output layer. It is obvious from Figure 9.13 that feedforward networks are fully connected in the sense that each unit is connected to every output from the preceding layer or one input from the outside world.

THE FUNCTIONING OF ANNS

Consider a three-layer network with a single output, k middle layer units and n inputs $(x_1, \ldots, x_n)$. The middle layer units j, where $j = 1, 2, \ldots, k$, receive the weighted sum of inputs, $\sum w_{ij}x_i$, where w_{ij} is the weight assigned to input i in unit j, as well as a bias term, x_0, which is equal to 1. The output signalled by this unit is represented by the equation

$$m_j = F\left(\sum_{i=1}^{n} w_{ij}x_i\right) \tag{9.17}$$

for $j = 1, 2, \ldots, k$ and $i = 0, 1, 2, \ldots, n$, such that w_0x_0 is the weighted bias term. F is the transfer function, which is normally and most frequently specified as the sigmoid or logistic function. As shown in Figure 9.14, this function provides an input–output mapping, and it is represented by the equation

$$F(q) = \frac{1}{1 + e^{-q}} \tag{9.18}$$

In a similar manner, the output unit receives the output of the middle layer units to produce the output given by the equation

$$y = H\left(\sum_{j=1}^{k} \nu_j m_j\right) \tag{9.19}$$

for $j = 1, 2, \ldots, k$, such that ν_0 is the weight assigned to the bias term, m_0, and H is the transfer function.

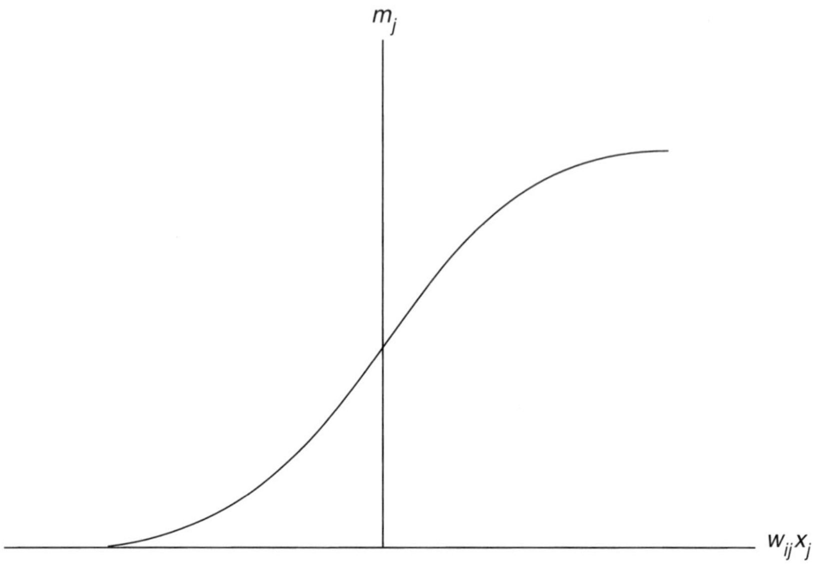

Figure 9.14 The sigmoid (logistic) transfer function

By substitution we obtain

$$y = H\left[\nu_0 + \sum_{j=1}^{k} \nu_j F\left(\sum_{i=0}^{n} w_{ij}x_i\right)\right] \tag{9.20}$$

which is obviously a nonlinear specification.

The most widely used training method of the ANN described above is error backpropagation. This is a recursive gradient descent method that aims at the minimisation of the sum of the squared errors by moving down the gradient of the error curve. The process works as described in Figure 9.15. The error is derived from the calculated output value and the actual value. A portion of this error is then propagated backwards through the network. At each unit the error is used to adjust the weights and the threshold values of the units. Next time, this makes the error in the network response less for the same input. The propagation process starts at the output level and by adjusting the weights of this layer. Once this has been done, the weights for the middle layer are adjusted and so on. When the sum of squares of errors has been reduced to the desired level the training process comes to an end and the network can be used for forecasting.

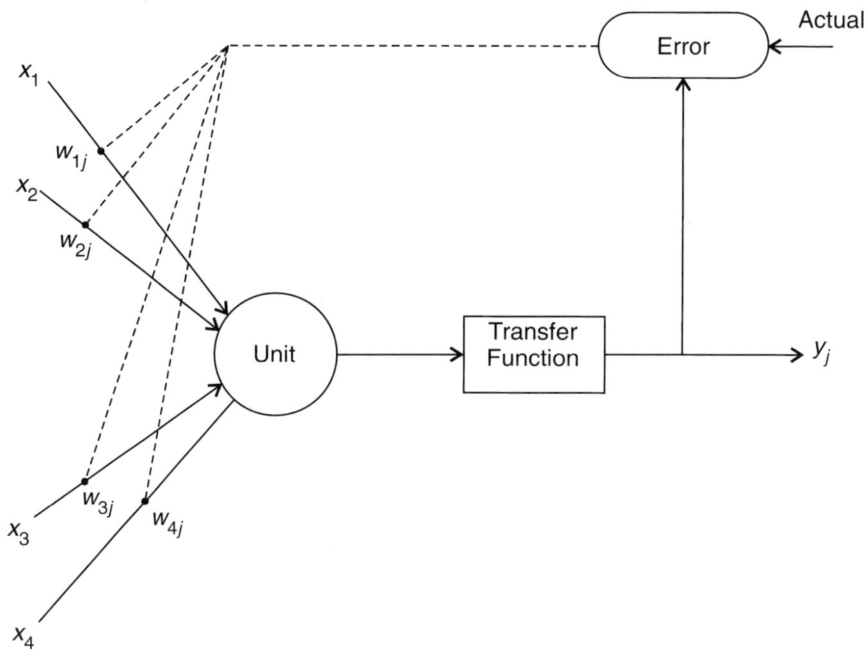

Figure 9.15 The training process in ANNs

APPLICATIONS TO EXCHANGE RATES: METHODOLOGY AND EMPIRICAL EVIDENCE

In economic and financial applications, the independent variable values enter as inputs, nonlinearities and discontinuties are handled by middle layer processing units and relative weighting of model components in the connections to the dependent variables in the output layer. The basic idea is to model the time series to be forecast in terms of the explanatory variables (the input). Lagged values of inputs and the output may also be used.

Let the variable to be forecast (the output) be the exchange rate. A linear exchange rate determination model may be written as an autoregressive distributed lag equation of the form

$$S_t = \sum_{i=1}^{p} a_i S_{t-i} + \sum_{j=0}^{q} \mathbf{X}'_{t-j}\mathbf{B}_j + \varepsilon_t \tag{9.21}$$

where **X** is a vector of explanatory variables and **B** is a vector of coefficients. Thus, the explanatory variables are the lagged dependent variables $S_{t-1}, \ldots, S_{t-p}$ and the other variables $\mathbf{X}'_t, \ldots, \mathbf{X}'_{t-q}$, including the bias term, which is the constant term. If there are k units in the middle layer, the model can be written as

$$S_t = w_0 + \sum_{j=1}^{k} w_j F(h_j) \tag{9.22}$$

such that

$$h_j = \sum \mathbf{Z}'_t \mathbf{A}_j \tag{9.23}$$

$$\mathbf{Z}'_t = S_{t-1}, \ldots, S_{t-p}, \mathbf{X}'_t, \ldots, \mathbf{X}'_{t-q} \tag{9.24}$$

where the w and the **A** are parameters (or weights) and $F(h_j)$ is a nonlinear function of the linear combination $\mathbf{Z}'_t\mathbf{A}_j$ which has the form

$$f(h_j) = \frac{1}{1 + e^{-h_j}} \tag{9.25}$$

The following question arises: how do we determine the set of explanatory variables to be included in the model? While economic theory may provide some guidance, conventional regression analysis can help in this respect. A conventional model can be used to identify trends and outliers and to determine the detrending method. Apart from this problem there are other problems associated with the application of ANNs. For example, there is no formal procedure whereby the optimal network structure can be determined. Another problem pertains to the interpretation of a trained ANN model.

Despite these problems, a large number of attempts have been made to forecast exchange rates and other financial prices by using ANNs. Kuan and Liu (1995) use neural networks to forecast five exchange rates against the US dollar. Their results reveal that, at least for two currencies, the models produce significant timing ability and/or significant lower out-of-sample forecasting errors. Similarly, Abu-Mostafa (1995) reports a significant improvement in forecasting power for four currencies. Hsu *et al.* (1995) report a better forecasting accuracy of the direction. However, Qi (1996) argues that these studies do not provide evidence in favour of the ability of ANNs to forecast exchange rates.

COMPUTER SOFTWARE AND FURTHER READING

Testing for chaos can be carried out by using the software package Chaos Data Analyzer (CDA) which is published by the American Institute of Physics. It is a collection of 14 programs that allows the user to analyse up to 16,328 data points with the objective of detecting chaos in random-looking data. If chaos is found to exist the program tries to determine properties of the equation underlying the behaviour of the time series and forecast the next few values. A number of software packages are also available to forecast by neural networks, one of which is Neuralyst. This is an Excel add-on program that is very user friendly.

Perhaps the best casual reading on chaos is Stewart (1990), which gives plenty of background material on the major researchers in the field. Gleick (1987) is even more casual and easier to read. Useful collections of readings are Cvitanovic (1989) and Anderson *et al.* (1988) as well as Barnett *et al.* (1989). For applications to exchange rates, see Brock *et al.* (1991). The literature on neural networks is plentiful. An interesting reading is Gurney (1997). See also the references provided by Qi (1996).

10: Measuring Forecasting Accuracy

INTRODUCTION

We have seen that forecasting is essential for decision making in situations when the outcome is contingent upon something that will happen in the future. Whether or not a decision to hedge payables or receivables is taken depends on the forecast exchange rate. Whether the outcome turns out to be favourable or adverse depends on the accuracy of this forecast. This argument is true for all other decisions requiring exchange rate forecasting. Forecasting accuracy is important, as erroneous forecasts could lead to decisions with disastrous consequences. We have seen how the failure of the Beecham Group and Laker Airlines resulted from bad financing decisions that could have been based on faulty exchange rate forecasts.

Whether the forecasting function is carried out in-house, bought from outside by subscribing to a forecasting service or both, the forecasts need regular monitoring and evaluation. If the forecasting function is performed in-house, evaluating the forecasting accuracy amounts to evaluating how well the forecasters do their job. If forecasts are obtained by subscribing to one or more services, evaluation is needed to assess the cost-effectiveness of buying the forecasts, to drop some forecasters and hire the services of others. If more than one forecasting service is subscribed to, or if the forecasting function is carried out internally as well as externally, then the objective may be to arrive at a consensus forecast by indulging in composite forecasting along the lines described in the previous chapter. In this case, the forecasting accuracy of the model is important to judge the superiority, or otherwise, of the composite forecast. Also, as we have seen before, combining the forecasts may be based on a weighting scheme where weights are derived from the accuracy of the individual forecasts. For various reasons, therefore, measures of forecasting accuracy are required.

SOME GENERAL CONSIDERATIONS

In this section some considerations pertaining to forecast evaluation are discussed. These include (i) the distinction between in-sample and out-of-sample forecasting; (ii) the benchmark models; (iii) the distinction between static and dynamic forecasting; (iv) the implication of serial correlation in the forecasting errors; (v) forecasting bias; (vi) the forecasting horizon and the date of forecast; and (vii) forecasting the magnitude and direction. These points are discussed in turn.

IN-SAMPLE AND OUT-OF-SAMPLE FORECAST EVALUATION

The evaluation of the forecasting power of a model at a particular point in time is, naturally, based on *ex post* forecasting. This is because the evaluation is based on the forecasting errors which are only available *ex post*. Hence, the evaluation can be based on in-sample (or within-sample) or out-of-sample forecasting results. An in-sample forecast implies that the exchange rate is forecast for points in time falling within the sample period used to estimate the model. An out-of-sample forecast, on the other hand, implies that the exchange rate is forecast for points in time falling outside the sample period used to estimate the model.

Suppose that the forecaster has n observations on the exchange rate and an explanatory variable, X. The pairs of observations are given by (X_1, S_1), (X_2, S_2), ..., (X_n, S_n). Let us assume that the underlying model is

$$S_t = a + bX_t + \varepsilon_t, \qquad t = 1, 2, \ldots, n \tag{10.1}$$

If the forecaster chooses to use the n available observations to estimate the model, then it is not possible at that point in time to estimate the out-of-sample forecasting power of the model, since observations $n+1$ and beyond are not available. It is only possible to evaluate the in-sample forecasting power on the basis of the individual errors which are given by

$$e_t = S_t - \hat{S}_t, \qquad t = 1, 2, \ldots, n \tag{10.2}$$

where $\hat{S}_t$ is the in-sample forecast value of the exchange rate, which is estimated from equation (10.1) as

$$\hat{S}_t = a + bX_t, \qquad t = 1, 2, \ldots, n \tag{10.3}$$

Notice that the difference between ε and e is that while the value of the former depends on the theoretical values of the parameters a and b, the latter is calculated from the estimated values of a and b.

Let us now assume that the forecaster chose to use the first k observations only to estimate the model. The k in-sample forecasts are given by

$$\hat{S}_t = a + bX_t, \qquad t = 1, 2, \ldots, k \tag{10.4}$$

while the $n - k$ out-of-sample forecasts are given by

$$\hat{S}_t = a + bX_t, \qquad t = k+1, k+2, \ldots, n \tag{10.5}$$

The in-sample forecasting power is then measured on the basis of the individual in-sample errors, which are given by

$$e_t = S_t - \hat{S}_t, \qquad t = 1, 2, \ldots, k \tag{10.6}$$

while the out-of-sample forecasting power is measured on the basis of the out-of-sample errors, which are given by

$$e_t = S_t - \hat{S}_t, \qquad t = k+1, k+2, \ldots, n \tag{10.7}$$

There is now a consensus view that out-of-sample forecasting accuracy is what matters. It is arguable that the in-sample forecasting accuracy is not relevant, simply because it tells us that the model fits the data reasonably well. The difference between in-sample and out-of-sample forecasting lies in the difference between the explanatory power and predictive or forecasting power of the underlying model. Some models may have a high explanatory power for the historical data but its forecasting power may be low. The trend has, since Meese and Rogoff (1983a, b), been to emphasise out-of-sample forecasting accuracy.

THE BENCHMARK MODELS

A decision maker may have some competing models of which he wants to choose the one that has the highest forecasting accuracy or the greatest forecasting power. What is done in this case is that a battery of measures of forecasting accuracy are calculated on the basis of the individual errors, and the model that is chosen is the one that has the highest accuracy or power. The situation may be such that the forecaster has one model only, and he wants to know whether or not this model generates good or bad forecasts. Being good or bad must be measured relative to something else, some sort of a benchmark. Two benchmarks are normally used, the random walk forecast and the forward rate forecast.

Consider the forecasting model represented by equation (10.1), which tells us that the exchange rate is determined by the explanatory variable X. This model produces a forecasting error that is given by

$$e_t = S_t - (a + bX_t) \tag{10.8}$$

The random walk model, on the other hand, tells that the best forecast of the exchange rate at a future point in time is its current value. Hence, the forecasting error of the random walk model is given by

$$e_t = S_t - S_{t-1} \tag{10.9}$$

Finally, the forward rate model (or the unbiased efficiency model) tells us that the best forecast is the current forward rate. Hence, the forecasting error of this model is given by

$$e_t = S_t - F_{t-1} \tag{10.10}$$

To evaluate the forecasting model given by equation (10.1) we have to measure its forecasting power on the basis of the forecasting errors and compare it with the same measures based on the forecasting errors of the random walk model and the forward rate model. If the model produces a higher level of accuracy than either of the two benchmark models, we say that the model outperforms or beats the random walk model and the forward rate model.

Notice that the need for a benchmark model arises even if there are several models under consideration. Suppose that we are trying to pick one of two models, a PPP model and an ARIMA model. We go through the exercise of measuring the forecasting accuracy of the two models based on their forecasting errors. If we find that the PPP model has a higher forecasting accuracy than the ARIMA model, can we jump to the conclusion that we should use the PPP model to generate forecasts? The answer is 'not necessarily'. It could be the case that while the PPP model is better than the ARIMA model, it is still bad, because it cannot outperform the random walk model or the forward rate model. Hence, the PPP model should also be dropped in preference for the random walk or the forward rate model. It is more appropriate, in this case, to say that the PPP model is 'less bad' than the ARIMA model. Both should be dropped, because it is cheaper, easier and more accurate to generate forecasts from the random walk model or the forward rate model. In the first case the forecast is the current period's spot exchange rate. In the second case it is the current period's forward exchange rate.

STATIC AND DYNAMIC FORECASTING

To illustrate the difference between static and dynamic forecasting we will utilise the simple autoregressive model

$$S_t = \alpha S_{t-1} + \varepsilon_t \tag{10.11}$$

Let us assume that the forecaster wants to generate out-of-sample forecasts. We start with static forecasting. The first out-of-sample static forecast is the one-step-ahead forecast calculated on the basis of the model estimated by utilising the first k observations. It is therefore given by

$$\hat{S}_{k+1} = \alpha S_k \tag{10.12}$$

The second out-of-sample static forecast is calculated by estimating the model using the first $k+1$ observations and then using this model to calculate the one-step-ahead forecast. Hence

$$\hat{S}_{k+2} = \alpha S_{k+1} \tag{10.13}$$

Likewise, the last out-of-sample static forecast is calculated by estimating the model using the whole sample except the last one and then using this model to calculate the one-step-ahead forecast

$$\hat{S}_n = \alpha S_{n-1} \tag{10.14}$$

Thus, static forecasting implies one-period-ahead forecasting. Let us now consider the generation of dynamic forecasts from the same model. In this case forecasts are generated for several periods ahead recursively by utilising the generated forecasts instead of the actual values. The first out-of-sample dynamic forecast is the same as the static forecast. It is the one-period-ahead forecast calculated as in equation (10.12). The second out-of-sample dynamic forecast is the two-period-ahead forecast, which is calculated from the one-period-ahead forecast as

$$\hat{S}_{k+2} = \alpha \hat{S}_{k+1} = \alpha^2 S_k \tag{10.15}$$

The last out-of-sample dynamic forecast is calculated from the previous forecast as

$$\hat{S}_n = \alpha \hat{S}_{n-1} = \alpha^n S_k \tag{10.16}$$

Obviously, a model is viewed more favourably if it forecasts well multi-step ahead than one-step ahead, that is, if it is judged on the basis of dynamic rather than static forecasts. In comparing the forecasting power of two or more models we have to make sure that we are comparing static forecasts with static forecasts and dynamic forecasts with dynamic forecasts.

What are the multi-step-ahead forecasts of the benchmark models described earlier? As we have seen in Chapter 5, the random walk model produces the same forecast, the current exchange rate, irrespective of the time horizon. Therefore, the forecast for any time horizon is S_k. The forward rate model produces different forecasts for different horizons. The one-

Table 10.1 Static and dynamic forecasts

Time	$k+1$	$k+2$	$k+3$	...	n
Autoregressive model					
Static	αS_k	αS_{k+1}	αS_{k+2}	...	αS_{n-1}
Dynamic	αS_k	$\alpha^2 S_k$	$\alpha^3 S_k$	...	$\alpha^n S_k$
Random walk model					
Static	S_k	S_{k+1}	S_{k+2}	...	S_{n-1}
Dynamic	S_k	S_k	S_k	...	S_k
Forward rate model					
Static	F_k^{k+1}	F_{k+1}^{k+2}	F_{k+2}^{k+3}	...	F_{n-1}^n
Dynamic	F_k^{k+1}	F_k^{k+2}	F_k^{k+3}	...	F_k^n

step-ahead forecast is the one-period forward rate, that is, the forward rate implicit in a forward contract initiated at time k for delivery at time $k+1$, F_k^{k+1}. Similarly, the two-step-ahead forecast is the two-period forward rate, F_k^{k+2}, and so on. Table 10.1 lists the various forecasts for the autoregressive model and the two benchmark models.

THE IMPLICATIONS OF SERIAL CORRELATION IN THE FORECASTING ERRORS

It is important that the forecasting errors do not display serial correlation, since this implies that the forecasts are not efficient in the sense that they do not utilise the information reflected in the regular behaviour of the errors. If this is the case then the information can be utilised to improve the forecasting power of the model.

Consider the following example. A forecaster is using the random walk model to forecast the exchange rate between the dollar and the pound (USD/GBP) over 10 points in time (1, ..., 10). Table 10.2 lists the actual values of the exchange rate as well as the dynamic and static forecasts derived from the random walk model.

The actual behaviour of the exchange rate shows a persistent appreciation of the pound until period 5, and depreciation afterwards. The dynamic forecast is the same for all points in time, standing at 1.6500, while the static forecast varies. Let us examine the behaviour of the forecasting error in both cases. The behaviour of the forecasting error associated with the dynamic forecasts is shown in Figure 10.1(a). It is obvious that the error is serially

Table 10.2 Static and dynamic forecasts of the random walk model

Observation	*Actual*	*Dynamic*	*Static*
1	1.6500	1.6500	1.6500
2	1.6600	1.6500	1.6500
3	1.6700	1.6500	1.6600
4	1.6800	1.6500	1.6700
5	1.6900	1.6500	1.6800
6	1.6700	1.6500	1.6900
7	1.6500	1.6500	1.6700
8	1.6400	1.6500	1.6500
9	1.6000	1.6500	1.6400
10	1.5900	1.6500	1.6000

correlated. Initially, the forecasting error is positive, then it turns negative. The autocorrelation function plotted in Figure 10.1(b) shows an obvious first-order serial correlation with an autocorrelation coefficient of 0.65. The same story goes for the errors associated with the static forecasts. Positive serial correlation is obvious from the behaviour shown in Figure 10.2. In this case, however, serial correlation is less severe as the first-order correlation coefficient stands at 0.44.

If a forecaster is faced with a situation like this, then the action that needs to be taken is to respecify the model to take into account the behaviour of the forecasting error. For example, a moving average component could be added to the model. If the errors are dependent on each other in a nonlinear fashion then an ARCH model can be specified. Let us see what happens when the model is respecified as an ARMA(1, 2) model. The behaviour of the forecasting error associated with this model is shown in Figure 10.3. We can see that the error now changes sign from positive to negative, it is smaller than previously and it is less serially correlated than before. The first-order autocorrelation coefficient is now 0.18.

If a forecaster uses a model that contains explanatory variables then serial correlation in the errors may be due to the omission of one or more of these variables. In his endeavour to generate accurate forecasts, the forecaster aims at capturing all of the systematic influences affecting the exchange rate, but this may be difficult to accomplish in practice. By examining the historical behaviour of the forecasting error the forecaster may be able to find out what he has missed. It is possible, however, that no matter how extensive the search is, the forecaster will be unable to locate the missing variable or variables. It is still possible in this case to utilise the pattern in the errors to improve the forecasts.

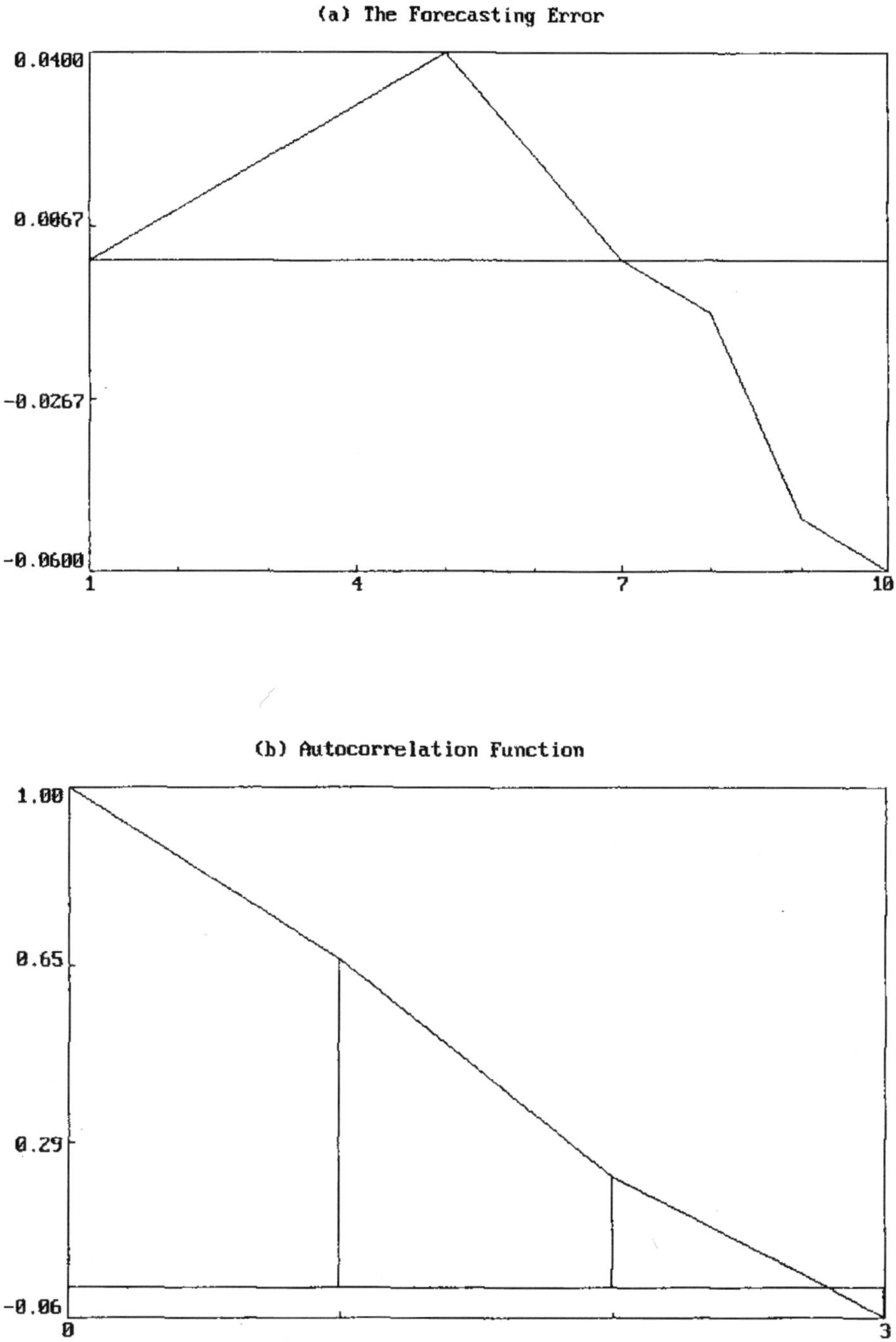

Figure 10.1 Dynamic forecasting error of a random walk model

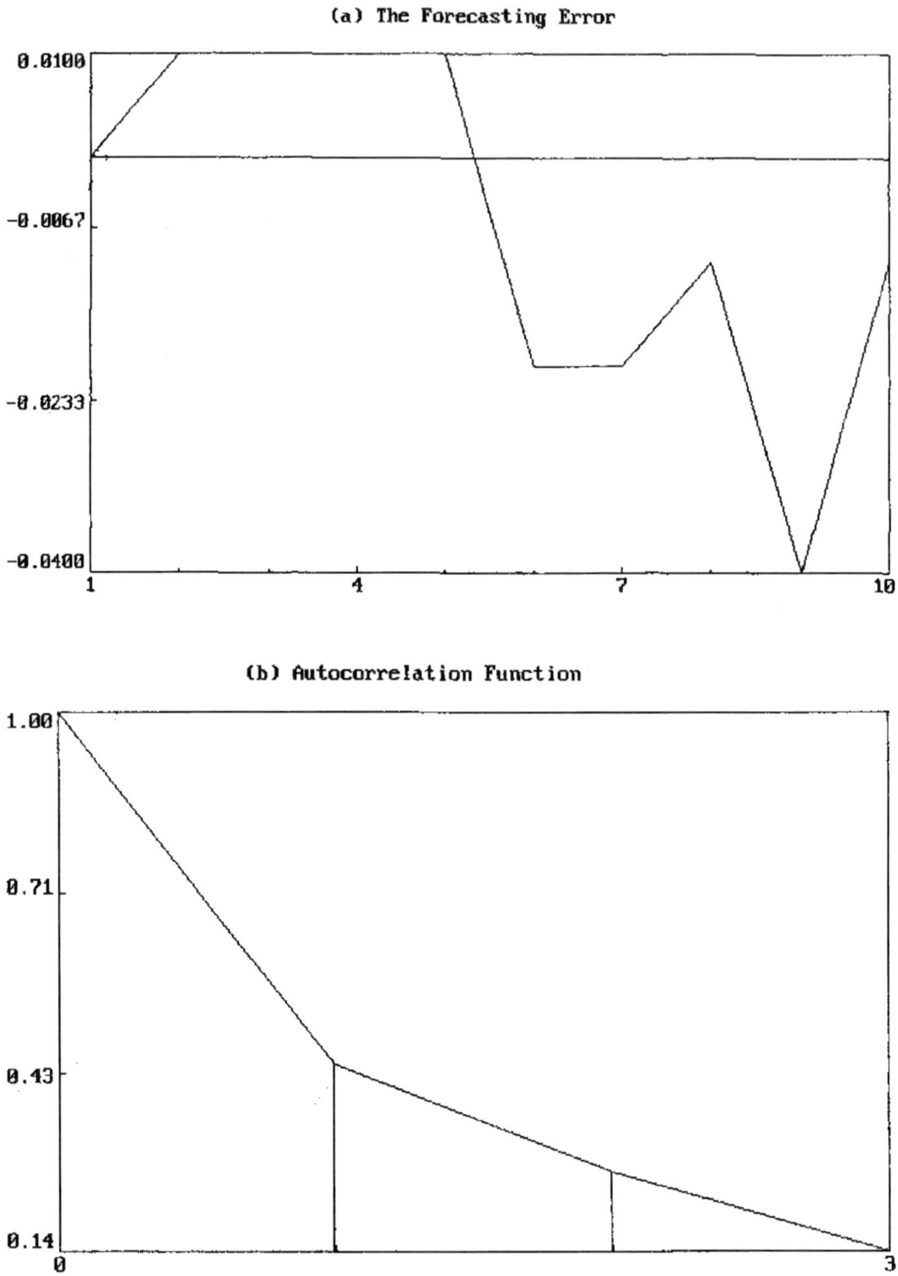

Figure 10.2 Static forecasting error of a random walk model

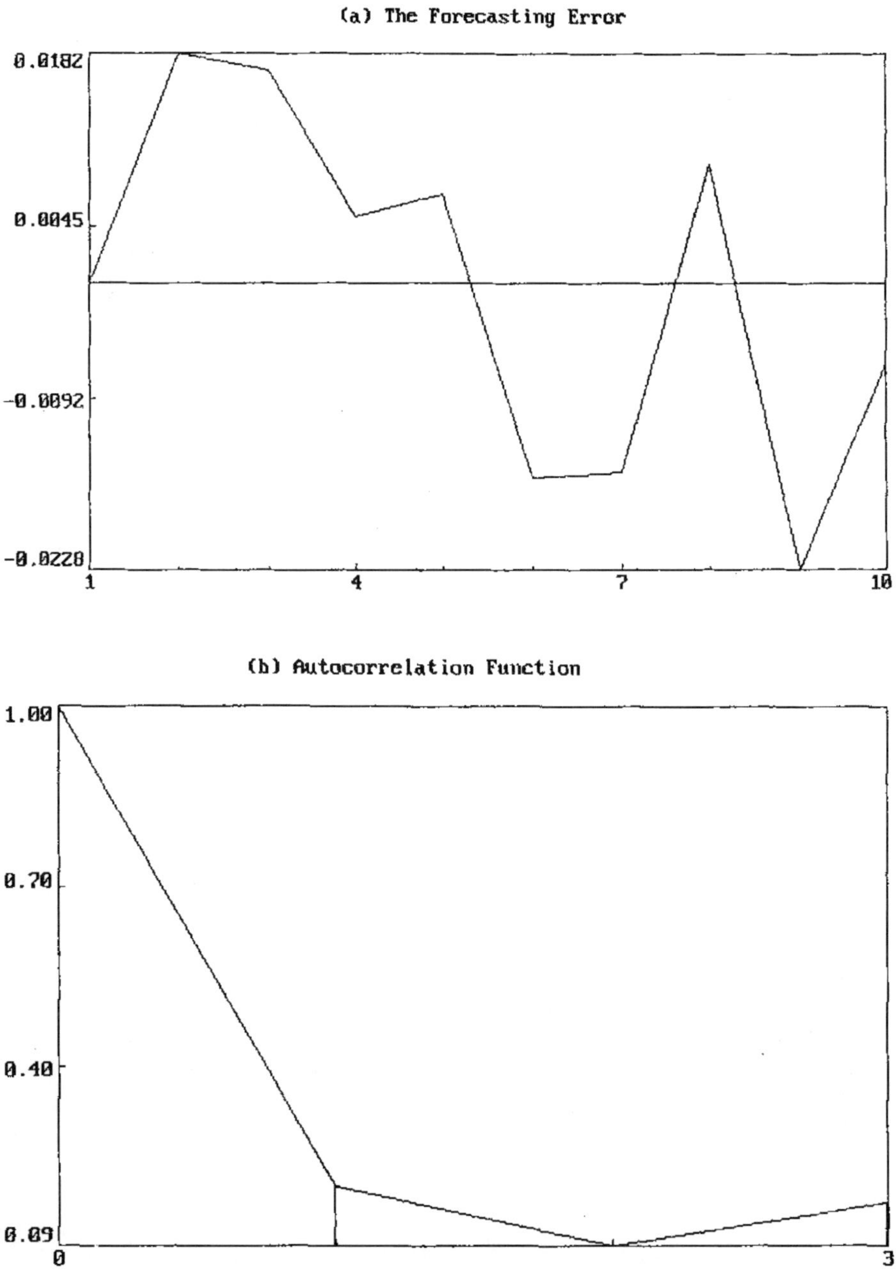

Figure 10.3 Forecasting error of an ARMA (1, 2) model

FORECASTING BIAS

A biased forecast is a forecast that consistently overestimates or underestimates the exchange rate. Bias does not necessarily imply lack of accuracy. Forecasts can be wrong, but as long as the forecasting error is not consistently positive or consistently negative these forecasts are not biased. What is required for unbiasedness is that on average the forecasting error is zero, that the model has equal tendencies to overestimate and underestimate the exchange rate. Accuracy and bias therefore do not go hand in hand. There is obviously a relationship between accuracy, serial correlation and bias but they are not the same. Consider the following example, which is shown in Table 10.3, involving three forecasters (A, B and C) for the USD/GBP exchange rate.

We examine the forecasts produced by forecaster A first. Obviously, these forecasts are biased as they are consistently above the actual values. The forecasts produced by B are also biased but in the opposite direction: they are consistently below the actual values. Forecaster C, on the other hand, does not produce biased forecasts. These forecasts alternate between being above and below the actual values.

Consider now Table 10.4, which shows the forecasting error measured as a percentage of the actual value. It is clear that A is more accurate than B. The unbiased forecasts of C are less accurate than any of the two sets of biased forecasts. Notice, however, that if we judge the forecasting accuracy by the average forecasting error, forecaster C would look the best forecaster, but we know that this is not true. This anomaly appears because the negative errors cancel out the positive errors. To avoid this anomaly we could calculate the mean absolute error or the mean square error as we are going to find out later.

Table 10.3 Bias and accuracy of forecasts

Observation	*Actual*	*A*	*B*	*C*
1	1.6500	1.6830	1.5675	1.8150
2	1.6600	1.6932	1.5936	1.5272
3	1.6700	1.7118	1.6049	1.8337
4	1.6800	1.7304	1.6178	1.6296
5	1.6900	1.7323	1.6292	1.8252
6	1.6700	1.7134	1.6116	1.6030
7	1.6500	1.6946	1.5989	1.7490
8	1.6400	1.6859	1.5826	1.5252
9	1.6000	1.6368	1.5408	1.7280
10	1.5900	1.6377	1.5359	1.4628

Table 10.4 Forecasting errors as a percentage of the actual values

Observation	*A*	*B*	*C*
1	−2.0	5.0	−10.0
2	−2.0	4.0	8.0
3	−2.5	3.9	−9.8
4	−3.0	3.7	3.0
5	−2.5	3.6	−8.0
6	−2.6	3.5	4.0
7	−2.7	3.1	−6.0
8	−2.8	3.5	7.0
9	−2.3	3.7	−8.0
10	−3.0	3.4	8.0

It is possible to test for unbiasedness formally on the basis of the proposition that unbiasedness implies a zero-mean forecasting error. The test statistic for the null hypothesis that forecasts are unbiased (the mean forecasting error is zero) is

$$\tau = \frac{\bar{e}}{\sqrt{\frac{1}{n}\sum_{t=1}^{n}(e_t - \bar{e})^2}} \tag{10.17}$$

where e_t is the forecasting error at time t and $\bar{e}$ is the mean value of the forecasting error. This test statistic has a t-distribution with degrees of freedom equal to the number of observations less one. The null hypothesis is rejected if the mean forecasting error is significantly different from zero, that is if the test statistic is greater than the critical value of the t-distribution.

Alternatively, unbiasedness can be tested on the basis of a regression model. To run the test, a regression equation is estimated relating the forecast values to the actual values. Thus, the regression equation takes the form

$$\hat{S}_t = \alpha + \beta S_t + \varepsilon_t \tag{10.18}$$

The null hypothesis of unbiasedness is represented by the coefficient restriction $(\alpha, \beta) = (0, 1)$. Because of the non-stationarity of exchange rates the model is more appropriately specified in first difference form as

$$\Delta\hat{S}_t = \alpha + \beta\Delta S_t + \varepsilon_t \tag{10.19}$$

The following specification is also valid

$$\hat{S}_t - S_{t-1} = \alpha + \beta(S_t - S_{t-1}) + \varepsilon_t \quad (10.20)$$

where $\hat{S}_t - S_{t-1}$ is the predicted change and $S_t - S_{t-1}$ is the actual change in the exchange rate. In both of these cases the coefficient restriction representing unbiasedness is the same.

FORECASTING HORIZON AND DATE OF FORECAST

The forecasting horizon measures how far in the future or out of sample is the point in time for which the forecast is made. Starting from a point in time, k, out-of-sample forecasts can be made for points in time ranging between $k + 1$ and n. If there are two competing models or forecasters, we have to judge their relative forecasting accuracy on the basis of similar time horizons, or the forecasting errors must be adjusted to reflect differences in the forecasting horizons. Naturally, we expect the forecasting power of a model to diminish, the longer the forecasting horizon. Because of differences in the forecasting horizon, a distinction arises between short-term, medium-term and long-term forecasting. Exchange rate forecasts can, for example, be daily over the next two weeks, weekly over the next three months, monthly over the next year, quarterly over the next three years and annual over the next 10 years.

Consider the following example. Two forecasters, A and B, have produced forecasts of the USD/GBP exchange rate one month ahead, three months ahead and six months ahead. The forecast values, the actual values and the forecasting errors as a percentage of the actual values are given in Table 10.5.

Table 10.5 Different forecasting horizons

	One Month	*Three Months*	*Six Months*
Actual	1.6500	1.6900	1.600
Forecasts			
A	1.6700	1.7325	1.6625
B	1.6825	1.7595	1.6400
Errors			
A	−1.2	−2.5	−3.9
B	−2.0	−4.1	−2.5

It is obvious that forecaster A is better than B for the forecasting horizons of one and three months, but B outperforms A over a forecasting horizon of six months. Who is better overall in the sense of having a higher accuracy? To answer this question the errors must be assigned weights, such that the shorter the horizon the heavier is the weight. Let us assign weights that reflect the length of the forecasting horizons in an inverse manner. Hence, the weights 6, 3 and 1 are assigned to errors associated with forecasting horizons of 1, 3 and 6 months respectively. This enables us to calculate a weighted average of the errors over the three horizons. These weighted average errors are −1.9 for forecaster A and −2.7 for forecaster B. Thus, A has a higher forecasting accuracy.

We could generalise this rule as follows. Assume forecasting horizons ranging from 1 to $n-k$, corresponding to out-of-sample forecasts for points in time $k+1$ to n. A schematic representation of this framework is presented in Table 10.6. For a particular forecaster or a model, the weighted average forecasting error is calculated as

$$e_w = \frac{\sum_{i=1}^{n-k} w_i |e_{k+i}|}{\sum_{i=1}^{n-k} w_i} \tag{10.21}$$

where

$$w_i = n - k - (i-1) \tag{10.22}$$

Notice that the absolute values of the errors are used so that negative and positive errors do not cancel out.

The second point that must be taken account of is the date of the forecast. Take, for example, a quarterly forecast prepared in the last quarter for the exchange rate in the current quarter. The question that must be asked, and answered, in this case is when the forecast was prepared. It could have been

Table 10.6 Forecasting horizons and weights

Time	$k+1$	$k+2$	...	n
Horizon	1	2	...	$n-k$
Forecast	S_{k+1}	S_{k+2}	...	S_n
Error	e_1	e_2	...	e_n
Weight	$n-k$	$n-k-1$	...	1

prepared at the end, the beginning or the middle of the last quarter. The evaluation of competing forecasts must take into account this factor either by making sure that the forecasts are prepared at the same point in time or by adjusting their weights. This is because forecasts prepared at the beginning of the quarter for the end of the following quarter effectively have longer horizons than those prepared at the end of the quarter for the end of the following quarter.

MAGNITUDE VERSUS DIRECTION FORECASTING

Suppose that the current level of the USD/GBP exchange rate is 1.65. Two forecasters, A and B, are then asked to forecast the exchange rate three months ahead. Forecaster A is bullish on the pound and his forecast for the exchange rate is 1.80. Conversely, forecaster B is slightly bullish on the US dollar, and so her forecast is 1.62. Three months later, the exchange rate turns out to be 1.68; which forecaster is better, A or B?

In terms of the absolute forecasting errors forecaster B is better, with an absolute forecasting error of 0.06 while the absolute forecasting error of A is 0.12. Thus, B is better at forecasting the magnitude of the change in the exchange rate. Notice that while the actual change in the exchange rate is 0.03 (1.68 – 1.65), the predicted change according to A is 0.15 and according to B it is –0.03. However, the exchange rate rose (the pound appreciated) when B's forecast indicated that it would fall (the pound would depreciate). This is an error of direction in B's forecast. A's forecast has no error of direction, however. A predicted that the pound would appreciate and it did, albeit by less than what A said it would.

A question that arises here concerns the relative importance of forecasting the magnitude and the direction. The answer is that it depends on the purpose for which the forecast is used. Speculative decisions, for example, hinge on the direction of the exchange rate. Hence, if a currency is forecast to appreciate, a long position on that currency is taken, while if it is forecast to depreciate a short position is taken. Consider the situation where these forecasts are the basis for taking such a speculative decision. A's forecast would lead to the right decision of taking a long position on the pound.

What if these forecasts are taken to be the basis for decisions to hedge pound payables in the forward market? In this case we need to know the magnitude of change, as the decision to hedge is taken only if the forecast is higher than the forward rate. If the current forward rate is 1.75 then following forecaster A leads to a hedge decision while following forecaster B leads to a no-hedge decision. In this case, B's forecast leads to the correct decision since under the no-hedge decision the pound can be bought spot at 1.68, while under the hedge decision it is bought forward at 1.75. If the current forward rate is 1.82, both forecasts will lead to the right no-hedge decision. Thus, for the purpose of taking the hedge/no-hedge decision, an accurate forecasting of the magnitude is necessary. In fact, even the decision concerning the choice of the hedge requires an accurate forecast of the magnitude of the change. For example, the decision to go for a money market hedge rather than a forward hedge or no hedge (of payables) at all is taken only if the forecast indicates that the future spot rate is higher than the forward rate, which in turn is higher than the interest parity forward rate. In fact, even the speculative decision may require an accurate forecasting of the magnitude of change. For example, it may not be worthwhile to take a decision to go long on a currency although it is forecast to appreciate if the appreciation is not significant enough to generate profit in excess of transaction costs.

Only when the two forecasters get the direction right is it possible then to judge the accuracy on the basis of the magnitude of the error. Imagine now that B is also bullish on the pound, and hence her forecast indicates that the exchange rate will rise to 1.70. The exchange rate turns out to be 1.74, in which case B is more accurate than A as the absolute forecasting errors are 0.04 and 0.06 respectively. Even in this situation there is no guarantee that the more accurate forecast will lead to a better decision. Consider the situation in which this forecast is intended to be used for taking a decision whether or not to buy a call option on the pound with an exercise exchange rate of 1.73. A's forecast would lead to a 'yes' decision while B's forecast would lead to a 'no' decision. Since the actual exchange rate turns out to be 1.74, net profit can be made by exercising the option, provided that the premium paid to obtain the option is less than 1 cent per pound. Hence, the less accurate forecast could lead to a better decision.

Consider now the following example, which shows that what matters is the absolute magnitude of the change in the exchange rate. Assume again that the current value of the USD/GBP is 1.65 and that a decision is being considered whether or not to take a long straddle position on the pound. This position is obtained by buying a call and a put on the pound with the same exercise exchange rate, which we will assume to be equal to the current rate of 1.65. The idea behind this position is that if the exchange rate ends up above or below the exercise exchange rate by more than the cost of the position, then one of the options can exercised at net profit while the other is left to expire. Assume that the cost of the call and the put is 2 cents, which makes the combined cost of the position 4 cents. This position will be profitable if the exchange rate ends up above 1.69 or below 1.61.

Assume now that A and B produce forecasts of 1.58 and 1.68 respectively. If the forecast of A is followed then the decision will be to take the position. If, on the other hand, the forecast of B is followed, then the decision will be not to take the position. Assume also that the actual exchange rate turns out to be 1.73. Obviously, A has made an error of direction, whereas B got the direction right. In terms of the absolute magnitude of change, A predicted that the exchange rate would change by 7 cents while B predicted that it would change by 3 cents, when in fact it changed by 8 cents. At 1.73, the position is profitable, as the call option can be exercised while the put option is left to expire, producing a net profit of 4 cents/pound. Thus, A's forecast has led to the right decision although A got the direction wrong and his forecast was far away from the actual value. What A is better at is predicting volatility, the extent of variation in the exchange rate, which is what is important for this decision.

What matters most may differ from one situation to another, and so a forecaster may have a loss function associated with the errors. For one forecaster underestimates may be less serious than overestimates. For another forecaster, large errors may be considered more serious than small errors irrespective of the direction. For yet another forecaster, it may not be important to consider errors smaller than a cutoff value.

TESTING THE SIGNIFICANCE OF THE DIFFERENCE BETWEEN ACTUAL AND FORECAST VALUES

Consider the exchange rate determination model represented by equation (10.1). Assume that the model is estimated using the first k observations then used to produce the first out-of-sample forecast, $\hat{S}_{k+1}$. It is possible to test if the difference between the actual and forecast values, that is the forecasting error, is statistically significant. In this case we test the null hypothesis

$$H_0 : S_{k+1} = \hat{S}_{k+1} \tag{10.23}$$

against the alternative hypothesis

$$H_1 : S_{k+1} \neq \hat{S}_{k+1} \tag{10.24}$$

The test statistic is given by

$$t^* = \frac{S_{k+1} - \hat{S}_{k+1}}{\sigma_\varepsilon \sqrt{1 + \frac{1}{k} + \frac{(X_{k+1} - \bar{X})^2}{\sum_{t=1}^{k} (X_t - \bar{X})^2}}} \tag{10.25}$$

where σ_ε is the standard deviation of ε. The test statistic is distributed as t with degrees of freedom equal to the sample size minus two. The difference between the actual and the forecast value arises for a number of reasons. The first of these is the rise of abnormal conditions during the period of forecast. It could be the case that at time $k + 1$ intense speculation in the foreign exchange market pushes the exchange rate to a level that is much higher than what is attributed to the effect of the explanatory variable. The second reason is that there could be an error in the measurement of the explanatory variable at $k + 1$. Another reason is a structural change in the relationship, so that at time $k + 1$ it is no longer an adequate representation of the process generating the exchange rate.

GRAPHICAL TECHNIQUES FOR MEASURING AND MONITORING FORECASTING ACCURACY

In this section two graphical techniques for measuring and monitoring forecasting accuracy are described. These are the control chart and the prediction–realisation diagram.

THE CONTROL CHART

We have seen that if the forecasts are unbiased then the sum of the errors tends to converge on zero as the negative errors cancel out positive errors. A control chart shows the behaviour of the cumulative sum of the forecasting errors, providing a warning signal when this sum exceeds an upper (positive) limit or a lower (negative) limit. These limits are defined by a multiple of the standard deviation of the forecasting error, where the multiple may be determined from the probability distribution of the forecasting error.

Figure 10.4 shows a control chart. As long as the cumulative sum of errors is within the range prescribed by the upper limit and the lower limit, there is no reason to worry. Once the cumulative error goes through the lower or upper limits and remains there for say two successive points in time, then this is a warning signal that something must be done about the forecasts. Thus, the control chart is a device for making sure that the forecasts are not biased in either direction.

THE PREDICTION–REALISATION DIAGRAM

We have seen that errors of direction, or turning point errors, can be more important than errors of magnitude. In fact, turning point errors are often taken to be symptomatic of basic flaws in the underlying models. Take, for example, the uncovered interest parity condition (or theory), which tells us that the exchange rate should change by a percentage that is equal to (or determined by) the interest rate differential of the two currencies comprising the exchange rate. If this model is valid, the currency offering a lower interest rate must appreciate and vice versa. Hence, if the interest rate on

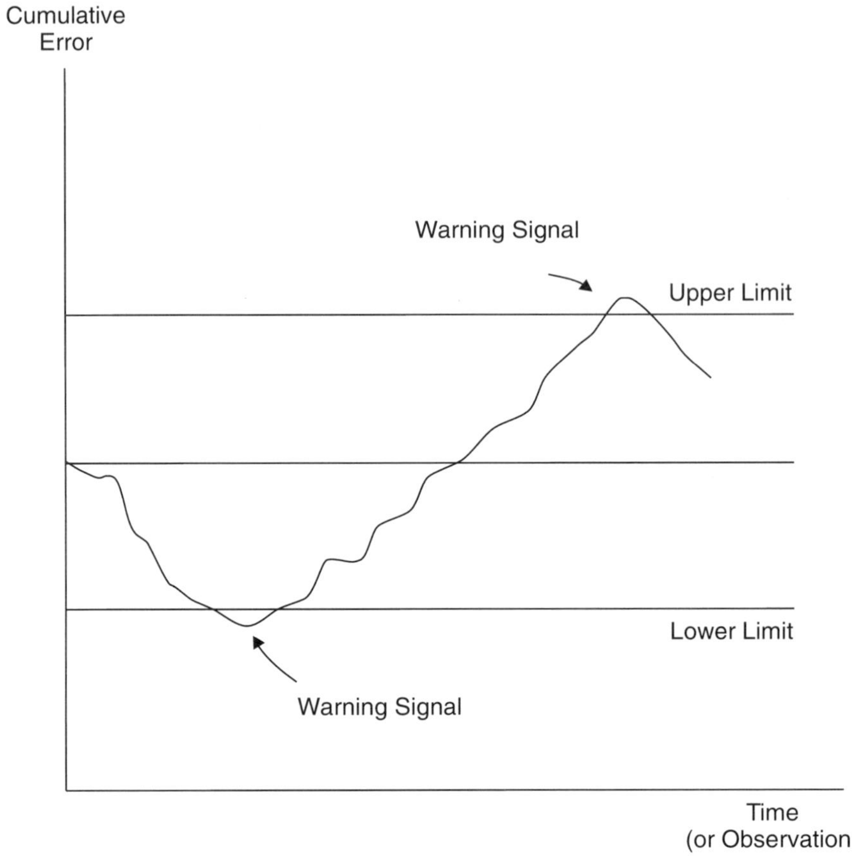

Figure 10.4 A control chart

currency x is higher than the interest rate on currency y, the exchange rate (x/y) must rise, implying an appreciation of y and depreciation of x. If the interest differential is 5 percentage points, then the model predicts that the exchange rate should rise by 5 per cent or something close to that. If the exchange rate rises by 10 per cent then there is a big forecasting error but the model correctly predicts a rise in the exchange rate. If, on the other hand, the exchange rate drops by 1 per cent then there is a direction or a turning point error, which is normally regarded as being more serious.

The prediction–realisation diagram is shown in Figure 10.5. The diagram is no more than the four-quadrant shape used in basic analytical geometry to define the coordinates of a point. On this diagram we plot points whose coordinates are the actual change in the exchange rate and the predicted change in the exchange rate. Thus the actual change, $S_t - S_{t-1}$, is measured on the horizontal axis while the predicted change, $\hat{S}_t - S_{t-1}$, is measured on the vertical axis. A 45-degree line passing through the origin is then plotted. This is the line of perfect forecast that has the equation $\hat{S}_t - S_{t-1} = S_t - S_{t-1}$, implying that $\hat{S}_t = S_t$. Point A falls exactly on the line, and so it represents a perfect forecast. Any point falling off the line represents a forecasting error measured by the distance from the line.

Let us now examine the various points scattered in the four quadrants of the diagram. In general, points falling in the first quadrant (A, B, C and D) as well as those falling in the third quadrant (F and G) indicate no turning point errors. Out of these points, only A (which falls exactly on the line) shows no error of magnitude. Points in the first quadrant imply that the model predicts a rise in the exchange rate when it actually rises. Points below the line (B and C) imply that the model predicts a smaller rise than what actually materialises. Points above the line (such as D) imply that the model predicts a larger rise than what actually materialises. Points in the third quadrant imply that the model predicts a fall in the exchange rate when it actually falls. Point G implies a larger fall than what actually materialises

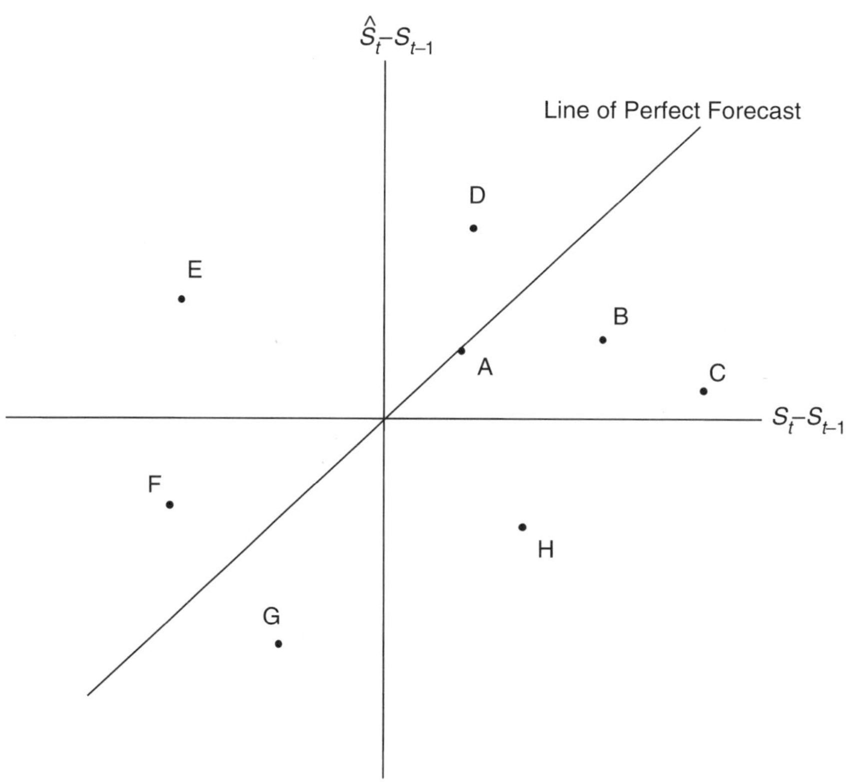

Figure 10.5 The prediction–realisation diagram

while point F implies a smaller predicted fall. Finally, points in the second and fourth quadrants (E and H) imply turning point errors. Point E shows that the model predicts a rise in the exchange rate when it actually falls, while point H has the opposite implication.

By examining the pattern of the points in a prediction–realisation diagram, we may obtain a rough idea about the forecasting accuracy of the model. Figure 10.6 shows the prediction–realisation diagrams for four models with different forecasting accuracy. Model (a) is the best because it shows no turning point errors and very small errors of magnitude. This is obvious because all of the points fall in the first or third quadrants, very close to the line of perfect forecast. Model (d) is the worst because on no occasion does it forecast the right direction of the change in the exchange rate. Model (b) is better than model (c) because the former does not have turning point errors, but model (b) is not better than model (a) since the latter has smaller (magnitude) errors.

Uncovered interest parity can be represented by the prediction–realisation diagram as in Figure 10.7. The forecast change is replaced by the interest rate differential while the actual absolute change is replaced by the actual percentage change. Points in the first and third quadrants indicate no turning point errors as a positive interest rate differential is associated with a rise in the exchange rate while a negative interest rate differential is associated with a fall in the exchange rate. Points in the second and fourth quadrants indicate the presence of turning point errors. Point D indicates that while the model predicts a rise in the exchange rate it actually falls, while point G indicates that the model predicts a fall in the exchange rate when it actually rises.

The prediction–realisation diagram can be more useful if it is turned 45 degrees to the right so that the line of perfect forecast becomes the horizontal axis. This is shown in Figure 10.8. In this case, the diagram is divided into six zones. Two of these zones (II and V) indicate turning point errors while the other four zones show overestimation and underestimation of positive and negative changes. Perfect forecasts would in this case fall on the horizontal axis.

The prediction–realisation diagram provides more information than the control chart but it includes no such device as the upper and lower limits in the control chart. Both of these graphical measures, however, do not provide a quantitative measure of forecasting accuracy, which are needed to compare the forecasting power of various models.

QUANTITATIVE MEASURES OF FORECASTING ACCURACY

Let us assume the availability of n forecasts and the corresponding actual values. Hence, the forecasts are $\hat{S}_1, \hat{S}_2, \ldots, \hat{S}_n$ and the corresponding

(a)

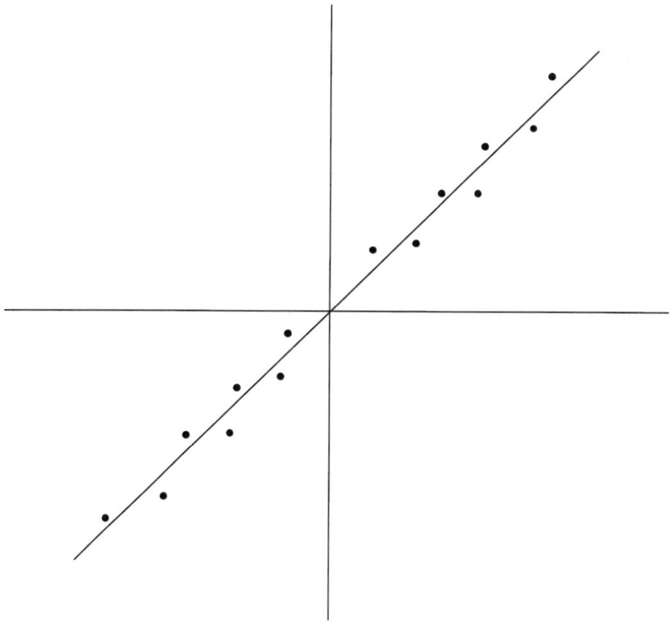

(b)

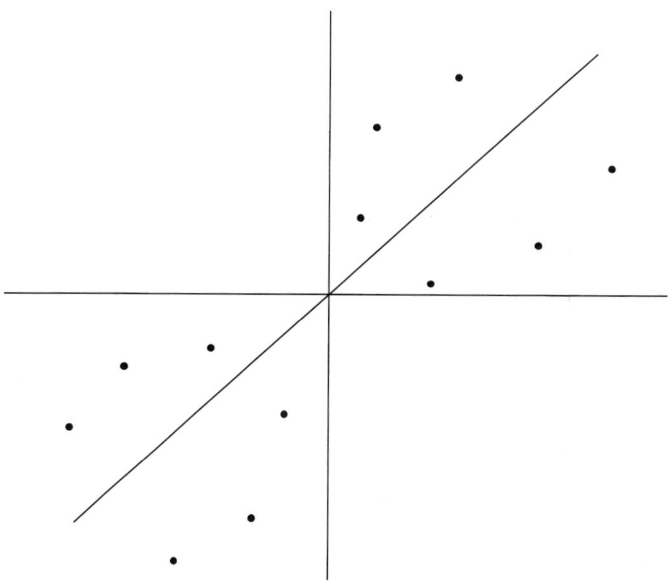

Figure 10.6 The prediction–realisation diagrams for models with different forecasting accuracy

(c)

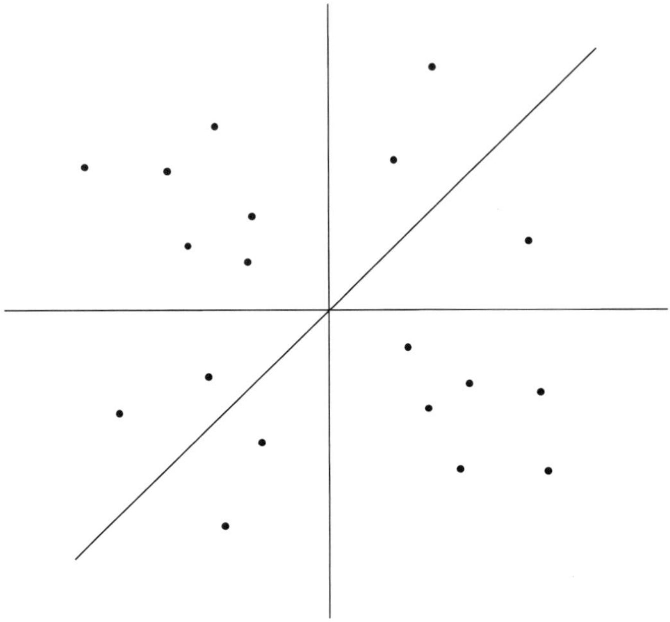

(d)

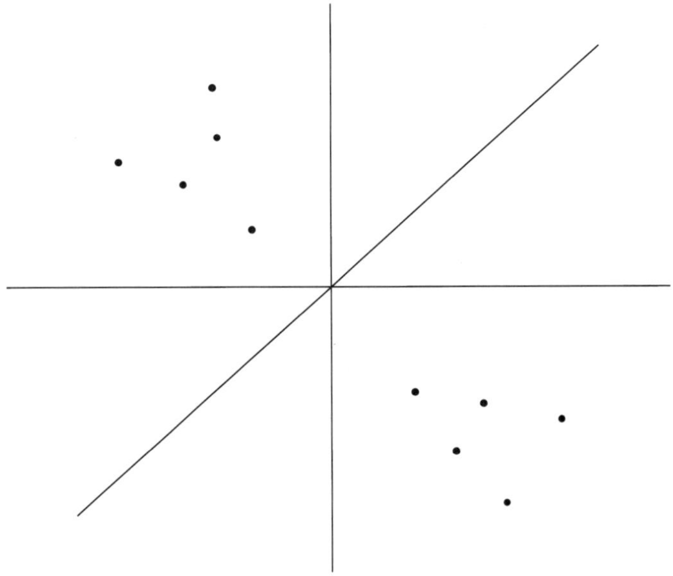

Figure 10.6 The prediction–realisation diagrams for models with different forecasting accuracy (cont.)

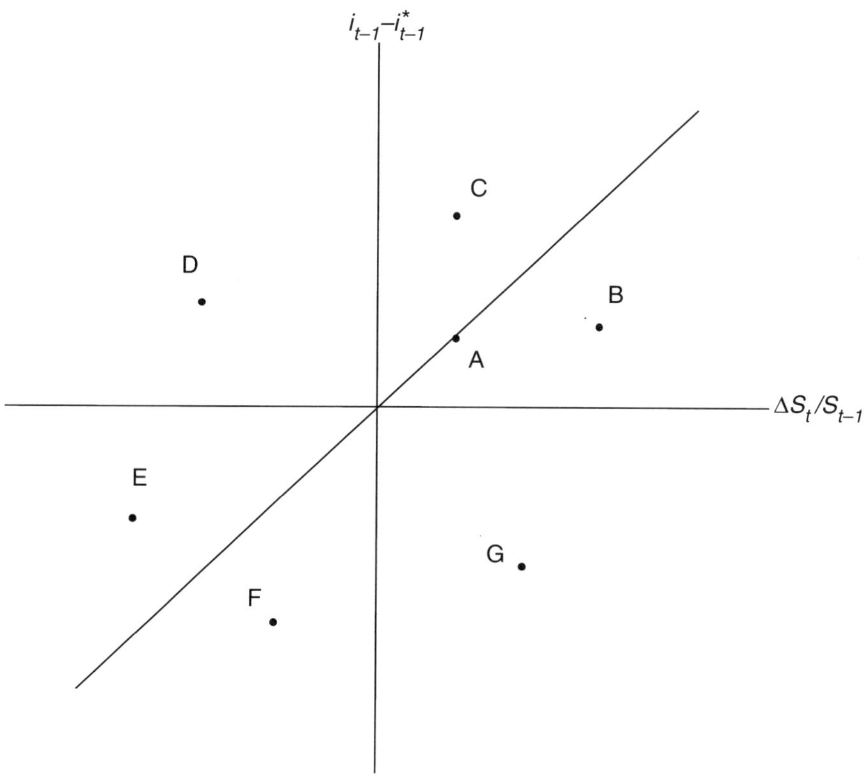

Figure 10.7 The prediction–realisation diagram for uncovered interest parity

actual values are $S_1, S_2, \ldots, S_n$. The forecasting errors are then $S_1 - \hat{S}_1$, $S_2 - \hat{S}_2, \ldots, S_n - \hat{S}_n$. The following quantitative measures can then be defined.

MEAN ABSOLUTE ERROR

The mean absolute error (*MAE*) is the average value of the sum of absolute errors. The reason why the absolute errors rather than the actual errors are summed is that a misleading result can be obtained when negative and positive errors cancel out. The *MAE* is calculated as

$$MAE = \frac{1}{n}\sum_{i=1}^{n}\left|S_i - \hat{S}_i\right| \tag{10.26}$$

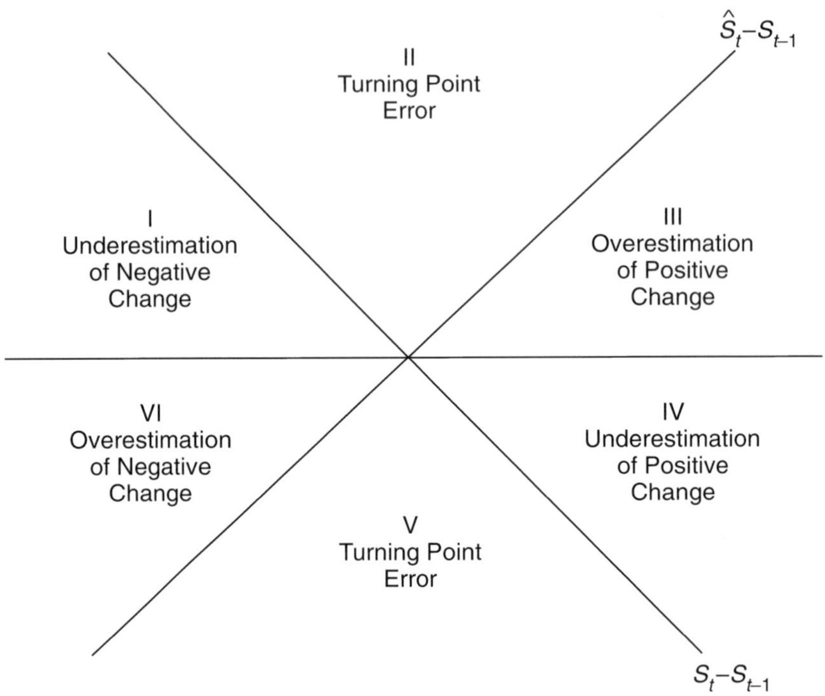

Figure 10.8 The modified prediction–realisation diagram

An alternative measure is the mean absolute percentage error, which is calculated as

$$MAE = \frac{1}{n}\sum_{i=1}^{n}\left|\frac{S_i - \hat{S}_i}{S_i}\right| \tag{10.27}$$

For a perfect forecast, $S_i = \hat{S}_i$ for all i, implying that $MAE = 0$.

MEAN SQUARE ERROR

The mean square error (*MSE*) is calculated from the sum of squares of the errors. Squaring the errors has two advantages. The first is that the problem of negative and positive errors cancelling out is avoided, while the second is that larger errors are penalised more severely. The *MSE* is calculated as

$$MSE = \frac{1}{n}\sum_{i=1}^{n}(S_i - \hat{S}_i)^2 \tag{10.28}$$

A related measure is the root mean square error (*RMSE*), which is the square root of the *MSE*. Hence

$$RMSE = \sqrt{MSE} = \sqrt{\frac{1}{n}\sum_{i=1}^{n}(S_i - \hat{S}_i)^2} \tag{10.29}$$

It is also obvious that for a perfect forecast, $S_i = \hat{S}_i$ for all i, implying that $MSE = RMSE = 0$. The *MSE* and *RMSE* can be calculated on the basis of the percentage errors, in which case we have

$$MSE = \frac{1}{n}\sum_{i=1}^{n}\left(\frac{S_i - \hat{S}_i}{S_i}\right)^2 \tag{10.30}$$

and

$$RMSE = \sqrt{\frac{1}{n}\sum_{i=1}^{n}\left(\frac{S_i - \hat{S}_i}{S_i}\right)^2} \tag{10.31}$$

Percentage errors are used for scaling, which is particularly useful in exchange rate forecasting. Suppose that we want to find out if a particular model does a better job in forecasting the exchange rate of the yen (JPY/USD) than the Australian dollar (AUD/USD). Suppose that the model produces the following forecasts for the two exchange rates at a particular point in time: 135 and 1.70, when the actual values are 140 and 1.80. The absolute errors are 5 and 0.10 respectively. Can we say that the model is more powerful in predicting the Australian dollar than the yen? The answer is obviously 'not necessarily' as these errors are not scaled, and hence they reflect differences in the par values of the two currencies. It is more appropriate to calculate the percentage errors relative to the actual values. The percentage errors are 3.6 per cent and 5.6 per cent. Hence, the model is more powerful in forecasting the yen. Scaling can be accomplished differently by measuring the root mean square error calculated from equation (10.29) as a percentage of the mean actual value of the exchange rate.

THE COEFFICIENT OF DETERMINATION

The coefficient of determination (R^2) measures the relationship between the sum of squares of errors and the sum of squares of deviations from the mean value of the exchange rate. It can be obtained by regressing the actual values on the forecasts. Alternatively, it is calculated as

$$R^2 = 1 - \frac{\sum_{i=1}^{n}(S_i - \hat{S}_i)^2}{\sum_{i=1}^{n}(S_i - \bar{S})^2} \tag{10.32}$$

where $\bar{S}$ is the actual mean value, which is given by

$$\bar{S} = \frac{1}{n}\sum_{i=1}^{n} S_i \tag{10.33}$$

For a perfect forecast, $S_i = \hat{S}_i$ for all i, implying that $R^2 = 1$.

THE CORRELATION COEFFICIENT

The correlation coefficient (r) measures the correlation between the actual and forecast values. It is calculated as

$$r = \frac{\sum_{i=1}^{n}(S_i - \bar{S})(\hat{S}_i - \bar{\hat{S}})}{\sqrt{(S_i - \bar{S})^2(\hat{S}_i - \bar{\hat{S}})^2}} \tag{10.34}$$

For a perfect forecast, $S_i = \hat{S}_i$ for all i, implying that $r = 1$. If the actual values and the forecasts are totally unrelated, their covariance will be zero and so $r = 0$.

THEIL'S INEQUALITY COEFFICIENT

Theil's inequality coefficient measures the forecasting power of a model relative to the random walk model. It is calculated by dividing the *RMSE* of the model by the *RMSE* of the random walk model. Hence

$$U = \frac{\sqrt{\frac{1}{n-1}\sum_{i=1}^{n}(S_{i+1} - \hat{S}_{i+1})^2}}{\sqrt{\frac{1}{n-1}\sum_{i=1}^{n}(S_{i+1} - S_i)^2}} \tag{10.35}$$

The denominator is calculated from the actual change in the exchange rate between i and $i+1$. The numerator is derived from the difference between the actual change and the predicted change which gives

$$(S_{i+1} - S_i) - (\hat{S}_{i+1} - S_i) = (S_{i+1} - \hat{S}_{i+1}) \tag{10.36}$$

where $(S_{i+1} - S_i)$ is the actual change and $(\hat{S}_{i+1} - S_i)$ is the predicted change. Another version of Theil's inequality coefficient is based on relative changes. Hence, it is calculated as

$$U = \frac{\sqrt{\dfrac{1}{n-1}\displaystyle\sum_{i=1}^{n}\left(\dfrac{S_{i+1} - \hat{S}_{i+1}}{S_i}\right)^2}}{\sqrt{\dfrac{1}{n-1}\displaystyle\sum_{i=1}^{n}\left(\dfrac{S_{i+1} - S_i}{S_i}\right)^2}} \tag{10.37}$$

Table 10.7 provides a summary of the implications of the numerical values of U.

Since the forward rate model is sometimes used as a benchmark model instead of the random walk model, another version of Theil's inequality coefficient can be written on the basis of the forward rate. Hence

$$U = \frac{\sqrt{\dfrac{1}{n-1}\displaystyle\sum_{i=1}^{n}(S_{i+1} - \hat{S}_{i+1})^2}}{\sqrt{\dfrac{1}{n-1}\displaystyle\sum_{i=1}^{n}(S_{i+1} - F_i)^2}} \tag{10.38}$$

where F is the forward rate.

Table 10.7 Implications of the value of Theil's inequality coefficient

Value	*Implication*
$U = 0$	The model produces perfect forecasts
$0 < U < 1$	The model provides less than perfect forecasts but outperforms the random walk model
$U = 1$	The model is as good as the random walk model
$U > 1$	The model is worse than the random walk model, and hence there is no point in using it for forecasting

It is possible, by decomposing Theil's inequality coefficient, to identify the sources of the forecasting error. This decomposition is similar to the decomposition of the total variance of any variable which is the basis of the analysis of variance. For this purpose the expression for the inequality coefficient is rewritten in terms of the predicted and actual changes as

$$U = \frac{\sqrt{\frac{1}{n-1}\sum_{i=1}^{n}(A_{i+1} - P_{i+1})^2}}{\sqrt{\frac{1}{n-1}\sum_{i=1}^{n}A_i^2}} \tag{10.39}$$

where A is the actual change and P is the predicted change. These are defined as

$$A_{i+1} = S_{i+1} - S_i \tag{10.40}$$

$$P_{i+1} = \hat{S}_{i+1} - S_i \tag{10.41}$$

The numerator can be decomposed into three terms, each of which shows a different source of error. Hence

$$\frac{1}{n-1}\sum_{i=1}^{n}(A_{i+1} - P_{i+1})^2 = (\bar{A} - \bar{P}) + (\sigma_A - \sigma_P)^2 + 2(1 - r_{AP})\sigma_A\sigma_P \tag{10.42}$$

where

$$\bar{A} = \frac{1}{n-1}\sum_{i=1}^{n}A_{i+1} \tag{10.43}$$

$$\bar{P} = \frac{1}{n-1}\sum_{i=1}^{n}P_{i+1} \tag{10.44}$$

$$\sigma_A^2 = \frac{1}{n-1}\sum_{i=1}^{n}(A_{i+1} - \bar{A})^2 \tag{10.45}$$

$$\sigma_P^2 = \frac{1}{n-1}\sum_{i=1}^{n}(P_{i+1} - \bar{P})^2 \tag{10.46}$$

$$r_{AP} = \frac{\sum_{i=1}^{n}(A_{i+1} - \bar{A})(P_{i+1} - \bar{P})}{(n-1)\sigma_A\sigma_P} \tag{10.47}$$

The three components which form the sources of the forecast error are called the partial inequality coefficients. The first component, which is called the bias component, shows that the cause of the discrepancy between the actual and predicted values is the difference between their means. The second component, known as the variance component, shows that the discrepancy is due to differences in the variances. The third component, known as the covaraiance component, attributes the error to the covariance between the actual and predicted changes.

The so-called inequality proportions can be obtained by dividing each of the components by the total forecast variation. Hence, the bias proportion is measured as

$$U_B = \frac{(\bar{A} - \bar{P})^2}{\frac{1}{n-1}\sum_{i=1}^{n}(A_{i+1} - P_{i+1})^2} \tag{10.48}$$

The variance proportion is

$$U_V = \frac{(\sigma_A - \sigma_P)^2}{\frac{1}{n-1}\sum_{i=1}^{n}(A_{i+1} - P_{i+1})^2} \tag{10.49}$$

and the covariance proportion is

$$U_C = \frac{2(1 - r_{AP})\sigma_A \sigma_{PA}}{\frac{1}{n-1}\sum_{i=1}^{n}(A_{i+1} - P_{i+1})^2} \tag{10.50}$$

It is obvious that

$$U_B + U_V + U_C = 1 \tag{10.51}$$

A related measure of forecasting accuracy is McLaughlin's (1975) batting average. The batting average (*BA*) is related to Theil's inequality coefficient as follows

$$BA = 100(4 - U) \tag{10.52}$$

The value of the batting average corresponding to $U = 0$ is 400, while the value corresponding to $U = 1$ is 300.

DIRECTION ACCURACY AND CONFUSION RATE

Direction accuracy (DA) is calculated as

$$DA = \frac{1}{n}\sum_{i=1}^{n} a_i \tag{10.53}$$

where $a_i = 1$ if $(S_{i+1} - S_i)(\hat{S}_{i+1} - S_i) > 0$ and $a_i = 0$ otherwise. This means that a takes the value 1 if the actual change and the predicted change have the same sign and 0 if they have the opposite signs. If $(S_{i+1} - S_i)(\hat{S}_{i+1} - S_i) > 0$ for all i, then the value of DA will be 1, implying that the model predicts the right change on all occasions. In this case there is a zero confusion rate, that is confusing the direction of the change in the exchange rate. In general, the confusion rate (CR) is related to the measure of direction accuracy as follows:

$$CR = 1 - DA \tag{10.54}$$

MEASURES INCLUDING HYPOTHESIS TESTING

It is possible to test the significance of the difference between the sums of squares of errors of two models. For this purpose, the Diebold–Mariano (1995) test is used. The hypothesis of independence between the actual and predicted directions can be tested by applying the Henriksson–Merton (1981) test or the Pesaran–Timmerman (1994) test.

MEASURES BASED ON IN-SAMPLE AND OUT-OF-SAMPLE FORECASTING ACCURACY

The Janus quotient is a measure of forecasting accuracy that is based on both the in-sample and out-of-sample forecasting power. We will define this measure in terms of the actual and predicted changes. Assume that the model is estimated using the first k observations of a total sample of size n. The Janus quotient is defined as

$$J = \frac{\sqrt{\dfrac{1}{n-k}\sum_{i=k}^{n}(S_{i+1} - \hat{S}_{i+1})^2}}{\sqrt{\dfrac{1}{k-1}\sum_{i=1}^{k}(S_{i+1} - \hat{S}_{i+1})^2}} \tag{10.55}$$

Thus it is a measure of the out-of-sample forecasting accuracy to the in-sample forecasting accuracy. If the structure of the model over the estimation period and out-of it are identical, the value of J should be approximately equal to 1. The higher the value of J, the poorer the forecasting power of the model. A value above unity is indicative of change in the structure of the model.

11: Selection, Implementation and Monitoring of Forecasts

THE TALE OF TWO EXCHANGE RATE FORECASTERS

Andrew and Liam are two young economists who have been employed by two major banks as exchange rate forecasters. They use their formal training in economics to provide judgemental forecasts based on extensive fundamental analysis of the underlying situation. Their job is to advise foreign exchange dealers who need an input on the possible direction of the exchange rate between the US dollar and the pound whenever some development takes place. At the end of each week, Andrew and Liam meet in a pub and talk about their favourite subject: exchange rate forecasting. They exchange notes on what took place in the previous week and what kind of forecasts they made in response to a certain development. The following is what these young economists said over a period of five consecutive weeks.

WEEK 1

The Bank of England announces that the money supply in the UK increased by 5 per cent in the previous month, which is a very high rate of monetary expansion. On the basis of this announcement, Andrew predicts that the pound would depreciate because the monetary model and the PPP theory predict this outcome. Liam, on the other hand, predicts that the pound would appreciate because the Bank of England would react by raising the level of interest rates, making pound-denominated assets more attractive. Andrew's reaction to Liam's prediction is that this is not necessarily the case because interest rates are after all determined by market forces, the supply and demand for liquidity. Hence, an increase in the money supply should be accompanied by a decline rather than a rise in interest rates. Liam in turn argues that interest rates should rise as a result of the monetary expansion even if the proposition that market forces determine interest rates is accepted. This is because a monetary expansion has four effects: a liquidity effect, an income effect, a price level effect and an inflationary expectations effect. Only the liquidity effect causes a fall in interest rates; the other effects cause a rise in interest rates. For example, a rapid monetary expansion leads to a higher level of inflationary expectations, and hence (via the Fisher effect) to a higher level of interest rates. This should cause an appreciation of the pound.

WEEK 2

The level of short-term interest rates on the pound increases by one percentage point. Andrew bases his opinion on the flow model of exchange rate determination, forecasting an appreciation of the pound. It is the normal argument that higher interest rates attract capital flows, consequently leading to currency appreciation. Liam, on the other hand, bases his view on stock rather than flow equilibrium. He thinks that the effect of a higher interest rate is transmitted to the exchange rate not through capital flows but rather through the supply and demand for money. Hence, a higher interest rate should lead to currency depreciation as predicted by the flexible-price monetary model. Andrew responds to this line of reasoning by arguing that even if the effect is transmitted through changes in the demand for money, a higher level of interest rates should cause an appreciation of the pound. This is the prediction of the sticky-price monetary model. Unlike Liam, Andrew views the level of interest rates as reflecting the liquidity situation in the money market. A higher level of interest rates implies a liquidity shortage which should lead to currency appreciation. Liam, on the other hand, views the level of interest rates as reflecting inflationary expectations. A higher level of interest rates reflects higher inflationary expectations, which is bad for the currency. The pound should, according to Liam, depreciate.

WEEK 3

The Treasury's forecasts show that the British economy would grow by 5 per cent in real terms during the coming year. This prediction is supported by private sector economists. Andrew predicts that the pound would appreciate. A higher growth rate means a stronger stock market and higher interest rates, attracting capital flows and leading to currency appreciation. Liam thinks that the pound would depreciate because a higher growth rate leads to a higher level of imports, leading to a deterioration in the current account of the balance of payments and consequently currency depreciation.

WEEK 4

It is announced that public debt would decline, with the ratio of the public sector borrowing requirements (PSBR) to GDP going down by one percentage point. Andrew thinks that this would lead to a depreciation of the pound because the government's demand for loanable funds would decline, relieving pressure on interest rates. A lower level of interest rates would lead to currency depreciation. Liam analyses the situation differently. A lower budget deficit, in the absence of a change in the domestic saving-investment balance, would be associated with a lower current account deficit. This would lead to currency appreciation.

WEEK 5

Energy economists expect the price of crude oil to rise. Andrew thinks that this would lead to an appreciation of the pound because it is a petrocurrency. Liam on the other hand, thinks that an increase in the price of oil would result in a rise in the demand for the US dollar, since it is the currency used to settle transactions involving crude oil. This would lead to an appreciation of the dollar and a depreciation of the pound.

THE MESSAGE

This tale of two forecasters gives a very strong message. Two forecasters using exactly the same forecasting technique (judgemental forecasting in this case), who have access to the same information, and who are equally technically capable produce exactly contrasting forecasts. This is an extreme case, because it is more likely the case that forecasters may agree on the direction but not on the magnitude of the change, particularly when a trend has been established. It is also highly likely that they will disagree on the timing of the turning points. So, the question that needs to be answered here is why forecasters disagree, and why they produce different forecasts. An attempt to answer this question is made in the next section.

WHY DO FORECASTERS DIFFER?

In this section we try to explain the differences in the forecasts generated by using formal models. A number of factors cause discrepancies in the forecasts provided by different forecasters. All of these factors are related to the judgement of the forecaster in choosing the model, the estimation method, the sample period, data frequency, definitions, values of the explanatory variables, and judgemental adjustment. These factors are discussed in turn.

DIFFERENT MODELS

Four different forecasters may use four different models. The following are examples:

$$S_t = a + bS_{t-1} + \varepsilon_t \tag{11.1}$$

$$S_t = a + bX_t + \varepsilon_t \tag{11.2}$$

$$S_t = a + bX_t + cZ_t + \varepsilon_t \tag{11.3}$$

$$S_t = a + bX_t^2 + \varepsilon_t \tag{11.4}$$

The first of these models is a univariate AR(1) model. The second model has one explanatory variable, X, while the third model has two explanatory variables, X and Z. The fourth model has one explanatory variable like the second model but it is nonlinear. These models are bound to produce different forecasts.

DIFFERENT ESTIMATION METHODS

Different estimation methods are likely to produce different estimates of the coefficients a and b, and hence different forecasts. Take, for example, the model represented by equation (11.2). One forecaster may assume that the variable X is exogenous, in which case the equation is estimated by OLS. Another forecaster may think that it is endogenous, in which case he resorts to instrumental variables. Generalised least squares may be resorted to and also one of the other methods dealing with the cases when the residuals do not satisfy the OLS assumptions. These methods involve the specification of some process for the residuals. Different estimation methods are likely to produce different estimates of the parameters a and b, leading to different forecasts.

DIFFERENT SAMPLE PERIODS

If two forecasters use equation (11.2) and both of them estimate it by OLS, they are very likely to get two different sets of estimated coefficients when they estimate the model using two sample periods. In fact, the estimation results are invariably more sensitive to the sample period than to the estimation method. For example, one forecaster thinks that it is better to use data going back to the early days of floating, say to 1973. Another forecaster may believe that the foreign exchange market today is different from what it was in the 1970s, as the behaviour of exchange rates has become more erratic since the 1980s. The second forecaster may, therefore, choose to start the sample period in 1980. Again, different forecasts are obtained by using different sample periods.

DIFFERENT DATA FREQUENCIES

A forecast of the exchange rate at the end of March 1999 may be based on a monthly model or a quarterly model estimated over the period 1980–1998. These two models are bound to produce different forecasts.

DIFFERENT DEFINITIONS

Assume that the model represented by equation (11.2) is the PPP model such that X is the price ratio. The price ratio may be measured in terms of consumer prices, wholesale prices, GDP deflators or other price indices. Two forecasters using different price measures will obtain different estimates of the PPP model and, therefore, different forecasts.

DIFFERENT VALUES OF THE EXPLANATORY VARIABLES

If the value of the explanatory variable for the point in time for which the variable is generated is not known the forecaster has to assume a value in order to generate forecasts. Two forecasters may have exactly the same estimated model, but because of the differences in the values of the explanatory variable different forecasts will be generated.

JUDGEMENTAL ADJUSTMENT

Two forecasters obtaining identical forecasts from a formal model may still end up with two different forecasts. One of the forecasters may think that the forecast is reasonable as it is, while the other thinks that it is not, in which case he uses his judgement to adjust the forecasts. Even if they both believe that judgemental adjustment is necessary, they are likely to disagree on the size of this adjustment. The result is once more two different forecasts.

THE POSSIBILITIES

Imagine a situation in which the following are available:

- Two different models, A and B.
- Two estimation methods, 1 and 2.
- Two sample periods, 1975–98 and 1980–98.
- Two data frequencies, quarterly (Q) and monthly (M).
- Two definitions for the explanatory variable, I and II.
- Two values for the explanatory variable, x and y.
- Two values for the size of the judgemental adjustment factor, α and β.

Given this menu, the possibility exists for 128 different forecasts to arise. These forecasts are obtained by various combinations of the these factors. The first 14 of these forecasts are shown in Table 11.1.

INTERNAL OR EXTERNAL FORECASTERS?

A decision that often arises concerns the choice between generating the forecasts internally by hiring one or more forecasters or to obtain the forecasts from external sources by subscribing to one or more forecasting

Table 11.1 Possibilities for forecast values

Model	*Method*	*Sample*	*Frequency*	*Definition*	*Value*	*Adjustment*	*Forecast*
A	1	75–98	Q	I	x	α	1
B	1	75–98	Q	I	x	α	2
A	2	75–98	Q	I	x	α	3
B	2	75–98	Q	I	x	α	4
A	1	80–98	Q	I	x	α	5
B	1	80–98	Q	I	x	α	6
A	1	75–98	M	I	x	α	7
B	1	75–98	M	I	x	α	8
A	1	75–98	Q	II	x	α	9
B	1	75–98	Q	II	x	α	10
A	1	75–98	Q	I	y	α	11
B	1	75–98	Q	I	y	α	12
A	1	75–98	Q	I	x	β	13
B	1	75–98	Q	I	x	β	14
⋮	⋮	⋮	⋮	⋮	⋮	⋮	⋮
⋮	⋮	⋮	⋮	⋮	⋮	⋮	128

services. The issue eventually boils down to the cost-effectiveness of these two alternatives. Some companies may not need external forecasters because they have sophisticated foreign exchange departments with staff recruited from financial institutions. This is naturally the case if the company believes that an external forecaster is unable to offer anything that cannot be made in-house.

Subscribing to a forecasting service may seem easier and cheaper than hiring one or more forecasters. Forecasting services may be able to offer their forecasts at a low cost because they have a large number of clients, enabling them to exploit the economies of scale. This may be appealing to small companies that find it expensive to run their own forecasting units or foreign exchange departments. Moreover, the personnel of the forecasting services do nothing but forecasting. Over time, they build up significant expertise that may not be available elsewhere. In a competitive market they are forced to keep on developing their forecasting techniques and offer better services. Another reason why hiring the services of an external forecaster is appealing is that this forecaster is more likely to provide independent and objective advice than an internal forecaster who wants to please his boss. While most big companies can utilise their staff to generate the products offered by external forecasters, it is easy to become biased and lose objectivity.

There are reasons, however, why subscribing to a forecasting service may not be appealing. First, the methodology, format and the frequency of the output may not be suitable for the needs of the client. The methodology pertains to whether the forecasting service uses fundamental or technical models. Format pertains to whether the forecasts are point forecasts or interval forecasts, whether they are short-term or long-term forecasts, and so on. Frequency of the output refers to the frequency of receiving the forecasts. This may sound as no problem because one is bound to find a forecasting service with the characteristics that are suitable to one's needs. However, it is a problem if the most suitable forecasting service does not have a good track record. These points will be discussed in more detail when we consider the factors determining the selection of an external forecaster.

Sometimes, it is argued that external forecasters do not have any responsibility for the advice they give, while huge losses could be incurred by following the wrong advice. However, this argument is equally valid for internal forecasters. Both have something to lose if they provide inaccurate forecasts: the internal forecaster could lose his job, while the external forecaster could lose a client or clients if the word gets around. But in either case, faulty forecasts do not constitute a criminal offence for which either the internal or the external forecaster can be prosecuted.

If a satisfactory external forecaster cannot be found, it may be better to generate the forecasts internally, particularly if this proves to be more cost-effective. At least the internal forecaster can do other things and is always on standby to respond to any need pertaining to forecasting and economic analysis. Sometimes, however, it may be found useful to employ a forecaster while subscribing to a forecasting service. This will be the case if the objective is to reach some sort of a consensus forecast. The internal forecaster may also monitor the track record of the forecasting services, providing some recommendation to the management on whether subscription is kept or terminated.

SELECTING AN EXTERNAL FORECASTER

Selecting the right external forecaster involves a decision that actually involves the forecasting of forecasters. The choice can be costly in terms of the fees charged and/or the losses incurred if the forecaster produces excessively erroneous forecasts. It is important to establish beforehand what one wants from a forecaster. After all, we pay for what we need (or what we want), and we do not pay for what we do not need (or want) even if it is extremely cheap.

Clients have different needs, which is obvious from the decision-making problems described in Chapter 2. Consider the following situations:

1. A straightforward currency speculator is interested in buy/sell signals.
2. A hedger is interested in knowing the direction and magnitude of the change in the exchange rate between the present time and the point in time when the payables or receivables become due.
3. A speculator on a European options position needs forecasts on the level of the exchange rate at a particular point in time (the time of expiry of the option).
4. A speculator on American options needs forecasts on the behaviour of the exchange rate between the time the position is taken and the time of expiry of the option.
5. A speculator on combined option positions, like a straddle, is interested only in the magnitude of change, that is in the volatility of the exchange rate, irrespective of the direction.
6. A decision maker addressing a capital budgeting problem involving foreign direct investment needs long-term forecasts over a period of, say, 10 years.

Given these possibilities, the client will be concerned with the methodology, format, timing and frequency of the release of the forecasts. Although forecasters are in the same general business, most of them do not compete head-on because they do not offer the same services and do not cater for the same clientele. Let us now examine what the clients described above need and what kind of product they seek.

A speculator who is only interested in buy/sell signals may choose a forecasting service using technical analysis. Such a speculator will be trading on a day-to-day basis, which makes daily updates rather important. Forecasts based on technical analysis are more suitable for this kind of client. The speculator will also look for a foreign exchange forecasting service that can deal with his needs around the clock.

A hedger, on the other hand, does not require these day-to-day updates because the hedger is only interested in where the exchange rate will end up on the date when the payables or receivables fall due. Thus, a forecaster who provides monthly or weekly updates may be suitable. The problem here is the timing, as the date on which the payables and receivables fall due may not coincide with the date for which the forecasts are prepared. In this case the frequency of releasing the forecasts does matter. It is more likely that the date on which the payables and receivables fall due is near a date for which forecasts are prepared when the forecasting frequency is weekly rather than monthly.

A speculator on European options will look for something similar to what a hedger looks for. But a speculator on American options would want a forecast of the level of the exchange rate between the time the position is taken and the date of expiry of the option. This is because American options can be exercised before maturity. Hence, even if a forecast of the end value of the exchange rate may indicate that the position is unprofitable, the exchange rate could behave in such a way as to make it profitable to exercise the option before maturity. Such a speculator would be interested in an output showing the forecast values of the exchange rate at discrete and close points in time between the present time and the date of expiry. Otherwise, a description of the time path of the exchange rate during this time period identifying the turning points will also be suitable. Thus, point forecasts with a commentary on the time path of the exchange rate will be useful.

A speculator on combined option positions, such as a straddle, is not interested in an exact level of the exchange rate by or on a particular date. Rather, this speculator is interested in the absolute magnitude of change in the exchange rate. What this speculator wants to know is whether the exchange rate will be above or below a certain level. In this case point forecasts are not necessary and interval forecasts will be just as useful. More appropriately, this speculator needs forecasts of several point values with associated probabilities.

Finally, a decision maker considering a foreign direct investment project needs long-term rather than short-term forecasts. Exchange rate forecasts at the end of each year over the next 10 years may be required to evaluate the net present value and the internal rate of return on the project.

The criteria used to select an external forecaster can be listed as follows.

THE METHODOLOGY

To start with, the methodology affects the description of the product as explained above. A forecaster using a PPP model cannot provide forecasts on a daily basis, while a forecaster using a technical model to generate buy/sell signals cannot provide the long-term forecasts needed to make a capital budgeting decision. The methodology may also affect the choice of the forecaster for 'ideological' reasons. For example, a client who thinks that technical analysis is some sort of 'witchcraft' is unlikely to choose a forecaster using technical models. Moreover, a client is more likely to choose a forecaster using methodology that sounds familiar or convincing. Other important aspects of the methodology pertain to how up to date it is, as well as the quality and the sources of the data used to estimate the model.

THE FORMAT

Like the methodology, the format also affects the characteristics of the product. These pertain to such aspects as whether the forecast is given in terms of buy/sell signals, point estimates or interval forecasts, with or without a commentary, and so on.

TIMING AND FREQUENCY OF THE FORECASTS

Again, these two criteria affect the characteristics of the product.

JUDGEMENTAL ADJUSTMENT

Some clients might believe that judgemental adjustment is subjective and inappropriate. This is why the size of judgemental adjustment may be an important factor in determining the selection of the forecaster.

MEANS OF TRANSMISSION

Forecasts are transmitted from the forecaster to the client by a number of means. These include mail delivery, fax, telephone and computer networks. The means of transmission is important for at least two reasons. First, it makes a difference for the time elapsing between the production and delivery of the forecasts, and hence between the availability of information and the utilisation of this information in decision making. Second, the means of transmission must be conducive to delivery without error and allows for the evaluation of a track record. Thus, mail and telephone delivery do not satisfy these requirements.

EXCLUSIVENESS OF THE FORECASTS

A client would feel more comfortable if the forecasts are not available to competitors. It may, however, not be possible to have access to information revealing the identity of other subscribers.

THE TRACK RECORD

The track record is very important because it shows the accuracy or otherwise of the forecasts. Two points must be borne in mind when the track record is considered. First, it is possible to falsify the track record. This can be done fairly easily as all it takes is to change the wrong forecasts when the track record is printed out of a computer. Thus, it is important to find out if the track record has been audited by an independent body. Second, the track record as such may not be as important as whether or not profits have been generated by following the forecasts. Evidence on this proposition may be obtained by simulating a strategy on the basis of historical forecasts, or from an existing client. Financial newspapers and magazines, such as *Euromoney*, often report useful information on the track record of the foreign exchange forecasting services.

THE COST

The cost comes last because what is important is cost-effectiveness, that is what is really obtained for the subscription paid. The cost factor cannot be considered independently of the other aspects of the contract, including support services. For example, does the subscription allow the client access to the forecaster to ask specific questions? If, so what is the extent of this access? Does the forecaster provide training for the client's staff? All of these aspects must be considered to determine the cost-effectiveness of a particular forecasting service. The appendix to this chapter provides a brief description of some of the services offered by forecasting services in practice.

FORECAST IMPLEMENTATION

Forecasts are generated in order to be implemented and used as an input in the decision-making process. Without implementing the forecasts they will not be used for this purpose. Forecasters want their forecasts to be implemented, which makes implementation as important as accuracy.

Schultz (1984) defines implementation as follows. A forecast is implemented when it changes the decision-making process. When it both changes and improves the decision-making process then it is successfully implemented. Therefore, this definition is based on improved decision making and consequently improved organisational effectiveness. Geistauts and Eschenbach (1987) define implementation differently. A forecast is implemented if the decision maker adopts the forecast in essence and continues to use it as long as the underlying conditions apply. The degree of implementation can vary from zero or negligible use to being the decisive element in the decision-making process. They also make a distinction between implementing a specific forecast and implementing a forecasting model. Implementation of a forecast necessarily requires a one-time implementation of the underlying model, but it does not automatically commit the decision maker to a long-term use of the model. Permanent implementation of a method generally heightens the degree of risk and places an extra burden on the implementation strategy. The implementation problem becomes more complicated when the users of the forecasts are not the decision makers. This may occur when higher-level management contracts for a forecast to be used by subordinates in their decision making. The subordinates may feel that the forecasts which are imposed on them are not that good.

Alter (1979) suggests that a set of implementation factors, which measure deviations from the ideal implementation situation, can be used to identify implementation stumbling blocks. The following are the major deviation categories:

- Non-existent or unwilling users
- Multiple users and implementers
- Disappearing users, implementers or maintainers
- Inability to specify purpose or usage pattern in advance
- Inability to predict and cushion impact on all parties
- Lack or loss of support
- Lack of prior experience with similar systems
- Technical problems and cost-effectiveness issues.

Schultz (1984) has applied the implementation profile developed by Schultz and Selvin (1983) to forecasting implementation. The factors considered are the following:

- Top management support
- Impact on job performance
- The user–forecaster-model designer relationship
- Impact on goal congruence
- The amount or degree of change
- The forecasting system or model format
- The system or model quality
- The implementation strategy
- Cost–benefit justification
- Implementer's resources
- Decision style
- Environmental events.

It has also been suggested (for example, Geistauts and Eschenbach, 1987) that the implementation problem can be analysed in terms of three basic measures: validity, credibility and acceptability. Validity refers to the accuracy of the forecasts. Credibility pertains to the perception potential users have of the reliability of the forecasts. Acceptability refers to the forecasts' implementarity from the decision maker's perspective.

MONITORING OF FORECASTS

Monitoring of forecasts is important for measuring the cost-effectiveness of the forecasts. This statement is valid whether the forecasts are generated externally, by subscribing to a forecasting service, or internally by establishing a forecasting unit. In both cases the objective of monitoring the forecasts is to answer the following two questions:

1. Have the forecasts been accurate? This question can be answered by evaluating the forecasts using the measures suggested in Chapter 10.
2. Has it been profitable to follow the forecasts? As we have seen, accuracy (defined in a certain way) does not necessarily lead to profitable operations. This question can be answered by considering what would have happened had the forecasts been followed or otherwise.

The objective of monitoring external forecasters is to carry out a periodic review to decide if the subscription is renewed or a new forecaster is sought. Companies often change the forecasting service they subscribe to for a variety of reasons. Objectively, however, a company will keep the subscription if there is a feeling that the forecasts are and have been contributing to the profitability of the business. Otherwise, the subscription will be terminated.

Monitoring internal forecasts is rather different. If the monitoring is carried out by someone other than the forecaster himself, then the objective is the same as in the case of the external forecaster, that is to make sure that the forecaster is worthy of his salary by providing the right advice. If, on the other hand, the monitoring is carried out by the forecaster himself, then the objective is to improve the accuracy of the forecasts. Monitoring in this case is part of the forecasting process.

Monitoring of the forecasts may be incorporated in the forecasting process by considering the various stages of the process. These stages are as follows:

1. Collection and examination of data.
2. Choice of the forecasting method.
3. Generating forecasts over the existing sample period (which can be in-sample or out-of-sample). If the accuracy is unacceptable, the data are re-examined and another forecasting method is chosen. If it is acceptable then the model is used to generate *ex ante* forecasts which are used in the decision-making process.
4. As time passes the forecasts are monitored for accuracy. If accuracy is acceptable, then no changes are introduced. If accuracy is unacceptable then the data are re-examined, using the extended sample period, and an alternative model may be chosen.

What this means is that monitoring refers to checking the accuracy of *ex ante* forecasts, after the model has been chosen. This is the second accuracy measurement exercise (step 4). The first accuracy measurement exercise is conducted using the initial sample period for the purpose of the initial selection of a forecasting model (step 3).

Appendix to Chapter 11: Foreign Exchange Forecasting Services in Practice

In this appendix we take a look at the range of services provided by foreign exchange services in practice. This information is not necessarily up to date because this is not meant to be a directory of foreign exchange forecasting services. Rather the objective is just to present an idea of the range of services provided by these forecasters.

BEST AND ASSOCIES

Forecasts are produced for horizons ranging between one week and 10 years. Advice is also tailored to the client's specific needs, utilising asset selection and risk analysis models.

BISSET, A G AND CO INC

Three kinds of services are provided for corporate clients: (i) market timing advice on when to buy and sell currencies over horizons ranging between two months and four years; (ii) hedging portfolio foreign exchange risk; and (iii) currency fund management.

BRIAN MARBER AND CO

A technical advisory service offering personal consultancy, reports and private access page on Reuters.

CAPITAL TECHNIQUES

A technical advisory service providing medium-term forecasts derived from a combination of technical models embodying Elliott wave theory and bar charts.

COMMODITY MANAGEMENT SERVICES CORPORATION

A technical model based on currency futures is used. The service includes a daily report of market position, stop-loss and re-entry points. Personal consultancy is also provided in which specific deals can be considered based on cycle analysis and other indicators.

COMPUCOM RESEARCH INC

A mix of technical and fundamental analysis is used. Trends are identified and volatility filters are applied. Two kinds of services are provided: a managed account service and a telex advisory service.

CORPORATE TREASURY CONSULTANTS LTD

Comprehensive consultancy on foreign exchange risk management. Services range from written studies analysing exposure and reviewing existing policies through the design of appropriate hedging strategies. Advice is specific to each client. Currency forecasts ranging from short-term to very long-term are based on fundamental rather than technical analysis.

CRANE INVESTMENT ANALYSIS LTD

Combined technical and fundamental consultancy. Advice is tailored to clients' individual requirements.

FINTECH (UK) LTD

Fund management services as well as other products including daily foreign exchange reports (updated hourly) and a monthly fundamental currency report. Customised forecasting and exposure management advice is provided. Technical analysis is provided as well as a forward contract management system and modules for pricing options.

FOREXIA (UK) LTD

Three kinds of products are provided: (i) an automatic on-line currency forecasting service containing fundamental and technical analysis; (ii) a daily service based on technical analysis for the four major currencies and their cross rates; and (iii) a daily telephone service.

FRIEDBERG COMMODITY MANAGEMENT

Forecasts are based on a model combining both fundamental and technical analysis. All major currencies as well as exotic currencies are covered.

FX CONCEPTS

A technical model is used that analyses short-term and long-term trend and contra-trend movements.

GAIACORP LIMITED

This company offers four products: (i) currency hedge funds; (ii) selective currency exposure management; (iii) discretionary accounts; and (iv) performance measurement of currency exposure decisions.

GLOBAL FINANCE AND CONSULTING (GFC)

A full range of tailor-made treasury services, ongoing foreign exchange consultancy and technical trend systems.

GOLDMAN SACHS

The service includes technical analysis for short-term forecasts and a portfolio balance model for long-run forecasts.

GROTE FINANCIAL FUTURES LTD

Two services are offered: the first focuses on US and European markets while the second is designed for Far Eastern customers. The services are based on daily reports with buy/sell signals as well support and resistance levels for each currency.

HANSEATIC

A technical system that provides buy/sell signals. The system is based on artificial intelligence to isolate high confidence market patterns.

HENLEY CENTRE FOR FORECASTING

Short-term forecasts are generated from technical models. Long-term forecasts are based on econometric models.

INTERNATIONAL TREASURY CONSULTING INC (ITC)

Short-term forecasts are generated through technical models. Long-term forecasts are provided in a monthly publication which includes economic analysis of 24 countries. ITC also provides fund management and offers foreign exchange software packages.

INVESTMENT RESEARCH OF CAMBRIDGE

A technical model is based on rate of change indicators and moving averages. Clients have access to telephone consultancy and receive a publication.

MORGAN GRENFELL

Forecasts are based on analysis of the economic and political fundamentals, market intelligence and technical analysis. Both long-term and short-term forecasts are provided.

MULTINATIONAL COMPUTER MODELS INC

The company offers a computer-based foreign exchange exposure management system. The system has different modules dealing with exposure analysis, hedging strategies, spot and forward contract management and accounting, futures contracts accounting, option contract accounting, and portfolio risk-return analysis. The system also offers daily technical analysis and long-term fundamental forecasting.

NP RECORD

A service is offered that provides cover equivalent to that given by currency options but at a lower cost.

PREDEX

Three technical systems as well as a fundamental vector autoregression model are used to generate forecasts.

PREVIEW ECONOMICS

A daily report provides buy/sell recommendations. The recommendations are based on technical analysis. Fundamental models are also used to forecast exchange rates up to 12 months ahead.

STOLL MOMENTUM SYSTEM

A selection of three models is available covering a number of currencies. Short-, medium- and long-term forecasts are provided.

TECHNICAL TREND ANALYSIS

This is a purely technical service providing trading, trending and hedging signals.

WALDNER AND CO

Services offered include: (i) foreign exchange management; (ii) exposure management strategies; (iii) design of exposure software; and (iv) hedging consultancy.

WHARTON ECONOMETRIC FORECASTING ASSOCIATES (WEFA)

Two services are provided. The first is based on an econometric model producing monthly and annual forecasts. The second is a momentum model providing buy/sell signals.

12: Case Studies

In this chapter five case studies are presented to demonstrate how exchange rate forecasting is used in the decision-making process. All of the case studies are fictitious but, with the exception of the first case, they are based on actual data.

CASE STUDY 1: ABC HOME FURNITURE LIMITED

ABC Home Furniture Limited is a British company established in 1998 to manufacture and sell wooden furniture in the UK and Europe. The company's objective is to distinguish its products from the products of other companies in the same line of business and capture a significant market share in a short period of time. To accomplish this objective, the company decided to use a special kind of timber that is only available in some Caribbean islands.

At the end of 1998, the company started negotiating with the governments of two Caribbean islands, St Kilda and Barbara, to sign an agreement with one of them to be the supplier of timber over the period 1999–2008. Since the timber produced by the two islands is of comparable quality, the company's choice would fall on the island supplying the cheaper timber in pound terms. Initially, the annual shipment of the timber is worth GBP500,000. The current exchange rates are GBP/SFR (0.25) and GBP/BFR (0.50), where SFR and BFR are the currencies of St Kilda and Barbara respectively. The initial values of the annual shipments from the two islands are SFR2,000,000 and BFR1,000,000 respectively. These values are calculated on the basis of a fixed-weight shipment to be imported over 10 years.

In order to calculate the cost of imported timber over the period of the contract the company's finance manager visits the two islands on a fact-finding mission. During the visit he collects the following information:

1. The inflation rate in St Kilda is expected to be 30 per cent per annum over the next 10 years. The price of timber in terms of the St Kilda franc (SFR) normally goes up by about two-thirds of the inflation rate, that is by 20 per cent per annum.
2. In Barbara, the inflation rate is expected to be 15 per cent per annum and the price of timber also rises by two-thirds of the inflation rate, that is by 10 per cent per annum.

3. The price of timber supplied in a given year (in the currencies of the two islands) is determined at the end of the previous year according to the inflation rate prevailing then.
4. The payment is made at the end of the year, such that the relevant currency conversion rate is the exchange rate prevailing on the payment date.

Upon his return to the UK the finance manager embarks on the task of calculating the total cost of timber in pound terms from the two islands over the period 1999–2008. The decision is to be based entirely on the cost of timber in pound terms, so that the island providing the lower cost will be chosen as the supplier. Given the information collected during the visit, the finance manager starts by calculating the expected price of timber in the two foreign currencies. The results are shown in Table 12.1. In both cases the calculations are based on compounding the initial value of timber at the rates of price rise (20 per cent and 10 per cent respectively).

What is important for ABC Limited, however, is the value of timber in pounds, which depends on the exchange rate prevailing at the end of the year when the payment is due. There are two reasons why hedging the position is not a contemplated course of action. The first reason is that forward contracts on the two currencies are unavailable. The second reason is that, given that both of the islands have high inflation rates, it is expected that their currencies will depreciate continuously, in which case remaining unhedged will be more advantageous even if hedging can be implemented.

The decision-making process, therefore, requires exchange rate forecasting. What is required is a forecast for the two exchange rates of the two currencies against the pound at the end of each year (GBP/SFR and GBP/

Table 12.1 Value of timber in foreign currency terms

Year	*St Kilda (SFR)*	*Barbara (BFR)*
1999	2,000,000	1,000,000
2000	2,400,000	1,100,000
2001	2,880,000	1,210,000
2002	3,456,000	1,331,000
2003	4,147,200	1,464,100
2004	4,976,640	1,610,510
2005	5,971,968	1,771,561
2006	7,166,362	1,948,717
2007	8,599,634	2,143,589
2008	10,391,561	2,357,948
Total	51,989,365	15,937,425

BFR). Given the high inflation rates in both islands and the long time period involved, the finance manager, acting as a forecaster, believes that it is reasonable to assume that PPP will hold. Hence, he embarks on calculating the forecast exchange rates from the exact PPP formula

$$\hat{S}_t = S_0 \left[\frac{P_t / P_0}{P_t^* / P_0^*} \right] \tag{12.1}$$

where $\hat{S}_t$ is the forecast exchange rate such that t is 1999, . . ., 2008, S_0 is the actual exchange rate at the end of 1998, P_t is the forecast price level in the UK over the 10-year period, P_0 is the price level in the UK at the end of 1998, and an asterisk denotes the corresponding variables for the two islands. Assuming that $P_0 = P_0^* = 100$, the calculations for the price levels in the UK, St Kilda and Barbara are given in Table 12.2.

Given the price levels that are expected to prevail, the application of the PPP equation produces the exchange rate forecasts. Given the forecast exchange rates, it is possible to calculate the value of the timber in pound terms for each year. Table 12.3 shows these calculations.

The results show that St Kilda would be a better choice as the value of timber imported over the 10-year period costs GBP3,038,172 compared with GBP3,978,996 for Barbara. This is the case despite the fact that the foreign currency price of the timber imported from St Kilda rises faster than the price of timber imported from Barbara. Since St Kilda has a higher inflation rate, its currency should depreciate faster than the currency of Barbara against the pound. The effect of currency depreciation seems to more than to offset the effect of the rising price of timber.

Table 12.2 Expected price levels

Year	*UK*	*St Kilda*	*Barbara*
1998	100.0	100.0	100.0
1999	102.0	130.0	115.0
2000	104.0	169.0	132.3
2001	106.1	219.7	152.1
2002	108.2	285.6	174.9
2003	110.4	371.3	201.1
2004	112.6	482.7	231.3
2005	114.9	627.5	266.0
2006	117.2	815.7	305.9
2007	119.5	1060.5	351.8
2008	121.9	1378.6	404.6

Table 12.3 The forecast exchange rates and pound values of imported timber

Year	*GBP/SFR*	*GBP/BFR*	*St Kilda*	*Barbara*
1999	0.1962	0.4435	392,400	443,500
2000	0.1539	0.3933	369,360	432,630
2001	0.1208	0.3489	347,904	422,169
2002	0.0947	0.3094	327,283	411,811
2003	0.0743	0.2745	308,137	401,896
2004	0.0583	0.2434	290,138	391,998
2005	0.0458	0.2159	273,516	382,480
2006	0.0359	0.1915	257,272	373,179
2007	0.0282	0.1699	242,509	364,196
2008	0.0221	0.1506	229,653	355,107
Total			3,038,172	3,978,996

CASE STUDY 2: DEF OFFICE EQUIPMENT LIMITED

It is the end of 1993, and DEF Office Equipment Limited is considering an expansion of operations to be financed by issuing straight bonds. The amount to be raised is USD5 million to be repaid over a period five years with semi-annual coupon payments. A decision is to be made concerning: (i) whether the currency of denomination is the US dollar or a foreign currency; and (ii) if the choice falls on foreign currency financing, then which foreign currency is to be chosen? Five different foreign currencies are under consideration: the Canadian dollar (CAD), the French franc (FFR), the German mark (DEM), the Swiss franc (CHF) and the British pound (GBP). The market conditions prevailing at the time dictate the coupon rates shown in Table 12.4. The table also reports the initial exchange rates, as at the end of 1993.

Table 12.5 reports the foreign currency amounts to be borrowed (that is, the principal which is USD5 million equivalent at current exchange rates) as well as the interest payments and the total repayment (principal plus interest).

What is important for this decision is not only the coupon rate but also the exchange rate, as these two variables will determine the amount paid out by the company in terms of the principal borrowed and the coupon interest payments. Since the payments will be made every six months over a period of five years between 1994 and 1998, the forecast values of the exchange rates at these payment dates are required so that a decision can be made.

Table 12.4 Coupon rates and exchange rates at the end of 1993

Currency	*Coupon rate*	*Exchange rate (USD/Currency)*
USD	4.45	–
CAD	5.20	0.7553
FFR	4.45	0.1696
DEM	5.40	0.5793
CHF	4.25	0.6759
GBP	5.50	1.4812

Table 12.5 Principal, interest payment and total repayment in various currencies

Currency	*Amount borrowed*	*Interest payment (semi-annual)*	*Total repayment*
USD	5,000,000	111,250	6,112,500
CAD	6,619,886	172,117	8,341,056
FFR	29,481,132	655,955	36,040,682
DEM	8,631,107	233,040	10,961,507
CHF	7,397,544	157,198	8,969,524
GBP	3,375,641	92,830	4,303,942

The company's economist then embarks on the task of preparing these forecasts. The actual behaviour of the exchange rates is shown in Figure 12.1. The forecaster decides to use the univariate version of Harvey's structural time series model, believing that it can capture the time series properties of the exchange rates, and hence it is capable of producing good forecasts. For this purpose the economist estimates the model using historical quarterly time series covering the period 1974–1993. The forecasts on the payment dates are given in Table 12.6. Given the forecasts reported in Table 12.6, the interest payments, principal repayment and total repayment are reported in Table 12.7 for all of the currencies.

Despite the fact that the pound has the highest interest rate, the forecast depreciation of the pound against the dollar makes it cheaper to issue pound-denominated bonds. Conversely, the currency offering the lowest coupon rate (the Swiss franc) provides the most expensive alternative due to the forecast appreciation of the Swiss currency against the dollar. The choice, therefore, is between borrowing in US dollars at the certain cost of USD6,112,500 and borrowing in pounds at a forecast cost of GBP5,780,482. The economist fancies his forecasts. Accordingly he recommends borrowing by issuing pound-denominated bonds.

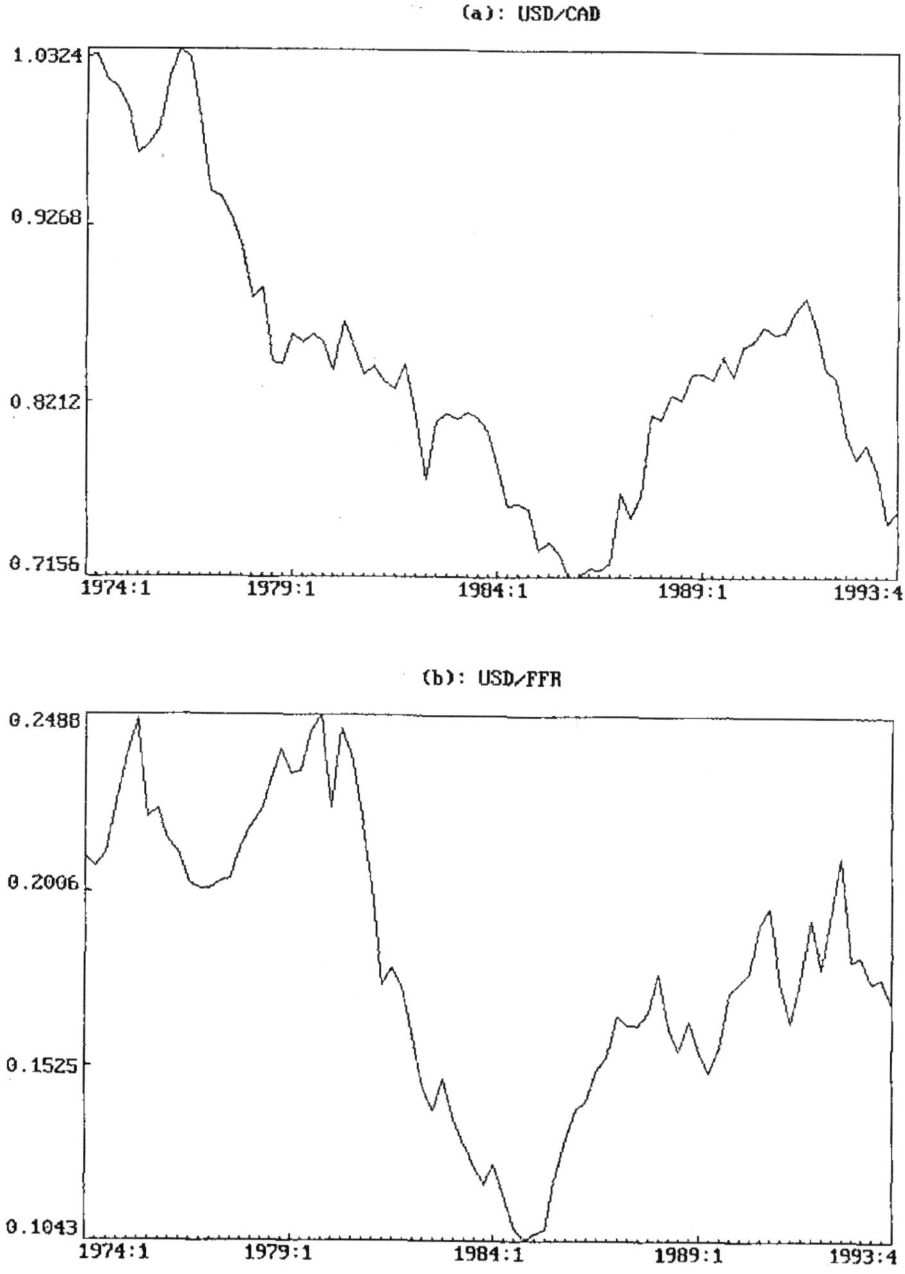

Figure 12.1 Quarterly exchange rates (1974–1993)

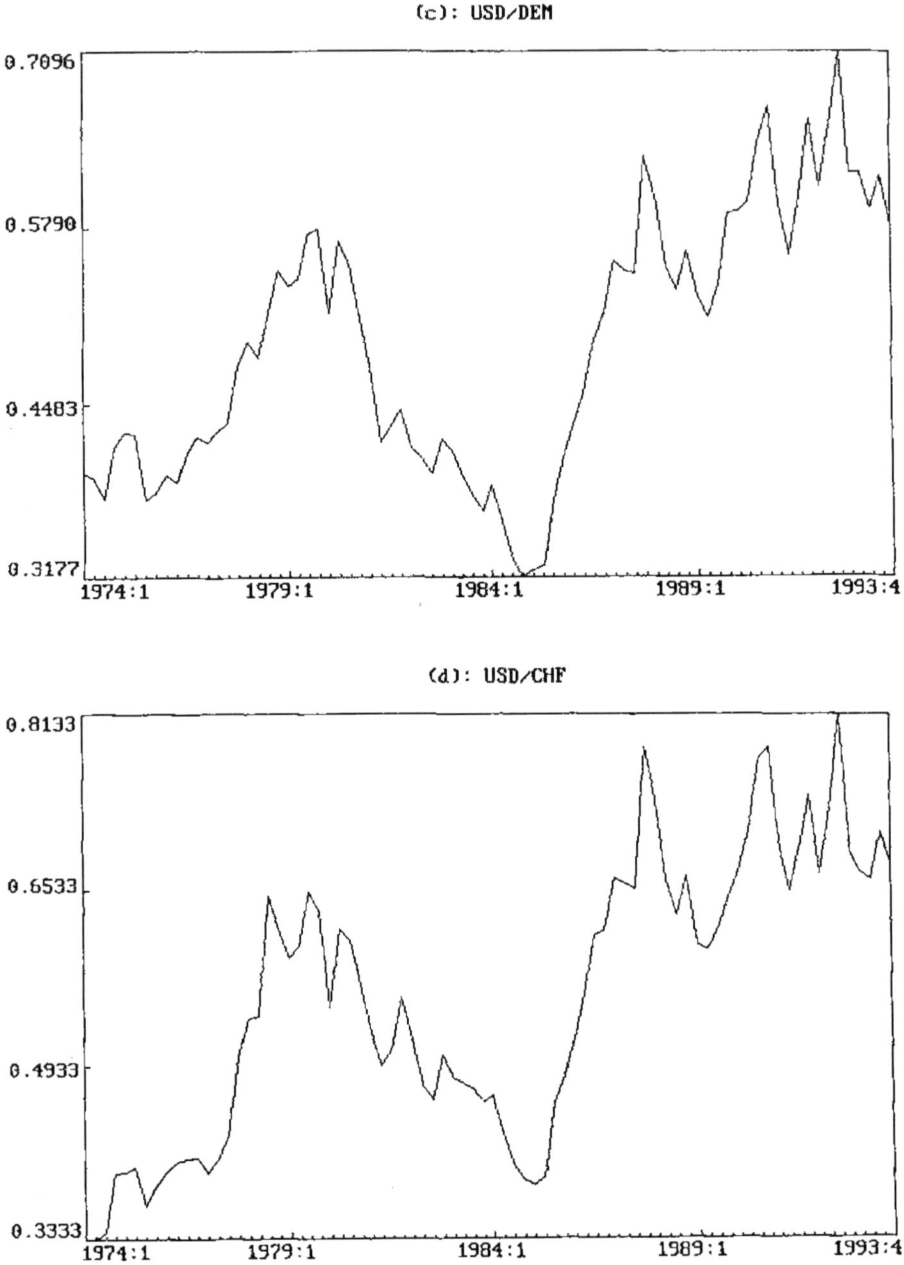

Figure 12.1 Quarterly exchange rates (1974–1993) (cont.)

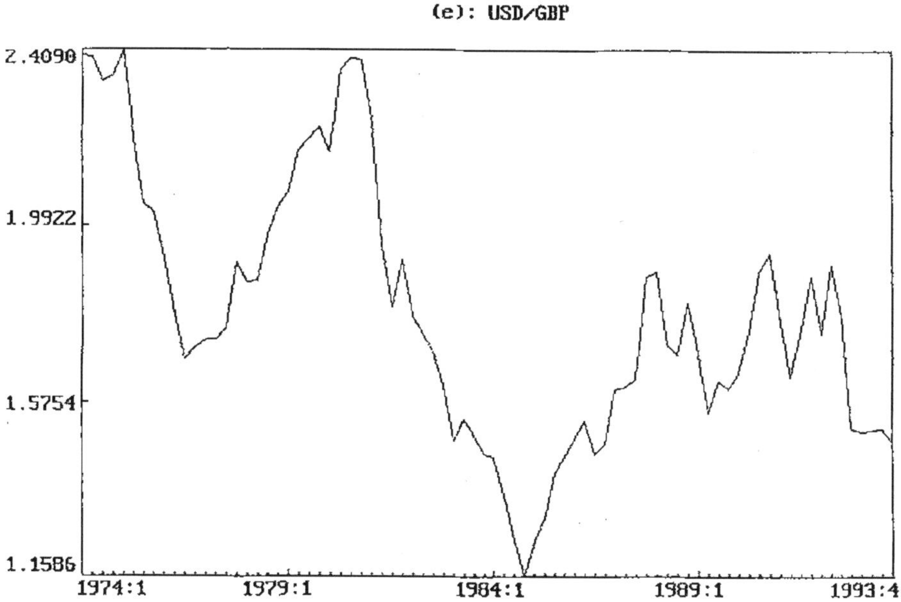

Figure 12.1 Quarterly exchange rates (1974–1993) (cont.)

Table 12.6 Forecast exchange rates (1994–98)

Date	*USD/CAD*	*USD/FFR*	*USD/DEM*	*USD/CHF*	*USD/GBP*
6: 1994	0.7804	0.1754	0.6047	0.6896	1.3664
12: 1994	0.7795	0.1799	0.5837	0.6734	1.3224
6: 1995	0.7791	0.1737	0.5946	0.6905	1.2260
12: 1995	0.7784	0.1782	0.5622	0.6897	1.2337
6: 1996	0.7729	0.1721	0.5882	0.7037	1.1886
12: 1996	0.7656	0.1765	0.5591	0.7201	1.2416
6: 1997	0.7564	0.1704	0.5864	0.7246	1.2306
12: 1997	0.7505	0.1748	0.5727	0.7573	1.3035
6: 1998	0.7464	0.1687	0.5888	0.7483	1.2973
12: 1998	0.7455	0.1731	0.5972	0.7819	1.3612

Table 12.7 Forecast interest payments and total repayments (USD)

Date	*USD*	*CAD*	*FFR*	*DEM*	*CHF*	*GBP*
6: 1994	111,250	134,320	115,055	140,919	108,404	126,843
12: 1994	111,250	134,165	118,006	136,025	105,857	122,758
6: 1995	111,250	134,096	113,939	138,566	108,545	113,809
12: 1995	111,250	133,976	116,894	131,015	108,419	114,524
6: 1996	111,250	133,029	112,889	137,074	110,620	110,338
12: 1996	111,250	131,773	115,776	130,293	113,198	115,258
6: 1997	111,250	130,189	111,775	136,655	113,906	114,237
12: 1997	111,250	129,174	114,661	133,462	119,046	121,004
6: 1998	111,250	128,468	110,660	137,214	117,631	120,428
12: 1998	111,250	128,313	113,546	139,171	122,913	126,360
Principal	5,000,000	4,935,125	5,103,183	5,154,496	5,784,139	4,594,923
Total	6,112,500	6,252,629	6,246,382	6,514,891	6,912,678	5,780,482

CASE STUDY 3: GHI FINANCIAL SERVICES LIMITED

It is late February 1998. GHI Financial Services Limited, a British company, has an offer to buy a call option on the US dollar expiring on 6 March. The following information is available:

Current Exchange Rate (GBP/USD)	0.61125
Exercise Exchange Rate	0.61130
Expiry Date	6 March 1998
Days to Expiry	10
Type of Option	American Call
Amount	USD50,000,000
Premium (per unit)	0.01 pence
Total Cost	GBP5,000

The decision whether or not to take the offer depends on one thing only: the behaviour of the exchange rate between the present time and the expiry date. Currently the exchange rate is 0.61125, which means that the option is out of the money. A decision to take the offer will be made only if the exchange rate goes above 0.61140 at any point in time within the remaining life of the option. The critical value of the exchange rate is obtained by adding up the exercise exchange rate and the premium. Obviously, daily exchange rate forecasts are needed.

Since a quick forecast is needed, the company starts to prepare the needed forecasts. The chief economist who embarks on the task chooses to prepare the forecasts from an analysis of the daily exchange rate movements over the past 90 days. He also chooses the following techniques to prepare the forecasts:

- Simple average
- 50-day moving average
- 25-day moving average
- Double moving average (of order 20)
- ARIMA(2, 1, 2) model.

By applying these methods to the sample data the forecast values reported in Table 12.8 are produced.

The forecasting results indicate that only the ARIMA forecasts show a value above 0.61140 to prevail on the expiry date. The economist seems to believe that ARIMA models produce more accurate forecasts than moving average methods, and accordingly he decides to go ahead with the decision to buy the option.

The following 10 days are very critical as the economist watches the behaviour of the exchange rate. Table 12.9 lists the actual values of the exchange rate over the 10-day period. On no day does the exchange rate reach the 0.61100 level. On the expiry date, however, the exchange rate is 0.61196. This is good news: the option can be exercised to make a net profit of GBP28,000. The right decision has been taken.

Having made the profit, the economist wants to learn from this experience. He wants to see whether or not the most accurate forecast (over the whole period) leads to the right decision. Therefore, he embarks on an analysis of the forecasting accuracy of the techniques he used, now that the

Table 12.8 Daily exchange rate forecasts

Day	*Simple*	*50-Day*	*25-Day*	*Double*	*ARIMA*
1	0.60465	0.60904	0.61007	0.60904	0.61111
2	0.60471	0.60915	0.61008	0.60994	0.61110
3	0.60478	0.60915	0.60099	0.60981	0.60820
4	0.60480	0.60926	0.60962	0.60975	0.60960
5	0.60484	0.60930	0.60951	0.60954	0.60974
6	0.60488	0.60914	0.60941	0.60876	0.60669
7	0.60486	0.60909	0.60959	0.60885	0.60870
8	0.60488	0.60909	0.60951	0.60871	0.60820
9	0.60489	0.60925	0.60940	0.60917	0.60894
10	0.60491	0.60950	0.60941	0.60983	0.61185

Table 12.9 Actual values of the exchange rate

Day	*Exchange rate*
1	0.61087
2	0.61087
3	0.60617
4	0.60846
5	0.60861
6	0.60350
7	0.60676
8	0.60588
9	0.60705
10	0.61196

actual data are available. The following measures of forecasting accuracy are employed:

- Mean absolute error (*MAE* measured in per cent)
- Mean square error (*MSE* measured in per cent)
- Root mean square error (*RMSE* measured in per cent)
- Coefficient of determination (R^2)
- Correlation coefficient (r)
- Theil's inequality coefficient (U)
- Direction accuracy rate (*DA*)
- Confusion rate (*CR*).

The calculations reveal the measures of accuracy reported in Table 12.10.

Overall, the results show that the ARIMA model produced the most accurate forecasts. The simple average and 25-day moving average methods seem to be inferior to the random walk model as indicated by Theil's inequality coefficient. On this occasion, therefore, the model generating the most accurate forecasts has led to the right decision. As we have seen, this may not always be the case.

CASE STUDY 4: JKL ELECTRONICS LIMITED

JKL Electronics Limited is a US company specialising in manufacturing some electronic components. The company supplies Europe with its products via its subsidiary in Scotland. It is the end of 1993 and the subsidiary approaches the parent company with a proposal to expand operations in Scotland starting with a 10-year joint venture with a Scottish electronics company located in Aberdeen.

Table 12.10 Measures of forecasting accuracy

Measure	*Simple*	*50-day*	*25-day*	*Double*	*ARIMA*
MAE	0.569	0.393	0.430	0.379	0.235
MSE	0.0045	0.0020	0.0020	0.0019	0.0008
RMSE	0.067	0.045	0.051	0.004	0.028
R^2	0.18	0.18	0.08	0.36	0.98
r	0.43	0.42	0.29	0.60	0.99
U	1.19	0.89	1.04	0.85	0.57
DA	0.56	0.44	0.33	0.44	0.44
CR	0.44	0.56	0.67	0.56	0.56

A feasibility study conducted by the subsidiary reveals that the joint venture will result in lucrative business. The feasibility study indicates that the project will be extremely profitable. The cost of the project is GBP1,000,000 but it is estimated that it will provide annual net profit of GBP200,000 over the next 10 years, and that it will have a liquidation value of GBP1,500,000. At a discount rate of 10 per cent, the net present value of the project is (GBP807,228). While the project is very profitable from the subsidiary's perspective, the parent company may have a different view. The most important factor leading to this difference is the exchange rate between the base currencies of the subsidiary and the parent company (the pound and the US dollar).

To evaluate the project from the perspective of the parent company the chief economist embarks on preparing some forecasts for the exchange rate between the dollar and pound (USD/GBP) over the period 1994–2003. The economist uses a sample of quarterly data covering the period 1974:1–1993:4 to estimate the following PPP model:

$$\Delta s_t = \alpha + \beta \Delta p_t^A + \gamma \Delta p_t^B \tag{12.2}$$

where Δs_t is the percentage change in the exchange rate, Δp_t^A is the US inflation rate and Δp_t^B is the UK inflation rate. The estimation produces the following equation:

$$\Delta s_t = -3.0861 + 1.2562 \Delta p_t^A - 0.60396 \Delta p_t^B \tag{12.3}$$

which shows that the US inflation rate has a greater impact on the exchange rate than the UK inflation rate. The economist then constructs four different scenarios for the behaviour of the inflation rates in the two countries over the forecast period. The economist believes that the US inflation rate will be

Table 12.11 The four scenarios

Scenario	*Probability*	*US inflation*	*UK inflation*	*Exchange rate (%)*
1	0.1	3	5	−2.34
2	0.2	3	6	−2.94
3	0.3	3	7	−3.55
4	0.4	3	8	−4.14

stable at 3 per cent and that the UK inflation rate will be consistently higher. The four different scenarios envisage that the UK inflation rate over the forecast period will be 5, 6, 7 and 8 per cent with probabilities of 0.1, 0.2, 0.3 and 0.4 respectively. According to the first scenario, the US inflation rate will be 3 per cent while the UK inflation rate will be 5 per cent. From the estimated PPP equation the exchange rate should fall (the pound should depreciate) at an annual rate of 2.34 per cent. Table 12.11 summarises the implications of the four scenarios.

The economist moves on to estimate the values of the cash flows and the net present value under the four different scenarios. These results are reported in Table 12.12. The net present value of the project ranges between USD1,537,969 under scenario 1 and USD1,268,342 under scenario 4. Thus,

Table 12.12 Exchange rates and dollar cash flows under the four scenarios

Year	*Scenario 1*		*Scenario 2*		*Scenario 3*		*Scenario 4*	
	Exch rate	*Cash flow*	*Exch rate*	*Cash flow*	*Exch rate*	*Cash flow*	*Exch rate*	*Cash flow*
1994	1.4466	289320	1.4377	287540	1.4286	285720	1.4198	283960
1995	1.4127	282550	1.3954	279086	1.3779	275576	1.3610	272204
1996	1.3797	275938	1.3544	270881	1.3290	265794	1.3047	260934
1997	1.3474	269481	1.3146	262917	1.2818	256358	1.2507	250132
1998	1.3159	263175	1.2759	255188	1.2363	247257	1.1989	239777
1999	1.2851	257017	1.2384	247685	1.1924	238479	1.1492	229850
2000	1.2550	251003	1.2020	240403	1.1501	230013	1.1017	220334
2001	1.2256	245130	1.1667	233335	1.1092	221848	1.0561	211212
2002	1.1970	239393	1.1324	226475	1.0669	213972	1.0123	202468
2003	1.1690	1987229	1.0991	1868443	1.0319	1754202	0.9704	1649730

the forecast depreciation of the pound against the dollar reduces the attractiveness of the project from the perspective of the parent company. The expected net present value of the project, calculated as a weighted average, is USD1,355,859.

When the top management of the parent company examines these figures, it is decided that the project is unacceptable. Another project in the US has a higher net present value of USD1,450,000. It is apparent that what makes the difference in this case is the exchange rate. If the forecast indicated that the pound will not depreciate by more than 2.34 per cent per year as in the first scenario, then the project would have produced an expected net present value of USD1,537,969, in which case it might have been accepted.

CASE STUDY 5: MNP TRADING COMPANY LIMITED

It is October 1993. MNP is a US trading company, exporting and importing from Europe. The company has an amount of GBP2,000,000 payable to a British company at the end of 1993. The current three-month forward rate (USD/GBP) is 1.4867, which means that if the company takes the decision to hedge the position in the forward market, then the amount payable is USD2,973,400. The company will take the decision to hedge the position only if the pound is forecast to appreciate.

The company hires the services of a consultant to advise the management on this matter. The consultant's job boils down to forecasting the USD/GBP exchange rate at the end of 1993. The consultant embarks on his task by collecting quarterly data on the exchange rate and some relevant variables over the period 1974:1–1993:3. The consultant's strategy consists of the following steps:

1. Estimating five different models: the random walk model, the unbiased efficiency model, UIP, PPP and an ARIMA model over the period 1974:1–1989:4.
2. Using the models as estimated in step 1 to forecast the exchange rate over the period 1974:1–1989:4, and calculating the *RMSE* for each model.
3. Re-estimating the models over the period 1974:1–1993:3, and using them to forecast the exchange rate at the end of 1993.
4. Calculating a composite forecast as a weighted average of the individual forecasts. The weights are proportional to the inverse of the *RMSE*.

Having executed these steps the consultant ends up with the results reported in Table 12.13.

Table 12.13 The forecasting models

Model	*Specification*	*RMSE*	*Forecast* $\Delta\hat{S}_{t+1}$
Random walk	$\Delta s_t = \alpha + \varepsilon_t$	0.071569	−0.0057142
Unbiasedness	$\Delta s_t = \alpha + \beta(f_{t-1} - s_{t-1}) + \varepsilon_t$	0.059842	−0.0036609
UIP	$\Delta s_t = \alpha + \beta(i_{t-1} - i^*_{t-1}) + \varepsilon_t$	0.057762	−0.0095634
PPP	$\Delta s_t = \alpha + \beta(\Delta p_t - \Delta p^*_t) + \varepsilon_t$	0.071504	−0.0023896
ARIMA(2,1,2)	$\Delta s_t = \alpha + \beta\Delta s_{t-1} + \gamma\Delta s_{t-2}$ $+ \varepsilon_t - \theta_1\varepsilon_{t-1} - \theta_2\varepsilon_t - 2$	0.065371	0.016534

Table 12.14 Forecasts generated by various models

Model	*Weight*	*Forecast* ($\hat{S}_{t+1}$)
Random walk	0.181	1.5021
Unbiasedness	0.216	1.5052
UIP	0.224	1.4962
PPP	0.181	1.5071
ARIMA(2,1,2)	0.198	1.5357
Composite		1.5090

The weights needed to generate the composite forecast are calculated from the *RMSE*s of the five models according to the formula

$$w_i = \frac{\dfrac{1}{(RMSE)_i}}{\displaystyle\sum_{i=1}^{5} \frac{1}{(RMSE)_i}} \tag{12.4}$$

in which case heavier weights are assigned to the forecasts generated from models with lower root mean square errors. Table 12.14 reports the weights as derived from equation (12.4) as well as the forecasts of the actual value of the exchange rate. It is obvious that all of the forecasts indicate that the exchange rate will decline but not to the extent that would take it below the level of the forward rate. Therefore, the decision to hedge is taken. This case study demonstrates how various models with different forecasting accuracies may lead to taking the same decision.

13: Concluding Remarks

RECAPITULATION

We have in this book tried to answer a number of questions pertaining to the generation, implementation, evaluation and monitoring of forecasts, with a particular emphasis on one of the most important macroeconomic variables, the exchange rate. This has not been an easy task, and we probably did not reach a clear-cut conclusion about at least some of the issues raised in this book. What makes this so much the case is the fact that the exchange rate is probably the most difficult financial variable to forecast, as it is generated by a complex interaction of variables involving forces from outside the domestic economy.

One of the extreme views is that exchange rate forecasting is a futile exercise because the foreign exchange market is efficient, because the exchange rate is determined by unpredictable news, or because it is generated by chaotic processes with a complex and unknown structure. This view cannot be taken for granted, since there is at best mixed evidence for efficiency and because the news approach to exchange rate determination has not found widespread acceptance. The last proposition is equally applicablc to chaos theory.

The other argument is that exchange rate forecasting is useful but, since the empirical evidence on the power of the forecasting models is not that sanguine, we will at least save the cost of obtaining forecasts by relying on the spot rate and the forward rate as forecasters. At a time which exchange rate forecasters want to forget about (the first half of the 1980s), a cynical view became widely accepted. This view was that 'the only way foreign exchange rate forecasters will get more accurate is if we return to fixed exchange rates'. Failure to predict the strength of the US dollar at that time led to the conclusion that 'no one knows where the exchange rate is going, and that if someone knew it, it would be pure luck'. This argument is again not convincing because some evidence indicates that it is possible to outperform the random walk model and the forward rate model. The problem is that the decision that requires the forecasts may involve a position worth millions or billions of dollars. Because we are rational, we have to do our best to get a forecast that we feel comfortable with. It may turn out to be wrong, but *ex ante* we thought it would be better than the toss of a coin.

An argument that can be put forward for forecasting is the fact that forecasting services have flourished despite the negative views on forecasting. A cynical explanation for this phenomenon is that some business managers want someone to blame when they (the managers) make the wrong decision. It is very convenient then to hire the services of an external forecaster. If the right decision is taken then the manager can claim the credit for himself or herself. If a wrong decision is taken the forecaster is hammered in the next board meeting with a promise from the manager to terminate this forecaster's services and seek another one. The story is repeated subsequently. While there may be cases like this, we cannot generalise this conspiracy-theory explanation. Rather we tend to view a business manager to be objective enough to be motivated by the cost-effectiveness of the forecasts only.

VITAL QUESTIONS

A large number of questions were raised, which we tried to answer in various chapters. The following are the main questions and some brief answers.

WHY DO WE NEED EXCHANGE RATE FORECASTING?

The need for exchange rate forecasting was discussed in Chapter 2. In general, we need exchange rate forecasting because the outcomes of some financial decisions are contingent upon the future values of the exchange rate. The real world provides a large number of examples demonstrating that accurate forecasting could mean the difference between a spectacular success and a total collapse. Sometimes it is claimed that exchange rate forecasting is not needed because it is always possible to hedge exposure to foreign exchange risk. This argument is not valid for a number of reasons. First, the argument mostly pertains to transaction exposure, not to economic exposure. Second, it may not be possible to hedge long-term transaction exposure because of the unavailability of long-term forward contracts and other hedging instruments. Third, even if it is possible to hedge an exposure, it may not be advisable to take such a course of action. The hedge decision is basically a speculative decision that depends on the exchange rate expected to prevail when payables and receivables are due. Exchange rate forecasting is required not only to decide whether or not to hedge but also to determine the hedging instrument.

WHAT ARE THE DECISIONS THAT NEED EXCHANGE RATE FORECASTING?

Table 13.1 provides a summary of some of the decisions that were described in Chapter 2. The decision rules pertain to a variety of financial operations involving more than one currency.

WHAT IS THE APPROPRIATE TIME HORIZON FOR FORECASTING?

The appropriate time horizon for forecasting differs from one situation to another. Some decisions, such as spot speculation, require forecasting on a day-to-day basis, while others, such as foreign direct investment, require forecasting possibly at the end of each year over a period of 10 years. A distinction, hence, must be made among short-term, medium-term and long-term forecasting.

HOW CAN WE FORECAST EXCHANGE RATES?

This book dealt with the general classes of the models and methods used to forecast exchange rates. In Chapter 3 we dealt with univariate time series techniques, while Chapter 4 dealt with multivariate models, including single-equation models and multi-equation models. Market-based forecasting, technical forecasting, judgemental forecasting and composite forecasting were also dealt with in Chapters 5, 6 and 7. It seems that there is a trend towards the use of both technical and fundamental models, and that the use of judgement and forecast combinations are common practices.

WHAT DATA ARE AVAILABLE? ARE THEY SUFFICIENT TO GENERATE THE NEEDED FORECASTS?

The availability of data determines which technique is used for forecasting. If no data are available then forecasting will be purely judgemental. If data are available on the exchange rate only, then a univariate model is used. Single-equation multivariate models use a larger amount of data than univariate models. Multi-equation models are the most demanding in terms of data requirement. Data requirement may pertain to more than what is needed to estimate the model, as data may be needed to write scenarios for *ex ante* forecasting.

WHAT IS THE ROLE OF JUDGEMENT IN EXCHANGE RATE FORECASTING?

The role of judgement in exchange rate forecasting was discussed in Chapter 6. This role may take any of a number of forms: the whole forecasting can be judgemental, or that judgement can be used to write scenarios to derive conditional forecasts. Even when the forecaster uses a formal econometric model to derive forecasts, the very choice of the model, the data, the estimation techniques, and so on involves judgement.

Table 13.1 Some decision rules requiring exchange rate forecasting

Decision situation	*Decision rule*
Spot speculation	Go long on y if $E(x/y)_{t+n} > (x/y)_t$. Otherwise, go long on x.
Spot speculation (with bid–offer spread)	Go long on y if $E(x/y)_{b,t+n} > (x/y)_{a,t}$ and long on x if $E(x/y)_{a,t+n} < (x/y)_{b,t}$.
Uncovered interest arbitrage	Go short on x and long on y if $E(\dot{S}_{t+n}) > i_x - i_y$. Otherwise, go short on y and long on x.
Uncovered interest arbitrage (with bid–offer spread)	Go short on x and long on y if $E(\dot{S}_{b,t+n}) > i_{xa} - i_{yb}$.
Spot-forward speculation	Buy currency y forward at time t and sell spot at $t+n$ if $ES_{t+n}(x/y) > F_t^{t+n}(x/y)$.
Spot-forward speculation (with bid–offer spread)	Buy currency y forward at time t and sell spot at $t+n$ if $ES_{t+n}(x/y)_b > F_t^{t+n}(x/y)_a$.
Forward speculation	Buy currency y on the two-period contract at t and sell the one-period contract at $t+2$ if $EF_{t+1}^{t+2} > F_t^{t+2}$.
Option speculation	Buy a call or sell a put on a currency that is expected to appreciate. Conversely, buy a put or sell a call.
Money market hedging of transaction exposure	Hedge payables if $\bar{F}_t < ES_{t+n}$. Otherwise, hedge receivables.
Short-term financing	Choose currency y rather than currency x if $i_y + E\dot{S}_{t+n} < i_x$. Otherwise, choose currency x.
Short-term investment	Choose currency y rather than currency x if $i_y + E\dot{S}_{t+n} > i_x$. Otherwise, choose currency x.
Long-term bond financing	Choose currency y rather than currency x if $\left(\frac{ES_{t+n}}{S_t}\right)(1+i_y)^n > (1+i_x)^n$. Otherwise, choose currency x.
Long-term investment (shares)	Choose foreign shares if $\left(\frac{ES_{t+n}}{S_t}\right)(1+d^*+a^*)^n > (1+d+a)^n$
Foreign direct investment	Accept a project if $-S_tX_t + \sum_{j=1}^{n} \frac{ES_{t+j}X_{t+j}}{(1+i)^j} > 0$

WHY DO WE COMBINE FORECASTS?

Composite forecasting is the act (or art) of combining forecasts. This topic was discussed in Chapter 6. There are two reasons for combining forecasts pertaining to efficiency and accuracy. The first is that different forecasters have different access to information and different capabilities. Hence, a composite forecast may be more efficient. Second, forecast diversification may reduce the forecasting error.

WHY DO FORECASTERS DIFFER?

The question why forecasters differ was answered in Chapter 11. Forecasters differ because of differences in model specification, estimation methods, sample periods, data frequencies, variable definitions, values of explanatory variables for the forecasting period and judgemental adjustment.

IS FORECASTING A USELESS EXERCISE, SINCE THE FOREIGN EXCHANGE MARKET IS EFFICIENT?

The implication of market efficiency for exchange rate forecasting was discussed in Chapter 5. If the foreign exchange market is perfectly efficient, then forecasting is useless in the sense that either the spot rate or the forward rate provide optimal forecasts. However, the evidence for market efficiency is at best mixed, which leaves some space for forecasting to be useful. Moreover, it has been shown that some econometric models can beat the spot rate and the forward rate in out-of-sample forecasting.

SHOULD WE USE FUNDAMENTAL OR TECHNICAL MODELS TO FORECAST EXCHANGE RATES?

The question on the choice between fundamental and technical models has been debated extensively. There seems to be a consensus view that while fundamental models are more useful for long-term forecasting, technical models are more appropriate for short-term forecasting. There has been a growing tendency for exchange rate forecasting services to use both technical and fundamental models to generate their forecasts.

ARE MECHANICAL TRADING RULES PROFITABLE?

The evidence on the profitability of mechanical trading rules is mixed. Given that the market is not fully efficient, trading rules should, at least theoretically, be profitable. One problem with trading rules is that they may or may not work for a particular combination of a specific rule and specific market conditions. Another problem is that it is not easy to determine the dimensions of a trading rule *ex ante*, that is it is not possible to determine the optimal filter size for a filter rule or the optimal order of the moving average for a moving average rule. Even more difficult is the determination of the right model for the right market conditions. Our only guide is the historical performance of the rule, and this is why a rule may or may not work.

HOW CAN WE EXPLAIN THE FAILURE OF EXCHANGE RATE FORECASTING MODELS AND THE POOR TRACK RECORD OF FORECASTERS?

A simple answer to this question is that the process of exchange rate determination is highly complex and not fully understood. The process may be highly stochastic and hence difficult to forecast. There could be a large number of factors at play at the same time, some of which are unidentified and some are unmeasurable. Failing to take into account these factors is bound to produce inaccurate forecasts. Another explanation is found in the news model of exchange rate determination. If the exchange rate is determined by news, then it is unforecastable because news is by definition unforecastable. Finally, the process determining the exchange rate may be a deterministic nonlinear process that produces a chaotic behaviour. If this process is unknown and because of the sensitivity to the initial condition, forecasting exchange rates can be difficult or impossible.

IS IT BETTER TO GENERATE FORECASTS INTERNALLY OR EXTERNALLY? IF EXTERNALLY, HOW CAN WE PICK AN EXTERNAL FORECASTER?

The selection of forecasters was discussed in Chapter 11. The decision concerning the choice between internal and external forecasters and the choice of the external forecaster depends on a number of factors. The situation boils down to a decision that is based on the cost-effectiveness of the choice.

HOW DO WE MEASURE FORECASTING ACCURACY?

Measuring forecasting accuracy was discussed in Chapter 10. It is important to emphasise that what we mean by accuracy differs from one case to another. In some cases getting the direction correct is more important than predicting the magnitude of the change. In other cases the reverse is true. What is important in general is that the forecast must lead to improved decision making.

WHERE DO WE GO FROM HERE?

One conclusion that can definitely be derived from this book is that exchange rate forecasting is needed to make decisions involving the expected value of the exchange rate. Tossing a coin is certainly not a viable alternative. It is true that the performance of foreign exchange forecasters has since the early 1970s been appalling, but this is no reason to give up. At one time our ancestors had a great difficulty forecasting the time it takes a falling object to hit the ground and whether or not rain was coming. Now, we can forecast precisely how long it takes a falling object to hit the ground, and significant advances have been made in forecasting weather conditions. True, the first of these two phenomena is governed by a precise physical law and this is why we can now forecast it precisely. Our ancestors did not know that. Weather conditions could be governed by chaotic processes, and this is why we cannot yet forecast the weather precisely. Until now, no one claims to know with a reasonable degree of certainty what kind of process determines exchange rates and other financial prices. This is more of a reason not to give up the search for the truth. Scientists have been frustrated by their inability to forecast earthquakes, but they have not given up. Great advances have been made in explaining earthquakes, and future research is bound to improve our understanding of earthquakes and, hopefully, lead to an improvement in our ability to forecast them. The same argument applies to hurricanes and indeed to exchange rates.

Our ability to forecast exchange rates may be improved by a continuation of high-quality research in three related areas: economic theory, econometrics and time series analysis, and mathematics.

Advances in economic theory will undoubtedly lead to improvement in our understanding of exchange rate determination. It is probably the case that the mainstream models of exchange rate determination that have been presented since the advent of floating exchange rates are inadequate. One can easily notice that exchange rates are too volatile to be explained by the smooth movements of macroeconomic variables such as the money supply, output and prices. The question whether or not exchange rate volatility is associated with macroeconomic factors has led some economists to look for other explanatory factors. In a recent paper (Williams *et al.*, 1998), a distinction is made between traditional fundamentals (such as those used in mainstream models) and virtual fundamentals which are derived from asset market data. This study provides results showing that virtual fundamentals exhibit similar volatility to 15 bilateral exchange rates while traditional fundamentals are much less volatile. Taking into account institutional factors may also help. Thinking along these lines has led to the development of a post-Keynesian model of exchange rate determination which is worthy of more attention than it has received (see Harvey, 1991, 1993a, b, 1995).

This does not mean that research along the lines of mainstream neoclassical economics should be discarded. Our understanding of a number of macroeconomic phenomena has increased tremendously over the last 20 years, simply because of the work of mainstream neoclassical economists. If these economists can produce breakthroughs in other areas of macroeconomics, there is no reason why the same thing could not happen in the area of exchange rate determination.

Advances in econometrics and time series analysis seem to go hand in hand with developments in economic theory. Developments in econometrics and time series methods have led to the rise and fall of structural forecasting with large-scale macroeconomic models. By the late 1970s it was clear that these models, at least traditionally implemented, were losing ground. A major development in the 1970s was the publication of a landmark book by Box and Jenkins, which gave birth to the ARIMA methodology (the most recent edition of the book is Box *et al.*, 1994). It was then shown that simple univariate models can outperform the complex structural models. Sims (1980) suggested an alternative that can handle multivariate relationships, coming up with the VAR methodology. Granger (1969) and Sims (1972) made important contributions by providing the tools for exploring causal relationships in multivariate systems. Further important contributions followed, with the development of the dynamic factor model of Sargent and Sims (1977), cointegration and error correction modelling (Engle and Granger, 1987), structural time series analysis (Harvey, 1989), regime switching models (for example, Hamilton, 1989) and nonlinear models (for example, Tong, 1990).

It is true that the accuracy of exchange rate forecasting models and developments in econometrics have not been highly correlated (and on occasions negatively correlated). Yet, any attempt that leads to better model specification and estimation methods that can capture the underlying time series properties of the data is potentially capable of leading to better forecasting. For example, a model that specifies a deterministic trend and/or deterministic seasonality when they are stochastic is bound to produce inaccurate forecasts (Harvey and Scott, 1994; Moosa and Kennedy, 1998; Lenten and Moosa, 1999). A model estimated by OLS when the coefficients are actually time varying will also produce less accurate forecasts than can be obtained from a model estimated within a TVP framework (Moosa and Kwiecien, 1999). And an unrestricted VAR without an error correction term is more likely to produce less accurate forecasts than the corresponding error correction model if the variables are cointegrated.

Developments in mathematics are important for at least two reasons. The first is that these developments serve both economic theory and econometric theory. The second reason is more specific. We have seen how the development of nonlinear dynamic models and topology has helped the development of chaos theory, which has been applied to exchange rate determination and forecasting. Further developments in this field will have positive slipovers on exchange rate forecasting. Diebold (1998b) makes the prediction that 'the hallmark of macroeconomic forecasting over the next 20 years will be the marriage of the best of non-structural and structural approaches, facilitated by advances in numerical and simulation techniques that will help macroeconomists to solve, estimate, simulate, and yes, forecast with rich models'.

The humiliation of exchange rate forecasting models has been blown out of proportion because economists were over-optimistic about the ability of these models to forecast such a volatile variable. The expectation that has led to over-optimism has been appropriately revised downwards. People, at least rational people, learn from their mistakes, and forecasters are no exception.

Glossary*

Absolute PPP A version of the PPP theory stipulating that the exchange rate at a point in time is equal to or determined by the price ratio.

Accumulation In technical analysis, an accumulation occurs when a bottom is followed by a reversal as a result of demand overcoming supply.

Adaptive expectations An expectations formation mechanism whereby the exchange rate is expected to change by a fraction of the current period's error.

Adaptive response rate single exponential smoothing (ARRSES) method A technique that allows for continuous changes in the smoothing parameter when exponential smoothing is used for forecasting.

Adjusted coefficient of determination ($\bar{R}^2$) The coefficient of determination adjusted for the degrees of freedom.

Akaike information criterion (*AIC*) A measure of goodness of fit calculated from the variance of the error terms.

American option An option that can be exercised on or before the maturity (or expiry) date.

Appreciation A rise in the value of a currency relative to other currencies under a system of flexible exchange rates.

Arbitrage A financial operation designed to make riskless profit by capitalising on anomalies in market prices.

Artificial neural network (ANN) A representation of a nonlinear nonparametric model based on the functioning of the human brain.

Attractor A smooth curve that represents the locus of points on a phase portrait.

Autocorrelation coefficient The correlation coefficient between the current value and the lagged values of a variable or a residual.

Autocorrelation function The relationship between the autocorrelation coefficient of a certain order and the lag length.

Autoregressive conditional heteroscedasticity (ARCH) A model due to Engle (1982) that fits financial time series well and is capable of explaining volatility clustering.

---

* Most of the concepts in this glossary are generic. Howerver, in the spirit of this book they are defined in relation to exchange rates and the foreign exchange market.

Autoregressive distributed lag (ADL) model A model in which the dependent variable is explained by its lagged value as well as the contemporaneous and lagged vales of the explanatory variables.

Autoregressive integrated moving average (ARIMA) model A model in which the dependent variable is an integrated variable, being a function of its lagged values as well as the current and lagged values of the error term.

Autoregressive model A model in which the dependent variable is a function of its lagged values.

Autoregressive moving average (ARMA) model A model in which the dependent variable is stationary and a function of its lagged values as well as the current and lagged values of the error term.

Average rate option An option that gives the right to sell the underlying currency at the exercise exchange rate if the average spot rate between two points in time is less than the exercise exchange rate.

Averaging methods Forecasting methods based on the assumption that fluctuations in exchange rates represent random departures from some smooth time path.

Bandwagon expectations See **extrapolative expectations**.

Bar chart A chart used by technical analysts to represent the movement of exchange rates and other financial variables. It shows the behaviour over time of the high, low and closing levels (and opening levels if available) of the exchange rate.

Batting average A measure of forecasting accuracy that is related to Theil's inequality coefficient.

BDS test A test for chaos based on the concept of the correlation dimension.

Benchmark model A model used as a benchmark to evaluate the forecasting accuracy of other models.

Bid exchange rate The exchange rate at which the quoting party is willing to buy the underlying currency.

Bid interest rate The interest rate at which the quoting party is willing to borrow funds.

Bid–offer spread The difference between the offer and the bid exchange and interest rates.

Bilateral exchange rate An exchange rate between two currencies, or the price of one currency in terms of another.

Black box problem A problem associated with reduced-form models arising because these models explain the value of the dependent variable in terms of other variables without telling us how the explanatory variables are determined. This problem can be avoided by using multi-equation models.

Bowman–Shenton test A test for the normality of the residuals based on the third and fourth moments of the frequency distribution.

Box–Jenkins methodology Also called ARIMA modelling, it is a modelling and forecasting methodology based the identification and estimation of autoregressive and/or moving average models.

Breakeven filter size A filter size producing neither profit nor loss.

Brown's method See **double exponential smoothing**.

Call option A contract that gives the right to buy a certain amount of a currency on or before a certain date at an exchange rate determined at the present time.

Central bank intervention The process whereby a central bank enters the foreign exchange market, by buying and selling currencies, in an attempt to affect exchange rates.

Chaos theory A theory that provides an analysis of deterministic processes that are too irregular to be predictable.

Chaotic process A deterministic nonlinear process that looks random.

Chartism See **technical analysis**.

Coefficient of determination (R^2) A measure of the goodness of fit calculated as the ratio of the explained sum of squares to the total sum of squares of the dependent variable.

Cointegration Variables are cointegrated if they are linked by a long-run relationship such that they cannot move away from each other without bounds.

Composite forecasting A procedure involving the combination of two or more forecasts derived from different models to produce the final forecast.

Conditional forecasting See **ex post forecasting**.

Confusion rate A measure of the direction accuracy of a forecasting model based on the number of times the wrong direction is predicted.

Consensus forecast A forecast that reflects the overall view of a number of forecasters.

Consolidation patterns See **continuation patterns**.

Continuation patterns Also called consolidation patterns. In technical analysis, a continuation pattern is a sideways movement that temporarily interrupts an upward or a downward move in the exchange rate. Examples are flags, symmetrical triangles and head and shoulders. In Japanese candlestick charts continuation patterns include window, upside tasuki gap, rising three methods, falling three methods, upside gap and downside gap.

Control chart A graphical device that is used to monitor the forecasting error, to make sure that the forecasts are not biased in either direction.

Correlation dimension A test for chaos based on the significant difference in the behaviour of a chaotic process and a stochastic process.

Correlation integral In testing for chaos this is the fraction of pairs of points that are not far away from each other by a certain small amount.

Covered interest arbitrage A financial operation whereby the arbitrager borrows funds in a certain currency and invests in another, while covering the long position in the forward market. It is triggered by the violation of covered interest parity.

Covered interest parity (CIP) An equilibrium condition that precludes covered interest arbitrage. It is obtained when the return on a currency position is equal to the covered return on a position in another currency, or when the interest rate differential is equal to the forward spread.

Cross hedging Hedging exposure to a particular currency by taking a position on another currency whose exchange rate against the base currency is highly correlated with that of the first currency.

Cross-sectional efficiency A concept implying that prices generated in two markets are not related to the extent that one price can be used to forecast the other.

Currency bubble A self-reinforcing movement of a currency that is unrelated to fundamental factors.

Currency substitution model A version of the monetary model of exchange rate determination that allows agents to hold domestic and foreign money.

Decision tree A technique used to consider all possible outcomes with their associated probabilities.

Delphi method A procedure that is used to arrive at a consensus forecast in situations in which the group effect may distort the forecast.

Depreciation A fall in the value of a currency relative to other currencies under a system of flexible exchange rates.

Destabilising speculation Destabilising speculation in the foreign exchange market occurs when speculators buy a currency when it is appreciating and sell it when it is depreciating, thus accentuating fluctuations in exchange rates.

Deterministic model A model in which the value of the dependent variable at a particular point in time can be determined precisely.

Devaluation A downward change in the value of a currency relative to other currencies under a system of fixed exchange rates.

Diagnostic tests Tests for things like serial correlation, normality and heteroscedastity that determine the validity of the model.

Direction accuracy A measure of the direction accuracy of a forecasting model.

Distribution In technical analysis, a distribution occurs when a top is followed by a reversal as a result of supply overcoming demand.

Double exponential smoothing Also called Brown's method. This is a forecasting technique based on calculating forecasts from single and double exponentially smoothed values.

Double moving average method A forecasting method based on calculating forecasts from a single and a double moving average.

Double moving average rule A trading rule that generates buy and sell signals from the points of intersection between two moving averages of different orders.

Dow theory A series of propositions on the movement of stock prices published in the *Wall Street Journal* between 1900 and 1902.

Durbin's *h*-statistic A test for the presence of first-order serial correlation when the model contains a lagged dependent variable. Under the null of no serial correlation it is distributed as a standard normal variate.

Durbin–Watson (DW) statistic A test for the presence of first-order serial correlation when the model does not contain a lagged dependent variable.

Dynamic forecasting Forecasting several periods ahead based on the actual and forecast values.

Econometric model A theory-based model that is estimated by an econometric method.

Economic exposure Exposure to foreign exchange risk that arises from the effect of changes in the exchange rate on non-contractual or unplanned cash flows.

Economic risk Risk arising from the effect of changes in the real exchange rate on a firm's costs and revenues.

Effective exchange rate Also called the multilateral exchange rate. The exchange rate of a currency against a group of the other currencies, normally the currencies of the main trading partners. It is measured as an index relative to a base period of time.

Effective financing rate The cost of borrowing funds in a foreign currency, taking into account the interest rate and changes in the exchange rate.

Effective rate of return The rate of return on a foreign currency position or asset, taking into account the nominal return and changes in the exchange rate.

Efficiency A forecaster is efficient if it is not possible to improve the forecast by utilising information.

Elliott wave theory A theory, developed by Ralph Elliott, that attempts to predict market reversals.

Endogenous variable A variable that is determined within an economic system.

Error correction model A model in which the previous period's deviation of the actual value of the dependent variable from its equilibrium value appears as an explanatory variable.

Error of direction Also called a turning point error. An error of direction occurs when a model forecast a rise (a fall), when the variable actually falls (rises).

Error of magnitude An error of magnitude occurs when a model predicts a smaller or a larger change than actually materialises.

Error propagation A training method in artificial neural networks. It is a recursive gradient descent method that aims at the minimisation of the sum of squared errors by moving down the gradient of the error curve.

European option An option that can be exercised on the maturity (or expiry) date only.

***Ex ante* forecasting** Out-of-sample forecasting when observations on the exchange rate and its determining variables are unknown over the forecasting horizon.

***Ex ante* PPP** A version of the PPP theory stipulating that the expected change in the exchange rate is equal to or determined by the expected inflation differential.

***Ex post* forecasting** Out-of-sample forecasting is unconditional forecasting when observations on the exchange rate and its determining variables are known with certainty over the forecasting horizon.

Exchange rate overshooting The tendency of the exchange rate to deviate significantly from its equilibrium value in the short run before converging on the equilibrium value in the long run.

Exercise exchange rate The exchange rate at which an option can be exercised, that is the exchange rate at which the underlying currency is bought or sold.

Exogenous variable A variable that affects the endogenous variables in an economic system but it is determined outside the system.

Expected value Also called the mathematical expected value. It is the weighted average of a variable assuming a number of values with assigned probabilities, the latter being used as weights.

Exponential smoothing A smoothing technique that assigns heavier weights to more recent observations.

Exponential smoothing adjusted for trend Also called Holt's two-parameter method. This is a smoothing method that is more suitable for trended data.

Exponential smoothing adjusted for trend and seasonal variation Also called Winter's method, it is a smoothing method that is more suitable for trended and seasonal data.

Exponentially smoothed moving average A weighted moving average such that each weight is a fixed proportion of the preceding weight.

Extrapolative expectations Also called bandwagon expectations. It is an expectations formation mechanism whereby the exchange rate is expected to change by a fraction of its the percentage change in the current period.

F-statistic A statistic that is used to test the significance of the estimated coefficient in a multiple regression model.

Fan In technical analysis, a fan is obtained by drawing three trendlines in a fan-like appearance.

Feedforward network See **feedforward propagation network**.

Feedforward propagation network Also called feedforward network, this is an artificial neural network that consists of layers of units with several inputs and a single output. The layers are the input layer, the output layer and the middle layers.

Filter rule An x per cent filter rule stipulates that a currency is bought when the exchange rate has risen by x per cent from its most recent trough and sold when it has declined by x per cent from its most recent peak. It is also possible to have an x–y per cent rule.

Filter size In a filter rule the filter size is the percentage of appreciation and depreciation from the trough and peak providing buy and sell signals.

Fixed exchange rate An exchange rate that is determined by the monetary authorities and not by market forces.

Flexible exchange rate Also called a floating exchange rate, it is an exchange rate that is determined in a free market by the forces of supply and demand.

Flexible-price monetary model A model in which the exchange rate is determined by the supply and demand for money within a setting characterised by perfect price flexibility such that PPP holds continuously.

Floating exchange rate See **flexible exchange rate**.

Flow model A model of exchange rate determination in which the exchange rate is determined by trade and capital flows.

Forecast combination The process of combining individual forecasts to obtain a composite or a consensus forecast.

Forecast encompassing A forecast is said to encompass another if it incorporates all the relevant information in the latter.

Forecast horizon The length of time over which forecast values are calculated.

Forecast implementation A forecast is implemented when it changes the decision-making process. It is successfully implemented when it changes and improves the decision-making process.

Forecasting A formal method of generating expectations.

Forecasting bias A biased forecast is a forecast that consistently overestimates or underestimates the variable to be forecast.

Forecasting event outcome Forecasting what will happen if a certain event materialises.

Forecasting event timing Forecasting the timing of an event of a once-and-for-all nature. It is mostly relevant to fixed exchange rates.

Foreign exchange risk Financial risk arising from the unanticipated changes in exchange rates on sales, prices, costs, profits, etc. It can be measured by deviations from uncovered interest parity.

Forward exchange rate The exchange rate applicable to transactions involving delivery of the currencies some time in the future.

Forward market hedging Hedging exposure to foreign exchange risk by buying and selling currencies in the forward market.

Forward rate bias The difference between the forward rate and the spot rate prevailing on the maturity of the forward contract.

Forward rate rule A fundamental trading rule whereby the buy and sell signals are determined by the deviation of the exchange rate from the lagged forward rate.

Forward speculation A profit-seeking operation that involves combining two offsetting transactions contracted at two different points in time for the same delivery date, that is by using two forward contracts with different maturities.

Forward spread The difference between the forward and spot exchange rates as a percentage of the spot rate.

Fundamental analysis The study of exchange rate determination in terms of some explanatory or determining variables.

Fundamental rules Trading rules providing buy and sell signals on the basis of deviations from an equilibrium level of the exchange rate.

General efficiency hypothesis A hypothesis stipulating that the forward rate is an efficient forecaster of the future spot rate while allowing for the presence of a risk premium.

General to specific methodology A procedure whereby the parsimonious specification of a model is obtained from a general ADL specification.

Generalised autoregressive conditional heteroscedasticity (GARCH) A generalised version of the ARCH model.

Goodness of fit measures Measures of how well the model explains variation in the dependent variable.

Hannan–Quinn criterion (*HQC*) A measure of goodness of fit calculated from the variance of the error terms.

Heteroscedasticity The property that the residuals of a model have changing variance over time.

Hodrick–Prescott (HP) filter A detrending technique that is used to split a time series into a trend and a cycle.

Holt's two-parameter method See **exponential smoothing adjusted for trend**.

Homoscedasticity The property that the residuals of a model have a constant variance over time.

Hooper–Morton model A version of the monetary model of exchange rate determination in which the cumulative current account balances appear as explanatory variables.

Hyperparameters In structural time series modelling these are the variances of the time series components as well as the amplitude and the damping factor of the cycle.

Inequality proportions Measure of the sources of forecasting inaccuracy obtained by dividing each partial inequality coefficient by the total forecast variation.

Initial condition The initial value assumed by a variable generated by a nonlinear chaotic process.

In-sample forecasting Also called within-sample forecasting, a forecasting exercise in which the forecasting model is used to forecast the exchange rate within the sample period over which the model is initially estimated.

Integrated variables Non-stationary variables due to the presence of unit roots or stochastic trends. An integrated variable becomes stationary by differencing.

Interest parity forward rate The equilibrium value of the forward rate that is calculated by adjusting the spot rate for a factor that reflects the interest rate differential.

Interest rate risk The risk arising from changes in interest rates.

Internal rate of return The discount rate that makes the net present value of a project equal to zero.

Interval forecasting A forecasting exercise that provides a range of values within which the forecast value is likely to fall.

Janus quotient A measure of forecasting accuracy based on in-sample and out-of-sample forecasting power.

Japanese candlestick charts Charts devised by Japanese traders several centuries ago describing various formations created by the behaviour of the high, low, opening and closing levels of prices.

Judgemental forecasting Also called qualitative forecasting, it is based on the forecaster's judgement or intuition. Although some mental processing of data or information is carried out, the process does not involve a model or a formula.

Kalman filter A procedure used in the estimation of models with time-varying parameters. The filter is used to update the estimates as more information becomes available.

Kurtosis The fourth moment of the frequency distribution.

Line chart A chart used by technical analysts to study the behaviour over time of the closing levels of the exchange rate.

Long position A long position in a certain currency arises when an investment is made in the currency or when there are more assets than liabilities in the currency.

Long straddle An options position obtained by buying a call and a put with the same exercise exchange rate.

Long-term forecasting Forecasting over a long horizon. Long-term exchange rate forecasting is required for long-term operations, such as foreign direct investment.

Lyapunov exponent test A test for the necessary and sufficient conditions for chaos, the necessary condition being nonlinearity while the sufficient condition is sensitivity to the initial condition.

Macroeconomic forecasting Forecasting macroeconomic variables such as exchange rate and inflation.

Managed floating A system whereby the exchange rate is determined by the forces of supply and demand in the foreign exchange market subject to occasional intervention by the central bank.

Market efficiency An efficient market is a market in which prices reflect all available information.

Market-based forecasting A procedure whereby the forecasts are provided by the spot and forward foreign exchange markets.

Mathematical expected value See **expected value**.

Mean absolute error (*MAE*) A measure of forecasting accuracy based on the absolute values of the forecasting error.

Mean square error (*MSE*) A measure of forecasting accuracy based on the squared values of the forecasting error.

Measurement errors Errors in the measurement of economic variables such as prices, output and the current account.

Microeconomic forecasting Forecasting variables specific to one company or one sector.

Mixed fundamental rule A fundamental trading rule whereby buy and sell signals are determined by the deviation of the exchange rate from its equilibrium level, the latter being determined by more than one criterion.

Model identification The first step in ARIMA modelling, involving the determination of the order of integration of the time series and whether it is an autoregressive, moving average or a mixed process.

Modified coefficient of determination (R_d^2) The coefficient of determination calculated on the basis of the first difference rather than the level of the dependent variable. It is arguably more appropriate for trended data.

Momentum oscillators Quantitative technical indicators designed to measure the speed or the rate of change of the exchange rate.

Money market hedging Hedging exposure to foreign exchange risk by borrowing and lending in the money market.

Moving average model A model in which the dependent variable is a function of the current and lagged values of the error term.

Moving average oscillator A quantitative technical indicator measured as the difference between two moving averages of different orders.

Moving average rule A trading rule based on the behaviour of one or two moving averages.

Multicollinearity A problem that arises in the estimation of multiple regression models when the explanatory variables are highly correlated.

Multi-equation economic models Also called simultaneous-equation models, they consist of a number of equations explaining variables in terms of each other and showing the interaction within some economic system.

Multilateral exchange rate See **effective exchange rate**.

Multivariate time series forecasting A forecasting exercise that is based on a data set that contains observations on the past values of the exchange rate as well as the variables that affect it. Alternatively, it refers to forecasting more than one exchange rate by using a model of jointly estimated equations.

Multivariate time series models Time series models in which the exchange rate is explained in terms of its lagged values as well as the current and lagged values of the explanatory variables. Alternatively, it refers to time series models that jointly determine a number of exchange rates.

Net present value (NPV) The sum of the discounted values of the cash flows generated by a project net of its capital cost.

Neuron The cell in the human brain or the unit in an artificial neural network.

News Unanticipated changes in economic fundamentals.

Nominal exchange rate An exchange rate (bilateral or effective) that is not adjusted for differences in inflation.

Non-stationarity A non-stationary time series is a time series that has a changing mean value. It tends to move without bounds over time.

Non-structural forecasting Forecasting that is not based on an explicit theory.

Offer exchange rate The exchange rate at which the quoting party is willing to sell the underlying currency.

Offer interest rate The interest rate at which the quoting party is willing to lend funds.

Open position A long position in a currency that is not covered, giving rise to foreign exchange risk.

Oscillator rule A trading rule whereby buy and sell signals are indicated by the points of intersection between the oscillator and the midway line.

Out-of-sample forecasting A forecasting exercise in which the forecasting model is used to forecast the exchange rate outside the sample period over which the model is initially estimated.

Partial autocorrelation coefficient The correlation coefficient between the current value and the lagged values of a variable or a residual when the other lagged values are unchanged.

Partial autocorrelation function The relationship between the partial autocorrelation coefficient and the lag length.

Partial inequality coefficients The three components into which Theil's inequality coefficient can be decomposed. They are the bias component, the variance component and the covariance component.

Peso problem A term devised to describe the situation surrounding the Mexican peso before its devaluation in 1976. Prior to what was an expected devaluation the forward rate appeared to be a biased forecaster of the future spot rate.

Phase portrait Also called the phase space, it is a scatter plot of the values assumed by a variable in one period on its value in the previous period.

Phase space See **phase portrait**.

Point and figure chart A chart used by technical analysts to show significant changes in the exchange rate without a time dimension.

Point forecasting A forecasting exercise in which single forecast values are obtained for each point in time.

Political risk The risk arising from changes in governments and/or possible changes in the rules and regulations governing foreign investment.

Portfolio balance model A model of exchange rate determination in which agents are allowed to hold bonds as well as money.

Predetermined variables These are normally the lagged values of the endogenous variables in a multi-equation model.

Prediction–realisation diagram A graphical device that is used to plot the actual change in the variable against the predicted change. It shows the magnitude and direction of the forecasting errors.

Primary trends Long-term trends in the movement of exchange rates and other financial prices.

Probability distribution A random variable has a probability distribution when it assumes a number of values with assigned probabilities.

Productivity bias hypothesis A hypothesis stipulating that the productivity differential is a factor determining the exchange rate in addition to prices as stipulated by the PPP theory.

Purchasing power parity (PPP) A theory stipulating that the exchange rate is determined by prices or inflation rates, such that a country that has a higher inflation rate than its trading partners tends to have a depreciating currency.

Purchasing power parity rule A fundamental trading rule whereby buy and sell signals are determined by the deviation of the exchange rate from its PPP level.

Purchasing power risk The risk arising from changes in the inflation rate.

Put option A contract that gives the right to sell a certain amount of a currency on or before a certain date at an exchange rate determined at the present time.

Qualitative forecasting See **judgemental forecasting**.

Qualitative variables Variables that cannot be measured but can affect the exchange rate, such as sentiment.

Quantitative forecasting Also called scientific forecasting, it is based on some sort of a formal model or a formula and requires processing of data.

Quantitative technical indicators Technical indicators providing buy and sell signals when their numerical values reach certain levels.

Random walk hypothesis A hypothesis that postulates that period-to-period changes in exchange rates are random and unpredictable.

Rate of change oscillator A quantitative technical indicator that measures the rate of change in the exchange rate over a certain time interval.

Rational expectations A hypothesis that postulates that in forming expectations agents gather and process all available information. As a result they do not make systematic errors and eventually they converge on the correct underlying model.

Real exchange rate An exchange rate (bilateral or effective) that is adjusted for differences in inflation.

Real interest differential model A version of the sticky-price monetary model in which the real interest differential appears as an explanatory variable.

Reduced-form models See **single-equation economic models**.

Regressive expectations An expectations formation mechanism whereby the exchange rate is expected to change by a fraction of the deviation of the current level from the equilibrium level.

Relative PPP A version of the PPP theory stipulating that the rate of change of the exchange rate is equal to or determined by the inflation differential.

Relative strength index (*RSI*) A quantitative technical indicator calculated from negative and positive changes in the exchange rate.

RESET test of functional form A test of linear versus quadratic specifications. The null hypothesis is that the specification is linear.

Resistance level A level of the exchange rate at which there is a significant supply of the currency, causing the exchange rate to stop moving upwards, moving downwards instead.

Retracement A retracement occurs when the exchange rate moves upwards or downwards for some time, then it moves in the opposite direction, correcting a portion of the previous move.

Revaluation An upward change in the value of a currency relative to other currencies under a system of fixed exchange rates.

Reversal patterns In technical analysis, a reversal pattern is identified when the exchange rate is changing direction either from upwards to downwards or vice versa. These include head and shoulders, triangles, rectangles, double tops, double bottoms, triple tops, triple bottoms, rising wedges, falling wedges and diamonds. In Japanese candlestick charts the bullish reversal patterns include hammer, bullish engulfing pattern, tweezer bottom, piercing line, morning star, bullish doji star, bullish harami, bullish harami cross and bullish meeting lines. The bearish reversal patterns include hanging man, bearish engulfing pattern, tweezer top, dark cloud cover, upside gap two crows, evening star, bearish doji star, shooting star, bearish harami, bearish harami cross and bearish meeting lines.

Risk aversion A term implying that agents require a risk premium to hold foreign assets in preference to domestic assets when they offer the same rate of return.

Risk neutrality A term implying that agents are indifferent between holding domestic and foreign assets if they offer the same rate of return.

Risk premium The extra return required by risk-averse agents to hold foreign assets in preference to domestic assets when they offer the same rate of return.

Root mean square error (RMSE) A measure of forecasting accuracy based on the squared values of the forecasting error.

RSI rule A trading rule whereby buy and sell signals are determined by the level of the RSI.

Scenario Scenarios are descriptions of alternative hypothetical futures that allow the forecaster to assess potential development.

Schwartz Bayesian criterion (*SBC*) A measure of goodness of fit calculated from the variance of the error terms.

Scientific forecasting See **quantitative forecasting**.

Secondary reactions Short-term movements that interrupt primary trends in financial markets.

Seemingly unrelated regressions (SUR) A systems estimation technique that utilises the information embodied in the cross-correlations of the residuals.

Seemingly unrelated time series equations (SUTSE) The time series equivalent of seemingly unrelated regressions. The equations contain the time series components and possibly explanatory variables.

Semi-strong efficiency A market is efficient in a semi-strong sense if the prices reflect all publicly available information.

Short position A short position in a certain currency arises when the currency is borrowed or when there are more liabilities than assets in the currency.

Short straddle An options position obtained by selling a call and a put with the same exercise exchange rate.

Short-term forecasting Forecasting over a short horizon. Short-term exchange rate forecasting is required for short-term operations, such as money market investment and financing operations.

Simple average method A forecasting method based on the simple average or the mean.

Simple efficiency hypothesis See **unbiased efficiency hypothesis**.

Simple moving average A moving average calculated by assigning the same weights to all observations.

Simultaneous equation models See **multi-equation economic models**.

Single moving average method A forecasting method whereby the forecast value of the exchange rate is a moving average of a given order.

Single moving average rule A trading rule whereby buy and sell signals are indicated by the points of intersection between the level of the exchange rate and the moving average.

Single-equation econometric models See **single-equation economic models**.

Single-equation economic models Also called single-equation econometric models or reduced-form models. Such a model consists of a single equation that is based on some economic theory and estimated by some econometric method.

Skewness The third moment of the frequency distribution.

Smoothing constant A parameter assuming values between zero and one used to calculate the forecast in exponential smoothing.

Smoothing methods Forecasting methods that aim at identifying a smooth curve representing the time path of the exchange rate and then project it into the future.

Speculation The deliberate assumption of risk with the objective of making profit.

Speed resistance lines Lines used to measure the rate at which a trend moves up or down.

Spot exchange rate The exchange rate applicable to transactions involving an immediate delivery of the currencies.

Spot speculation Speculation in the spot foreign exchange market by buying and selling currencies on the basis of expected changes in the exchange rates.

Spot-forward speculation An operation that involves buying and selling currencies in the spot and forward markets in order to make profit.

Stabilising speculation Stabilising speculation in the foreign exchange market occurs when speculators buy a currency when it is depreciating and sell it when it is appreciating, thus dampening fluctuations in exchange rates.

State space form A model is written in state space form when it is specified in terms of two equations: a measurement equation and a transition equation. Once a model is written in state space form it can be estimated by maximum likelihood with the Kalman filter used to update the estimates when more information becomes available.

Static expectations An expectations formation mechanism whereby the expected exchange rate is the same as its current level.

Static forecasting Forecasting based on the actual values only.

Stationarity A stationary time series is a time series that tends to return to its mean value and fluctuate around it.

Sticky-price monetary model A model in which the exchange rate is determined by the supply and demand for money within a setting characterised by sticky prices such that PPP holds in the long run only. The model predicts exchange rate overshooting in the short run.

Stochastic model A model in which the value of the dependent variable at a particular point in time cannot be determined precisely due to the presence of a stochastic error term.

Stochastics A quantitative technical indicator that measures the velocity of exchange rate changes.

Stochastics rule A trading rule whereby buy and sell signals are determined by the behaviour of the stochastics.

Strong efficiency A market is efficient in a strong sense if the prices reflect all publicly available information as well as insider information.

Structural changes Changes that affect the estimated parameters of a model, causing them to change over time.

Structural forecasting Forecasting based on an explicit theory.

Structural time series model A model in which the dependent variable is determined by its time series components with or without explanatory variables.

Support level A level of the exchange rate at which there is adequate demand for the currency to stop it from moving downwards, moving upwards instead.

Technical analysis Also called chartism, it is the study of the movement of historical prices to deduce the future trend.

Technical rules Trading rules providing buy and sell signals on the basis of possible trend reversals.

Theil's inequality coefficient A measure of forecasting accuracy based on a comparison between the root mean square of the forecasting model and the root mean square error of the random walk model.

Three-point arbitrage An arbitrage operation that is triggered when the cross exchange rates between three currencies are inconsistent.

Time series A sequence of values gathered at regular intervals of time.

Time series decomposition A forecasting technique that involves the decomposition of a time series into four components (trend, cycle, seasonal component and random component), forecasting the individual components and then adding up the forecast components to obtain the forecast total series.

Time-varying parametric (TVP) estimation Estimation methods that allow the estimated coefficients to vary over time.

Tracking system A setup whereby the forecasting error is monitored with the objective of changing the smoothing constant in exponential smoothing.

Trading rules Rules used by traders in financial markets to obtain buy and sell signals according to some predetermined criteria.

Transaction exposure Exposure to foreign exchange risk arising from the effect of changes in the exchange rate on the domestic currency values of assets, liabilities and profits.

Translation exposure Exposure to foreign exchange risk arising from the effect of changes in the exchange rate on the domestic currency values of the items in consolidated financial statements.

Trend channel A range formed by the trendline and a parallel line connecting the tops and bottoms of exchange rates.

Trendline A line connecting the tops or bottoms of exchange rates.

Tuning parameter The coefficient on the right-hand side of a logistic nonlinear function that can be used to generate chaotic processes.

Turning point error See **error of direction**.

Two-point arbitrage An arbitrage operation that is triggered when exchange rates are not equal across financial centres.

Unbiased efficiency hypothesis Also called the simple efficiency hypothesis, it stipulates that the forward rate is an efficient and unbiased forecaster of the future spot rate.

Unbiasedness A forecaster is unbiased when it does not consistently overestimate or underestimate the variable to be forecast.

Uncovered interest arbitrage A financial operation whereby the arbitrager borrows funds in a certain currency and invests in another currency, without covering the long position.

Uncovered interest parity (UIP) An equilibrium condition that precludes uncovered interest arbitrage. It is obtained when the return on a currency position is equal to the uncovered return on a position in another currency, or when the interest rate differential is equal to the expected change in the exchange rate.

Uncovered interest parity rule A fundamental trading rule whereby buy and sell signals are determined by the deviation of the exchange rate from its UIP level.

Univariate time series forecasting Forecasting based on an information set that only contains the past history of the exchange rate only.

Vector autoregression (VAR) model A model in which all variables are jointly determined without making a distinction between endogenous and exogenous variables. The model is theory free.

Weak efficiency A market is efficient in a weak sense if the prices reflect the information embodied in their past history.

Weighted moving average A moving average calculated by assigning heavier weights to more recent observations.

Winter's method See **exponential smoothing adjusted for trend and seasonal variation**.

Within-sample forecasting See **in-sample forecasting**.

References

Abu-Mostafa, Y.S. (1995) Financial Market Applications of Learning from Hints, in Refenes, A.P. (ed.) *Neural Networks in Capital Markets*, Chichester, Wiley.

Agnew, C.A. (1985) Bayesian Consensus Forecasts of Macroeconomic Variables, *Journal of Forecasting*, **4**, 363–76.

Alexander, S.S. (1961) Price Movements in Speculative Markets: Trends or Random Walks, *Industrial Management Review*, **2**, 7–26.

Alexander, S.S. (1964) Price Movements in Speculative Markets: Trends or Random Walks, Number 2, *Industrial Management Review*, **5**, 25–46.

Allen, F. and Karjalainen, R. (1999) Using Genetic Algorithms to Find Technical Trading Rules, *Journal of Financial Economics*, **51**, 245–71.

Allen, H.L. and Taylor, M.P. (1989) Chart Analysis and the Foreign Exchange Market, *Bank of England Quarterly Bulletin*, November.

Allen, H.L. and Taylor, M.P. (1990) Charts, Noise and Fundamentals in the London Foreign Exchange Market, *Economic Journal*, **100**, 49–59.

Allen, H.L. and Taylor, M.P. (1993) Chartist Analysis, in Newman, P., Milgate, M. and Eatwell, J. (eds) *The New Palgrave Dictionary of Money and Finance*, London: Macmillan.

Alter, S. (1979) Implementation Risk Analysis, in Doktor, R., Schultz, R.L. and Selvin, D.P. (eds) *The Implementation of Management Science*, Amsterdam, North-Holland.

Anderson, P.W., Arrow, K.J. and Pines, D. (1988) *The Economy as an Evolving Complex System*, Reading, MA: Addison-Wesley.

Arize, A.C. (1995) The Effects of Exchange Rate Volatility on U.S. Exports: An Empirical Investigation, *Southern Economic Journal*, **62**, 34–43.

Armstrong, J.S. (1989) Combining Forecasts: The End of the Beginning or the Beginning of the End? *International Journal of Forecasting*, **5**, 585–92.

Baillie, R.T. and Bollerslev, T. (1989) Common Stochastic Trends in a System of Exchange Rates, *Journal of Finance*, **44**, 167–81.

Bajo-Rubio, O., Fernandez-Rodiguez, F. and Sovilla-Rivero, S. (1997) Chaotic Behaviour in Exchange Rate Series: First Results for the Peseta–U.S. Dollar Case, *Economics Letters*, **39**, 207–11.

Balassa, B. (1964) The Purchasing Power Parity Doctrine: A Reappraisal, *Journal of Political Economy*, **72**, 584–96.

Barnett, W.A., Geweke, J. and Shell, K. (1989) *Economic Complexity: Chaos, Sunspots, Bubbles and Nonlinearity*, Cambridge: Cambridge University Press.

Batchelor, R.A. (1990) All Forecasters are Equal, *Journal of Business and Economic Statistics*, **8**, 143–4.

Bera, A.K. and Jarque, C.M. (1981) An Efficient Large Sample Test for Normality of Observations and Regression Residuals, *Australian National University Working Papers in Econometrics*, No. 40.

Bewley, R.A. (1979) The Direct Estimation of the Equilibrium Response in a Linear Model, *Economics Letters*, **3**, 357–61.

Bilson, J.F.O. (1978) The Monetary Approach to the Exchange Rate: Some Empirical Evidence, *IMF Staff Papers*, **25**, 48–75.

Bilson, J.F.O. (1981) The Speculative Efficiency Hypothesis, *Journal of Business*, **54**, 435–51.

Bollerslev, T. (1986) Generalised Autoregressive Conditional Heteroskedasticity, *Journal of Econometrics*, **31**, 307–27.

Boothe, P. and Glassman, D. (1987) Off the Mark: Lessons for Exchange Rate Modelling, *Oxford Economic Papers*, **39**, 443–57.

Boughton, J.M. (1984) Exchange Rate Movements and Adjustment in Financial Markets: Quarterly Estimates for Major Currencies, *IMF Staff Papers*, **31**, 445–68.

Boughton, J.M. (1987) Tests of the Performance of Reduced-Form Exchange Rate Models, *Journal of International Economics*, **23**, 41–56.

Bowerman, B.L. and O'Connell, R.T. (1987) *Time Series Forecasting: Unified Concepts and Computer Implementation* (2nd edn), Boston: Duxbury Press.

Bowman, K.O. and Shenton, L.R. (1975) Omnibus Test Contours for Departures from Normality Based on $\sqrt{b_1}$ and b_2, *Biometrika*, **62**, 243–50.

Box, G.E.P., Jenkins, G.W. and Reinsel, G. (1994) *Time Series Analysis, Forecasting and Control*, Englewood Cliffs, NJ: Prentice Hall.

Breusch, T.S. and Pagan, A.R. (1979) A Simple Test for Heteroskedasticity and Random Coefficient Variation, *Econometrica*, **50**, 1287–94.

Brock, W. (1986) Distinguishing Random and Deterministic Systems (abridged edn), *Journal of Economic Theory*, **40**, 168–195.

Brock, W., Dechert, W. and J. Scheinkman, J. (1987) A Test for Independence Based on the Correlation Dimension, Working Paper, University of Wisconsin at Madison.

Brock, W.A., Hsieh, D.A. and LeBaron, B. (1991) Nonlinear Dynamics, Chaos and Instability: Statistical Theory and Economic Evidence, Cambridge, MA: MIT Press.

Brock, W., Lakonishok, J. and LeBaron, B. (1992) Simple Technical Trading Rules and the Stochastic Properties of Stock Returns, *Journal of Finance*, **47**, 1731–64.

Burke, M. L. (1990) *Three-Point Reversal Method of Point and Figure Construction and Formations*, New Rochelle, NY: Chartcraft Inc.

Chang, P.H.K. and Osler, C.L. (1995) *Head and Shoulders: Not Just a Flaky Pattern*, Federal Reserve Bank of New York Staff Reports, No. 4.

Chappell, D. and Eldridge, R.M. (1997) Non-linear Characteristics of the Sterling/European Currency Unit Exchange Rate: 1984–1992, *European Journal of Finance*, **3**, 159–82.

Clemen, R.T. (1989) Combining Forecast: A Review and Annotated Bibliography, *Journal of Forecasting*, **5**, 559–83.

Clyde, W.C. and Osler, C.L. (1997) Charting: Chaos Theory in Disguise, *Journal of Futures Markets*, **17**, 489–514.

Colby, R.W. and Myers, T.A. (1988) *The Encyclopedia of Technical Market Indicators*, Homewood, IL: Business One Irwin.

Cootner, P.H. (ed.) (1964) *The Random Character of Stock Market Prices*, Cambridge, MA: MIT Press.

Copeland, L.S. (1991) Cointegration Tests with Daily Exchange Rate Data, *Oxford Bulletin of Economics and Statistics*, **53**, 185–98.

Copeland, L.S. (1994) *Exchange Rates and International Finance* (2nd edn), Wokingham: Addison-Wesley.

Cornell, W.B. and Dietrich, J.K. (1978) The Efficiency of Markets for Foreign Exchange Rates, *Review of Economics and Statistics*, **60**, 111–20.

Curcio, R. and Goodhart, C.A.E. (1991) Chartism: A Controlled Experiment, Working Paper, London School of Economics, September.

Cuthbertson, K., Hall, S.G. and Taylor, M.P. (1992) *Applied Econometric Techniques*, London: Phillip Allan.

Cvitanovic, P. (1989) *Universality in Chaos* (2nd edn), Bristol: Adam Hilger.

De Grauwe, P. and Vansanten, K. (1990) Deterministic Chaos in the Foreign Exchange Market, *CEPR Discussion Papers*, No. 370.

Diebold, F.X. (1998a) *Elements of Forecasting*, Cincinnati, OH: South-Western College Publishing.

Diebold, F.X. (1998b) The Past, Present and Future of Macroeconomic Forecasting, *Journal of Economic Perspectives*, **12**, 175–92.

Diebold, F.X. and Mariano, R.S. (1995) Comparing Predictive Accuracy, *Journal of Business and Economic Statistics*, **13**, 253–63.

Diebold, F.X. and Nason, J. (1990) Nonparametric Exchange Rate Prediction? *Journal of International Economics*, **28**, 315–332.

Dominguez, K.M. (1986) Are Foreign Exchange Forecasts Rational? New Evidence from Survey Data, *Economics Letters*, **21**, 277–81.

Domowitz, I. and Hakkio, C.S. (1985) Conditional Variance and the Risk Premium in the Foreign Exchange Market, *Journal of International Economics*, **19**, 47–66.

Dooley, M.P. and Shafer, J.R. (1976) Analysis of Short-Run Exchange Rate Behavior: March 1973 to September 1975, *International Finance Discussion Papers*, No. 76, Federal Reserve System.

Dooley, M.P. and Shafer, J.R. (1983) Analysis of Short-Run Exchange Rate Behavior: March 1973 to November 1981, in Bigman, D. and Taya, T. (eds) *Exchange Rate and Trade Instability*, Cambridge, MA: Ballinger.

Dornbusch, R. (1976) Expectations and Exchange Rate Dynamics, *Journal of Political Economy*, **84**, 1161–76.

Ducot, C. and Lubben, G.H. (1980) A Typology for Scenarios, *Futures*, **12**, 51–7.

Dungey, M. (1998) How Important are Meteor Showers and Heat Waves in Exchange Rate Volatility, Working Paper, La Trobe University.

Dwyer, J.G.P. and Wallace, M.S. (1992) Cointegration and Market Efficiency, *Journal of International Money and Finance*, **4**, 361–72.

Eldridge, R.M., Bernhardt, C. and Mulvey, I. (1993) Evidence of Chaos in the S and P 500 Cash Index, *Recent Advances in Futures and Options Research*, 6.

Engle, C. and Hamilton, J.D. (1990) Long Swings in the Dollar: Are They in the Data and Do Markets Know it? *American Economic Review*, **80**, 689–713.

Engle, R.F. (1982) Autoregressive Conditional Heteroscedasticity with Estimates of the Variance of U.K. Inflation, *Econometrica*, **50**, 987–1007.

Engle, R.F. and Granger, C.W.J. (1987) Cointegration and Error Correction: Representation, Estimation and Testing, *Econometrica*, **55**, 251–76.

Fama, E.F. (1970) Efficient Capital Markets: A Review of Theory and Empirical Work, *Journal of Finance*, **25**, 383–417.

Fama, E.F. (1984) Forward and Spot Exchange Rates, *Journal of Monetary Economics*, **14**, 319–38.

Fama, E.F. (1990) Efficient Capital Markets II, Unpublished Paper, University of Chicago.
Fama, E.F. and Blume, M.E. (1966) Filter Rules and Stock Market Trading, *Journal of Business*, **39**, 226–41.
Frankel, J.A. (1979a) On the Mark: A Theory of Floating Exchange Rates Based on Real Interest Differentials, *American Economic Review*, **69**, 601–22.
Frankel, J.A. (1979b) A Test of the Existence of the Risk Premium in the Foreign Exchange Market vs the Hypothesis of Perfect Substitutability, *International Finance Discussion Papers*, No. 149.
Frankel, J.A. (1982) In Search of the Exchange Risk Premium: A Six-Currency Test Assuming Mean-Variance Optimisation, *Journal of International Money and Finance*, **1**, 255–74.
Frankel, J.A. and Dornbusch, R. (1988) The Flexible Exchange Rate System: Experience and Alternatives, in S. Boner (ed.) *International Finance and Trade*, London: Macmillan.
Frankel, J.A. and Froot, K. (1987) Using Survey Data to Test the Standard Propositions Regarding Exchange Rate Expectations, *American Economic Review*, **80**, 181–5.
Frankel, J.A. and Froot, K.A. (1990a) Exchange Rate Forecasting Techniques, Survey Data and Implications for the Foreign Exchange Market, *NBER Working Papers*, No. 3470.
Frankel, J.A. and Froot, K.A. (1990b) Chartists, Fundamentalists and the Demand for Dollars, in Courakis, A.S. and Taylor, M.P. (eds) *Private Behavior and Government Policy in Interdependent Economies*, Oxford: Oxford University Press.
Frenkel, J.A. (1976) A Monetary Approach to the Exchange Rate: Doctrinal Aspects and Empirical Evidence, *Scandinavian Journal of Economics*, **78**, 200–24.
Froot, K.A. and Frankel, J.A. (1986) Interpreting Tests of Forward Discount Bias Using Survey Data on Exchange Rate Expectations, *NBER Working Papers*, No. 1963.
Froot, K.A. and Frankel, J.A. (1989) Forward Discount Bias: Is it an Exchange Risk Premium? *Quarterly Journal of Economics*, **104**, 139–61.
Gandolfo, G., Padoan, P.C. and Paladino, G. (1990) Exchange Rate Determination: Single-Equation or Economy-Wide Models? A Test against the Random Walk, *Journal of Banking and Finance*, **14**, 965–92.
Geistauts, G.A. and Eschenbach, T.G. (1987) Bridging the Gap between Forecasting and Action, in Wright, G. and Ayton, P. (eds) *Judgmental Forecasting*, Chichester: Wiley.
Geschka, H. and Reibnitz, U. (1983) Die Szenario-Technik – ein Instrument der Zukunftsanalyse und der Strategischen Planung, in Tlpfer, A. and Afheldt, M. (eds) *Praxis der Unternehmensplanung*, Frankfurt.
Gleick, J. (1987) *Chaos: Making a New Science*, London: Cardinal Books.
Godfrey, L.G. (1978a) Testing against General Autoregressive and Moving Average Error Models when the Regressors Include Lagged Dependent Variables, *Econometrica*, **46**, 1293–301.
Godfrey, L.G. (1978b) Testing for Higher Order Serial Correlation in Regression Equations when the Regressors Include Lagged Dependent Variables, *Econometrica*, **46**, 1303–10.

Goodhart, C.A.E. (1988) The Foreign Exchange Market: A Random Walk with a Dragging Anchor, *Economica*, **55**, 437–80.
Goodman, S.H. (1979) Foreign Exchange Rate Forecasting Techniques: Implications for Business and Policy, *Journal of Finance*, **344**, 415–27.
Goodman, S.H. (1980) Who is Better than the Toss of a Coin, *Euromoney*, September, 80–4.
Granger, C.W.J. (1969) Investigating Causal Relations by Econometric Models and Cross-Spectral Methods, *Econometrica*, **37**, 424–38.
Granger, C.W.J. (1986) Developments in the Study of Cointegrated Economic Variables, *Oxford Bulletin of Economics and Statistics*, **48**, 213–28.
Granger, C.W.J. and Newbold, P. (1974) Spurious Regression in Econometrics, *Journal of Econometrics*, **2**, 111–20.
Granger, C.W.J. and Ramanathan, R. (1984) Improved Methods of Forecasting, *Journal of Forecasting*, **3**, 197–204.
Grassberger, P. and Procaccia, I. (1983) Characterization of Strange Attractors, *Physical Review Letters*, **50**, 339–68.
Gurney, K. (1997) *An Introduction to Neural Networks*, London: UCL Press.
Hamilton, J.D. (1989) A New Approach to the Economic Analysis of Nonstationary Time Series and the Business Cycle, *Econometrica*, **57**, 357–84.
Hamilton, J.D. (1994) *Time Series Analysis*, Princeton: Princeton University Press.
Harvey, A.C. (1985) Trends and Cycles in Macroeconomic Time Series, *Journal of Business and Economic Statistics*, **3**, 216–27.
Harvey, A.C. (1989) Forecasting, *Structural Time Series Models and the Kalman Filter*, Cambridge: Cambridge University Press.
Harvey, A.C. (1993) *Time Series Models* (2nd edn), London: Harvester Wheatsheaf.
Harvey, A.C. and Scott, A. (1994) Seasonality in Dynamic Regression Models, *Economic Journal*, **104**, 1324–45.
Harvey, J.T. (1991) A Post Keynesian View of Exchange Rate Determination, *Journal of Post Keynesian Economics*, **14**, 61–71.
Harvey, J.T. (1993a) The Institution of Foreign Exchange Trading, *Journal of Economic Issues*, **27**, 679–98.
Harvey, J.T. (1993b) Daily Exchange Rate Variance, *Journal of Post Keynesian Economics*, **15**, 515–40.
Harvey, J.T. (1995) The International Monetary System and Exchange Rate Determination: 1945 to the Present, *Journal of Economic Issues*, **29**, 493–502.
Hendry, D.F. (1980) The Simple Analysis of Single Dynamic Econometric Equation, London School of Economics, Mimeo.
Hendry, D.F., Pagan, A.R. and Sargan, J.D. (1984) Dynamic Specification, in Griliches, Z. and Intriligator, M.D. (eds) *Handbook of Econometrics*, Amsterdam: North-Holland.
Henriksson, R.O. and Merton, R.C. (1981) On Market Timing and Investment Performance II, Statistical Procedures for Evaluating Forecasting Skills, *Journal of Business*, **54**, 513–33.
Holtfrerich, C.L. (1986) *The German Inflation 1914–1923: Causes and Effects in International Perspective*, New York: Walter de Gruyter.
Hooper, P. and Morton, J. (1982) Fluctuations in the Dollar: A Model of Nominal and Real Exchange Rate Determination, *Journal of International Money and Finance*, **1**, 39–56.

Hsieh, D. (1989) Testing for Nonlinearity in Daily Foreign Exchange Rate Changes, *Journal of Business*, **62**, 339–68.

Hsu, W., Hsu, L.S. and Tenorio, M.F. (1995) A Neural Network Procedure for Selecting Predictive Indicators in Currency trading, in A.P. Refenes (ed.) *Neural Networks in Capital Markets*, Chichester: Wiley.

International Monetary Fund (1984) *Exchange Rate Volatility and World Trade*, IMF Occasional Papers, No. 28.

Jarque, C.M. and Bera, A.K. (1980) Efficient Tests for Normality, Homoscedasticity and Serial Independence of Regression Residuals, *Economics Letters*, **6**, 255–9.

Jungermann, H. and Thuring, M. (1987) The Use of Mental Models for Generating Scenarios, in Wright, G. and Ayton, P. (eds) *Judgmental Forecasting*, Chichester: Wiley.

Khan, H. (1965) *On Escalation: Metaphor and Scenarios*, New York: Praeger.

Kirman, A.P. (1991) Epidemics of Opinion and Speculative Bubbles in Financial Markets, in Taylor, M.P. (ed.) *Money and Financial Markets*, Oxford: Blackwell.

Koopman, S.J., Harvey, A.C., Doornik, J.A. and Shephard, N. (1995*) STAMP 5.0: Structural Time Series Analyser, Modeller and Predictor*, London: Chapman & Hall.

Krasker, W.S. (1980) The Peso Problem in Testing the Efficiency of Forward Exchange Markets, *Journal of Monetary Economics*, **6**, 269–76.

Krugman, P. (1993) Recent Thinking about Exchange Rate Determination and Policy, in Blundell-Wignall, A. (ed.) *International Trade and Balance of Payments*, Sydney: Reserve Bank of Australia.

Kuan, C. and Liu, T. (1995) Forecasting Exchange Rates Using Feedforward and Recurrent Neural Networks, *Journal of Applied Econometrics*, **10**, 347–64.

Kugler, P. and Lenz, C. (1991) Chaos, ARCH and the Foreign Exchange Market: Empirical Results from Weekly Data, paper presented at the European meeting of the Econometric Society, Cambridge.

Lahiri, K. and Teigland, C. (1987) On the Normality of Probability Distributions of Inflation and GNP Forecasts, *International Journal of Forecasting*, **3**, 269–79.

Lane, T.D. (1991) Empirical Models of Exchange Rate Determination: Picking Up the Pieces, *Economia Internazionale*, **44**, 210–26.

LeBaron, B. (1991) Technical Trading Rules and Regime Shifts in Foreign Exchange, Working Paper, University of Wisconsin, Social Systems Research Institute.

Lenten, L.J.A. and Moosa, I.A. (1999) Modelling the Trend and Seasonality in the Consumption of Alcoholic Beverages in the United Kingdom, *Applied Economics* (forthcoming).

LeRoy, S.F. (1989) Efficient Capital Markets and Martingales, *Journal of Economic Literature*, **27**, 1583–621.

Levine, R. (1989) The Pricing of Forward Exchange Rates, *Journal of International Money and Finance*, **8**, 163–79.

Liao, S.L. (1997) Nonlinear Dynamics and Chaos in Foreign Exchange Markets, Paper Presented at the Sixth Conference on the Theories and Practices of Security and Financial Markets, Kaohsuing, Taiwan, December.

Lim, G.C. and Martin, V.L. (1995) Regression-Based Cointegration Estimators with Applications, *Journal of Economic Studies*, **22**, 3–22.

Liu, P.C. and Maddala, G.S. (1992) Rationality of Survey Data and Tests for Market Efficiency in the Foreign Exchange Markets, *Journal of International Money and Finance*, **11**, 366–81.

Ljung, G.M. and Box, G.E.P. (1978) On a Measure of Lack of Fit in Time Series Models, *Biometrika*, **65**, 297–303.

Logue, D.E., Sweeney, R.J. and Willett, T.D. (1978) Speculative Behaviour of Foreign Exchange Rates during the Current Float, *Journal of Business Research*, **6**, 159–74.

Lucas, R.E. (1982) Interest Rates and Currency Prices in a Two Country World, *Journal of Monetary Economics*, **10**, 335–60.

Lui, Y.H. and Mole, D. (1998) The Use of Fundamental and Technical Analyses by Foreign Exchange Dealers: Hong Kong Evidence, *Journal of International Money and Finance*, **17**, 535–45.

MacDonald, R. (1992) Exchange Rate Survey Data: A Disaggregated G-7 Perspective, *The Manchester School of Economic and Social Studies*, 58-229-41.

McLaughlin, R.L. (1975) The Real Record of Economic Forecasters, *Business Economics*, **10**, 28–36.

McNees, S.K. (1987) Consensus Forecasts: Tyranny of the Majority? *New England Economic Review*, Nov/Dec, 15–21.

McNees, S.K. (1990) The Role of Judgment in Macroeconomic Forecasting Accuracy, *International Journal of Forecasting*, **7**, 287–99.

Mahmoud, E. (1989) Combining Forecasts: Some Managerial Issues, *International Journal of Forecasting*, **5**, 599–600.

Makridakis, S., Wheelright, S.C. and McGee, V.E. (1983) *Forecasting: Methods and Applications*, New York: Wiley.

Malkiel, B.G. (1990) *A Random Walk down Wall Street* (5th edn), New York: Norton.

Meese, R.A. and Rogoff, K. (1983a) Empirical Exchange Rate Models of the Seventies: Do They Fit out of Sample? *Journal of International Economics*, **14**, 3–24.

Meese, R.A. and Rogoff, K. (1983b) The Out-of-Sample Failure of Empirical Exchange Rate Models: Sampling Error or Misspecification?, in Frenkel, J.A. (ed.) *Exchange Rates and International Macroeconomics*, Chicago: Chicago University Press.

Meese, R. and Rose, A. (1990) Nonlinear, Nonparametric, Nonessential Exchange Rate Estimation, *American Economic Review*, **80**, 192–6.

Meese, R. and Rose, A. (1991) An Empirical Assessment of Nonlinearities in Models of Exchange Rate Determination, *Review of Economic Studies*, **58**, 603–19.

Merville, L.J. and Pieptea, D.R. (1989) Stock Price Volatility, Mean-Reverting Diffusion, and Noise, *Journal of Financial Economics*, **24**, 193–214.

Mills, T.C. (1990) *Time Series Techniques for Economists*, Cambridge: Cambridge University Press.

Mitchell, R.B., Tydeman, J. and Georgiades, J. (1979) Structuring the Future Application of a Scenario Generation Procedure, *Technological Forecasting and Social Change*, **14**, 409–28.

Moosa, I.A. (1994) The Monetary Model of Exchange Rates Revisited, *Applied Financial Economics*, **4**, 279–87.

Moosa, I.A. (1998) *International Finance: An Analytical Approach*, Sydney: McGraw-Hill.

Moosa, I.A. and Bhatti, R.H. (1997) *International Parity Conditions: Theory, Econometric Testing and Empirical Evidence*, London: Macmillan.

Moosa, I.A. and Kennedy, P. (1998) Modelling Seasonality in the Australian Consumption Function, *Australian Economic Papers*, **37**, 88–102.

Moosa, I.A. and Kwiecien, J. (1999) The Nominal Exchange Rate as a Predictor of Inflation: A Re-examination of the Underlying Model, *Applied Financial Economics* (forthcoming).

Neftci, S.N. (1991) Naïve Trading Rules in Financial Markets and Weiner-Kolmogorov Prediction Theory, *Journal of Business*, **64**, 549–71.

Nison, S. (1991) *Japanese Candlestick Charting Techniques: A Contemporary Guide to the Ancient Investment Techniques of the Far East*, New York: New York Institute of Finance.

Papell, D.H. (1988) Expectations and Exchange Rate Dynamics after a Decade of Floating, *Journal of International Economics*, **25**, 303–17.

Pentecost, E.J. (1991) Econometric Approaches to Empirical Models of Exchange Rate Determination, *Journal of Economic Surveys*, **5**, 71–96.

Pesaran, M.H. and Pesaran, B. (1997) *Working with Microfit 4.0: Interactive Econometric Analysis*, Oxford: Oxford University Press.

Pesaran, M.H. and Timmerman, A. (1994) Forecasting Stock Returns: An Examination of Stock Market Trading in the Presence of Transaction Costs, *Journal of Forecasting*, **13**, 333–67.

Phillips, L.D. (1987) On the Adequacy of Judgmental Forecasting, in Wright, G. and Ayton, P. (eds) *Judgmental Forecasting*, Chichester: Wiley.

Phillips, P.C.B. and Loretan, M. (1991) Estimating Long-Run Equilibria, *Review of Economic Studies*, **58**, 407–36.

Pilbeam, K. (1995) The Profitability of Trading in the Foreign Exchange Market: Chartists, Fundamentalists and Simpletons, *Oxford Economic Papers*, **47**, 437–52.

Pindyck, R.S. and Rubinfeld, D.L. (1991) *Econometric Models and Economic Forecasts*, New York: McGraw-Hill.

Pretcher, R.R. (ed.) (1980) *The Major Works of R.N. Elliott*, Gainesville, GA: New Classics Library.

Prechter, R.R. and Frost, A.J. (1990) *Elliott Wave Principle: Key to Stock Market Profits* (expanded edn), Gainesville, GA: New Classics Library.

Pring, M.J. (1991) *Technical Analysis Explained: The Successful Investor's Guide to Spotting Investment Trends and Turning Points* (3rd edn), New York: McGraw-Hill.

Qi, M. (1996) Financial Applications of Artificial Neural Networks, in Maddala, G.S. and Rao, C.R. (eds) *Statistical Methods in Finance*, Amsterdam, Elsevier Science.

Rhea, R. (1932a) *Dow Theory*, New York: Barrons.

Rhea, R. (1932b) *Dow Theory* (abridged edn), New York: Barrons.

Saikkonen, P. (1991) Asymptotically Efficient Estimation of Cointegrating Regressions, *Econometric Theory*, **7**,1–21.

Sargent, T.J. and Sims, C.A. (1977) Business Cycle Modeling without Pretending to Have Too Much a Priori Theory, in Sims, C.A. (ed.) *New Methods of Business Cycle Research*, Minneapolis: Federal Reserve Bank of Minneapolis.

Savit, R. (1988) When Random is not Random: An Introduction to Chaos in Market Prices, *Journal of Futures Markets*, **8**, 271–89.

Sayers, C. (1991) Statistical Inference Based upon Non-linear Science, *European Economic Review*, **35**, 306–12.

Schinasi, G.H. and Swamy, P.A.V.B. (1989) The Out-of-Sample Forecasting Performance of Exchange Rate Models when Coefficients are Allowed to Change, *Journal of International Money and Finance*, **8**, 375–90.

Schnader, M.H. and Stekler, H.O. (1991) Do Consensus Forecasts Exist? *International Journal of Forecasting*, **7**, 165–70.

Schultz, R.L. (1984) The Implementation of Forecasting Models, *Journal of Forecasting*, **3**, 43–5.

Schultz, R.L. and Selvin, D.P. (eds) (1983) The Implementation Profile, *Interfaces*, **13**, 87–92.

Schwager, J.D. (1984) *A Complete Guide to the Futures Markets: Fundamental Analysis, Technical Analysis, Trading, Spreads, and Options*, New York: Wiley.

Sheimo, M.D. (1989) *Dow Theory Redux: The Classic Investment Theory Revised and Updated for the 1990s*, Chicago: Probus.

Sims, C.A. (1972) Money, Income and Causality, *American Economic Review*, **62**, 540–52.

Sims, C.A. (1980) Macroeconomics and Reality, *Econometrica*, **48**, 1–48.

Sims, C.A. (1984) Martingale-like Behaviour of Asset Prices and Interest Rates, Unpublished Paper, University of Minnesota.

Sims, C.A., Stock. J.H. and Watson, M.W. (1990) Inference in Linear Time Series Models with Some Unit Roots, *Econometrica*, **58**, 113–44.

Somanath, V.S. (1986) Efficient Exchange Rate Forecasts: Lagged Models Better than the Random Walk, *Journal of International Money and Finance*, **5**, 195–220.

Stekler, H.O. (1987) Who Forecasts Better? *Journal of Business and Economic Statistics*, **5**, 155–8.

Stewart, I. (1990) *Does God Play Dice*? London: Penguin Books.

Stock, J.H. and Watson, M.W. (1993) A Simple Estimator of Cointegrating Vectors in Higher Order Integrated Systems, *Econometrica*, **61**, 783–820.

Surajaras, P. and Sweeney, R.J. (1992) *Profit-Making Speculation in Foreign Exchange Markets*, Boulder, CO: Westview Press.

Sweeney, R.J. (1986) Beating the Foreign Exchange Market, *Journal of Finance*, **41**, 163–82.

Sweeney, R.J. (1988) Some New Filter Rule Tests: Methods and Results, *Journal of Financial and Quantitative Analysis*, **23**, 285–300.

Sweeney, R.J. and Lee, E.J.Q. (1990) Profits in Forward Market Speculation, *Advances in Financial Planning and Forecasting 4* (Part A), 55–79.

Taylor, M.P. and Allen, H.L. (1992) The Use of Technical Analysis in the Foreign Exchange Market, *Journal of International Money and Finance*, **11**, 304–14.

Taylor, S.J. (1994) Trading Futures Using a Channel Rule: A Study of the Predictive Power of Technical Analysis with Currency Examples, *Journal of Futures Markets*, **14**, 215–35.

Tong, H. (1990) *Non-linear Time Series*, Oxford: Clarendon Press.

Tronzano, M. (1992) Efficiency in the German and Japanese Foreign Exchange Markets, *Weltwirtschaftliches Archiv*, **128**, 1–19.

Weiss, M.D. (1991) Nonlinear and Chaotic Dynamics, *Journal of Agricultural Economics Research*, **43**, 2–17.

Wickens, M.R. and Breusch, T.S. (1988) Dynamic Specification, the Long Run and the Specification of Transformed Regression Models, *Economic Journal*, **98**, 189–205.

Wilder, J.W. (1978) *New Concepts in Technical Trading Systems*, McLeansville, NC: Trend Research.

Williams, G., Parikh, A. and Bailey, D. (1998) Are Exchange Rates Determined by Macroeconomic Factors, *Applied Economics*, **30**, 553–67.

Wolff, C.C.P. (1987a) Forward Foreign Exchange Rates, Expected Spot Rates and Premia: A Signal Extraction Approach, *Journal of Finance*, **42**, 395–406.

Wolff, C.C.P. (1987b) Time Varying Parameters and the Out-of-Sample Forecasting Performance of Structural Exchange Rate Models, *Journal of Business and Economic Statistics*, **42**, 395–406.

Zarnowitz, V. (1985) Rational Expectations and Macroeconomic Forecasts, *Journal of Business and Economic Statistics*, **3**, 293–311.

Index